THE INSIDERS' GUIDE® TO
Florida's Great Northwest

THE INSIDERS' GUIDE® TO
Florida's Great Northwest

by
Robin Rowan
and
Clark Perry

THE INSIDERS' GUIDE®

The Insiders' Guides, Inc.

Co-published and marketed by:
Tallahassee Democrat, Inc.
227 N. Magnolia Drive
Tallahassee, FL 32302-0990
(904) 599-2100

Co-published and distributed by:
The Insiders' Guides, Inc.
P.O. Box 2057 • Highway 64
Manteo, NC 27954
(919) 473-6100

•

FIRST EDITION
1st printing

•

Copyright ©1994
by Tallahassee Democrat, Inc.

•

Printed in the United States
of America

•

All rights reserved. No part of this book may be reproduced in any form without permission, in writing, from the publisher, except by a reviewer who wishes to quote brief passages in connection with a review in a magazine or newspaper.

•

ISBN 0-912367-53-9

Tallahassee Democrat, Inc.

Sales and Marketing Manager
Thomas Tomasi

Account Executives
Sally Richardson
Barbara Reker
Marcia Richardson

Artists
Marilyn J. Biwer, Stephanie Weinard, Tali Rodin and Kelly Broderick

The Insiders' Guides, Inc.

Publisher/Managing Editor
Beth P. Storie

President/General Manager
Michael McOwen

Creative Services Director
Michael Lay

Partnership Services Director
Giles Bissonnette

Distribution Manager
Julie Ross

Fulfillment Coordination
Gina Twiford

Controller
Claudette Forney

Preface

Pull up a chair and let us tell you a little about this place; in our estimation, one of the most beautiful in America. Biased? Perhaps. Even though we weren't born and raised here, we've lived here long enough to feel like we're "dug in," giving us a unique perspective on the area as we've moved from being "outsiders" to "insiders."

We remember fondly when our friends from "up north" would call and say, "We're coming to Florida to visit Disney World next month; any chance you can meet us halfway for lunch?" Sure, we'll just hop the next *plane*. If you look at a map of the United States, Northwest Florida is closer to New Orleans, Atlanta, Memphis and Nashville than it is to Miami. From Pensacola, Key West and Chicago are about equidistant.

Yet, the farther north you travel in Florida, the more southern it gets. You hear more Southern accents here. See more grits served as a side dish in place of hash browns or baked potatoes. But it's not *all* slow drawls and porch-settin'. An influx of military families and "transplants" from other places gives a cosmopolitan feel to most larger resort areas. It's a good blend of past and present, the old ways and the new ways, tradition and progress.

Here, too, is so much more of Florida the way it "used" to be — verdant, expansive woodlands of slash pine, live oak and magnolia; preserved coastal wetlands that make better homes for herons and alligators than for people.

But above everything else, surpassing Southern charm and down-home cooking and even a rich and colorful past, there's the main attraction that visitors can't quite seem to get enough of: endless expanses of snow-white beaches and dunes framing glittering gulf waters in hues of emerald and aquamarine. More miles of beachfront are preserved here than any other place in Florida. And when you roll up your pants legs and wade into still-warm gulf water in mid-November, look behind you at white, rolling dunes, ahead at a school of playful dolphin . . . well, that, my friend, is why we stay.

Florida's Great Northwest stretches from Pensacola to Tallahassee, and there's a lot of diversity between the two cities. In fact, you're likely to see a wider range of people and places along this stretch than you will anywhere else in the state.

We've tried to reflect this diversity in the book by geographically dividing the northwest into five large

PREFACE

areas that include surrounding communities and points of interest. These are:

Pensacola area — Pensacola, Pensacola Beach, Gulf Breeze, Navarre Beach, Milton, Perdido Key;

Fort Walton Beach/Destin/Beaches of South Walton — Fort Walton Beach (Niceville, Valparaiso, Shalimar), Destin, Beaches of South Walton (Sandestin, Seaside, Grayton Beach, Point Washington);

Panama City area — Panama City, Panama City Beach;

Florida's Forgotten Coast — Mexico Beach, Port St. Joe, Cape San Blas, St. Vincent Island, Apalachicola, Eastpoint, St. George Island, Carrabelle;

Tallahassee area (including inland areas east of Panama City to Tallahassee) — Tallahassee, Chipley, Marianna, Wakulla, St. Marks.

We also include information about Thomasville, Georgia, in the Tallahassee Daytrips section because its close proximity to the Capitol City invites many residents and visitors to sample its annual events, shopping districts and fine restaurants. For the same reason, you'll also find a chapter on Mobile, Alabama.

Our experience tells us that vacationers move freely throughout one area, but there isn't a great amount of crossover from one area to the next. Although it only takes around three hours to drive from Pensacola to Tallahassee, there's such an incredible amount of things to see and do in between that most visitors may find it simply too exhausting and demanding to explore all five areas at once.

You should note that street numbering is not used consistently except within city limits, so directions such as "along the beach road" or "near the intersection of..." may be more helpful than street addresses.

Keeping all this in mind, we must say that the best way to use this guide is just to read it. Then pick a place and go. No matter where it is, we've been there, too, and we can help you find the magic.

About the Authors

Robin Hill Rowan wanted to speak more than write at first; she got her early experience as a disc jockey while a Speech major at the University of Wisconsin - Eau Claire. While "marking time" in between radio jobs, she landed a position with a Chicago-based incentives company, writing about places she'd never been. Rio de Janeiro, Cozumel, the Swiss Alps, South Africa — the pieces she produced were meant to inspire salespeople to win fabulous trips to exotic destinations.

But the urge to play d.j. was still stronger than the one to write, and in 1982, Rowan headed, sight unseen, to Pensacola, Florida, where she'd been hired as the all-night country d.j. Simultaneously, she was also voicing commercials for an ad agency's production studio. Before long, she was running the studio and soon started writing commercials. Working two full-time jobs left little time for sleep, so Rowan went full-time at that agency, then another, and finally to a full-time writing career in 1988.

Rowan's credits include state vacation guides for Florida and Alabama, and travel videos for Southeastern markets — New Orleans, Atlanta, Key West and Florida's Great Northwest. She continues writing advertising, p.r. and travel while making a permanent home in Pensacola with her husband, Michael, and daughter, Rachel, 4.

Clark Perry was born in the hills of Alabama but has called Florida his home for nearly a decade now. He has worked as a soda jerk, photographer, dishwasher and obituary clerk, all with varying degrees of success. He attended the University of North Alabama and Michigan State University, and graduated from the University of Tampa in 1988 with a bachelor's degree in Writing.

Since that time, he's worked mainly as a free-lance writer, with work appearing in magazines and newspapers such as *Creative Loafing, Tampa Tribune, The Silver Web* and *Starlog*. As a technical writer, he's also produced user manuals for several software companies.

His hobbies include technology and the arts, especially those areas where the two converge. Although he's basically a happy and upbeat fellow who enjoys sunshine and the beach, Clark has been known to acknowledge his dark side through his writing. His sometimes horrific short stories can he found in several anthologies, including *Young Blood* (Zebra, 1994), edited by Mike Baker, and *Ghosts* (Pocket, 1994), a Horror Writers Association anthology edited by Peter Straub.

Acknowledgments

Robin...

Special thanks to the following people who helped make this book possible:

Andy Witt, Executive Director, and The Arts Council of Northwest Florida, publishers of the *Northwest Florida Cultural Directory*. The information provided in the directory was accurate, complete and saved me a month of research!

J. Earle Bowden, Editor of the *Pensacola News Journal*, whose 40 years experience at the paper proved invaluable, since many of the articles I used for historical information on Pensacola were written by Mr. Bowden in the '50s and '60s. He was also kind enough to read my history chapter and make corrections and clarifications;

Sandra Johnson and her staff at the Pensacola Historical Society for checking my facts for accuracy and providing me with a wealth of material and photographs for the book;

Dr. William Coker, retired history professor at the University of West Florida, for his insights into the colonial period in Pensacola;

Jerry Eubanks, Superintendent of Gulf Islands National Seashore and his staff (and especially Mary Jones) for providing missing pieces of the puzzles throughout the GINS, sending slides and checking the chapter on the Seashore;

Sheilah Bowman, Director of the Pensacola Convention and Visitors Center, who is a walking Rolodex of contact people and phone numbers;

Karen Lee Tucker of the Florida Park Service, for providing information and photos for Northwest Florida's scenic state parks;

Andrea Mathews of Geiger & Associates, Tallahassee, for sending zillions of photos and assisting with information on the Beaches of South Walton;

Davis Company and Beach TV for sending me oodles of information on cities up and down the coast, and especially to Toni Davis, who first gave me the opportunity to research and write about Florida's Great Northwest;

and, most of all, to my husband Michael, fellow adventurer, writing critic ("That metaphor doesn't really work for me"), patient listener and steadfast supporter.

Clark...

My sincerest thanks go to the following for their invaluable assistance and advice in the preparation of this book:

Coleen David, Director of Pro-

ACKNOWLEDGMENTS

grams and Services for the Tallahassee Area Convention and Visitors Bureau;

Helen E. Rouse of the Monticello Opera House;

Eleanor B. Hawkins, Jefferson County Clerk of Circuit Court;

Phyllis C. McVoy, Education Specialist with the Knott House Museum;

Kathy Anderson, Festival Director for Springtime Tallahassee;

Shari Hubbard, Senior Account Supervisor with Geiger & Associates Public Relations;

Clifton L. Maxwell of the Florida Department of Environmental Protection;

Kim McCray of the Destination Thomasville Tourism Authority;

Catherine Cameron of the Wakulla County Chamber of Commerce;

Sally Richardson of Apalachicola;

Cindy Clark of Bay Media Services in Apalachicola;

Chuck Spicer, publisher of the *Coastline* in Apalachicola;

Paula Pate of Thomasville, Ga.;

the Tallahassee Historical Society, whose voluminous writings and accounts were invaluable during the preparation of this book;

Dr. James W. Covington, professor emeritus of the University of Tampa, whose wonderful book *The Seminoles of Florida* and stimulating conversation shed much light on Tallahassee's turbulent, controversial and always fascinating history;

the helpful gang at The Insiders' Guides, Inc.;

and last but not least my fiancé Donna, whose love and encouragement proved to be the most valuable resource of them all.

Structures such as this gazebo are among the highlights of the community of Seaside.

Table of Contents

Preface v
About the Authors vii
Acknowledgments viii

OVERVIEW
Getting Around 1
General Beach Information 5

PENSACOLA
History 13
The Pensacola Area 24
Restaurants and Nightlife 28
Accommodations 43
Shopping 50
Attractions 55
Festivals and Special Events 73
Parks and Recreation 89
Arts and Culture 98
Higher Education 110
Real Estate 112
Retirement 121
Health Care 125
Military 130

GULF ISLANDS NATIONAL SEASHORE 135

FORT WALTON BEACH/DESTIN/ BEACHES OF SOUTH WALTON
History 142
Restaurants and Nightlife 146
Accommodations 159
Shopping 174
Attractions 181
Festivals and Special Events 191
Parks and Recreation 200
Arts and Culture 216
Higher Education 219
Real Estate 221
Retirement 230
Health Care 233
Military 238

PANAMA CITY
History 241
Restaurants and Nightlife 244
Accommodations 251
Shopping 259
Attractions 263
Festivals and Special Events 275
Parks and Recreation 281
Arts and Culture 292
Higher Education 296
Real Estate 298
Retirement 303
Health Care 306
Military 309

FLORIDA'S FORGOTTEN COAST 311

TALLAHASSEE
History 351
The Tallahassee Area 367
Getting Around 371
Restaurants 375
Nightlife 383
Accommodations 388
Shopping 395
Kidstuff 400
Historic Sites and Attractions 402
Festivals and Special Events 409
Parks and Recreation 417
Golf and Hunting 437
Spectator Sports 439
Arts and Culture 441
Higher Education 450
State Government 455
Real Estate 460
Retirement 464
Medical Care 467
Daytrips 473
Mobile 487
Index of Advertisers 503
Index 504

Directory of Maps
Regional Overview .... inside front cover
Tallahassee 372

Fish flock to this spot at the St. Andrews jetties.

Photo: Florida Park Service

Inside
Getting Around

Getting here is almost as important as getting around, and we'd like to assist you in doing so without eating up days (and dollars) from your vacation. If you're coming in from more than 400 miles away, the quickest trip is by air, with the greatest number of flights coming into Pensacola. But, be warned that there's no such thing as a non-stop flight from that distance. You'll have to make connections in Atlanta, Charlotte, Memphis or Nashville. If time isn't a problem, the Amtrak is comfortable and ambles its way right through Northwest Florida. Buses seem to stop at every place that has a pay phone, and a 400-mile trip could seem like *days*. If you can wait until you get to Florida to rent a car, it's the best way to get around. Weekly rates are still some of the best in the country, and the rental agencies have gotten away from plastering their cars with rental bumper stickers that scream "Tourist!" from 100 paces. This section covers the area from Pensacola to Panama City Beach; Please see the Tallahassee section for "Getting Around" information east of Panama City Beach.

By Car

Florida, geographically, is somewhat isolated from the rest of the United States, surrounded almost completely by water. For the first time, Northwest Florida got the recognition it deserved from the state with the slogan "See Florida Coast to Coast to Coast," meaning the Atlantic Coast, and the Western and Northern Gulf Coasts.

There are only two ways in by car; from the west and from the north. Pensacola, the first city of any size from the west on Interstate 10, has been nicknamed "The Western Gate to the Sunshine State." Because of its proximity to Alabama, the area has also been dubbed "L.A.," or Lower Alabama, a moniker locals have tried to dispel for years. From I-10, the main east-west route ending in Jacksonville, you won't notice much difference in the scenery, but the landscape along the Alabama-to-Florida beaches on Highway 292 changes dramatically. For some reason, the sand changes from light brown to brilliant white, and if it weren't for the two miles of Perdido Key that Florida gave away over a monetary dispute some years ago, you'd know immediately you were in Florida by that alone.

Welcome Centers greet Florida visitors from three entry points: from the west on I-10 near Pensacola; from

GETTING AROUND

the north on U.S. 231 near Campbellton; and inside the Capitol Building in Tallahassee. This might be a good place to start your trip through Florida's Great Northwest (and have a complimentary glass of Florida orange or grapefruit juice).

The most direct route from Pensacola to Tallahassee is on I-10, but it's also one of the most boring drives in the state. Infinitely more scenic, but also much longer (but you're not in a hurry, are you?) is the beach route, which mostly follows Highway 98 except on Perdido Key, Pensacola Beach and Navarre Beach.

If you're coming into Florida on I-65, there's no good way to get into Pensacola right now. You can get here from there, but you'll have to veer off the interstate way before you reach Florida, where it's small towns and mostly two-lane highways for the remainder of the trip. After you pass Evergreen, Alabama, on I-65, look for the Flomaton exit (113). This two-lane country road dead-ends after a few miles; turn right and follow the signs for Highway 29 south. Make a quick left at the Hardee's and you'll be on the right road. Follow Highway 29 into Century, Florida, then continue through several rural communities until you reach Pensacola (it's about an hour's drive from the turnoff at Highway 29). A few miles into Pensacola, there's an I-10 interchange going east (to the beaches, the I-110 spur, the University of West Florida and Tallahassee), and west (to Naval Air Station Pensacola and Mobile). There's been much talk about connecting I-10 with I-65 via the I-110 spur, which would make everybody's life easier, but this is still years away. Sigh.

Now a few words about traffic: To say that drivers in Northwest Florida are a little . . . casual . . . about the rules of the road is an understatement. Only Boston drivers can relate. Since it goes on all year long we can't blame the tourists. Just be extra careful at stoplights and stop signs. For some reason, drivers here refuse to pull into the intersection when turning left, causing cars behind them to wait through another light, and most are completely unfamiliar with turn indicators! *Most* locals will show a bit of added courtesy to cars with out-of-state license plates (we call them "tags" here).

There's a bit of the Old South left in us, too. In Pensacola and a few other scattered communities, all traffic stops to allow funeral processions to pass.

If you're from a large city, you're probably already used to the summer's heavy traffic, but serious backups can occur on the Three Mile Bay Bridge from Gulf Breeze into Pensacola from about 3 until 7 PM every day in the summer months. Accidents and stalled vehicles can make it an even longer wait. The stretch of Highway 98 between Fort Walton Beach and Destin is slow going from about 3 until 6 PM all year long, although the new Mid-Bay Bridge over Choctawhatchee Bay has alleviated that somewhat.

By Air

PENSACOLA REGIONAL AIRPORT
Airport Blvd. at 12th Ave.   435-1745

Northwest Florida's largest airport is in Pensacola, with 45 daily

GETTING AROUND

departures spread over eight carriers, more than any of the other airports. Delta, US Air, US Air Express, Continental, American Eagle, ComAir and Atlantic Southeast (Delta's commuter carrier), serve Pensacola Regional. The new terminal, opened in 1990, now has several jetways, allowing passengers to board and deplane without walking outside, as was previously the case. From Pensacola, non-stop flights go to Atlanta, Charlotte, Dallas, Houston, Memphis, Mobile, Nashville, New Orleans, Orlando, Tallahassee and Tampa. If you need to go any farther than that, you'll have to change planes, most likely in Atlanta.

You may save yourself some headache if you can make a connecting flight from either Charlotte or Memphis, which are much smaller airports than Atlanta and not as spread out, avoiding that last-minute dash through three terminal sections to make a flight. Pensacola Regional Airport is located smack in the middle of town at Airport Boulevard and 12th Avenue near Cordova Mall and Pensacola Junior College.

Shuttle service is provided to the Pensacola Grand Hotel downtown and the Holiday Inn University Mall on the north end of town; call individual hotels to inquire about other shuttles to and from the airport. There are always several taxis lined up in front of the terminal waiting for fares; this may be the simplest way to get to your hotel in town. Taxi fares to the beach are steep; it may be in your best interest to find other travelers going that way and double up, or rent a car yourself. Right across from baggage claim are the following rental agencies:

Avis	433-5614; (800) 331-1212
Hertz	432-2345; (800) 654-3131
Dollar	474-9000; (800) 800-4000
National	432-8338; (800) 227-7368

OKALOOSA COUNTY AIR TERMINAL
Hwy. 85 between Niceville and Fort Walton Beach   651-7160

Okaloosa is serviced by Atlantic Southeast (Delta connection), American Eagle, US Air Express and Northwest Airlines. National, Hertz, Budget and Avis rental car agencies are located right in the terminal. Budget's toll free number is (800) 527-0700. For other toll free numbers, look under Pensacola.

PANAMA CITY-BAY COUNTY MUNICIPAL AIRPORT
Lisenby Ave.   763-6751

Panama City is also equipped with a small airport, recently designated an international airport, with 27 daily incoming flights. Delta, ASA, Northwest Airlink, USAir Express and ComAir all service the airport. Cross the Hathaway Bridge as you come into town, go about two miles to Lisenby Avenue and turn left. Lisenby dead-ends at the airport. Car rental agencies in the airport terminal are Avis (769-1411), Budget (769-8733) and Hertz (763-6673). Toll free numbers are listed under the Pensacola Regional Airport.

Pensacola Aviation at Pensacola Regional Airport (434-0636), Bob Sikes Airport in Crestview (on John Gibbons Road off of Airport Road, phone 682-6395), and Miracle Strip Aviation in Destin (Airport Road off of Highway 98, phone 837-6135)

• 3

GETTING AROUND

handle charter service, private planes and corporate jets.

By Train

After 20 years, Amtrak has started up passenger service through Northwest Florida, closing the last gap on a Los Angeles to Miami run. The Sunset Limited began three-times-weekly service in April of 1993. If you never understood why people would pay almost as much as an airplane ticket to ride something almost as slow as a bus, you may just have to see for yourself. The seats are gigantic and terribly comfortable with plenty of leg room, you can get up and stretch at anytime, visit the dining car, the lounge/observation car, the smoking lounge, or just take a walk through the entire train, upstairs and downstairs.

The trip from Pensacola to Tallahassee on the Sunset Limited takes about an hour longer than driving it yourself (about 4½ hours), and remember, you'll lose an hour traveling east. Don't expect to see some of Florida's most beautiful scenery, however; this is the CSX railroad line, made for freight trains. The Sunset Limited passes through mostly rural sections of inland Florida where the major attractions are swamps, rivers and small-town communities. The prettiest section of the entire trip is in Pensacola: The train crosses over Bayou Texar, then winds its way around Pensacola Bay along the wooded red-dirt Bay Bluffs, then over Escambia Bay. Unfortunately, the ride occurs at about 5 or 6 in the morning when it's usually too dark to see. The Sunset Limited makes stops in Pensacola, Crestview, Chipley and Tallahassee.

Pensacola's Amtrak Station is off of 14th Avenue, near Gregory Street close to downtown. For other locations, see the Tallahassee Getting Around chapter. For information and reservations, call (800) 872-7245.

By Sea

Major waterways, and especially the Intracoastal Waterway, stay fairly busy all year, packed with pleasure boats, barges, foreign cargo ships, shrimpers, trawlers, fishing charters and sailboats. Short jaunts, say from Pensacola to Destin, offer spectacular scenery and relative safety within the confines of the shipping channel. Just be sure you're comfortable with the navigation of your watercraft, weather conditions and regulations before shipping out.

By Bus

The Escambia County Transit System (436-9383) runs a fleet of 27 buses to get you around the Pensacola area. Intra-city service is provided by Greyhound-Trailways. Pensacola station: 505 W. Burgess Road off Highway 29 (476-4800); Fort Walton Beach/Destin station: Chestnut Avenue and Highway 98 in Fort Walton Beach (243-1940); Panama City station: 917 Harrison Avenue (785-7861).

Inside
General Beach Information

Miles and miles and miles of white-sand beaches and dunes . . . crystalline gulf waters . . . gentle gulf breezes and a sun that shines 340 days a year. Kind of makes you want to jump in the minute you first lay eyes on it. And do, by all means, but *please* take a few moments to read over this section first. Information contained here pertains mostly to Gulf of Mexico beaches, but some is pure common sense to use *wherever* you swim. We're not trying to scare you or dissuade you from enjoying our beautiful beaches. But it is absolutely essential that newcomers and vacationers know what to expect in unfamiliar waters. And this information really *could* save your life.

Tides: Two a day, low and high, about twelve hours apart. Check the local papers' front section back page; times should be listed. At low tide the current is going out to sea; high tide means the water is coming into shore. If you're out swimming, floating, or snorkeling in the gulf, pay particular attention to tides. You could be carried far from shore in a matter of minutes. This author is all-too-familiar with that scenario; as a newcomer from the North and naive about water conditions, I was carried out on a raft to where I couldn't see land (that's at least seven miles)! So grateful was I to have made it back alive, I made it a point to learn more about my environment (and now *never* go out alone!).

Undertows: Sometimes a clue that an undertow's not far from shore is a bowl-shaped indentation in the shoreline (many people are more familiar with the term "riptide"). The surf may also appear flatter here. If you do get caught in an undertow, don't panic. Drownings occur when people try to swim against them, with unfortunate results. An undertow will only carry you about 30 yards out; *out* but not *under*. Your best bet is to swim parallel to the shoreline until you feel you are past the pull of the water. Can't swim? Just turn on your back, close your mouth and float.

Lifeguards: Many of the public beaches are protected by lifeguards for a good part of the day during peak months. If you're visiting the beach with small children, an extra pair of eyes and ears is always a good idea. In some areas, swim flags are posted in lieu of lifeguards, advising of current water conditions. Since the beaches are so vast, lifeguards and park rangers cannot hope to patrol the entire area. *Never* swim, surf, snorkel or dive by yourself. Period.

GENERAL BEACH INFORMATION

Keep an eye on the kids: Perhaps the best tip here is to only swim where and when lifeguards are on watch. If children get a little too adventuresome, they're called back into an area where a lifeguard can reach them quickly. Good places for young children are Quietwater Beach on Santa Rosa Sound (Pensacola Beach), Big Lagoon State Park near Perdido Key, Okaloosa Island at the Gulf Islands National Sea Shore (on Choctawhatchee Bay), and the "kiddie pools" at the jetties in St. Andrews State Recreation Area (Panama City Beach).

Marine life: Jellyfish make their annual appearance around July every year and stay for about a month. There are many, many different kinds, from flat bluish disks to the long-tentacled Man-O'-War. Not all will sting, but moving to a less infested area of the beach or switching from the gulf to the sound side may save you from painful stings. If you do encounter a jellyfish sting, neutralize it with ammonia, then sprinkle on some Adolph's Meat Tenderizer (regular or seasoned!) or make a paste of baking soda and water. If none of these remedies is immediately handy, put some beach sand on the sting until you can get first aid. Sometimes very hot water works well, too. With all the above, only sprinkle the remedy on; don't rub it onto the skin. Rubbing will make the sting worse.

Other than jellyfish, there's not too much to be concerned about in the gulf. The abundant marine life is mostly harmless, and much more terrified of you than the other way around. Still, a good rule to follow is: If you don't know what it is, don't pick it up!

What to leave at home: Glass containers and pets. Neither is permitted on the beaches at any time, and fines are imposed on offenders.

We don't want it either: When the signs say "Take only pictures. Leave only footprints," they mean it. Please clean up after yourself; and it would be nice if you would pick up an extra piece of litter on your way out.

Swimming and alcohol: A bad mix anytime, but especially in the ever-changing conditions of the Gulf of Mexico. High summer temperatures and equally high humidity can dehydrate a sober person quickly; alcohol will intensify the effect. Jumping into the bathwater-warm gulf will not sober a person up, it will only make that person tired.

Tanning tips (if you must): Florida sun is hotter and much more intense than just about any other place in the United States. Add to that reflection off the gulf and the white sand and you could be headed for trouble. Take note of these precautionary measures:

1. Start out with small amounts of sun instead of one long stretch. Just an hour of sun during peak periods can burn you enough to ruin an entire week's vacation.

2. Use sunscreen, no matter if you were "born to tan" or not. Lather up on "hot spots"—nose, lips, top of the ears, shoulders, hair part and any place that hasn't seen the sun for awhile.

3. Peak sun hours are 10 AM until 2 PM. Use at least a 15 SPF sunblock or stay out of the sun altogether

Seaweed:
Can you eat this stuff, or what?

It's a gorgeous day in early June. You pack up the family, head for the Gulf of Mexico, and there, clogging the water and spread out for miles on the beach like giant mounds of Brillo pads is — SEAWEED! The annual migration of Sargassum seaweed, like the ebb and flow of the tides, is an inevitable but natural part of the Gulf Coast environment.

This sandy-colored seaweed was first described in the journal of Christopher Columbus while sailing the Sargasso Sea. Nineteen ninety-one was perhaps the worst year for the weed here in Northwest Florida. Violent winter storms kept the gulf in constant motion throughout the winter months, causing the weed, which grows on the sandy gulf bottom, to be uprooted and sent sometimes hundreds of miles towards the shore. Bulldozers were used to move gigantic mountains of the weed away from public swimming areas. Besides spoiling an otherwise pristine view, the odor of dead fish permeated the air, sending beachgoers fleeing to inland waterways.

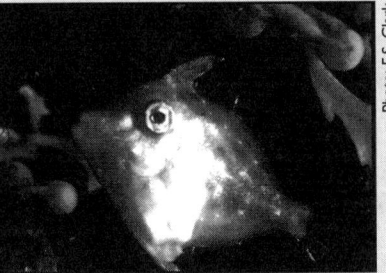

A file fish finds a safe haven among clumps of sargassum weed.

Swimmers and surfers find Sargassum weed to be merely a nuisance, but the real threat is to boaters. Motors can become suddenly entangled in the weed, stopping them dead. If Sargassum weed has been spotted in the gulf, boaters are warned to steer clear.

But microbiologists, coastal scientists, and park rangers see the weed as an asset to coastal ecology. The weed provides protection for hundreds of species of tiny fish, shrimp, baby sea turtles and other organisms. Marine creatures will lay their eggs in the weed, knowing the young have a better chance at survival if hidden from predators' view.

And the weed could one day provide a benefit to humans: Navy and Coast Guard trainees are instructed to seek out patches of Sargassum weed and fill their helmets. Just that amount of weed can provide enough nourishment from the instant supply of fish, shrimp and other edibles to keep a person alive until rescued.

GENERAL BEACH INFORMATION

Grayton Beach is hailed as the No. One beach in the United States.

during these hours.

4. If you see any red or pink on your skin at all, it's time to get out of the sun. You're burned.

5. Post-sun skin care: After a warm, soapy shower, apply an aloe-based lotion. If you do burn, take the heat off with a cloth soaked in vinegar. You'll smell like a salad, but you'll feel much better!

What to wear: Casual and comfortable is the rule of the day at all but the fanciest restaurants and resorts. Shirts and shoes are required in just about every establishment, although you can get away with only swimsuits and flip flops. From May through October, shorts and short-sleeved shirts are the accepted mode of dress. You may want to pack a light jacket or sweater for occasional "cold snaps" or restaurants that keep the temperature on "deep freeze." The rest of the year, and especially for windy beach walks in January, you'll need warmer attire, with temperatures dipping sometimes into the 40s. We call it "fireplace weather," and northern vacationers still think it a far cry from

8 •

GENERAL BEACH INFORMATION

snow and sleet and gray skies.

Always wear shoes unless you're actually *on* the beach. Trying to cross the dunes in bare feet is a bad idea, since sand spurs will always find the most tender flesh to stick. The South is also blessed with dreaded fire ants that build mounds in front yards, public parks and on beaches. They look harmless enough, but their bite is painful and leaves a nasty-looking blister. Shoes and socks won't prevent fire ants from attacking, but will offer better protection than bare feet.

Seasons: Unlike our neighbors to the south, Northwest Florida has four distinct seasons. Although snow is nearly unheard of, we get a flurry or two every few years. Rainiest months are January and July, but don't let it change your vacation plans; showers along the Gulf Coast rarely last more than twenty minutes at a time. Camellias and Japanese magnolia make their showing in December and January, and most everything stays green all year, so although it might be cold, it doesn't really *seem* like winter.

Azaleas herald the spring's return, beginning as early as late February. The dogwood's showy blossoms follow close behind, and even the humblest of homes appears grander when framed by mounds of bright flowers. The temperature cranks up in earnest by May, although flocks of Spring Breakers and surfers have been lining the beaches since March.

We won't try to gloss over summer: it's HOT, HOT, HOT. On some days you'll feel like you were sealed in Tupperware. Take a 95-degree day, add a brief afternoon rainshower for added humidity, and you'll probably want to relax in your air-conditioned condo. There *is*, however, one saving grace if you're on the beach — an almost constant ocean breeze that can make the heat a little easier to take. June 1 through November 30 is also hurricane season, but not to worry; if a storm is headed our way (the last big hit was in 1926), you'll have at least 24 hours' warning, and hurricane evacuation routes are well marked.

Summer stays with us right through September, but by early October, we can look forward to highs only(!) in the 80s. No frost on the pumpkin here. Fall is, weather-wise, the very best time of the year in Northwest Florida. Gulf waters are still quite warm, the huge crowds have thinned and fishing and arts festivals abound.

Time Zones: Northwest Florida covers two time zones, Central and Eastern. From its western entry point in Pensacola and for about two hours into Florida, you're on Central Time. The jump ahead to Eastern Time occurs around Marianna (just before Apalachicola on the beach road); there are highway markers notifying you of the exact moment to set your watch ahead one hour.

Area Codes: Every phone number in Northwest Florida is in the 904 area code. When calling from Pensacola to Fort Walton Beach or from Panama City to Tallahassee, you must first dial the area code before the number, even though you are in the same area code. The phone number, preceded by a "1" (for toll calls) is no longer in operation.

• 9

GENERAL BEACH INFORMATION

Photo: Robin Rowan

The beaches near Pensacola are characterized by white sand and sea oats as far as the eye can see.

Boating Safety

Whether chartering a boat for deep-sea fishing, tooling around the bay in a pontoon boat or feeling the wind in your face at the helm of your own sailboat, getting out on the water offers a delightfully different perspective on the area and its many surrounding waterways. Water in Northwest Florida is so popular, in fact, that a quick lesson in boating safety is essential for both captain and crew.

Leave a list of all members of your party with someone back on land, plus your intended destination, route and expected time of return. Even if you're renting a boat from a reputable concessionaire, take a few minutes to inspect safety equipment before leaving the dock.

One Coast Guard-approved life vest is required for each person on board. Many marinas have special child-size vests for children under 50 pounds. Make sure that children wear their safety vests at all times, as well as all those adults who can't swim. A life preserver ring is also a good backup.

For motor or sailboats less than 20 meters in length, a ship's bell or whistle, audible up to a quarter mile, is required. If you plan to be out on the water between sundown and sunrise, your boat will also need navigation lights. The last piece of equipment is a good, strong anchor, capable of staying the boat in severe weather.

Pontoon boats probably require the least amount of nautical know-how, with motor boats and sailboats

10 •

next. If you're a first-time captain, however, be sure to ask for a demonstration of boat operation and safety features. Since many accidents are caused by improper boat handling, take a few moments to review these safety precautions:

1. Do not attempt to "outrun" another boat. Sailboats are at the mercy of the wind, and always have the right of way. It is sometimes impossible to tell how fast a distant boat is going, and you may not be able to get out of the way in time.

2. Pick up a *Florida Boater's Guide* at any Marine Patrol Office. Knowing speed limits, identifying buoy markers and learning on-the-water courtesy will help prevent accidents!

3. Stay in the shipping channel to avoid running aground. Water close to shore can change suddenly and dramatically.

4. Never drink while operating any boat. The Coast Guard reports that 60 percent of all boating accidents involve alcohol or drugs.

5. Keep passengers off of elevated surfaces, especially the bow or casting platforms. Sunbathers could easily roll off should you hit a wake or sudden high seas.

6. And finally, respect your fellow boaters and the environment. Please don't throw *anything* overboard! Save your trash to dispose of back on shore. Now go out there and enjoy yourself, relax and stay safe!

PENSACOLA — HISTORY

Giant red snapper like this made Pensacola "the red snapper capital of the world."

Pensacola Area History

Pensacola ought to be pretty good at hosting visitors by now. They've been doing it for more than 400 years, longer than almost anyone in America. This scenic area, with its wide, sugar-white beaches, abundant marine life, and natural deep-water port, became a brass ring for countries vying for their stake in the New World. Seventeen times Pensacola would change flags, batted about like a volleyball among French, Spanish, British, Confederate, and finally U.S. forces.

Although Native Americans had occupied Northwest Florida for more than 10,000 years, no written account exists of their lifestyle, only the numerous artifacts now on display in local museums. So it was the Spanish who "officially" laid claim to *La Florida*, or "Land of the Flowers." It was they, too, who gave names to the early tribes: Apalachee, Choctaw, Coosa, Chickasaw, Creek, Mobile, Pensacola (or *Panzacola*, meaning "long-haired people").

We Were First

Early in the 16th century, a few Spanish explorers sailed to Pensacola (which was called "Ochuse" until the 18th century), remarking on her beauty, natural harbor, and their desire to establish a fortress here. But it wasn't until August 14, 1559, that Spaniard Don Tristan de Luna made landfall along the shores of Pensacola (the exact spot is widely disputed) with an entourage of 1,400 colonists, among them women, children, blacks, and Indians. Their mission: to beat out the French in establishing the first crown-sponsored settlement in the land explored earlier by Hernando de Soto, to build a defensible fortress, and to bring Christianity to the Indians.

Not much was accomplished in the first days after the landing; the new settlers enjoyed some leisure time, swimming and fishing and racing boats. But before any building was begun in earnest, a massive hurricane ripped through Pensacola, sinking or destroying most of the dozen or so ships and drowning the livestock. The expedition was a disaster, the colonists shipwrecked in a strange land.

For about eighteen months the discouraged Spanish colonists wandered inland in search of food. Luna was finally fired, and in the spring of 1561, a new team sailed in with fresh supplies and an energetic crew of officers and Catholic friars. Since the colonists didn't care to plant and harvest the land, choosing instead to trade with Indian tribes and exploit existing resources, the settlement was doomed to fail. By summer of that year, the entire colony was abandoned. And so it is that St. Augustine, established six years later in 1565, holds the title of "America's oldest city." What they certainly have over Pensacola is permanence, since another attempt at settlement wasn't made in Pensacola for 139 years.

Today's Governing Country Is . . .

By the time another Spanish expedition set out to colonize Pensacola in 1698, the French had made some attempt to settle West Florida, which at that time included lands clear over to the Mississippi River. The two countries became uneasy neighbors, the Spanish in Pensacola, the French in Mobile. They did a bit of trading but mostly stayed out of each other's way.

The Spanish started with a fort settlement at the present-day Naval Air Station. By 1719, a second Spanish fort went up near present-day Fort Pickens on Santa Rosa Island. This crucial year saw Pensacola change flags four times in six months between French and Spanish forces. Finally, the French lost Pensacola to the Spanish in a 1722 treaty.

Spain lost no time in establishing yet another settlement on Santa Rosa Island, which ended 30 years later (1722-52) when nature's hand again intervened: A powerful hurricane sent them scurrying back to the mainland. In 1757, the King of Spain officially named the town "Panzacola." England was next in line to claim the prize from Spain in the Treaty of Paris. During this British period (1763-1781), Englishman Elias Durnford surveyed the city, drawing up a grid plan that is today's Seville Historic District. Homeowners each received a corresponding garden plot at the northern edge of town for planting flowers and vegetables (today's Garden Street).

Expansion of British West Florida brought more immigrants, many families, even a few educated people into the area, but it also brought problems with fresh drinking water, garbage, and illness. But, those everyday annoyances seemed insignificant once General Bernardo de Galvez marched into Pensacola with 4,000 soldiers in March of 1781. The siege of Pensacola lasted about 60 days, with the Spanish emerging victorious.

The new Spanish government saw to it that most vestiges of British rule were eliminated. Although the street grid remained intact, street names were one significant change; Prince, Granby, Charlotte and George streets became Romana, Intendencia, Alcaniz and Palafox.

Soon the War of 1812 fell upon the country, with Spain and Britain aligning themselves against the U.S. After Andrew Jackson's victory over the Creeks in the Battle of Horseshoe Bend two years later, the U.S. controlled all land in present-day West Florida, save for Pensacola and St. Marks.

Let Me Do My Job and Let Me Leave . . .

Perhaps feeling the flush of newly found power, Jackson was outraged that the Spanish had allowed the British to use their forts and harbor to train the Creeks for battle, and quickly moved in. He drove the British out, leaving the Spanish disgraced, then departed as quickly as he had come. Jackson's attacks had no authorization from President James Monroe, however, so to placate the Spanish, Pensacola was returned to them. But it no longer played the vital role of military stronghold it once had. A treaty signed by both Spain and the U.S. handed the remaining land over to the U.S. The transfer was officially completed in a somber ceremony in Plaza Ferdinand on July 17, 1821. Andrew Jackson was sanctioned to accept the territory from Spain and become its first provisional governor.

Jackson performed his duties with remarkable precision and leadership. Within a week, he'd appointed a local governing body and organized Escambia County. But both he and his wife Rachel were less than happy during their stay in Pensacola. They disliked the heat, disliked the squalor and lack of morality of the residents, disliked the cabinet President Monroe had chosen to help govern. Rachel spoke of the filthy streets and the disorderly and unholy residents. By October of that same year, the Jacksons packed their belongings and headed off to Jackson's native Tennessee, never to return.

Pensacola Gets a Leg Up

Despite the Jacksons' feelings about the area, the city's groundwork had been well laid. Pensacola's future as a thriving city with strong military backing and a busy port was virtually assured. President John Quincy Adams authorized federal monies for development of a Navy yard in 1825. A location was chosen about seven miles southwest of the city. Through local petitioners, Adams also became convinced that this city on the Gulf of Mexico was easily defensible, warranting a major military presence. Money poured in to begin construction of three military fortifications, completing a triangle guarding the entrance to Pensacola Bay.

Captain William H. Chase of the U.S. Army Corps of Engineers was assigned to oversee the fort-building concern. A well-respected leader, the veteran military engineer and entrepreneur helped turn brickmaking into Pensacola's first industry. Forty million bricks were needed to construct Fort Pickens at the tip of Santa Rosa Island, Fort McRee on Foster's Island (now Perdido Key), and the expansion of Fort San Carlos de Barrancas.

The real problems with building the massive forts were not in brickmaking. Scarce free labor forced Chase to contract for supply slaves through local owners, in essence expanding slavery where there had previously been very little. Although built during the 1820s and 1830s, the forts saw negligible action until the Civil War.

• 15

"You Have Opened the Gates of Hell"

In 1861, Florida was the third state to secede from the Union. And Pensacola, having a major strategic impact because of its supply base and shipyard, became a volatile place. Shots were fired at Fort Barrancas four months before the war-opening shots at Fort Sumter. The exchange took place when Federal guards at Fort Barrancas fired on Confederate soldiers on a reconnaissance mission.

Deciding that perhaps Fort Barrancas might be a weak link, Federal troops instead occupied Fort Pickens, leaving Barrancas and the Navy Yard to the Confederacy. After a lengthy standoff, where the Union refused to surrender to Confederate forces, a truce was reached; no additional Union forces would be sent to Fort Pickens if the Confederacy agreed not to attack.

This arrangement was short-lived, however, when General Winfield Scott ordered reinforcements at Fort Pickens. The war droned on for soldiers on both sides, who might have preferred a gun battle to months of suffocating heat, mosquitoes and dysentery.

A "grand and sublime" artillery exchange shook Pensacola to its rafters on November 22, 1861. The three forts, plus two Union vessels in the bay, fired upon one another for the better part of two days. Only the thick smoke, darkness, and a drenching rain silenced the guns, but even as dawn crept over the horizon, shelling began anew. The Union ships, the *Niagara* and the *Richmond*, both concentrated their fire on Fort McRee, reducing it to ruins in a matter of hours and sufficiently crippling its capacity to return fire.

Even though the fort was destroyed, most cannon fire missed its mark. Either the ships couldn't get close enough to their targets (Forts McRee and Barrancas) and kept running aground at low tide, or the cannon were not large or powerful enough to hurl the balls the two miles across the bay. Small numbers on both sides were killed and wounded. But no one bothered to count the greatest number of casualties — the thousands of mullet floating belly-up in the bay!

Weeds and Charred Remains

Prior to the North-South conflict, Pensacola was the largest city in Florida, with nearly 3,000 residents. By the time the Confederate troops moved out in May of 1862, most of the residents had already left. Weeds grew in the streets, buildings and homes were abandoned, and Southern troops saw to it that what was left was of no use to the North; sawmills, brickyards, and ships were torched. Most of the city lay in ruins. It wasn't until war's end that families, merchants, and soldiers quietly moved back, looking for anything salvageable and beginning the painstaking process of rebuilding.

Surprisingly, free blacks fared better in Pensacola than in many other Southern cities, and for the most part were treated fairly in the county courts. Much of the attitude that prevailed may have been attributed to former U.S. Senator Stephen Mallory, a highly respected leader whose opinions about treatment of former slaves were echoed by many. Several hundred blacks were employed at the Navy Yard, which had been left in ruins by fleeing Confederates.

So the citizens turned their attention away from the military and ahead to more profitable ventures — lumber and shipping. Harvesting the vast tracts of yellow pine had already proved lucrative in the decades before the war. There certainly seemed to be enough to go around, and the demand for it in Europe and South America was tremendous. Great ships were built to carry it off; wharves sprang up at the foot of Palafox, Commandancia and Tarragona streets. There was work for every able-bodied person either aboard the ships, in the sawmills, or among the pines.

Money, Northern investors, and new residents came streaming in. What had been a virtual ghost town at the close of the war was now a bustling city of 8,000. But again the population waned as the Yellow Fever epidemic of 1873-74 sent the unacclimated scurrying for northern climates, quarantined every boat coming into port, and caused a general panic in the streets. More than 80 people succumbed to the disease; hundreds more were afflicted.

The Naples of America

Almost nothing, not wars nor disease nor dissension, could stop this city. Why, it was paradise on earth with its mild winters, bustling downtown, and prosperous lumber and shipping trades. And there was no better person to promote the advantages of Pensacola than W.D. Chipley. The Civil War veteran turned railroad magnate sought to expand the Pensacola and Louisville Railroad line to Northern markets and the Atlantic coast. He got his reward in 1881, when the Florida legislature incorporated the Pensacola and Atlantic Railroad Company, handing over millions of acres of land. Chipley became the railroad's vice president and general manager.

To build up the passenger railroad business, Chipley published a booklet on the benefits of the area called "Pensacola: The Naples of America":

> ...Pensacola offers more stir, variety, and reality of life than any city in Florida ... The resident of a colder and less congenial clime will enjoy the most perfect transformation ... Winter and summer its healthfulness is marvelous, except during epidemics....

Lumber was Pensacola's yellow gold. Lumber, shipping, and railroad families amassed obscene wealth and loved to show it off. Architectural styles, mostly from Europe, were incorporated into homes owned by the "new rich." The North Hill Preservation District, a 60-block neighborhood north of downtown, is one of the most eclectic mixtures of architectural styles in the country.

Most of the lumber passed through the Port of Pensacola. At times, ships from such exotic ports of call as Denmark, Norway, Italy, and Australia were lined up three deep waiting to dump their ballast and take on timber.

It was during the last part of the century, too, when two Northern entrepreneurs realized that the possibilities for even greater wealth lay right at their feet in offshore waters. The Gulf of Mexico harbored a vast assortment of tasty delicacies, the most abundant and prized among them the Red Snapper. So many snapper could be caught at one time that ever larger ships were needed to carry them back to Pensacola. One-hundred-foot, 100-ton schooners sometimes spent weeks in the gulf, packing their catches in the tons of ice they'd brought with them.

Two huge fishing fleets, belonging to the Warren Fish Company and E.E. Saunders and Company, prospered with little or no competition for nearly eighty years, until over-fishing made this commercial venture unprofitable. At its peak, between 1900 and 1920, ten million pounds per year were caught and shipped fresh by rail to markets all over the U.S.

Flying High

You might guess that it was rather a fine time to live in Pensacola. The city was a cultural gumbo of lifestyles, languages, and religions, and because of it, people here seemed to have quite a tolerance for diversity.

Despite all the affluence, Pensacola was dealt a major blow when the U.S. Navy ordered the closing of the Navy Yard in 1911. In ruins since the Civil War, the Navy had never made any attempt to restore buildings or send troops to be stationed here. But just three years later, the surprised residents of Pensacola learned that their fair city was to become the new home of the fledgling Naval Aeronautic Service.

Within a very short time, the aviation unit transferred from Annapolis and began training in Pensacola. The move was to have a significant impact on the city for decades, as Naval Air Station Pensacola became the largest flight training center in the country. Since its inception in 1914, Pensacola NAS and the city have worked hand-in-hand creating thousands of jobs, constructing housing for the influx of personnel and their families and bringing prosperity to many of its citizens.

End of the Trail

The Depression years hit Pensacola hard, but three major hurricanes in 1906, 1916, and 1926 did their best to wipe her out even before economics became a factor. By the late 1920s, nearly all of the usable pine had been clear cut, with very little reforestation left in its wake. Many families followed the last of the lumber out of town, presumably to start over somewhere else. The fishing industry hit rock bottom as well, causing more people to flee.

For the next few decades, Pensacola was a desolate place. There was virtually no industry; abandoned buildings were left to decay; families left the city for "modern" subdivisions in outlying areas.

The First Tourist Attraction

A train arriving at the Louisville and Nashville depot on October 25, 1886, was causing quite a stir. A huge crowd had gathered downtown to catch a glimpse of the train's cargo: seventeen Apache men, among them the famed medicine man Geronimo. The group was to be incarcerated at Fort Pickens for their "crimes," skirmishes with the U.S. Army in the Southwest.

Even before the new prisoners had settled in, Geronimo gained instant celebrity stature. Boatloads of people sailed over from the mainland just to get a distant look at the fierce Apache; others came by rail from New Orleans. Once the women and children joined their men at the fort (a condition of the Apache surrender), more of the curious followed.

For the next year and a half, Geronimo's presence at the fort was fodder for newspaper gossip columns. He began selling buttons off his shirt to willing takers for $1.00 apiece. When the boatload ferried back to the mainland for more passengers, he'd sew on a few more buttons in preparation for the next wave. He also learned to write his name at the fort, and made a tidy profit selling signed flat stones or shells to onlookers.

But without any warning, Geronimo, along with the other Apaches, were moved out under cover of darkness to Mobile, and then to Mount Vernon, Alabama. The people stopped coming.

Apache medicine man Geronimo was incarcerated at Fort Pickens for 18 months.

But it wasn't all bad news for those who chose to wait out the hard times. A couple of bright spots in development gave locals and visitors easy access to tourist areas. The 1920s saw the construction of Gulf Beach Highway joining Pensacola and Perdido Key. In the decade that followed, a three-mile-long bridge spanning Pensacola Bay brought the

PENSACOLA — HISTORY

communities of Pensacola and Gulf Breeze together for the first time.

A New and Thriving Industry

The outbreak of World War II turned things around for Pensacola, at least temporarily. Pilots streamed into the Navy base for flight training. The demand for talented pilots was so great that the program was shortened from fourteen to just seven months. Foreign trainees were welcomed to the air station as well, among them 3,000 British and a smaller entourage of French pilots.

The Navy newspaper, *The Gosport*, sent out the call for hundreds of civilian personnel to work as engineers, riggers, electricians, and others. Many positions were filled by area women until after the war, the Navy even establishing ferry service to help them get to and from work.

Expansion plans were quickly initiated for auxiliary bases at Corry Station and Saufley Field. Realignment of the command created the Naval Air Training Center at Pensacola. With the vast amount of personnel either in training or employed as support workers, the bases enjoyed regular visits by entertainers and other notables such as Jack Dempsey, Helen Keller, Mary Pickford, Tyrone Power and Bob Hope.

Being far from home during the war, many local blacks became increasingly irritated at continued segregation in the South. Blacks were allowed, however, to serve as jurors in Escambia County and the local Tolerance Club pushed hard for full citizenship for its black residents, including the right to vote.

The Push for Pensacola

By the 1950s, so many "outsiders" from all over the world had visited Pensacola, that the word of her friendly residents and sparkling beaches became widespread. The time was ripe for promotional efforts to begin in earnest.

One of the city's first endeavors was to commission a sign pointing the way to the "World's Whitest Beaches." The neon fish sign has become an area landmark (see sidebar). Both locals and out-of-towners carved out their little piece of paradise on the beach. Very quickly, dozens of cinder block homes rose from the dunes to be used by families as summer cottag-

> **Insiders' Tips**
> South of Main Street in downtown Pensacola are 60 acres of "made" land jutting out into Pensacola Bay, created from the ballast of steamboats and square-riggers from ports all over the world. The shoreline in this part of town is made up of red granite from Sweden, blue stone from Italy, broken tile from France, and dredging material from the River Thames and the Scheldes of The Netherlands.

PENSACOLA — HISTORY

An early Marine Corps aviator takes off in a Curtiss AH-3 in 1915.

es. The homes were built as cheaply as possible, since no hurricane or flood insurance existed. To have their home swept away in a storm would be no great loss to the owners.

Through the '50s and '60s, the downtown area stagnated as subdivisions spread northward and malls sprang up to service them.

Local history buffs seemed undaunted by what was happening around them. They persuaded the Chamber of Commerce to put a challenge to Pensacola residents: It's history we've got, and it's history that will bring people here. Let's give them something to come for.

The movement to preserve the city's heritage, though, was a long and arduous process. Residents had yet to see any value in the dilapidated homes in the Seville area and would have just as soon seen them replaced.

One of the first hopeful signs of the preservation effort came in the 1960s, when The Pensacola Historical Society moved into Old Christ Church on Seville Square, transforming it into a history museum. Following that, the Pensacola Heritage Foundation sought to preserve the Seville District, the oldest section of Pensacola, with the help of local businesses and residents. The Historic Pensacola Preservation Board served as a liaison between business and community groups for restoration efforts.

In 1972, the North Hill Preservation District got a listing in the National Register of Historic Places, spurring renovations of grand homes north of downtown. By 1980, a third area downtown, the Palafox Place Historic and Business District,

• 21

PENSACOLA — HISTORY

South Palafox Street in downtown Pensacola was a bustling place in the 1920s. Many of these buildings are still in place.

was created for restoration of commercial establishments.

For the Enjoyment of Future Generations

Santa Rosa Island had become popular for beachgoers and campers, but haphazard development, heavy public use, and a lack of cohesive efforts to preserve and maintain the pristine shoreline stepped up the push for the creation of the Gulf Islands National Seashore in 1972. In Northwest Florida, the move successfully protected much of Santa Rosa Island, including Fort Pickens, portions of the Navy base on the mainland, the Naval Live Oaks Preserve in Gulf Breeze, and Perdido Key to the west.

In the '90s, the downtown sector is again filled with activity. Visitors stroll Palafox Street, North Hill, and the Seville District with self-guided tour books in hand, marveling at the beautifully restored buildings and stories and legends of ghosts, pirates, soldiers and privateers. Picnics in Plaza Ferdinand featuring live entertainment bring downtown workers outside for lunch, and the public turns out for numerous festivals, theatrical performances, concerts and fishing tournaments in record numbers. Those who've chosen Pensacola as their home push hard for change in the schools, change in the government, change in whatever they find that needs fixing, preserving the best of what we already have and making the community the best place it can be for all its citizens.

Sure it's a neon nightmare, but you gotta love it.

It's tacky. It's kitschy. It's out of style and out of date. But the 40-foot-high neon monstrosity near the foot of the bridge crossing onto Pensacola Beach is a slice of Pensacola history, and dear to the hearts of both visitors and locals.

The neon billfish is a Pensacola landmark.

Built by Lamar Advertising's neon shop in the 1950s, the sign was commissioned by The Santa Rosa Island Authority to direct downtown tourists to the beaches. The gigantic billfish originally towered over most downtown buildings atop Escambia Motors at Gregory and Palafox streets (now the Civic Inn parking lot).

Once the Bob Sikes Bridge opened up traffic to the beach from Gulf Breeze, the fish sign was relocated in 1960. "That sign breaks every code in the book," says Lamar representative Bobby Switzer. "You couldn't build a sign like that today." And, after dark, as you make the wide swing to the right, ready to cross the beach bridge, there it is, like a beacon, its orange and yellow neon stripes lighting up "Turn Right — Pensacola Beach" and its fish's skinny proboscis pointing the way. No ... no, you really couldn't build a sign like that today. . . .

Inside The Pensacola Area

Pensacola, Pensacola Beach, Gulf Breeze, Navarre Beach, Perdido Key and Milton

The Pensacola metro area is easily the largest in Northwest Florida, covering 50 miles and two counties from east to west with something like 300,000 year-round residents. Beginning with Perdido Key at the state's western entrance and moving east, it includes Pensacola, Gulf Breeze, Pensacola Beach, and Navarre Beach. Milton is a town about 15 miles north of Pensacola but is of interest because of its proximity to the area's many scenic rivers.

From white-sand beaches and dunes to bayfront mossy oaks to bustling downtowns brimming with history, this geographically diverse portion of Northwest Florida is grouped together around its anchor city, Pensacola. The city of 65,000 is a major transportation hub, and is the largest Florida city for two hundred miles.

"... we say put your money in your pockets and come see us.... To the invalids, we offer our seabreezes and the gushing spring water, to the sportsman, a bay crowded with fish, and a forest crowded with game, to the pleasures of man our billiard rooms, to the athlete our nine pin alleys & to all, the safest blandest air that ever breathed upon the cheek of beauty."
— **Pensacola newspaper promoting tourism, 1850s**

The words may be written differently today, but the message is the same. We are fortunate enough to live in a place that gets better with time; a place where the beaches are so dazzling, the gulf waters so clear, the fish so abundant, the climate so mild, and the people so friendly that we're spreading the word: we'd like to share it.

And share it we have. There is no definitive method for counting the number of tourists visiting the Pensacola area, but we do know that nearly 3½ million cars drove over the Bob Sikes Bridge onto Pensacola Beach in 1992. But we're not Ocean City or Coney Island. You needn't fight for a spot of sand on the beach. Even at the height of the season you can find a secluded spot along the miles of open shoreline.

Pensacola is a really big small town. For the most part, locals are friendly and accommodating and are fiercely proud of the few who have achieved celebrity status. Middleweight boxing champion Roy

Need A Little R & R & R? There's Not A Better Time Or Place.

Located on Santa Rosa Island in Northwest Florida and bordered on either side by the Gulf Islands National Seashore, Pensacola Beach is just the place for rest, relaxation, and recreation. Enjoy water sports, visit forts and museums, dine on fresh seafood, or just relax and enjoy the beauty of our seashore.

Pensacola Beach is a year-round vacation island, so plan to revitalize with us. For information about our island and accomodations, call 1-800-635-4803.

Pensacola Beach
THE REAL FLORIDA

Santa Rosa Island Authority • P.O. Drawer 1208 • Pensacola Beach, FL 32562

Jones, Jr. and Dallas Cowboys running back Emmitt Smith are both nationally known, but still find time to do some community service work or just hang out with friends and family in Pensacola.

But all the scenic beauty and neighborliness aside, Pensacola seems to have more than its share of — well, weirdness. Like a drive-in funeral parlor. A train that travels up the middle of a downtown street with traffic rolling along on either side. A 22-minute church service for people in a hurry. And enough sightings of strange shapes and beams of light in the night sky for 27 Arthur C. Clarke novels.

Over the past few decades, Pensacolians have come to realize

Insiders' Tips

The staff at the Florida Welcome Center on I-10 west of Pensacola keeps track of their visitors in a most unique way: They count the number of used orange juice cups, which totalled nearly 350,000 in 1992.

• 25

Visitor Information

Pensacola Convention & Visitors Information Center
1041 E. Gregory St.
Pensacola   434-1234
(800) 874-1234, in Florida (800) 343-4321

Pensacola Beach Chamber of Commerce/Visitors Information Center
735 Pensacola Beach Blvd.   932-1500
Pensacola Beach   (800) 635-4803

Perdido Key Area Chamber of Commerce
15500 Perdido Key Dr.
Perdido Key   492-4660

Navarre Beach Area Chamber of Commerce
8543 Navarre Pkwy.   939-3267
Navarre   (800) 480-7263

South Santa Rosa Welcome Center
8543 Navarre Pkwy., Navarre 939-2691

Gulf Breeze Area Chamber of Commerce
1170 Gulf Breeze Pkwy.
Gulf Breeze   932-7888

Pensacola Area Chamber of Commerce
117 W. Garden St., Pensacola 438-4081

Santa Rosa County Chamber of Commerce
501 Stewart St., S.W.
Milton   623-2339

that what they have here is unique. Battles of wits and words were waged at the local, state, and national levels to protect huge tracts of our pristine shoreline from development and to keep 18th- and 19th-century homes and commercial buildings from the wrecking ball. All the words and fund-drives and bonds and bake sales couldn't save the old San Carlos Hotel, however. The once glorious downtown landmark, which stood at the corner of Palafox and Garden streets since 1912, was laid to rest by a wrecking crew in 1993.

But there are plenty of success stories, too. In 1990, city workers installing a new sewer line in the oldest part of the city unearthed part of a brick foundation and called the university's archaeological team to investigate. Underneath the streets, homes, and commercial buildings stretching from Plaza Ferdinand to Seville Square (about four blocks) were the remnants of a British fort. After a brief dig for artifacts, the site had to be bricked over until a state grant could be awarded to unearth the site, connecting it to others like it via the Colonial Archaeological Trail.

Divers have known for decades about the wealth of sunken wrecks in Pensacola and Escambia bays. But in 1992, preserved under centuries of silt, a ship was discovered that could change history. At this writing, underwater archaeologists' best guess is that it is Spanish, 16th century, and possibly a galleon; the same type of ship Don Tristan de Luna and 1,400 colonists sailed into the bay in 1559 to establish America's first settlement. Whether its the genuine article or not, the ship's discovery has generated enough support to establish an underwater archaeological park out in the bay.

Pensacola is a little offbeat, sometimes tacky, often surprisingly sophisticated. It's the combination of those things that makes it such an extraordinary place to live.

Pensacola Area Restaurants and Nightlife

We're skipping over the Shoney's, the Red Lobster, the Showbiz Pizza, the Whataburger, the Chuck E. Cheese, the Steak and Ale, etc., etc., etc. You probably have them in your own hometown, as do most cities of any size in America. Therefore, we prefer to concentrate here on those dining establishments that are one-of-a-kind — the best of local cuisine.

Our pricing code is set up to offer you a *general* idea of what a dinner for two will cost, including appetizer, entree, beverage and dessert. What's *not* included are cocktails, 7% sales tax (higher on the beach) and gratuity. As a general rule, dinner at an in-town restaurant will cost less than one on the beach with a view of the water.

One especially nice aspect of dining out in the Pensacola area is that there is literally no place requiring ties or even coats. It's a beach resort area, for heaven's sake, where the only dress code is — be comfortable! Again, take your cues from the write-ups; while bikinis and bare feet may be acceptable at a beach bar, they're definitely taboo for most sit-down restaurants.

Most of the restaurants listed accept major credit cards; exceptions are noted.

Price codes for the Pensacola area are as follows:
Under $20	$
$21 to $40	$$
$41 to $60	$$$
More Than $60	$$$$

Pensacola

STREGA NONA'S BAKERY & CAFE
Tower East, 1010 N. 12th Ave.
Pensacola 433-3055
$$

Yeah, it's kind of a sprout place, but there are enough good-tasting items on the menu for regular people, too. (And, besides, plenty of "regular" folks are looking for healthy meals these days.) Another plus is its location in what used to be Sacred Heart Hospital, a formidable-looking stone structure dating to 1915. Strega Nona's is in the basement, with giant casement windows, lots of plants, and colorful wall murals depicting the story of the witch Strega Nona.

Don't overlook the "Flipper-safe" tuna salad, nachos (meatless with red beans and organic tortilla chips), homemade soups and tantalizing baked goods. Strega's has recently opened for dinner, where nightly specials like cashew ginger stir-fry or bean and rice burritos will cost a buck or so more than luncheon dishes. The meatless pizzas are outstanding, smothered with ingredients like black olives, feta cheese, red onions, mushrooms and spinach. Late nights, Strega's offers a full plate of live entertainment, from acoustic music to story and poetry readings. Open 6 AM until midnight Monday through Friday; 24 hours on the weekends. Reservations for dinner are welcome.

HOPKINS HOUSE
900 N. Spring St., Pensacola   438-3979
$

Located in the lovely old North Hill Preservation District, eating at Hopkins House is a local tradition. More than likely you'll have to wait out on the huge wrapped veranda for a table, but there are lots of porch swings and rockers to make the wait more pleasant.

Once inside, your party will be seated at a table with people you don't know, but they won't remain strangers for long. Hopkins is known for its family-style, "pass-me-the-grits" meals, which consist of black-eyed peas, squash, sweet potato pie, greens, corn bread muffins, roast beef and gravy and some of the best fried chicken you ever put a lip-lock on. It's also a Hopkins tradition that diners take their dishes to the kitchen when they're done!

Menus change daily, and no reservations are taken. No alcohol is served, either. Open 7 to 9 AM for breakfast, 11 to 2 for lunch, and 5 to 7 for dinner. Closed Saturday and Sunday night, and all day Monday. Hopkins takes cash and local checks only.

SKOPELOS ON THE BAY
670 Scenic Hwy., Pensacola   432-6565
$$$$

Skopelos has been here for years, although a move from West Cervantes Street to the current location on Pensacola Bay some years ago has doubled its space and its clientele. This is a favorite "special occasion" place for lots of insiders; the decor is a little eccentric with its mirrors and twinkly lights, but it's first-class dining in every respect. Specializing in both steaks and seafood, Skopelos is also famous for nightly seafood specials and Greek-inspired dishes.

The restaurant is built atop the bluffs overlooking Pensacola Bay, and the view is every bit as nice as at the beach. After lunch or dinner, walk around the nicely landscaped grounds to the edge of the bluffs. As you might expect, the lawn is a perfect setting for outdoor weddings and receptions. Reservations are recommended. Open for dinner Tuesday through Saturday from 5 to 10:30 PM; for lunch on Friday only from 11:30 to 2:30.

NEW WORLD LANDING
600 S. Palafox St., Pensacola   434-7736
$$$

New World Landing made a most successful transformation from 19th-century warehouse to elegant restaurant, inn and meeting hall. Oversized bay windows in the restaurant overlook a flowering courtyard with fountains and brick walkways; inside, peach and white linens and sparkling crystal grace the tables. Other dining and meeting areas reflect Pensacola's rich history through old photographs, enlarged to cover half the wall.

New World restaurant serves gourmet continental cuisine, so your favorite steaks and seafood are there, but also dishes with some new twists. Chicken Escambia is a boneless breast of chicken stuffed with veal and basil, then wrapped in a pastry and baked. Try your steak blackened with Cajun spices or a delicate filet mignon. Pensacola's favorite red snapper can be made your way, or for a meatier white fish, try grouper topped with crab, mushrooms, shrimp and artichoke hearts. Open for lunch Tuesday through Friday from 11 to 2 with a daily buffet from 11:30 until 1:30. Dinner is served Tuesday through Saturday from 5:30 to 9:30.

NORMA'S CAFE
Inside the Pensacola Cultural Center
400 S. Jefferson St., Pensacola   436-2101
$

The historic Court of Records building opened as the Pensacola Cultural Center in 1992, accommodating theater, music, dance and literary groups. Norma's Cafe sits right in the middle of the building, with a three-story open atrium above. Now you can dine in a historic building, eat a great lunch and hobnob with actors, musicians and literary types. Fortunately, Norma's reasonable prices encourage these folks, as well as local business people, to dine there.

Glass-topped tables for two are tiny — there's barely room for the plates — but the food is commendable. Crepes are a specialty, filled with chicken and broccoli, shrimp and mushroom, ham and asparagus, primavera . . . go ahead, go off your diet. They come with a fruit salad, so you can think you're eating healthy. Sandwiches come on croissants, in pita pockets, on French bread, rye, English muffins or poppyseed bread. Doesn't that sound plain irresistible? They do a terrific job on salads of all descriptions, too and, actually, most of the food has at least the perception of being "light." A full menu is served Monday through Friday from 11 AM to 3 PM; a limited menu is offered from 3 PM to 5 PM.

SCOTTO'S RISTORANTE ITALIAN
300 S. Alcaniz St., Pensacola   434-1932
$$

Scotto's is simply the finest Italian restaurant Pensacola has to offer. The atmosphere is quiet and intimate for a business lunch or a romantic evening out for two.

All your favorite Italian dishes are here, such as Chicken Parmesean, lasagna, antipasto and spaghetti. A sampling of appetizers will get you into the mood for more: spaghetti marinara, ravioli, fettucine alfredo, Oysters Florentine. Scotto's makes all its own pasta; combine that with fresh seafood catches and you've got something really special. Stuffed snapper combines the delicate, slightly sweet taste of fresh red snapper with seasoned crabmeat dressing, then adds a side of pasta. Fettucine Scotto sautes crabmeat and shrimp in butter, then covers them with a light cream and Parmesean cheese sauce over homemade fettucine. Try a bottle of wine with your meal in the historic surroundings of Seville Square. Open for lunch from 11 to 2 Monday through Friday; dinner is served Monday through Saturday from 5:30 until 10 PM.

BODENHEIMER'S
304 S. Alcaniz St., Pensacola   434-5588
$$

You'll find this charming spot right on Seville Square next to Scotto's in the heart of the historic district. This German-inspired restaurant takes you to another place and time with its dark polished wood, lace curtains and a wall of cubbyholes under the stairs displaying beers, wines, mugs and other German memorabilia.

The dining room is big enough for only about 10 tables, its centerpiece a pre-20th-century double hearth fireplace, which is kept stoked up during the cooler winter months.

German mugs hang from long pegs overhead, and at Christmas are replaced with hand-dipped candlesticks. German background music does more for overall ambiance than for constant listening, but helps to carry off the Old World feel. Your luncheon menu is posted on a sign and brought to your table, since it tends to change daily. Soups are robust and homemade, sandwiches like sausage and sauerkraut or corned beef are ample. Do try the ginger vinaigrette salad dressing. Dinners range from sauerbraten and wiener schnitzel to fish and pasta specialties. For a tourist area, prices are pretty good — dinners start at $5.00 and run up to $13.00. Open Tuesday through Saturday for lunch from 11 until 2; dinner is from 5 until 9:30 or 10 PM. Bodenheimer's accepts cash and checks only.

JAMIE'S FRENCH RESTAURANT
424 E. Zaragoza St., Pensacola   434-2911
$$$$

Jamie's has been named as one of Florida's Top 100 Restaurants over and over, has won the Golden Spoon Award for excellence in restaurant food and service, and the list of accolades continues to grow. This restaurant is a place all the locals know about and will be quick to recommend. The intimate restaurant is in one of the renovated Seville Historic District homes. Inside, the decor is as tastefully prepared as the food: muted peaches, burgundies and ivories mesh with dark wood antiques and fireplaces in each of the dining rooms.

Seafood selections change daily, but the preparation and presentation make this a memorable meal. Breast of chicken, char-grilled filets, veal medallions, pork tenderloin, French cut lamb chops and Norwegian salmon dishes are expertly pre-

---

Watching the sun sink into the bay at Chris' Seafood Grille is a favorite Insider activity; it's the best seat in the house for the nightly show.

pared with different sauces by chefs Mike Liebeno and owner Gary Serafin. Wines are recommended with each dish. Magnifique! Open for lunch from 11:30 to 2:30 Tuesday through Saturday; for dinner from 6 to 10 PM Monday through Saturday.

SEVILLE QUARTER
130 E. Government St.
Pensacola 434-6211
$$

This dining and entertainment complex was one of the first to open in the wake of the downtown restoration movement. Bob Snow, who also owns Church Street Station in Orlando, has long since sold the place, but its reputation is so well established that it's still *the* place to go for nighttime entertainment in Pensacola. The Palace Oyster Bar has a full menu of appetizers, dinners such as fresh seafood, barbecued shrimp, fried oysters, Chicken Parmesan and New York strip steak in a turn-of-the-century setting. A "Good Eats" menu is available in other parts of the complex as well, which is mainly sandwiches, burgers and appetizers. Of course, *all* the lounges and restaurants serve every drink imaginable. Enjoy the foot-stompin' show at Rosie O'Grady's featuring a Dixieland band and cancan dancers, acoustic music at the End O' the Alley outdoor courtyard, jazz in Apple Annie's, or high-energy dance music in Phineas Phoggs. A $2.00 cover is charged after 8 PM. Membership cards are available. Open 11 AM until 2:30 AM every day.

TRADER JON'S
511 S. Palafox St., Pensacola 433-7113
$

The world-famous bar has been a favorite of naval aviators since the Second World War. Order up a bottled beer and take a tour of the inside—you've never seen so much Navy memorabilia that wasn't in a museum. Photographs of Trader Jon with Blue Angels pilots, astronauts and other rich and famous visitors crowd the walls, while miniature planes, flags and garage sale finds hang from the ceiling. Prince Andrew, Bob Hope and Brooke Shields have all stopped by to pay their respects. It's a local landmark, as is Trader Jon himself with his ball cap and mismatched socks.

Trader's hosts bands of all sorts on the weekends, but leave the kids at home; it can get pretty raunchy at times. Open from 12 PM until 3 AM every day.

THE ALE HOUSE
Harbour Village at Pitt Slip Marina
Pensacola 435-9719
$$

This is a favorite lunchtime spot and after-hours social gathering place for local business people, with its hearty fare served in an atmosphere of fun overlooking the marina. The Ale House serves up homemade soups, sandwiches (these are BIG), steamed veggies and seafood, burgers, steaks, hot dogs, salads and more than a dozen appetizers. There's a children's menu, too.

The Mighty Mudsharks are the house band, playing jazz, blues and popular favorites several nights a week. Open Sunday through

PENSACOLA — RESTAURANTS

Jamie's French Restaurant in Pensacola's Seville Historic District takes top honors for Florida restaurants year after year.

Wednesday 11 AM until 1 AM; Thursday through Saturday 11 AM until 2 AM.

McGuire's Irish Pub and Brewery
Gregory St. (Hwy. 98) Between the Bay Bridge and the Civic Center
Pensacola 433-6789
$$$

One of the biggest tourist draws in the area, McGuire's is a spot everybody eventually gets to, so the crowds are huge, the wait is long and, recently, McGuire's began dispensing beepers to tell you when your table's ready. And what do you get for all that waiting? Huge USDA Certified Prime steaks, fine ales, porters and stouts brewed on the premises, and the best Irish entertainment south of Boston. More than 90,000 dollar bills are signed and stapled to the ceilings, the walls and the bar, with more coming in every day. Lighter fare is available as well, with a full complement of salads, sandwiches and burgers. Open daily for lunch, dinner and well into the wee hours.

Jerry's Drive-In
2815 E. Cervantes St.
Pensacola 433-9910
$

It's old, cheap, greasy and the locals love it. Jerry's has been in Pensacola longer than Baptists have been in the South. You want local color? Jerry's provides every hue imaginable with its roadhouse atmosphere — pennants, posters, old snapshots and framed witticisms cover the walls; the rigid bright orange vinyl booths, droopy ceiling tiles and ragged curtains may have never been updated, at least, not in our lifetime.

But what's important to know about Jerry's is this: cheeseburgers. Huge, thick, juicy and greasy

• 33

enough to soak through twelve napkins, Jerry's cheeseburgers are cholesterol-packed diet-busters. There's not one menu item that would qualify as remotely "light," so don't even ask. The menu is down and dirty — chili dogs, grilled cheese, Dixie Dog on a Stick, barbecue, boiled shrimp, fried chicken gizzards, milk shakes, beer. Try it once; you'll be hooked. The grill starts cranking up for breakfast at 8:30 and doesn't cool down until 11:30 PM every day but Sunday. Bring a little bit of cash — it's all you'll need and all they take.

MARINA OYSTER BARN
505 Bayou Blvd., Pensacola   433-0511
$

Not too far from Jerry's is another local hangout, and by locals we mean people *and* pelicans. The Marina Oyster Barn can be spotted from the Cervantes Street bridge across Bayou Texar (Te-HAR), but to get there, go to the first light (Perry Street), turn left, then veer off to the water. It's easier by boat — just tie up at the dock.

The decor is spare, with all-around windows for that unparalleled view. Seafood dominates the menu selections; get it baked, fried, broiled or gumboed. Fish chowder and chicken dumplings are specialties of the house. If the weather's fine, take your meal out on the deck, where flocks of seagulls and pelicans create a pleasant diversion. Beer and wine are available. Open at 11:00 Tuesday through Saturday, closes at 8:45 Tuesday, Wednesday and Thursday; stays open an hour later on the weekends.

THE YACHT RESTAURANT
Harbor Village at Pitt Slip
Pensacola   432-3707
$$$$

How about dining on a yacht tonight? This 153' grand lady has been converted into a floating restaurant. It doesn't go anywhere, but it doesn't need to with Seville Square, Pensacola Bay and the Pitt Slip Marina providing the scenery.

Impeccable service is the hallmark of the glass-enclosed dining room. Tuxedoed waiters make sure your water (and wine) glasses are constantly filled, and in every way, make you feel like a VIP. Chicken, steaks and seafood are prepared in traditional and gourmet dishes. This author especially remembers a grouper dish stuffed with crabmeat that was quite exceptional. Most seafood is local, but for visitors who long for a taste of home, try the Atlantic Salmon, dusted in Caribbean spices, seared, then placed on a painted plate of raspberry Bordelaise and spiked with Hollandaise sauce or grilled and served in a pool of champagne cream.

After dinner, take in a breathtaking sunset in the Topside Lounge, where bay breezes stir the imagination. Alternate menu items are available from 4:30 until midnight Tuesday through Saturday and from noon to sundown on Sunday. A special Sunday brunch, offering Eggs Florentine, Hunard and Benedict, roast beef, ham, Seafood Newberg and a variety of desserts, soups, salads and side dishes begins at 11:30 and lasts until 2:30. Open from 6 to 10 PM for dinner; closed Monday.

Founaris Bros. Greek Restaurant
1015 N. 9th Ave.
Pensacola   432-0629 or 432-0639
$

This is one of those restaurants you probably wouldn't give a second thought to unless someone told you to go there. So we're telling you to go there! Short on atmosphere, long on good eating, Founaris Bros. makes a mean Greek pizza (feta cheese, Greek olives, peppers, gyro meat — you pick the ingredients) and an even meaner Greek salad. Sure, you'll smell like feta cheese for three days, but it'll be worth it! Ever try Greek lasagna? There's quite an assortment of house specialties. It's a local favorite, been here for years, and in a seasonal resort town, if you can't get the locals to come during the off-season, you won't stay in business. Open Monday through Thursday 11 to 9; Friday and Saturday 11 to 10.

Coffee Cup
520 E. Cervantes St.
Pensacola   432-7060
$

The Coffee Cup serves old-fashioned "fast food" in a 1940s diner. Cooks sling eggs, pancakes, sandwiches, grits and burgers behind the counter while waitresses, many who've been here for 30 years, sing out orders. It's noisy with all that chatter, clanging pots and dishes, and ringing cash register, but it's cheap, good and the coffee is exceptional. Recently, the Coffee Cup's reopened for late-night dining beginning at 10 PM and lasting all night. Open for breakfast and lunch Monday through Sunday 5:30 AM until 1:30 PM. Cash only, please.

Perry's Seafood House and Gazebo Oyster Bar
Corner of Barrancas and Pace Blvd.
Pensacola   434-2995
$$

We like this place more for the location and the old house than the food, but Perry's is one of those places that's been here forever. It's right at the drawbridge on Bayou Chico, so you can walk down and watch the ships passing, or watch work at the drydock in one of the shipyards. A brick walkway leads you around the grounds dotted with huge live oaks; the centerpiece is an old fountain.

The restaurant's interior is filled with old photographs of fishing and Pensacola history. Bring the kids and don't worry if they spill; it's casual and comfortable. More than 40 seafood entrees are made fresh daily. Most of the seafood is fried and comes with french fries and coleslaw. A lounge in the gazebo serves up raw oysters and camaraderie. Hours are 11 to 10 every day but Tuesday; open an hour later on weekends.

Mesquite Charlie's
5901 N. "W" St., Pensacola   434-0498
$$

You almost *have* to love country music if you come to Mesquite Charlie's, since there's live entertainment every night, invariably country. The steaks are hanging-off-the-plate huge; the smallest one is 8 oz. (filet mignon), the largest 32 oz. (porterhouse). Steaks, chicken and

PENSACOLA — RESTAURANTS

The Yacht Restaurant offers fine dining on a 153-foot luxury yacht once owned by Carl Fisher.

ribs are all cooked over an open mesquite grill and seasoned with Charlie's natural spices.

The exterior is built like an old western town, but it's all one huge restaurant inside with high ceilings, balconies and a huge stuffed moose in the corner. There's a little cowpokes menu available and a big bowl of barbecued beans to go with your steak. Make reservations for this popular restaurant. Open Sunday through Thursday 5 until 10 PM; Friday and Saturday until 11 PM.

JERRY'S CAJUN CAFE & MARKET
9th at Creighton in the K&B Shopping Center, Pensacola   484-6962
$$

Although Jerry's has only been open for a short while, the word is spreading of the best Cajun food anywhere in the area. Pensacolians like to travel to New Orleans for good Cajun cooking (which is actually closer to here than Tallahassee!), so imagine their delight at finding the real thing so close to home! Gobble down a plateful of Boudin, red beans & rice, Crawfish Etouffé, or a giant oyster po-boy. Nobody does a Muffuletta like Jerry's — ham, Genoa salami, mortadella and provolone cheese are drenched in the authentic New Orleans' Central Grocery Olive Salad, then slapped on what looks like an overgrown English muffin. A whole one feeds two people easily. Take home a six-pack of Dixie Black Voodoo beer, Zapp's potato chips or one of the many deli items available. Open 11 AM until 8 PM Monday through Thursday; until 9 PM on Friday and Saturday.

PENSACOLA — RESTAURANTS

Gulf Breeze

CHRIS' SEAFOOD GRILLE
47 Gulf Breeze Pkwy.
Gulf Breeze   934-3500
$$

Swing a right turn just as you come over the Pensacola Bay Bridge and you'll be in Chris' parking lot. This wonderful little restaurant used to be called Pier I, and since the name change, it's every bit as nice if not better. Obviously seafood is the prime catch here — shrimp, seafood gumbo, oysters, mullet, crab, amberjack or whatever the catch of the day might be. This might be a good place to experiment with some of the local seafood; the prices are reasonable, so if you don't like it, you won't be out a lot of money. (We put our money on the amberjack every time.) If you enjoy fishing while you're here, Chris' will cook your catch to your liking (just be sure it's dressed).

If you're not a seafood lover (stick around here long enough, you'll turn into one), or if you've had seafood vacation overkill (it can happen), there are also fine steaks, sandwiches, pasta, veggies, even tacos. Pull up to Chris' in your boat and park in one of the slips out back. Open 11 to 8:30 Sunday through Thursday; 11 to 9:30 on weekends.

BAY WINDOW DELI
911 Gulf Breeze Pkwy.
Gulf Breeze   932-0817
$

Just before you make that right turn to the beach at the giant fish sign, look to your right for the big bay window, then stop in for great variety, good prices, and homemade everything. Soups are rich and hearty, sandwiches like chicken and tuna salad, reubens and clubs come with an extra half (to take home?!), and the selection of breads is too good to be true, from pumpernickel to rye to pita pockets to English muffins to croissants. Order a sampler plate and try a little taste of everything including one of the excruciatingly sinful desserts!

The interior of the Bay Window Deli is somewhat spare with wooden tables and chairs and baskets hanging overhead. Fresh flowers grace every table, and shelves along one wall are lined with gourmet groceries and coffees. If you can find room, the Bay Window serves Ben & Jerry's ice cream treats.

Save one Thursday for "Latin Nights" at the Bay Window. Owner Connie Simmons whips up a Caribbean feast beginning with an entree of chicken marinated in tropical fruit juices and herbs and served over rice, fried plantains with black bean dip, and guava cheese cake. The whole thing is just ten bucks and that includes tax. The Bay Window Deli is open for breakfast at 7 AM and stays open until 11 PM every day.

Pensacola Beach

BOY ON A DOLPHIN
400 Pensacola Beach Blvd.
Pensacola Beach   932-7949
$$$

Greek legend or not, this is a strange name for a restaurant. The Greek-inspired steaks, seafood and pasta dishes are superb, though, so

• 37

PENSACOLA — RESTAURANTS

hopefully visitors don't dismiss it out of hand. Boy On A Dolphin is a classy place right on the water — cloth napkins, peach and ivory decor, a little gazebo in the restaurant's center and huge windows to catch the view. Fish dishes depend on what's been caught that day, but the traditional Greek preparation comes highly recommended. Chef's recommendations are starred (*) on the menu; if you can't decide, try one of the house specialties. Hours are 4 to 11 PM Monday through Saturday; Sunday from 11 to 11.

SANDSHAKER LOUNGE, PACKAGE STORE & SANDWICH SHOP
731 Pensacola Beach Blvd.
Pensacola Beach   932-2211 (Lounge)
*   932-0023 (Sandwich Shop)*
$

Serving up really tasty sandwiches with equally tasty prices, the Sandshaker Sandwich Shop is a nice complement to the Sandshaker Lounge, which has been in place at the corner of Pensacola Beach Boulevard and Fort Pickens Road for nearly two decades. Clubs, open-face, subs and many other varieties of sandwiches are offered for just $3.75 (you get a pickle with that). For the same price, pick one of the daily specials (a full meal except for beverage) such as chicken spaghetti, meat loaf or a taco salad for $3.75.

Next door, the tiny Sandshaker Lounge is a beach landmark, made famous by the creation of Pensacola's own local concoction, the Bushwacker, which tastes something like a milkshake (an *adult* milkshake, that is, since the alcohol content in two of these could put you in a haze for days). The place is barely big enough to stand up and turn around in, but worth a stop for this sinfully sweet and frothy treat. The sandwich shop is open daily at 11:00, and closes at 9:00 PM Monday through Wednesday, 10:00 PM the remainder of the week.

For Insiders only, the "secret" recipe, courtesy of the Sandshaker Lounge.

Bushwacker
1 part Kahlua or coffee liqueur
1 part white Creme de Cocoa
½ part Cream of Coconut
2 parts whole milk
1 part rum
blend with ice

JUBILEE TOPSIDE
Quietwater Beach Boardwalk
Pensacola Beach   934-3108
$$$$

From an Insiders' perspective, Jubilee Topside is one of the finest restaurants anywhere in the area, period. Bring your charge card, though; since it's the beach, you'll pay tourist prices. But oh, what a meal! Start with crab claws delicately sauteed in garlic butter, Oysters Rockefeller or soft-shell crab and pasta topped with honey-roasted nuts swimming in a garlic beurre blanc and sauce Bearnaise.

A special treat at Jubilee is the bread and butter service, where a "baker's helper" comes around to your table two, three, maybe four times to deliver fresh-baked rolls and an array of butters — whipped, garlic and one specialty (chocolate butter... sounds strange, but ooooohhh, it's melt-in-your-mouth good!).

Ready for the entree? It's Florida cuisine, through and through, with some Cajun twists. Blackened grouper is served over seasoned rice, topped with sauteed mushrooms, then finished with a red wine sauce and lemon beurre blanc. Grouper Chardonnay is pan-sauteed with vegetables in a light lobster cream sauce, then finished with Parmesean cheese and broiled to a golden brown. Land-

The "Art" of Beachside Dining

Sheilagh Foster, owner of Foster's Fine Art Studio in Pensacola, tranformed Jubilee Beachside on Pensacola Beach into a Caribbean retreat for diners.

At Jubilee Beachside, the comfortably bright, Caribbean atmosphere is the work of local interior artist Sheilagh Foster. Owner June Guerra chose three unusual fabrics to cover the bar stools and chairs; Foster recreated the patterns, hand-painting the designs on different parts of the walls. Portions of the multicolored lower wall are covered in a staggered yellow "integrated plaster" texture to give a feeling of age.

Small exotic and primitive characters are painstakingly drawn, and then painted, on each of the mahogany dining tables. And to pull the colors, the patterns and the figures together, Foster created a giant polystyrene pink hibiscus, five feet across, which is suspended from the ceiling.

Asked why she chose to commission an artist instead of employing an interior designer, Guerra says she wanted something really unusual to bring people in, something that no one else was doing, something that was custommade specifically for *this* restaurant in *this* location. After viewing Foster's

> impressive portfolio of interior work, Guerra hired her on the spot. Right outside the windows on a 30-foot-high wall, Foster is set to paint a giant mural. Through research and visual interpretation, a Caribbean street market scene will begin to unfold, blending nicely with the tropical plants and beach backdrop for outdoor Beachside Cafe diners. The "outdoor gallery" should be in progress throughout the summer of 1994.

lubbers might go for hand-cut Angus Filets Roland, sauteed with artichokes, lump crabmeat and white wine, topped with sauce bearnaise, or Steak "Dano," a filet mignon wood-grilled over an open flame, served over fresh angel hair pasta, finished with blackened shrimp and scallops with a light beurre blanc and sauce Bearnaise.

The decor is elegant with big, comfortable chairs, stained glass, an open-beam ceiling and dining on two levels. The view — and the service — are outstanding. This successful restaurant is poised to expand, both upstairs and downstairs. In the works is a $1.3 million two-story, open-air deck, increasing seating capacity and banquet facilities, and expanding both kitchens. Construction begins in August 1994, and should be completed by December.

Open for dinner at 6:00 PM Sunday through Thursday, 5:00 PM on weekends. Sunday brunch is served from 9:00 AM until 3.

JUBILEE BEACHSIDE
Quietwater Beach Boardwalk
Pensacola Beach   934-3108
$$$

Downstairs at Jubilee, you'll find the atmosphere a little "beachier" and the prices a bit easier to handle. Hand-painted walls and tables offer diners something to contemplate while they eat (see sidebar). Some menu items ditto the ones upstairs and are every bit as scrumptious. Salads, sandwiches, burgers and deli selections are good anytime. For dinner, try shrimp scampi, blackened amberjack, or chicken and broccoli fettucini. A kid's menu is available. Open daily at 11:00; closing is seasonal. You'll enjoy the live entertainment Wednesday through Sunday and the great view everyday.

FLOUNDER'S CHOWDER & ALE HOUSE
At the traffic light on
Pensacola Beach   932-2003
$$$

Don't you love it when a business is good enough to poke fun at itself? Flounder's has fun with everything from the menu to the decor to the food. "Eat, drink, and Flounder" is the motto, and several other "famous" quotes appear in the menu, slightly askew, such as "Better to have Floundered and Lost, Than Never to Have Floundered at All" — Alfred, Lord Flounder.

The folks who've done such an outstanding job with McGuire's run

PENSACOLA — RESTAURANTS

"Feasting, Imbibery and Debauchery" — only at McGuire's Irish Pub, a local landmark.

this place too, so the same fresh seafood, prime steaks and quality service apply.

Florida seafood is presented almost three dozen ways; steaks start at 10 oz. if you're not hungry and grow to 16 oz. if you are! Chowders, salads, light pasta dishes, poultry, burgers and sandwiches offer everybody something they like, including Julius Flounder, who says: "I Came, I Saw, I Floundered." Open 11 to 11 weekdays; 'til 12:30 on weekends. There's live entertainment Fridays and Saturdays.

> **Insiders' Tips**
>
> Visit the Flora-Bama Lounge at the Alabama state line on Perdido Key for its pure "honky-tonk" atmosphere and some of the best music on the Gulf Coast. The Flora-Bama has hasted regional and nationally-known performers playing about every musical style imaginable on multiple states. Try to overlook the funkiness of the place, order up a long neck, and kick back with a mixed crowd of bare feet, bikinis, biker gear and cowboy hats.

• 41

PENSACOLA — ACCOMMODATIONS

The 1912 Louisville & Nashville Train Depot now serves as the lobby for the Pensacola Grand Hotel.

Photo: Robin Rowan

Pensacola Area
Accommodations

Step out your back door onto Gulf of Mexico beaches . . . peer down from your window onto manicured gardens . . . spread out in a rental vacation house that sleeps 16 . . . snuggle into a sleeping bag surrounded by nothing but stars and tall pines . . . or enjoy sweeping panoramas from a ninth-floor beachfront balcony. Condos, high-rise hotels and private villas on the beach offer many modern conveniences, while in-town bed and breakfasts and historic hotels slow the pace a bit, reminiscent of a time when tradition and family took center stage. If it's a "back to nature" vacation you want, commune with wildlife and rough it under the stars in a serene wooded campground.

If you've spent vacations at Disney World or anywhere in South Florida, you'll be thrilled to find that even at the peak of the season, Pensacola area rates are surprisingly low. A five-bedroom house with full kitchen, living room and three baths across the street from the gulf rents for as little as $800 a week! Similar deals can be found through area rental agencies.

Hotels and Motels

If you've absolutely, positively *got* to have the surf coming in your door, then the beaches are the place and that's that. But for the rest of you, check into downtown, north or near-the-airport properties. You could be paying less and getting more and still end up with a nice view.

We're providing a general pricing guide to help you plan what accommodation best fits your needs. Price structure is based on double occupancy for one night and does not include tax, which can add up to 12.2 percent to the final bill.

Have a great night's rest!

$60 or less	$
$61-85	$$
$86-99	$$$
$100 or more	$$$$

Perdido Key

COMFORT INN
13585 Perdido Key Dr.
Perdido Key   492-2755, (800) 554-8879
$

New, inexpensive, right on the key, near the beach, and no extra charge for up to four people in a room, the Comfort Inn caters to families who need room, but who also have to watch what they spend. There's an outdoor pool and a children's playground. All guests may use the indoor Jacuzzi, the out-

PENSACOLA — ACCOMMODATIONS

door grills, and take advantage of a daily continental breakfast, which comes with the price of the room. All rooms feature queen beds, and close by are some good restaurants. Ask about the "Just Off Base" military special if you qualify.

Pensacola

EXECUTIVE INN
6954 Pensacola Blvd. (Hwy. 29)
Pensacola   478-4015
$$

A favorite overnight spot for corporate travelers, the Executive Inn has 36 spacious units, some with microwaves and refrigerators; all have cable TV with HBO and remote control. Take a refreshing swim in the pool and enjoy complimentary coffee in the morning. Double rooms have two full-size or one king bed and sitting areas. Nonsmoking and handicapped accessible rooms are available.

HOLIDAY INN UNIVERSITY MALL
7220 Plantation Rd.
Pensacola   474-0100
$$ (800) HOLIDAY

A truly outstanding Holiday Inn in north Pensacola features Coconuts Comedy Club, Coconut Bay Lounge and Bon Appetit Cafe & Bakery in addition to airport shuttles, in-room movies, complimentary coffee and a newspaper with your wake-up call. Believe it or not, this Holiday Inn allows small pets in the room with you — but no pets in the pool. Sorry. Nonsmoking and handicapped accessible rooms are available. The property is right across the street from University Mall.

HOSPITALITY INN
6900 Pensacola Blvd. (Hwy. 29)
Pensacola   477-2333
$$$ (800) 321-0052

The Hospitality Inn is a full-service hotel convenient to the airport with a spacious multistory lobby. Mini-suite kitchens have private patios. Guests may take advantage of the pool, a complimentary breakfast buffet, an exercise room, laundry, barbecue grills and handicapped facilities.

NEW WORLD LANDING
600 S. Palafox St.
Pensacola   432-4111
$$

Surprisingly affordable rooms offer lots of little extras at this motel in the heart of the downtown historic district. All 16 rooms are decorated in antique reproductions and overlook a landscaped courtyard with fountains or Palafox Street to the bay. Complimentary continental breakfast comes with your room. A full-service restaurant provides views of the lovely courtyard.

THE PENSACOLA GRAND HOTEL
200 E. Gregory St.
Pensacola   433-3336
$$-$$$$ (800) 348-3336

Formerly the Pensacola Hilton, this 15-story beauty is directly across the street from the Pensacola Civic Center, so naturally, many performers stay here while in town. The lobby is the old Louisville & Nashville train depot (1912), remarkably restored into shops, restaurants and convention space. Gorgeous antiques and period fixtures grace the lobby, lounges and restaurants. A glass atrium connects the depot to the main hotel. Room rates go up incrementally — the higher the floor, the higher the rate — but remain the same year round.

RAMADA BAYVIEW
7601 Scenic Hwy.
Pensacola 477-7155
$$ *(800) 282-1212*

This gorgeous new facility has 150 rooms overlooking Escambia Bay in north Pensacola. In-room whirlpools are a favorite. All guests can enjoy the outdoor pool and a complimentary newspaper in the morning. The restaurant features live entertainment, a seafood buffet on Fridays and a jazz brunch on Sundays.

Pensacola Beach

BEACHSIDE RESORT & CONFERENCE CENTER
14 Via de Luna Dr.
Pensacola Beach 932-5331
$$$$ *(800) BEACH-16*

Formerly the Sunset Lodge, which was formerly the Howard Johnson's (things change so fast in a resort area!), this newly expanded and renovated resort sits right on the gulf and right in the hub of beach activity. Owned now by the Innisfree Hotels, the 116 rooms are getting a facelift with casual, contemporary furnishings and bright colors. Gulf-front suites provide kitchenettes; handicapped rooms are also available. On site are a large pool, a children's pool, a beach volleyball net, a cookout area, a restaurant and meeting rooms for up to 700.

CLARION SUITES RESORT & CONVENTION CENTER
20 Via de Luna Dr.
Pensacola Beach 932-4300
$$$$ *(800) 874-5303*

The Clarion all-suite resort looks more like a village of beach cottages than a hotel. The 86 luxury one-bedroom suites have living and dining areas, a master bedroom, a kitchenette with refrigerator, microwave, toaster oven and coffee maker, two TVs and complimentary continental breakfast. Families and couples will especially like the extras: a swimming pool, beach pavilion, children's play area, fitness room and a location right on the gulf.

THE DUNES
333 Fort Pickens Rd.
Pensacola Beach 932-3536
$$$$ *(800) 83-DUNES*

The priciest luxury hotel on the beach, The Dunes hosted Michael Jackson for a month while he was in town rehearsing for his "Dangerous" tour. Rooms are decked in beach peach and seafoam green with tropical wallpaper, bedspreads and

---

Insiders' Tips

Never take the first price offered to you by hotels. It's always the highest. Ask again if the hotel has any other rates — family rates, business rates, seniors rates, weekend rates, military rates — you're bound to fit into one of those categories, and the savings can be as much as 50 percent!

PENSACOLA — ACCOMMODATIONS

pictures. Double rooms offer a king-size or two queen beds; prices jump $10 on weekends. Penthouse suites are available with two rooms, a full kitchen (no stove), a four-person Jacuzzi, and either a rooftop terrace or double balcony overlooking the gulf. Penthouse suites start at $215 a night.

HOLIDAY INN PENSACOLA BEACH
165 Fort Pickens Rd.
Pensacola Beach   932-5361
$$$-$$$$ (800) HOLIDAY

This Holiday Inn was the first high-rise hotel on Pensacola Beach and has been here for years. Renovations have come at regular intervals, so expect your room to be as nice as new. Rooms look either east or west along the beach ($90.00) or overlook the gulf ($100.00); first-floor rooms are $10.00 extra. All have private balconies. A pool, tennis courts, gift shop, game room and the Casino Restaurant are right on the property, and the ninth-floor Penthouse Lounge offers spectacular views from every side.

Navarre Beach

HOLIDAY INN NAVARRE BEACH
8375 Gulf Blvd.
Navarre Beach   939-2321
$$-$$$$

Walk out your back door and onto the sugar-white sands of the gulf — that's how close you'll be in a gulf-front room. This older Holiday Inn has been revamped and is looking great. The Holidome pool is the center of activity; game rooms, guest rooms and snack bars surround it. An open staircase leads to the second floor reception area with floor-to-ceiling windows overlooking the emerald waters of the gulf on one side and the cool blue of the pool on the other. The three-story-high ceiling over the pool creates something of an echo chamber, but it isn't bothersome. Room rates remain fairly inexpensive here since Navarre Beach is a little out of the way. Most rooms offer two double beds, but you can get king-size beds for a little extra. A lounge and a restaurant on the property take care of most of your needs; the Sunday brunch is one of the best in the area.

Bed and Breakfast Inns

NORTH HILL HIDEAWAY
903 N. Barcelona St.
Pensacola   438-4806
$$

If you're looking for an unusual place to stay, this historic third-floor guest room in a 1904 Victorian charmer offers 1,000 square feet of living space in the North Hill Preservation District. Besides the huge peaked ceilings, guests have a queen-size bed, a seating area with an entertainment center and wet bar, a separate reading nook and a hammock! One or two meals per day can be included, if you wish, and are served just a block away at Hopkins Boarding House (see chapter on Pensacola Restaurants). For business travelers, the North Hill Hideaway provides a private telephone, fax machine, answering machine and secretarial services. Rates are just $70 a night with two meals provided, and children are welcome.

Condos/Townhomes/ Vacation Cottages

Condominiums are, for the most part, individually owned, meaning that each will be furnished differently. Ask about specific properties when you call. Prices reflect the weekly cost of a two-bedroom/two-bath condo or house during the peak summer season. Most rental agencies want a deposit up front which can be up to a third of the week's rental. The rest is due upon check-in. Prices do not include tax.

$500 or under	$
$501-750	$$
$751-999	$$$
Over $1000	$$$$

PENSACOLA BEACH PROPERTIES, INC.
1200 Fort Pickens Rd.
Pensacola Beach 932-9341
$$ (800) 826-0614

PBP manages the rentals for the 15-story Tristan Towers condominiums on Santa Rosa Sound. Every room has either a view of the sound or the Gulf of Mexico, which is right across the street (the island is only half a mile wide). Besides 24-hour security, guests have access to the Olympic-size swimming pool, lighted tennis courts, a clubhouse, gazebo and a boardwalk to the beach (sound side). Be sure to ask for a corner condo, which is the same price as a regular condo, but has a wraparound balcony for panoramic views. Condos rent weekly only from mid-June to mid-August.

PENSACOLA BEACH REALTY, INC.
Pensacola Beach Blvd.
Pensacola Beach 932-5337
$$-$$$ (800) 874-9243

More than 150 condominiums, townhomes, and private homes are offered by Pensacola Beach Realty. Portside Villas (two-story townhomes with first-story parking), Gulf Winds (gulfside condos, four stories), and Sans Souci (high-rise condos, gulfside) are a few examples on Pensacola Beach. Prices can vary by up to $200 for a two-bedroom/two-bath unit depending on location, size of the units and amenities.

NAVARRE AGENCY, INC.
8512 Navarre Pkwy. (Hwy. 98 near the bridge)
Navarre 939-2366
$$-$$$ (800) 821-8790

All townhomes and condos are gulfside on Navarre Beach, some have pools, most have two cable TVs. Navarre Villas and San Dollar are townhomes; Emerald Surf is a mid-rise with a pool, and Sun Dunes is a high-rise. Half of the weekly rental is due within 10 days of the reservation.

Insiders' Tips

One short scene in *Jaws II* was filmed on the white shores of Navarre Beach.

PENSACOLA — ACCOMMODATIONS

PROFESSIONAL REALTY OF PENSACOLA BEACH
Quietwater Beach Boardwalk
Pensacola Beach 934-4333
$$$ (800) 239-4334
The Palm Beach Club condos are the newest on the beach with views of both the sound and the gulf. Master bedrooms and living rooms have separate private balconies overlooking the beaches, a two-person Jacuzzi in the master bath, 24-foot cathedral ceilings, fireplaces, wet bars and security. Share a pool and a 16-person hot tub with 15 of your closest friends.

EDEN CONDOMINIUM
16281 Perdido Key Dr.
Perdido Key 492-3336
$$$$ (800) 523-8141
This unusual stepped condominium on Perdido Key is the epitome of a luxury vacation resort. Huge units feature private gulf-front balconies, full kitchen, washer and dryer, whirlpool tub and wet bar. West wing units are slightly larger (and consequently more expensive) than their eastern counterparts. You could say Eden has pools, but that's like saying the Taj Mahal is a house. The 176' pool overlooking the gulf is surrounded by lush tropical foliage, fake rocks and waterfalls, and is all lit up for late-night dips. The outdoor landscape pools are filled with Japanese Koi fish. Indoors is a heated solarium pool and more tropical gardens. Add to that a fitness center, two lighted tennis courts and a private 24-slip boat dock, and you might never want to go anywhere else.

SOUNDSIDE HOLIDAY BEACH RESORT
19 Via de Luna Dr.
Pensacola Beach 433-5701
$$$ (800) 445-9931
You're right in the center of the beach action in one of these 28 waterfront condos on Santa Rosa Sound. All are two-bedroom/two-bath with kitchens, towels, linens, fireplaces, Jacuzzis and washer/dryer. An outdoor hot tub, pool and tennis courts make this a great family retreat.

PERDIDO SUN CONDOMINIUMS
13753 Perdido Key Dr.
Perdido Key 492-2390
$$$$ (800) 227-2390
Treat yourself to luxury living on the white sands of Perdido Key with views of the gulf or the Intracoastal Waterway all around. Perdido Key is a less frenzied atmosphere, more suitable for enjoying the natural amenities the area has to offer. Manmade amenities at the Sun include a 24-hour front desk, heated indoor pool and outdoor pool, hot tub, sauna and fitness room. Big Lagoon State Park and Johnson Beach, part of the Gulf Islands National Seashore, are nearby.

Campgrounds and RV Parks

ADVENTURES UNLIMITED
Tomahawk Landing
Milton 623-6197
The place that made Northwest Florida's inland rivers famous goes one better with overnight accommodations at Tomahawk Landing, also known as canoe trip central. Spa-

cious wooded campsites on the water with a full hookup are just $15.00. Rustic treehouse-style cabins on either Coldwater or Wolfe Creek have screened-in porches and porch swings outside, and nothing more than a bed and a lantern inside. A campfire ring, picnic tables and grills are centrally located, with the restroom and bathhouse nearby. These are just $29 a night for two people. Slightly larger and with more amenities are the rustic camping cabins in Pine Forest. These have porches, too, but inside offer relief from summer's heat with ceiling fans and air conditioning for $39 a night. One-bedroom cabins with room for four are $59 per night, and a one-bedroom cottage (sleeps four) with a fireplace and fully equipped kitchen is $65. Granny Peaden's cabin is a relic, now completely restored to sleep four with two bedrooms, bath, kitchen and air conditioning.

NAVARRE BEACH FAMILY CAMPGROUND
9201 Navarre Pkwy. (Hwy. 98)
Navarre   939-2188

This older park has ninety-nine shady and grassy sites on Santa Rosa Sound; many of those are taken up by year-round residents. The sound side offers shallow, safe swimming for young children, and the woodsy backdrop is terrific for a break from the sun. Sites have full hookups (including cable TV!) and pull-throughs. A pool, pier, boat ramp, playground, four bathhouses, a laundry and a store are right on the grounds. Overnight fees are $16 to $18 depending on the view. Weekly rates are $96 for six days, with the seventh day free.

Pensacola Area Shopping

Two large malls, 70-plus strip shopping centers, tiny boutiques, art galleries, surf shops, antique stores, flea markets and one-of-a-kind shops in renovated historic homes highlight offerings in the Pensacola area. Spend some time downtown and on the beaches to find antiques, handmade and specialty items unique to this area.

UNIVERSITY MALL
Davis Hwy. at I-10
Pensacola 478-3600

More than 70 stores feature Sears, JC Penney and McRae's department stores, plus six theaters and the new Foodworks food court. Open Monday through Saturday 10 to 9; Sunday 12:30 to 5:30.

CORDOVA MALL
Ninth Ave. at Bayou Blvd.
Pensacola 477-5355

Over 140 specialty shops make Cordova one of the Southeast's largest, with anchors Gayfers, Dillard's, Montgomery Ward and Parisian. Four inside theaters, a food court, puppet shows and entertainment year round make this a fun place to shop. Open Monday through Saturday 10 to 9; Sunday 12:30 to 5.

RIVIERA CENTRE FACTORY STORES
Hwy. 59 S. (205) 943-8888
Foley, Alabama (800) 5-CENTRE

Let's hit those cheaper than retail outlets! This is one of our favorites, with over 80 factory-direct outlet stores about an hour's drive from Pensacola and a short trip if you're staying on Perdido Key. Savings up to 75% off retail make it possible to buy twice as much as you came there for. Make a day of it! It's just 10 minutes north of Gulf Shores and Orange Beach, Alabama. Open Monday through Saturday 9 to 9; Sunday 10 to 6.

TOWN & COUNTRY PLAZA
3300 N. Pace Blvd.
Pensacola 432-7766

Pensacola's original shopping center has covered walkways connecting its 27 stores. Gayfers is the main department store, but there are banks, a frame shop, a post office, a fabric shop, a computer store, jewelry stores and several others at the intersection of Pace Boulevard and Fairfield Drive. Most stores open 10 to 9; some close at 6 PM.

ALVIN'S ISLAND TROPICAL DEPARTMENT STORE
400 Quietwater Beach Rd. at Quietwater Beach Boardwalk
Pensacola Beach 934-3711

Two stories of everything for the

PENSACOLA — SHOPPING

beach are featured at Alvin's, including beachwear, swimwear, sportswear, gifts, souvenirs and airbrush art. Open Memorial Day to Labor Day 9 AM to 11 PM; off-season hours are 9 AM to 6 PM.

J.W. Renfroe Pecan Company
2400 W. Fairfield Dr.
Pensacola   438-9405, (800) 874-1929

The Renfroe family has been around for many years selling nuts and gifts for all occasions. Jake Renfroe oversees the operation himself, allowing only top-quality pecans into his shelling factory. Pecans come shelled and unshelled. The gift shop also tempts buyers with cashews, almonds, walnuts, pistachios, peanuts, natural food mixes, pecan candy and homemade fudge. The Renfroe Pecan Shelling Plant is just a block north of the retail shop, where pecans are shelled, roasted and salted daily. Mail orders are welcome. Open Monday through Saturday 8 to 5.

Artesana Inc.
242 W. Garden St.
Pensacola   433-4001

A stunning collection of basketry, hand-painted china, specialty books and cookbooks, exotic wrapping paper, children's toys, herbs and spices, candles, housewares, linens and many gift items is found at Artesana. At certain times during the year, Artesana offers shoppers glasses of iced tea or mulled cider; there's always a delicious aroma hanging in the air. Open Monday through Saturday 10 to 5:30.

Page & Palette
106 S. Palafox St.
Pensacola   432-6656

More than 60,000 titles grace the floor-to-ceiling shelves of this downtown bookstore. And that's just the front room. The middle room is filled with wonderful cards, stationery, and gift wrap for all occasions, and in the back find artist's supplies — canvas, palettes, brushes, paints and accessories. Book signings are held here regularly for local and regional authors. Open 9:30 to 5:30 Monday through Friday; 9:30 to 5 on Saturday.

My Bookstore
112 S. Palafox Place
Pensacola   436-2096

Debbie Hagler and her staff will assist you in selecting books for "tots to teens." Just two doors down from Page & Palette, My Bookstore specializes in selling books that are not usually available in the chain bookstores. Special orders are welcome. Open Monday through Friday 9:30 to 5:30; Saturday 9:30 to 4.

Bayou Country Store
Corner of 9th Ave. and E. Jackson St.
Pensacola   432-5697

Although the Bayou Country Store sells antiques such as rockers and benches and tables, it's also a wonderful place for finding old kitchenware like washboards, sifters, rolling pins and mixing bowls. Located in the "West East Hill" neighborhood, the store features handmade items and lots of folk art. Christmas time is an especially good time to shop, when hand-carved ornaments, wreaths, and mantle

• 51

PENSACOLA — SHOPPING

decorations are offered for sale. Open 10 to 5 every day but Sunday.

CLELAND ANTIQUES
412 E. Zaragoza St.
Pensacola   432-9933

Cleland's is an established and reputable antiques dealer located in a renovated home in the Seville Square Historic District. The shop specializes in 18th-century antiques, both formal and primitive. Most furniture and furnishings are restored. Look upstairs for everything from four-posters to spinning wheels. Cook Cleland was a Thompson Trophy winner in the 1930s; the plane he flew is on display at the National Museum of Naval Aviation. Open Monday through Saturday 10 to 4.

STORYBOOK GALLERY
505 S. Adams St.
Pensacola   438-0075

In the heart of the Seville Historic District is this little find, featuring children's books, original art works, prints and many other "treasures," big and small. Be sure to see the unusual works by Michael Parkes, who taught at Pensacola Junior College from 1968 to 1972, and the whimsical original watercolors and pig art, titled "Out of My Mind," by owner/artist Dick Winkowski. Find the Storybook Gallery in the string of shops just across the street from Old Christ Church on Seville Square. It's open some time around 10 AM, surely by 10:30, and stays open until some time around 5 PM every day but Sunday.

JOE PATTI'S SEAFOOD CO.
South of Main St. on "A" St.
Pensacola   434-3193

A wonderful local experience for visitors, Joe Patti's is an institution in Pensacola. Where "A" Street deadends, a gazebo and lively recorded music welcome you to one of the area's most popular seafood markets. When you step inside, you'll most likely be overwhelmed by the smell of fish, but not to worry; after a few minutes you'll hardly notice it. Laid out before you is a breathtaking array of fresh seafood — about six different sizes of shrimp, oysters, live crawfish, flounder, red snapper, triggerfish, amberjack, mullet, even shark! Buy them whole or filleted. The fishing fleet backs right up to Joe Patti's docks, where pelicans and seagulls abound. It's a commercial fishing area, so you won't see many pleasure craft here; these are hard-working fleets that look like they've been around a few years.

"T" STREET, PENSACOLA

"T" Street, off Fairfield Drive on Pensacola's west side, is an antique and bargain-hunter's dream. Start

---

Insiders' Tips

Visit the seafood markets along the Pensacola waterfront, where the fishing fleets dock at the markets' back doors. You won't find fresher fish anywhere!

52 •

at one end and stop anywhere along the way for everything from old hubcaps to beautifully restored antiques. There are plenty of junk shops here, but a keen eye can spot a diamond in the rough. Searching through the cluttered shelves might reveal a porcelain doll, an old railroad lantern or a vintage hand-cranked Victrola.

ALLAN DAVIS SEASHELLS & SOUVENIRS
E. Hwy. 98
Gulf Breeze 932-2151
Here's a little Gulf Coast history, right in the middle of Gulf Breeze. The locals pass by this place every day and never give it a second thought, but it's become a local landmark. For the area's many visitors, Allan Davis is like a sideshow of beach mania: carved shell nightlights, little figurines made of shells, T-shirts, jewelry boxes with shell motifs, inexpensive kid's toys and thousands, maybe millions, of seashells of every description offered for sale. But Allan Davis isn't like most other souvenir shops, first, because it opened here in 1950 and became more of an attraction than a place to shop, and second, because it has a fantastic collection of shells on display. These shells are definitely *not* for sale; the shells under glass throughout the store represent a lifetime of collecting from all over the world. That alone makes the shop more like a museum, but wait — there's more. Lining some of the shop's walls are specimens of the deep floating in formaldehyde — tiny squids, octopi, sea robins and creatures that were captured so long ago the name on the jar has worn off. Allan Davis is open every single day from 8 AM until 6:30 PM; Sundays 9 to 6:30. Go take a look.

THE FLEA MARKET
5760 Gulf Breeze Pkwy.
Gulf Breeze 934-1971
This brand new flea market across from The ZOO is one of the largest in the area with more than 400 exhibit spaces. Scout for bargains on clothing, plants, jewelry, artwork, antiques and garage sale finds in the gigantic outdoor marketplace. Open weekends from 9 to 5.

THE NEW AGE SHOP
#19 Harbourtown Shopping Village
Gulf Breeze 932-1779
Crystals, new age CDs, self-improvement books, herbs and incense might all be expected from a shop like this, but The New Age Shop has some of the most unique greeting cards and gifts of any place we've seen. Not everything in the store is necessarily "New Age," whatever that means. The staff is really friendly and encourages browsing; some of the jewelry sold here is truly one-of-a-kind. Open 10 to 7 Monday through Friday; 10 to 6 Saturdays; 11 to 6 Sundays.

FARLEY'S OLD AND RARE BOOKS
5855 Tippin Ave.
Pensacola 477-8282
Looking for a first edition of *Gone With The Wind*? How about an original copy of a Hemingway classic? Owen and Moonean Farley will gladly assist you in finding a special book, which can include a computer search of all editions currently available. Farley's is great fun for brows-

PENSACOLA — SHOPPING

ing, with a collection of vintage magazines, newspapers, postcards, even original copies of Dr. Seuss! Book cleaning, repair and restoration are available. Open Monday through Saturday 10 to 5.

LADS & LASSIES CONSIGNMENT
1339 E. Creighton Rd.
Pensacola 477-8748
We've always thought it was a little crazy to spend a lot of money on our children's clothing when they're just going to grow out of it in a month or two. So, this shop is a great place for finding incredible prices on pre-owned clothing for infants through adult women. Used toys, books, shoes and accessories are also offered for sale. Open 10 to 5 Monday through Saturday.

QUAYSIDE MARKET
712 S. Palafox St.
Pensacola 433-9930
Books, antiques, handmade linens and clothing, jewelry, candies, gourmet coffees and more are offered at this one-of-a-kind indoor marketplace in historic downtown Pensacola. Open Wednesday through Saturday 10 to 5; Sundays 12 to 4.

Pensacola Area Attractions

Beaches, beaches, beaches. State beaches, national seashore beaches, nude beaches, gulf beaches, gay beaches, sound beaches, bay beaches, crowded beaches, secluded beaches. They're the number one attraction throughout Northwest Florida, and almost always the reason given by first-time visitors for why they come.

But next to those, most of the best sightseeing and family fun is on the mainland in the Pensacola area. And you don't want to spend *all* your vacation getting a sunburn . . . do you?

Here's a quick rundown on how to get to the areas described in this chapter:

Perdido Key — A barrier island 15 miles west of Pensacola. From downtown, follow Garden Street West (Highway 98), which turns into Navy Boulevard. Turning right from Navy Boulevard onto Gulf Beach Highway will get you there, but you'll travel through some fairly shabby areas. You can also take Highway 98 West straight on through to Blue Angel Parkway (Highway 173). Turn south (left) on Blue Angel to Highway 292. Turn right (west) and follow the signs to Perdido Key.

Pensacola — The city and surrounding communities are built around the water — Pensacola Bay and Escambia Bay, Bayou Texar and Bayou Chico, Grand Lagoon and the Intracoastal Waterway. I-10 is a quick north-south route; however, there's no easy (or fast) way to get from east to west. Your best bet to the west (toward Perdido Key and the Naval Air Station) is to follow the water as closely as possible from downtown.

Milton — This area is easily accessed from Pensacola via Highway 90 (also Scenic Highway) or on I-10 going east. After you cross the bridge over Escambia Bay, take the first exit (Avalon Boulevard), turn left, and travel north to the intersection of U.S. 90. Downtown Milton is to your right.

Gulf Breeze — Jump on the Pensacola Bay Bridge from downtown (17th Avenue and Bayfront Parkway at the Visitor Information Center) and 3 miles later you're there. Keep traveling east on Highway 98 (Gulf Breeze Parkway) for Navarre Beach and The ZOO.

Pensacola Beach — From Gulf Breeze, turn right at the neon fish sign and continue over the Bob Sikes Bridge ($1 toll).

Attractions that are fun for families with kids will be denoted by an asterisk (*). Before you tackle one of the area's varied attractions, you may want to stop at the Pensacola Tourism and Convention Center at

• 55

PENSACOLA — ATTRACTIONS

The Old Water Battery is part of Fort Barrancas at Pensacola Naval Air Station.

the foot of the Three Mile Bridge for information on prices, times and special programs.

*GULF ISLANDS NATIONAL SEASHORE
934-2600

Please see our separate chapter on the Gulf Islands National Seashore (GINS) for complete information.

FORT PICKENS AREA
Fort Pickens Road, Santa Rosa Island

The pre-Civil War-era fort is the highlight of this part of the GINS. Guided tours are available, as well as park programs in the Fort Pickens Museum. Some of the area's most exquisite beaches await your discovery along this seven-mile strip of Santa Rosa Island. Camping, picnic shelters, concessions, a campground store, and hiking and biking trails provide enough diversions to keep the family busy for a week!

SANTA ROSA DAY-USE AREA
Between Pensacola Beach and Navarre Beach

Picnic pavilions, concessions, showers and indoor exhibits take up a small part of this seemingly endless stretch of white dunes, beaches, scrub and freshwater ponds spanning both sides of the highway.

NAVAL LIVE OAKS AREA
East of Gulf Breeze

These few miles of dense oak forest were set aside by President John Quincy Adams in 1828 for the sole purpose of shipbuilding. Trails lead you through the moss-draped woods along the bay where Native American encampments thrived thousands of years ago. Exhibits and a slide show on how the wood was used in shipbuilding are provided at the Visitor Center, which also serves as the Seashore Headquarters.

FORT BARRANCAS AND THE ADVANCED REDOUBT
Naval Air Station Pensacola

Two fortifications built for coastal defense are open for exploration and guided tours. Hike through the surrounding woodlands or enjoy the area's quiet beauty in the small picnic area. While you're here, you might also enjoy a trip to the historic lighthouse on the NAS property.

*NATIONAL MUSEUM OF NAVAL AVIATION
Pensacola Naval Air Station   452-3604

It's not only one-of-a-kind, it's one of the three largest air and space museums in the world. Pensacola became the country's first Naval Air Station back in 1914, and up through World War II, every Navy pilot got his training here. The 250,000 square feet of museum space packs in more than 100 Navy, Marine Corps and Coast Guard aircraft, and traces the history of naval aviation from biplanes to the space age. There's a gigantic NC-4, the first aircraft to cross the Atlantic, the first F-14 Tomcat (flown in the movie *Top Gun*), and a Navy F-18 fighter jet.

The seven-story Blue Angel Atrium, used for social events and military ceremonies, features four Blue Angels' Skyhawks suspended in formation from the ceiling. In the works are plans to build an IMAX theater, with an over-your-head multiple-story screen and about 70 speakers. If you've ever seen a short film in one of these theaters, you know what a boost it will be to the museum and the entire area.

This is one terrific museum whether you're in the military or even know anything *about* the military, and kids really like the hands-on cockpit and other "touchables." The museum is open daily from 9 AM to 5 PM except Thanksgiving, Christmas and New Year's Day. Admission is free.

*PERDIDO KEY STATE RECREATION AREA
Off State Rd. 292, Perdido Key   492-1595

This small beach area (1½ miles of gulf-front), smack in the middle of the Key off State Road 292, is part of a 247-acre preserve spanning both sides of the two-lane highway. There are picnic shelters between the gulf and Old River on the north. If you're coming for the beach, there's a parking lot behind the sign for public beach access. If you plan to walk through the preserve, however, you'll find it rough going. There aren't any trails, boardwalks or roads. Remember, too, that in Florida, nobody *owns* the beach, so feel free to walk the shoreline past the fancy condos and private residences lining the key. Open 8 AM to sunset all year. There is a $2.00 honor fee per vehicle.

The Florida Park Service is now issuing vacation passes good for up to 15 days. A Family Entrance Permit (up to eight people) covers admission to any of Florida's State Parks and costs $20.00. The new passes can be purchased at any Florida State Park.

PENSACOLA — ATTRACTIONS

*BIG LAGOON STATE RECREATION AREA
12301 Gulf Beach Hwy.
Pensacola 492-1595

Big Lagoon is a personal favorite spot, since it combines many different landscapes and habitats, from marshlands to grassy beds to white sand beaches and pine forests, all centered around Big Lagoon (what they call the Intracoastal Waterway here). The park is beautifully maintained, very clean and nicely laid out. Two highlights are the natural wood outdoor amphitheater and the 40-foot observation tower at East Beach.

From the top of the tower, you'll get a feel for the diversity of the park — herons bob for fish along the sandy shore, while brown thrashers, red-winged blackbirds and towhees hide among the marsh grasses. Look out across Big Lagoon to the beach area at Gulf Islands National Seashore. From this perspective, too, you'll see how fast the area is developing; homes now hug the outer boundaries of the park, sharing the area's wetlands.

For the most part, Big Lagoon is buffered by the barrier island (Perdido Key), but is still subject to harsh coastal conditions. Vegetation looks twisted and stubby; yellow pine "swales" (long troughs parallel to the dune line) thrive in waterlogged soil, with surrounding scrub buffeted and shaped into an impenetrable thicket of vines and gnarled branches.

Boardwalks lead to picnic shelters, the amphitheater, the observation tower and right down to the beach. The Long Pine, Youpon and Grand Lagoon hiking trails offer an opportunity for close-up nature study of surrounding vegetation, wetlands and wildlife. Gray foxes, raccoons, skunks and opossums have been known to cross paths with patient observers. More than 75 campsites, both for RV and primitive camping, are located right in the center of the park on a sand pine ridge. Seasonal programs, guided nature walks, and interpretive exhibits add an even richer dimension to your visit.

A boat ramp right along the main loop road provides easy access to Big Lagoon. Picnic areas and a swimming beach are nearby. Other picnic and designated swimming areas (no lifeguard provided) are near the amphitheater and west of the observation tower. You can fish here, too; anglers catch redfish, bluefish, flounder and mullet as well as crabs.

Please remember that all plant and animal life is protected. You may take seashells, but first be sure there's nobody "home." Dogs are prohibited almost everywhere, and so is alcohol.

The park is open year-round from 8 AM until sunset. Entrance fee for cars (up to eight people in one vehicle) is $3.25 (good for one day); bike and foot traffic is $1.00 per person. Big Lagoon State Recreation Area is on County Road 292A, about 10 miles southwest of Pensacola.

PENSACOLA GREYHOUND TRACK
Hwy. 98 at Dog Track Rd.
Pensacola 455-8595

"Here . . . comes . . . Swifty!" Greyhound racing seems to have taken off as fast as these dogs burst

PENSACOLA — ATTRACTIONS

"Lap dogs" compete at Pensacola Greyhound Track.

out of the starting gate, providing an enjoyable afternoon or evening's entertainment (whether you wager on your favorite hound or not). Dine in the Kennel Club, sip a cocktail in the lounge, or sit in the grandstand outdoors for a close-up view of the action! Live and instant replay televisions are provided throughout the complex. When no races are scheduled, you may still enjoy simulcast thoroughbred racing. Children younger than 12 are admitted to the races, but they have to be 12 or older to have dinner in the restaurant. Rain or shine, greyhound races take place nightly at 7:00 PM, with matinee races on weekends at 1:00 PM. Call for post times. General admission is $1.00; Kennel Club and Restaurant $2.50; seniors are free. Visitors are admitted free with a hotel or motel key (up to four people).

FIVE FLAGS SPEEDWAY
7450 Pine Forest Rd.
Pensacola   944-0466

This ½-mile track has attracted racing greats such as Darrell Waltrip and Rusty Wallace as hundreds of fans turn out to cheer on their favorite drivers. Annual events such as the Snow Ball Derby and Winston Cup All-Pro races draw record crowds. Regular season runs March to September; Friday night races are $8.00 for adults, $3.00 for children 6 to 12. Admission prices vary at other times. Call for race dates and times.

*WILDLIFE RESCUE AND SANCTUARY
105 N. "S" St., Pensacola   433-9453

Foxes, raccoons, deer, eagles, owls, armadillos, alligators, herons, pelicans, snakes and many other species have put in a stay at the sanctuary. It's a unique place in the middle of the city where abandoned, sick and injured wildlife are brought

PENSACOLA — ATTRACTIONS

The 1871 Clara Barkley Dorr House in the Seville Historic District reflects the opulence of the period with its Victorian trim, brick piers and "jib" windows. In the 1890s, the Dorr House served as a private school for affluent families.

for treatment. Some of the residents may have been exotic pets that got too large, or may have ended up here because they were simply unwanted. Other birds and animals were accidentally shot by hunters, hit by cars or, in the case of several pelicans, got such a bad case of frostbite one year that many had to have beaks, wings or legs amputated.

Not all of the wildlife can be released into the wild; the pelicans can't survive on their own, so have become permanent residents of the sanctuary. The Wildlife Rescue and Sanctuary relies almost solely on donations; park volunteers do a terrific job of caring for the animals and love to talk about "their" animals to everyone who comes by. The Sanctuary is off the beaten path a couple blocks behind the Gulf Power Company building at Pace and Garden streets on "S" Street. No admission is charged, but donations are welcome.

THE WALL SOUTH AND VETERAN'S MEMORIAL PARK
Bayfront Pkwy., Pensacola   433-8200

A 1/3-scale traveling version of the Vietnam Veterans Memorial in Washington, D.C. came through Pensacola several years ago, making such an impact that the Vietnam Veterans of Northwest Florida started a push to build a permanent half-scale replica of The Wall here in Pensacola. With community support and an awful lot of fish fries, The Wall South and the Veteran's Memorial Park opened to great fanfare in 1992. Eventually, the park will include a memorial for every

PENSACOLA — ATTRACTIONS

war from WWI to the present. The location is in downtown Pensacola along Bayfront Parkway. No admission is charged.

SEVILLE HISTORIC DISTRICT
Downtown Pensacola 444-8905

Here is a rare neighborhood, fairly intact, dating from the early 19th century. Most of the homes are simply constructed and well adapted to the climate. The Frame Vernacular, Folk Victorian and Creole homes are some of the oldest in Florida (listed on the National Register of Historic Places). There's an excellent self-guided tour brochure of the three historic districts available at the Visitor Information Center. The district is located between the bayfront and north to Wright Street, and Tarragona Street east to Florida Blanca Street.

While you're in this area, stop by St. Michael's Cemetery on Alcaniz Street. Graves date back 200 years; 3,000 people are buried there, from slaves to nobility. Land for the cemetery was deeded by King Philip of Spain in the early 18th century. There is no admission.

*HISTORIC PENSACOLA VILLAGE
Zaragoza St. at Tarragona in the Seville Historic District, Pensacola 444-8905

Several homes and commercial buildings within the Seville Historic District have been carefully restored to reflect West Florida's coastal history. The Museum of Industry features machinery from the Piney Woods Sawmill used during Pensacola's lumber boom. The Museum of Commerce recreates a streetscape of the late 19th century. The Lavalle House, Julee Cottage, Dorr House, Quina House, Lear House and Weaver's Cottage depict early life in West Florida through their architecture and period furnishings, while the grand dame of the Seville district, the Barkley House, serves as the official residence of Pensacola.

Also included as part of the Village is the Colonial Archaeological Trail, which leads past sites of the recently uncovered British fort of Pensacola. Pensacola's old City Hall is the new home of the T.T. Wentworth, Jr. Florida State Museum.

Tickets for Historic Pensacola Village are $5.50 for adults, $4.50 for seniors and children 4-16. Un-

---

Insiders' Tips

Insiders' like playing the Florida lottery, which has become almost as popular as the beaches. Even though the odds of winning the weekly millions are even greater than the likelihood of an airplane crash-landing in your front yard (about 14 million to one), it still doesn't keep folks from playing their lucky numbers, or driving in from other states to buy tickets when the jackpot swells (it's been as high as $100 million!).

PENSACOLA — ATTRACTIONS

A living history guide gives a demonstration in the Creole-style Lavalle House.

Photo: Historic Pensacola Preservation Board

less you're a real fan of history or architecture or love spending hours in museums, you may want to take in the village in small doses, since your tickets are good for seven days. Museums and historic homes are open Monday through Saturday from 10 AM to 4:30 PM; also open Sundays from 1 PM and 4:30 PM between Easter and Labor Day. Tickets may be purchased at the Wentworth Museum or in the central ticketing office (The Tivoli High House) on Zaragoza Street in Historic Pensacola Village.

PALAFOX HISTORIC DISTRICT
Palafox St. Area, Pensacola   434-5371

The downtown business district was the very heart of this thriving port city. Several old wooden hotels, the Pensacola Opera House, and the San Carlos Hotel have been lost to hurricanes, fires and demolition, but the downtown area retains a large number of its historic commercial buildings. As you drive through this area, notice the intricate ironwork balconies, reminiscent of New Orleans architecture. This locally ordinanced historic district begins at Palafox Pier and continues up Palafox Street to Wright Street; on the west, Reus Street is the boundary, and Tarragona Street divides the Palafox district from the Seville district.

THE CIVIL WAR SOLDIERS MUSEUM
108 S. Palafox Place
Pensacola   469-1900

This museum provides an absolutely fascinating encounter with the names and faces of soldiers, generals, doctors, photographers and just plain folk. From John Brown and Frederick Douglass to the last Civil War veteran to die in 1959, this

62 •

museum chronicles every facet of the war and is absolutely top-notch in every respect. Recorded remembrances and letters bring these long-forgotten soldiers to life again. The Pensacola Room records the significant people and events during the war in Pensacola, including a 23-minute video presentation,*Pensacola and the Civil War*, which may be more than you ever wanted to know, but certainly history buffs and locals will get a lot out of it.

One wall is devoted entirely to the more grizzly side of the war — primitive surgical procedures and equipment, early anesthesia (such as a musket ball with teeth marks!), amputations and some rather disturbing photographs. The man responsible for the museum, Norman Haines, is a local doctor, so naturally he devoted a good bit of space to an area in which he has a particular interest.

In all, though, the museum is spacious, well documented, nicely laid out and worth a few hours of your time. The museum bookstore offers 500 titles on the Civil War, from fiction to biographies, histories and letters. Admission is $4.00 for adults; $2.00 for children 6 to 12, with yearly memberships available. The Civil War Soldiers Museum is open Monday through Saturday from 10:00 AM until 4:30 PM.

PENSACOLA HISTORICAL MUSEUM
405 S. Adams St., Pensacola   433-1559

The oldest church building in Florida (1832) houses a history of the City of Pensacola in artifacts and a research library. The church itself, built in the romantic Norman Gothic Revival style, features huge hand-hewn heart pine beams in the ceiling and beautifully carved and highly decorated *botonee* crosses over the arched side doors. Federal forces used the church during the Civil War as a barracks, a prison, a hospital and a military chapel. Beginning with ancient fossils, the history of the area is traced through Indian pottery, maps, Civil War exhibits, materials used during the lumber and snapper fishing periods and household items. Walk through the museum yourself or take one of the guided tours. Admission is $2.00 for adults, $1.00 for children. Open Monday through Saturday, 9 AM to 4:30 PM; closed Sundays and holidays.

PENSACOLA MUSEUM OF ART
407 S. Jefferson St., Pensacola   432-6247

Here is a showcase of both local and traveling art exhibits in the old City Jail (1906). Some of the old cell blocks are still intact, with barred doors and windows, but it lends an atmosphere of history to the visual pieces. Photography, old Dutch masters, Chinese porcelain, contemporary arts and many other fascinating shows are presented each year. Donations are accepted.

NORTH HILL PRESERVATION DISTRICT
1½ miles north of downtown, north of Wright St. and west of Palafox St.   444-8905

Maybe it doesn't have the impact of Charleston or New Orleans' Garden District, or even some areas of Mobile, but the North Hill district is still a visual treat. The upper-middle

PENSACOLA — ATTRACTIONS

class neighborhood developed between 1870 and 1930 with the rise, and eventual bust, of lumber. Of the 50 blocks and 500 homes, some 400 of the homes contribute to the character of the district.

Several architectural styles are represented as wealthy families all tried to outdo each other. You'll find turreted and gingerbreaded Queen Annes, as well as Craftsman bungalows, Neoclassical, Tudor Revival, Art Moderne and Mediterranean Revival. Nearly all of the homes are private residences, so may only be enjoyed from the sidewalk unless a friendly resident is willing to give you a tour, which happens on occasion. Pick up a copy of the brochure "A Historical Tour of Pensacola" at the Visitor Center for walking tour highlights.

West East Hill Preservation District
Cervantes St. to Wright St. and
9th Ave. to Haines St. 433-1559

Newly protected under a Pensacola city ordinance in December of 1993, the neighborhood west of another called "East Hill" began around 1870 as a community of middle- and upper-class railroad workers. The Pensacola & Atlantic Railroad came through the city, connecting it with the rest of the state for the first time. Before the railroad, Pensacola was not easily accessible because of its many rivers and no bridges.

Many of the lovely Victorian homes, subdivided into apartments when the neighborhood began to decline in the 1930s, are being restored to their original splendor. A few old brick streets still remain. There is much work to do in the area, but a drive through will provide you with an overall feeling for what the neighborhood once was and, with diligence, will be again.

Scenic Highway Historic Trail
Scenic Hwy. (Hwy. 90)
Pensacola 477-7155

1993 marked the 20th anniversary of Scenic Highway's designation as a state scenic parkway. First opened in 1929, the original route may have been an Indian trail, then part of the Spanish Trail trade route between El Paso, Texas, and Jacksonville, Florida. This beautiful 10-mile drive along the scenic bluffs and bayfront will soon acquire historic site markers.

Beginning at the point where Cervantes Street becomes Scenic Highway is Emanuel or English Point (#1). Not far from the shoreline

---

Insiders' Tips

While you're visiting Pensacola Beach, take a walk out onto the Pensacola Beach Fishing Pier, which juts more than 1,000 feet into the Gulf of Mexico. Anglers can hook some mammoth catches from the pier's southernmost point, and the sheer abundance and variety of fish caught on the pier is interesting and educational.

here are the remains of a 16th-century Spanish ship. Site #2 is Magnolia Bluff and Beach, one of the first city beach areas, now developed as East Pensacola Heights. Bay Bluffs Park (#3) provides a scenic overlook and wooden stairways down to the foot of the bay.

Gaberonne Point (#4) was once the site of one of the many brick-making companies along the bluffs. Bricks made here were shipped to construct Fort Jefferson in the Dry Tortugas and Fort Taylor in Key West before the Civil War. The 30-foot-high brick chimney is all that's left of an 1854 steam-powered sawmill at Bohemia (#5). The sawmill was torched by Confederate soldiers as they evacuated Pensacola in 1862.

Gull or Diablo Point (#6) isn't readily seen from the highway, but several homes were constructed on this 732 acres jutting out into the bay. Stony or Rock Point (#7) marks the spot where the Escambia River Bridge opened in 1926. The British operated the first brickyard below the point as far back as the 1770s.

Lora or Laura's Point (#8) marks the opening of the first bridge across Escambia Bay in 1882. And the last marker is at River Gardens or Campbell Town (#9), which was first settled in 1766 by French Protestants. It later became another brickyard.

*EDWARD BALL NATURE PRESERVE AT THE UNIVERSITY OF WEST FLORIDA
University Pkwy., Pensacola   474-3000

The entire UWF campus sits on a 1,000-acre nature preserve on the Escambia River north of town, providing a scenic wooded landscape for university buildings. The nature preserve takes up a good portion of wetlands on the university's property. A 3/4-mile wooden boardwalk meanders through prime hardwood swamp and over a small fork of the Escambia River (Thompson's Bayou), where turtles and alligators are spotted regularly. Visitors to the preserve often stop along the way to feed bread to the turtles and fish, who seem to congregate in areas where they know food is plentiful. Picnic areas are provided in a clearing shaded by old mossy oaks. No admission is charged. The preserve is located down the hill behind Building 13 off Blue Parking Lot 20.

*THE ZOO
5701 Gulf Breeze Pkwy.
Gulf Breeze   932-2229

It claims to be "The World's Friendliest," and after a trip, you might agree. This small zoo, 10 miles east of Gulf Breeze, packs in an impressive collection of animals, like the white Bengal tiger, but it's the layout and atmosphere here that will win you over. Impeccable landscaping, a botanical garden filled with exotic species, a farm where children may pet and feed the animals, and a nursery and incubator room for zoo babies are just a few highlights.

The Safari Line Train ($1.25 ad-

PENSACOLA — ATTRACTIONS

These exotic white tigers have found a new home at The ZOO in Gulf Breeze.

mission) chugs through 30 acres of free-roaming animals in re-created habitats. Look for pygmy hippos, Florida alligators and an amazing assortment of birds and horned creatures from all corners of the world. Want to see a giraffe up close? Climb to the top of the Giraffe Feeding Tower and get a slimy lick from a 12-inch black tongue! Yecch! Ellie the African elephant takes visitors on rides, and wildlife demonstrations are staged daily at the outdoor amphitheater.

The ZOO's star attraction, Colossus, the largest gorilla in captivity, is now on loan to the Cincinnati Zoo for breeding purposes. The ZOO tried playing matchmaker, but Colossus never hit it off with his chosen mate, Muke (MOO-key). She stayed; he's been temporarily replaced with a couple of other gorillas who are still plenty of fun to watch.

The ZOO is open daily, weather permitting, from 9 AM to 5 PM; the park closes an hour earlier during the winter months. Admission charge is $8.75 plus tax for adults, $5.25 for children 3 to 11, $7.50 for seniors. You may also purchase a yearly membership for $50.00 (individual) or $95.00 (family).

MILTON HISTORIC DISTRICT
Hwy. 90, Downtown Milton   626-9830

Milton was once a thriving lumber town with a port of entry on the Blackwater River. The many lovely historic homes date mostly to the late 19th century, and downtown commercial buildings have some real history packed into their walls.

The 1913 Exchange Hotel on Elmira Street was intended for use as a telephone exchange, but when the phone office moved next door, the building became a hotel. Accu-

PENSACOLA — ATTRACTIONS

rately restored in the 1980s, it spent time as a bed and breakfast, but now sits vacant.

The Imogene Theatre and Milton Opera House (1912) is the only three-story building in the city. The second floor has a tiered balcony on three sides. It is occasionally used as a theater, but full-time as Santa Rosa Historical Society headquarters and a museum of local history.

The Milton Depot (1909) has always been a favorite. Its architecture is reminiscent of a quaint, small town, and even though trains haven't run through here since the 1960s, if you stand on the platform, you can imagine what a busy place it once was. The inside has been converted into the West Florida Railroad Museum with plenty of model train displays to make a child's (and an adult's) eyes shine.

Though not part of the historic district, there's an effort afoot to preserve the Old Brick Road in Santa Rosa County, known as old Highway 90. It's the earliest (1919) and the only brick highway in Northwest Florida. Preservationists hope to incorporate the road into the county's historic and recreational trails program.

BAGDAD HISTORIC DISTRICT
C-191 and Bagdad Hwy.
Bagdad 623-8493

Very old, very rural, very Southern, the tiny village of Bagdad is a charmer. Glorious antebellum mansions sit near trailer homes with chickens in the front yards. The trees make this a sight in itself — live oaks eerily decked out in Spanish moss supply the old homes, and even the newer ones, with their "down-home" character.

Many of the most striking homes line Forsyth Street. Owners restoring the 1847 Thompson House found graffiti made by a burnt stick on an interior wall — left there by a Union soldier in 1864.

Where Forsyth Street dead-ends, a panoramic view unfolds of the Oakland Basin and Blackwater Bay. The only structure here is a derelict abandoned home. You might wonder why no one has snatched this land up to build on. It once was a park where residents went "courtin'," and perhaps the locals aren't ready yet for the change that comes with tourism. A self-guided tour brochure is in the works; check at the museum in the Imogene Theatre in Milton or with the Santa Rosa County Chamber of

---

Insiders' Tips

The old Pensacola Bay Bridge, which runs parallel to the new bridge connecting Pensacola with Gulf Breeze, is one of the world's longest fishing piers. Day and night, rain or shine, the bridge is filled with rod-and-reel-wielding locals hoping to get lucky. And they usually do. The problem is keeping watchful herons and pelicans from stealing the catch!

PENSACOLA — ATTRACTIONS

Clear, cool water, white sand banks and lush woodlands make Northwest Florida's inland rivers delightful for canoeing, tubing, camping or sunbathing.

Commerce on Highway 87.

*ADVENTURES UNLIMITED
Tomahawk Landing, Hwy. 87
Milton   623-6197

Talk about fun! If you've never canoed one of inland Florida's scenic rivers, you're missing out on another aspect of this area's beauty. Adventures Unlimited provides canoes, giant inner tubes (for a more leisurely float) and cooler tubes (to drag your cooler along behind you!), camping supplies, cabins, you name it, to make your trip as safe and comfortable as possible.

Each of the four rivers offers its own scenic diversions, and three are relatively shallow for first-time canoe enthusiasts. Take a short trip, day trip, or 1- or 2-day trip down the Coldwater, Blackwater, Perdido or Sweetwater-Juniper. This author has canoed each of the rivers, and, in my own opinion, the Sweetwater-Juniper offers the most stunning scenery (although it is also the shortest river); the Perdido the most challenging ride. The Perdido is wide and *deep*, and is probably best left to veteran canoe handlers, since amateurs tend to tip over a lot.

One word of caution: the Coldwater and Blackwater are the most popular rivers, and therefore the most crowded. On a Saturday in early summer, you won't feel much seclusion as one group after another passes you on the river. It might be prudent to ask the folks at Adventures Unlimited, if you truly desire a calm and quiet trip, what days of the week or months of the year are not quite so popular.

PENSACOLA — ATTRACTIONS

Overnight camping on the rivers opens a whole new world to the first-time visitor. Paddle gently through the tea-colored water, stopping often for a dip in the river, a walk through the woods, a picnic lunch. About two hours before dark, scope out one of the many *white* sandbars (yes, the sandy bottom is white), pull your canoe out, and make camp. You may build a fire in the sand, just be sure you're far enough away from the woods so errant sparks from your campfire don't burn anything else! During dry periods, campfires may be prohibited, so be sure to bring a campstove (or lots of bologna sandwiches!). Each of the rivers is spring-fed, ensuring their purity (feel free to brush your teeth in the water) and constant cool temperature.

Another option for roughing it, if you don't care so much for *really* wide open spaces, is rental cabins. You'll find just about all the comforts of home here — showers, refrigerators, air conditioning, fireplaces — all strewn along Wolfe Creek (an offshoot of the Coldwater), or scattered deeper in the woods. Tent and hookup sites are also available at Tomahawk Landing.

Tubing or canoeing these wild rivers really is an adventure not to be missed! More detailed information on campsites and cabins is included in the chapter on Pensacola Accommodations.

*BLACKWATER RIVER STATE PARK
Off U.S. 90, Holt   623-2363

The Blackwater River is still considered one of the purest sand-bottom rivers in the world, mostly preserved in its natural state. The shallow river is terrific for canoeing, tubing and swimming (see Adventures Unlimited above or the chapter on Pensacola Recreation). Almost 200,000 acres are teeming with wildlife in this under-utilized state park. Camping, nature and horse trails, boating, picnicking, and hunting are all offered, though some are seasonal. The park is open from 8 AM until sunset year round. There's a $2.00 entrance fee for cars. No pets are allowed. Blackwater is located 15 miles northeast of Milton off U.S. 90 in Holt.

Insiders' Tips

The entire North Hill Preservation District sits atop a vast battlefield where Spaniard Don Bernardo de Galvez and 4,000 troops snatched Pensacola from the British in a bloody two-month-long battle in 1781. North Hill residents still find cannon balls, coat buttons and other artifacts while digging in their gardens! Historical markers on Spring Street and Barcelona Street fill you in on Fort San Bernardo and the battlefield site.

Lights in the Night Sky

Craft hovering above a road in Gulf Breeze.

Look there! Is it a bird? A plane? No, it's just another UFO sighting, which have become almost as common as sand dollars. Of the 111 unsolved reports of UFO sightings in Florida over the past five years, about 85% come from Escambia and Santa Rosa counties. The watchdog group MUFON (Mutual UFO Network) has its hands full with the study of Ufology, or sending out State Section Directors and Field Investigator Trainees to write up reports when a sighting is called into their hotline. At this point, about 90% of the *total* sightings are attributed to other phenomenon (military aircraft, weather surveillance equipment, satellites). The other 10%, which can't be explained away, are sent to the deputy director of investigations in Texas, who reviews the reports, calling in other experts when necessary. Before being filed in the MUFON archives, each report is marked as to its significance.

Several reports, called "greatly significant" by MUFON, and "greatly controversial" by some locals, are those of Ed and Frances Walters of Gulf Breeze, chronicled in great detail in their book *The Gulf Breeze Sightings*. Ed Walters happened to have a video camera or a Polaroid handy to document several of the sightings, which raised the eyebrows of local skeptics. But MUFON stands behind its investigations, even providing the Walters' with stereo cameras for capturing crafts.

And, to give Ed and Frances and MUFON some credibility, reports of UFO sightings have come in from tourists, police officers, other reputable residents, even politicians, giving real credence to the mysterious lights in the night sky.

Circle of scorched earth behind Gulf Breeze High School taken by members of MUFON (Mutual UFO Network).

So why so many sightings in Northwest Florida? According to Charles Flannigan, MUFON's Executive Director, there are two reasons. First, there are more UFO watchers — groups congregate regularly to gaze heavenward at Shoreline Park in Gulf Breeze and at the foot of the Three Mile Bridge over Pensacola Bay. The other reason, says Flannigan, is the ease of reporting a UFO sighting. If you're driving across the Three Mile Bridge one night and happen to spot mysterious lights or shapes in the sky that you can't identify, get out the video camera, then call MUFON's hotline number: (904) 438-3313.

PENSACOLA — FESTIVALS AND SPECIAL EVENTS

A sax player warms up before a performance by The Airmen of Note at the Pensacola Jazz Festival.

Pensacola Area
Festivals and Special Events

You pick the time of year to be here, and the Pensacola area will do its best to provide a full plate of activities. When we talk about Pensacola area festivals and events, sometimes we just can't help but include a few events happening on the other side of the state line. Mobile is only as far to the west of Pensacola as Destin is to the east. Besides, we don't want you to miss out on *anything!*

Listed here are events that occur *annually.* Seasonal festivities, concerts, poetry readings, special museum exhibits or anything we've left out can be tapped into by contacting the Pensacola Convention & Visitor Information Center at 434-1234 or by checking the local paper. One more note: the names Pensacola Beach and Santa Rosa Island are used interchangeably at times. Pensacola Beach is *part* of Santa Rosa Island, and Quietwater Beach and Casino Beach are also *part* of Pensacola Beach. Confused? Sometimes, so are we. But, it's a small area out there, so if you drive around a bit, you're sure to find what you came for. Also remember that you'll pay a $1.00 toll to drive onto the beach from Gulf Breeze; coming in from Navarre Beach, the toll is a quarter.

January

POLAR BEAR DIP
Flora-Bama Lounge at the Florida-Alabama line, Perdido Key 492-0611

OK, so it isn't Minnesota, but the folks who participate are still crazy for donning swimsuits and splashing around in the Gulf of Mexico on New Years' Day — what a way to start the year! After the dip, the participants run into the Flora-Bama and start drinking heavily to warm up. You can watch or participate for free.

WINTER BIRD COUNT
Big Lagoon and Perdido Key State Recreation Areas, Perdido Key 492-1595

After a big party on New Year's Eve, many insiders can't think of anything they'd rather do than be at one of the parks at 6:00 AM to watch for the annual winter migration of birds — hey, some people think this is *big* fun. You'll be in good company with members of the Audubon Society, and you'll actually be part of a scientific study. Avid birders will want to bring binoculars, and everybody needs to dress for the weather.

SNOW FEST
Quietwater Beach Boardwalk Pensacola Beach 932-2259

Some local kids have never seen snow, so here's their opportunity to

• 73

PENSACOLA — FESTIVALS AND SPECIAL EVENTS

see (and feel) what it's like. The Santa Rosa Island Authority sponsors the two-day fest, with lots of artificial snow, food vendors, crafts and ice and sand sculpture contests.

MARTIN LUTHER KING JR. PARADE
Downtown Pensacola   434-2431

This annual parade begins at Government and Spring streets at 11:00 AM and winds its way around downtown, ending at the Martin Luther King Jr. Memorial Plaza on Palafox Street. The parade is a tribute to the civil rights leader and to all African-Americans.

February

BRIDGE TO THE BEACH RUN
At the foot of the Bob Sikes Bridge
Gulf Breeze   434-2800

It's a quickie... from the foot of the bridge up and over to Pensacola Beach, where runners are met with food, refreshments and live entertainment. The run is sponsored by the Pensacola Sports Association with help from the Santa Rosa Island Authority.

BLUE ANGEL MARATHON
Naval Air Station Pensacola   452-2843

This grueling 26.2 mile run is a qualifier for the big one in Boston. Skaters, bikers and walkers also join in the fun through the most scenic places on the Navy base starting in front of Building 632, out onto Barrancas Avenue, then into downtown and back again. Whew! There's a smaller 5K run in the morning, and together, about 1,700 runners take the challenge.

MARDI GRAS
Pensacola Beach   932-2259

A champagne breakfast and street dance, a street parade and a huge pot of red beans and rice for all are just a few of the annual events sponsored by the Krewe of Wrecks of Pensacola Beach.

MARDI GRAS CELEBRATION
Downtown Pensacola   934-0337

The Krewe of Lafitte Parade, the Grand Mardi Gras Parade, and the Fat Tuesday celebration all take place downtown. Mardi Gras Balls for the most part are by invitation only, but everyone can participate in the costume contests and the Priscus Procession, a drink-'til-you-drop bar hop.

March

SPRING BREAK
Beaches at Pensacola,
Navarre and Perdido Key   932-2259

When some Florida cities that traditionally hosted the annual migration of college students turned their attention elsewhere, Northwest Florida beaches welcomed them heartily. In past years, free concerts by Bruce Hornsby, Starship and Toto brought 100,000 people to Pensacola Beach. Over-stressed residents nixed the concert idea, but Spring Breakers can still fill their days and nights with activities and entertainment of all sorts.

MOBILE HISTORIC HOMES TOUR
Mobile, Ala.   (205) 438-6936

Each March, when the city's decked out in azaleas and dogwoods for spring, the doors to some of

Mobile's finest homes open to welcome visitors. The two-day event features more than twenty homes representing architectural styles from Creole cottages and Federal-style townhomes to Greek Revival mansions and turn-of-the-century Victorian and Neo-Classical homes. Day and evening candlelight tours offer varying perspectives on the homes; homeowners are your tour guides. Tour prices vary from $10 to $40; some include progressive dinners.

GALLERY NIGHTS
Downtown Pensacola   432-9906

The Arts Council of Northwest Florida sponsors this thrice-yearly celebration of the arts in Pensacola. Downtown art galleries, frame shops, bookstores, art supply stores, dance troupes, poets, literary groups and even a few advertising people put on the dog for locals and visitors. Buses take gallery-goers to each of the sixteen or so stops along the tour route; or you may park your car and walk with a self-guided tour map. Most businesses serve refreshments and offer some type of entertainment, from string quartets to poetry readings. Merchants pick up the tab for the whole thing. All you have to do is show up!

ELBERTA SAUSAGE FESTIVAL
Elberta City Park
Elberta, Ala.   (205) 986-5987

For some reason Elberta has attracted a large contingent of German residents; the downtown looks like something out of an Old World picture book. But this twice-yearly festival attracts people from all over, and they come for one thing — German sausage. Not just any German sausage, *this* foot-long, locally made variety could just be the best you've ever eaten.

Giant outdoor grills are set up in an open area near downtown and the lines for sausages never seem to get any shorter. Maybe because people return three and four times! And while you're standing in line, or while you're trying your best to eat this monstrosity without getting *too* much mustard on your chin, there are cloggers and jug bands and clowns and arts and crafts and other silly and fun entertainment. It's more a celebration of sausage than German heritage, but nobody seems to mind.

Elberta is about an hour's drive from Pensacola along Highway 98 West. Cross over the Lillian Bridge (Lillian, Ala.) and Elberta is another 15 to 20 minutes.

ST. PATRICK'S DAY CELEBRATION AND KITE CONTEST
Pensacola Beach   932-2259

The beach bars, of course, have their annual Pub Crawl, complete with green beer. A kite decorating contest is now incorporated into the walking parade and other various celebratory functions.

SCRATCH ANKLE FESTIVAL
Riverwalk, Downtown Milton   623-9418

Okay, so the name's a little funny. This is an annual spring celebration of Milton's heritage, going back to a time when Milton was called "Scratch Ankle" for the numerous stickers and sand spurs that infested the area. Food vendors, arts and crafts and live entertainment are part of what is probably Milton's largest annual festival.

The T.T. Wentworth, Jr. Florida State Museum houses a collection of more than 20,000 artifacts, mostly from Northwest Florida.

PRE-EASTER EGG HUNT
Casino Beach
Pensacola Beach   932-2259

Here's one for the kiddies, sponsored by the beach merchants and the Island Authority. The hunt is held to the right of the Casino Beach bathhouse.

DO IT IN THE SAND VOLLEYBALL
Pensacola Beach   944-4091

One volleyball tournament a month is held at Casino Beach from March through September. This is a chance to see some great playing, while the sand flies.

April

BRITISH CAR SHOW
Casino Parking Lot
Pensacola Beach   478-3171

A group of British car enthusiasts loves to show off its classic British motor cars at shows and in parades; this particular show may become an annual event.

SATURDAY IN THE PARK CONCERT SERIES
Big Lagoon State Recreation Area
Near Perdido Key   492-1595

The first of four concerts in April features jazz bands, symphonies and local choirs in the scenic splendor of the Big Lagoon amphitheater. Call the park's main number for more information on performers and tickets.

SPRINGFEST
Downtown Pensacola   477-8998

The warm weather's arrived for good, the flowers are blooming, the sun is shining and the streets of downtown Pensacola are alive with

PENSACOLA — FESTIVALS AND SPECIAL EVENTS

music, dancing and people! SpringFest marks its third year in 1994, billed as a musical and cultural celebration, and each year seems to get better. The first year showcased the performances of local jazz, blues, rock and acoustic performers, and the response was so positive, the SpringFest sponsors brought in some heavy-hitters for the 1993 celebration: The Fabulous Thunderbirds, Roger McGuinn (lead singer of The Byrds), Bo Diddley, and Maria Muldahr in addition to the local groups. A Fine Arts & Masters Show adds another facet to this weekend-long event. More than 70,000 are expected to attend SpringFest, which closes off all major thoroughfares in downtown to set up huge sound stages. SpringFest may turn out to be one of Pensacola's very best offerings.

PICNICS IN THE PARK
Plaza Ferdinand
Downtown Pensacola   434-5371

The Picnics in the Park series got its start as a way to lure downtown workers out into the sunshine during lunchtime to enjoy the beautiful weather and live entertainment. A different local band or entertainer is featured every Friday through mid-May, and the entertainment's free.

JAZZ JAM
Quietwater Beach Boardwalk
Pensacola Beach   932-2259

Jazz Jam offers a two-day festival at "the shell" featuring the best in local and regional live jazz and blues bands.

FRIENDS OF THE LIBRARY BOOK SALE
Bayfront Auditorium
Downtown Pensacola   444-7696

Once a year, the local library cleans out the stacks, replacing old volumes with new, updating reference materials, and weeding out books that are just plain worn out. Those books are offered for sale at a fraction of their original cost—some books can be bought for as little as a dime. Maps, artwork and other collectibles are also on sale as part of this yearly fund-raiser.

PENSACOLA JAZZFEST
Seville Square
Downtown Pensacola   474-2327

Sponsored by the local public radio station, WUWF-FM and other corporate sponsors, the three-day festival brings in the best of local and regional jazz and blues acts. This is an intimate, top-quality production for all ages. Seating is limited, so you may want to bring your own lawn chairs. The kickoff is Friday evening, where sponsors are recognized, and a party atmosphere prevails. Tickets for Friday only are $3.00. Cost is $5.00 for either Saturday or Sunday, and if you want to attend both Saturday and Sunday, tickets are $9.00.

EARTH DAY CELEBRATION
Quietwater Beach Boardwalk and
Island-wide, Pensacola Beach   932-2259

If you're concerned for Mother Earth, this celebration provides you with a chance to help. Listen to live music, visit environmental displays, eat health food, sign petitions against oil drilling in the Gulf or get involved with causes like preserving

• 77

PENSACOLA — FESTIVALS AND SPECIAL EVENTS

This strolling New Orleans street band is a highlight of the Pensacola Jazz Festival.

the last public beach acreage (plans are to put a golf course there!). Betcha if you spend 30 minutes here, you'll find out something you didn't know. You'll also see lots of long hair and tie-dyes, but it's the beach, man! No admission is charged.

EARTH DAY CELEBRATION
Big Lagoon State Recreation Area
Near Perdido Key   492-1595

Guided tours by park rangers, environmental exhibits, nature walks and more will teach you about this delicate coastal environment and about one of Florida's most scenically diverse parks. Admission is $3.25 per vehicle.

MULLET TOSS
Flora-Bama Lounge
Perdido Key at the State Line   492-0611

The wacky locals are at it again, trying to make the *Guinness Book of World Records* by tossing mullet across the state line from Florida to Alabama. Unfortunately, Guinness refuses to recognize mullet tossing as a viable record for the book, so the pure enjoyment of the sport will have to suffice for the Flora-Bama crowd. As you might expect, these antics are free to the public.

May

ASSOCIATION OF VOLLEYBALL PROFESSIONALS MILLER LITE PRO-BEACH VOLLEYBALL TOURNAMENT
Casino Beach
Pensacola Beach   932-2259

These are the real pros, who provide plenty of action for spectators. The event is also nationally televised. Hi, Mom! It's also free.

PENSACOLA — FESTIVALS AND SPECIAL EVENTS

CINCO DE MAYO
Quietwater Beach Boardwalk and
Island-wide, Pensacola Beach 932-2259

This Spanish-influenced festival features Latin performers, arts and crafts and, of course, FOOD! Admission is free.

SATURDAY IN THE PARK CONCERT SERIES
Big Lagoon State Recreation Area 492-1595

A variety of entertainers perform at the park's open amphitheater. Call for featured entertainers and tickets.

FIREMATICS COMPETITION
Casino Parking Lot
Pensacola Beach 932-2259

This frenetic competition pits fire department teams against each other in a series of timed events. In the fire brigade competition, teams must try to put out a simulated burning building — by handing buckets of water down a line and throwing them on the fire! The busted hose competition means that the hose springs a "leak;" each team must find, clamp and replace the hose, get the water back on and hit a target before time runs out! Aside from being good for a few laughs, the competition helps to train both paid and volunteer fire departments. Trophies are awarded. There is no fee.

BRITISH FESTIVAL
Seville Square
Downtown Pensacola 456-5474

The British Festival is a celebration of Pensacola's British heritage with native foods, crafts and music — all for free. Crumpet, anyone?

CAMPFIRE PROGRAM
Big Lagoon State Recreation Area 492-1595

After the "Saturday in the Park" performances, right around sunset, park rangers put on their own shows covering a variety of topics on natural Florida. Programs are held after the concerts May through June. Admission charge to the park is $3.25 per vehicle.

JUBILEE'S LOBSTER FEST
Quietwater Beach Boardwalk
Pensacola Beach 934-3108

How do I love thee, lobster? Jubilee Restaurant, sponsors of the annual event, believes there are enough serious lovers of the popular crustacean that they go to a great deal of trouble for this event. Live Maine lobsters are shipped here on a special flight. A refrigerated truck meets it on the runway in Pensacola, where the lobsters are taken to the restaurant and kept very cold until cooking time. The live lobsters (about 1½ pounds each) are stuffed into net bags along with baby new potatoes, corn-on-the-cob, fresh clams and Andouille Cajun sausage, and tossed into a Cajun boil. To complement your meal, there's live entertainment and children's activities. Proceeds go to a local children's charity.

PARADE OF HOMES
Selected sites around Pensacola 476-0318

Don't you just love going into other homes to get decorating and design ideas? Here's a tour for you featuring homes in the area's newest neighborhoods, showcasing exceptional designs and interiors, including the "American Dream

• 79

PENSACOLA — FESTIVALS AND SPECIAL EVENTS

Home." Ahhh . . . dream on we do. The event is sponsored by the Home Builders Association and is free.

June

FIESTA OF FIVE FLAGS
*Various locations throughout
the Pensacola area   433-6512*
Pensacola's own celebration of a rich heritage under five flags (Spanish, French, British, Confederate and United States) might be more fun for locals than visitors, but there are plenty of parades, contests and balls to go around. A British Street Party, fishing tournaments, the Fiesta Mass, a yacht parade, a Confederate Encampment, outdoor concerts and treasure hunts highlight the 10-day festival. And all the while, a tacky 10-foot statue of Don Tristan de Luna, held to the ground with painfully visible buckets of concrete and ropes, peers out at festival-goers from a downtown median. Most events are free. A treasure hunt nets the finder $5,000 in cash and prizes. Wow, that's worth practicing for!

DE LUNA LANDING, FIESTA OF FIVE FLAGS
*Quietwater Beach
Santa Rosa Island   433-6512*
Don Tristan de Luna, a Spaniard, and a contingent of 1,400 colonists disembarked at Pensacola in August of 1559, hoping to build the first settlement in the New World. After just a few days, a hurricane ripped through here, destroying most of the ships and the provisions. However, the fate of the mission isn't important. What *is* important is that we were first, a fact of which Pensacolians are fiercely proud, whether or not it happens to be true. A loosely historical reenactment of the landing is fun for both the actors and the onlookers, and is free.

CHILDREN'S TREASURE HUNT AND SANDCASTLE CONTEST
*Quietwater Beach
Santa Rosa Island   433-6512*
What fun for the kids! Building sand castles and finding treasures on the beach could win them some prizes. The contests are part of the Fiesta of Five Flags celebrations.

PENSACOLA INTERNATIONAL BILLFISH TOURNAMENT
*Bayfront Auditorium
Downtown Pensacola   453-4638*
The Pensacola Big Game Fishing Club sponsors this tournament, held over the July 4th weekend. Prizes are awarded to the largest catch in several divisions: Billfish (blue marlin, white marlin, sailfish); Tuna, Wahoo and Dolphin; Ladies; and Junior Anglers. Although participating in the tournament must be great fun, the weigh-ins at the Auditorium are the real crowd-pleasers. Spectators gather around sunset to watch the huge charter boats dock and unload the day's catches, which are hoisted up on the scales for everyone to ogle.

EVENINGS IN OLDE SEVILLE SQUARE
Seville Square, Pensacola   438-6505
Come enjoy a superb series of outdoor concerts under the oaks in historic Seville Square. Jazz, country, bluegrass, blues and many other types of music are presented every Thursday throughout the summer

months. Many concert-goers come early, bring a picnic and make a night of it. The concerts are well attended, so bring your blankets and lawn chairs and arrive early. Some of the concerts are simulcast on the local public radio station, WUWF-FM. This is a wonderful family evening of entertainment that's absolutely free.

BATTLE OF MOBILE BAY REENACTMENT
Fort Gaines Historic Site
Dauphin Island, Ala.   (205) 861-6992

"Damn the torpedoes! Full speed ahead!" was the battle cry of Admiral David Farragut during the famous battle. See it recreated before your eyes and enjoy a special candlelight tour of the fort while you're there. Admission to Fort Gaines is $2.00 for adults, children 7 to 12 $1.00, and younger than 7 are free.

July

JULY 4TH FIREWORKS
Casino Beach, Santa Rosa Island   932-2259

Come early and bring lawn chairs and a cooler. Better yet, bring your boat and watch the fireworks from the water. Also bring a boom box, if you have one, since one of the radio stations plays patriotic music, which is supposed to be synchronized with the fireworks. It only sort of works, but it's nice to have the musical accompaniment, anyway. There's no admission fee.

SERTOMA'S JULY 4TH
Seville Square
Downtown Pensacola   476-0042

Local Sertoma Clubs put together this two-day family celebration, culminating with the fireworks show on the 4th. One spectacular show is held at the beach and the other in the historic district downtown for folks who don't want to travel all the way to the beach. The two fireworks shows are staggered; when the show on the beach ends, the show in town begins. The in-town show (along the bayfront) is also accompanied by patriotic music on one of the local radio stations. All this sparkling entertainment is free.

RIVERFEST
Riverwalk Park and Willing St.
Milton   994-0811

Milton's historic downtown along the beautiful Blackwater River is the setting for free water skiing shows, a children's festival, a boat parade, arts and crafts and plenty of food. The Riverwalk Park is a fairly recent addition to downtown. Now visitors can stroll along wooden boardwalks to a covered gazebo right on the water.

PENSACOLA BEACH AIR SHOW WITH THE BLUE ANGELS
Gulfside, Pensacola Beach   452-2583

Thousands congregate to witness the aerial artistry of the Pensacola-based Blues stunt-flying team. It's quite a good show (and free to boot), but be warned that you'll be stuck in traffic for a while afterwards. Better to plan a day at the beach so you won't have to move from your spot on the sand.

GALLERY NIGHTS
Downtown Pensacola   432-9906

Come be a part of this Friday

evening celebration of the arts in downtown Pensacola. Shops stay open until 9 PM and invite the public in for a free tour, refreshments and entertainment.

Wine Festival
Quietwater Beach Boardwalk
Pensacola Beach   934-3108

Pay one price and get your fill of over 175 different wines from 150 wineries worldwide. Several winery representatives are on hand to talk to patrons about the wines. Each winery donates a magnum of wine with a signed label to be auctioned off, with all proceeds going to charity. In 1993 several thousand dollars was donated to the Red Cross for hurricane and earthquake disaster relief.

August

Bushwacker Festival
Quietwater Beach Boardwalk
Pensacola Beach   934-3108

The Bushwacker is a local drink that tastes something like a milkshake with a kick (there are a few kinds of alcohol tossed in). It's cold, frothy and refreshing, and that's about all you need to build a festival around. Pull in some local entertainers, print up a few souvenir cups, add a few events such as the 5K Capt'n Fun Run for charity, invite 33,000 of your closest friends, and voila! A festival is born. More than 78,000 Bushwackers were served during the 1993 festival.

Bar-B-Q Rib Burnoff
Pensacola Civic Center
Pensacola   432-0800

What can people be thinking? Fifteen barbecue grills all cranked up and cooking at once in the asphalt parking lot of the Civic Center in August? If you love barbecue *so* much that you're willing to put up with the heat, then don't miss this one. There'll be children's activities (hopefully in a grassy area) and a raffle. There is no admission charge.

September

Santa Rosa Fair
Santa Rosa Industrial Park
Milton   623-5055

The big draw to this fair is the two-day rodeo, where bronco-busting and calf roping elicit plenty of whoops and hollers from the enthusiastic audience. Carnival rides, food and live entertainment fill out the six-day celebration.

Labor Day Fireworks
Casino Beach, Santa Rosa Island   932-2259

Pick a beach or a boat for fireworks-watching the Sunday before Labor Day—you can see the display from all over the beach area. This event is sponsored by the Santa Rosa Island Authority.

International Billfish Tournament
Orange Beach Marina
Orange Beach, Ala.   (205) 981-4207

Even if you don't care a whit for fishing, the Orange Beach Marina is a spectacle in itself, and moreso during a fishing tournament. Slips are jammed with multi-million-dollar yachts and pleasure boats of all descriptions. Men and women run around in Izod polos sporting plenty of gold jewelry. In short, it's a tour-

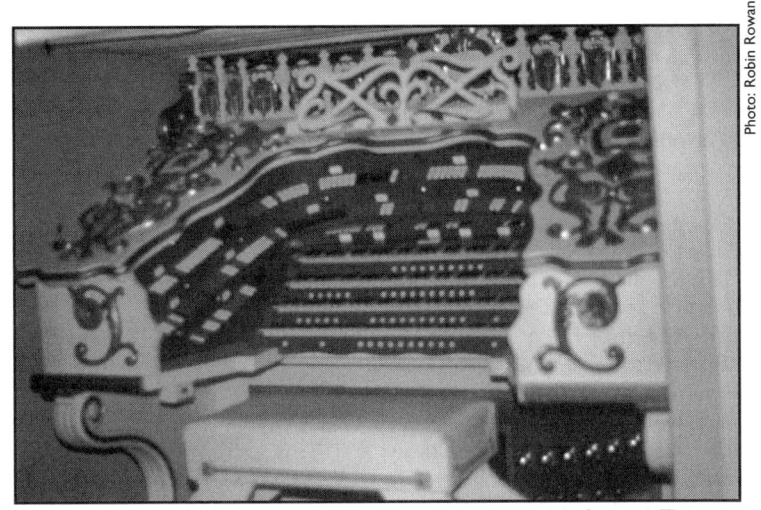

This magnificent 1925 Robert Morton pipe organ at Pensacola's Saenger Theatre was originally designed to accompany silent films.

nament for the well-heeled and a spectator sport for the rest of us.

FAMILY EXPO
Pensacola Civic Center
Pensacola   432-1222

This is a trade show for families. Pick up information on various family-related topics, fill a shopping bag with giveaways, ask questions about particular services, sit in on demonstrations and short seminars. Topics range from "How to Talk to Your Teenager" to "Family Stress: Keeping it Under Control." Kids have a variety of activities of their own to keep them busy — costumed characters stroll around talking to children, and a special celebrity makes an appearance. Day care is provided. The response to the first Expo was overwhelming, so the plan is to expand it in upcoming years. To make it even more family-friendly, the whole expo is free.

BEACH AND SHORE CLEAN-UP
Big Lagoon State Recreation Area
Pensacola   492-1595

Dedicated volunteers arrive at various coastal locations throughout Northwest Florida to pick up trash and learn more about the preservation of our delicate coastal environment. It may not sound like much fun, but it really can be. The park rangers keep track of how many bags of trash are collected and from where, what are the most unusual items collected, etc. The media almost always shows up to talk with volunteers and park rangers, and a very upbeat, positive atmosphere prevails. It's a great way for children to learn about ecology and how to preserve our most precious natural resource.

PENSACOLA — FESTIVALS AND SPECIAL EVENTS

JUBILEE LOBSTER FEST
Quietwater Beach Boardwalk
Pensacola Beach   934-3108
This is a mini-version of the blowout in June, featuring live Maine Lobsters cooked to perfection. Yummmm.

SEAFOOD FESTIVAL
Quietwater Beach Boardwalk
Pensacola Beach   433-6512
The person who thought that setting up a bunch of food booths and barbecue grills in an asphalt parking lot on a hot September weekend was a good idea needs to have his (or her) head examined. Yet, people still flock to the beach by the thousands for this event, perhaps to enjoy the weather and the free live entertainment. It doesn't cost anything to go, and if you get too hot, you can always jump in the water, which is never very far away.

SEAFOOD FESTIVAL
Seville Square, Pensacola   433-6512
Now, for folks who don't necessarily groove on the heat, this is more like it — shade, giant oak trees and the pleasant and historic atmosphere of Seville Square. Bands set up in the quaint gazebo in the park, and folks tend to linger a little longer at the many arts and crafts booths when they're out of the hot sun. Besides the fresh seafood cooked many wonderful ways, there's a children's activity area, an antique show and a 5K run.

October

ST. ANNE'S ROUND-UP
St. Anne's Catholic Church, 5200 Saufley Rd., Pensacola   456-5966
Why this church's fund-raiser has become so popular is a mystery, but it must have something to do with good p.r. The grounds of the church are *enormous*, big enough to build an entire little western town on, called Bellview Junction, where most of the Round-Up activities take place. During the three-day event, you can witness shoot-outs, stuff yourself with lots of rich food or listen to the many entertainers, one of whom is a moderately famous TV star. Heather Locklear and John Ritter have graced the stage in past years. All it costs is a buck for parking.

GULF SHORES SHRIMP FESTIVAL
Gulf Shores, Ala.   (205) 968-7511
Barbecued, braised, broiled, buttered, battered and on-a-stick — eat shrimp to your heart's delight at this festival on the public beach area at the dead-end of Highway 59 in Gulf Shores. Entertainment, arts and crafts, a parade and other beach activities are interspersed between bouts of overeating. The activities are free.

HISPANIC HERITAGE FESTIVAL
Quietwater Beach Boardwalk
Pensacola Beach   932-3560
You'll enjoy this free festival with everything Latin — food, music and crafts, celebrating Pensacola's Hispanic heritage.

ELBERTA SAUSAGE FESTIVAL
Elberta City Park
Elberta, Ala.   (205) 986-5997
If you missed it in the spring, here's one more opportunity to savor the best German sausage in the South! Continuous live entertainment, dancing, and arts and crafts are featured — for free.

84 •

PENSACOLA — FESTIVALS AND SPECIAL EVENTS

BEATLES ON THE BEACH FALL FESTIVAL
Pensacola Beach 932-2259

Buttons, T-shirts, old records, Beatles look-alike contests, entertainers playing Beatles tunes and touring Beatles sound-alike bands highlight this free event.

INTERNATIONAL FALL FESTIVAL
St. Rose of Lima Parish
515 W. Park Ave., Milton 623-3600

This festival with its international flavor attracts hundreds of people from all over the area. Sample food from several countries, try your skill at Scottish or Greek games, listen to traditional music from other countries, or pick your merry way through the throngs of people to the crafts booths. No admission is charged.

GRAND FESTIVAL OF ART
Marriott's Grand Hotel, Hwy. 98
Point Clear, Ala. (205) 928-2228

This is a celebration of art, with quality works for sale. There are also fun children's activities. Both the beautiful drive over from Pensacola and the historic Grand Hotel on Mobile Bay are worth the trip.

PENSACOLA INTERSTATE FAIR
Pensacola Fairgrounds, Mobile Hwy.
Pensacola 944-4500

More than just prize cattle and beets with thyroid conditions, this fair features an amazing number of rides for all ages, games of chance and skill, plenty of sweets and fatty foods, exhibit buildings and nationally known entertainers (mostly country acts). Lee Greenwood, The Judds, Kenny Rogers, Waylon Jennings, Ray Stevens and Diamond Rio have all performed in past years. Admission charge is $5.00 for adults, $3.00 ages 3-11, $1.00 for parking. All proceeds go the Florida Highway Patrol. 600,000 people a year attend the 10-day fair.

HAUNTED HOUSE WALKING TOUR OF SEVILLE SQUARE
Seville Historic District
Downtown Pensacola 433-1559

This walking tour of the district's haunted places will send chills up your spine whether the weather outside is frightful or not. Listen to the tales of the Charbonier House (1885), whose family members suffered "rage, lunacy, and torment." The local Jaycees, who used the house for their Halloween haunted house, reported doors closing, floating and exploding lights, and other mystifying occurrences. At his house on Seville Square, the spirit of John Gray paces the floors and drags his old sea bag up and down stairs. The architectural firm now occupying the house reports chairs rolling across the floor by themselves, strange smells, footsteps on the stairs and doors opening. Find out more by taking the tour, sponsored by the Pensacola Historical Society. Tickets are $3.00 for adults, $1.50 for children. Reservations are necessary for this popular tour!

November

GREAT GULFCOAST ARTS FESTIVAL
Seville Square, Pensacola 438-4081

This is absolutely the finest arts festival Northwest Florida has to offer. Two hundred artists are chosen from across the country for this juried show to display their wares in historic Seville Square. Artists are chosen for the quality of their work as well as for variety. On display are handmade instruments and furniture pieces, exquisite jewelry, torn rice paper pictures, photography, ceramics — it's more diverse than most any other show on the Gulf Coast, and a good time to start your Christmas shopping! Food, a children's area and continuous live entertainment could keep you there all day. If you choose only one festival to attend this year, make this the one. The three-day festival is free.

VETERANS' DAY PARADE
Pensacola Beach   932-2259

Saluting veterans from World War I on, the parade is sponsored by the Pensacola Beach Elks Lodge and the Santa Rosa Island Authority.

GALLERY NIGHTS
Downtown Pensacola   432-9906

Downtown arts-related businesses open their doors to the public for a celebration of arts and culture. Free buses take gallery-goers to each stop along the tour. There is no admission charged.

POARCH CREEK INDIANS THANKSGIVING DAY POW WOW
Poarch Reservation
Near Atmore, Ala.   (205) 368-9136

The Poarch Creek and other regional tribes congregate on the Poarch Reservation to cook Thanksgiving dinner for visitors and share their culture, their songs and their dances. More than 8,000 showed up for the 1993 Pow Wow, where tribes competed against one another for $5,000 in cash prizes. It's a rare opportunity to witness a culture vastly different from our own, enjoy the beautifully detailed costumes, and cheer on the dancers.

Several booths are set up selling handmade jewelry, handwoven ponchos, toys and crafts. Tickets for the festivities are $3.00 for adults, with children 6 and younger admitted free. If you'd like to have Thanksgiving dinner, it's $4.50 for turkey and dressing, $3.00 for a chicken dinner. Seating is often a problem for dinner, so the festival organizers suggest you bring your own lawn chairs. There's free parking and shuttle service provided.

After a 5K run at 8 AM, the gates for the Pow Wow open at 9 AM. The festival continues until 5 PM. Take Highway 29 north into Atmore and turn left at the Church's Chicken (Jack Springs Road). The reservation is on your left.

DEPOT DAYS
Henry Street at the Railroad Tracks
Milton   623-8493

The two-day, free festival gets bigger every year with the resurgence of interest in the restored Milton Depot as the West Florida Railroad Museum. Besides pony rides, continuous musical entertainment, crafts, a kiddie carousel and the Orbitron space exerciser, a restored L&N boxcar is open for public viewing. Three other railroad cars near the Depot await restoration funding.

BLUE ANGELS HOMECOMING AIR SHOW
Sherman Field
Pensacola Naval Air Station   452-2583

The Blues perform on their own

PENSACOLA — FESTIVALS AND SPECIAL EVENTS

turf every November, a free show that concludes their season. The show begins at 11 AM, but is tied in to other activities on the base, including a display of over 60 military aircraft.

BAYOU HILLS RUN
Bayview Park, Pensacola 432-1768

The 10K course winds its way around Bayou Texar (pronounced Ta-HAR) beginning at 8 in the morning. If you're not that ambitious, there's a two-miler at 9:30 AM. The run benefits the Creative Learning Center.

THE FRANK BROWN INTERNATIONAL SONGWRITERS' FESTIVAL
Various Locations Along the Florida and Alabama Gulf Coasts (205) 981-7325

The week-long event celebrates noted songwriters (some Grammy winners) and many local writers performing at local lounges. Two Songwriters' Seminars are sponsored by BMI and ASCAP, a "Legends of Songwriters" concert is held at the end of the week, and two songwriters' contests award cash and college scholarships. What began as an event for local lounge lizards has exploded into a nationally recognized event. Sponsored by chambers of commerce of the Perdido Key Area, the Greater Gulf Coast, and Orange Beach.

MARKETBASKET
*Bayfront Auditorium
Pensacola 438-4040*

It's a fund-raiser for the Junior League of Pensacola, but the show is a veritable wonderland of Christmas gifts. More than 50 local and national merchants display food items (lots of sampling), jewelry, art work, books, clothing and holiday decorations. If yours is one of the first 50 children to arrive, he or she will be treated to breakfast with Santa on Saturday. Tickets are $3.00 for adults, $1.00 for children 6 to 12, younger than 6 free.

December

CHRISTMAS ON THE ISLAND
Island-wide, Pensacola Beach 932-2259

Highlights of this celebration are the annual Christmas Parade, a decorated Boat Procession, and the Residential/Commercial Outdoor Decorating Contest. Call the Santa Rosa Island Authority for a complete schedule of events.

BLACKWATER HERITAGE TOUR
*Milton Opera House, Willing St.
Milton 623-8493*

The Heritage Tour takes you inside some of the restored businesses downtown as well as private residences throughout Milton's historic district. The first tour (5:00 PM) ends at the Imogene Theatre next to the Opera House, where a lavish dinner and live entertainment finish out the evening. The second tour begins at 2:00 PM Sunday. Tickets are $15.00 for both members of the Santa Rosa Historical Society and nonmembers.

MUSIC AT CHRIST CHURCH
Christ Episcopal Church, Wright and Palafox Sts., Pensacola 432-5115

This free music series started in 1975, providing concerts of local and traveling performers. Although

• 87

concerts are scheduled throughout the year, locals seem to flock to the annual Christmas concert series. Small orchestral ensembles, instrumental and vocal soloists, and the Christ Church choir perform in the ethereal surroundings of this turn-of-the-century church. Donations are accepted and appreciated for the continuation of the concert series.

CHRISTMAS WALK
Seville Historic District
Pensacola   434-1234

The Seville area restaurants and merchants are decked out in Christmas finery to welcome visitors. Many feature great bargains, and most offer coffee, mulled wine or cider and cookies. The Pensacola Historical Museum is open to the public at no charge during the walk, as are some of the homes in the Pensacola Historic Village.

DECEMBERFEST
Gulf Shores, Ala.   (205) 968-7511

You can get in shape for all the holiday partying at this month-long celebration featuring a Christmas tree lighting, fashion shows, boat parades and the Taste of the Tropics, a collection of food booths and tasty delights from several area restaurants.

CHRISTMAS PARADES
Downtown Pensacola, Gulf Breeze and
Milton   434-1234

With downtowns decorated with twinkling lights and shop windows all aglow, the annual Christmas parades make their trek through downtown streets featuring marching bands, dance troupes, gaily decorated floats, gobs of parade throws and, of course, Santa.

PENSACOLA'S NUTCRACKER BALLET
Saenger Theatre, Pensacola   444-7686

A yearly event, the *Nutcracker* is a family favorite, performed by members of local dance troupes and other individuals fortunate enough to be selected in open auditions. The music, dancing and pageantry of the traditional holiday story will delight all ages.

Pensacola Area
Parks and Recreation

Taking on a subject as wide-ranging as recreation is, for a resort area, a rather daunting task. It seems any answer you'd get to "So, what do you do for fun around here?" qualifies for a listing. Herein, some of the top picks for outdoor and indoor fun, which is by no means an exhaustive list. Some equipment rentals have been included to give you an idea of the vast amount of activities available to visitors.

Golf

CLUB AT HIDDEN CREEK
3070 PGA Blvd., Holley-By-The-Sea
Navarre   939-4604

This semiprivate 18-hole, par 72 course with very little water is open to the public and is located off Highway 98 inside the Holley-By-The-Sea subdivision. Avail yourself of the pro shop, driving range, the restaurant and the snack bar. It's open from 6:30 AM to 6 PM every day.

CREEKSIDE GOLF
2355 W. Michigan Ave.
Pensacola   944-7969

Creekside is a fairly new 18-hole course on Pensacola's west side. Marcus Creek winds through the length of the course with oaks, cedars, pines and native wildlife all around. Creekside is open to the public starting at 8 AM every day, and features a practice green, snack bar and a pro shop.

MARCUS POINTE GOLF CLUB
2500 Oak Pointe Dr.
Pensacola   484-9770

Tee off on 18 holes of championship golf, spread over 600 acres of rolling woodlands of pine and oak, with Bayou Marcus Creek bordering much of the course. Marcus Pointe hosted both the 1991 and 1992 PGA Pensacola Open. The full-service facility has practice greens and a clubhouse restaurant. The course is located off Highway 29 just 10 minutes north of downtown. The pro shop opens at 6 or 6:30 in the morning; tee times start at 7 AM.

THE MOORS
3220 Avalon Blvd.
Milton   995-4653

The Moors is one of the area's newest public golf courses, located one mile north of I-10 at the Avalon exit just 10 minutes from Pensacola. The Scottish- and Florida-style golf course features broad fairways and native grasses. The par 71 course is open to the public on a daily-fee basis every day except Christmas. There's a driving range and a lavish Tudor-style clubhouse with a pro shop, locker rooms and banquet facilities. Call three days in advance for tee times on weekends. The pro shop opens at 6:30 AM; tee times begin at 7 AM.

PERDIDO BAY RESORT
One Doug Ford Dr.
Pensacola   492-1223, (800) 874-5355
Home of the prestigious PGA Pensacola Open from 1978-1987, Perdido Bay Resort is just this side of Perdido Key. The resort encompasses a huge tract of land on the bay, an ideal setting for golf or just about anything else. Three of the back nine holes on this 7,154-yard tournament course were picked as some of the toughest on the 1987 PGA tour. Perdido Bay's pro shop opens at 6:30; the practice range, putting and pitching greens, and a snack bar are open starting with the first tee time at 7 AM.

TIGER POINT GOLF & COUNTRY CLUB
1255 Country Club Rd.
Gulf Breeze   932-1333
East and west facilities off Highway 98 offer 36 holes on Santa Rosa Sound. The newer east course highlights an island green on the fifth hole. The west course provides the nicest views and is especially challenging on the back nine. The country club facility has two practice greens, a driving range, a pro shop and a good restaurant, all open to the public; tee times begin at 6:45 AM.

SCENIC HILLS COUNTRY CLUB
8891 Burning Tree Rd.
Pensacola   476-0611
An older semiprivate course recently updated by Jerry Pate, Scenic Hills is located in an attractive residential area. Mature trees keep the links fairly shady even in the dregs of summer. The 6,689-yard, 18-hole course offers four sets of tees for all skill levels. A driving range, golf shop, clubhouse, swimming pool, children's pool and tennis courts are available to members and guests. Located off of 9-Mile Road in northeast Pensacola, the course is open to the public with the first tee time at 6:30 AM.

Golf Supplies and Equipment

EDWIN WATTS GOLF SHOP
5705 N. Davis Hwy.
Pensacola   477-0519
Nationally advertised pro-line golf equipment is Edwin Watts' forte. A golf expert is on staff to offer advice. Open Monday through Friday 9:30 to 6; Saturday 9 to 3.

PLAY IT AGAIN SPORTS
6601 N. Davis Hwy., Tradewinds Shopping Center
Pensacola   477-7407
Buy, sell or trade new and used equipment for golf and many other sports at Play It Again. Open 10 to 7 Monday through Friday; 10 to 6 on Saturdays.

Charter Boats

SCUBA SHACK CHARTERS
719 S. Palafox St.
Pensacola   433-4319
Charter fishing trips, dive trips and moonlight excursions are offered courtesy of the 50' *Wet Dream* docked at Baylen Slip right behind

the Scuba Shack. Trips are available year-round, weather permitting. Scuba Shack provides rod and reel, bait, ice and stringer for trolling or bottom fishing. Cost for a six-hour trip is $50 per person; an eight-hour trip is $55. Pre-certified divers make visits to several sites out in the bay and the gulf. A typical two-tank dive is around $50 per person.

PERDIDO PASS MARINA
Hwy. 182 E. at Alabama Point Bridge
Orange Beach, Alabama   (205) 981-8499,
(800) 981-4499

The *Moreno Queen* party boat takes anglers out for Gulf of Mexico, back bay fishing, trolling, bottom and inshore fishing for individuals or groups. They supply everything you need to fish. Food and drink can be purchased on board. Half-day trips start at $30 for adults, $20 for children. If you don't care to fish, come along for the ride at the child's fare.

CHULAMAR
Docked at Boy On A Dolphin restaurant at the foot of the Pensacola Beach Bridge
Pensacola Beach   434-6977

Trips leave daily for individuals or groups. The *Chulamar* offers day and night fishing, party and moonlight cruises. All equipment and bait are furnished for fishing trips. During the winter months, full-day trips are required to get you far enough out to where the fish are biting. The 7 AM to 5 PM trip is $45 per person; $25 for children. The *Chulamar* will take your family or party out on a private chartered cruise for $250 for two hours; each additional hour is $75.

LO-BABY
Docked downtown at Pitt Slip Marina
Pensacola   934-5285

Fish, dive, cruise or frolic with the dolphins on this 22-passenger vessel. Captain G.K. Lough has been in the business for more than 20 years and loves to tell sea stories to his guests! Boating charters are tailor-made for your enjoyment. On board in the air conditioned cabin, you'll find music, a microwave and a coffee maker. From two-hour boat rides to day-long fishing charters, the 40-foot *Lo-Baby* is ready to go. Capt. Lough recommends the 8- to 9-hour trolling and bottom fishing trip since it takes a few hours just to ride out to the reefs. There, try your luck for snapper, grouper, triggerfish, Spanish mackerel, ling, ladyfish, bluefish and many others. There's enough room in the front of the ship for "fifteen people who really like each other." All cruises are based on demand.

Insiders' Tips

Biking along the beach path down to Fort Pickens on Santa Rosa Island is a wonderful way to spend an afternoon. From Pensacola Beach, it's about a 9½-mile journey, but the surroundings are exceptional, with both beachfront and wooded landscapes.

PENSACOLA — PARKS AND RECREATION

ROCKY TOP
Downtown at Pitt Slip Marina
Pensacola   432-7536
   This one is especially for family fun, offering bottom fishing for king and Spanish mackerel, blue fish and little tunny. Half-day and all-day rates provide fishing for up to six passengers. Fishing license, bait and tackle are all included in the price. The *Rocky Top* runs spring to fall only; call for rates.

Amusement Centers

FAST EDDIES FUN CENTER
505 Michigan Ave. at "W" St.
Pensacola   433-7735
   Get ready for a day your kids will thank you for. This is Pensacola's complete family fun park — rides, games, prizes, parties, food and snacks. Three go-kart tracks, a gameroom with pool tables, air hockey and video games award high-scorers with redemption tickets that can be traded in for prizes. Open during the summer months from noon until midnight; winter hours are 3 to 10 PM. There's no admission charge, just a cost to ride and play games.

Canoeing/Tubing

ADVENTURES UNLIMITED
Tomahawk Landing, 12 miles north of Milton, then 4 miles off Hwy. 87
Milton   623-6197, (800) 239-6864
   You're really missing out on some of the best parts of Northwest Florida if you skip a trip down one of the inland rivers. Adventures Unlimited provides canoes, life jackets, paddles, camping gear, ice, refreshments and just about everything you could ever possibly need on a one-day or overnight canoe trip. Cabins on Wolfe Creek and campsites are available for overnight stays; see the chapter on Pensacola Accommodations for all the details. Canoe rentals start at $11.00 per person for a short trip; to completely outfit you for an overnight stay on the river is $40.00 per person.

BOB'S CANOES
On Munson Hwy. at the Coldwater Creek Bridge
              623-5457, (800) 892-4504
   In business for more than two decades, Bob's Canoes sends you down the river in canoes, tubes, paddleboats and kayaks. Choose from Coldwater Creek, the East Fork of the Coldwater, Juniper Creek or the Blackwater River — all clear, cool and relatively shallow freshwater streams, perfect for beginners. A large waterfront pavilion at rental headquarters is available for picnics. Bob's provides canoes, paddles, life jackets, seat cushions and a trip up the river to your starting point. Rates start at $11.00 per person for a short trip, $12.00 for a day trip. Tube floats are $7.00 each; $4.00 for a cooler tube. Paddle boats, kayak trips and group rates are available.

BLACKWATER CANOE RENTAL
9 miles east of Milton off Hwy. 90
              623-0235, (800) 967-6789
   Canoe, tube or kayak for a half-day or up to a three-day camping trip on the beautiful Blackwater River. Blackwater Canoe Rental provides all the necessities for getting you there; you supply your own

PENSACOLA — PARKS AND RECREATION

Pull your boat up to one of Perdido Key's many marinas to refuel the boat and the family — many full-service marinas offer on-site restaurants and convenience items.

camping equipment, eats and drinks. A short trip (1½ hours paddling time plus stops) is $11.00 per person; a day trip (four hours paddling) is $12.00. Children 12 and younger are free with two adults in one canoe. Overnight trips start at $17.00 per person. Call for reservations and directions.

Watersport Rentals

WAVERUNNER & JET SKI RENTALS
17100 Perdido Key Dr.
Perdido Key   492-7656

Rates here are by the hour and half-hour, and the staff will deliver to you! They're closed in the winter months.

CURIOSITY RENTALS
17100 Perdido Key Dr.
Perdido Key   492-2516 or 492-1188

You may be curious about what some of these strange contraptions are, but the folks at Curiosity Rentals will explain all before you rent. Take the family out on a pontoon or ski boat, or pack the car for an outing with rods and reels, boogie boards and beach umbrellas. They offer one-stop rentals for outdoor adventure by the hour, half-day and daily. Open 9 to 7 daily; earlier by appointment.

KEY SAILING
Quietwater Beach Boardwalk
Pensacola Beach   932-5520

Key Sailing is the watersports headquarters on the beach for parasailing, waverunners, pontoon and sailboats. Pick up a brochure from the Pensacola Beach Visitor Information Center (right across the street) and get $5.00 off your rental. They close up shop in the winter.

• 93

Bike Rentals

**PARADISE SCOOTER
& BICYCLE RENTAL**
715-A Pensacola Beach Blvd.
Pensacola Beach   934-0014
   We call these bikes "beach cruisers," since they're especially made for the terrain on the beach, kind of short and squat with big tires. Bike paths cover all of Pensacola Beach up to the Gulf Islands National Seashore boundaries. Riding into the Fort Pickens area comes highly recommended for some outstanding scenery and solitude. Motorized scooters are also available. Paradise is closed during the winter months; call for new rates by the hour, day or week.

Concert Tickets

TICKETMASTER OUTLETS
Pensacola Civic Center Box Office	433-6311
Sound Shop Records	
University Mall	476-2533
Saenger Theatre Box Office	438-2787
NAS-Pensacola	452-4229

Community Centers

   Many of these public recreational centers offer classes in dance, music, arts, crafts, sports or self-improvement. Most are located within area parks; all are available to residents. Please call 435-1770 for schedule information or hours of operation.

BAYVIEW COMMUNITY CENTER
Bayview Park, 20th Ave. and Lloyd St.
Pensacola   435-1788
   With a gorgeous view of Bayou Texar and a location right on the water in Bayview Park, this community center is popular for its dance classes (featuring jazz, tap, ballet, ballroom, and belly!), gymnastics program, oil painting, after-school arts and crafts, and Taekwondo classes, plus many special events like the annual Easter Egg Hunt.

BAYVIEW SENIOR CITIZENS CENTER
Bayview Park, 20th Ave. and Lloyd St.
Pensacola   435-1790
   Right next to the community center, this senior center gets its members from AARP, Retired Railway Employees, and other retiree groups but is open to all seniors aged 50 and older. The building houses meeting rooms, a pool room (that's billiards), an art room, a music room, a social hall and a library/lounge area. Several programs and classes in activities such as stitchery, ballroom dancing, and aerobics are offered.

BEACON CLUB
119 E. Church St., Pensacola   435-1791
   The Beacon used to be a teen hangout in the '50s and '60s, and many high schools and social clubs use the old refurbished hall for reunions. The club, located in the heart of the downtown historic district (across the street from Seville Quarter) has a large dance floor, a bar, kitchen, ice machine, giant-screen TV with VCR hookup and a pool table. Rental is only $100.00 for a night.

E.S. COBB COMMUNITY CENTER
6th Ave. and Mallory St., Pensacola   435-1792
   Tumbling, cooking and baking, tennis, ceramics, Black History studies and Kid's Movie Nights are some

PENSACOLA — PARKS AND RECREATION

Numerous festivals, from seafood to jazz to art, center around oak-shaded Seville Square in Pensacola.

of the activities available at this community center. Everybody can enjoy the free daily activities like volleyball, shuffleboard, ping pong, skating, basketball, and video games. Call about Cobb's many sports programs and special events.

CORINNE JONES CENTER
600 W. Government St., Pensacola   435-1793

This small center presents many programs for senior citizens, including ceramics, senior exercise, sewing and walking.

EAST PENSACOLA HEIGHTS CENTER
3208 E. Gonzalez St.
Pensacola   435-1794, 435-1770

Some of the classes offered here are adult aerobics, folk dancing, quilting, art study and round dancing. The facility is also available for parties, meetings and receptions.

FRICKER CENTER
1121 W. DeSoto St., Pensacola   435-1795

Get fit with regular activities such as aerobics, jogging, weight training, karate, tumbling and basketball. Other offerings are arts and crafts for children, gospel singing, adult basic education and bingo.

GULL POINT CENTER
7140 Old Spanish Trail (at Creighton Rd.)
Pensacola   478-4301

Ladies' exercise, Walk for Life, Kenpo Karate, Cheerleading and Modeling are just as few of the offerings at Gull Point. Call about classes in art, special parents' nights out and recitals by the Gull Point Dancers.

SANDERS BEACH CENTER
913 S. "I" St., Pensacola   435-1798

With a beautiful view overlooking Pensacola Bay, Sanders Beach is in an older part of town with a public

• 95

PENSACOLA — PARKS AND RECREATION

beach and picnic facilities nearby, two lighted tennis courts, a volleyball court, boat ramp and a pier. Soccer classes, as well as classes in country and western dancing, tennis and ballroom dancing are available at the center.

SCOTT TENNIS CENTER
4601 Piedmont Dr. at Summit Blvd. Pensacola   432-2939

Eighteen courts with lights, a pro shop, restrooms, lessons and major tournaments are all available to locals at this exceptional tennis facility in the Cordova Park area.

MALCOLM YONGE CENTER
925 E. Jackson St., Pensacola   435-1796

The Yonge center offers youth basketball, football, girls' slow pitch softball and many other youth programs throughout the year.

City Parks

There are nearly 100 parks within the city limits, featuring everything from old fort sites to swimming pools to scenic overlooks on the bay. Below, just a few of our top picks.

BAYVIEW PARK
20th Ave. and Mallory St., Pensacola

This 30-acre park overlooks Bayou Texar and is probably the city's very best park, located in the heart of East Hill. Three separate playground areas provide enough equipment for a hoard of kiddies; covered picnic pavilions with barbecue grills are just perfect for family reunions or Sunday outings. There are four tennis courts lit for night play, a boat ramp, a huge over-the-water deck with piers (these are great for either fishing or duck feeding) and a recreation center.

CECIL T. HUNTER MUNICIPAL POOL
200 E. Blount St., Pensacola   435-1797

This public pool under the I-10 spur is open daily May through September from noon until 8 PM. Lessons are offered during the summer by Red Cross-certified instructors. Admission fee to the pool is $1.00 for adults (18 and older), 50¢ for children 4 to 17, and free for children younger than 4. Children younger than 10 must be accompanied by an adult. Season passes are available.

ADMIRAL MASON PARK
9th Ave. and Romana St., Pensacola

Wide and open and right on the bayfront, Admiral Mason is tops for kite flying. It is here, too, where you'll find the Wall South, the half-scale replica of the Vietnam Veteran's Memorial in Washington, D.C.

PLAZA FERDINAND
Bounded by Government, Palafox, Zaragoza and Jefferson Sts., Pensacola

Plaza Ferdinand is the very centerpiece of the downtown historic district. It was here in a somber ceremony in 1821 that Andrew Jackson accepted Florida from Spain. This "passive" park (meaning there's no ball fields or playground equipment) with its lovely fountain also hosts "Picnics in the Plaza" each Friday during lunch in October and May.

SEVILLE SQUARE
Bounded by Government, Adams, Zaragoza and Alcaniz Sts., Pensacola

The original city square, the Seville area is a virtual hub of festival activity throughout the year with its charming gazebo, giant oaks and shady sidewalks.

BARTRAM PARK
South of Seville Square, Pensacola

The small bayfront park just south of the main park at Seville Square is used primarily for smaller festivals such as the Crawfish Festival, and as an overflow for larger festivals like the Great Gulfcoast Arts Festival.

BAY BLUFFS PARK
Scenic Hwy. and Summit Blvd., Pensacola

Pensacola is fortunate enough to be the only city in Florida with its own bluffs — most likely because most of Florida is *completely flat!* These bluffs are gorgeous, though, and now have scenic overlooks and stairs built all the way to the foot of the bay (huff, huff).

JOHN HITZMAN/OPTIMIST PARK
Langley Ave. and Buford, Pensacola

This is a fine 16-acre park in northeast Pensacola with plenty of room to run. Since the Optimists had a hand in funding this park, the playground equipment is really first-class; ball fields with stadium bleachers and lots of large trees beckon visitors to linger.

EXCHANGE PARK
Lakeview Ave. and Watson, Pensacola

National softball tournaments are held at this large fenced-in park complete with good playground equipment, rest rooms and a concession stand.

FORT GEORGE
Palafox and LaRua Sts., Pensacola

This is more of a historic site than a park, but it's worth a stop to read about the great 61-day siege of Pensacola in 1781, part of which took place right under where you're standing. Only a tiny portion of the land was saved, and a few representative parts of the original fort are reproduced. The view of the entire downtown area to the bay from here gives you an idea of why this location was chosen to build a fort.

Pensacola Area
Arts and Culture

Since so many Pensacolians have moved here from other places, and many from major metropolitan areas, they are used to attending the ballet, the opera, and the symphony. Our cultural awareness has been expanded by these new residents who see the need for a particular group, and so take it upon themselves to start one.

How very fortunate we are, too, to have the facilities and the savvy to attract Broadway productions, top-name entertainment and nationally recognized musicians and soloists to perform with our many choral, opera, and symphonic groups.

We acknowledge the assistance of the Arts Council of Northwest Florida for its permission to reprint the groups as listed in its 1993 edition of the *Northwest Florida Cultural Directory*. Note: There really *are* this many cultural groups in the Pensacola area. We are not making this up.

Crafts

GULF COAST WEAVERS GUILD
9200 Chisholm Rd., Pensacola   477-0240
This guild provides an opportunity to learn or further your knowledge of weaving, spinning and basket-making through workshops, demonstrations and community exhibitions. Call for class schedules.

Dance

EXPRESSIONS IN DANCE
9708 N. Palafox St. (Ensley)
Pensacola   478-4749
Want to move those feet in graceful, joyous fashion? Then this group can help with dance instruction in tap, ballet and jazz for dancers from 4 years to adult.

GULL POINT PERFORMING DANCERS, INC.
Gull Point Community Center, 7140 Old Spanish Trail Rd.
Pensacola   432-8965, 478-4301
Between 10 and 20 students, ages 10 to 17, are either invited or recommended to become part of this performing troupe, which is privately funded. The Gull Point Dance program serves its members by offering dance instruction in a variety of styles and educational and performance opportunities. Instruction at the Gull Point Community Center paves the way for three scheduled performances each year, one of those in conjunction with the Pensacola Junior College Dance Theater. All performances are free and open to the public.

PENSACOLA — ARTS & CULTURE

Traditional and contemporary dance performances thrill audiences of the Northwest Florida Ballet.

KALEIDOSCOPE DANCE THEATRE/ BALLET PENSACOLA
400 S. Jefferson, Pensacola   432-9546

This nonprofit school, headquartered at the Pensacola Cultural Center, seeks to educate its young dancers in a variety of dance styles, offering performances through Ballet Pensacola. Performances are held three times a year at the Saenger Theatre. Kaleidoscope also offers classes for your budding ballerinas from age 3 on up.

PENSACOLA JUNIOR COLLEGE DANCE THEATRE
1000 College Blvd., Pensacola   484-1330

Students may earn college credit while they learn about dance as a performance art and have the opportunity to perform themselves. Call the number above for registration information.

OLD WORLD FOLKDANCERS
1218 E. Moreno St., Pensacola   433-1405

Revival of recreational folk dancing with an emphasis on Eastern Europe is the thrust of this teaching group. Folkdance demonstrations are held at various festivals and events throughout the year.

PENSACOLA SPECIAL STEPPERS, INC.
P.O. Box 11313, Pensacola   455-6052

This square dance club is specifically set up for people who are mentally handicapped. The Special Steppers have performed at many national conventions and have received recognition for their efforts, including a Presidential Citation.

• 99

PENSACOLA — ARTS & CULTURE

**ST. ANDREW'S SOCIETY
OF PENSACOLA SCOTTISH
COUNTRY DANCERS**
5642 Leesway Blvd., Pensacola   477-7136
The Society offers weekly classes for beginners and more advanced dancers, and was organized to maintain the standards set up by the Royal Scottish Dance Society of Edinburgh, Scotland.

Ethnic/Cultural

**AFRICAN-AMERICAN
HERITAGE SOCIETY, INC.**
400 S. Jefferson St., Pensacola   469-1299
Besides its yearly festival, this group seeks to promote and encourage the development of African-American cultural heritage in Northwest Florida. *When Black Folks Was Colored*, a collection of memoirs and poems by local African-Americans, was a 1993 highlight. The Society meets monthly at the Pensacola Cultural Center.

**HANSA CLUB/GERMAN-AMERICAN
SOCIETY OF PENSACOLA**
P.O. Box 552, Gulf Breeze   932-2326
Camaraderie and a chance to practice your German is offered to those of German-American, German, Austrian and Swiss heritage.

**ITALIAN CULTURAL SOCIETY OF
NORTHWEST FLORIDA, INC.**
*P.O. Box 4142, 6555 Mobile Hwy.
Pensacola   839-9443*
This group is trying to organize an Italian-American museum to promote Italian heritage. It offers grants, scholarships and endowments to Italian-Americans or to groups promoting Italian-American culture. The group usually meets for lunch, but is not on a regular schedule. Call for meeting place and time

**ITALIAN CULTURAL SOCIETY
OF PENSACOLA, INC.**
P.O. Box 1811, Pensacola   932-7062
This cultural society promotes the Italian culture through nonprofit activities and scholarships.

**THE JAPAN CULTURAL SOCIETY
OF NORTHWEST FLORIDA, INC.**
P.O. Box 11512, Pensacola   944-1164
The Japan Cultural Society promotes understanding of Far Eastern culture through a series of cultural events.

**NORTHWEST FLORIDA
CREEK INDIAN COUNCIL**
3300 North Pace Blvd., Pensacola   444-8410
The Creek Indian Council is set up to ensure that every Creek Indian and his or her descendants takes advantage of all state, local and federal benefits currently available. Group members also offer educational programs for schools and civic groups.

PHILIPPINE CULTURAL SOCIETY, INC.
8113 Westbourne Dr., Pensacola   453-9240
Filipino-Americans interested in becoming more involved with Escambia County schools and cultivating native customs through exhibits, a performing arts series and presentations will find this group helpful.

**ST. ANDREW'S SOCIETY OF
PENSACOLA, FLORIDA, INC.**
302 Camellia St., Pensacola   932-3605
Monthly dinner meetings are

PENSACOLA — ARTS & CULTURE

held the second Friday of the month at the Seville Inn. Discussions center around promotion of Scottish culture and heritage.

Literary

FRIENDS OF THE PENSACOLA PUBLIC LIBRARY
200 W. Gregory St., Pensacola   435-1760

The Friends is a volunteer non-profit group promoting library services to the community. The group's annual book sale raises money for the continuation and enhancement of library services.

WEST FLORIDA LITERARY FEDERATION, INC.
Pensacola Cultural Center
400 S. Jefferson St., Suite 212
Pensacola   968-9344

This diverse group offers several sub-groups in the promotion of West Florida writers. The Readers Showcase performs local and well-known writers' works at the Pensacola Cultural Center. The Back Door Poets meet once a month in a coffeehouse atmosphere to read their poetry, and the Writer's Workshop and Student Writer's Network meet monthly to develop the writing technique of published and unpublished authors. Another program, Writers in Service to Education, puts local writers in the public schools to talk about their craft. The federation publishes an annual anthology, the *Emerald Coast Review*, containing the best works of West Florida writers.

WEST FLORIDA REGIONAL LIBRARY
Headquarters: Pensacola Public Library
200 W. Government St.
Pensacola   435-1760, 435-1763

The library system serves residents of Escambia and Santa Rosa counties with branches in Northwest Pensacola, Milton, Gulf Breeze and Jay. Bookmobile and Outreach Van service reach the more rural areas of Escambia County. There's even a Sub-regional Talking Books Library for visually and physically handicapped residents.

Music

AMERICAN THEATRE ORGAN SOCIETY
Saenger Theatre, 118 S. Palafox Place
Pensacola   444-7696

A magnificent 1925 Robert Morton pipe organ, built especially to accompany silent movies at the Saenger Theatre, now comes out of storage for recitals and concerts by prominent organists.

THE CHORAL SOCIETY OF PENSACOLA
1000 College Blvd., Pensacola   484-1800

This group performs "serious"

Insiders' Tips

It's great to have the opportunity to see the ballet, the symphony, the theater and a wealth of fine concerts — all without leaving town!

PENSACOLA — ARTS & CULTURE

music in grand style, both at Pensacola Junior College's Ashmore Fine Arts Auditorium and at the Cokesbury Methodist Church right across the street. The Choral Society focuses on all musical styles and periods, often accompanied by the Pensacola Symphony Orchestra. Locals look forward to the stirring annual performance of Handel's "Messiah" at Easter or Christmas.

THE EARLY MUSIC CONSORT
5106 Treahna Rd., Pensacola   455-1500

This recorder group performs traditional and contemporary works, many times in period costume, for festivals and private functions.

GULF COAST CHORALE
412 Dolphin St., Gulf Breeze   932-9248,
932-6209

Limited to 40 members, the Gulf Coast Chorale's four yearly concerts (in mid-October, mid-December, mid-March and the end of April) focus almost entirely on the classics: Mozart, Bach, Haydn, Beethoven, Handel. Vocalists must audition for a slot in the Chorale; membership dues are $40 yearly. Performances are at St. Anne's Catholic Church, 100 Daniels Drive in Gulf Breeze.

JAZZ SOCIETY OF PENSACOLA, INC.
P.O. Box 18337,
Pensacola, Fla. 32523-8337   433-8382

The Jazz Society founded the Pensacola JazzFest, a weekend festival held each April in Seville Square combining local, regional and national jazz performers. Group members also make themselves available to schools and civic groups for lectures, discussions and performances.

JOE OCCHIPINTI'S BIG BAND
P.O. Box 4068   (800) 447-8532
Pensacola, Fla. 32507-0068   433-6287

Strictly a performance band (that means for hire), the five-piece ensemble's repertoire is all the best of the Big Band era.

MUSIC AT CHRIST CHURCH
18 W. Wright St., Pensacola   432-5115

Sit back, relax and enjoy organ, vocal and chamber music presented in the gilded opulence of Christ Church downtown. Performances are held throughout the year, with groups and soloists brought in from all over the world. The highlight of the year is the Pensacola Summer Music Festival, which showcases the church's Gabrial Key pipe organ. All concerts are open to the public. There is no admission charge, but donations are accepted to continue these outstanding programs.

MUSIC STUDY CLUB OF PENSACOLA
400 Jefferson St., Pensacola   434-3770

The Music Study Club seeks to enhance the love of music by encouraging young musicians to hone their skills and perform publicly. The club meets monthly at the Pensacola Cultural Center.

PENSACOLA FIESTA BARBERSHOP CHORUS
8349 Pilgrim Rd., Pensacola   476-5922

These delightful gentlemen, clad in festive red-and-white-striped vests, perform traditional and contemporary barbershop tunes every time they get the chance. They are part of a larger organization called The Society for the Preservation and Encouragement of Barbershop

PENSACOLA — ARTS & CULTURE

The Great Gulfcoast Arts Festival brings the talents of 200 artists from across the country to historic Seville Square each November.

Quartet Singing in America, or SPEBSQSA for short(!).

PENSACOLA JUNIOR COLLEGE GUITAR ASSOCIATION/PENSACOLA GUITAR ENSEMBLE AND SOCIETY
Department of Music and Drama - PJC
1000 College Blvd., Pensacola   484-1805

Under the direction of Joe Stallings, the Association sponsors concerts and recitals throughout the community, sometimes bringing in outside masters to enhance student's education. The classical Guitar Ensemble performs a wide range of music, from Renaissance to contemporary. Call for scheduled concert information.

PENSACOLA MUSIC TEACHERS ASSOCIATION
726 Bay Blvd., Pensacola   433-5206

There are the folks to call to set up lessons for your child prodigy. Area music teachers in piano, voice and other instruments teach applied music, sponsor sonata contests and work with students who must audition for scholarships. Stop into Reynalds Music House (Garden and Jefferson streets in Pensacola) or Dollarhide Music Center (Palafox Place in Pensacola) for listings of music teachers who take students as young as 6 or 7 right up to college age. Other members of the association can be contacted through the University of West Florida or Pensacola Junior College.

PENSACOLA SYMPHONY CHILDREN'S CHORUS
400 S. Jefferson St., Pensacola   434-7760

Weekly rehearsals are held at the Pensacola Cultural Center for children ages 9-13. The competition is fierce for placement in the group,

• 103

PENSACOLA — ARTS & CULTURE

and only the most musically talented are accepted. But, the benefits are great: These kids get to sing with the Pensacola Symphony Orchestra, and the results will take your breath away. They're good.

PENSACOLA SYMPHONY ORCHESTRA
321 S. Palafox St., Pensacola   435-2533
This very professional volunteer group seeks to promote symphonic music by bringing it to the people several times yearly. Yearly auditions are held. The orchestral performances, all at the Saenger Theatre, at times combine with the talents of the Pensacola Symphony Children's Chorus, The Choral Society or nationally known guest soloists and conductors for many memorable evenings of first-rate entertainment. Tickets are available at the Saenger Theatre box office.

Science/History

ESCAMBIA AMATEUR ASTRONOMER'S ASSOCIATION
c/o Professor Wayne Wooten, Sponsor
6235 Omie Circle, Pensacola   484-1152,
477-8859
Search out shooting stars, meteor showers and other strange lights in the sky at public stargazings, offered at area schools and during the summer at Fort Pickens on Santa Rosa Island. Regular meetings are in the Geology Lab at Pensacola Junior College the last Friday of the month. The Science & Space Theatre at Pensacola Junior College is the site of the association's monthly labs, but it also holds regular planetarium shows, which are open to the public Thursday through Saturday. Admission charge is $3.00 for adults; $2.00 for students; children younger than 5 are not admitted. Call 484-1150 for a complete schedule of shows.

HISTORIC PENSACOLA PRESERVATION BOARD
120 E. Church St., Pensacola   444-8905
This lavish Art Deco office (formerly home to a very "hip" ad agency) seems an odd home base for a group interested in the preservation of historic landmarks. But the HPPB has accomplished some remarkable feats, first among them the Pensacola Historic Village (see listing under Pensacola Attractions). If you live in the North Hill or Seville Historic Districts, you may be able to locate and search through a file with your home's address to find original blueprints, old photographs of your house and a listing of all former owners and their occupations.

NATIONAL MUSEUM OF NAVAL AVIATION
Naval Air Station, Pensacola   453-2389
Here is a one-of-a-kind museum, and even for nonmilitary personnel, a "must see." Pensacola got the first-ever Naval Air Station, hence yet another nickname, "The Cradle of Naval Aviation." But the museum is crammed with fascinating displays, exhibits and rare full-sized aircraft incorporating Navy, Marine Corps and Coast Guard Aviation. The new Blue Angel Atrium, used for concerts and lectures, displays four of the retired planes hanging overhead in perfect formation.

PENSACOLA — ARTS & CULTURE

PENSACOLA HISTORICAL SOCIETY
*405 S. Adams St., Pensacola   433-1559,
                                434-5455*

Pensacolians find this phone number easy to memorize — it's the date when Don Tristan de Luna first landed on Pensacola shores (1559). The historical museum is housed in Old Christ Church, the oldest church in Florida (1832). Its many displays and artifacts detail life from the earliest tribes of Native Americans through the lumber boom of the late 19th century and beyond. Open 10 to 4:30 Monday through Saturday; admission is $2.00.

Theater

MINI-MASQUERS, INC.
4241 Morelia Pl., Pensacola   432-2042

Performing twice yearly in the fall and spring at the Pensacola Little Theatre, the Mini-Masquers' focus is family entertainment. Two recent productions were the musical *Meet Me In St. Louis* and the children's production of *Beanstalk*.

PENSACOLA LITTLE THEATRE, INC.
*186 N. Palafox St.
Pensacola   432-2042, 432-8621 or 434-6703*

The Little Theatre, now in its 57th season, cranks out eight shows a year: Musicals, comedies, dramas, you name it. Whatever the group performs, the community attends in force to support it. Once the third phase of the Pensacola Cultural Center is completed (around 1995), the PLT will have a new permanent home with a 600-seat theater. The Pensacola Little Theatre Guild is the fund raising arm, and staffs the box office.

PENSACOLA MINING AND WATER BALLET AUTHORITY
*P.O. Box 10570
Pensacola, Fla. 32514   474-0034*

Marc Peterson and his troupe of happy revelers produce plays, one acts and reviews for special events, as well as improvisational theater. Recent productions are *Three Men Naked From the Waist Down* (dinner theater) and a one-man show on Christopher Columbus.

The troupe doesn't have a real home, but performs at several locations, among them the Imogene Theater in Milton, the Pensacola Cultural Center, First Night Pensacola on New Year's Eve, and last Christmas they performed *How the Grinch Stole Christmas* on the front lawn of a private residence.

PENSACOLA OPERA, INC.
321 S. Palafox St., Pensacola   433-6737

Here is a group of real opera aficionados who saw a need to bring good opera performances to the people, so started this group. They do more than just perform, however; one goal of the Opera is to provide an opportunity for students and other talented individuals to perform in complete opera productions. The group has a performing arts series, provides lectures, demonstrations, workshops and tours of its Scenic Design Studio. This year, the opera performs *Rigoletto, The Barber of Seville* and *La Traviata* at the Saenger Theatre in downtown Pensacola.

PUPPET FACTORY
8804 Jernigan Rd., Pensacola   484-8494

Yes, they perform traveling pup-

• 105

PENSACOLA — ARTS & CULTURE

pet shows, but what the group enjoys doing most is workshops for children from kindergarten through the 8th grade on designing and building puppets and stages and learning how to become puppeteers. Find them at the weekly "Picnics in the Plaza" at Plaza Fredinand in the fall and spring, at the First Night Pensacola Celebration on New Year's Eve, at the Family Expo at the Pensacola Civic Center in the spring, and at many schools and other events all year long.

ST. MARY'S PRODUCTIONS
8019 Coronet Dr., Pensacola   484-1400

Yet another Pensacola-based theater group, St. Mary's produces one show per year (usually a musical) at the Saenger Theatre, with auditions open to the public.

UNIVERSITY THEATRE/ THEATRE DEPARTMENT
University of West Florida
11000 University Pkwy., Pensacola   474-2146

This is a thriving theater community, staging three or four full productions annually, student productions, and the Playwright's Repertory Festival during the summer, which produces three or four productions from a single playwright.

Visual Arts

ARTEL GALLERY
22 N. Palafox St., Pensacola   432-4080

Local artists exhibit their work here, as well as hold exhibitions of local, regional and national contemporary art. All artwork is offered for sale.

CASA DE COSAS
210 E. Garden St., Pensacola   433-5921

This candy factory-turned-gallery in the heart of downtown features several rooms filled with paintings, pottery, jewelry, sculpture and crafts.

FLORIDA FIVE
4535 LaVallet Lane, Pensacola   434-7398

Florida Five is a group of talented artists whose sole purpose is to bring their combined knowledge to the schools and the community through exhibitions, classes, lectures and demonstrations.

GARTH'S ANTIQUES & AUCTION GALLERY
3930 Navy Blvd., Pensacola   456-7192

Winston Garth and his staff conduct fine arts showings four times yearly for school children and arts charity auctions at his shop on Navy Boulevard.

GULF BREEZE ARTS, INC.
312 Smith Circle, Gulf Breeze   932-5691

A group of artists got together five years ago and now are 50 strong. Monthly meetings are held at the Gulf Breeze Library; speakers lecture on some aspect of the visual arts. Gulf Breeze Arts members award a scholarship each year to a deserving high school student, and every October exhibit their work at the Santa Rosa Recreation Center.

NORTHWEST FLORIDA PORCELAIN ARTISTS
P.O. Box 34405
Pensacola, Fla. 32507   492-9501

Here is a unique art form that this group seeks to expand by learning how to better create it. The em-

PENSACOLA — ARTS & CULTURE

The Pensacola Little Theater is one of several area groups performing musicals, dramas and comedies throughout the year. The PLT will occupy a new 600-seat theater in the Pensacola Cultural Center in 1995.

phasis on their work is china painting, but members create other art pieces as well. The porcelain is displayed once a year in November at the East Pensacola Heights Center and at the Garden Center on Ninth Avenue in Pensacola. Meetings are moved around so no one always has to travel; they are held the second Friday of each month. Dues are a paltry $5.00 a year.

PENSACOLA MUSEUM OF ART
407 S. Jefferson St., Pensacola   432-6247

This is the old City Jail building, where art pieces are exhibited in cell blocks with bars on the windows. The surroundings are nearly as interesting as the exhibits. Some of the art is local, and monthly exhibitions showcase some outstanding work. The museum also brings in really terrific exhibitions from all over the world — Chinese porcelain, Dutch Masters, photography and contemporary art.

SANTA ROSA ART ASSOCIATION
P.O. Box 4256
Milton, Fla. 32572   623-6686, 623-1256

These artists enjoy promoting their craft in any way they can: by bringing in guest artists for workshops, by exhibiting at their annual Members' Show (held at the Milton Depot during November's Depot Days Festival), and by getting their work selected for the juried Riverwalk Fine Arts Show in Milton, held in late March or early April. Regular meetings are the last Saturday of the month at the Milton Depot on Henry Street.

UNIVERSITY OF WEST FLORIDA ART GALLERY
11000 University Pkwy., Pensacola   474-2482

Since this is a university studio, it calls for diversity. And that's what you'll find — to educate, to keep an

• 107

PENSACOLA — ARTS & CULTURE

eye on new trends, to display the avant garde.

UNTITLED II
1904 E. Moreno St., Pensacola   438-1572

Untitled II is comprised of feminist artists who provide programs of readings and critiques on current issues and topics. Once a year, the group exhibits its work in the University of West Florida art gallery.

Multidisciplinary

THE CREATIVE GUILD
106 E. Gregory St., Pensacola   433-2400

Now here's a diverse group: Photographers, illustrators, copywriters, graphic artists, fine artists, sign artists, sculptors, video and audio production people, voice talent, you name it. The Guild is an organization of creative professionals brought together to promote their creative abilities, to network with other creative folks, and to let businesses know they're out there, waiting to be hired. The Creative Guild recently put up an advertising exhibit during one of the DADA Tours (see below), calling themselves "The Creative Liberation Front," sporting fatigues and berets, and staged dramatic readings of advertising copy. They meet the first Thursday of every month.

DOWNTOWN ARTS DISTRICT ASSOCIATION (DADA)
P.O. Box 731
Pensacola, Fla. 32594   432-9906

Organized to increase awareness of the arts in downtown Pensacola and sponsored by the Arts Council of Northwest Florida, the Downtown Arts District Association puts on the ritz three times a year (March, July and November) with a gallery tour. Pottery shops, photography studios, bookstores, frame shops, art galleries and studios, museums and music stores provide exhibitions, entertainment and refreshments to the public free of charge.

FIRST NIGHT PENSACOLA
803 N. Palafox St., Pensacola   434-2724

Looking for an alternative to the traditional New Year's Eve celebrations? This alcohol-free family entertainment might be just the ticket. Events and entertainment take place all over downtown Pensacola, featuring storytellers, musicians, dancers, actors, singers, magicians and mimes.

GREAT GULFCOAST ARTS FESTIVAL
P.O. Box 731
Pensacola, Fla. 32584   432-9906

An annual event for more than two decades, the GGAF might just be the best festival in Northwest Florida. The juried show attracts artists from all over the country to exhibit in historic Seville Square. Only the top 200 are chosen in a wide variety of mediums from ceramics to torn rice paper to woodworking. Dance and musical performances, a children's area and heritage arts are also part of this popular celebration.

WEST FLORIDA ADVERTISING COUNCIL
P.O. Box 12491
Pensacola, Fla. 32573   478-6011

This council is a group of advertising folks who get together once a month over lunch to hear one of their peers speak about some aspect of "the biz." Once a year, the Advertising Council stages the ADDY Awards, to reward the best in local advertising.

PENSACOLA HERITAGE FOUNDATION
P.O. Box 12424
Pensacola, Fla. 32582   438-6505

Started almost 30 years ago, the Heritage Foundation promotes the history and preservation of this area through entertainment and recreational fund raisers.

PENSACOLA JUNIOR COLLEGE LYCEUM
Music and Drama Department
1000 College Blvd., Pensacola   484-1800

Throughout the school year (September-May), the artist series holds regular exhibitions either at the PJC Ashmore Fine Arts Auditorium on campus or the Saenger Theatre downtown.

SANTA ROSA HISTORICAL SOCIETY, INC.
814 Caroline St. SE
Milton   623-8493, 626-9830

The historical society oversees the preservation and restoration of several historical buildings and sites. The Milton Opera House (home to he Imogene Theatre, the Historical Society's headquarters and Museum of Local History), the Milton L&N Depot and the Arcadia Mill are all properties owned by the society.

SOCIETY FOR CREATIVE ANACHRONISM
SCA c/o 10279 Sugar Creek Dr,
Pensacola, Fla. 32514   479-1680

Need a historical reenactment? These are the folks to call, but only if you need something from the Medieval Period (600-1600 AD). But lots of people do, so the society gets out into the community to provide it with exhibitions, classes, lectures and demonstrations (jousting, perhaps?).

Pensacola Area Higher Education

Widely diverse and ever-expanding, the Pensacola area is filled with educational opportunities for part-time and full-time students wishing to obtain degrees, complete course work for career promotion, or simply to expand their knowledge. Both the university and the junior college are well regarded within the community; it seems as if nearly every resident takes a class at one time or another. Art classes, computer workshops and creative writing programs appeal to most students seeking to try something fun or improve their skills outside of the workplace.

UNIVERSITY OF WEST FLORIDA
11000 University Pkwy.
Pensacola 474-2000

UWF is a regional, four-year, fully accredited liberal arts institution located within a 1,000-acre nature preserve in north Pensacola. Comprehensive undergraduate, graduate and continuing education programs in environmental resource management, marine biology, coastal zone studies and archaeology, plus more than 100 traditional business, science, arts, social sciences and education disciplines are offered on the main campus or off-campus centers. About 8,000 students attend the main campus either full- or part-time, with 1,000 more attending satellite classes at Okaloosa-Walton Community College, the UWF Fort Walton Beach Center, and the Eglin Air Force Base Center (see the chapter on Fort Walton Beach Area Higher Education for more information). The local public radio station, WUWF (88.1 FM), broadcasts from new facilities at the university, playing classical, jazz and alternative music, as well as sponsoring or cosponsoring numerous community events such as the annual Jazzfest, Springfest, and the Great Gulfcoast Arts Festival.

PENSACOLA JUNIOR COLLEGE
Main Campus, 1000 College Blvd.
Pensacola 484-1000
Naval Air Station Center, Bldg. 679, West Wing
Pensacola Naval Air Station 453-7526,
 452-4520
Downtown Center, 19 W. Garden St.
Pensacola 434-8411
Warrington Campus, 5555 W. Hwy. 98
Pensacola 457-2200
Milton Campus, 1130 U.S. Hwy. 90 West
Milton 626-1010

An integral part of the Pensacola community since 1948, Pensacola Junior College reaches into every level of continuing education. Classes and associate degrees are offered in over 200 major areas of study including advanced technology and vocational programs. The new Baroco

PENSACOLA — HIGHER EDUCATION

Center for Science and Advanced Technology is a real boon to the entire area. The Center supports the sciences, business, computer science and computer integrated manufacturing. The regional public television station, WSRE (Channel 23), broadcasts from the campus, and in 1994 will move into superb expanded facilities for educational and community enrichment.

GEORGE STONE AREA VOCATIONAL-TECHNICAL CENTER
2400 Longleaf Dr.
Pensacola   944-1424

Just off Pine Forest Road northwest of Pensacola, George Stone provides programs for vocational and technical training for students aged 16 and older in preparation for a career, retraining, supervisory training or supplementary preparation. High school students may earn three elective credits for completion of a one-year program. Adults completing programs and passing state-required basic skills tests in math and language are eligible for a Vocational Certificate of Completion. More than 70 percent of students completing course work at George Stone find placement in their field of study or a comparable field. Programs offered include Business and Office Technology; Building Trades; Technology Education; Automotive, Engine and Body Repair; Health & Personal Services; Public Service; Agribusiness & Natural Resource Education; Welding; Upholstery and Furniture Refinishing; Cooperative Education; and Apprentice Training.

PENSACOLA CHRISTIAN COLLEGE
250 Brent Lane
Pensacola   478-8496

Pensacola Christian's stunning, sprawling campus features state-of-the-art everything, including its own bowling alley, skating rink, television and radio studios, production facilities and publishing company for PCC's Worldwide Ministry. This independent, private school began 20 years ago with 100 students; that number has grown to include students from every state in the U.S. and 40 foreign countries. Education here is based on the Christian traditional approach as opposed to the humanistic, progressive systems offered in public schools. Every facet of the student's life is impacted by the school, from education to religious training to social behavior. Students are expected to conform absolutely to the beliefs and philosophies the school imparts or risk forced withdrawal. Students may earn Bachelor's, Associate's, Master's and even a few Doctoral degrees in more than sixty areas.

• 111

Pensacola Area Real Estate

Buy yourself a fixer-upper for $25,000 or build a palace on the beach for millions. Strange, isn't it, that the two can be within a few minutes' drive of each other. If you're one of the fortunate few with wealth to spare, or have had to forego eating out for three years just to make a down payment, you can buy a whole lot more house for your money in the Pensacola area. Mainland neighborhoods such as the North Hill Preservation District and East Hill are undergoing regentrification; old Pensacola families are selling off (or in some cases, giving away) huge tracts of land that have been in the family for generations. And young professionals who like city life and the cosmopolitan feel of a nearby downtown are waiting in line to snatch it up.

Whenever possible, new uses are being found for historic buildings. Two such successes are the old Sacred Heart Hospital on 12th Avenue in East Hill, now converted into restaurants, offices and shops; and the P.K. Yonge School on Palafox Street in the North Hill neighborhood. The building, which sat empty and vandalized for years, will enjoy a facelift and a new life as home to the Florida Department of Law Enforcement.

With this new trend toward revamping and redoing, one would tend to rethink putting in something as useful as sidewalks and streetlights, but, no, what would seem to be standard in most parts of the country just hasn't found much popularity here. I remember when I lived outside the city limits, I called my county commissioner to request that the county install a streetlight at the corner of my street, which intersects one of Pensacola's busiest roads. It was so dark at night I'd passed it up three times! He suggested I get a bunch of my neighbors together and all pitch in to buy one! I have streetlights in my city neighborhood, but sidewalks are still an unlikely tax hike away.

Pensacola has been built up around the water, and there seems to be enough waterfront property for everyone who can afford it with the Gulf of Mexico, Escambia, Pensacola and East bays, Santa Rosa Sound, four rivers and maybe more bayous than that. Still, if that weren't enough, homeowners in Villa Venyce east of Gulf Breeze can park their boats in their backyards on a series of man-made canals.

Hot new areas for subdivisions are in Pace, north of Pensacola, and east Gulf Breeze, stretching to Na-

PENSACOLA — REAL ESTATE

varre and beyond. What ten years ago was wilderness and acres of pine forest is now an ever-expanding population base, essentially blurring the divisions between "here" and "there."

Perdido Key

What's nice about Perdido Key is that it hasn't been spoiled by too much development and is still a tiny, neighborly community that just happens to sit on some of the world's most beautiful beachfront. A walk along the shoreline will yield huge scallops, whelks and sand dollars. What's different about the beach here is that there are no sand bars to trap the shells like on Pensacola Beach. Condominiums were a fairly recent addition to the key when building took off in the early '80s. Completely surrounded by water, Perdido Key just can't get any bigger. So it just keeps getting better.

LAND'S END
13335 Johnson Beach Rd.
Perdido Key   492-9819

One of Perdido Key's early condominiums, Land's End is located just east of where Highway 292 (Perdido Key Drive) takes a huge swerve to the right. Just look for the mini-waterfall out front. This ultra-fancy high-rise has all the amenities of a world-class resort: elevated and lighted tennis courts, a large heated pool and sundeck, high-speed elevators, a clubhouse, exercise room, covered parking and its own boardwalk to the beach. The units are huge — only 30 occupy the 10-story building. These three-bedroom units feature deluxe kitchens with Euro-style cabinets; luxury master baths with oversized whirlpools, a separate glass shower enclosure and a bidet; large walk-in closets; separate dressing areas; a screened lanai with a ceiling fan and summer kitchen; insulated and tinted floor-to-ceiling windows; and a gorgeous gulf-front panorama from every unit.

EDEN
16281 Perdido Key Dr.
Perdido Key   492-3336, (800) 523-8141

Was it Mae West who said "Too much of a good thing . . . can be wonderful!" Around every corner, inside and out, is another undiscovered feature, another glorious view not yet taken in. From its architecture modeled after luxury hotels along the French Riviera to its exotic landscaping and waterfalls, nothing has been left out of these one-, two- and three-bedroom gems. For more information on Eden, look under Pensacola Accommodations.

Insiders' Tips

Pick up a Sunday edition of the *Pensacola News Journal;* the "Homefinder" section highlights a different residential area each week, lists completed sales and classifieds, and offers tips on building and buying.

• 113

PENSACOLA — REAL ESTATE

Photo: Robin Rowan

Grand turn-of-the-century homes such as this one sprang up as a result of Pensacola's lumber boom.

PERDIDO SUN
13753 Perdido Key Dr.
Perdido Key   492-2390, (800) 227-2390

You came here for the sun — now have it all year long with a luxury one-, two- or three-bedroom furnished condo unit. With the gulf just steps from your back door, imagine the thrill of waking up to the sound of the surf *every day!* Perdido Sun features a large outdoor pool on the gulf side with a hot tub nearby, a glass-enclosed heated indoor pool for year-round swimming, an exercise room and a sauna.

Real Estate Companies

LEIB & ASSOCIATES REALTY
14620 Perdido Key Dr.
Perdido Key   492-0744, (800) 553-1223

Leib & Associates offers sales, vacation rentals and management of properties on Perdido Key exclusively. From luxury high-rises like Eden (see listing above) to the Perdido Dunes Victorian-style townhomes to single-family residences, Leib & Associates knows Perdido Key better than many who've lived here for years.

AQUATIC REALTY
14508 Perdido Key Dr.
Perdido Key   492-4632, (800) 881-RENT

Vacation properties abound on Perdido Key, and Aquatic Realty handles sales of some of the best: Perdido Shores (three-bedroom townhomes with fireplaces on the gulf), Perdido Sun (with indoor/outdoor pool, sauna and lots of extras), Spinnaker (two-bedroom low-rise units on the gulf) and Molokai Villas (gulfside villa townhouses).

PENSACOLA — REAL ESTATE

Key Concepts
13880 Perdido Key Dr.
Perdido Key 492-5462

Qualified agents can assist you in finding a home, condo, townhome or lot in Pensacola or on Perdido Key, one of "America's Top Beaches." Condos are available at Land's End (see listing above), Sandy Key and Sea Spray (both high-rises on the gulf), and in the new Parasol gulf-front, single-family community.

Pensacola Beach

Funky little cinder block homes that were thrown up here in the '50s for about $5,000 now sell for more than $100,000. It's the land on the half-mile-wide island, not the house, that makes the difference. Pensacola Beach, part of Santa Rosa Island, is the developed area including Quietwater and Casino beaches, east to the Gulf Islands National Seashore Santa Rosa area, and west to Fort Pickens gate. Most of the stores and commercial buildings are confined to the area around Casino Beach, leaving many quiet pockets of residential development.

Tristan Towers
1200 Fort Pickens Rd.
Pensacola Beach 932-9341

The two- and three-bedroom/two-bath condos may not be directly on the gulf, but the 16-story high-rise offers water views from every unit! Waters in Santa Rosa Sound stay a bit warmer and much calmer than the gulf, but if you wish, the gulf is just across the street. Water in the Olympic-size swimming pool is *always* calm and ready when you are, day or night. Two elevators, two lighted tennis courts, a clubhouse, security, plus the best views on the beach make Tristan Towers as popular for year-round residents as it is for vacationers.

San de Luna
1350 Fort Pickens Rd.
Pensacola Beach 932-9723

These three-story townhouse units are exceptional for their privacy, their layout, and their size. You won't feel crowded into these one-, two- and three-bedroom/two-bath units with their large decks, ample windows and generous closets. Living space is on the second and third floors, connected by a spiral staircase. The first floor is reserved for covered parking and storage. On the top floor, vaulted ceilings make rooms appear even larger. In the one-bedroom units, the master bedroom and bath take up the entire third-floor space, and all units feature a whirlpool bath, separate shower stall and dressing room. Barbecue grills, a large swimming pool and tennis courts are communal amenities.

Starboard Village
1111 Fort Pickens Rd.
Pensacola Beach 932-0988

Large rooms, covered parking and stone fireplaces welcome you to your private paradise. These two-, three- and four-bedroom condos with their stark white exteriors and red roofs almost seem to sell themselves. Have morning coffee on your private balcony as your senses

PENSACOLA — REAL ESTATE

awaken to sunshine and sea air. A large swimming pool on the gulf side and a private beach walkover will make you believe that this beach is all yours.

Real Estate Companies

TRISTAN REALTY, INC.
1010 Fort Pickens Rd.　　　932-7363
Pensacola Beach　　　(800) 445-9931

Located right in front of Tristan Towers, Tristan Realty can help you choose one of the two- and three-bedroom/two-bath units in the towers or in one of its other properties. San de Luna, a soundfront townhome community, has one- and two-bedroom units available; the new Palm Beach Club located at Fort Pickens gate and the entrance to Gulf Islands National Seashore features covered parking, whirlpool tubs, wet bars and fireplaces; and at Sabine Yacht & Racquet Club, a one-bedroom condo on the bayside sleeps six and comes with a boat slip.

PENSACOLA BEACH REALTY
649 Pensacola Beach Blvd.　　932-5337
Pensacola Beach　　　(800) 874-9243

Discover resort property sales and rentals from the folks who know the beach best. From the beach cottages scattered along Via de Luna and Panferio Drive to condo communities and private villas to big-bucks investments at exclusive addresses like Sugar Bowl (a dozen or so mansions near the entrance to the Gulf Islands National Seashore), PBR will find you what you need and what you can afford.

REAL ESTATE HOUSE INC.
U.S. 98 and College Pkwy.
Gulf Breeze　　934-8700, (800) 239-4346

Nine top real estate agents are available to help with property on Pensacola Beach, Navarre Beach or in Gulf Breeze. Schools are excellent, services are convenient and waterfront property is plentiful.

Gulf Breeze

Right between Pensacola and Pensacola Beach (you *have* to go through it to get to either), Gulf Breeze is on a peninsula with Santa Rosa Sound on one side and Pensacola Bay on the other. Unlike Pensacola Beach, neighborhoods are heavily wooded with a good amount of open space left. New shopping centers, grocery stores and movie theaters have finally made a daily trip into Pensacola unnecessary. Schools in the area are exceptional, and real estate prices land somewhere between Pensacola and the beach. One drawback you'll hear from residents again and again — on a sunny weekend during tourist season, traffic can back up all the way through Gulf Breeze and over the bridge to the beach, which can sometimes be frustrating!

BAHAMA BAY CLUB
201 Pensacola Beach Rd.
Gulf Breeze　　　　　　932-2200

You wouldn't know these places were here unless you got off the main road and drove in. These older two-story townhomes are set far enough off the main road to have a buffer from the traffic, but they're convenient to everything in Gulf

PENSACOLA — REAL ESTATE

Breeze, and just this side of the bridge to the beach. The whole area is heavily wooded; many of the trees put here when Bahama Bay Club was new have grown large enough to shade both the courtyard area and the parking lot. Two-bedroom/two-bath units are well maintained and very affordable. Bahama Bay is located just behind Harbourtown Shopping Center.

BAY WOODS
Off Hwy. 98, east of Gulf Breeze

Elegant homes, many on Pensacola Bay, are tucked into this densely wooded area. Carved out of a mature forest, Bay Woods is really the best of two worlds — the pristine views of waterfront living plus the cool shade of overhanging trees. Homes are beautifully landscaped with two- and three-car garages; some have pools.

QUAIL RIDGE LANDING
Off Hwy. 98, east of Gulf Breeze

Brand new homes on wooded lots are causing a stir in an area popular with young families. These starter homes are filled with charm — dormer windows, gabled rooflines, oval etched glass in the front door and privacy fences. Quail Ridge is located within a short walk of the public boat landing on the Intracoastal Waterway.

Real Estate Companies

MONTGOMERY REALTORS
1388 Country Club Rd.
Gulf Breeze   932-9228, (800) 445-2507

Let these professionals tell you about their favorites places — Gulf Breeze, South Santa Rosa County and the beaches. They'll soon be your favorites as well, since the staff at Montgomery Realtors can speak knowledgeably and enthusiastically about schools, recreation, city parks, hospitals, shopping and the unequalled natural beauty of this area.

CENTURY 21 FOUR WINDS REALTY
2507 Gulf Breeze Pkwy.
Gulf Breeze   932-3513

Right in the hub of the Gulf Breeze home-buying market, Four Winds has up-to-the-minute listings of waterfront, golf course land and resort property sales, and they'll manage your investment property if you don't plan to live there year round. With Century 21's national relocation service, learn all about the area *before* you make that first visit to look for a home.

Navarre Beach

Take a gorgeous beach, add a few condos, some colorful homes, sparkling gulf waters and friendly neighbors. That's Navarre Beach, and unlike its neighbors Pensacola Beach and Fort Walton Beach, it has remained small, uncluttered and fairly unpopulated. Residents like to get together at Juana's for an ice cold beer on a hot day and speculate about who might be moving into the big peach house being built just down the road, or talk about the great buffet they had last Friday at the Fish House, or where the fish are biting. Navarre Beach does have a Holiday Inn, a few good restaurants and a couple of shops, but it seems determined to remain small, with

PENSACOLA — REAL ESTATE

Photo: Robin Rowan

The North Hill Preservation District is on the National Register of Historic Places.

enough space between homes to feel uncrowded, and enough open beach for everyone to take in the view. The town of Navarre stretches along Highway 98 farther inland.

HOLLEY BY THE SEA
6846 Water St.
Navarre   939-2371

Fountains inside man-made lakes shoot water ten feet into the air at the entrance to Holley By The Sea — you can't miss it along Highway 98. The residential community, called The Estates at Hidden Creek, offers golf course homes and homesites sprinkled around The Club at Hidden Creek, a country club and golf facility. Naturally, these homes are large, built with classic designs suited for Florida living with high ceilings, lots of windows and drought-resistant landscaping. Membership at the recreation center is extended to all property owners, which includes eight clay tennis courts, two heated pools and a workout center.

Pensacola

The city proper is pretty well built up, with something like 6% of available land undeveloped. If living in a home convenient to downtown and all of its festivals and waterfront amenities appeals to you, there's an abundance of gorgeous older homes on the market. That doesn't necessarily mean historic (more than 50 years old), unless you're intent on restoring one of the charming Seville or North Hill district homes, which can be as old as 150 years! Newer subdivisions along Spanish Trail and across the Santa Rosa County line in Pace seem to attract two-income couples and families with young children.

PENSACOLA — REAL ESTATE

MONTAGE
Spanish Tr. and Langley, Pensacola

A barrage of subdivisions has hit the Spanish Trail area, once just a dirt road that nobody much used. Neighborhoods are trendy and upscale, like this one at Montage, although except for new subdivision signs every couple of hundred feet or so, all of this new construction looks pretty much alike. If you don't like a lot of yardwork, Montage has the solution — small fenced yards that are fully landscaped (meaning not much sod to water and fertilize). Home exteriors will be either vinyl or brick with square footage between 1,400 and 2,000 square feet. Gourmet kitchens, spacious master bedrooms and a two-car garage add to Montage's appeal.

CORDOVA PARK
North Summit Blvd., Pensacola

There's got to be something pretty special about a neighborhood where kids grew up, moved away, then returned to raise their own children. But that's what has happened many times over in the Cordova Park area. Since construction began in 1950, trees and shrubbery have reached maturity, lending a shady, pleasant air to these mostly three-bedroom/two-bath homes. Professional couples with children enjoy the quiet, safe streets, the neighbor-helping-neighbor attitude, and one of the best elementary schools in the county.

EAST HILL
9th Ave. east to Bayou Texar and Texar Dr. south to Escambia Bay

The dividing lines are somewhat blurry, but this area is one of the nicest in Pensacola (and I'm not saying that just because I live there). The homes nearest Bayou Texar (te-HAR) are mostly large and expensive, as you might imagine, but the majority of the neighborhood offers charming, affordable residences, even if this is your first home. The oldest homes tend to be between the entrance to Bayou Texar (at Escambia Bay) and north to Blount Street. Most of these are charming wood-frame buildings with overhanging porches and all-around windows built before the advent of air conditioning in the '30s and '40s. Keep going north and homes get newer; a great many are red brick with three bedrooms and two full baths on shady, comfortable lots. There's a lived-in "hometown" feel to East Hill; the flat, shady streets find joggers, bikers and dog-walkers out at all times of the day.

MILESTONE
Nine Mile Rd. at Pine Forest Rd.
Pensacola   434-2244

Here's your chance to get in on the ground floor of this ultra-planned community on 200 acres, located within a mile of I-10. Two-acre homesites are available if you'd like to build a horse stable behind your property(!); most buyers will probably go for the 100' x 150' lot built around common areas such as jogging trails and bike paths, a "town square" with a gazebo and bandstand, parks and ball fields, and retail shops. Hey, they've even planned in *sidewalks!* A business park will come later, so many of the residents will be able to walk to work.

Inverness
Off Bayou Blvd., Pensacola

This self-contained neighborhood features several cul-de-sacs to keep through-traffic to a minimum. For that reason, children can ride bikes and play safely in the 1980s-style subdivision. A yearly fee of $55 pays for maintenance of common areas and electricity for street lights. Lot sizes range from 90' x 150' to half an acre.

Pebble Ridge
Avalon Blvd., Milton

Thirty-five different floor plans are available from the builders of Pebble Ridge, or choose one of the dozen or so homesites left in the development. Most homes are modest, with brick or vinyl exteriors, vaulted ceilings, garden tubs and separate showers. Upgrades of the basic house package include extra insulation in the walls and ceiling, extra energy-efficient heating and cooling units, tiled foyers and special ceiling and wall treatments. Many of the residents of Pebble Ridge are retirees who were attracted by Pebble Ridge's proximity to The Moors, a new championship golf course.

Real Estate Companies

1 First Choice Realty of Pensacola
7200 N. 9th Ave., Suite A-1
Pensacola   476-2154, (800) 405-HOME

1 First Choice Realty puts the Better Homes and Gardens "Home Marketing System" to work for you when you're ready to sell, making your home more attractive to prospective buyers. The 11-member team deals primarily with single-family residential property in Pensacola, Gulf Breeze, Pace, Pensacola Beach and Navarre Beach. Through Better Homes and Gardens Military Relocation Assistance program, First Choice can hook you up with all sorts of information about this area from wherever you are now; even overseas!

Joseph M. Endry Realty Company
22-A Via de Luna Dr.
Pensacola Beach   932-5300
3232 Gulf Breeze Pkwy.
Gulf Breeze   932-1000
4301 Spanish Trail Rd.
Pensacola   432-5300
5601 Woodbine Rd., Pace   994-6128

You'll see many JME signs all over town. The agency does quite a business, specializing in sales and rentals of residential homes, weekly beach rentals, resort real estate and waterfront property. That about covers everything except JME's relocation service, which, of course, is free.

Connell & Manziek Realty Inc.
2107 Airport Blvd.
Pensacola   478-4141

Let Connell & Manziek make buying a home easy for you (like they've done for innumerable insiders). As a member of the Multiple Listing Service, daily printouts keep you informed of current and new listings in your price range and in your neighborhoods of choice.

Pensacola Area
Retirement

The positive side of so many military personnel constantly coming through Pensacola for a two-, three- or four-year tour of duty is that when they leave, they take the good word about Pensacola with them. Nearly all of them return at some point, for a military reunion or a vacation. Or they come to find their place in the sun to retire. With plenty of sunshine, plentiful housing, an affordable cost of living and water at every turn for fishing or boating, the Pensacola area seems an ideal place for empty nesters to put down permanent roots. Although many retirees opt for beach condominiums, some like the comfort and camaraderie afforded by retirement communities. The carefree lifestyle frees up time spent on yard maintenance, household repairs and a host of mundane chores for relaxation, a wealth of planned activities and time to get to know their neighbors.

Retirement Communities/ Independent Residential Facilities

THE ELITE GUEST HOUSE
1120 N. Palafox St.
Pensacola 438-8368

You'll fall in love with this turn-of-the-century Queen Anne home the moment you see it. The 1909 Elite Guest House is located in Pensacola's North Hill Preservation District, and the owners have done a magnificent restoration job, doubling the size of the original house a few years ago with an attached addition in back. Original stained and leaded glass windows, turned balusters and a gazebo connected to the shady front porch bring back memories of simpler times. It's only about two miles from Baptist Hospital, and less than that from the heart of downtown. Choose from 18 private or semiprivate rooms or two-room suites with cabinets, a sink, a microwave and a small refrigerator. Residents have their medications supervised and administered, menus are individually planned with special dietary needs in mind, and the home has a wander-guard system for Alzheimer residents.

AZALEA TRACE
10100 Hillview Rd.
Pensacola 478-5200

This 56-acre campus in north Pensacola offers more choices in residential units than any other retirement community in the area (25 floor plans!). It is near Escambia Bay and a population center with excel-

• 121

PENSACOLA — RETIREMENT

lent medical facilities and shopping malls. Towering pines, nature trails, a pond and four seasons of flowering plants provide a well-tended and relaxing environment away from the bustle of the city.

Choose the type of unit that suits your lifestyle, from master studios to spacious two-bedroom units in the Garden, Midrise or Terrace apartments. All feature complete kitchens, safety-equipped baths, security and complete privacy. If you'd like to prepare a gourmet meal for close friends, you have the facilities at your disposal. If you choose not to cook, have your meals in the comfortable dining area, and invite your friends if you wish. On the grounds are a library, a sewing room, a woodworking shop and an indoor swimming pool. Azalea Trace's Health Care Center offers 24-hour emergency, recuperative and unlimited long-term care.

BAY BREEZE NURSING & RETIREMENT CENTER
3375 Gulf Breeze Pkwy.
Gulf Breeze   932-9257

Freedom, privacy and independent living are the keys to the Bay Breeze lifestyle. This adult congregate living facility is spacious and decorated with contemporary furnishings in warm pastels. In addition to pleasant surroundings, Bay Breeze provides social and recreational activities, a comfortable, airy dining facility and assistance with medication, bathing, dressing and housekeeping on a daily basis or as needed. Physical therapy, occupational therapy and speech therapy are also offered as part of the rehabilitation program.

If further care is needed, the Bay Breeze Nursing Center, adjacent to the retirement center, is available for 24-hour restorative nursing care. A registered dietician plans all meals with regard to physician recommendations for each patient. The facility is a member of the Florida Health Care Association.

CARPENTER'S CREEK COMMUNITY
5918 N. Davis Hwy.
Pensacola   477-8998

Ninety-six one-bedroom, efficiency and studio units center around an attractive Southern-tinged facility in the heart of Pensacola. A tin-roofed main building with a cupola and weather vane, wrapped porches, arched windows and vaulted ceilings lend an air of comfort and hospitality. Mennonite-style cooking is a favorite of the residents. In addition to a full country breakfast each morning, Carpenter's Creek serves full Southern meals such as country fried steak, fried mullet, fried chicken and short ribs, greens, hushpuppies and

---

The average age of Pensacola area residents is 44 years.

PENSACOLA — RETIREMENT

okra with homemade bread, rolls and desserts daily.

Private baths, small in-room refrigerators, a 24-hour snack and juice bar and CCC's own country store are just a few of the special touches that make it feel more like home. Rentals are by the month with no endowment fees. Ten assisted living units for residents and nonresidents provide 24-hour medical assistance, private baths, cable TV connections and rentals by the day, week or month.

BAYOU VILLAS
201 S. Stillman St.
Pensacola   434-1504

Tranquil waterfront retirement living is the hallmark of this facility on the shore of Bayou Chico, one block off of Navy Boulevard on Pensacola's west side. Private and semiprivate units are available with or without waterfront views. Two-room suites have separate living and bedroom accommodations and are specially suited to couples. Enjoy the company of friends and a lovely view of the bayou in the large dining room. A full-time recreation director provides for field trips, shopping, arts and crafts, lectures, movies and special social hours, among other activities. Limited nursing services provide assistance with bathing, grooming, dressing and medications on a 24-hour basis. Counseling is offered to residents for respiratory therapy, physical therapy and speech therapy.

THE HOMESTEAD VILLAGE
7830 Pine Forest Rd.
Pensacola   944-4366, (800) 937-1735

Although fairly new, this well-planned development is already one of the most popular retirement communities in the area. It could have something to do with the delicious Mennonite recipes used in the dining area or the fresh breads and rolls made right here daily. Several living options are available to residents. Choose from a large custom-designed two-bedroom, two-bath patio home at The Homestead Estates; a studio, one- or two-bedroom, two-bath unit with a Jacuzzi at The Homestead Garden Apartments; one of the new Homestead Villas with nine spacious floors plans in one, two or three bedrooms with access to the dining room and common areas and a 24-hour nurse call; or one of four apartment styles in The Homestead Retirement Center, a cluster design building featuring special 24-hour assistance with personal care, medications and recuperation. Fees are by the month with no endowment.

Homestead Village is also licensed to provide extended care, should the need arise. They're so certain you're going to love it that they've extended an invitation for a free lunch and a tour of the grounds; just call for an appointment.

Senior Support Services

ESCAMBIA COUNTY COUNCIL ON AGING, INC.
21 S. Tarragona St.
Pensacola   432-1475

The Council on Aging coordinates everything from Meals on Wheels (hot meals delivered to elderly people) to a retired senior volunteer program to a foster grandparent and senior companion program. Staff members can assist with home care services, Alzheimer's respite care, transportation or choosing a retirement community. The Council truly provides full-service support to all residents of the county aged 55 or older. Satellite offices offer many of these services in Cantonment and Century.

AMERICAN ASSOCIATION OF RETIRED PERSONS
904 N. 57th Ave.
Pensacola   455-3794

Assistance with everything from tax forms to travel, the AARP has become a powerful voice for seniors. Get an AARP card for discounts on hotels, tickets to special attractions and even restaurants. The Pensacola Chapter 3564 will guide you to the special services and programs available in this area.

Pensacola Area Health Care

The Pensacola area is indeed fortunate to have three top-quality medical facilities in the area. Residents need look no further than one of these excellent hospitals for special facilities and services in women's health, cardiac care and cancer care, and for many high-tech services such as laser surgery, MRI and CT Scans.

Hospitals and Medical Centers

SACRED HEART HOSPITAL
5151 N. 9th Ave.
Pensacola   474-7000

A Daughters of Charity hospital in business for more than 75 years, Sacred Heart has a reputation for being both "high-tech" and "high-touch," providing 21st-century technology and equipment while offering dignity and respect to all of its patients. Sacred Heart was the first hospital to perform open heart surgery in Northwest Florida, the first to do laparoscopic abdominal surgery, and the first to perform a coronary atherectomy (removal of plaque from narrowed heart arteries).

A major expansion is underway for a new Children's Hospital and Women's Hospital. The Children's Hospital at Sacred Heart is already widely known throughout Northwest Florida for its neonatal intensive care unit and unique and specialized services for children. Recent expansions include the Ann L. Baroco Center for Women's Health, the James H. Baroco Center for Cancer Care, a new magnetic resonance imaging facility, new facilities for the diagnosis and treatment of heart disease, and an outpatient Center for Diagnostic Services.

BAPTIST HOSPITAL
1000 W. Moreno St.
Pensacola   434-4011

Baptist Hospital is affiliated with Baptist Health Care, a network of hospitals, nursing homes and retirement centers throughout Northwest Florida and South Alabama. It operates the Life Flight helicopter ambulance service within a 100-mile radius of Pensacola, which has proven invaluable in getting critically injured patients the care they need more quickly. Added to these are other innovative programs and services such as behavioral medicine, The Women's Resource Center, a health and wellness program, the Special Delivery program for families-to-be, and Mobile Diagnostics, providing CT Scanning, mobile mammography and mobile EEGs for smaller hospitals affiliated with Baptist Health Care.

GULF BREEZE HOSPITAL
1110 Gulf Breeze Pkwy.
Gulf Breeze   934-2000
This is an acute-care facility affiliated with Baptist Health Care serving Gulf Breeze, Pensacola Beach, Holley-Navarre and South Pensacola. A 24-hour emergency department is there when you need it.

WEST FLORIDA REGIONAL MEDICAL CENTER
8383 N. Davis Hwy.
Pensacola   494-4000
Northwest Florida's largest healthcare facility provides care to residents of Northwest Florida, south Alabama, and south Georgia. This Hospital Corporation of America (HCA) hospital offers 547 total beds, 400 of which are in the hospital, 58 in the rehab facility, and the remainder in the mental health and outpatient cancer treatment centers. WFRMC specializes in cardiology, neurology, ophthalmology and orthopedics, among others. On the grounds of the hospital in north Pensacola are The Rehabilitation Institute of West Florida for general rehab and head and spinal cord injuries; The Pavilion, providing substance abuse treatment, inpatient geriatric services, and outpatient programs; the West Florida Cancer Institute for comprehensive diagnosis and treatment; and the Medical Center Clinic, P.A., a group of 140 practicing physicians representing all major specialties.

Immediate Care Centers

Got a bad cold? Need a flu shot? Maybe your daughter's developed a rash while on vacation. These centers offer full-range physician services for non-emergency illnesses or injuries on a onetime or temporary basis. Appointments are taken but are not necessary.

CARRIAGE HILLS FAMILY CARE CENTER
4929 Mobile Hwy., ½ mile north of Fairfield Dr.
Pensacola   453-3281
Open 8 AM to 9 PM, seven days a week.

PERDIDO BAY FAMILY CARE CENTER
13139 Sorrento Rd., one mile north of the Intracoastal Waterway Bridge near Perdido Key   492-0543
Open 8 AM to 6 PM, Monday through Friday; Saturdays from 8 to 1.

PENSACOLA BOULEVARD FAMILY CARE CENTER
6950 Pensacola Blvd., north of Car City
Pensacola   478-4357
Open 8 to 8 Monday through Saturday; Sundays 2 to 8 PM.

PINE FOREST FAMILY CARE CENTER
7284 Pine Forest Rd., ½ mile south of I-10
Pensacola   944-4686
Open 7 to 6 Monday through Friday; 8 to 1 on weekends.

TIGER POINT FAMILY CARE CENTER
3370 Gulf Breeze Pkwy., across from Pizza Hut
Gulf Breeze   932-9251
Open 8 to 7 Monday through Friday; weekends from 8 to 1.

PENSACOLA — HEALTH CARE

NORTH DAVIS FAMILY MEDICINE CENTER
6330 N. Davis Hwy.
Pensacola   478-3336
Open 8 to 6 Monday through Saturday.

WARRINGTON PRIMARY CARE
4045 Barrancas Ave.
Pensacola   455-0314
Open 9 to 5 Monday through Friday.

NAVARRE FAMILY MEDICINE CENTER
7964 Navarre Pkwy.
Navarre   939-6110
Open 8 to 5 Monday through Friday.

SCENIC HIGHWAY FAMILY MEDICINE CENTER
8105 Scenic Hwy.
Pensacola   484-9435
Open 7:30 to 5:30 Monday through Friday.

WEST SIDE FAMILY MEDICINE CENTER
6715 Hwy. 98 W.
Pensacola   453-6737
Open 8 to 5 Monday through Friday.

SPANISH TRAIL FAMILY MEDICAL CENTER
4601 Spanish Tr.
Pensacola   433-9911
Open 8 to 5 Monday through Friday.

GULF BREEZE FAMILY MEDICAL CENTER
85 Baybridge
Gulf Breeze   932-2251
Open 8 to 5 Monday through Friday.

WARRINGTON FAMILY MEDICAL CENTER
30 S. 3rd St.
Pensacola   455-4516
Open 8:30 to 4:30 Monday through Friday; ½ day on Wednesday.

CANTONMENT FAMILY MEDICAL CENTER
748 Hwy. 29, ¼ mile north of Champion Paper Mill
Cantonment   968-0763
Open 7 to 5 Monday through Friday.

WEST PENSACOLA MEDICAL CENTER
321 S. Fairfield Dr.
Pensacola   456-6696
Open 7:30 to 5 Monday through Friday.

Support Services

THE HEALTH PERFORMANCE CENTER
1601 Airport Blvd.
Pensacola   474-6150

The center offers health and fitness training in addition to cardiovascular stress testing, evaluation and monitoring, nutrition counseling and weight loss programs for adults, teens and children.

PEDIATRIC EXTRA HOURS AT SACRED HEART
Children's Medical Services Building
5177 N. Ninth Ave.
Pensacola   474-7299

Do you have a sick child but also a must-do business schedule? Then call this after-hours pediatric service that accepts kids from infancy through 18 years. It's open Monday through Friday 5 to 10 PM; weekends from 2 to 9 PM.

SACRED HEART SURGICAL CENTER
5151 N. 9th Ave.
Pensacola   474-7120

Sacred Heart offers a variety of surgical procedures, enabling patients to go home the same day. Some of those services include eye, dental/oral, ear/nose/throat, gynecology, orthopedic, pediatric, recon-

• 127

PENSACOLA — HEALTH CARE

structive, podiatry, urology and vascular surgery. A new surgical center will open above the existing Ann L. Baroco Center for Women's Health in late summer 1994.

THE REHABILITATION INSTITUTE OF WEST FLORIDA
8391 N. Davis Hwy.
Pensacola   474-5358

Comprehensive rehabilitation services are offered here, such as rehab nursing for disabled patients, physical therapy, occupational therapy, therapeutic recreation, speech-language pathology and audiology, pulmonary rehabilitation, social work and psychological and vocational services. The institute's Work Performance Rehabilitation Program is designed to get an injured worker back on the job as quickly as possible through an intensive program of stress management, biofeedback and relaxation training, job modification, nutrition management and energy conservation.

MEDICAL CENTER CLINIC, P.A.
8333 N. Davis Hwy.
Pensacola   474-8000

This physician-owned group practice of 140 physicians represents every major specialty.

SURGICARE
1000 W. Moreno St.
Pensacola   469-2169

A state-of-the-art outpatient surgery center at Baptist Hospital, SurgiCare allows patients to go home the same day, reducing costs, inconvenience and stress!

THE NORTH FLORIDA SURGERY CENTER
4600 N. Davis Hwy.
Pensacola   494-0048

This is a surgical center where prep, surgery and recovery takes place all in one day. Patients go home the same day, which is particularly helpful for small children.

Physician Referral Services

If you're new in town or just visiting, a physician referral service can be invaluable. If you need a doctor for a non-emergency vacation-related injury or illness, if your prescription runs out and you're only halfway through your vacation, or if you have a health concern that won't wait, make a call to one of these *free* services. Affiliated with area hospitals, referral staff members will be happy to call to make you an appointment while you're still on the line.

CALL SACRED HEART
Offered by Sacred Heart Hospital   474-7500
Open 8 to 4 Monday through Friday.

MDLINE
Offered by Baptist Health Care   434-4080
Open 9 to 5 Monday through Friday.

PHYSICIAN ON CALL
Offered by West Florida Regional
Medical Center   474-8200
Open 8 to 4:30 Monday through Friday.

Substance Abuse/Mental Health/Geriatric Services

TWELVE OAKS
2068 Healthcare Ave.
Navarre   939-1200, (800) 622-1255

Located midway between

Pensacola and Fort Walton Beach, this five-acre campus sits on Santa Rosa Sound in a serene wooded area. Programs are individualized for the special needs of each patient, but the Twelve Steps of AA are used as the program base. Six buildings centered around a wooded park area create a homelike atmosphere conducive to recovery.

THE PAVILION
2191 Johnson Ave.
Pensacola   494-5000
Inpatient, outpatient and partial hospitalization for substance abuse treatment are part of the services offered at The Pavilion. Clients also can receive psychiatric inpatient treatment and geriatric evaluations and screening on an inpatient basis. Assistance and referrals are taken on a 24-hour basis.

BEHAVIORAL MEDICINE CENTER
1000 W. Moreno St.
Pensacola   434-4866
Mental health services are provided on an inpatient and outpatient basis. Specializing in stress treatment for adults, children and adolescents, and adult psychiatric treatment, the center provides 24-hour admissions.

LAKEVIEW CENTER INC.
1221 W. Lakeview Ave.
Pensacola   432-1222
One of the largest mental health programs in the Southeast, Lakeview Center provides outpatient counseling, emergency and stabilization services, substance abuse programs and many types of vocational training programs. Its 24-hour crisis counseling hotline is open seven days a week. The Trauma Recovery Center/Rape Crisis Center also has its own 24-hour crisis line providing counseling, advocacy and referral services to victims of sexual assault and other crimes.

THE FRIARY OF BAPTIST HEALTH CARE
4400 Hickory Shores Blvd.
Gulf Breeze   932-9375, (800) 332-2271
The Friary is a residential drug and alcohol and co-dependency treatment center on the shores of Pensacola Bay. The site was once a retreat for retired Franciscan friars. An eight-week outpatient treatment program is available through centers in Pensacola and Mobile, Alabama.

Pensacola Area
Military

When people in Pensacola tell you to keep watching the skies, they could be referring to flying saucers. Then again, it's more likely they're talking about the military aircraft you can spot zooming across the blue expanse.

The military is a key player in the Pensacola area and everyone knows it. Eglin Air Force Base and the Naval Air Station are known around the world as high-tech facilities that are very important to the nation's defense.

They are rich in history, which you can sample at their museums. These facilities also have quite an economic impact on the Pensacola area — combined, they contribute more than half a billion dollars to the economy here.

Pensacola residents are rightly proud of this area's military heritage. And their presence here just might explain why so many people keep seeing strange lights in the sky. . . .

Naval Air Station

They call Pensacola the "Cradle of Naval Aviation," and the Naval Air Station is the reason why. Its impact on America's defensive readiness is almost immeasurable, especially in light of its long and colorful history.

The station shares land with the pre-Civil War Fort Barrancas, the third fort built here. The area's strategic position was recognized by President John Quincy Adams, who ordered the construction of a naval yard in 1826 to help suppress piracy and the slave trade that flourished in the Gulf of Mexico and Caribbean Sea.

The Naval Air Station has seen a lot of action since then. During the Civil War when Confederate troops fell at New Orleans, they retreated to the naval yard and burned everything down. The yard was rebuilt after the Civil War but was destroyed again in 1906 when a hurricane and tidal wave flattened the new buildings. Attempts to rebuild after this disaster were slowed by an outbreak of yellow fever, and in 1911 construction was halted indefinitely.

Thanks to the Wright brothers and other aviation pioneers, the airplane soon proved to be a valuable instrument in peacetime as well as war. The very first aircraft carrier appeared in 1911, and when the Navy brass gathered in San Francisco to watch the first plane land on its wooden decks, they knew they had to support the concept of naval aviation.

In 1914, the abandoned naval

PENSACOLA — MILITARY

Photo: United States Navy

The air space around Whiting Field in Milton is the busiest in America, boasting more than 2½ million takeoffs and landings per year (that's one every eight seconds).

yard at Pensacola became the site of the first U.S. Naval Air Station, which immediately proved its worth by training over 1,000 aviators who served in World War I. By the time World War II rolled around, military experts were already calling the station the "Annapolis of the Air." The base expanded in preparation for American's entry into WWII, and pilots trained at the Naval Air Station displayed a stunning 14-to-1 air superiority over Japanese planes.

After the war, the station was actively involved in furthering the field of naval aviation, and soon jets and helicopters filled the skies along with airplanes. The Naval Air Station has played an important role in such conflicts as the Korean War, the Vietnam War and more recently the Persian Gulf War.

The National Museum of Naval Aviation is one huge time capsule displaying the history of the station. It's one of the largest air and space museums in the world, and over half a million visitors pass through its doors each year. You can see the entire lineage of aircraft here, from WWI-era biplanes to advanced spacecraft and everything in between, including a replica of a WWII flight deck, the NC-4 Flying Boat and F-14 Flying Tomcat. The Flight Adventure Deck gives kids the chance for some hands-on exploration of flight.

The museum is open daily from 9 AM to 6 PM except on Thanksgiving, Christmas and New Year's Day. There's a museum shop and admission is free.

There are many squadrons based at the station, but the best-known is

• 131

PENSACOLA — MILITARY

These T-34 Turbo Mentor training aircraft are based at Whiting Field in Milton.

probably the U.S. Navy Demonstration Squadron, known popularly as the Blue Angels, home-based at Sherman Field. Though this elite squad of fighter pilots is based here, they're often on the road — or in the air — traveling around the country with their fantastic air show. They usually return for a special demonstration in Pensacola in November, and have been known to buzz the beach in July, as well. You might want to check and see if they're going to be taking their thrilling aerial ballet to the skies when you visit. You can call the Blue Angels' Public Affairs Officer at 452-4784.

Other squadrons at the Naval Air Station include Training Air Wing Six, Training Squadrons Four, Ten and Eighty-six. Some of the commands here include the Naval Education and Training Command, the Naval Audit Office, the Navy Comptroller Program Management Office, the Naval Education and Training Security Assistance Field Activity, the Naval Criminal Investigative Service, the Joint Analysis Program Technical Support Center, the Naval Aviation Schools Command and the Navy Recruiting Orientation Unit.

The Naval Aviation Depot, which has a work force of nearly 3,000 people, is the station's largest tenant, providing ground support maintenance for many fleets and units from each branch of the armed services. When the depot is officially closed down in 1995, the repercussions will be felt far and wide throughout the Pensacola area.

The Pensacola Naval Air Station makes a huge contribution to the area's economy, employing nearly

10,000 military personnel and 9,000 civilians. Though the current trend towards military downsizing will certainly have effects on the Naval Air Station, its presence is certain to remain strong and able in the years to come.

Other Military Facilities in the Pensacola Area

The U.S. Coast Guard Station, located on Big Lagoon just west of Pensacola Pass, is officially a subunit of the Coast Guard Group in Mobile, Ala., but they're also an important player at the Naval Air Station.

There are several nearby fields and stations associated with the Naval Air Station, including Corry Field, which graduates nearly 7,000 naval students each year in the fields of cryptology, electronic warfare and opticalman/instrumentman training. Saufley Field is home to the Naval Education and Training Program Support Activity, the Naval Training Systems Center, the Naval Reserve Center as well as a Federal Prison Camp.

Whiting Field

Just because it's located seven miles north of Milton in Santa Rosa County certainly doesn't belie its importance to the military. Whiting accounts for fully 10 percent of all Navy and Marine flight operations, doing about 80 percent of its fixed-wing training and *all* of its helicopter training. Navy pilots break in on the T-34 "Turbo Mentor" aircraft; helicopter pilots learn the ropes on the TH-57 "Sea Ranger" helicopter. This is *the* busiest air space in America; more than two *million* takeoffs and landings take place at Whiting every year. Locals are trying hard right now to keep the operation here; the government is looking to consolidate helicopter training at Fort Rucker, Alabama.

GULF ISLANDS NATIONAL SEASHORE

Photo: Robin Rowan

A coastal dweller searches for supper.

Inside
Gulf Islands National Seashore

Stretched out from Perdido Key on the west to Mexico Beach on the east is almost 100 miles of coastline. In the past few decades, much of what hadn't been snatched up by the military had become industrial waterfront or had fallen to haphazard development. Gulf Coast residents became anxious over places like Port St. Joe, its coastline almost completely given over to the timber industry, and Pensacola Beach, where blocks of cheap cinder block homes were hastily constructed as "summer cottages" in the 1950s.

By the 1960s, more and more people were discovering Gulf Coast beaches — people who needed places to stay and places to eat and other diversions besides the beaches. Not only was encroaching development threatening the remaining pristine shoreline, but Fort Pickens on Santa Rosa Island and Fort Barrancas on Pensacola Naval Air Station were in shambles. A prehistoric Indian site at the Naval Live Oaks Reservation near Gulf Breeze had been vandalized.

Finally, spurred by radio and newspaper editorials in Pensacola, U.S. Representative Bob Sikes introduced a bill to create a national seashore. President Richard Nixon signed the bill into law in January 1971.

The Gulf Islands National Seashore effectively preserves portions of islands and keys from Horn Island in Mississippi to Okaloosa Island near Destin — a stretch of 150 miles. Fifty-two of those miles are in Northwest Florida, the largest tract of protected shoreline in the state. Twelve more miles will be added when the Air Force vacates its property at Eglin between Fort Walton Beach and Navarre.

The Seashore, with its historic forts, white beaches, hiking trails and campgrounds, is a destination in itself; therefore, all facets of the park will be discussed here (one exception: detailed camping information can be found in the section on Pensacola Accommodations).

Beaches

Visitors are finally discovering what locals have known all along: Northwest Florida has some of the best beaches in the U.S. Early in 1994, a Maryland researcher surveyed top geographers and coastal experts to compile a list of the top 20 beaches based on 50 environmental criteria. Not surprisingly, five of the top 12 were in Northwest Florida:

St. Andrews State Recreation Area, Panama City Beach, #4

GULF ISLANDS NATIONAL SEASHORE

St. Joseph Peninsula State Park, Port St. Joe, #5
St. George Island State Park, Apalachicola, #9
Perdido Key State Recreation Area, Perdido Key, #12.
And the #1 beach in the United States? Grayton Beach State Recreation Area in South Walton County.
Come to our beaches. Wiggle your toes into the powdery white sand. Gaze out over the waves crashing at sea, then breaking gently on the shore. Listen to the surf, the seagull cries, the wind whistling through the dune grasses and sea oats and you'll come to understand why we've worked so hard to preserve this natural splendor.

All Gulf Islands National Seashore beaches are open to the public year round. At the Fort Pickens and Perdido Key areas, there is an admission charge of $4.00 per car, $2.00 for bicycles and foot traffic (good for seven days). A yearly pass can be bought for $10.00. All other areas are free.

Perdido Key

Almost seven miles of gulf-front on Perdido Key is part of the Gulf Islands National Seashore; 9½ more miles line Big Lagoon. A two-mile paved road allows visitors direct access to the beach. Beyond that, five additional miles of shoreline bar all but foot and water traffic. There's a picnic area with shelters and showers, a nature trail, restrooms and a boat launch for very small sailboats and skiffs. Perdido Key is off Gulf Beach Highway 15 miles west of Pensacola.

Santa Rosa Island

The entire western tip of Santa Rosa Island, called the Fort Pickens Area, is under GINS jurisdiction, and what a magnificent piece of property it is. The drive toward Fort Pickens is nothing short of spectacular — huge grass and scrub-covered white dunes frame emerald and turquoise gulf water. A few miles down the road, ancient batteries jut from the landscape, nearly covered over with vegetation sculpted by the wind. And out of the brilliant white sand grow magnolias and slash pines, lending an appearance of a forest after a snowfall.

For preservation of the dunes and beach grasses, you're encouraged to use boardwalks and dune walk-overs whenever possible. There are plenty of parking areas along the road, but if you must park on the shoulder, watch that powdery sand!

As you near the western end of Santa Rosa Island, Fort Pickens looms out of the tall grasses and pines. There's ample parking here,

Insiders' Tips

The Gulf Islands National Seashore remains one of America's most popular parks, attracting 5.5 million visitors annually.

GULF ISLANDS NATIONAL SEASHORE

Coastal scrub vegetation is shaped by the harsh winds at Fort Pickens.

so pick your spot and start walking. On the sound side, about 100 yards east of the fishing pier, is some of the best snorkeling in the area. Leftover concrete chunks from fort construction were left along the shoreline, attracting scads of unusual marine life. It's best to bring gloves and a net for poking around — the gloves are handy for holding onto a piece of rock when the current's strong. On the other side of the fishing pier is a favorite dive spot, but be aware that the current coming from Pensacola Pass is much too strong for even the best swimmers without a weight belt. The shoreline at the pass is terrific both for watching the sun sink into the watery depths and for spotting schools of dolphin.

The next tract of National Seashore is a few miles east of the main public beach (locals still call it "Casino Beach" for a structure built here in the '30s). Just keep driving until you run out of houses. The coastline here is the longest continuous stretch of protected beach in Northwest Florida — some 16 miles (if you count both gulf and sound sides) between Pensacola Beach and Navarre Beach. Although the gulf side is what sunners and swimmers prefer, the soundside offers plenty of natural sub-tropical wilderness for anyone in a mood to explore. Dunes on this side tend to be taller and laden with more vegetation, since they are better protected from harsh winds and tidal action (and feet) than their sisters across the highway. These are some wide-open spaces perfect for birders and shutterbugs.

Along Route 399 (the beach road) is the Santa Rosa Day-Use Area with picnic pavilions, a snack bar, showers (inside and outside) and an

• *137*

GULF ISLANDS NATIONAL SEASHORE

exhibit room with displays of natural and cultural history. Open 8 AM until sunset every day.

Okaloosa Island

Okaloosa Island is really just another name for the eastern end of Santa Rosa Island, but the flavor of this area is far removed from the remoteness of the beaches farther west. Besides an expanse of public beach on Choctawhatchee Bay, the Okaloosa Area of GINS, located on U.S. Highway 98 just east of Fort Walton Beach near the Eglin Air Force reservation, offers picnic tables, restrooms and outdoor showers. There is no admission charge.

Naval Live Oaks Area

This 1400-acre tract of gnarled live oaks along Highway 98 east of Gulf Breeze was set aside in 1828 by then-President John Quincy Adams. The wood from the oaks, called "ironwood," is much stronger than most other types of timber and its natural curves are more easily shaped for hulls and bows in shipbuilding.

The Naval Live Oaks Area (which is also the Seashore headquarters) offers peaceful walks through dense woodlands and along the sound, which harbor abundant marine, animal and bird life. Remember that here, as well as in other preserved areas, all plants, animals and artifacts are protected by the National Park Service and must not be disturbed.

A visitor's center displays Indian artifacts plus runs a free orientation slide show on the Gulf Islands National Seashore. Several nature trails and a shady picnic area make this area a delightful respite from all that bright sand and sun.

The Forts

Around the 1820s and 1830s, three forts were constructed forming a triangle to guard the entrance to Pensacola Bay: Fort Pickens at the tip of Santa Rosa Island, Fort Barrancas at the Naval Air Station and Fort McRee on Perdido Key. In ruins after a Civil War battle and due to shifting sands over a century, Fort McRee has crumbled into the water, but Pickens and Barrancas remain intact and still have many fascinating stories to tell. More detailed information is included in the chapter on Pensacola History.

Fort Pickens

The most colorful fort historically of the three mentioned above, Fort Pickens made a name for itself

---

Insiders' Tips

Ever notice the squeaking sound the sand makes as you cross the dunes? Insiders call it "barking" sand.

Salt air, intense heat and lots of bugs were a way of life for Civil War soldiers at Fort Pickens.

during the Civil War (Union troops had control of Pickens, while McRee and Barrancas stayed under Confederate command) and during the incarceration of Apache medicine man Geronimo (again, see the Pensacola History chapter for more information).

After the National Park Service took over, Fort Pickens received a heavy overhaul to repair the decades of neglect and constant battering by harsh sun, wind and salt air. One corner of the fort, blown to bits by an exploding magazine in 1899, was never rebuilt.

The fort is open from 9:30 AM to 5 PM daily from April through October; from November through March hours are 8:30 AM to 4 PM. Park rangers narrate guided tours Monday through Friday at 2 PM and at 11 AM and 2 PM on weekends. The tours are free and come highly recommended. After a tour, be sure to take some time to explore on your own — the fort is chock-full of dark, damp passageways, small rooms and underground tunnels that aren't part of the tour.

Just inside the main fort entrance is the Visitor Center. In the clump of green and white buildings near the fishing pier you'll find the Fort Pickens Museum (same hours as the fort) and the Fort Pickens Auditorium, which shows a movie or provides some type of program on the fort, the island, weather, local history, marine life or the like, at scheduled times during the year. For more information on the Gulf Islands National Seashore, call 934-2600.

Near the fort is an exceptionally good fishing pier, and within a few

GULF ISLANDS NATIONAL SEASHORE

This crumbling wall at Fort Pickens resulted from a magazine explosion in 1899.

miles are picnic shelters, swimming areas, nature trails, RV dump stations and campgrounds.

Just past the red-roofed ranger's station and up until the fort pops into view are several strangely shaped concrete structures poking out of the brush. These eight concrete batteries scattered throughout the area were built much later to house various types of gunnery for coastal defense during the Spanish-American War and the two World Wars.

Fort Barrancas and the Advanced Redoubt

The fort that sits proudly overlooking the bayfront at Pensacola Naval Air Station played a vital part in Pensacola's coastal defense, but was the last of a string of forts built on that site. The Spanish take credit for the first fortification, Fort San Carlos de Austria, built at the end of the 17th century, east of the current

> **Insiders' Tips**
>
> The stunning white sand along Northwest Florida shores gets its color and texture from pure white quartz, which once was granite from the Appalachian Mountains. Over time, the mud was separated from the quartz crystals and landed on the beach, where wave action rounded the particles, making them soft and fine.

fort. That fort was destroyed when the French took possession of Pensacola just over 20 years later. Some ruins of this early fort may have recently been located.

French occupation was brief (only three years), and the Spanish were again in control when another country sought the strategic coastal position. The British docked at Pensacola after signing the Treaty of Paris in 1763. They built their own fort on top of a mainland bluff, or "barranca," first called Red Cliffs, then renamed the British Royal Navy Redoubt. You guessed it, this one didn't last either. And neither did the Brits. They were ousted by the Spanish in 1781, changing the fort's name to Fort San Carlos de Barrancas. After just 25 years, this structure was decaying badly, so a new Fort San Carlos de Barrancas was built on the bluff (barranca), with a water level battery, Bateria de San Antonio, below it.

The British returned in the War of 1812, destroying the fort. Not to be intimidated, the Spanish charged ahead with a third Fort San Carlos de Barrancas in 1817. Four years later the American flag was raised over this fort, but the entire fort was razed in 1838 to make way for the present Fort Barrancas, which was actually built into the bluff this time. Bateria de San Antonio was somehow spared, and is now connected to Fort Barrancas by an underground tunnel.

Early in 1861, a few musket shots were fired by Federal troops, which some claim were the first shots of the Civil War. For the remainder of the War, though, Federal troops moved to Fort Pickens; Barrancas was held by the Confederacy until their departure in May of 1862. Adjacent to Fort Barrancas is the Advanced Redoubt, a small fortification built between 1845 and 1859, designed to protect Fort Barrancas from land attack.

Today the fort makes a great place for exploration, open from 9:30 AM to 5 PM daily April through September. From here on in hours get fairly complicated; call 934-2600 for hours during the remainder of the year (guided tour times tend to vary as well). Outside the visitor's center, a ranger does a program on artillery at 9:30 AM. The 65 acres surrounding the forts contain forests of oak and pine, a picnic area and nature trail. Fort Barrancas is on Naval Air Station Pensacola and is free to the public.

Both the USS *Constitution* and the USS *Constellation* were constructed with the hard wood from the Naval Live Oaks Preserve, called "ironwood," giving the *Constitution* the nickname "Old Ironsides."

Insiders' Tips

Inside
Fort Walton Beach/ Destin/Beaches of South Walton

Huddled together smack in the middle of Northwest Florida, these three coastal resort areas are separated by only a few miles yet differ immensely in atmosphere. Beach activities range from rowdy Spring Breakers swilling beer and engaging in a rousing game of volleyball to a family oriented arts festival to a classy wine-tasting extravaganza complete with a concert pianist. It is rife with amusement parks and T-shirt shops, multi-million-dollar yachts and penthouse condos, peaceful gardens and seaside cottages.

To experience the real flavor of the place, you have to get off the main road. Highway 98 is the fastest way to travel from Point A to Point B, but it's also the most commercial. Savor the little inland communities, the beach hamlets along 30-A. It's scenic, engaging and worth the time to discover your own favorite spots.

Fort Walton Beach

Although only 10 miles separate Fort Walton Beach from Destin, the two resort destinations have distinct personalities, catering to a different clientele. Fort Walton Beach had a rather bawdy upbringing, and is still looked upon as the stepchild in an area recently dubbed the "Emerald Coast."

First named Camp Walton during the Civil War for a military outpost there, by the turn of the century, the tiny town was already gaining a reputation as a pleasant vacation retreat. No matter that the number of black bears outnumbered the year-round residents, people flocked here for the fishing, stayed in rental cottages or the two downtown hotels and ferried across Santa Rosa Sound to the beach.

Real promotion of the area's amenities began in earnest by the

> **Insiders' Tips**
>
> You might notice that the air is a little thinner in northern Walton County. That's because you've reached the highest point in Florida — a whopping 345 feet above sea level!

1930s, prompting a name change to Fort Walton. U.S. Highway 98 and the Brooks Bridge brought more automobile traffic in, but dirt roads and wayward livestock still made getting around a bit tricky.

But forward-thinking locals had a desire to offer visitors more than simply a place in the sun. They needed an attraction, something people would come back for again and again. They found it in gambling. Slot machines appeared in general stores, hotels, gas stations and restaurants. It brought the people in, all right, but with them came a sleazy reputation as a "Little Las Vegas." After some bad press from South Florida newspapers, the slot machines, and the entire gambling industry, faded into history.

But better news waited on the horizon, which would expand and define this little town perhaps even more than tourism. Until the 1930s, when Eglin Field was established as a bombing and gunnery base, much of Fort Walton was still wilderness. A good-sized expansion after World War II, plus the addition of a Climatic Laboratory, solidified Eglin's notoriety as a test center, pulling in military families and defense contractors.

By the late '40s and early '50s, tourism was in full swing. Fort Walton's population swelled between Memorial Day and Labor Day, and locals could barely keep up with construction of new restaurants and hotels and cottages to accommodate them all. "Beach" was added to the city charter about the same time an enterprising newspaperman began calling the area the "Miracle Strip." Over the next twenty years, Fort Walton Beach saw a population surge, but the little town had no place to expand.

Today, Fort Walton Beach is a jumble of residential areas, souvenir shops, military bases and strip shopping centers. Wayward development of past decades has been reined in with local zoning ordinances for both commercial and residential construction. Still, the downtown area with its many wooded parks, pink buildings and neon signs has a real feeling of the "Old Florida" — a town on the brink of a tourism explosion. The bridge onto Okaloosa Island (the *beach* part of Fort Walton Beach) carries you over to the city's alter-ego — resort hotels, beach bars, mini-golf courses, amusement parks and the Gulfarium, one of north Florida's oldest attractions.

Visitor Information

EMERALD COAST CONVENTION & VISITORS BUREAU
P.O. Box 609, Fort Walton Beach, 32549
651-7131, (800) 322-3319

FORT WALTON BEACH CHAMBER OF COMMERCE
P.O. Box 640
Fort Walton Beach, 32549   244-8191

CRESTVIEW AREA CHAMBER OF COMMERCE
502 S. Main St.
Crestview, 32536   682-3212

NICEVILLE-VALPARAISO-BAY CHAMBER OF COMMERCE
170 John Sims Pkwy.
Valparaiso, 32580   678-2323

Destin

Destin was the last beach area in Northwest Florida to make a name for itself as a resort destination. The reason could be that until a bridge was erected over Destin Pass in the 1930s, it was literally cut off from the rest of the world. The families who lived here thrived on the bounty of the gulf, and, until word reached the outside about the "World's Luckiest Fishing Village," it seemed enough.

There's no complete written history of Destin, so the real story of exactly how and when the town started depends on who you talk to. What *is* known is that Leonard Destin left New England to settle along the East Pass peninsula sometime around 1850. He hired young men from all over to build fishing seines and learn the life of the sea. The names of those that settled here themselves are well-known to Destin residents: Marler, Melvin, Jones, Maltezos. The town's name pays homage to Leonard Destin, the man who provided many men with lifelong skills and a love for this area.

Now, the identity of the first boat captain to turn from commercial fishing to sport charter fishing is a little fuzzy. There are a few old-timers left who remember the boats taking tourists out fishing in the '20s and '30s, but they all seem to remember it in a different way. No matter. A new industry was born in Destin, and sport fishing is still what makes it such a popular place to vacation.

The view of the Pass, with its emerald waters, white sand, high-rise condos, and sea of charter boats may be one of the prettiest in Florida.

Beaches of South Walton

Cross the Walton County line and almost right away you'll feel a change in atmosphere. One reason is that it's more spread out; the toe-to-toe development drops off dramatically. Gone are the amusement parks, the bungee jumping. The Beaches of South Walton are mostly that — 26 miles of pure white sand with scattered beach communities dotting the piney landscape.

Most communities sprang up in the last 20 years (the internationally acclaimed village of Seaside is less than 10 years old). But in parts of the county, such as Seagrove Beach,

---

Insiders' Tips

According to an article in the *Northwest Florida Daily News*, visitors came to Camp Walton (now Fort Walton Beach) looking for the fish camp of Issac Walton, one of the world's best-known anglers, who never lived here and may have never even visited. Henry Dobson, author of *A History of Okaloosa County*, explains the continuing confusion: "People first came looking for a camp that didn't exist, and after the name was changed to Fort Walton, they came looking for a fort that didn't exist. After 1953 (when "Beach" was added to the city's name), they came looking for a beach that didn't exist."

Our Beaches Separate Us From All Others And You From The Crowd.

Each year, the powder white sands and clear turquoise waters of The Beaches of South Walton are rated among the top in the United States. Come, discover the pleasures. You'll find The Beaches of South Walton uncrowded between Destin and Panama City. Call for your free vacation guide. 1-800-822-6877

Beaches of South Walton
IN NORTHWEST FLORIDA

You'll Love Our Unspoiled Nature

Point Washington and Grayton Beach, pockets of weather-worn cottages and historic community buildings provide the essence of the seaside lifestyle of decades past.

Point Washington started as a sawmill community in the latter part of the last century, built up around the Wesley Lumber Company. The Wesley mansion is now the centerpiece of Eden State Gardens.

Santa Rosa (not to be confused with Santa Rosa Beach) remains sparsely populated, although it once had about 1,000 residents. Citrus groves brought families in to grow oranges; around 1915, an outbreak of citrus canker meant the trees had to be destroyed. The industry, and the community, went with them.

Grayton Beach is probably the oldest community in South Walton, starting with just one house around 1880. That house is still standing. The Louisville & Nashville Railroad did its part to advertise the beauty and appeal of South Walton County by printing up postcards featuring fashionably dressed couples with hats and parasols strolling Grayton Beach.

The railroad line extended 25 miles north into DeFuniak Springs, which, perhaps because of its accessibility (and a few land concessions from railroad magnate W.D. Chipley), became the winter assembly of the Chautauqua. More likely, though, one of the residents of Lake Chautauqua, New York, owned a piece of land near here and started a southern version of the cultural and educational festival. The Chautauqua Festival continues in DeFuniak Springs each year on Lake de Funiak.

Rails and roads brought more people to the area, and by the '50s and '60s, some small communities offered year-round diversions for vacationers. By the '70s, developers caught wind of this magnificent piece of Florida that was just *sitting* there! One by one, condominiums, resorts and golf courses began filling the empty acres. Development here, though, seems to be more tightly controlled, so natural beauty still reigns.

• 145

Fort Walton Beach/Destin/ Beaches of South Walton
Restaurants and Nightlife

Salt air, saltwater, and fresh seafood... the mix provides for some of the finest eating anywhere. Try some of the local favorites like grouper, amberjack, blue crab, and red snapper. Come down to the docks near sunset when the fishing fleets return from their day's work. Watching crews unload and huge catches being taken directly from the boat to the restaurant's back door gives you an idea of what fresh really is.

Casual dress is the mode of the day, all day, all year in most restaurants in the area (the exceptions are noted), so relax and have a great time.

The pricing code below is to use as a general guide to a dinner for two. Prices listed include appetizer, entree, beverage and dessert, but not cocktails, sales tax or gratuity.

Under $20	$
$21-40	$$
$41-60	$$$
More than $60	$$$$

Fort Walton Beach

FUDPUCKER'S BEACHSIDE BAR & GRILL
On Okaloosa Island across from the Holiday Inn 243-3833
$$

Fudpucker's is about as far from serious as you can get — dressed up in weathered wood with early attic accessories inside and out, Fudpucker's offers diners a choice of dining on several levels, bands featuring classic rock 'n' roll, cool jazz and reggae, and a tabloid newspaper menu filled with silliness. Seafood, burgers, steaks and sandwiches make up the standard beach fare, with plenty of cold drinks to wash them down. Kids menu, too. You can come away from Fudpucker's spending a lot or a little, since most everything is a la carte. The owners (and the patrons) seem to enjoy the funky atmosphere, which blends in well with the beach party crowd. Open every day at 11 AM until "real late."

TEXAS SALOON AND DANCE HALL
West of the Brooks Bridge on
Eglin Pkwy. 664-6255
$

Round up the cowpokes, pardner, and head on down to Texas! The two-steppin', foot-stompin', hand-clappin' nightspot has become one of the more popular nightspots on the coast. Get a lesson in country dancing on Tuesdays and Thursdays from 8 to 10 PM. Drinks are just a buck from 8 to 11 PM and there's no cover charge on those nights. There are only two requirements necessary to pay a visit to Texas; one, that you're at least 18 years old to party, 21 to drink, and the second, that you *love* country music! Texas hosts some of the hottest country acts in the U.S. Call the concert line at 664-5255. One night a week is Family Night, where kids of all ages are welcome. Learn to dance, rope a calf or feast on pizza, hot dogs, nachos and non-alcoholic specialty drinks. Open daily at 8 PM until real late daily; Sundays open 6 to 11 PM.

JUDY'S GARDEN CAFE
334 N. Eglin Pkwy. 862-6210
$$

Judy's is a lunch place, which makes it popular with business folks who need a great place to take clients but have to get in and out in a reasonable amount of time. The restaurant decor makes you feel as if you're in a garden setting, with lots of cool blues and greens, open-backed wrought iron furniture, and plants, plants and more plants. Salads, soups and sandwiches are typical lunchtime fare. Sandwiches are served on fresh bread and rolls; salads are topped with one of ten house dressings. Weekly specials include muffelettas (a giant New Orleans-style concoction of cheeses and meats with olive dressing) and chicken fettucine. Open 11 AM to 2 PM Monday through Friday.

THE SOUND RESTAURANT AND LOUNGE
108 W. Hwy. 98 243-2722
$$$

Great sunsets, seafood, dining and dancing are yours for the taking at this Fort Walton Beach landmark across from City Hall. Begin your evening with cocktails in the lounge as sunset colors paint the water and cast golden light through the large windows. For dinner, you'll feel as comfortable in a dinner jacket as you will in walking shorts and polos as you settle into large rattan chairs with oversize cushions. Shrimp, scallops, snapper, grouper and softshell crab are absolutely fresh and cooked just the way you like. Or give in to temptation and order a sizzling chargrilled steak or cut-to-order prime rib. Linger a little over dessert, then head back to the lounge for late-night dancing and romancing on the water. Open seven days a week from 11 AM until 9:30 or 10 at night.

PERRI'S ITALIAN RESTAURANT
300 Eglin Pkwy. 862-4421
$$$

Perri's is off the main drag, but word-of-mouth regulars will tell you it's worth finding. Both Northern and Southern Italian favorites offer diners enough choices for many return visits. For the uninitiated, South-

---

Do as the locals do: dine on the harbor in Destin at sunset and watch the fishing fleets unload the day's catch.

ern Italian cooking is probably most familiar to you; lasagna, spaghetti, rigatoni and tortellini are served with a rich meat sauce that's been cooking for hours to blend the ingredients perfectly. Entrees from Northern Italy pride themselves on being a bit lighter: sauces are cooked on the spot and served immediately. Both are outstanding, but you're not required to buy a one-way ticket to Italy just to eat here. Fresh gulf seafood is on every good Gulf Coast menu, as are chargrilled steaks, cooked just the way you like. Open for dinner at 5; reservations are suggested.

HIGHTIDE RESTAURANT, LOUNGE & OYSTER BAR
At the foot of the Brooks Bridge
Okaloosa Island   244-2624
$$

Walk in off the beach and please — don't dress up! Here's where to get your FRESH shucked oysters, absolutely ice cold, falling-off-the-plate burgers, and all types of fresh seafood steamed, fried or chargrilled. A tall icy mug of brew goes down good with this "barefoot" atmosphere. Nightly entertainment and drink specials make Hightide appealing after dark, too. Open at 11 AM daily just over the bridge from Fort Walton Beach on the island.

HOG'S BREATH SALOON & CAFE
1239 Siebert Ave.
Okaloosa Island   243-4646
541 E. Hwy. 98
Destin   837-5620
$

"Hog's Breath is better than no breath at all" and, if you believe that, you're in for a fun evening out at this giant lounge on the island and in Destin. It's all in fun, and what a time you'll have with $5.00 lunch and dinner specials, live entertainment and friendly clientele. Take home a Hog's Breath souvenir T-Shirt (they're world famous, you know). Suck in a little Hog's Breath Monday through Thursday between 11 AM and 10 PM; open late on the weekends.

THE MELTING POT
225 Miracle Strip Pkwy.   664-7685
$$$

Do you fondue? Dunking and dipping are required at The Melting Pot, and so are about three hours to cook and eat your meal! Choose an appetizer of bread, carrots and apples dipped in a blend of beer and cheeses. Next, order up your batter-dipped chicken or beef entree, then have fun cooking it yourself at your table, interspersing bites with quiet conversation. The decor is dark wood with several private booths; The Melting Pot staff *expects* you to take your time. Fondue can be a welcome change of pace from standard steak and seafood fare, and lots of fun besides! Open for a traditional lunch from 11:30 AM; fondue dinners begin at 5 PM.

Destin

Destin restaurants do not require any special type of dress, so come on in, bring the family, dress casually and settle in for some great Gulf Coast hospitality.

Bellissimo Pasta & Pizza
707 Hwy. 98 E.   654-3838
$

Forget that diet! Come sample (oh, alright, pig out on) great local pizza with at least 30 toppings to choose from! Check these out: artichoke hearts, goat cheese, pine nuts, amberjack, broccoli, pineapple and cauliflower! Or try one of Bellissimo's own concoctions, like New Orleans Spicy Shrimp Pizza with marinated fresh shrimp, onions, garlic, peppers and jalapenos. The South of the Border Pizza is heaped with refried beans and chili, tomato sauce (with or without beef), cheddar and Monterey jack cheese, and lettuce and tomato.

In just a few years, Bellissimo has risen to the top for favorite pizza spots in the area, but don't overlook the other great offerings — sandwiches and subs, pastas and entire dinners of chicken, amberjack, shrimp and pork chops. Bring the kids for a hearty, affordable meal. Carry out and free delivery also are available. Open for lunch from 11 to 2:30 Monday through Saturday; open again for dinner starting at 4:30 every day until 9:30 weekdays, 10:30 on weekends.

Fudpucker's Beachside Bar & Grill
Hwy. 98 two miles east of
downtown Destin   654-4200
$$

Fudpucker's likes to have fun, and the folks who own the place don't know the meaning of the word serious! It's kind of tacky inside with junky old toys and rusty bikes and weathered wood. Dine on one of several levels, groove to live bands featuring classic rock 'n' roll, cool jazz and reggae, and chuckle at the tabloid newspaper menu filled with silliness. Seafood, burgers, steaks and sandwiches make up the standard beach fare, with plenty of cold drinks to wash them down. Kids get a menu, too. You can come away from Fudpucker's spending a lot or a little, since most everything is a la carte. The owners (and the patrons) seem to enjoy the funky atmosphere, which blends in well with the beach party crowd. After lunch or dinner, step outside to cheer on the bungee jumpers! Open every day at 11 AM until "real late."

Harry T's Boathouse
320 E. Hwy. 98   654-6555
$$

Harry T's is as legendary as the man himself, a former circus performer. The restaurant overlooks the Destin Harbor, one of the prettiest views in all of Florida's Great Northwest. Harry T. the man owned the boat house back in the 1920s; some of his own collection of circus memorabilia plus shipwreck salvage graces the interior, making for interesting conversation pieces. The food is worth writing home about as well, with over 120 menu items! Sandwiches, seafood, steaks, soups, salads and more are complemented by live music most nights. Kids eat free between 4 and 5 PM Sunday through Thursday; dinner entrees can be as inexpensive as $5.95 and run up to $14.95. Lunch is served every day starting at 11, which is when the bar opens. Sunday brunch is another local experience — what a selection! Come and stuff yourself between 10 AM and 2 PM. Harry T's is one of the local favorite haunts, so you know the food is good. No reservations are taken, and dress is always "off the beach" casual. Look for Harry T's one mile east of the Destin bridge at the Destin Yacht Club.

HARBOR DOCKS
538 Hwy. 98 E. *837-2506*
$$$

Perched on a bluff overlooking Destin Harbor, you can't beat Harbor Docks for the view. On chilly winter evenings, they stoke up the potbellied stove, adding to the already warm atmosphere. Nautical antiques and historic photos line the walls that *don't* have a view; no spot is wasted at Harbor Docks with plants and partitions and different levels to create an intimate dining experience.

Harbor Docks has its own fish market (next door), so while you dine you can watch the fishing fleet unload. Chefs Long and Dang dish up such delicacies as sauteed red snapper with artichoke hearts, broiled red snapper with lemon caper sauce and chargrilled marinated yellowfin tuna, as well as sizzling steaks and Thai specialties. The downstairs Sporting Club is filled with the strains of live jazz, where you can belly up to the Sushi Bar. Come by land or by sea, there are boat slips to tie up to, and valet parking. Open seven days for lunch and dinner from 11 AM to 11 PM.

AJ'S SEAFOOD & OYSTER BAR
Hwy. 98 E. *837-1913*
$$

There's always a party going on at AJ's, located in the heart of Destin

Seafood Facts

A quick guide for those who haven't yet been initiated:

• Grouper, triggerfish, snapper, amberjack and mahi-mahi are considered to be whitefish — fleshy, meaty, and "un-fishy."

• Shrimp can be about any size, from the microscopic ones in your shrimp salad (sometimes these can be *canned*, be sure to ask) to the super deluxe jumbo gulf shrimp that are half as big as your arm. If you're buying them to take home and boil, use Zatarain's or any type of Cajun boil (use sparingly) to bring out the flavor.

• Crawfish are not usually local, but if you see them alive before they appear on your plate, they're nice and fresh.

• Mullet appears on lots of menus, but it's an acquired taste. Breaded in cornmeal and almost always fried, mullet is what you'll get at almost every fish fry you attend in Northwest Florida.

• Oysters are still a bargain everywhere, but warning signs are now posted at all raw oyster-serving establishments that they can possibly carry some strain of bacteria that could ruin your vacation. You're safe if you order them fried, broiled, Rockefellered or cooked in some way.

on the harbor. Watch the boats unload their catches, then have a seat inside or out to enjoy the gulf's bounty — seafood comes chargrilled, fried, steamed or raw. Landlubbers and kids can order up sandwiches and burgers. Upstairs is Club Bimini with a complete hibachi menu. AJ's is about as comfortable as you can get, and the kids will really like all the saltwater aquariums. Things can get pretty wild on the weekends during the summer months, especially upstairs in the area's largest outdoor lounge, where bands perform seasonally. Open 11 AM until . . . every day.

Marina Cafe
404 Hwy. 98 E.　　　　　　837-7960
$$$

Park your own boat at the back door and enjoy the remarkable view. Inside and out, the Marina Cafe blends with its waterfront surroundings. Colorful underwater sculptures and a mosaic tile archway lend a seafaring air to this comfortable dining area centered around a two-story lighthouse sculpture. Entrees can be as kid-pleasing as pizza, as gourmet as Classic Creole or Pacific Rim cuisine. Open for dinner daily from 5 until 10 PM. Reservations suggested.

The Back Porch
Old Hwy. 98 E.　　　　　　837-2022
$$

The restaurant dates back 20 years when it was no more than a concession stand; customers had to order at a tiny window. Now that it's doubled in size, there's room for the throngs of diners looking for great views, great prices and great seafood, and is Destin's only "open air" full service restaurant. Upstairs, the Appetizer Bar serves lighter menu items such as seafood nachos and freshly made cold smoked tuna dip, as well as delicious frozen concoctions. It doubles as a fine place to wait for dinner seating.

By day, walk in right off the beach and have a casual lunch. Watch carefully out the huge open windows for schools of dolphin playing in the surf. By night, the seafood is sensational. The Back Porch originated chargrilled amberjack, now a staple item on the Gulf Coast. Heart Healthy entrees use only pure vegetable oil and are either broiled or chargrilled. Everything from sauces to salads to desserts are made fresh every day in the Back Porch kitchen. And they haven't forgotten the kids! They have their own menu, and waitpeople are sure to fuss over them to make sure they're having as much fun as mom and dad! Open every day from 11 AM until 9:30 PM.

The Crab Trap
At James Lee Park, Beach Rd. 98
between Destin and Sandestin　654-2722
$$

A crab-lover's delight—soft shell crab sandwiches, She-Crab soup, snow crab, tender crab claws, New Orleans-style crab cakes, crab salad, gumbo (with crab, naturally!). But don't turn your back on this restaurant if you're *not* particularly fond of the little crustacean. There's "fresh-off-the-boat" shrimp, broiled in a butter and garlic sauce with Cajun spices, juicy burgers, hearty sandwiches and a souvenir sports

Take in the spectacular view of sand, surf and sea oats, from many of the area's waterfront restaurants.

bottle filled with your favorite daiquiri! The Crab Trap caters to the younger set, serving favorites like shrimp and fries, burgers and hot dogs in a souvenir beach pail complete with a shovel! (No, the shovel's not to *eat* with, kids.) They'll stay busy with coloring books and crayons, giant ice cream cones, something sweet from The Parrot Sweet Shop or a Destin souvenir from Boardwalk Gifts. Dine inside or out, in one of the tropical gazebos, or get it to go and eat on the beach! Open every day from 11 AM until 10 PM.

Captain Dave's Restaurant & Marina on the Harbor
314 E. Hwy. 98   837-6357
$$$

Yep, there really *is* a Captain Dave ... Captain Dave Marler, a gruff old salt who grew up on the water here. He turned in his rig for a restaurant long ago, but Captain Dave's is still the oldest seafood restaurant around; in fact, you may have seen it in *Jaws II*. The movie crew liked the atmosphere with its stuffed trophy fish, nautical knickknacks and historic photos, and shot several scenes here. They also liked the food, returning again and again to savor huge overflowing platters of shrimp, oysters, scallops, fish and deviled crab. Captain Dave still oversees his fleet behind the restaurant, ensuring that only the freshest, top-quality catches wind up on diner's tables. Steaks, prime rib and chicken dishes will ensnare non-seafood lovers. Open every day for lunch in the Oyster Bar from 10 to 3; dinner is served from 4:30 until 10 PM. Closed from December to mid-February.

Captain Dave's on the Gulf
3796 Old Hwy. 98   837-2627
$$$

A Destin original, this restaurant built in the '50s still has the old tunnel built under the highway for customers crossing from the parking lot. Setting off the gorgeous gulf view are old curved greenhouse windows. A rustic Oyster Bar is outside downstairs, a casual spot for gulping oysters, peeling boiled shrimp and sipping cocktails and beer. For the main attraction, try chargrilled tuna with a green chile salsa, Snapper Dijon or fresh swordfish and scallops marinated in teriyaki sauce. Open daily for dinner from 5 to 10 PM. Closed between December 1 and mid-February.

Louisiana Lagniappe
775 Gulf Shore Dr. at Sandpiper Cove, Holiday Isle   837-0881
$$$

"Lagniappe" (lan-yap) is a Cajun word meaning "a little something extra." From the seafood gumbo, where the seafood is cooked and added just before serving, to the authentic Cajun recipes to the homemade bread pudding with whiskey, Louisiana Lagniappe is noted for its attention to detail. The chargrilled tuna steak is wrapped in bacon and topped with flaky white jumbo lump crabmeat, then finished with a splash of Hollandaise. Grouper Pontchartrain takes a heapin' helpin' of pan-sauteed grouper filet, tops it with a fried jumbo softshell crab, honey-roasted nuts and Hollandaise. Is your mouth watering yet? This is a casual, family-style restaurant, where shorts are fine,

FORT WALTON BEACH AREA — RESTAURANTS AND NIGHTLIFE

smiles are plentiful and service is exceptional. Open daily for dinner from 6 to 10; 5:30 to 10 on weekends from March through October. No reservations are accepted.

NIGHTOWN
Two blocks north of
Palmetto Plaza   837-6448
$

It's a jumpin' joint featuring a variety of entertainment every night of the week. The "Other Bar" has a New Orleans feel, where live entertainment cranks out nearly every night. Play pool or foosball in a room bedecked in shipwreck salvage. The Beer Bar offers beer from around the world. And the main attraction, The Main Room, sports a 1958 Mack Truck in it's own garage overlooking the massive dance floor. This is the party room, where a sound and light extravaganza keeps you on your feet. Check out the surfboards, sailboards, jet skis and *real records* lining the walls. A ferris wheel hangs from the ceiling, as does another dance floor, nine feet over your head, surrounded by neon palms.

Two island bars in the Main Room offer cocktails, and the Smart Bar specializes in nonalcoholic drinks for the Designated Drivers. Let's see . . . a Foreign Bar with domestic and imported beer, lava lamps, a French Fry Bar, a comedy club . . . Yikes! You'll just have to come and see the rest for yourself. There's a cover charge, and it opens at 8 PM every night of the week.

FISH HEADS
543 Hwy. 98 E. across from
Harbor Docks   837-4848
$

Are you up past midnight on a regular basis? Then, this is probably just the spot you've been looking for to mingle with the other night owls. Nightly specials, daily happy hour, a d.j. playing top hits for dancing, an outdoor patio deck . . . what more could you want? Open at 11 AM for lunch.

DESTIN DINER
Hwy. 98 at Airport Rd.
Destin   654-5843
$

Right out of a '50s flashback, the Destin Diner is a burgers-and-maltedskind of place. It's a real chrome diner with vinyl-covered stools and booths and jukeboxes. Prices aren't quite out of that era,

---

Insiders' Tips

In April of 1927, a distress call went out that a luxury liner was sinking off the coast of Destin. A circus trapeze artist was first to heed the call. His fast thinking and tireless heroics saved every one of the 2,000-plus passengers. Afterwards, the Big Top star opened a restaurant bearing his name. Harry T's Boathouse is furnished with salvaged furniture and fixtures from the ship, the reward for his amazing efforts.

but they're not bad. The diner serves up omelets (12 varieties), breakfast sandwiches like ham and egg served with two pickle slices, pancakes, soups, shakes, burgers, Coke floats and even banana splits!

You can eat here fairly cheaply — the most expensive menu item is a complete country-style dinner for $5.75. Choose from grilled pork chops, roast beef with gravy, chicken fried steak with gravy, grilled liver and onions or a grilled chicken breast, then add on two vegetables (corn, fries, greens, green beans, cole slaw or mashed potatoes), and soup or salad. The food is out of the days when you didn't even know what cholesterol was, so don't worry about it now. Pop a quarter in the jukebox (or is it 75¢ now?) and hearken back to the days of tail fins and saddle shoes. The Destin Diner is serving up great food 24 hours every day.

Beaches of South Walton

Fast food restaurants are about as scarce as snowstorms in South Walton County. What you will find, however, are several cozy "gathering places" — stop in not just for hearty homemade fare, but news and gossip from the locals. South Walton also prides itself on some of the best gourmet restaurants in Northwest Florida, impeccably presented against a backdrop of white dunes and emerald waters.

Some of the fancier restaurants will allow patrons to wear collared shirts and dressy walking shorts in lieu of coats and ties; those will be noted. Shirts and shoes are required everywhere.

BAYOU BILL'S CRABHOUSE
Hwy. 98 E., Santa Rosa Beach   267-3849
Hwy. 30-A, Seagrove Beach   231-1400
$$

Two locations along the Beaches of South Walton serve up heaps of blue crabs and steaming seafood buckets. The Seagrove Beach location on Eastern Lake has a special oyster bar. Any place that serves a crustacean that has to be hand-cracked and peeled and dipped and eaten with the fingers is bound to be unpretentious. Bayou Bill's welcomes all comers to its friendly and comfortable surroundings. Open 11 AM, with dinner served from 5 to 10 PM daily.

BUSTER'S OYSTER BAR & GRILL
Delchamps Plaza near Sandestin   837-4399
$$

Buster's specializes in seafood — fried, chargrilled, steamed or broiled — in a casual hometown lounge atmosphere. Giant sandwiches, frosty spirits and a big-screen TV keep the locals happy. Lunch and dinner specials are daily features, ranging from oyster dishes to juicy steaks. Buster's won the first Great Southern Gumbo Cookoff, so its gumbo is sure to be a winner. There's an oyster happy hour from 11 AM until 6 PM daily; restaurant opens at 11 AM daily.

CRIOLLA'S
County Rd. 30-A
Grayton Beach   267-1267
$$$$

Called one of the America's Top Ten Restaurants in 1991 by *Florida Trend* magazine, Criolla's unique Creole/Caribbean cuisine is a gourmet's delight and unbelievably wonderful, even for someone who's pretty picky (like yours truly). Some of the menu items are unpronounceable and fairly exotic, so you might want to ask your server to recommend something. How about the Criolla Colado, grilled tenderloin chili between layers of masa, steamed in banana leaves and served with ancho tomato sauce? A favorite at Criolla's is the Crabmeat Quesadillas, flour tortillas filled with jumbo lump crabmeat and muenster — mmmmm! Pick pan fried pompano, fresh soft shell crabs, or wood-grilled tuna mignon. Muted shades of melon and dark green, antiques and paintings and Caribbean-flavored-what-have-yous all around create a warm and pleasing environment for diners to hunker down and prepare for an evening they'll long remember. Resort dress attire is requested. Open 5:30 to 10 Monday through Saturday.

ELEPHANT WALK
Hwy. 98 E. at the Sandestin
Beach Resort　　　　　*267-4800*
$$$$

Save the Elephant Walk for a really special night out, like a night when you can get a babysitter. It's all candlelight and crystal and linen and four-waitpeople-per-table service, where you wouldn't want to worry about less than perfect behavior from your offspring. So, now that you've settled into the business of eating, start with an appetizer of chargrilled shrimp and scallops with lump crabmeat, served chilled on a bed of lettuce with a brandy cocktail sauce, or twin cakes of lump crabmeat seasoned with fresh herbs. Since a dinner at the Elephant Walk constitutes an entire evening out (expect to spend a couple of hours enjoying this meal), feel free to walk out on the deck in between courses. The building itself was modeled after a plantation home in the 1954 movie *Elephant Walk*.

Ready for the main course? Try the Grouper Elizabeth, a sauteed filet with seasoned jumbo lump crabmeat with toasted almonds and a white wine cream sauce, a chargrilled filet of beef with Bearnaise sauce served with potato cakes, or Georgia mountain trout (one of the nightly specials) stuffed with crawfish tails and red onions served with black bean and okra sauce. Coats and ties are not required, but most folks like to dress up to dine in such splendor. Open Tuesday through Saturday from 5 to 10 PM; open Mondays during the summer season.

BUD & ALLEYS
County Rd. 30-A, Seaside　　*231-5900*
$$$

One of the original Seaside eateries, Bud & Alley's features its own herb garden, so you know you're getting the freshest ingredients possible. An old 1955 Airstream trailer attached to the main dining area houses the restaurant's grill. You can enjoy live jazz on weekends in the summer. Lunch is served 11:30 to 3:00; dinner is from 6 until 9:30 Sunday through Thursday, open half an hour later on weekends. Closed Tuesdays in the off-season.

SHADES
County Rd. 30-A, Seaside　　*231-1950*
$$

Look for the neon shades in the

window. It's upbeat, frivolous and about as laid-back as Seaside gets. Ribs, crab cakes, barbecued shrimp, burgers and indoor and outdoor seating set the mood; shoes are not required. Open 11 to 9 every day but Sunday; open an hour later in summer; Sundays open 11 to 3.

JOSEPHINE'S DINING ROOM
Inside Josephine's Bed & Breakfast
Seaside   231-1939
$$$$

Since the bed and breakfast is so tastefully decorated, the turn-of-the-century charm so thick, the southern style so elegant, Josephine's Dining Room has a tough act to follow. But from the moment you step into this comfortable oasis, Bruce and Judy Albert, your evening's hosts, will make you feel like you've arrived someplace very special. Rich burgundies, deep greens and dark wood set the mood for dining on fresh seafood, thick steaks, lamb and chicken entrees.

Try something as offbeat as Key West fish, lightly dusted in seasoned flour, then served on a bed of capellini pasta with a Key lime chutney and fresh fruit couli. Chefs Olivier Petit and Deborah DiPietrantonio (Chef Deborah for short) stir up a kettle of soup daily featuring handpicked herbs with fresh vegetables and a stock they prepare fresh daily. All dinner entrees come with a mixed green salad with some unusual but tasty tarragon vinaigrette dressing, sauteed vegetables and a potato du jour. Expect to spend the better part of your evening partaking of all of this splendor. At Seaside, there's no need to rush. A full wine list is available; ask your server for recommendations. Reservations are suggested. Except for Mondays and Tuesdays, Josephine's is open for dinner 5:30 to 9:30.

BASMATI'S
Downtown Seaside   231-1366
$$$

Looking for some place that's really *intimate?* Basmati's only has room for 22 guests, so you're sure to get some individualized attention here. Basmati's takes popular Asian-Pacific cuisine and gives it a Gulf Coast twist with *lots* of fresh seafood. One spin on a local favorite is lump crabmeat stir-fried with asparagus, basil and somen noodles. Or try a meaty filet of pompano pan-seared in ginger with a fig sweet and sour sauce, and served with a combination of Chinese rice noodles, shrimp, scallops, spinach and plum tomatoes. Very unusual, but folks staying in this neck of the woods are open to new tastes, which makes Basmati's quite popular. No credit cards are accepted but reservations are. The entire dining room is nonsmoking. Open every evening at 5:30; closed Wednesdays.

SILVER BUCKET
On the Gulf, Seaside   231-1190
$

Silver Bucket replaced the Sip-N-Dip, so gone are some of the best New Orleans muffalattas you ever ate. But replacing them are inexpensive treats for quick meals or midday snacks. Six different sandwiches include Vermont Cheddar with sliced green apple on sourdough bread, smoked turkey with roasted pepper and coarse grain mustard on multigrain bread, and grilled marinated chicken breast with lettuce and fresh pesto on a baguette. Nothing run-of-the-mill for this place, except for the kid-size grilled cheese and peanut butter and jelly sandwich buckets. Stop in for takeout every day but Monday.

LeBleau's Cajun Kitchen
Hwy. 98 E. near Sandestin   267-3724
$

Inexpensive and good, this might be the best deal in the area. Terrific breakfasts and daily specials are under $5.00, and all are served with a Cajun flair. Stop in for breakfast to catch up on the local news; LaBleau's is a prime gathering spot for coffee and conversation. Open 6 AM to 9 PM every day but Tuesday.

Donut Hole II Cafe & Bakery
32459 Hwy. 98 E.
Santa Rosa Beach   267-3239
$

As you might imagine, doughnuts are a specialty (and at 44 cents apiece are a good deal), but fresh-baked muffins and stacks of flapjacks will lure you in again and again. "Country dinners" are hearty, tasty and about 5 bucks, and sandwiches and soups are stick-to-your-ribs yummy. A full bakery features danish, fruit cobblers, cookies, pies and fresh breads daily. Open 6 to 11:30 AM for breakfast; dinner starts at 11:30 AM and lasts until closing (around 9 PM) daily. Bring cash 'cause it's all they take.

The Grayton Corner Cafe
Off County Rd. 283 on the corner
Grayton Beach   231-1211
$

These folks practically have a corner on the market, since there are only about two restaurants in all of Grayton Beach. The atmosphere is fairly nil (except that it's directly across the street from that beautiful beach), the sandwiches pretty basic (I recommend the fish sandwich, but what kind of fish it is remains elusive), but this is Grayton Beach, a wonderfully old seaside community without much flash, and that's why people like it. An example of the "mañana" spirit of the town is a sign posted outside the Grayton Corner Cafe: "Hours may vary depending on the quality of the surf": but generally it's Tuesday through Sunday, 11 AM until 9:30 PM. In winter, the cafe opens Wednesday and Thursday 11 to 2:30; Friday and Saturday 11 to 8:30. Cash only is the policy.

Goatfeathers Raw Bar & Restaurant
Hwy. 30-A between Dune Allen and
Blue Mountain Beach   267-3342
$$

Steam buckets, steak, soups, sandwiches and kid's baskets fill tummies and warm hearts at this fun and friendly eatery. The open-air deck offers spectacular gulf views, and the seafood comes from downstairs at Goatfeathers' own seafood market. Open 11:30 to 10 daily; until 9 PM in the off-season. It's another cash only place.

Fort Walton Beach/Destin/ Beaches of South Walton
Accommodations

Residents of Fort Walton Beach and Destin may wince at this, but it's quite likely that Florida's Great Northwest is becoming more well known because of Seaside. Articles on the little village's architecture, its planned community, its ambience, have appeared in hundreds of national and international magazines. As far as getting good press goes, Seaside could be right up there with Disney World. But what's been good for that little community has been good for the entire area — new visitors from all over the United States and many foreign countries are trying us on for size — and liking the fit.

Along this 30-mile stretch of Highway 98, visitors can shop around for good deals before they ever leave home. Fort Walton Beach caters to singles and families, and probably offers more hotel and motel accommodations than the other destinations. Destin is condo heaven, with most high-rises right on the water. The Beaches of South Walton is a mix — interior-designed cottages and backwater cabins.

Put your money down on cottage and resort reservations; most require a deposit before your reservation can be confirmed. Before you sign on the dotted line, ask about added costs such as a pet deposit or a post-visit flea spray (although most do not accept pets), bed taxes and cleaning fees.

Fort Walton Beach

Fort Walton Beach doesn't try to be all things to all people. Compared to Panama City Beach, it's peaceful; compared to Destin or Seaside, it's affordable. Stay on Okaloosa Island and you're near all the action — amusements, beaches, recreation. Families especially will find Fort Walton Beach a friendly and accommodating place where locals love to stop and chat with out-of-towners and take great pride in the place they call home.

Note: Okaloosa Island properties are just over the Brooks Bridge from Fort Walton Beach.

Hotels and Motels

The giant Holiday Inn and Ramada Resort on Okaloosa Island are just what you'd expect — large, spacious rooms, restaurants and lounges on the grounds, beautiful lobbies, atriums and a high-rise view of the gulf. But if you'd rather spend your money taking a charter fishing trip or dining in a gourmet restaurant, we've included a few of the local motels, too, which maybe don't have fancy shampoos and blow dryers, but they're inexpensive, and nice enough to at least offer the basics. Price structure is based on double occupancy for one night and does not include tax.

$80 or less	$
$81-100	$$
$101-150	$$$
$151 or more	$$$$

HOLIDAY INN - OKALOOSA ISLAND
1110 Santa Rosa Blvd.
Okaloosa Island 243-9181
$$$ (800) 732-GULF

A full-service, 385-room hotel right on the gulf, this all-inclusive property offers four swimming pools, two lighted tennis courts, a poolside snack bar and a restaurant. Children's activities and seasonal beach rentals are available through the hotel's resort services. Double room rates depend on location, and range from $105 (parking lot view) to $130 (gulf view) per night. Junior suites and executive suites face the gulf, include more amenities and cost extra.

BLUEWATER BAY RESORT
1950 Bluewater Blvd.
Niceville 897-3613
$-$$$ (800) 874-2128

Residents and guests are welcome to enjoy 36 holes of golf, 21 tennis courts, a 120-slip marina, swimming pools, playgrounds, a bayside beach, bike and nature trails. Both nightly and weekly rates are available on three-story hotel units, condominiums and villas. Since lots of folks live here year round, you get in on all the luxuries they enjoy every day. Bluewater Bay is a Northwest Florida gem; the units are spacious, the grounds immaculate and the sunset views across the bay outstanding.

BEACHMARK INN
573 Santa Rosa Blvd.
Okaloosa Island 244-8686
$$ (800) 433-7736

One-bedroom suites overlooking the gulf include separate living and bedroom areas and kitchens. All rooms have sliding patio doors leading to private patios or balconies; interiors are contemporary with beach-inspired pastels. You're within walking distance of restaurants, shopping, nightlife and amusements on Okaloosa Island. These units are pleasant and functional without the high price.

PIRATES' BAY CONDO & HOTEL MARINA
214 Miracle Strip Pkwy.
Fort Walton Beach 243-3154
$$$ (800) 356-1861

Studio and one-bedroom suites are geared to both tourists and business travelers. All units have sofas and work areas, microwaves and refrigerators, private wraparound balconies and offer free local calls. Slip your boat into the 121-slip marina, or dive into one of two large free-form pools. Pirates' Bay is located on the Intracoastal Waterway in the heart of Fort Walton Beach.

CONQUISTADOR INN
74 Venus Ct.
Okaloosa Island 244-6155
$-$$ (800) 824-7112

The Conquistador Inn gives its guests plenty of options when it comes to accommodations with eighty-seven units, both double ho-

KOKOMO Motel & Marina

KITCHENETTES • BOATSLIPS ON HARBOR

- **CUSTOM 37' SPORTFISH**
- Fast Twin Turbo Diesel
- Team Daiwa Equipped
- Tournament entered
- Destin Cobia tournament
- All Day, 1/2 Day
- Fly Fishing
- Live Bait

- **SNORKELING $20.00**
  (gear included)
- USCG Approved
- 49 Passenger
- 50 Ft. Custom-Built Boat

SUNSET HARBOR CRUISE $10

500 HWY 98 • DESTIN • (904) 837-9029

---

tel rooms and one and two-bedroom condos on the gulf. All rooms are Old Florida tropical in shades of aqua and pastels. A pool, boardwalk to the beach and volleyball courts are on the property.

RAMADA BEACH RESORT
1599 Miracle Strip Pkwy. (Hwy. 98 E.)
Okaloosa Island   243-9161
$$-$$$ (800) 874-8962

With 454 rooms, the Ramada offers everything a vacation is meant to include: pools indoors and out, a hot tub/whirlpool, kiddie pools, three restaurants, two lounges, a courtyard garden area, a health spa, tennis courts, a picnic area and it's all handicapped accessible. Room rates depend on location; choose from a parking lot view ($95) up to a room right on the gulf ($125).

LEESIDE INN & MARINA
1350 Hwy. 98 E.
Okaloosa Island   243-7359
$ (800) 824-2747

An older hotel on the bay side, Leeside has been upgraded to be handicapped accessible. With 107 units, every other room offers a small kitchenette; that is, a small refrigerator, two-burner stove and service for four. Rooms have either two queen- or one king-size bed. Nothin' fancy, but if you plan to spend your days taking in the sights of the area, all you'll require at night is a comfortable place to sleep!

FORT WALTON BEACH AREA — ACCOMMODATIONS

Condominiums/ Townhomes/Vacation Cottages

Gulfside, bayside, or soundside, just about every condo in a two-county area is on the water, affording splendid all-around views. Check the neighbors to the east (that's Destin and The Beaches of South Walton) for additional accommodations. Prices reflect the average weekly cost of a two bedroom/two bath condo or house during the peak summer season and do not include tax.

$500-750	$
$751-900	$$
$901-1100	$$$
$1101 and over	$$$$

BLUEWATER BAY RESORT
1950 Bluewater Blvd.
Niceville 897-3613
$-$$ (800) 874-2128

Bluewater Bay masterfully melds residential community and resort. The 2,000-acre property on Choctawhatchee Bay takes special care to leave some spaces in their natural state, to insist upon stringent building codes and to preserve every tree possible.

Spacious condominium units offer many extras; each is individually owned and suited to the owner's taste and lifestyle. Resort extras abound; see the listing under hotels for a rundown.

EMERALD ISLE CONDOMINIUM
770 Sundial Ct.
Okaloosa Island (800) 336-GULF
$$$$

By the day, the week or the month, Emerald Isle is a favorite of vacationing families. Located gulfside, this seven-story high-rise is nicely landscaped with private beach boardwalks, a large pool with sundeck and tennis courts. All rooms have private balconies; indoors, look for all the comforts of home.

SEA OATS CONDOMINIUM
1114 Santa Rosa Blvd.
Okaloosa Island (800) 336-GULF
$$-$$$$

With views of the gulf or the Intracoastal Waterway from every room, Sea Oats is on that spit of land over the bridge from Fort Walton Beach known as Okaloosa Island. You're close to all the best stuff — The Gulfarium, mini-golf, amusement parks, restaurants, shopping. Tennis and shuffleboard courts, pool, game room and 24-hour security are all on-site.

SEASPRAY CONDOMINIUMS
1530 Hwy. 98 E.
Okaloosa Island 244-1108
$$-$$$ (800) 428-2726

These one-, two- and three-bedroom low-rise townhomes front the gulf on Okaloosa Island. The units are arranged in a horseshoe design with a courtyard opening on the gulf beach. Athletic club, sauna and large courtyard pool provide recreational opportunities. Some pets are welcome, but check first. This is a family-oriented property, meaning no Spring Breakers or student groups. Nightly and monthly rates are available.

Destin

Next to the remarkably emerald green water and huge fleets of fishing boats, one of the first things

FORT WALTON BEACH AREA — ACCOMMODATIONS

FREE FL RESORT CATALOG!
Destin • Ft. Walton • So. Walton Beaches

Abbott Resorts offers you the best of over 1,500 beach vacation condos, townhomes, B & B's, and individual beach homes along FL's Emerald Coast. Call for your **FREE** 78 pg. Resort Catalog with color photos, descriptions and rates!

24-HR. Central Reservations:
1-800-336-4853
We Sell Resort Property Too!
Call Sales: 1-800-547-0805

Please send me a FREE Resort Catalogue! MIGX
Name: _____
Address: _____

Abbott
REALTY SERVICES INC.   City/St./Zip: _____

Abbott Resorts: 35000 Emerald Coast Pkwy. Destin, FL 32541

---

you'll notice upon crossing the Destin Bridge is the tall rows of shimmering condos lining the water in every direction. The success of charter fishing brought tourism and a resort lifestyle along with it, issuing in a new era more suitable to the comfort and convenience of visitors.

The reasonable year-round rates get even better in the slower fall and winter seasons, with some rates dropping by one-third after Labor Day; lower than that in the winter months.

Check both the Fort Walton Beach and Beaches of South Walton listings for an even wider range of prices and unit availability.

Hotels and Motels

One of the hotel chain's slogans is "The Best Surprise Is No Surprise," and if you make reservations at a hotel you're already familiar with, you won't be disappointed when you get there. Condos are king in Destin, but the chain hotels provide a nice alternative for much less money.

DAYS INN - DESTIN
1029 Hwy. 98 E.
Destin   837-2599
$-$$

One of the newest motels in Destin, the Days Inn offers regular rooms, suites and efficiencies with in-room Jacuzzis and cable TV with

• 163

FORT WALTON BEACH AREA — ACCOMMODATIONS

Herons are frequent visitors to Grayton Beach.

Showtime. There's a nice pool here, but you won't need it, since you're right across from the gulf. Both non-smoking and handicapped accessible rooms are available. A continental breakfast of coffee, doughnuts and orange juice comes with the price of a room. Call for special corporate, military, AAA & senior discounts.

CLUB DESTIN RESORT
1085 Hwy. 98 E.
Destin   654-4700, (800) 326-1223
$$-$$$

This timeshare resort also offers nightly rates on hotel rooms and efficiencies. The entire resort encompasses 4½ acres near Sandestin with a large heated swimming pool, a putting green, shuffleboard courts and Stoney's restaurant and lounge. Club Destin is brand new, so expect upbeat, contemporary furnishings and lots of little extras.

SUMMERSPELL
3881 Scenic Beach Hwy. 98 E.
Destin   654-4747, (800) 336-9669
$$$

All the comforts of a privately owned condominium are found at Summerspell, with the affordability of an in-town hotel. Although rentals by the week and the month are available, these are all one-bedroom, one-bath units, so for our purposes are included in the hotel listings. French doors open onto balconies, affording gulf views. A heated pool, gazebo, on-site laundry and beach service (in season) are available to guests, as well as nonsmoking units. Each unit is designed to sleep six.

Bed and Breakfast Inns

HENDERSON PARK INN
2700 Scenic Beach Hwy. 98 E.
Destin   (800) 336-GULF
$$$$

Still just getting broken in, the Queen-Anne-style Henderson Park Inn is celebrated as the Emerald Coast's first bed and breakfast. Thirty-nine suites and apartment villas provide all of the daily necessities, but the structure oozes Victorian charm, featuring shaker-style siding, a cupola and a widow's walk. Complimentary breakfast, evening social hour, heated pool, sundeck, beach gazebo, outdoor grills and beach rentals in season are all part of the package. Most rooms in the main building come with Jacuzzis. Weekly rentals are available.

Condos/Townhomes/ Vacation Cottages

Condominiums and cottages, with their full kitchens and multiple bedrooms, seem perfect for families who don't want to eat out every night, or couples desiring a romantic respite from workaday pressures.

Prices reflect the weekly cost of a two-bedroom/two-bath condo or house during the peak summer season. Since prices are a bit higher than in the Fort Walton Beach area, the pricing structure below reflects that increase. Most rental agencies want a deposit up front, which can be up to a third of the week's rental. The rest is due upon check-in. Prices do not include tax. Please be sure to check both Fort Walton Beach and

FORT WALTON BEACH AREA — ACCOMMODATIONS

the Beaches of South Walton accommodations for a full area listing; many realty companies offer properties throughout the entire area.

$750-950	$
$951-1100	$$
$1101-1500	$$$
$1501 and over	$$$$

ABBOTT REALTY SERVICES, INC.
35000 Emerald Coast Pkwy.
Destin   837-4853, (800) 336-4853
$-$$$$

Abbott is one of the largest realty companies in the area, offering over 80 resort properties from high- and low-rise condominiums to townhomes and beach cottages throughout the Fort Walton Beach, Destin and Beaches of South Walton area.

EDGEWATER SERVICES, INC.
Palm Plaza, 5160 Hwy. 98 E.
Destin   654-1113, (800) 322-7263
$$$

Edgewater manages units in 12 properties in Destin and the Beaches of South Walton. Since they're smaller, you might get more individualized attention. Some of the properties available are at Edgewater Beach Resort, the unusual stepped structure, which provides a nice family atmosphere, Hidden Dunes, which has both high-rise and secluded low-rise units and the Beachside Towers at Sandestin. Nightly and weekly rates are available, as are monthly rentals in the off-season.

SHORELINE TOWERS
Off Hwy. 98, Holiday Isle
Destin   837-6100
$$$

Streamlined high-rises set on 500 feet of gulf-front, these two and three-bedroom condominiums are huge — 1,400 and 1,600 square feet. Guests have a clubhouse, tennis and racquetball courts, and a swimming pool at their service. Some units have fireplaces; all have private balconies.

DESTIN HOLIDAY BEACH RESORT
1006 Hwy. 98 E.
Destin   (800) 874-0402
$$$

Your own private beach highlights this all-inclusive resort. Boardwalks, pool, an outdoor hot tub, lighted tennis courts, an exercise room, shuffleboard courts, a putting green, a kiddie pool and outdoor grills make for a great family place to play. There's a $200 deposit required; nightly rates are available.

HENDERSON PARK TOWNHOMES
2701 Scenic Beach Hwy. 98 E.
Destin   (800) 336-GULF
$

Newly renovated, these rustic-style townhomes are on the eastern boundary of Henderson Beach State Park and across from the Henderson Inn B&B. Many floor plans and square footage layouts are available. The view from the third floor decks is nothing short of spectacular. If you don't like paying for health clubs and golf courses that you'll never use anyway, these townhomes are a perfect alternative, and are only a short walk to the beaches.

SUNDESTIN
1040 Hwy. 98 E.
Destin   654-4747, (800) 336-9669
$$$

Another of Destin's sun spots, this high-rise condo-hotel beach resort on the gulf offers one-, two- and three-bedroom floor plans with a full palate of amenities. Exercise equipment, a steam room, sauna, whirlpool, shuffleboard and a party room are part of the all-inclusive health club; there's an outdoor and an indoor heated pool; on-site restaurant and lounge; and in-season beach service. You're close to everything in Destin and right across the street from Big Kahuna's Water Park.

SANDPIPER COVE
775 Gulfshore Dr.
Destin   837-9121
$$

Sandpiper cove is a Destin landmark on Holiday Isle, popular because of its homey low-rise look and the zillion and one extras offered with your rental. Start with studio, one- or three-bedroom gulf-front, gulf view or street side units, a private beach boardwalk with gazebo, six tennis courts (three night lighted), four pools open 8 AM to 10 PM, beach equipment, a marina and boat ramp, picnic pavilions and barbecue pits, a nine-hole, par 3 golf course, a beach bar and restaurant... shall we go on? Talk about your full service! Needless to say, you'll probably like it.

Beaches of South Walton

Views, luxury, golf and tennis galore and quaint charm all describe the variety of accommodations in the Beaches of South Walton. You'll see more Mercedes, BMWs, and Jaguars on the road here, too; affluent visitors from the Midwest and East Coast are discovering Florida's last frontier and wondering why they ever bothered going farther south!

The Beaches of South Walton

We talk about them often enough, but do you really know how *many* beaches there are in South Walton? Try eighteen! And heeeerrre they are:

Frangista Beach	dune Allen
Seascape	Blue Mountain Beach
Surfside	Gulf Trace
Edgewater	Grayton Beach
Miramar	Seaside
Mainsail	Seagrove Beach
Hidden Dunes	Camp Creek
Sandestin	Inlet Beach
Tops'l	Santa Rosa Beach

Three of the properties at Sandestin Resort rise out of the emerald landscape like sun-kissed jewels.

Resort Properties

With all this sprawling, undeveloped beachfront, why opt for just a hotel room when you can have golf, tennis, spas, fitness centers and restaurants right at your fingertips?

So you won't have to refer back to the price code chart at the start of this chapter, here it is again:

$80 or less	$
$81-100	$$
$101-150	$$$
$151 or more	$$$$

SANDESTIN RESORT
5500 Hwy. 98 E.
Destin				267-8000
$$$$

Spanning both sides of the highway and fronting both the Gulf of Mexico and Choctawhatchee Bay, Sandestin is a city unto itself. 2,300 acres offer both hotel rooms and villas, 45 holes of golf, 14 tennis courts, a 98-slip marina, 10 swimming pools, bike and watersport rentals, two full-service restaurants, an upscale festival marketplace, children's programs and its own spa and salon. If you're looking to really live it up on your vacation, you can't beat it for a place to be pampered!

SANDESTIN BEACH HILTON GOLF & TENNIS RESORT
5540 Hwy. 98 E.
Destin				267-9500
$$$$

Towering over almost everything in the resort, the all-suite Hilton rises above the gulf within the confines of the Sandestin Beach Resort. All 400 junior suites have gulf views, a bunk-bed area, wet bars and private balconies. Heated indoor and outdoor swimming pools, a gourmet restaurant and all the amenities of the Sandestin Resort (above) are included. Room rates begin at $195 per night for a partial beach view and go up from there; the most expensive is a room facing the gulf. A $5.00 per night resort fee is added to the price of any room.

SEASCAPE RESORT & CONFERENCE CENTER
100 Seascape Dr.
Destin   837-9181, (800) 874-9141
$$$

Seascape is a nicely landscaped, 230-acre beach resort with an 18-hole championship golf course, five swimming pools, eight tennis courts and one full-service restaurant. These one-, two- and three-bedroom condos with private balconies and all the trimmings offer either golf course or beach views.

Bed and Breakfast Inns

JOSEPHINE'S BED AND BREAKFAST
101 Seaside Ave.
Seaside   231-1940, (800) 848-1840
$$$-$$$$

Like everything at Seaside, Josephine's does an exquisite job of capturing the mannerly Southern feel of a seaside retreat. Every room is perfectly furnished in period antiques or reproductions, topped off with balloon curtains, Battenburg lace comforters, settees, fireplaces and clawfoot tubs. No cookie-cutter hotel here, though; each room has its own color scheme — and its own surprises. All include wet bars, coffee makers and small refrigerators. Brunch is included in the comfort and privacy of your room (perhaps on your own veranda?) or Josephine's private dining room. The dining room is open for breakfast, lunch and dinner daily.

A HIGHLANDS HOUSE
10 Bullard Rd.
Dune Allen Beach   267-0110
$

Sit back and enjoy this taste of the Old South — a summer home with wide porches and gentle gulf breezes right on the beach. Rooms are individually furnished with four-poster rice carved beds, wing-backed chairs and wicker furniture on outdoor porches. An expanded continental breakfast comes with your room, served in the dining room. Children under 10 stay free with parents. Credit cards are not accepted. A Highlands House hearkens back to the time when families rented tiny cottages along the beach, and there were maybe two restaurants, one store and one gas station within 30 miles. It's pretty far out there, but it's quiet, the beach is beautiful and the price is great!

Condominiums/ Townhomes/Vacation Cottages

Please be sure to check Destin accommodations for a full area listing; many realty companies offer properties throughout the entire area. Prices, which follow the same code as those in Destin, reflect the average weekly cost of a two-bedroom/two-bath condo or house during the peak summer season. Most rental agencies want a deposit up front which can be up to a third of the week's rental. The rest is due upon check-in. Prices do not include tax.

FORT WALTON BEACH AREA — ACCOMMODATIONS

ABBOTT REALTY SERVICES, INC.
35000 Emerald Coast Pkwy.
Destin   837-4853, (800) 336-4853
$-$$$$

Abbott is one of the largest realty companies in the area, offering over 80 resort properties from high- and low-rise condominiums to townhomes and beach cottages. If you're not sure exactly *where* in the area might be best for you and your entourage, Abbott can explain the huge variety of options, both beachfront and inland, family-friendly or couples only, luxury at every turn or basic lodgings.

EDGEWATER BEACH CONDOMINIUM
5000 Hwy. 98 E.
Destin   837-1550, (800) 882-4929
$$$

All units were decorated by designers, so each has its own special touches in addition to marble baths, views of the gulf and private balconies. Three swimming pools, a wading pool, hot tub, shuffleboard, a putting hole and a playground are available to guests.

TOPS'L BEACH & RACQUET CLUB
5550 Hwy. 98 E.
Destin   267-9222, (800) 476-9222
$$$$

Lose yourself in 52 acres of rolling dunes and hills with two- and three-bedroom gulf-front and tennis villa accommodations. Twelve tennis courts, three swimming pools (one indoor/outdoor), a fitness center, a full-service salon and a 1.7-mile nature and fitness trail are surrounded by some of the area's best natural woodlands.

RIVARD OF SOUTH WALTON
2100 Magnolia St.
Santa Rosa Beach   231-4446
$$-$$$$ (800) 423-3215

A wealth of private home, condominium and townhouse rentals throughout the many communities of South Walton County are managed by Rivard. Many offer water views or are directly at the foot of the gulf. Where your rental unit sits in relation to the water can make hundreds of dollars of difference in the price. If the view doesn't matter all that much, be sure to ask for one a bit inland. The beach is never far away.

MONARCH REALTY AT SEASIDE
At Josephine's Bed & Breakfast, Seaside
Cottages   (800) 475-1841
Josephine's   (800) 848-1840
$$$-$$$$

Monarch has rentals on all sorts of pristine cottages and townhomes at Seaside, which can't be beat for ambience and seaside resort atmosphere. Park your car and leave it for the length of your stay; all shops, restaurants and the beach are just steps away. But there's a price for all that "atmosphere" — a two-bedroom/two-bath cottage starts at $1495 for a week. Reservations for Josephine's Bed & Breakfast can also be made through Monarch.

HIDDEN DUNES
5394 Hwy. 98 E.
Destin   837-3521
$$-$$$

A great getaway place, Hidden Dunes features secluded one-, two- and three-bedroom condos centered around man-made tiled pools with fountains. Private screened

FORT WALTON BEACH AREA — ACCOMMODATIONS

Interiors of Seaside Cottages are well adapted to their coastal environment with high ceilings, hardwood floors and paddle fans.

FORT WALTON BEACH AREA — ACCOMMODATIONS

porches with ceiling fans keep out the bugs while letting you enjoy relaxing or dining in comfort. Hidden Dunes is a large property (27 acres), but was designed with privacy and relaxation in mind; walkways lead you around, but not *to* the units (main entrances face the parking lot), and you're never face-to-face with someone else's bathroom window. Strolling around the grounds at night is peaceful, well-lit and safe. On the grounds are swimming pools, Jacuzzis and one high-rise condo on the gulf, if that's your style. Other buildings are two-stories.

SEASIDE
County Rd. 30-A between Grayton Beach and Seagrove Beach, Seaside 231-1320
$$$$

A tiny beach community rising out of the scrub on the Gulf of Mexico, Seaside is an architect's dream. Brightly painted cottages sport wrapped porches with swings and rockers, widow's walks, gazebos and gingerbread of every description. White picket fences mark property lines, and community playgrounds and beach pavilions allow residents and visitors to meet and mingle.

Northwest Florida is fortunate and privileged to have this internationally acclaimed community in its midst. The word is out, the trend has caught on, and copycat communities have sprung up throughout the area and the Southeast. But Seaside was the first, and people still flock here to buy vacation homes, or just spend a week or two in this idyllic setting.

People from Atlanta, New Jersey, New York and just about every other place have bought property here — people who are used to paying high prices. Consequently, Seaside is one of the most expensive places to stay in Northwest Florida. A two-bedroom/two-bath cottage for a week at high season will run you somewhere between $1555 and $3311. The difference in price is not the space — most cottages are fairly small — but the location, whether directly on the gulf or not.

RV Parks/Campsites

EMERALD COAST RV RESORT
Hwy. 30-A
Santa Rosa Beach 267-2808
(800) BEACH-RV

Plain and simple, this is the prettiest, cleanest RV park you may ever lay eyes on, with more amenities than some luxury resorts. Try these on for size: concrete pads with patios, a heated pool, cable TV, phones, LP gas, tennis, a laundry, country store, clubhouse, picnic tables, security gate, nature trails and fishing in stocked lakes. A complimentary shuttle takes you to the beach from May through September. No tents or pop-ups are allowed since this is strictly an RV resort. Summertime daily rates start at $23.00; add $2.00 apiece for electric and cable. Weekly rates are $140.00, plus $12.00 each for electric and cable.

GRAYTON BEACH STATE RECREATION AREA
County Rd. 30-A near
Grayton Beach 231-4210

This exquisite state park with its rolling white dunes and forests of pine is perfect for camping, picnicking, swimming and hiking on the nature trail. Canoes are available for rent. No pets are allowed. RV hookup sites are $10.76 until March 1; without electricity $8.64. In-season rates are $16.00 and $14.00 respectively, which includes tax. Some of the 37 sites back up to the freshwater Western Lake, just a stone's throw from the gulf.

HOLIDAY TRAVEL PARK
5380 Hwy. 98 E.
Destin 837-6334

Camp right on gulf beaches or in grassy, shaded sites. 250 RV and primitive sites are available. Off-season rates are terrific, just $10 a night for any site, $50 a week or $200 a month. From March 1 through November, the park charges per-night fees of only $27 for water and electric hookups, $29 for a full hookup, and $37 if you want to camp on the beach. A pool and convenience store are on the grounds.

Fort Walton Beach/Destin/Beaches of South Walton
Shopping

Beach Ts, souvenirs, airbrush art, swimwear, footwear, beachwear and enough little sculptures, nightlights, boxes and bangles created from the gulf's treasures to leave you "shell" shocked. Most everyone gets a new hat, swimsuit or pair of sunglasses from one of these shops, and boy, they're out there. In fact, they're everywhere. But so is some terrific outlet shopping in Fort Walton Beach, Destin and Graceville; gorgeous restored antiques, boutiques and original works of art throughout the Beaches of South Walton; and some pretty unusual finds in between.

Fort Walton Beach

ALVIN'S ISLAND TROPICAL DEPARTMENT STORES
1204 E. Hwy. 98 on the corner of Santa Rosa Blvd.
Okaloosa Island 244-3913

You'll find everything you could ever want in the way of beachwear, airbrush art, postcards, souvenirs and jewelry. Open every day from 9 to 5:30.

MANUFACTURERS OUTLET CENTER
127 SW and 255 Miracle Strip Pkwy.
Fort Walton Beach 244-2744

In the mood for some real outlet shopping, with savings of 30% to 70%? Sure, who isn't? You can choose from Russell, Van Heusen, Converse, Corning/Revere, Bass Shoes, Carter's and many more. And since they're open seven days a week, you can shop to your heart's content. The stores here expanded so rapidly that a second Manufacturers Outlet Center had to be built about a mile and a half down the road, hence the two addresses. There's a free trolley that runs between the two; for now, it just runs on weekends.

SANTA ROSA MALL
300 Mary Esther Blvd.
Mary Esther 244-2172

One of the more popular area malls, Santa Rosa Mall has 120 shops including anchors Gayfers, McRae's, Sears and JC Penney. Shop here for fashions, sporting goods, footwear, books, toys, music and electronics, eyewear, jewelry, cellular phones, furniture, flowers... have we missed anything? Oh yes, FOOD — there are sit-down restaurants, snack shops and a fast-food food court mecca of eleven eateries. Open 10 to 9 Monday through Saturday; Sundays 12 to 5.

FORT WALTON BEACH AREA — SHOPPING

ISLANDER'S SURF & SPORT
Hwy. 98, downtown
Fort Walton Beach   244-0451

Islander's offers a most excellent selection of beach and swimwear including Patagonia, Nike, Quicksilver, Oakley and more. T-shirts, flops, tanks and plenty of accessories, too. When the surf's up, Islander's Surf Shops is ready with a great selection of surf boards and boogie boards for sale and for rent. Open 10 to 6 daily; 10 to 5 Sundays.

SMITH'S
123 Miracle Strip Pkwy. SE
Fort Walton Beach   243-1714, 243-6215

Clothing and accessories catering to women only, Smith's is as trusted as an old friend in Fort Walton Beach. Find not just sportswear and beachwear, but a full line of shoes, hosiery, lingerie, jewelry, formals and unique gifts for your favorite lady (even if that's *you*!). Smith's will be looking for you from 9 to 6 Monday through Saturday and on occasional Sundays.

BEACH AVE. T-SHIRT FACTORY
196 Miracle Strip Pkwy. SE
Fort Walton Beach   664-6765

Along Highway 98 (called Miracle Strip Parkway here) is a short strip of shops, many of them geared to tourists. Strategically placed *before* you hit the beach, the "Miracle Strip" can get you just about anything you might need, and sometimes for a lower price than you'll find on the island. This store you can't miss, and not just because it's *purple*. Here are T's of every sort, screen printed, airbrushed or from a hand-picked, custom transfer. The T-Shirt Factory also has plenty of those coordinated pants-and-tunic sets with tropical motifs, mostly birds. Souvenir T's can be sought from 10 to 8 every day.

VF FACTORY OUTLET
950 Prim Ave., Ste. 12
Graceville   263-3207

Is it worth going well out of your way to save up to 50% on everything you buy? Let's do a little name dropping: Lee, Health-Tex, Jantzen, Vanity Fair, Wrangler. There are many more. Happy shopping! Open Monday through Thursday 9 to 7; Friday and Saturday 9 to 8; Sunday noon to 6.

THE SHOWTOWN SWAP SHOP & FLEA MARKET
Two miles north of the Mary Esther cutoff on Beal Pkwy.
Fort Walton Beach   863-9034

Flea markets are big in Northwest Florida. If you've never been to one, you owe it to yourself to go just to see the incredible array of stuff offered at ridiculously low prices. It's fun to browse and bargain, even if you end up with something you can't possibly use, but just had to have! Open Saturday 7 AM until and Sunday from 8 AM until.

Destin

SHORELINE VILLAGE MALL
Hwy. 98 and Gulf Shore Dr., Destin

Several specialty shops center around a courtyard and The Lighthouse Restaurant. The Mole Hole (837-8070) offers an assortment of unique gift items. Maxine's of Destin (837-0770) sells beach sportswear and collectibles such as lead crystal,

• 175

Floppy hats, funky jewelry and hand-painted attire dress up the open air marketplace at Seaside.

Dickens village and Andrea Sadek pieces. An airbrush artist is on staff for custom T's, visors and car tags. Tooley Street (837-8008) is a rather pricey contemporary clothing store for women, while Destin T-Shirt & Supply Co. (654-6988) is more low-key for casual and beach wear. Lindz's A Place of Christmas (837-7211) lets you browse through a winter wonderland all year long. Streetwear (654-1432) is another clothing shop for men and women with casual styles and affordable prices.

BUMIN' IN THE SUN BEACHWEAR
1655 E. Hwy. 98
Destin   654-4622

The stuff inside is as good as the name — beachwear, swimwear, jewelry, beach accessories and just about everything you could want to outfit you for vacation. You've just got to splurge on yourself once during your visit, maybe with a new hat, a daring swimsuit, or a night-on-the-town sundress. Bumin' in the Sun is the place to find it from 9 to 9 every day. They're located right across the street from The Back Porch Restaurant.

ALVIN'S ISLAND TROPICAL DEPARTMENT STORES
1079 E. Hwy. 98, Destin   837-5178

Alvin's carries everything you could ever want in the way of beachwear, airbrush art, postcards, souvenirs and jewelry. Open every day from 9 to 5:30.

SILVER SANDS FACTORY STORES
5101 Hwy. 98 E., one mile west of Sandestin

Adjacent to Sandestin Beach Resort, Silver Sands tends to be more upscale that its in-town counterparts, with 85 fashion outlet stores including Adrienne Vittadini (654-4006), J. Crew (654-5565) and Donna Karan

(654-3356). There's housewares, linens, accessories, sportswear and evening attire. Open 10 to 9 Monday through Saturday; 11 to 6 Sunday.

ISLANDER'S SURF & SPORT
Shoreline Village Mall in Destin   837-5735

Anyone who is really into sports knows the name brands carried here quite well—Patagonia, Nike, Quicksilver, Oakley and more. There's T-shirts, flops, tanks and plenty of accessories, too. The shop is open daily from 10 to 6; Sundays 10 to 5.

GALLERY OF FINE ART
Palmetto Plaza at the corner of Hwy. 98 and Palmetto
Destin   837-3993, 837-3488

Richard and Dorothy Williams invite you to come in and browse through their collection of fine art by local and nationally known artists. An artist's studio is upstairs, where watercolor classes are taught by Richard during the winter months. The Gallery of Fine Art will not only help you select a painting, but assist in framing it as well. Open 9:30 to 5:30 every day except Sunday.

THE CANDYMAKER
Old Hwy. 98 E. across from The Back Porch Restaurant
Destin   654-0833

You not only get to sample some of the finest saltwater taffy, creamy fudge, walnut toffee and juicy caramel apples north of the Gulf of Mexico, but you get to watch them make it! The Candymaker may be more of an attraction than merely a place to shop. Passersby can stop in front of the huge front window and watch in fascination as the taffy-pulling machine works its magic. Hand-dipped ice cream cones, frozen yogurt, floats and shakes will make you save a trip to The Candymaker for a scrumptious dessert! Open 11 to 5; closed Tuesdays.

SANTA FE DEPOT
Shoreline Village Mall, Gulf Shores Dr. and Hwy. 98
Destin   654-0909

Native American and primitive arts and crafts steeped in culture and heritage are almost exclusively handmade. Look over the array of earrings, accessories, pottery, even leather bikinis! Santa Fe Depot takes orders for custom leathers, hides and stone. Navajo rugs, hides and wall hangings can turn your home into a Southwestern design showplace. Talk to Lois, owner of Santa Fe Depot, who specializes in Southwestern interior design; she'll be happy to assist you with your selections. Open Monday through Saturday from 10 to 5; Sunday 1 to 5.

DESTIN ICE SEAFOOD MARKET
Hwy. 98, half a mile east of the Destin Bridge
Destin   837-8333

Fishing put Destin on the map, so here, laid out before you, is the abundance of the sea, done in fine fashion by Destin Ice Seafood Market. This started 25 years ago as a little business supplying ice to commercial fishing vessels, and now they've entered the seafood business themselves, supplying seafood to many of the area's fine restaurants.

If you've never bought fresh fish before, try a mild, white flaky fish like grouper, triggerfish, red snapper, scamp or flounder. If you buy it already filleted, about a half-pound a person is the rule. This kind of fish is best broiled, baked or fried. For backyard grilling, try amberjack, yellowfin tuna, cobia, swordfish or — shark! Shrimp, a Gulf Coast favorite, is available in several sizes, either with "heads-on" or "heads-off," depending on your preference. Crab meat and lobster come in many varieties, and the Destin Ice Seafood Market has all the accompanying spices and sauces to make your meal complete. They can even pack fresh seafood for shipping! Open 8 to 6 daily.

Marine Supplies

Yachties'
200 Hwy. 98 E.
Destin 837-4900

It's affordable because it's been used before! This is a classy, quality place for used marine equipment, nautical clothing and other items on consignment. Gifts, jewelry, accessories, discount new marine supplies and everything nautical. Located a half-mile east of the Destin Bridge, they're open 9 to 5 Monday through Saturday.

The Ships Chandler
646 Hwy. 98 E.
Destin 837-9306

This marine store is also a complete boating equipment and fishing tackle shop. Get a good buy on safety equipment, marine paints, topsider shoes and nautical sportswear. Rod and reel repair, fishing information and guide service make it a one-stop shop. Open in the off season from 7 AM until 5 PM Monday through Saturday; in season from daylight to dark seven days a week.

Beaches of South Walton

Beach Bums
Hwy. 98 west of Sandestin 837-7111

The incredibly PINK building that you can't miss, Beach Bums has between 5,000 and 10,000 swimsuits. Even if you're only looking for one, Beach Bums is a fun place to browse. Open 8 AM until "real late."

Islander's Surf & Sport
Hwy. 98 at The Market at
Sandestin 654-4144

As with the other Islander's in Fort Walton Beach and Destin, this store carries a big selection of beachwear, name brand footwear, jewelry, Ts and visors. Open 10 to 9 daily.

Seaside
County Rd. 30-A, Seaside

Spanning both sides of the two-lane highway, Seaside offers an eclectic collection of outdoor markets, gourmet food shops and galleries. Beginning with the gulfside shops, there's Sue Vaneer's (231-2497), selling all forms of Seaside memorabilia, which, of course, sells like crazy! Beach reading is popular at Seaside, and Sundog Books (231-5481) provides great Southern literature, children's books and timeless classics. Whimsical clothing describes 4 Kids (231-1733), with a full complement of accessories, toys and novelties.

Donna Burgess' watercolors grace the homes of many a Seaside visitor and resident, and one can be yours by stopping by Artz (231-5781), Burgess' Seaside gallery. No animals were harmed to create the line of skin care products and cosmetics at

Patchouli's (231-1447). And, Patchouli's can create a custom fragrance to blend with your body's own chemistry. Per-spi-cas-ity (231-5829) might be hard to pronounce, but it's not hard to find something wonderful in this outdoor marketplace, filled with casual clothing, baskets, glassware and accessories.

Jump across the highway to Central Square and begin your shopping adventure with iii s (231-1000), featuring designer eyewear. Azure (231-4044) is for men, with sports and casual wear and accessories. L. Pizitz & Co. is the "purveyor of Seaside style" (read: pricey) in dinnerware, handpainted pottery and linens. Some antiques, some new pieces, jewelry, pewter and sterling, all hand-picked for you are at Fernleigh Ltd. (231-2240). And don't miss an opportunity to see some outstanding watercolor work by artist Nina Fritz. Her interpretations of jazz musicians and singers are dead-on perfect; her style is that of a well-seasoned, first-class pro. Travel a ways down Ruskin Place to the artist's colony. The Martha Green Gallery (231-1467) offers fine art and interior furnishings, jewelry, hand-blown glass and many other home furnishings, all handmade. Works by well-known and emerging artists are featured at Newbill Collection by the Sea (231-4500), and The Keeping Room (231-2410) sells popular Folk Art and American reproductions.

PATRONE'S
Off Hwy. 98, Grayton Beach

This is one of those unusual gems in Walton County that seems interesting enough from the road to stop and take a closer look. It's *kind* of an artist's colony mixed in with several animals on display in a giant pen, a barbecue place and a pretty view of the water. An artist that used to create huge wood carvings (some were used in the film *The Lost Boys*) evidently has found fame (if not fortune) and moved out, but he's left a few carvings behind to draw folks in to other artist's shops. Much of the work being done here, like custom-made cypress and whimsical handpainted furniture, handpainted children's clothing, Florida paintings, jewelry and hats, is of wonderful quality, offered at *very* reasonable prices, and the artists are ready to bargain. Open 9 to 5 daily. Ask to look at the delightful overnight cottages; staying in one of these could be a good introduction to this quirky part of Florida's Great Northwest.

THE MARKET AT SANDESTIN
Sandestin Beach Resort, Hwy. 98

Twenty-eight exclusive shops including Benetton international fashions, Black-n-White clothing (yes, it's all black and white), Classic Cargo (fine porcelain and crystal) and Tarzana's (trendy swimwear) make up this shopping area. It's located at the entrance to Sandestin Beach Resort, and hours are 10 to 9 daily.

CLEMENT'S ANTIQUES
Hwy. 98   837-1473

Although there are numerous antique shops throughout the Beaches of South Walton, this is the largest, specializing in estate quality antiques and some of the best 17th- and 18th-century antiques in the state. Open 9 to 5 Monday through Saturday.

FORT WALTON BEACH AREA — ATTRACTIONS

Take only pictures, leave only footprints.

Fort Walton Beach/Destin/ Beaches of South Walton
Attractions

So you maybe thought that all Northwest Florida had going for it was a couple of pearly-white beaches? Insiders have spread out far and wide, traversing east and west and north to find you, our reader, absolutely up-to-the-minute data on the area's many attractions. Here, all in one place, your guide to the ordinary, the unusual, and the downright strange — diversity galore. Attractions marked with an asterisk (*) are centered around family fun.

Fort Walton Beach

*THE GULFARIUM
Hwy. 98 on Okaloosa Island   244-5169

Florida, 1955 . . . before Disney World, Busch Gardens and world-class resorts, opening day at The Gulfarium was making front-page news. As the second oldest marine show aquarium in the world, The Gulfarium's focus is primarily on family entertainment, but also serves as an introduction to the wonders of marine life. Dolphin shows demonstrate the grace and agility of these gentle creatures, and educate audiences on the dolphins' eco-locators (to find food or fellow dolphins when it's too dark to see) and their uncanny eyesight and strength.

Sea lions are visitors from the "left" coast, but have adapted well to their more humid surroundings. As they slap and splash and clap and howl, trainers explain how the bristly whiskers allow them to balance objects in or out of the water.

Enter the dark arena of "The Living Sea," where a trained diver glides through a 10,000-gallon tank for a close encounter with alligator gars, sting rays and sharks as well as colorful tropical fish and a loggerhead turtle well over a century old!

The diverse services offered by The Gulfarium include a captive breeding program, environmental education, and The National Marine Mammal Stranding Network (see sidebar). The Network is set up to rescue and care for stranded dolphins, whales, turtles and birds. Admission charge is $12.00; $8.00 for children 4-11, plus tax.

*THE FOCUS CENTER
139 Brooks St.
Fort Walton Beach   664-1261

Here's a "touchy-feely" museum, but not in the way you parents might think. Touchable, workable exhibits demonstrate natural phenomena and basic scientific principles. Kids can make a gigantic four-foot bubble and believe they're just having fun instead of experimenting with fluid

Kiwi: A Happy Ending to a Fatal Stranding

Labor Day weekend, 1993: Five Atlantic spotted dolphins strand themselves in shallow water on Pensacola Beach. Volunteers take turns pouring water over them until help arrives. A crew from The Gulfarium in Fort Walton Beach carts in equipment for moving the dolphins to the EPA station across the island on Little Sabine Bay. Sadly, only two of the five survive the short journey — a female adult and a baby, who volunteers quickly dub "Kiwi."

"Kiwi"

A call goes out through the media, on local talk shows, in the newspaper and on TV that volunteers are needed to keep a vigil on the two surviving dolphins. It's not a pretty job; volunteers must don wet suits and wade waist-deep into the murky water, watching, waiting for signs of change. There is an immediate outpouring of support for the dolphins — hundreds of people call, sign up and send donations to help.

After three days of 'round-the-clock surveillance, the female adult succumbs. The dolphins may have had some sort of viral infection, but the actual cause of death is never determined. Kiwi, however, remains disease-free, drinking formula from a bottle and slowly regaining her strength. The media remain active, reporting on the baby dolphin's condition. But days turn into weeks and weeks into months. Only the hard-core volunteers are left as the days grow cool and the water chilly. On Halloween, after nearly two months, The Gulfarium determines that Kiwi is finally strong enough to be transferred to a holding pen at its facility.

At The Gulfarium, Kiwi has grown to 60 pounds from just 28 when she was first stranded. She's been put on a solid diet and may soon be placed with an adult female dolphin. A determination on releasing her into the wild will have to be made by the National Marine Fisheries.

Although the fight to save Kiwi garnered plenty of media attention, The Gulfarium has rescued and rehabilitated many species of dolphin and whales, as well as sea turtles and all forms of injured wildlife. If you witness a stranding, whether the animal is alive or dead, please call the Florida Marine Patrol in Pensacola at 444-8978.

FORT WALTON BEACH AREA — ATTRACTIONS

dynamics and surface tension. Come face-to-face with yourself in skeleton form to learn about bones and joints and how they are adapted to work together on command. There's a Try On A Career Room where youngsters can climb into a space suit or fire-fighting garb. Traveling exhibits such as the Starlab, a mini-planetarium dome, rotate with other exhibits on a yearly basis. Schedule your child's birthday party at The FOCUS Center and Focusaurus, the museum's mascot, may stop in for a visit. During the school year, the FOCUS Center is open on weekends only from 1 to 5 PM; summer hours are 1 to 5 PM daily. Admission is $2.00; younger than 3 free.

*ROCKY BAYOU STATE RECREATION AREA
State Road 20, Niceville   833-9144

Mature sandpine forests tower over scrub vegetation and shade Rocky Bayou, an offshoot of Choctawhatchee Bay. This area was a favorite of long-ago Native Americans; exhibits attest to their occupation. A mile of bayou shoreline runs within the park, which is especially nice for saltwater fishing and boating. There's freshwater fishing in Puddin Head Lake, where Rocky Creek flows into the bay. (Please remember that licenses are required for either type of fishing.) Three nature trails are explained in a self-guided booklet available at the park, and ranger-guided walks and campfire programs are offered seasonally. Admission is $3.25 per vehicle (up to 8 people); $1.00 for bikers or walkers.

DOOLITTLE MEMORIAL
193 John Sims Pkwy., Valparaiso

A memorial marks the site where "Doolittle's Raiders," headed up by General James Doolittle, trained for bombing missions over Japan in WWII.

*HISTORICAL SOCIETY MUSEUM
115 Westview Ave., Valparaiso   678-2615

Start with an exhibit of stone tools found right here in Northwest Florida, used by Paleolithic and Archaic Indians more than 8,000 years ago. More recent local history displays huge iron kettles and pots slung by pioneer women in the 19th century and instruments of the turpentine industry of the 1920s. Heritage craft classes teach old-time methods of quilting, tatting, bobbin lace and needlepoint. A "Youth Settlers" program introduces pioneer life to 9- and 10-year-olds. Over a two week session, they learn to fashion corn husk dolls, dip candles and weave as well as doing without the conveniences of modern life. The museum is open Tuesday through Saturday from 11 AM until 4 PM, and admission is free.

*INDIAN TEMPLE MOUND MUSEUM
Hwy. 98, Downtown
Fort Walton Beach   243-6521

Exhibits and dioramas of Native American tribes date back 10,000 years. All 4,000 Native American artifacts were found in a 40-mile radius of downtown. Designated a National Historic Landmark, the temple mound, just outside the museum, was used by Native Americans for political and religious ceremonies and has been restored to its

FORT WALTON BEACH AREA — ATTRACTIONS

Henderson Beach is Florida's newest state park.

original configuration. Admission is $.75 for adults; kids are free. The museum is closed Mondays.

FORT WALTON BEACH ART MUSEUM
38 Robinson Dr. SW
Fort Walton Beach   244-5319

This is a pleasant place to spend an hour or so, examining the American paintings and sculptures, many by local artists, and the Thai and Cambodian relics. The museum is open Sundays from 1 to 5 PM and weekdays by appointment, and admission is free.

*WATERWORLD OF OKALOOSA ISLAND
Hwy. 98, Okaloosa Island Bayside 243-9738

You could spend all day (or, at least, the *kids* could) at this fun spot featuring seven waterslides, an activity pool, go-karts, jet skis, parasailing, jet-boats, sailboats, windsurfing, dive shop with lessons, and an arcade. They're open Memorial Day to Labor Day. Call for admission prices and times.

*AIR FORCE ARMAMENT MUSEUM
West gate of Eglin AFB on State Rd. 85
near State Rd. 189   882-4062, 882-4063

The SR-71 Blackbird, the fastest

plane ever built, welcomes you to the museum. Inside, look for four full-size aircraft representing WWII, the Korean Conflict and Vietnam. For those interested in weaponry, you'll find a huge exhibit of bombs, missiles, rockets and guns. A 32-minute movie, *Arming the Air Force*, is shown continuously. Other aircraft and missiles are located around the museum grounds. Open daily from 9:30 to 4:30; closed Thanksgiving, Christmas and New Year's. Admission is free.

*PLEASURE ISLAND WATERPARK
Hwy. 98 on Okaloosa Island   243-9978

In the heat of summer, there's no better way to cool off! Seven waterslides, an activity pool, parasail rides, and wave runners let you and the kids float, slide, and splash to your heart's content. Go-karts, an arcade, an ice cream shop, restaurant and gift shop let you cool off out of the water. Open Memorial Day to Labor Day. Call for admission prices and times.

Destin

Fishing is right at the top of the charts in Destin, and most activities center around the water. Since it's a resort area, some family-type attractions are slowly creeping in, which is to be expected — and welcomed. Be sure to check the Recreation chapter for Destin as well; charter boat fishing and sightseeing offer a unique perspective on this scenic area, as do Destin's historical museums.

*THE GLASS BOTTOM BOAT II
Capt. Dave's Marina, 304 E. Hwy. 98
Destin   654-7787

Billed as "A Sightseeing Adventure," *The Glass Bottom Boat II* offers scenic wonders above — and below — the surface! Your adventure begins with a pleasant sojourn through Destin Pass and Choctawhatchee Bay as you head into the Gulf of Mexico. Be sure to bring your camera, not only to capture that emerald water (the folks back home won't quite believe it), but the remarkable scenery and flocks of seagulls and pelicans escorting the boat to sea (and anticipating a handout!). Schools of dolphin, almost as if on command, appear alongside the vessel, racing and jumping and having almost as much fun as the people on board.

Get set for a close-up encounter with fish, crabs, rays and other creatures of the deep through the large viewing window as the boat glides over the shallows of Choctawhatchee Bay and the pass. The captain and crew will point out the different species and tell you a little about them. Shrimp nets or crab traps may be pulled on board to show guests the intricacies and varieties of marine life, as well as the different methods of obtaining tonight's dinner!

As soon as the weather's warmed up a bit (as early as January), *The Glass Bottom Boat II* is off and running on Wednesdays and Saturdays with trips from 1 to 3:15 PM. Cost is $12.00 for adults, $7.00 for children. Call for summer cruises.

Killer Trash

Your fishing line gets tangled around a floating log. You snip the line off and start fresh. You finish your six-pack and toss the plastic rings into the water. You dump your bag of ice into the cooler and leave the bag on the beach. If you've ever done any of these things, you could be a killer.

Marine debris contributes to the higher-than-normal death rates for seals, seabirds, turtles and many species of fish. Uncaring, or in some cases simply unknowing, people dump plastic nets and lines off of boats or near the shore, a lethal trap for all inhabitants of the coastal environment. Turtles that become entangled in fishing line are unable to break free and quickly drown. Ospreys, gulls and other birds sometimes collect pieces of line for nesting material, creating death traps for their young. Beyond the threat to sealife, fishing line can easily become wrapped around boat propellers, crippling the vessels.

Plastic bags can be mistaken for jellyfish by turtles who ingest them and suffocate, a slow and agonizing death. Plastic six-pack rings are a threat to all kinds of marine animals. Fish, birds and sea lions have been found entangled in the rings.

Since these items are created and used only by people, it is up to all of us to dispose of them properly. It is illegal to dump *any* type of debris over the side of a boat, and it's so simple to save your trash until you get back to shore.

Northwest Florida is fortunate to be blessed with a thriving marine ecosystem and a wealth of natural beauty. We all need to take the steps necessary to help preserve the gulf and beaches, not only for ourselves, but for the creatures who inhabit them.

*THE TRACK FAMILY RECREATION CENTER
Hwy. 98, Destin   654-4668

A clean, affordable family place, The Track is loaded with entertainment for teens, tots and even grown-ups. Go-karts, bumper boats and the Surfin' Safari Mini-Golf courses will appeal to everybody, the teens will love to "hang" at the arcade, and the tiniest among you will thrill to "Kids Kountry" with its pint-sized Rio Grande Railroad, small-fry Ferris wheel, swing ride, spinning top (like a small-scale Tilt-A-Whirl), and Noah's Lark (a giant swinging boat ride). Books of 18 tickets are $21.00; 48 tickets will cost you $50.00. The Track is open from 10 AM until 10 PM from March to September; 9 AM to midnight in the summer; and 10 AM to 5 PM in the winter.

*MUSEUM OF THE SEA AND INDIAN
*Eight miles east of Destin on
Beach Hwy.   837-6625*

This one plays strictly for fun, one of those delightfully tacky old-Florida tourist attractions. Strange and unusual marine exhibits have

FORT WALTON BEACH AREA — ATTRACTIONS

been amassed from all corners of the world (if you believe the signs). Look for the drunken fish, the walking catfish, the mola mola (all head-no brains), Indian exhibits and a spook house. For the kids, there's a little zoo, but these creatures are not for petting — alligators, peacocks and monkeys are among the assemblage. This unique place is open 8 AM until 7 PM daily in the summer; 9 AM to 4 PM in winter. Admission is $3.75 for adults, $3.45 for seniors and $2.00 for kids 5 to 16.

*HENDERSON BEACH STATE PARK
17000 Emerald Coast Pkwy.
Destin   837-7550
Over 200 acres of beachfront were acquired for this new park as part of the "Save Our Coast" program. A nature trail winds through the white sand, dotted with Southern magnolias and native wildflowers. Six dune walkovers put you almost toe-to-toe with the gulf, while two tin-roofed picnic pavilions and bathhouses with outdoor showers provide families with all the amenities to enjoy a day at the beach. The site is handicapped accessible. Admission is $3.25 per vehicle (up to eight people); $1.00 for bikers and walk-ins.

The Florida Park Service is now issuing vacation passes good for up to 15 days. A Family Entrance Permit (up to eight people) covers admission to any of Florida's State Parks and costs $20.00. The new passes can be purchased at any Florida State Park.

---

*OLD DESTIN POST OFFICE MUSEUM
Stahlman Ave. across from the
Destin Library, Destin   837-8572
Artifacts and photos tell the story of early culture and standards of area pioneers. Destin's first post office was set up in the parlor of a private home in 1897. Admission is free, and guided tours are available. The museum is open Monday and Wednesday 1:30 to 4:00 PM.

*DESTIN FISHING MUSEUM
Moreno Plaza, one block east of
Destin Bridge, Destin   654-1011
Old photographs and fishing artifacts demonstrate how Destin became the fishing capital of the world. Most of the museum is a "dry" underwater scene, complete with lighting and sound effects. It's open Tuesday through Sunday 11 AM until 4 PM, and there is no admission charge.

*BIG KAHUNA'S WATERPARK
1007 Hwy. 98 E., Destin   837-4061
Big Kahuna's is chockfull of water slides, one with a multilevel activity pool with a "Shamu" the killer whale slide. It's water fun for everyone. Older kids will thrill to the new Tunnel of Doom and Cave of No Return! The Grand Prix racetrack and tropical golf course are open 10 AM until 10 PM; the water park is open until 5 PM. Open Memorial Day to Labor Day. Call for admission prices.

Beaches of South Walton

Beaches and leisure-time activities are the top draw along the Beaches of South Walton. You'll find no chain hotels, fast-food restaurants or

FORT WALTON BEACH AREA — ATTRACTIONS

Even more fun than touring the Chautauqua Winery and learning how wine is made is the free tasting session at the end!

"honky-tonk" bars along these beaches. Folks spend their time playing golf, tennis and croquet. Shopping in South Walton's many boutiques can net the bargain hunter some one-of-a-kind finds.

EDEN STATE GARDENS
Off Hwy. 98, Point Washington   231-4214

These neatly manicured grounds no longer echo with the laughter of children, the drone of a buzz saw, or the chorus of voices intermingled with the sounds of a busy lumber mill. The old Wesley mansion, once the hub of the twelve-acre site, stands majestically framed by gnarled oaks, colorful azaleas and garden walks of camellias. A century ago, the Wesley Lumber Company did a brisk business in yellow pine, building a dock out into Tucker Bayou for loading the lumber onto barges. From here the pine traveled to northern and western states, Europe, and parts of South America. At its peak, the acreage was filled with a saw mill, planer mill, dry kiln, about 20 company-owned houses for employees and their families, and a company commissary. The home is open for tours daily (admission is $4.00), and the gardens and picnic area are open from 8 AM until sundown. Peak flowering season is around mid-March, but Eden is a delightful spot to "set a-spell" any time of year. Admission to the park is free.

*GRAYTON BEACH STATE RECREATION AREA
*State Road 30-A near
Grayton Beach   231-4210*

You cannot leave South Walton County without standing on the beach that was rated #1 in the U.S.! Wide and flat, with scrub-covered rolling dunes, Grayton Beach is a Northwest Florida gem. After a visit, you may not want to leave at all. The park is heavily wooded with pine flatwoods and scrub oak. An inland lake is ringed by a salt marsh, a perfect nesting habitat for shorebirds and sea turtles. Camping and nature trails are offered in the park. Admission is $3.25 per vehicle (up to eight people); $1.00 for bikers and walkers.

CHAUTAUQUA VINEYARDS
*I-10 at U.S. 331
DeFuniak Springs   892-5887*

It's out of your way, but worth the drive, not only for a winery tour, but for the lovely historic town of DeFuniak Springs nearby. The several varieties of wines grown, produced and bottled here are made from muscadine grapes, giving the wines an unusual flavor. Although the winery is small and has been in operation only a few years, several Chautauqua wines have racked up top honors at international wine competitions. The tour is really fascinating; you may ask questions of the people who actually *make* the wine (called vintners). Now comes the fun part. When the tour is over, you may spend some time in the tasting room deciding which of the several varieties you like best. Most visitors buy at least one souvenir bottle if only for the tastefully-designed label; there's a discount on cases. Admission is free.

Rev up your Nikes for November's Sportfest, South Walton's largest. Compete in the 10K run, the half-marathon or numerous other events.

Fort Walton Beach/Destin/ Beaches of South Walton
Festivals and Special Events

Balmy weather emphasizes outdoor frolicking, so both visitors and locals take to the beaches and the water for year-round pleasure-hunting. Seasonal events add some extra zest to the good-times recipe. Note that a few of our festivals and events are located in north Walton County, a pleasant day trip away from the beaches, with plenty of scenic and historic diversions along the way.

Fort Walton Beach

APRIL

EGLIN AIR SHOW
Eglin AFB, Hwy. 85 north of Fort Walton Beach

Eglin is the free world's largest military installation, and once a year it opens its gates to the public. Watch the aerial acrobatics of the Thunderbirds, simulated dogfights from the Desert Storm 33rd Tactical Fighter Wing, and flightline displays of military power.

AMERICAN INDIAN SPRING FESTIVAL
E-CHOTA Cherokee Reservation at Mossy Head   892-4030

Native American (Cherokee) arts and crafts, intertribal dancing, native dance competitions and demonstrations combine to make this spring event fun as well as educational. Admission is just $1.00.

OLD SPANISH TRAIL FESTIVAL
Spanish Trail Park, Crestview   689-6783

A rodeo, arts and crafts, food booths, trail rides, beauty pageants, carnival rides, a parade and musical entertainment commemorate the area's heritage and the 16th-century trade route between El Paso, Texas, and Jacksonville, Florida.

SATURDAY IN THE PARK
Perrine Park, Valparaiso   678-2323

Sponsored by the Okaloosa-Walton Historical Society, the free festival attracts thousands from surrounding communities to shop at arts and crafts booths, listen to continuous live entertainment, watch demonstrations of pioneer crafts and eat!

JUNE

BILLY BOWLEGS FESTIVAL
Fort Walton Beach Landing
Fort Walton Beach   244-8191

A 500-boat parade brimming with costumed ruffians "captures" the

• 191

Butterflies stop to rest at Grayton Beach State Park during the annual monarch migration.

Emerald Coast to celebrate the landing of the notorious pirate Billy Bowlegs. Fireworks, a triathlon, volleyball, food booths, crafts, a torchlight parade and many other fun activities highlight the week-long event.

July

Niceville/Valparaiso Fireworks Display
Boggy Bayou, Niceville   678-2323
The beautiful Boggy Bayou is the setting for this annual pyrotechnic display. Fireworks-watchers line the bayou or anchor out in the water for free entertainment of the bright kind.

October

Oktoberfest
Niceville   897-3338
Doesn't *every* community have its own version of this German celebration? Niceville hosts this yearly bash with authentic German beer, music, ethnic foods, beer, arts and crafts and, of course, beer. Admission is free.

Festa Italiana
Fort Walton Square
Fort Walton Beach   243-9055
Festa Italiana is a one-day festival celebrating Columbus and everything Italian — an Italian-flavored parade, Italian cuisine and continuous live entertainment. No admission is charged.

Boggy Bayou Mullet Festival
Old Sawmill Site, Hwy. 85 N.
and College Rd., Niceville   678-1615
Mullet is considered a "trash fish" by Northerners, but the folks down here find the mighty mullet good eatin' fried up in cornmeal batter.

FORT WALTON BEACH AREA — FESTIVALS AND SPECIAL EVENTS

About eleven tons of the plentiful fish are consumed each year. Sixty food booths, eighty arts and crafts vendors, clown shows, pony rides and live entertainment should keep the family busy for at least one of the two festival days. Billy Ray ("Achy-Breaky Heart") Cyrus was '93's headliner — which, for some people, made the fact that there is no admission fee for this festival even more appealing.

DECEMBER

NICEVILLE/VALPARAISO CHRISTMAS PARADE
John Sims Pkwy., Niceville　　678-2323

The main street of downtown Niceville provides an idyllic hometown setting for marching bands, scouts, dance classes, drill teams and float-riders throwing candy to spectators.

CHRISTMAS FESTIVAL
Okaloosa Courthouse
Crestview　　682-3212

This one-day festival is a highlight for Crestview residents. Centered around a bazaar with arts, crafts, wares, food and entertainment, a grand parade marches past the courthouse, elementary school choruses sing their hearts out at the Courthouse Terrace, and everybody enjoys the music and steaming cups of cocoa. There's a special Kid's Korner where grown-ups are not allowed; children can shop here for special gifts for mom, dad and other favorite people at prices especially suited to the younger than-12 set. No admission is charged.

Destin

Almost every one of Destin's events is some sort of fishing tournament, as well it should be for the "World's Luckiest Fishing Village." Grab a rod and reel and try your own luck, or just enjoy the spectacle of million-dollar fishing rigs pulling into the harbor at sunset. Check listings for Fort Walton Beach and the Beaches of South Walton, too; they're close by and ready for a festival almost anytime you are!

MAY

MAYFEST
Destin　　837-6241

It's a celebration of spring, centered around the arts. This Cajun-flavored festival features enough spicy food and music to make a bayou-dweller feel right at home.

JUNE

HARBOR DOCKS SUMMER OPEN
Harbor Docks Restaurant, Hwy. 98
Destin　　837-2506

This is a small tournament with regard to boat entries (about 20 boats participate), but anglers vie for prizes of up to $2,000 for the elusive blue marlin.

JULY

DESTIN FIREWORKS
East Pass, Destin　　837-4242

Here's another extraordinary fireworks spectacle, held at the pass for landlubbers and boaters. And, the sky-full of entertainment is even free.

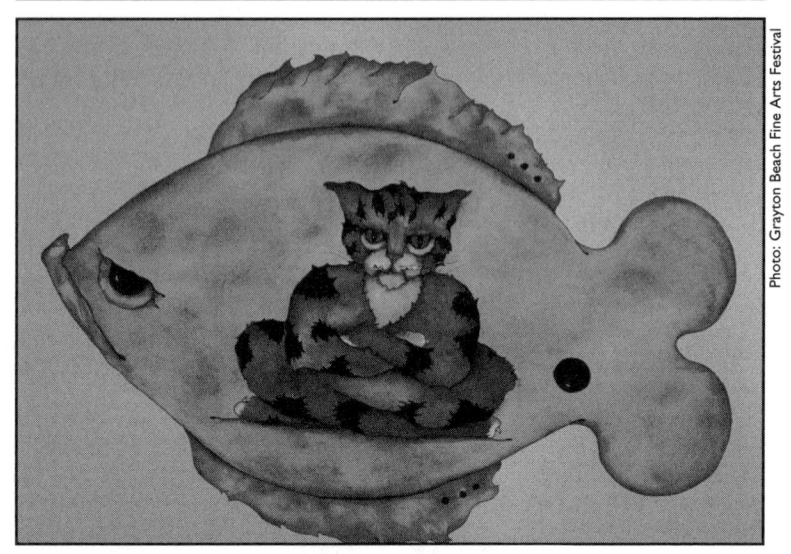

FORT WALTON BEACH AREA — FESTIVALS AND SPECIAL EVENTS

This whimsical mixed-media piece by artist Samuel Ruder was displayed at the Grayton Beach Fine Arts Festival.

DESTIN SHARK FISHING TOURNAMENT
Destin   654-1011

This is like a real fishing tournament, only . . . sharks are the main catch. Now, some people actually *eat* shark and, hopefully, many of these fearsome fish will end up on somebody's plate. You might guess the shark-infested docks attract a wild crowd; some catches weigh in at over 800 pounds!

AUGUST

DESTIN KING MACKEREL TOURNAMENT
Destin   654-1011

Sponsored by the Destin Fishing Museum, anglers fan out into the gulf for three days, fishing for the silver-striped king of the deep. Weigh-ins are held at Harbor Docks Restaurant.

OCTOBER

DESTIN SEAFOOD FESTIVAL
Kelly Trust property at the foot of Destin Bridge, Destin   837-6241

It's the kickoff to the fishing rodeo, a warm-up for the fresh catches yet to be caught. Alligator, crawfish, shrimp, shark, mullet, amberjack, pompano and a zillion varieties of marine life are barbecued, kabobed, fried, battered and broiled to the accompaniment of beach bands and a backdrop of the picturesque Destin harbor. While the food isn't free, admission is.

DESTIN FISHING RODEO
Kelly Docks, Destin   837-6734

Hook 'em, little doggie! Leave your spurs and chaps at home and pick up a rod and reel, 'cause this is the big one . . . a month-long inshore, offshore, bay and bayou frenzy where everybody can vie for prizes in over 100 categories and more than $100,000 in cash and prizes. The rodeo started more than 40 years ago, and the dock parties have become legendary. While private and charter boats head out hoping to reel in the "big one," those left on shore can partake in parades, regattas, dances, art shows and much more.

Beaches of South Walton

Perhaps more than anywhere else in Northwest Florida, the Beaches of South Walton have got something cooking. Sporting events, writer's retreats, wine tasting and arts festivals, the pleasure of these man-made diversions are heightened by the quiet surroundings of some of the world's most scenic beaches.

JANUARY

GREAT SOUTHERN GUMBO COOK-OFF
Market at Sandestin
Sandestin Resort   267-1216

Northwest Florida restaurants compete for the best gumbo and recognition by their peers in this deliciously enticing event. Tickets are $5.00 per person; $7.00 the day of the event.

ESCAPE TO CREATE
Seaside   231-2421

Is that creative urge surging? Then attend this week-long writing, composing and artistic retreat designed to further writings, scores and artistic endeavors in progress and offer community service.

FEBRUARY

ESCAPE TO CREATE
Seaside   231-2421

This is a weekend version of the artistic retreat in January.

MARCH

EMERALD COAST CHEF'S TASTING
Sandestin Beach Resort
Hwy. 98 East   267-1216

Some of the area's finest culinary delights are prepared for discriminating palates at this tasty event. Proceeds benefit the American Cancer Society. Call Sandestin Resort for ticket information.

CAMP SEASIDE ADVENTURE PROGRAM
Seaside   231-2222

Camp Seaside provides this weekend Spring Break program for kids, teens, families and even college students. Three days of nonstop activities include a basketball tourney, a treasure hunt, a kid's night out (sorry, mom and dad), bike trips and more. Other programs are held throughout the year.

APRIL

CHAUTAUQUA FESTIVAL
Around Lake de Funiak
DeFuniak Springs   892-9494

The Florida version of the New York Chautauqua began on Lake de Funiak in 1885. Since most Americans were sadly lacking in formal education and school was not mandatory, the Chautauqua emphasized religious training and educational activities for both children and adults. The three-week "intellectual summer camp" focused on "philosophy, theology, art, music, elocution and cookery."

That festival ended in the mid-1920s, but local residents are working to revive a contemporary version of the Florida Chautauqua. For now, this one-day family festival includes arts, crafts, food, an antique and classic car show, a parade, a children's activity area, live entertainment and a fireworks show over the lake at day's end. A $1.00 donation is charged.

WHITE WINE AND MUSIC FESTIVAL
Seaside   231-5424

Jazz and blues performers provide the musical backdrop for aficionados of fine wines to sample, swirl and select from vineyards throughout the Southeast. Saturday is the wine tasting, but Sunday is reserved for the music — blues, jazz and soul. Tickets for Saturday only are $20.00; $10.00 for Sunday only; and $25.00 for a weekend package.

MAY

SANDESTIN WINE FESTIVAL
The Market at Sandestin
Sandestin Resort   267-8000

More than 2,000 people have attended these weekend festivals in years past. More than twenty wineries from throughout the U.S. are represented, entering into the stiff competition for best wines. Tickets are on sale at all stores in the Market at Sandestin.

GRAYTON BEACH FINE ARTS FESTIVAL
Grayton Beach   267-1216

This old Florida resort community has grown into a haven for the arts and artists. There are many historic buildings in the tiny town, which is so small you can park and just walk to your heart's content. Artists from throughout the U.S. will have works on display and for sale, and all attendees may vote on their favorites for the People's Choice Award. Admission is free.

MEMORIAL DAY SAILING REGATTA
Sandestin Beach Resort
Hwy. 98 East   267-8150

Hoist the sails, mate, and join in the fun for the coveted Sandestin Cup. Fort Walton Yacht Club is the cast-off point, and the race ends at Sandestin's Baytowne Marina. After the race, everyone can enjoy the many "home from the sea" activities.

SANDESTIN PROFESSIONAL GRASS COURT TOURNAMENT CHAMPIONSHIPS
5500 Hwy. 98 E. at
Sandestin Beach Resort   267-7060

Avid tennis aficionados hit it off on the sprawling grass courts of Sandestin in both singles and doubles divisions. The event is free to spectators.

JULY

FOURTH OF JULY WEEKEND CELEBRATION
Sandestin Beach Hilton Golf &
Tennis Resort, Hwy. 98 East 267-9500

Grab the troops for a weekend of

FORT WALTON BEACH AREA — FESTIVALS AND SPECIAL EVENTS

The Grayton Beach Fine Arts Festival is a juried show, accepting only the very best of local artists' works.

star-spangled fun! Start with a July 4th cookout on the pool deck with live entertainment, a giant seafood buffet, and to top it off, a fireworks extravaganza on the beach.

BEACH BARBECUE AND DANCE PARTY

Seaside   231-5424

Not to be outdone by all this patriotic flag-waving, Seaside puts on a party of its own, a beach barbecue with "all the fixings," topped off with a beach dance party.

TURTLE WATCH

Grayton Beach State Recreation Area
Grayton Beach   231-4210

This watchdog volunteer group monitors nesting loggerhead sea turtles from July through August. The tiny newborns are subject to predators, vandals and a host of other dangers. Anyone spotting a nest or an egg-laying female is encouraged to immediately report it to one of the park rangers so protective measures can be taken.

WALTON COUNTY FOURTH OF JULY

Lake DeFuniak
DeFuniak Springs   892-2821

Beginning with a parade around the lake at 5:00 PM, the celebration includes music, food and a fireworks display over the lake. Admission is free.

AUGUST

NATIONAL & U.S. OPEN WATER SKI TOURNAMENT

Shortline Lake off Hwy. 98
South Walton County   267-1216

World-class skiers compete for top honors in this flashy and excit-

• *197*

FORT WALTON BEACH AREA — FESTIVALS AND SPECIAL EVENTS

ing event sponsored by the Tourist Development Council and Shortline Water Ski Club. Shortline Lake is on Sugar Drive off of Highway 98, just west of the Emerald Coast Plaza.

ELEPHANT WALK TRIATHLON & BAY TOWNE BIATHLON
Sandestin Resort, Sandestin   267-1216

This competition has grown into one of the most popular sporting events (maybe next to fishing) in the area. More than 500 men and women from across the United States sign up for the event, part of the Grand Prix Series Events.

SEPTEMBER

SEASIDE CONCERT SERIES
Seaside Amphitheater, Seaside   231-4224

Nationally acclaimed singers and musicians perform each weekend in September and October. Call Seaside for dates and season tickets.

OCTOBER

SEEING RED WEEKEND
Seaside   231-5424

This is a one-day wine tasting festival (you guessed it, *red* wine this time), centered around jazz and blues performers and an art exhibition. Stick around for the fancy fund-raising dinner for the Seaside Institute, or just come back the following day for more music and art.

MONARCH MIGRATION
Grayton Beach State Recreation Area
Grayton Beach   231-4210

Each year, tens of thousands of Monarch butterflies migrate from northern states to Mexico, stopping off in Northwest Florida for a week or so every October. The Monarchs seem particularly attracted to Grayton Beach's salt myrtle bushes, where thousands might cover one particular bush at a time. Monarchs have been spotted throughout Northwest Florida during this time, at Fort Pickens and other places along the coast in late October. Call the parks to find out approximate dates . . . and don't forget your camera! Admission to the park is $3.25 per car.

SEASIDE WRITER'S CONFERENCE
Seaside   231-2421

What perfectly inspirational surroundings for aspiring screenwriters, novelists and playwrights! A real novelist (most likely one who's been published) peeks over your shoulder during workshops. Lectures and evening public readings are also part of the weekend.

NOVEMBER

SOUTH WALTON SPORTFEST WEEKENDS
Various locations throughout the Beaches of South Walton   267-1216

Held on three consecutive weekends in November, Sportfest is South Walton's biggest event; participants double in number every year. Events include a triathlon, biathlon, 10K run, half-marathon, bike races, century bike tour, water ski and volleyball tournaments and a beach to bay walk. The event is free to spectators.

DECEMBER

CHRISTMAS BY CANDLELIGHT
Eden State Gardens
Point Washington　　　　　*231-4214*

The stately Wesley mansion, formerly part of the Wesley Lumber Company property, is decked out in holiday splendor for candlelight tours. There is a $4.00 admission to the house; there is no charge to tour the gardens.

CHRISTMAS BY THE SEA PROGRAM
Seaside　　　　　*231-5424*

Spend a spectacular season sunning at Seaside. Special packages for families are offered during this time, plus a full calendar of activities such as the Christmas tree lighting ceremony, a Christmas parade and special Christmas programs.

Fort Walton Beach/Destin/ Beaches of South Walton
Parks and Recreation

Northwest Floridians love spending their leisure time outdoors enjoying the area's natural as well as man-made attractions. Where the sun shines more than 340 days a year and there's no snow (well, *hardly* ever), locals take advantage of recreational pursuits by creating their own playgrounds.

This entire area from Fort Walton Beach to the Beaches of South Walton is only about a 20-mile drive, so don't limit yourself! Check listings in the other sections; many overlap or may be listed twice because of locations in more than one area. Some activities, such as for charter boat cruises, may be listed as attractions, so be sure to skip around *here* before you venture out in your car.

Fort Walton Beach

Golf

BLUEWATER BAY GOLF CLUB
2000 Bluewater Blvd.
Niceville   897-3241

Recently named one of the 25 top courses in Florida by *Golfweek* magazine, Bluewater Bay is a golfer's dream—dense woodlands, marshes and alternating rolling and flat terrain running along Choctawhatchee Bay create opportunities for challenging play. The four nine-hole courses were home to the Bluewater Bay International Invitational, welcoming players from 18 countries. Open every day from 7:30 until dark. The pro shop opens at 7:15 AM and closes at 5 PM.

EGLIN AIR FORCE BASE
John Sims Pkwy.
Niceville   882-2949

Located within Eglin Air Force Base, these 18 holes are open to those with active and retired military ID. A driving range, pro shop and snack bar are part of the facility. Open 6:30 to 5:30 daily.

FOXWOOD COUNTRY CLUB OF CRESTVIEW
Antioch Rd. off State Road 85
South of Crestview   682-2012

An 18-hole semiprivate course (public welcome) where water comes into play on six holes. The country club offers its own driving range, restaurant, and snack bar. The course and the pro shop open at 7 AM; closing is one hour after the last golfer leaves the course, usually around 6 or 7.

Fort Walton Beach Municipal Course
Off Lewis Turner Blvd.
Fort Walton Beach   862-3314

Located across from the fairgrounds, this city course has two public 18-hole courses, two putting greens and a driving range. Golf aficionados agree it's one of Florida's finest municipal courses appealing to the average golfer. Open daylight until dark daily; pro shop open from 6:30 AM to 6 PM.

Hurlburt Air Force Base
On Hurlburt AFB
Fort Walton Beach   884-6940

The Hurlburt course is open to active and retired military with government ID. Water surrounds 14 holes, interspersed with forests and bunkers. The course is open from 6:30 AM to 5 PM daily. Other facilities for your convenience include a driving range, putting greens and a pro shop.

Island Golf Center & Lost Lagoon Mini-Golf
1306 Miracle Strip Pkwy. (Hwy. 98)
Okaloosa Island   244-1612

This huge complex includes nine holes of pitch-n-putt, two 18-hole mini-courses, nine-hole and par 3 courses lit for night play. Lost Lagoon features 36 holes of miniature golf and a game room with a pool table and videos. This family oriented attraction is good for at least a few hours of your vacation time. Open 7:30 AM until dark.

Shalimar Pointe Golf and Country Club
2 Country Club Rd.
Shalimar   651-1416, (800) 964-2833

The rolling dunes and stands of magnolia, pine and oak make for tricky setups; keep your eyes peeled on the 11th and 17th holes. A driving range, putting green, snack bar and a restaurant are part of the Shalimar Pointe package. *Golfweek* magazine calls this course "One of the Southeast's Top 50 Development Courses." The pro shop is open from 6 to 6 every day; tee times start at 6:30 AM.

Shoal River Country Club
1104 Shoal River Dr.
Crestview   689-1010

Semiprivate, the 7,000-plus yard Shoal River course changes elevation constantly. Natural landscaping of trees and grasses creates navigational problems throughout. The country club has a lounge, snack bar, putting green and practice green for your additional enjoyment. Open 7 'til dark; pro shop closes around 6 PM.

Insiders' Tips

Eglin Air Force Base is home to several threatened and endangered species: the red-cockaded woodpecker, the Florida black bear, the Okaloosa darter, the least tern, loggerhead and green sea turtles, the gopher tortoise, alligators and the indigo snake. And you say you want to go *camping* there?

FORT WALTON BEACH AREA — PARKS AND RECREATION

Tennis

FORT WALTON RACQUET CLUB
23 Hurlburt Field Rd.
Fort Walton Beach   862-2023
Nine courts, both clay and hardcourts, are open to all. Since many players prefer to wait out the heat of the day to play, four courts are lit for night play. Open 8:30 to 9 Monday through Friday; 8:30 to 6 on weekends.

BLUEWATER BAY TENNIS CENTER
Bay Dr. at Bluewater Bay Resort
Niceville   897-3664
Twelve courts are located at the tennis center, and seven others are sprinkled throughout the resort. Clay courts are $7.50 per person per hour; hardcourts at Bay Drive are $3.50 an hour per person. The tennis center is open daily from 8 AM until 9 PM.

FORT WALTON BEACH MUNICIPAL TENNIS CENTER
45 W. Audrey
Fort Walton Beach   243-8789
Twelve lighted Laykold surfaced courts and four practice walls are open to the public on a first-come, first-served basis. The clubhouse has lockers, showers and a lounge area. Open Monday through Thursday 8 AM to 9 PM; 8 to 5 Friday and 9 to 5 Saturday and Sunday.

SHALIMAR POINTE TENNIS CENTER
2 Country Club Rd.
Shalimar   651-8872
In addition to its lavish golf facilities, Shalimar Pointe offers six outdoor rubico courts, four of them lighted. Lessons are also available and must be set up in advance. Fees are $8.00 per person per hour, then $4.00 for every hour additional for nonmembers. Open 8:30 AM until, depending on the weather.

Scuba/Snorkeling Trips

CHUCK'S DIVE WORLD
116 Meadow Woods Ln.
Niceville   897-3405
Once they teach you the open water PADI certification, you can scuba dive in a crystal clear spring where the fresh water fish are tame enough to eat from your hand. The dive shop offers flexible scheduling, they supply dive gear, and financing is available.

Watersport Rentals

ADVENTURE WATERSPORTS
Next to Toucans
Okaloosa Island   244-5222
Water toys abound! A three-seat Sea-Doo zips across the water at lightning speed. The Waverunner takes you on a two-hour excursion with a guide. Sailboats and wet or dry parasailing also are available.

PARADISE WATERSPORTS
Six locations on Hwy. 98 in
Fort Walton Beach and Destin   664-7872
Why not learn a new watersport while you're here? Rent jet skis, Waverunners, sailboats, pontoon boats, jet boats, sailboards and water trikes. The rental staff will instruct you on their safe operation before you head out. Parasailing on the bay and the beach is probably best reserved for the more adventurous. Paradise Watersports locations are

Take a canoe adventure on one of Northwest Florida's many scenic rivers.

at the seawall between Destin and Fort Walton Beach; The Hut (across from The Ramada on Okaloosa Island); the Destin Bridge; behind Water World; behind the Back Porch; and the parasail beach pickup.

PONTOON BOAT RENTALS
Hwy. 98, one mile west of Fort Walton Beach in Mary Esther at Consigned RVs   243-4488

For a true insider, this is the only way to go. It's a little noisy, but it's easy, flat and sturdy, and *you're* the captain! Bring a few friends and make it a fun and inexpensive day on the water. An 18-foot pontoon boat rents for $70.00 for a half-day; all day rental is $120 (up to four passengers). Twenty-footers go for $90 (half-day) and $150 (all day), taking up to eight passengers. The two largest are 24- and 28-feet, and will accommodate wheelchairs. Those rates are $110 and $175, respectively. You pay for fuel, bring a cooler, lots of friends and family and have a ball!

Canoeing/Tubing

ADVENTURES UNLIMITED
Tomahawk Landing, 12 miles north of Milton, then four miles
off Hwy. 87   623-6197, (800) 239-6864

You're really missing out on some of the best parts of Northwest Florida if you skip a trip down one of the inland rivers. Adventures Unlimited provides canoes, life jackets, paddles, camping gear, ice, refreshments and just about everything you could ever possibly need on a one-day or overnight canoe trip. Cabins on Wolfe Creek and campsites are available for overnight stays (see the chapter on Pensacola Accommodations). Canoe rentals start at $11.00

per person for a short trip; to completely outfit you for an overnight stay on the river is $40.00 per person.

BOB'S CANOES
On Munson Hwy. at the Coldwater Creek Bridge   623-5457, (800) 892-4504
In business for more than two decades, Bob's Canoes sends you down the river in canoes, tubes, paddleboats and kayaks. Choose from Coldwater Creek, Juniper Creek or the Blackwater River — all clear, cool and relatively shallow freshwater streams, perfect for beginners. A large waterfront pavilion at rental headquarters is available for picnics. Canoe trips start at $11.00 per person. Paddle boats, kayak trips (one person per kayak) and group rates are available.

BLACKWATER CANOE RENTAL
Nine miles east of Milton off Hwy. 90   623-0235, (800) 967-6789
Canoe, tube or kayak for a half-day or up to a three-day camping trip on the beautiful Blackwater River. Blackwater Canoe Rental provides all the necessities for getting you there; you supply your own camping equipment, eats and drinks. A short trip (1½ hours paddling time plus stops) is $11.00 per person; a day trip (four hours paddling) is $12.00. Children 12 and younger are free with two adults in one canoe. Overnight trips start at $17.00 per person. Call for reservations and directions.

EGLIN RESERVATION
Entry gate at Jackson guard on Hwy. 85 N. Niceville   882-4164
Freshwater lakes, the Yellow River and several other canoe and dirt bike trails are located inside the base. You must get permits to enter and use the facilities.

Bottom Fishing

OKALOOSA ISLAND PIER
Okaloosa Island east of Fort Walton Beach
Cast off from this extra-long pier, which juts 1,261 feet into the gulf.

Destin

Golf

EMERALD BAY GOLF CLUB
40001 Emerald Coast Pkwy.
Destin   837-5197
Wound around and through a residential community, Emerald Bay's semiprivate 18-hole championship course features pine-rimmed fairways and a tough slope rating of 135 from the championship tees. The pro shop hours are 7 AM to 5:30 PM; tee times begin at 7:30 and last until it's too dark to see the ball!

THE GARDEN
40091 Emerald Coast Pkwy.
Destin   837-7422
Lush landscaping surrounds the nine-hole lighted executive golf course (seven par 3s and two par 4s). The practice range is 10 acres with putting greens, a sand trap and a driving range. Open seven days a week, 7:30 AM to 4 PM off-season; 7:30 to 9 in-season.

INDIAN BAYOU GOLF AND COUNTRY CLUB
Off Hwy. 98 and Airport Rd.
Destin   837-6192
Indian Bayou is predominantly a

flat course with undulating greens and seven water holes. All nine holes of the Creek course wind through natural swamp surrounded by a residential community. Semiprivate, Indian Bayou has 27 holes of golf, a driving range, putting greens and a restaurant. Open 6:45 AM all year; closing is seasonal, usually around 5:30 or 6:00 PM.

Tennis

DESTIN RACQUET & FITNESS CENTER
995 Airport Rd.
Destin   837-7300

This is an all-inclusive center, with six rubico courts; four of them lit for nighttime play. Guest fees are $10.00 per person for singles and $8.00 per person for doubles, which will get you about 1½ hours on the courts. If you'd like to avail yourself of the fitness center, there's a full range of Nautilus equipment, stationery bikes, StairMasters, aerobics classes and racquetball courts. The one-time fee for equipment use and courts is $10.00 per person. Open from 6 AM until 9 PM.

Charter Boats

EAGLE HORIZONS, INC.
96 Yacht Club Dr., Unit #4
Fort Walton Beach   837-3700, 837-4986

The tops'l steel schooner *Flying Eagle* sets sail daily from the docks at Capt. Dave's Restaurant and Marina in Destin Harbor. Boarding is a half-mile east of the Destin Bridge on Hwy. 98. The Flying Eagle takes up to three 2½ hour cruises daily on a space available basis; reservations are preferred. Beer, wine coolers and T-shirts are all available on board. Tickets are $25 per person for adults; younger than 15, $15; and younger than three, free.

THE LADY EVENTHIA
Half-mile east of the Destin Bridge
Destin   837-6212 or 837-8729

Go fishing or sightseeing on *The Lady Eventhia*, a 70-passenger deep sea fishing party boat. Electronic equipment for locating running fish, a ship's galley and an indoor lounge offer guests every convenience for a day on the water. Six-hour fishing trips are $34.00 for adults, $16.50 for ages 12 and younger; eight-hour trips cost $39.50 and $16.50 respectively. Just want to ride? That's only $11.00 for either trip.

MOODY'S
194 Hwy. 98, Destin   837-1293

Tom Moody captains the *America II* for five-hour fishing trips year round. Charters and cruises are available as well. Refreshments and an indoor area that's either heated or air conditioned are de rigueur for most boats, but this one throws in free fish cleaning as one of its services. Trips are $35.00 (pick up a panel card at many local hotels or the Emerald Coast Tourist Development Council for a $10.00 discount).

SAILING SOUTH
Hwy. 98 at Benning Dr.
Destin   837-7245

Take an afternoon or sunset sail for $35.00 per person (a captain is included, of course). Private parties can rent out the *High Noon* for $175.

Sailing South rents 19-, 25- and 30-foot sailboats for $35 an hour or $200 a day.

BLACKBEARD SAILING CHARTERS
Quarter-mile east of the Destin Bridge behind AJ's Restaurant
Destin   837-2793

Welcome aboard, me hearties! This 54-foot gaff rigged schooner sails three times daily at 11, 2 and 5 just for the thrill of the wind in your face, the salt in your hair and a unique perspective on the Gulf Coast as seen from the water. The luxury sailboat accommodates up to 25 people, with the trip lasting about 2½ hours. Tickets are $25.00 per person; $15.00 for kids 4 to 12.

CAPT. DUKES PARTY BOAT
Destin Harbor, Destin   837-6152

For fishing or sightseeing, the *Capt. Dukes* will be happy to take you where you want to go. This 65-foot charter boat, with its own galley and lounge, heads out for half-day or all-day fishing trips starting at $300 for six people. Fish cleaning, bait and tackle are included. Sightseeing excursions of the harbor, bay and gulf start at $27.00 per person.

MISTY
Capt. Dave's Restaurant, Hwy. 98
Destin   267-3852, 837-3277

The 38-foot Delta Sportfisherman *Misty* hits the high seas for trolling or bottom fishing, accommodating up to six passengers. You don't have to be a pro; the crew will show you how to hook 'em, and even help you do it. Bring your own drinks, snacks and plenty of sunscreen! No fishing license is required. The *Misty* runs seasonally; call for dates, times and prices.

LIN-C-ANN
East Pass Marina
Destin   864-3880, 654-2022

For deep sea fishing, trolling, bottom fishing, billfishing, dive trips or sightseeing tours, the *Lin-C-Ann* is your ticket to over- and underwater fun. No license is required, but certification is necessary for dives. The boat runs seasonally; call for dates, times and prices.

OLIN MARLER'S CHARTER SERVICE
Kelly Docks, Destin   243-1769

All types of fishing are offered on a fleet of charter boats. Bottom fishing for snapper, grouper and amberjack is popular in the cooler months, and eight-hour trips are required to get far enough out to where the fish are biting. Bait, ice, tackle and fishing license comes with your ticket. Bring your own food and drink. Eight-hour trips are $97.00 per person; half-day trips cost $48.00.

Insiders' Tips

"The World's Luckiest Fishing Village" really *is* lucky, and here's why: There's an offshore shelf that dips straight from Destin's East Pass to 100-foot depths within 10 miles of shore — the speediest deep-water access on the Gulf of Mexico!

Hobie Cats, sailboats, pontoon boats and just about every description of water sports equipment are available at hourly, half-day and weekly rates.

SWEET JODY 5
Quarter-mile east of the Destin Bridge next to AJ's Restaurant
Destin   837-2222, 654-0088
(800) 531-9386

It's a fishing boat, it's a party boat, it's a private charter, it's whatever you want it to be. This 65-foot beauty of the sea is fully equipped with navigational and fish-finding electronics, a snack bar and an observation deck. Half-day trips are $27.00 for grown-ups; $13.50 for kids and riders (plus tax). During the summer months, the *Sweet Jody 5* runs a $22.00 special for a 2:30 PM to 6:30 PM trip; kids and riders are $11.00. They'll clean your fish for you, keep your drinks on ice for you, and pick up the tab for the fishing license.

SEA SCREAMER
#2 Hwy. 98 E. at Boogie's Restaurant
Destin   654-2996

Here's something everyone in the family can enjoy. The *Sea Screamer*, the world's largest speedboat, is docked under the Destin/Fort Walton Beach Bridge. You get two rides in one: first, a narrated cruise of the Destin Harbor and Choctawhatchee Bay, where birds, dolphins and other marine life are clearly visible in the air or through the crystal waters. Then, the *Sea Screamer* revs up for an exhilarating flight through the open waters of the gulf! Casual clothes or swimsuits are preferred for this venture because you may get wet! The *Sea Screamer* departs April 1 through May 27 at noon, 2 and 4 PM every day but Monday and Tuesday. From May 28 through Sept. 12, trips go out at 10, noon, 2, 4 and 6 every day. September 13 through October 31, trips are at noon, 2 and 4; closed Monday and Tuesday. Cruises last about an hour. Tickets go on sale at the dock 30 minutes prior to departure. Cost is $9.00 for adults; $6.00 for children 6 to 12; 5 and younger free.

Marine Supplies

YACHTIES'
200 Hwy. 98 E., Destin   837-4900
It's affordable because it's been used before! Yachties' is a classy, quality place for used marine equipment, nautical clothing and other items on consignment. Gifts, jewelry, accessories, discount new marine supplies and everything nautical are also there for the choosing. Located half a mile east of the Destin Bridge, it's open 9 to 5 Monday through Saturday.

THE SHIPS CHANDLER
646 Hwy. 98 E., Destin   837-9306
This marine store is also a complete boating equipment and fishing tackle shop. Get a good buy on safety equipment, marine paints, topsider shoes, and nautical sportswear. Rod and reel repair, fishing information, and guide service make it a one-stop shop. Open in the off-season from 7 AM until 5 PM Monday through Saturday; in season from daylight to dark seven days a week.

Scuba/Snorkeling Trips

FANTASEA SCUBA HEADQUARTERS
At the foot of the Destin Bridge
Destin   837-0732, 837-6943
Week-long courses allow you to become certified while on vacation. Daily dive trips are offered with all gear included. Snorkeling gear comes with a map for just $10. Non-divers are welcome to snorkel, sunbathe or sightsee.

AQUANAUT SCUBA CENTER, INC.
24 Hwy. 98, Destin   837-0359
Family owned for more than 20 years, the Aquanaut Scuba Center takes passengers out on daily dive trips, sunset cruises and snorkeling cruises; instruction and weeklong classes get you into the world of diving while you're still on vacation. Snorkeling tours are $20 per person; the sunset cruise is $10.

ADVENTURES ON THE KOKOMO
500 Hwy. 98 E. at the Kokomo Motel
& Marina, Destin   837-9029, 837-6171
Two boats are offered, a 50-foot, 49-passenger or a cigarette boat that holds six. Snorkeling trips are $20 with gear included; sunset cruises are $10. Capt. Brown has been diving these waters since 1957 and promises a delightful, fun time for everyone.

EMERALD COAST SCUBA SCHOOL
127 Hwy. 98 E., Suite 10A
Destin   837-0955
The one-day resort course promises you'll get your first taste of diving in just one afternoon! A three-hour session includes a pool lesson, your scuba dive and an underwater photo to show the folks back home. Regular four-day certifications, rescue, advanced and specialty courses are also offered.

Choctawhatchee Bay is almost shallow enough to cross on foot!

Scuba Tech
5371 Hwy. 98 E., a half-mile west of Sandestin
837-1933

Explore the wonders underwater or learn how to dive aboard the 45-foot *Sea Cobra*, which accommodates up to 29 passengers. On board are tank racks, bench seats, drop down ladders and giant stride entry points. Pick up your rental equipment from the main store (address above) or at the *Sea Cobra*, docked at Captain Dave's on the Harbor, 312 E. Hwy. 98, half a mile east of the Destin Bridge. Four diving charters are available daily: a four-hour, two-tank reef or wreck dive (65- to 90-foot depth); a six-hour, two-tank reef or wreck dive (65- to — gulp — 110-foot depth); an eight-hour, three-tank reef or wreck dive (same depth as the 6-hour dive); and a one-tank reef or wreck night dive. If you want to go diving at night with all that — stuff — out there, you go right ahead. These dive trips are fairly popular all year long, but remember you can't just go renting equipment and jump in. Prior certification is required, and Scuba Tech can help with that, too.

Watersport Rentals

Harbor Cove Charters
Behind AJ's on Destin Harbor
Destin   837-2222

You take the boat, you navigate, you go where you want to go — cruising, crabbing, fishing, snorkeling, swimming for a few hours, a half-day or a full day. Rates start at $25.00 per hour.

Boogie's Watersports
At the foot of the Destin Bridge
Destin   654-6043

Waverunners (jet skis), jet-n-cats

(rides three), winch boat parasails, pontoon boats, sailboats, cruises and champagne sunset cruises, and dive trips make Boogie's practically one-stop for beach fun — just add water! Take a "Discover Dive" with no experience necessary!

Paradise Watersports
Six locations on Hwy. 98 in
Fort Walton Beach and Destin   664-7872

You've reached Paradise — now get out there and enjoy it! Rent jet skis, waverunners, sailboats, pontoon boats, jet boats, sailboards or water trikes. The friendly staff will be happy to show you the safe operation of all equipment. Parasailing combines the best of water skiing and sky diving, with takeoff locations on the bay and the beach. Locations: The seawall between Destin and Fort Walton Beach; The Hut (across from The Ramada on Okaloosa Island); the Destin Bridge; behind Water World; behind the Back Porch; and the parasail beach pickup.

Bungee Jumping

Stateline Bungee
Hwy. 98 next to Fudpucker's
Destin   837-8197

Imagine the thrill of tying a bungee cord around your legs then diving off a huge platform into thin air! Sound like fun? Good — you go first! Rates start at $30.00 per person, payable *before* you jump!

Bottom Fishing

Destin Bridge Catwalk
Hook tonight's dinner along 3,000 feet of catwalk on the south side of the East Pass Bridge.

Beaches of South Walton

These little gulfside beach communities can range from really ritzy to downright down home. Some resorts don't look that different from ones on Hilton Head, South Carolina, or the Outer Banks in North Carolina. Other areas, like Seaside and Grayton Beach, are one-of-a-kind.

You'll keep seeing the name "Sandestin" crop up in directions. Sandestin is not a town, but a gigantic, sprawling resort along Highway 98. The street address for Sandestin Resort, the Sandestin Beach Hilton, etc., is Destin, but we've broken it out here under the Beaches of South Walton because it's actually over the Walton County line. It was a bit confusing for us deciding which Destin addresses to include where, but it won't be for you, since most everything is right along Highway 98.

Golf

Sandestin Beach Resort/ Sandestin Beach Hilton
5500 Hwy. 98 E., 12 miles east of Destin

Both courses are open to the public; however, priority is given to resort guests. Baytowne (267-8155) has 27 holes, open 7 AM to 7 PM daily; the Links Course (267-8144), has 18 holes, open 7 to 6 daily.

Santa Rosa Golf & Beach Club
County Rd. 30-A
Santa Rosa Beach   267-2229

This eighteen-hole course is open to the public. Driving range, putting

FORT WALTON BEACH AREA — PARKS AND RECREATION

green, pro shop and a snack bar add to the enjoyment. Open 7 AM to 7:30 PM daily.

SEASCAPE GOLF & RACQUET CLUB
100 Seascape Dr., Old Hwy. 98
Two miles west of Sandestin   837-9181
Here's a short, tight public 18-hole course with driving range and putting greens. Open from 7:30 AM to 6 PM daily.

EMERALD BAY GOLF & COUNTRY CLUB
241 Ellis Dr., Ste.15
Destin   837-5197
Emerald Bay gives you a beautiful, eighteen-hole course six miles east of Destin. It's open to the public, and hours are from 7:30 in the morning until 6:30 in the evening daily.

THE GARDEN
Hwy. 98, two miles west of
Sandestin   837-7422
This nine-hole executive course also offers a driving range and is open from 7 AM until 10 PM daily.

Tennis

HIDDEN DUNES
5394 Hwy. 98 E., a half-mile west of
Sandestin   837-3521
Six Rubico courts are lighted for night play and open to guests only. There's a resident tennis pro and a pro shop. Hidden Dunes is open from 8 AM to 10 PM daily.

SANDESTIN TENNIS CENTER
5500 Hwy. 98 E., Emerald Coast Pkwy.
Destin   267-7060
One of the America's top 50 tennis resorts, according to *Tennis* magazine, Sandestin offers 14 grass, hard and clay courts. The facility is open to the public, but resort guests get top priority. Hours are 8 AM to 7 PM daily.

SANTA ROSA GOLF & BEACH CLUB
County Rd. 30-A
Santa Rosa Beach   267-2229
Two hard courts are open to the public from 7 to 7:30 daily.

SEASCAPE GOLF & RACQUET CLUB
100 Seascape Dr., Destin   837-9181 ext. 3535
Eight clay and hard courts provide play from 8:30 AM to 6:30 PM.

SEASIDE
County Rd. 30-A, Seaside   231-4224
At these six clay and hard courts, Seaside guests play for free. If you want to get out there early, it opens at 7:30 in the morning and stays active until 6 in the evening on a daily basis.

TOPS'L BEACH AND RACQUET CLUB
5500 Hwy. 98 E., Destin   267-9222
Ten Rubico and two hard courts, plus three racquetball courts will keep you slappin' a little ball around to your heart's delight. Fees are included in membership or guest room rates. Hours depend on court availability. Tournaments, Round Robins, group and individual clinics and lessons and a pro shop make this a fun and active spot.

Beach/Bike Rentals

CABANA MAN
C-30A, Village of Seaside   231-5046
The Cabana Man will take care of all your beach needs, from chairs

• 211

and umbrellas to sailboats and boogie boards. Weekly rentals are available.

SANDESTIN BIKE RENTAL
Sandestin Resort near
Elephant Walk Restaurant   267-7077
Two-wheel it for $5.00 per hour for the public, $4.00 per hour for resort guests. Open 8 AM to 7 PM daily.

SEASIDE BIKE RENTAL
County Rd. 30-A, Seaside   231-2214
Located at the north end of Savannah Street, Seaside Bike Rental's fees are $4.00 per hour; $10.00 for four hours. They're open 7:30 to 8 daily.

SEAGROVE VILLAS BIKE RENTAL
County Rd. 30-A, a half-mile west of
Seaside   231-1535
This spot offers bike rentals for $10.00 per half-day; $15.00 per 24 hours. Go see them between 9 to 5 daily.

SANDESTIN RESORT RENTALS
Baytowne Marina at
Sandestin Resort   267-7777, 267-8166
Waverunners, ski boats, Bayliner deck boats, Hobie Cats, aqua-cycles, boogie boards — if you want to be on the water, they have a way to get you there. The marina location is open from 7 AM to 7 PM daily; off-season hours vary. The beach location is open 9 to 5 daily.

SANDESTIN BEACH
HILTON RESORT RENTALS
Sandestin Resort on Hwy. 98   267-9500
They've got 'em all — Hobie cats, waverunners, kayaks, aqua-cycles and boogie boards. Daily hours are from 9 to 5; winter hours vary.

SEASIDE BEACH RENTALS
County Rd. 30-A, Seaside   231-2214
Seaside also offers Hobie Cats, kayaks, aqua-cycles and boogie boards. They're open 9 to 6 in the summer; 9 to 5 in the spring and fall. (Open March through November 15.)

Hiking/Horseback Trails

GRAYTON BEACH
STATE RECREATION AREA
County Rd. 30-A, near
Grayton Beach   231-4210
Encounter native Northwest Florida terrain in the pine flatwoods, sand dunes and scrub of the Grayton Beach Nature Trail in the park. Pick up a self-guided tour brochure as you enter. Open daily from 8 AM to sundown. Admission is $3.25 per vehicle.

CASSINE GARDENS
County Rd. 30-A, near
Grayton Beach   231-5721
Explore the nature trail by foot or on horseback. A portion of the trail, located behind the Cassine Gardens townhomes, is on a raised boardwalk over marshland, bringing visitors eye-to-eye with waterfowl and native vegetation, like the garden's namesake, the "Ilex Cassine," or holly tree. There's no charge for this brush with nature.

Community Centers

Classes in dance, crafts and music, as well as competitive sports come in adult and child versions at the

One of Florida's most scenic wild rivers is the beautiful Blackwater.

city's five recreation centers. Call Vicki, Recreation Coordinator, at 243-3119 for a schedule of classes and events.

THEO DOCIE BASS RECREATION CENTER

54 Ferry Rd. NE, Ferry Park, Fort Walton Beach (off Hollywood Blvd.) 243-8911

The gym and meeting room host a soccer program, after school program, a Tot's Time program and many special events including the Greater Fort Walton Beach Talent Contest, the Annual Track Meet, a Halloween Carnival and a Kid's Day Out.

FORT WALTON BEACH CIVIC AUDITORIUM

Hwy. 98, Fort Walton Beach 243-3119

This auditorium, right in the heart of town, is home to the Okaloosa Symphony Orchestra and hosts many other concerts and school productions.

FRED B. HEDRICK RECREATION CENTER

132 Jet Dr. (take Beal Pkwy. to Hollywood Blvd., then west on Hollywood to Jefferson), Fort Walton Beach 243-3119

This center is headquarters to the Parks and Recreation Department, and also has a gym, a ceramic workshop, exercise room and two meeting/classrooms.

CHESTER PRUITT RECREATION CENTER

24 Carson Ave.
Fort Walton Beach 244-0534

Inside are a gym and two meeting rooms for a variety of classes and activities; outside is a playground area. There's a summer recreation program at the center every year.

FORT WALTON BEACH AREA — PARKS AND RECREATION

CREATIVE SENIOR CENTER
31 Memorial Pkwy. S.W.
Fort Walton Beach   244-1511

Classes, programs, special activities and luncheons are held here for residents aged 55 and older. The center's facilities are extensive, including a meeting hall, a pool room, library, shuffleboard courts, a ceramic workshop and horseshoe pits!

City/County Parks

JOHN BEASLEY WAYSIDE PARK
Hwy. 98, Okaloosa Island

Located right on the gulf, this public beach area comes with picnic tables, barbecue grills and restrooms.

BRACKIN WAYSIDE PARK
Hwy. 98, Okaloosa Island

Just down Highway 98 on the gulf side, the public beach area provides beachgoers with picnic tables, barbecue grills, a bathhouse with showers and dressing rooms, and rest rooms.

BRIARWOOD PARK
Briarwood Circle, Fort Walton Beach

On Briarwood Circle off Beal Parkway on Cinco Bayou, the small park has playground equipment and its own "tot lot."

FERRY PARK
Ferry Rd. and Hughes St., Fort Walton Beach

In addition to the Bass Recreation Center (see above), the park has a Little League field and four tennis courts lit for night play.

FORT WALTON LANDING
Brooks St., Fort Walton Beach

Just off Highway 98, this is another waterfront park with a boardwalk, a stage area, gazebo, picnic tables and a boat ramp.

GARNIER'S BEACH PARK
Beachview Dr. (off Eglin Pkwy.), Fort Walton Beach

Right where Cinco Bayou empties into Choctawhatchee Bay is a great public beach area with 240 feet of waterfront, a boat ramp, a playground and, of course, restrooms.

HOLLYWOOD AND MEMORIAL PARK
Hollywood Blvd. and Memorial Pkwy., Fort Walton Beach

This is just a teeny weeny park with a few benches for watching the world go by.

LIZA JACKSON PARK
Hwy. 98 next to the Howard Johnson's, Fort Walton Beach

This large city park sits on Santa Rosa Sound and is one of the first things you see as you drive into Fort Walton Beach. It's got 1,000 feet of waterfront, boat ramps, a fishing pier, open-air pavilions for picnicking, barbecue grills and lots of playground equipment and large shady trees.

JET DRIVE PARK
Jet Dr. and Holmes Blvd., Fort Walton Beach

Just past the Hedrick Recreation Center, the small park has a fenced playground area, basketball and tennis courts.

MARIER MEMORIAL PARK
Okaloosa Island

Marier is on the bay side of the island off Santa Rosa Boulevard and offers picnic tables, barbecue grills, a boat ramp and a bathhouse.

Mimosa Park
Mimosa St., Fort Walton Beach

Named for the flowering tree, not the drink, this small park near the bayou has picnic tables and a playground.

Chester Pruitt Park
Hollywood Blvd., Harbeson Ave. and McGriff St. next to the Head Start Center, Fort Walton Beach

With the recreation center as its focal point, this large park also provides a basketball court, tennis courts, a playground area, a softball field and two picnic pavilions.

Vesta Heights Park
Memorial Pkwy., Fort Walton Beach

This little neighborhood park within the Vesta Heights subdivision has a jogging track, two playground areas, picnic tables and park benches.

Villa Russ Park
Elliott Rd., Fort Walton Beach

This little triangular park is not more than a block or two from the bay going either east or south. You'll find park benches and playground equipment here.

Seabreeze Park
Memorial Pkwy., Fort Walton Beach

Travel north on Memorial Parkway from Highway 98 to find this small park, which may not be close enough to the water to catch a sea breeze, but does provide a playground, picnic tables and restroom facilities.

Fort Walton Beach/Destin/ Beaches of South Walton
Arts and Culture

Most of the cultural activities in this area are headquartered in the Fort Walton Beach area, but check this entire coastal region for some offbeat performances. One of the area's highlights is the outstanding Chautauqua Festival in DeFuniak Springs in North Walton County, a celebration of art, music, history and literature around Lake DeFuniak each April. Although not a separate cultural group per se, the village of Seaside provides visitors and residents with year-round cultural activities, from writer's retreats to fine art shows. Check the Beaches of South Walton section of this chapter for more information.

Dance

NORTHWEST FLORIDA BALLET
P.O. Box 964
Fort Walton Beach, Fla. 32549   664-7787

This professional ballet company performs throughout Northwest Florida and offers a training program for gifted students seeking a career in dance.

Music

THE CHORAL SOCIETY OF NORTHWEST FLORIDA
121 Bayou Dr.
Fort Walton Beach, Fla. 32547   863-1718

Although auditions are held for membership in the Choral Society, the group is mostly for fun and fellowship. These are folks who enjoy singing for the pure joy of it, but occasionally they will perform at public functions.

EMERALD COAST CONCERT ASSOCIATION
P.O. Box 815
Fort Walton Beach, Fla. 32549   243-3359

This is a nonprofit volunteer group dedicated to bringing the best possible local, regional and national entertainment into the area. Concert tickets are sold at several locations throughout Destin and Fort Walton Beach.

FORT WALTON BEACH COMMUNITY CHORUS
P.O. Box 2221
Fort Walton Beach, Fla. 32549   863-3900

Besides performing twice yearly, the 50-to-75-member Community Chorus sponsors a scholarship for

FORT WALTON BEACH AREA — ARTS & CULTURE

Photo: Arts Council of N.W. Florida

Several young dancers create a "sculpture garden" of form and movement.

high school or college students interested in becoming professional singers.

NORTHWEST FLORIDA SYMPHONY ORCHESTRA
100 College Blvd.
Niceville   729-5283

The orchestra is made up of members of all ages and skill ranges from the Okaloosa and Walton County areas who perform quality music at five annual concerts.

OKALOOSA SYMPHONY ORCHESTRA
P.O. Box 2109
Fort Walton Beach, Fla. 32649   244-3308

This year marks the 17th season of the orchestra, the last six as paid professionals. The 50-plus members perform four times per year at the Fort Walton Beach Civic Auditorium under the direction of Brian Sullivan, a talented young conductor from Orlando who travels to the area for several intensive rehearsals prior to each performance. The Symphony League is set up as a fundraising organization; the remainder of the annual budget comes from grants and donations from public and private sources.

Visual Arts

ARTIST'S SHOWROOM
542 Hwy. 98 E.
Destin   837-7606

More than 2,500 oil paintings and other artwork (much of it by local artists) are displayed in this wholesale/retail gallery on the harbor.

ARTS & DESIGN SOCIETY (ADSO)
P.O. Box 4963
Fort Walton Beach, Fla. 32549   244-1271

The nonprofit artist's group holds exhibitions, demonstrations,

• 217

FORT WALTON BEACH AREA — ARTS & CULTURE

workshops and art shows to educate the community and enhance appreciation of art in its many forms. The gallery is open Sundays from 1 to 4 PM.

CULTURAL ARTS ASSOCIATION
P.O. Box 4958
Santa Rosa Beach, Fla. 32459   231-5141

The Association funds and awards scholarships in the visual arts and provides after-school arts experiences for children. They sponsor the Grayton Beach Fine Arts Festival in May, Scholarship Arts and Crafts in October, and a Beaux Arts Ball in November.

THE PASTEL SOCIETY OF NORTH FLORIDA
P.O. Box 5133
Fort Walton Beach, Fla. 32549   581-2550

Soft colors are the emphasis of this chapter of the Pastel Society of America, now in its sixth year. April is the one time of the year when the group gets to shine — the "Pastel '94" exhibition at the Fort Walton Beach Art Museum showcased the pastel work of artists from 45 states. This year, artist William Schultz will be on hand for workshops. The local chapter meets infrequently for lunch, so if you'd like to be invited or need information about upcoming exhibitions, contact the Pastel Society of North Florida for inclusion on their mailing list.

Multidisciplinary

CHAUTAUQUA FESTIVAL
P.O. Box 847
DeFuniak Springs, Fla. 32433   892-9494

Years ago, some folks moved from upstate New York (where the original Chautauqua is held every year) to DeFuniak Springs and decided to start a smaller version of the festival here. Chautauqua, held around Lake DeFuniak in the historic district, promotes the heritage of Walton County with a flurry of educational and cultural activities — dances, lectures, poetry readings and storytelling, among others. It is now a one-day festival in April each year, but has grown steadily. The name "Chautauqua" has been linked to many other cultural events held at Lake DeFuniak throughout the year. Please see the Beaches of South Walton section of the Fort Walton Beach Area Festivals and Special Events chapter for additional information.

OKALOOSA FILM COMMISSION
P.O. Box 4097,
Fort Walton Beach, Fla. 32549   651-7374

This is the local liaison office to try to bring film productions into Northwest Florida. The commission works with location scouts and provides technical and talent assistance.

Fort Walton Beach Higher Education

Because of the excellent facilities in Fort Walton Beach and surrounding communities, people seeking continuing education or advanced degrees need not ever leave the area. Satellite branches of the University of West Florida and the area's own community college provide local residents with top programs in a multitude of disciplines.

OKALOOSA-WALTON COMMUNITY COLLEGE

1000 College Blvd., Niceville 678-5111
OWCC/UWF Fort Walton Beach campus, 1170 Freedom Way, Bldg. 1, Room 106
Fort Walton Beach 863-6501
OWCC/UWF Eglin Center, Bldg. 251
Eglin AFB 678-1717
OWCC Hurlburt Center, Bldg. 90309
Hurlburt Field 884-6296
OWCC at Chautauqua Neighborhood Center, U.S. Hwy. 90 W.
DeFuniak Springs 892-8100

This community college maintains several campuses where students may receive one of 60 associate degrees, both on and off campus, transferable to major four-year institutions. Also offered are GED competency courses, adult basic education and continuing education for enrichment and enhancement.

UNIVERSITY OF WEST FLORIDA

Fort Walton Beach campus, 1170 Freedom Way, Bldg. 1, Room 114
Fort Walton Beach 863-6565
Eglin Center, Bldg. 251
Eglin AFB 678-3727

These UWF branches offer junior, senior and graduate level studies in engineering, 18 undergraduate and eight graduate degrees through its in-district program with Okaloosa-Walton Community College. Evening courses are available to accommodate working students.

TROY STATE UNIVERSITY

Florida Regional Branches at Eglin Air Force Base Education Center, Bldg. 251 678-1865
Hurlburt Field, Bldg. 90312 581-3162

Based in Troy, Alabama, TSU offers two-year associate degrees in science, bachelor of science degree programs and one graduate program with no out-of-state fees.

Vocational-Technical Schools

Each of these schools offers a variety of training programs to prepare students to enter the workplace.

FORT WALTON BEACH AREA — HIGHER EDUCATION

BAY AREA VOCATIONAL-TECHNICAL SCHOOL
1976 Lewis Turner Blvd.
Fort Walton Beach   833-3500

CRESTVIEW VOCATIONAL-TECHNICAL CENTER
1306 N. Ferdon Blvd, Crestview   689-7276

WALTON COUNTY VOCATIONAL-TECHNICAL SCHOOL
850 N. 20th St.
DeFuniak Springs   892-8105, 892-8106

Fort Walton Beach/Destin/ Beaches of South Walton
Real Estate

What's it *really* like to live along Florida's northern Gulf Coast? Just ask the folks that do: The retirees who vacationed here with the kids for years and now want that same "on vacation" feeling all year long; the military family stationed here in the '70s who, after that tour of duty, could live anywhere they wanted and chose Northwest Florida; the couple from Atlanta invited once by friends who went back home just long enough to pack their belongings. Ten million of thirteen million Floridians are now from someplace else, and you'd think that with 1,500 new residents every week, all of Florida would be as populated as Miami and Orlando. Maybe some people can only feel like they're in Florida if they can see orange groves or can go swimming in the gulf in December. We're happy to let them. What we offer here is sun, water and ... space. Dig your toes into the sand, put down some roots, and enjoy one of the least populated parts of Florida.

Fort Walton Beach

The living is easy, the weather's unbeatable, and the fish are always biting here along the Emerald Coast, where the gulf and the sound provide a rather spectacular backdrop for high-rises and residential communities. Fort Walton Beach may seem a bit less organized as far as the newer subdivisions go, since up until 1974, it didn't have much in the way of zoning. But there's a positive side for homebuyers — most of the city proper is developed, so if you purchase a home in one of the older residential neighborhoods, you can rest assured that you won't ever have a high-rise condo or an apartment complex built in your backyard. Although it *is* a resort community, and you can't help but be somewhere *near* the water, prices for Fort Walton Beach homes are still usually less than comparable neighborhoods in Destin or the Beaches of South Walton. Once you hit the resort scene on Okaloosa Island, though, real estate prices take a hefty jump.

Many developments in outlying areas front Choctawhatchee Bay; with the opening of the new Mid-Bay Bridge, the drive into Fort Walton Beach or Destin from Niceville or Valparaiso is a snap.

Residential/Resort Communities

BLUEWATER BAY
1950 Bluewater Blvd.
Niceville   897-2879, (800) 874-2128
Preservation of the natural landscape is paramount in this residential

• 221

and resort community on Choctawhatchee Bay. More than 2,000 families call Bluewater Bay home, and most are content with all the restrictions and codes imposed on development. After all, they want to enjoy the area's unspoiled beauty, too, and the rules at Bluewater Bay ensure not only preservation of the environment, but unmarred views. Bluewater Bay controls setbacks, outbuildings, fences, garages and the removal of trees. Residents can't hang their laundry outside, rent rooms out in their homes or put up satellite dishes. On the 2,000-acre site are 36 holes of golf, 21 tennis courts, a 120-slip marina, swimming pools, playgrounds, a bayside beach and several bike trails meandering through the various residential communities and acres of natural wilderness.

INDIAN SHORES
Safe Harbor Dr.
Valparaiso 678-1900

The few lots left in this small development (62 lots on 40 acres) are all waterfront, so if you're a boat owner, build yourself a dock or a boathouse on the deep-water Weekley Bayou. If you're interested in the waterfront lot at Channel Marker 2, while it's the most expensive, your house will sit right at the confluence of Weekley and Boggy Bayous, with panoramic views. The narrow white sand shoreline gives way to dense vegetation, so if you like your privacy, leave as much of it intact as you need (but don't forget about leaving room for a view!). All lots are offered through Ruckel Properties, Inc., 17 John Sims Parkway, Valparaiso. Phone 678-2223 or (800) 258-LOTS.

ISLAND ECHOS CONDOMINIUM
676 Santa Rosa Blvd.
Fort Walton Beach 243-3191

You're so close to the water you can feel the spray from your balcony in this well-kept seven-story condo on Okaloosa Island. All 90 one-, two- or three-bedroom units have private balconies overlooking the gulf. Challenge a neighbor to a fast set of tennis on the lighted courts, or let the kids frolic in the heated swimming pool while you grab some rays on the sundeck. Covered parking, a barbecue area and beach service up the ante to make this a popular family getaway.

SURF DWELLER CONDOMINIUM
554 Coral Ct.
Fort Walton Beach 664-1113
 (800) 354-1113

Immerse yourself in the luxury of these two- and three-bedroom condos directly on the gulf on Okaloosa Island. The stark whiteness of the seven-story building blends with the dazzling sands of the Emerald Coast, creating a playland all your own. From more than 400 feet of private beachfront to elevated tennis courts to the big and little people's pools to those unmatched views, Surf Dweller takes the best of the beach and intertwines it with a fun and comfortable vacation home.

Real Estate Companies

CARRIAGE HILLS REALTY, INC.
1821 John Sims Pkwy.
Niceville 678-5178, (800) 874-8929

Carriage Hills services this entire area, from bayfront resort developments like Bluewater Bay to gulf-

FORT WALTON BEACH AREA — REAL ESTATE

Stay At Sea Level. Ideal vacations on the white sands of dune-Allen Beach between Sandestin and Seaside. Gulf front homes and condos. Rentals and sales. Free color brochure.

dune-Allen Realty Inc.
5200 W. Hwy. C-30A
Santa Rosa Beach, FL 32451

1-800-423-7433

side retreats in Destin and Fort Walton Beach. A free area video relocation packet is available on request.

VILLAGE REALTY EAST
4400 Hwy. 20 E. #109
Niceville   897-5000, (800) 525-6006
Located in Bluewater Bay's "Merchants Walk," Village Realty of course handles property in Bluewater Bay, but also in other areas of Niceville and Rocky Bayou, plus homesites and homes convenient to both Eglin and Hurlburt. Call for a free video and relocation package. Village Realty East is a member of the Multiple Listing Service; phones are answered 24 hours a day.

SUNDANCE AGENCY INC.
1150 John Sims Pkwy, Unit 1
Niceville   678-1156, (800) 874-0144
You'll find these real estate agents in the Oak Creek Shopping Center when they're not out showing and selling property in Bluewater Bay, Rocky Bayou, Eglin AFB, Niceville or Valparaiso. Sundance offers free relocation information and will gladly send you a free area video on request.

AMERICAN REALTY OF NORTHWEST FLORIDA, INC.
1270 N. Eglin Pkwy.
Shalimar   651-2454, (800) 372-0044
As members of "ERA," American can help you with sales and rentals of property in Fort Walton Beach, Niceville, Crestview and Destin/ South Walton. They consider themselves to be military relocation specialists, and if you're career military, you know how helpful that can be. Learn about schools, health care, higher education and retirement communities in the area before you start looking for your new home.

ABBOTT REALTY SERVICES, INC.
676 Nautilus Ct. at
Island Echos Condominium
Fort Walton Beach   243-3191
Trust Abbott for full-service real

• 223

FORT WALTON BEACH AREA — REAL ESTATE

Wide, shady porches, tin roofs and meticulous detailing characterize homes at Seaside.

estate assistance with sales and rentals of investment properties, property management and market analysis. This particular office deals with property and land in Destin, Fort Walton Beach, South Walton and Bluewater Bay. Abbott is a member of the Multiple Listing Service.

Destin

Feel like you're on vacation all year with a home or condo in this glittering resort town on the gulf. Although year-round residency is still rather low (condo owners preferring instead to rent their units for most of the year), some well-planned residential communities are popping up, offering enough amenities and a genuine community atmosphere to get new home owners to put down some roots. Land and resort property is still the number one buy in Destin, and the choices are practically endless.

Residential/Resort Communities

St. Martin Beachwalk Villas
Hwy. 98 E. across from Big Kahuna's
Destin 654-9444

These two- and three-bedroom villas are still offered at pre-construction prices. The 40 spacious villas have been designed with a Caribbean feel, with bold, bright colors, a pool and clubhouse and gulf views with a private beach walkover. Prices begin in the $80s.

Emerald Bay
40001 Emerald Coast Pkwy.
Destin 837-4455

If you're looking for class, look no farther than this very, very fancy neighborhood on 350 acres at the

Okaloosa-Walton County line. Previous home owners spared no expense when it came to designing their dream homes. Now, some of those are for sale featuring deluxe master suites, 20-foot ceilings and an average of 2,000 square feet. Most lots are about 100' wide by 150' deep. At the time of this writing there were two lots left on the bay starting at $178,000.

SANDPIPER COVE
775 Gulf Shore Dr.
Destin   837-9121
Located in the heart of Holiday Isle, these rustic and charming condominiums come in studio, one, two or three bedrooms with three choices of view. Dock your boat at the private marina, tee off on the nine-hole, par 3 golf course, take advantage of six tennis courts (three of them lighted), a swimming pool or the private beach boardwalk with a gazebo. If you want to take the night off from cooking, spend it at Louisiana Lagniappe, a superb Cajun restaurant right on the premises.

TOPS'L BEACH MANOR
5554 Hwy. 98 E.
Destin   267-9222, (800) 476-9222
There aren't enough adjectives to describe this 55-acre beachfront resort; suffice it to say it is luxury at every turn. Surrounded by tracts of protected beachfront on the grounds of Tops'l Beach and Racquet Club, the stepped high-rise Beach Manor offers two- and three-bedroom luxury beach and tennis villas complete with a heated pool, fitness room, oversized Jacuzzis, security and covered parking.

HIDDEN DUNES
5394 Scenic Beach Hwy. 98 E.
Destin   837-3521, (800) 535-3521
The designers of Hidden Dunes did more than just create another cookie-cutter condo on the beach. They went out of their way to do something special. In fact, the end result turned out so well that we wouldn't be a bit surprised if some of them bought property here. Hidden Dunes is peaceful and secure by day or by night. The two-story natural wood buildings with one-, two- and three-bedroom units overlook many different courtyard areas, some with a swimming pool and picnic area, some with decorative tiled pools with fountains. The effect of the underwater lights is spectacular at night. But really the best part of living at Hidden Dunes is the privacy. No unit directly faces another, but instead are set off by the pools. Large screened porches with ceiling fans are partially masked from public viewing by heavy landscaping or natural preserve. Walkways steer strollers away from windows and porches; front entrances face the parking lot. Gulfside condos rise twenty stories above the dunes, offering two- and three-bedroom and penthouse units. Beach Villas are two stories with three and four bedrooms overlooking Hidden Dunes Lake.

EDGEWATER BEACH CONDOMINIUM
5000 E. Hwy. 98
Destin   837-1550
You may do a double-take when passing this condo; its unusual

stepped architecture is a real attention-grabber. Units offered for sale are one and two bedrooms, and since the structure doesn't face the gulf, but gently curves around the three swimming pools, just about everybody gets a great view from the private balconies. Empty nesters and families especially love the surprisingly laid-back feel of Edgewater. The number above is for the condominium association, which handles some sales; other real estate companies throughout the area handle the rest, which can be said about most of the larger resort properties.

DESTIN BEACH CLUB CONDOMINIUM
1150 Hwy. 98 E.
Destin   837-3985

These condominiums are close to everything — tennis, golf, fishing, shopping, restaurants — and they have a location right on the gulf! All 47 units contain one bedroom, but all have built-in bunk beds for children or extra guests. Every condo has its own private balcony with a gulf view. There's a large pool tucked in between the building and the gulf, and a glass-enclosed hot tub overlooking the water for year-round relaxation.

Real Estate Companies

HOLIDAY ISLE PROPERTIES, INC.
904 Hwy. 98 E.
Destin   837-0009

Many of these properties are on Holiday Isle, a long and winding spit of land surrounded by waters of the gulf and Destin Harbor. Some offerings for second-home buyers might be a condominium at Holiday Surf & Racquet Club, a custom home on Holiday Isle with its own boat slip, or a fairway villa on a lake at Sandestin.

LINDA WATSON REALTY INC.
106 Benning Dr., Ste. 7
Destin   837-3111

A member of the Multiple Listing Service, Ms. Watson can lock in on hundreds of properties, prices and amenities with just a few computer keystrokes. Her own company's listings are mostly private homes within the Destin and Sandestin area.

ABBOTT REALTY SERVICES, INC.
35000 Emerald Coast Pkwy.
Destin   (800) 547-0805

The first name in vacation rentals is also the first name in home sales! Abbott handles both with panache, with an amazing assortment of single-family homes, homesites, condominiums and townhomes. Abbott sells units in many of the properties it manages for rentals, such as East Pass Towers and Waterview Towers Yacht Club on Holiday Isle; SunDestin Resort and Destin Towers on Highway 98; Oceanside Townhomes at the western boundary of Henderson Beach State Park; or the Crystal Villas just east of Destin right on the Gulf of Mexico. For a complete resort catalog, please call the number above.

NEWMAN-DAILEY RESORT PROPERTIES, INC.
5050 Hwy. 98 E., Ste. #210
Destin   837-1071, (800) 225-7652

For your own private vacation retreat or as a lifetime investment, Newman-Dailey can find you the perfect resort property on or off

FORT WALTON BEACH AREA — REAL ESTATE

the beach. If you choose to occupy your second home for part of the year, these folks can handle rental and management of your property as well.

REALTY ONE SERVICES INC.
114 Palmetto
Destin   837-5447, (800) 548-8026

The staff at Realty One has the expertise to match buyers with just the right vacation home, all up and down the beach. Properties include two-bedroom low- or high-rise units at Hidden Dunes; three-bedroom units at Mainsail, a high-rise fronting the gulf; and lakefront two- or four-bedroom Beachwalk Villas at Sandestin Resort. Talk to Jan Barrett about relocating or purchasing a second home in Florida's Great Northwest.

DESTIN REALTY INC.
1150 Hwy. 98 E.
Destin   837-3484, (800) 633-7846

Destin Realty provides on-site condominium management for the Destin Beach Club (see listing under Residential/Resort Communities) in addition to condominium resales, second home and rental properties, new condominium development sales and land and lot sales. The list of current offerings includes Indian Bayou, Holiday Isle, Tops'l, Sandestin Beach Resort, Hidden Dunes and many others.

Beaches of South Walton

The eighteen tiny communities that make up the Beaches of South Walton are immaculate, glittery little jewels stretched out like pearls in a necklace rimming the Gulf of Mexico. Planned communities are still at a premium in some places, but in others, entire subdivision homesites were sold out two days after they went up for sale! In more remote areas such as Blue Mountain Beach or Grayton Beach, you'll find a tranquil retreat in one of the rustic cottages cozied up against white dunes. Take an hour's walk on the beach without passing more than a handful of people. Or not. If resort living is what you're hankering for, you can live the good life overflowing with amenities at any number of plush resorts.

Residential/Resort Communities

BAYSIDE
Hwy. 98 E.
Destin   837-7020

This private residential community is rather unusual for South

---

Insiders' Tips

The beautiful pass at Destin was completely man-made — by accident. In 1927, with Choctawhatchee Bay at flood level, four men took their shovels and started digging a ditch across Okaloosa Island (about a half mile wide) to drain off some of the water. Two hours after the "ditch" was completed, it took on a life of its own; the swirling, raging water expanded from two feet to its current width — 100 yards!

• 227

Walton County. Single-family homesites with waterfront, bayview or interior views combine a close-knit neighborhood atmosphere with the preservation of wild and scenic areas fronting Choctawhatchee Bay. A gas-lit entryway signals more unique amenities within, such as a central park with its own pond, jogging and bike trails winding through nature preserves, a gazebo surrounded by lush gardens and underground utilities.

SANDESTIN
5500 Hwy. 98 E.
Destin   (800) 277-0801

You may already be familiar with Sandestin as one of the area's premiere resorts, but this sprawling acreage on both the Gulf of Mexico and Choctawhatchee Bay has to be one of the more diverse settings for residential homesites, homes and condominiums. All are within the secure confines of Sandestin Beach Resort where every imaginable amenity lies within walking distance or a short drive. Below, you'll find an overview of what's available at some of the newer developments at Sandestin:

BAYPINE COTTAGES

Settle into one of these charming two- and three-bedroom cottages in a wooded area on Choctawhatchee Bay overlooking Horseshoe Island. The tall pines shade rooftops and porches surprisingly well. Rustic lap siding with cedar accents blends with the wooded setting. Inside, you'll appreciate the head and leg room: large bedrooms and living areas, nine-foot ceilings and a spacious screened porch.

CLUB DRIVE

Homesites with bayfront and golf course views come with an added bonus — membership to the Burnt Pine Golf Club of Sandestin, a Rees Jones-designed, 18-hole championship course which will be ready for tee-offs by October of 1994.

GRAND HARBOUR

Low-rise, three-bedroom villas of up to 2,200 square feet are grand in every sense of the word. Arched windows, screened verandas, ten foot ceilings on the ground floor and vaulted ceilings up top combine with architectural detailing and beautiful harbor views.

LEGEND CREEK GOLF VILLAS

Right on the fifth fairway of Baytowne's Harbor golf course, these two- and three-bedroom villas offer quiet, carefree living with a private outdoor courtyard. New homes are designed with a Mediterranean flair featuring red-tile roofs and stucco exteriors awash in pastels. Homesites on the golf course lake are available as well.

SOUTHWINDS

Two-, three- and four-bedroom units offer unimaginable extras in this high-rise, gulf-front condo. Private covered parking, nine-foot ceilings, crown moldings, large balconies and limitations on rentals create a peaceful lifestyle for a retirement or second home.

TIVOLI TERRACE

Adjacent to the Tivoli condominiums, these three-bedroom townhomes line the fifth fairway of the

Dunes Golf Course on the gulf side of Sandestin. The stucco and tile-roofed villas are open and airy inside. Outside, you'll like the two-car garages and easy beach access.

THE VILLAS AT VANTAGE POINTE

Choose from either golf, bay or sunset views in these handsome three- and four-bedroom, 3½-bath townhomes. During the winter, your fireplace will make everything inside cozier; in summer, you'll get plenty of use out of your large screened-in porches and decks.

SEASIDE
County Rd. 30-A 231-4224, (800) 635-0296

Nearly every possible piece of property at Seaside has been bought up by people who know a good thing when they see it. A handful of lots remain in this quaint village, where all shopping, leisure and recreational activities are within walking distance. More and more, Seaside is adding cultural events to its calendar—wine festivals, piano recitals and art exhibitions round out the variety of opportunities available to residents. Homebuilders must abide by a fairly stringent set of rules to keep homes within the character of the neighborhood. Lots are small, but when you drive up 30-A and get your first look at all of those pastel hues rising out of the scrub, you'll feel far from the world you left behind.

Real Estate Companies

ABBOTT REALTY SERVICES, INC.
Rt. 2, Box 4820
Santa Rosa Beach   267-2693

Abbott is one of the largest real estate companies in the area, managing rental units at more than 80 properties as well as home, condominium and townhome sales. There's an office in Santa Rosa Beach, but Abbott's main headquarters are in Destin.

CARRIAGE HILLS REALTY SOUTH, INC.
Hwy. 98 W.
Santa Rosa Beach   267-2424
(800) 521-2951

Carriage Hills handles sales of homes and land all up and down the coast, covering all of South Walton County to Inlet Beach at the Bay County line.

GULF FRONT REALTY
Six miles east of Seaside/Seagrove Beach on Scenic Rd. 30A   231-1300
(800) 624-2055

Just like the name implies, Gulf Front Realty specializes in gulf-front and gulf-view lots and homes. In order to give you an idea of just how diverse South Walton County is, lots can range from less than $18,000 to a whopping $330,000 (remember, that's *without* the house!).

MONARCH REALTY AT SEASIDE
At Josephine's Bed & Breakfast
Seaside   231-1938
Cottages   (800) 475-1841
Josephine's   (800) 848-1840

Monarch's main offices are in Tallahassee, and that's who you'll talk to if you call its toll-free number. They maintain a small office inside Josephine's Bed & Breakfast to provide information on real estate lots and sales and cottage rentals at Seaside (they manage about 40 cottages there).

Fort Walton Beach/Destin/ Beaches of South Walton Retirement

When you make a decision to retire in Florida's Great Northwest, you'll find much more than clean and comfortable retirement communities and new friends who share your enthusiasm for the good life. There are a host of services offered to seniors to make the transition to retirement living go smoothly.

Retirement Communities

WESTWOOD RETIREMENT COMMUNITIES
1001 Mar-Walt Dr.
Fort Walton Beach   863-5174

Westwood spends a lot of time promoting itself as a rental community focusing on independent living. Residents live privately in their own studio and one- or two-bedroom apartments, available on a yearly lease. No endowment or large entry fees are required. Amenities include restaurant-style dining, free scheduled transportation, recreational and social activities, a library, beauty and barber salon, swimming pool, country store, greenhouse, 24-hour security, maintenance and housekeeping. Westwood is next door to Fort Walton Beach Medical Center.

WHITE SANDS MANOR
40 Windham Ave. SE
Fort Walton Beach   244-7162

White Sands is an HUD-subsidized retirement apartment project designed specifically for elderly residents. Ninety-five one-bedroom apartments are available with an emergency call system.

BOB HOPE VILLAGE
30 Holly Ave.
Shalimar   651-5770

TERESA VILLAGE
321 Woodrow St.
Fort Walton Beach   862-8778

Both of these retirement villages are set up primarily for widows of Air Force enlisted personnel. Bob Hope Village has 256 one-bedroom apartments and Teresa Village offers 123 one-bedroom units, both with scheduled transportation and activities. The facilities are operated by the Air Force Enlisted Men's Widows and Dependents Home Foundation, Inc., 92 Sunset Lane, Shalimar, 863-4113 or 863-4114.

CRYSTAL COVE AT SANDESTIN
2400 Crystal Cove Ln.
Destin   267-1600, (800) 359-7809

This sprawling retirement community centers around the spring-fed Crystal Lake eight miles east of Destin between the Gulf of Mexico

FORT WALTON BEACH AREA — RETIREMENT

A bird's-eye view captures the picturesque beauty of Seaside.

and Choctawhatchee Bay. The 2,600-acre property has several stocked lakes with fountains, a gazebo and walking paths. Other resort amenities such as 45 holes of championship golf, tennis courts, a 98-slip marina, a clubhouse, restaurants and shopping are within easy reach inside the Sandestin Beach Resort. Apartments in each of the three-story buildings come with fully equipped kitchens, washer and dryer hookups, cable TV, smoke detectors, spacious balconies and an emergency response system. Services provided with your lease fees include meals, housekeeping, linen service, security, maintenance, utilities and transportation. Adjacent to Crystal Cove is an assisted living facility, Sandcastle Shores, for a higher level of personal care.

EDGEWOOD TERRACE
State Road 393
Santa Rosa Beach 267-1755

Still in the development stages, this unusual retirement community will one day be filled with double-wide manufactured homes. Buy the land only or choose from a two- or three-bedroom model (a few of these are already in place). Each home comes complete with driveway, carport, screened-in porch, skirting, landscaping and maintenance.

Senior Support Services

FORT WALTON BEACH SENIOR CITIZEN'S CENTER
31 Memorial Pkwy. SW
Fort Walton Beach 244-1511

Classes in handicrafts, ceramics, oil painting, crochet, aerobics, Danse Orientale, Mah Jongg and bridge are fairly popular all year long.

• 231

FORT WALTON BEACH AREA — RETIREMENT

Weekly Bible study, bingo, bowling, bridge tournaments, square dancing and shuffleboard keep minds alert and bodies active, plus provide avenues for lasting friendships. Monthly parties, covered dish luncheons and pool tournaments add more fun to the social schedule. Call for a list of monthly scheduled activities.

Air Force Enlisted Widows Home Foundation
92 Sunset Lane
Shalimar   651-9422

Exclusively for widows of Air Force enlisted personnel, the foundation provides a safe and comfortable home for women 55 and older.

Okaloosa Coordinated Transportation
833-9173; bus rides, 833-9168

This system provides transportation to all programs receiving state or federal funds for transporting clients. Transportation arrangements must be made at least 24 hours in advance.

Okaloosa County Council on Aging
207 N.E. Hospital Dr.
Fort Walton Beach   833-9165
Crestview Senior Center
198 S. Wilson St., Crestview, 689-7807
Valparaiso Senior Center
268 Glenview Ave., Valparaiso, 833-9210

The Council on Aging provides a range of services to encourage independence and preserve dignity to all people over 55.

State of Florida Aging and Adult Services
417 Racetrack Rd.
Fort Walton Beach   833-3700

Services for adults and the disabled include elderly home care, adult foster care and placement in a retirement community.

Fort Walton Beach/Destin/ Beaches of South Walton
Health Care

Fortunately for the people who live here, good health care and a wealth of excellent facilities can be found within these many small communities. Three hospitals serve residents and visitors in the tri-county area (Okaloosa, Santa Rosa and Walton counties). For these small towns, it is rare to find the quality of doctors, specialists and facilities offered not only by hospitals, but medical clinics, nursing facilities and treatment centers.

Hospitals/Medical Centers

FORT WALTON BEACH MEDICAL CENTER
1000 Mar-Walt Dr.
Fort Walton Beach   862-1111

Formerly Humana Hospital, the Fort Walton Beach Medical Center provides inpatient and outpatient care to residents of Okaloosa, Santa Rosa and Walton counties. Special services include Women's Services, dedicated to women's health; the Psychiatric Treatment Center; newly renovated and equipped Intensive Care, Coronary Care and Progressive Care units; and 24-hour Emergency Room Service.

To fill other community needs, a six-room surgical suite, outpatient surgery, a pediatric unit, diagnostic radiology services, a pathology lab and physical therapy are also offered by the hospital.

New programs include The Senior Association, a nonprofit organization for adults 50 and older, set up to deal with every aspect of life from medical to financial to social. The Sports Medicine Program sends out a doctor to work as a liaison between the hospital and high school athletes in Okaloosa County high schools and at the Okaloosa-Walton Community College. Besides evaluations, referrals and treatment recommendations, the Sports Medicine Director is available to cover games.

NORTH OKALOOSA MEDICAL CENTER
151 Redstone Ave. SE
Crestview   682-9731

Serving both Okaloosa and Walton County residents, the North Okaloosa Medical Center is a 110-bed hospital offering echocardiography, laparoscopic surgery, magnetic resonance imaging, women's and children's services, 24-hour emergency services and a clinical laboratory.

HCA TWIN CITIES HOSPITAL
Hwy. 85 N. at College Blvd.
Niceville   678-4131

Attracting residents from both

• 233

Okaloosa and Walton counties, HCA Twin Cities Hospital is a 75-bed general acute care facility affiliated with the Hospital Corporation of America, a privately owned corporation out of Nashville, Tennessee. This full-service medical facility offers 24-hour emergency service, EEG/EKG, a CT Scanner, Intensive Care/Coronary Care, Physical Therapy, Radiology, Surgery, Pharmacy, Laboratory and Outpatient Services. Special services include a Wellness Center for topical programs, workshops, support groups and stress management; a Seniority health care program providing screenings, insurance claim filing, seminars, physician referral, travel discounts and social events; a Cardiac Rehab program for heart patients; and Alliance, offering injured workers fast, efficient treatment.

DESTIN HOSPITAL
996 Airport Rd.
Destin 654-7600

Patient care is what sets this 50-bed acute care hospital in the heart of Destin apart from larger facilities. Its small, family type atmosphere seems conducive to faster healing for its community patients. A special classroom promotes health education for employees, physicians and members of the community with year-round programs. High-tech equipment and services available at the hospital include an Intensive Care/Cardiac Care Unit, a fluoroscopy room in the Radiology Department, a CT Scanner, Ultrasound room and mammography unit. The 24-hour Emergency Room keeps a group of physician specialists on call to assist with consultations.

Support Services

WHITE-WILSON MEDICAL CENTER
1005 Mar -Walt Dr.
Fort Walton Beach 863-8100

A multi-specialty medical group of 40-plus physicians provides a full range of diagnostic services. Open Monday through Friday 8 AM until 5 PM; Saturday 8 AM until noon; 24-hours a day by phone.

DESTIN WHITE-WILSON MEDICAL CENTER
1000 Airport Rd.
Destin 837-3848

Convenient to Destin residents, this group of five doctors provides care in internal medicine, OB/GYN and pediatrics. Open 8 to 5 Monday through Friday; not all doctors are available every day.

DESTIN MEDICAL CENTER
623 Hwy. 98
Destin 837-5181

With offices in Destin and a satellite office in Santa Rosa Beach, also on Highway 98 (phone 267-3303), this group of physicians provides specialty care in pediatrics, gynecology, dermatology, geriatrics and internal medicine. Doctors also oversee hospital care, perform minor surgeries and have their own lab and x-ray facilities. Walk-ins are welcome. The center is located next to the Donut Hole.

AMERICAN HOMEPATIENT
99 Eglin Pkwy. NE, Ste. 8
Fort Walton Beach 243-9400

American Homepatient, located

in Fort Walton Square shopping center, provides in-home infusion and intravenous therapy, oxygen and respiratory equipment, and durable medical equipment such as wheelchairs, walkers and electric beds on a daily, weekly, monthly or yearly basis as needed. Trained RNs make this type of therapy easier on the patient than having to travel back and forth to a doctor's office or hospital.

NORTHWEST FLORIDA HOME HEALTH AGENCY
1326 Lewis Turner Blvd.
Fort Walton Beach   863-1161

Nurses provide care in patients' homes with a doctor's order, which can be from daily to once a month visits. Home health aides are available for patient baths, grooming and/or light housekeeping. The agency is JCAHO accredited and Medicare certified.

DELTA MED OF FLORIDA
426 Government St.
Valparaiso   678-1832

Delta Med provides necessary medical equipment (wheelchairs, walkers, beds, etc.) on a weekly, monthly or longer-term basis.

PHYSICIANS' HOME CARE
922 Mar-Walt Dr.
Fort Walton Beach   862-3240

This comprehensive rental and retail sales company provides many types of medical equipment, including oxygen, food supplements, IV therapy, nursing services, diabetic and ostomy supplies. The company is a certified fitter for breast prosthesis and compression garments.

PHC bills Medicare and insurance companies direct. It's located near Fort Walton Beach Medical Center.

GULF COAST IMMEDIATE CARE CENTER
420 Miracle Strip Pkwy. SW (U.S. Hwy. 98)
Mary Esther   244-3211

The doctors will see you now — they're available for all non-emergency injuries and illnesses, flu shots and physicals for school or work. Open 8 to 8 Monday through Thursday; 8 to 5 Friday; every 1st and 3rd Saturday from 8 until noon.

Physician Referral Services

If you're new in town, or are just visiting, a physician referral service can be invaluable, not just for non-emergency vacation-related injuries and illnesses, but for providing names and credentials of a specialist when your asthma kicks up or your luggage will be delayed — with all your medications in it. These services are affiliated with area hospitals, and staff members can tell you which kinds of insurance are accepted and even make an appointment for you.

THE PHYSICIAN AND SERVICE REFERRAL

A service of Fort Walton Beach Medical Center, 863-7568.

PHYSICIAN HEALTHLINE/REFERRAL

A service of North Okaloosa Medical Center, 682-9731, ext. 106.

PHYSICIAN INFORMATION SERVICE

A Destin Hospital service, 654-7680.

FORT WALTON BEACH AREA — HEALTH CARE

Physician Referral

A service of HCA Twin Cities Hospital, 729-7433.

Treatment Centers

Bridgeway Center
728 N. Ferdon Blvd.
Crestview   689-7845

Serving the entire Fort Walton Beach area, Bridgeway provides comprehensive mental health services, marriage and family counseling, crisis stabilization, children's services, alcohol/drug detoxification and rehab, and psychological and psychiatric evaluations. Services are offered through Human Resource Services in downtown Crestview (689-7900). A crisis line (682-0101) operates 24-hours a day.

Harbor Oaks Hospital
1015 Mar-Walt Dr.
Fort Walton Beach   863-4160

This 79-bed psychiatric facility meets the special needs of children and adolescents. Four psychiatrists and 130 trained therapy-related personnel are available in three areas: the Children's Unit for 5-to-13-year-olds, the Acute Care Unit, and the Chemical Dependency Unit plus long-term treatment.

Rivendell
1015 Mar-Walt Dr.
Fort Walton Beach   (800) 543-2919

Programs are specially designed for young people and adults such as residential treatment, acute inpatient services, eating disorders and sexual trauma. Open 24 hours a day, seven days a week.

Nursing and Convalescent Centers

Bay Heritage Nursing and Convalescent Center
Hart St., one block south of Twin Cities Hospital
Niceville   678-6667

A superior rated facility by the state of Florida, the center provides 24-hour registered nurse coverage, therapeutic diets and a full range of social and recreational activities. Bay Heritage is primarily a long-term care facility.

Fort Walton Beach Care Center
1 LBJ Senior Dr.
Fort Walton Beach   863-2066

A 120-bed skilled nursing center, Fort Walton Beach Care Center provides speech therapy, social services and activities, and round-the-clock nursing care.

Gulf Convalescent Center
114 Third St.
Fort Walton Beach   243-6134

This 120-bed skilled nursing geriatric facility is staffed by 105 employees and on-call physicians. Physical and speech therapy are included, as well as a full-time social and activities director.

Village at Sandestin
5851 Hwy. 98 E.
Destin   267-2887

For more than 25 years, the Village at Sandestin has offered services from occasional assistance to complex skilled nursing care. The top-quality facility provides priority nursing care, therapeutic and respite care programs as well as recreational and social activities for its residents.

SANDCASTLE SHORES AT SANDESTIN
2400 Crystal Cove Lane
Destin   267-1600, (800) 359-7809

Right next door to the Crystal Cove independent senior community, Sandcastle Shores provides an alternative to a nursing home. The staff assists with daily routines such as bathing, dressing and medication reminders for frail elderly adults. Respite care is also available. The monthly fee includes a one-room apartment with utilities and cable, 24-hour emergency response, housekeeping, laundry, meals, daily assistance, scheduled transportation and daily activities.

Fort Walton Beach/Destin/ Beaches of South Walton
Military

Eglin Air Force Base spreads over more than 450,000 acres in Okaloosa County, making its operations, its personnel and its economic impact of utmost interest to the people in this area. Unlike some military installations, Eglin allows the public to use its vast resources — we're not talking high-tech weaponry now, we're talking *natural* resources for hunting, fishing, camping, canoeing, hang gliding, you name it. Whatever disassembling the government decides to do with the military in the next several years, Eglin will probably always remain.

Eglin Air Force Base

Eglin Air Force Base is the largest base in the free world and a crucial player in America's national defense system. Insiders are quick to point out the economic and social value of having such a massive military base in the area, one whose presence is felt in almost every aspect of life. On the fiscal side of things, Eglin's total payroll amounts to over half a billion dollars each year, much of that going to the local and state economy. On the social front, consider not only the 10,000 active military personnel stationed there, but also their 8,000 children who are schooled and raised in Pensacola. Throw in the 30,000 military retirees drawn here by the attractive climate and facilities, stir in the nearly 5,000 civilians employed by the base, and you'll see why Eglin's impact on the area cannot be overestimated.

The base was established in the early 1930s and occupied a total area of fewer than 2,000 acres. It was named Eglin Field in 1937 after Lt. Col. Frederick I. Eglin, a U.S. Air Corps officer who died in an airplane crash.

During World War II, Eglin became an extremely important testing ground for aircraft and munitions. As the field's strategic importance grew, so did its size: in 1940 the War Department was given control of Florida's Choctawhatchee National Forest, whose land and water boundaries contained nearly 800 square miles.

Eglin served as one of the sites in March 1942 for Lt. Col. James H. Doolittle to prepare his B-25 crews for their legendary raid against Tokyo. On April 18, the 16 airplanes were launched from the carrier *Hornet* and flew 800 miles to drop their bombs on Tokyo and other cities. Though the actual physical damage was minimal, this was the first Allied air raid against Tokyo and had a chilling effect on Japanese morale — and, needless to say, gave Americans a much-needed boost.

Throughout the 1940s and 1950s, Eglin served as a vital test site for new advances in aircraft and weaponry, including the ground-breaking field of guided missiles. Several major defense programs were established at Eglin during the 1950s and 1960s, mostly in response to the Cold War. Many of these have grown into the Air Force Development Test Center, whose wide range of missions includes research and development, testing and acquisition of non-nuclear air armaments, electronic combat systems and navigation/guidance systems.

During the Vietnam War, Eglin housed and processed more than 10,000 Vietnamese refugees in a tent city. In 1980, Eglin did the same for over 10,000 Cuban refugees who fled to America.

During the Persian Gulf War in early 1991, Eglin played a large part in the success of that operation. The base sent fighter planes and over 2,000 people to the Middle East.

Today Eglin remains an influential and valuable asset to America's defense. Among the 50 tenant units stationed there are the 728th Control Squadron, the Army's 6th Ranger Training Battalion, the 33rd Fighter Wing, the 919th Special Operations Wing and the 20th Space Surveillance Squadron, whose football field-sized radar tracks over 85 percent of all objects currently orbiting our planet.

There are ten air fields on the Eglin reservation, but only three are active: Eglin Main, which contains the main testing, administrative and living facilities along with the major airfield; Duke Field, which serves the 728th Tactical Control Squadron and 919th Special Operations Wing; and Hurlburt Field, home to the Air Force Special Operations Command and the 1st Special Operations Wing.

Eglin's Armament Museum offers a stirring and educational look into the base's military history and accomplishments. It's a must for aviation buffs. Outdoor exhibits include the sleek SR-71 Blackbird, a B-52 bomber, a Russian MIG-21 fighter and the gigantic B-17 Flying Fortress Eagle. Inside you can see a P-51 Mustang that blazed the skies during World War II, an F-80 Shooting Star and even a restored World War II flight simulator. There's also a display of aircraft armament dating from World War I to the present.

The museum is open seven days a week from 9:30 AM to 4:30 PM. It's closed on Thanksgiving, Christmas and New Year's Day. Admission is free, and don't forget to stop by the Gift Shop and browse the great selection of airplane models, books and other related items.

Hurlburt Field

Hurlburt's main gate is five miles west of Fort Walton Beach right on Highway 98; you can't miss it if you're coming in from Pensacola. Most of these buildings have been here since it opened in 1940, and a fresh paint job can only slightly mask that fact. Hurlburt, on the Eglin property, is headquarters of the Air Force Special Operations Command. Personnel from the first Special Operations Wing took part in the aborted attempt in 1980 to rescue the hostages from Iran; five of the eight who died there were members of the 1st SOW at Hurlburt. Just a few years back, you might remember the AC-130 Gunship that crashed during Operation Desert Storm in the Persian Gulf; all 14 crew members of the 16th Special Operations Squadron died. We're not trying to be morbid here; Hurlburt personnel represent the most active wing since the end of the Vietnam War. There's a small chapel on the Hurlburt property housing a memorial to the Hurlburt heroes who gave their lives for their country.

Inside
Panama City Beach Area

Savvy, Southern, and sandy... Panama City Beach stretches out over more than 25 miles of shimmering, glittering beachfront. If you came to Florida for beaches, look no farther than Panama City Beach. Driving in from northern states, it's the shortest trip to any Florida beach.

The Panama City Beach area is almost completely surrounded by water — St. Andrew Bay, West Bay, North Bay, East Bay, St. Andrew Sound, Grand Lagoon, the Gulf of Mexico and dozens of bayous. Anglers visit from all over to take advantage of the gulf's "Loop Current" for catching marlin and sailfish, and fishing tournaments seem to be held nearly every weekend from May until October.

With so much waterfront property, commercial ventures such as shops and restaurants are spaced farther apart than they seem on your first drive through; in other words, the tightly packed string of tourist-oriented businesses goes on for miles on the gulf, thinning out only slightly when you hit Thomas Drive, Back Beach Road and in town on 15th and 23rd streets.

Spring Breakers have found a new home in Panama City Beach, and for about a month in the spring, merchants welcome the thousands of rowdy college students with open arms. MTV now features Panama City Beach every year as the new "Spring Break Capital," bringing international exposure to Northwest Florida. Residents greet the publicity with mixed reactions, but nobody can deny its impact on the area's economy.

There's much more to see in the area if you can drag yourself off the beach for a day or two. Panama City is flush with cultural offerings in theater, music, dance and visual arts. There's a new Arts District downtown featuring works of both locals and artists who are nationally known. Take in a concert in McKenzie Park, lunch on oysters and Cokes in the

---

Insiders' Tips

Up until the early part of this century, school in Panama City only went as far as the seventh grade. If you wanted to get any smarter than that, you had to go clear to Georgia.

The Miracle Strip is a glittering expanse of Panama City Beach.

bottle at Hilda's in Southport, or drive up to Vernon to tour an ostrich farm.

It's kind of a quirky thing with the locals, but "beach" people don't cross the bridge into town, and "city" people stay on their side of the bridge. Consequently, both sides are missing out on a wealth of opportunities for culture, recreation and, let's face it, neighborliness. Panama City Beach is a huge resort area overrun with visitors, while Panama City is a small Southern town that remains uncrowded even during peak business hours; the marina area is downright deserted. Can these two distinct environs ever find happiness together? They can in this book, and they can if *you* help break the mold by crisscrossing the bridge many times during your visit.

As a resort area, Panama City Beach goes back as far as the big tourist meccas down south. The Miracle Strip Amusement Park recently celebrated its 30th birthday. In town, performances at the Martin Theatre were wowing crowds long before Tyndall Air Force Base began gearing up for World War II. And families like the Andersons, whose descendants once provided fish to Confederate forces stationed here, may have piqued visitors' interest in charter fishing. The Andersons remain one of the area's most successful families, having stakes in both commercial and charter fishing.

Although it may be difficult to see past the resorts and visitor-related offerings, other equally influential forces are commercial fishing and the military. The three have grown up together and remain eternally intertwined, providing the ideal balance for both residents and visitors.

Visitor Information

**PANAMA CITY BEACH CONVENTION
& VISITORS BUREAU**
P.O. Box 9473
Panama City Beach   234-6575

**PANAMA CITY BEACHES
CHAMBER OF COMMERCE**
12015 Front Beach Rd.
Panama City Beach   234-3193

**BAY COUNTY TOURIST
DEVELOPMENT COUNCIL**
P.O. Box 9473, Panama City   233-5070

**BAY COUNTY
CHAMBER OF COMMERCE**
235 W. 5th St.
Panama City   785-5206

Panama City Beach Area
Restaurants and Nightlife

A laid-back beach bar with servers who are never in a hurry . . . a thumping, bumping dance club with palm trees growing up through the floor and elbow-to-elbow crowds . . . down-and-dirty oyster bars where slurping off the shells is expected and encouraged . . . elegant oceanside dining with high standards and prices to match . . . the Panama City Beach area's restaurants and lounges are as diverse as the people who fill them. Seafood is the favorite again, followed by steaks, then sandwiches. And because all Insiders need to know, you're going to have a heck of a time finding a nice restaurant on the beach that's open for lunch. Fine dining establishments do a great dinner business, but won't budge for lunch, even during Spring Break! Oyster bars, snack and sandwich shops, however, do most of the lunch business, so steer yourself to those. Just about every single dinner place takes major credit cards, but many of the more popular spots shy away from reservations, so ask about both when you call.

Two more words about the beach — nothing fancy. Dress casually, wear that spaghetti-strap sundress and sandals or that loud Hawaiian-print shirt you just bought, brush the sand off your feet, and come on in!

Price codes for the Panama City Beach area, for a basic dinner for two, are as follows:

Under $20	$
$21-40	$$
$41-60	$$$
More than $60	$$$$

Panama City Beach

Hamilton's Seafood Restaurant & Lounge
5711 N. Lagoon Dr., overlooking Grand Lagoon
Panama City Beach   234-1255
$$$

Mesquite grilling of steaks, ribs and seafood bring folks back here time and time again. Try Hamilton's Shrimp Christo, with grilled shrimp over angel hair pasta laden with fresh stewed tomatoes, onions, Feta cheese and spices. All the ingredients are fresh, fresh, fresh, and nothing is prepared ahead of time. Hamilton's uses only pure virgin olive oil, creamery butter, fresh cheeses and herbs, top choice meats and "from-the-dock" seafood. If you order scallops here, know that you're getting real Florida bay scallops; some restaurants try to pass off cut outs from stingray wings as "sea scallops." These tiny *real* scallops are so tasty and slightly sweet that they don't need any accompanying sauces. That mesquite grilling brings out their full flavor — real melt-in-your-mouth. The desserts, sauces, soups, even salad dressings are made fresh from Hamilton's own recipes.

The decor and unique atmosphere can't be overlooked. Inside, find polished wood, stained glass, period antiques and old photographs of Panama City and the beach. Watch your meal being cooked from a huge display window, or step onto the covered deck for cocktails and a sunset view. You can even eat outside, if you wish. Enjoy live jazz in the lounge nightly and remember, children are always welcome. Open daily from 4:00 until 10 PM, later in the summer. Reservations are *not* necessary.

THE TREASURE SHIP
3605 Thomas Dr.
Panama City Beach   234-8881
$-$$$$

You'll probably have to stop at The Treasure Ship just to see what the heck it is. What it is is a *huge* restaurant complex, a replica of Sir Frances Drake's *Golden Hind* with a gift shop and lounges on four levels. The Hold Gift Shop is the first thing you see upon entering, so take a few minutes and look for nautical and beach souvenirs. The Brig is here, too, with music and dancing and live entertainment until the wee hours. All of Level Two is the main dining room with big, comfortable booths and exquisite bay views. The Captain's Quarters and The Pirate's Pleasure can be found on Level Three, the first for cocktails and the second for more casual dining in a 17th-century atmosphere. There's outside dining available on The Decks way up at the top of The Treasure Ship, or for more romantic dining, try the delicate French cuisine created for you tableside at the Top of the Ship.

Dine early (between 4:30 and 6:00 PM) and pick up on some great savings. The Treasure Ship also hosts a truly gluttonous Sunday Brunch from 10 AM until 2 PM, and that's when you're likely to spot a few renegade pirates scouting about the ship. You're invited to stay awhile and tour the many levels or stroll the decks. Open daily at 4:30; reservations are not accepted.

BREAKERS
12627 Front Beach Rd.
Panama City Beach   234-6060
$$$

Not *Spring* Breakers . . . this place is upscale. It must be doing a fairly brisk business to be able to stay open for 23 years, but the view of the gulf, the warm, tropical atmosphere, won-

---

For a complete rundown of many of the beach's best restaurants, nightclubs, lounges and hot spots, tune in to Beach TV on cable channel 5 or 7. Beach TV is the Panama City Beach area's visitor information station.

derfully prepared food and nightly entertainment make Breakers a special night out. Chef Debra Griffin will be cooking up the day's catch in a number of your favorite ways, but try a lean cut of prime rib, baked fish with a lemon herb crust, or the shrimp and scallops primavera for a healthy alternative without a healthy price: all just $10.95. Woody Green is the house entertainer, singing and playing a mean piano for your listening or dancing pleasure from Monday through Saturday, 5 until 9:30 PM.

Capt. Anderson's
Dockside on Grand Lagoon, Thomas Dr.
Panama City Beach   234-2225
$$$

The "Golden Spoon" Award is a prestigious honor given annually by *Florida Trend* magazine, and for 13 years, Capt. Anderson's Restaurant has been named one of Florida's top 20 restaurants. Jimmy and Johnny Patronis, owners of Capt. Anderson's, take their seafood seriously. You might find them out on the docks, talking and bartering with the local fleet captains about the day's catch. When it's personally selected by the restaurant owners, you can be assured that only top-quality seafood ends up on your plate!

In keeping with the nautical decor inside Capt. Anderson's (named for the Anderson fishing fleet, incidentally, which is one of the Southeast's best), the emphasis is on seafood, and plenty of it. Get yours charcoal-grilled, broiled, fried or served any number of wonderful ways. Try a feta-packed Greek salad, or some fresh bread or desserts made right here in the Anderson's bakery. There's no better place to watch the fishing fleets unload the day's catch, either in the dining room, or in the Topside Lounge overlooking the lagoon. Open from January through October beginning at 4 PM every day but Sunday. Come early for dinner; no reservations are taken.

Schooner's
On the east end of Thomas Dr.
Panama City Beach   235-9074
$$$

It's the last local beach club, but nobody will tell us why. Is it the last one before you leave the beach, maybe? That seems more likely, with all the mom-and-pop places all along the beach. There isn't a great deal of atmosphere at Schooner's, just a lot of neon beer signs and old wood paneling. This is *one* of the fine beach establishments that welcomes you in for lunch, so gorge yourself on giant burgers, grilled grouper, salads and sandwiches, washed down with an icy cold beer. For lunch, outdoor dining is best, since the inside tends to be dark and, well, empty. But what's really earned Schooner's its reputation happens at dusk. Now things get a little bit nicer, with open-air dining and tablecloths and candles and live entertainment. You can still get your hushpuppies and your oysters on the half-shell, you just have to eat them a little more demurely. Not! This is a laid-back place, and nobody, but nobody, is going to tell you which fork to use, we promise. Open 11 AM until 3 AM every day but Sunday.

Dine out tonight — outside, that is! Many of Panama City Beach's restaurants offer "open air" seating.

MONTEGO BAY
On the curve of Thomas Dr.
Panama City Beach   234-8686
$$

It's a place for shuckin' and slurpin' and licking butter off your fingers. It's the beach, mon! Montego Bay has something of a Jamaican atmosphere, meaning everything is, well, colorful, including the clientele! Prices are really pretty good for all you get, like the "Captain's Catch," a seafood platter with a cup of gumbo; chargrilled amberjack; or Jamaican Grilled Chicken, all for less than 10 bucks. Lunch specials start at $4.00. Visit Montego Bay's four other locations: at the intersection of Middle Beach, Front Beach and Thomas Drive (235-3585); at the Shoppes at Edgewater (233-6033); at the Y (233-2900); and Montego Bay downtown, Highway 77 across from the mall (872-0098).

CAPTAIN DAVIS DOCKSIDE RESTAURANT & LOUNGE
At Captain Anderson's Marina
5550 N. Lagoon Dr. and Thomas Dr.
Panama City Beach   234-3608
$$$

Something about the lull of dining on the water, watching the boats, the sunset, the fishing fleets . . . tends to make a person hungry! It may be romantic, but you may also have your three children in tow! They'll like this place, too, since it's fun to watch the boats come in, and Captain Davis's friendly staff is always happy to see families. Fresh seafood can be grilled, broiled, blackened or fried. Thick-cut steaks, prime rib and delicious frosty cocktails provide enough variety for a few meals out during your vacation stay. Open Monday through Friday 5 to 10 PM; weekends 4 to 10 PM; closed Wednesday.

• 247

PANAMA CITY BEACH — RESTAURANTS AND NIGHTLIFE

BOAR'S HEAD
17290 Front Beach Rd. just west of Hwy. 79
Panama City Beach   234-6628
$$$

The Boar's Head is supposed to be Old English-style, but we're not talking Shepherd's Pie or crumpets or any of that bland-but-authentic food. The atmosphere is Old English, and the food is out of this world — roasted and chargrilled steaks and seafood, succulent prime rib, baby back pork ribs, fresh fish and shellfish creations, plus some served with pasta. Try the Garlic Shrimp with Cream Sauce and Pasta for a real treat. The shrimp are sauteed in fresh garlic and olive oil, then finished with a light cream sauce and served over fresh fettucine. There's the Grouper and Crayfish (or crawfish) Meuniere, which maybe you can't pronounce, but you can sure appreciate: a broiled grouper filet topped with crayfish tails in a Paul Prudhomme-inspired meuniere sauce (he's the famous New Orleans chef).

The children's menu is extensive, offering more choices than most (eight entrees). Nightly dinner specials start at just $9.95. Reservations are accepted, but not required. Enjoy live entertainment in The Tavern every weekend. The Boar's Head is open at 4:30 daily for dinner; they're closed Monday.

PINEAPPLE WILLIES BAR & GRILL
9900 S. Thomas Dr.
Panama City Beach   235-0928
$

It had to happen sooner or later — a nightspot designed especially for Baby Boomers. By day, Pineapple Willies caters to families, with seafood, ribs and deli specialties. Let us tell you a little about these ribs before you let your 8-year-old order them: They're coated with a "secret" Texas rub, slow cooked for eight hours, then basted with some sort of a special sauce featuring Jack Daniels. Okay, so most of the alcohol probably burns off. What's left is pure perfection. Food is served from 11 AM until 8 PM, when the entertainment starts cranking up and the crowd changes to people who actually remember all the words to the 1910 Fruitgum Company's hits. There's a $5.00 cover charge.

SPINNAKER
8795 Thomas Dr.
Panama City Beach   234-7892

If you're a member of Generation X, Spinnaker is a custom fit. Live concerts, a beachfront playground, nightly contests, live rock 'n' roll, something for the ladies, something for the men, great drinks and after-dark dancing to today's music in a colorful, rhythmic sound and light show fill the bill for the under-30 set. Spinnaker sometimes has two or three bands playing all at the same time! They have a swimming pool where pool volleyball is quite popular, 12 different levels, 19 different bars, a Panama Jack Miss Spinnaker contest on Saturdays, A Wet T-Shirt contest every Sunday, volleyball contests, male and female revues, jet ski and Hobie Cat rentals, Ladies' Night every Thursday, great deli food, music, lights, dancing — WHEW! No wonder it's called the "World Famous Beach Club." You have to be 18 to party, 21 to drink.

Cover charge is $3.00 if you're 21 and over; $5.00 for ages 18 to 20. Open every day 11 AM until 4 AM.

Panama City

THE GREENHOUSE RESTAURANT
443 Grace Ave. in the Grace Ave. Mini-Mall
Panama City   763-2245
$$

Let us give you yet another reason to cross over the bridge into town. The prices are nice, the crowds are nonexistent, and the food is worth the trip. This little mini-mall has little cobblestone streets and archways; the Greenhouse Restaurant is right at the end of the "road." Inside, several small rooms separated by trellises and stucco walls make for intimate dining; bare trees covered with tiny white lights give the feeling of dining outdoors.

The luncheon menu has a few unusual offerings: chargrilled chicken teriyaki, a chicken chimichanga, fried fish and Marie's Famous Crab Cakes (snow and lump crab). You can get away easily for under $10.00. For dinner, which is served from 5 to 10 PM every day but Sunday, order sauteed scallops in butter and herbs finished with white wine and heavy cream and served over fettucine. The catch of the day can be blackened to order, or you might try a beef tenderloin, sauteed to order with sauce Bernaise. All chicken, fish and shrimp can be ordered baked with wine and lemon if you're one of the health-conscious. The Greenhouse is open for lunch from 11 to 2.

CANOPIES
4423 W. Hwy. 98 on St. Andrew Bay
Panama City   872-8444
$$$

This elegant restaurant is in town, still on the water and features the same gorgeous sunsets. But no beach restaurant can hope to match Canopies' graceful atmosphere inside a home built in 1902 and framed by ancient oaks, or a lush lawn sloping to the water's edge.

Now, get ready for the feature attraction. How about a hearty slab of New Orleans Andouille sausage, sauteed with fresh gulf shrimp and served over fettucine alfredo? Or a couple of succulent St. Andrew Bay blue crabs simmering in rich cream and sherry for a steaming bowl of she crab soup? If you're needing a seafood break long about half way through vacation, order up a juicy chicken breast stuffed with feta cheese, mozzarella and fresh herbs, covered with marinara sauce, and served with pasta and a fresh vegetable. Other entrees let your taste decide with grilled tuna, gulf grouper, roast pork tenderloin, filet mignon and many others. Order one of the superb pastas as an appetizer or a main course. All entrees come with a house salad, a loaf of still-warm homemade bread and strawberry and herb butter. Yum!

Save room for whatever they're making for dessert that night and one of their numerous coffee creations. Open every evening with "Twilight Dining" from 5 to 6 PM, which means entrees go for between $8.95 to $10.95.

The Cheese Barn
425 & 440 Grace Ave.
Panama City   769-3892 (restaurant)
              763-4466 (bakery and deli)
$$

Here's another of those delightful out-of-the-way places that makes you feel like you alone have discovered it. As an insider, it's a place you need to know about. Here, take your choice: French crepes, German knockwurst, Cajun Jambalaya, Italian manicotti, pizza, salads, an incredible array of sandwiches (including a rather superb Muffeletta on a poppyseed bun), nachos, steaks, quiche and — CHEESE! Many of the sandwiches feature The Cheese Barn specialty cheeses, such as the Downtown Philly with Swiss and Cheddar, the Che' Che' Cheddar Beef, the Submarine and Super Duper with provolone, and plenty of others. The variety of domestic and imported beers is staggering, as is the selection of wines, wine coolers and champagnes and sparkling wines. This charming little spot has a European feel to it with its aged stucco walls, white tablecloths, several small dining rooms and dim lights, even during the day. Be sure to visit the bakery for a take-home dessert! The Cheese Barn is open Monday through Thursday from 11 to 8:45; Fridays and Saturdays from 11 to 9:45.

Taxi's Diner
23rd and Beck
Panama City   763-5025
$

Hooray! A place with good grub that's open 24 hours a day! Taxi's advertises "Cheap Fare — Speedy Service." They're slinging Hubcap Pancakes there in the back (ever had beer with breakfast long about 3 AM?), the Big Tipper Redeye, and Checker's Chili, all in a slick chrome-polished, jukebox-playing, malt-shop-mixing diner atmosphere. Take-out is available during the same hours, like *all the time.*

Thunderbirds
One mile east of the Hathaway
Bridge on Hwy. 98
Panama City   785-7444
$

Sometimes grown-ups need their own place, so Thunderbirds was invented to let big people have their own fun. Your kids wouldn't like that "old" music, anyway, but you'll be boogeyin' 'til the cows come home! Once a week is "Comedy Zone," with national touring comedians you may have seen on David Letterman or The Tonight Show. Thunderbirds also has a once-a-week "Sadie Hawkins" night, where the gal who asks the most guys to dance gets $100 in Thunderbucks! Oh, and *all* ladies, shy or not-so-shy, get free drinks from 7 until 10 PM. There's "Two Buck" night, "Casino Night," crazy giveaways in cash and prizes on the weekends, and Thunderbirds has just about run out of nights! Don't forget about the fabulous free buffet Monday to Friday from 5 to 7 PM and Saturdays from 6 to 8 PM, and two-for-one Happy Hour for *three* hours, 5 until 8 PM Monday through Friday. Open from 5 PM until. Hop in your Thunderbird (or more likely, your mini-van), and bop 'til you drop!

Panama City Beach Area Accommodations

Sleep cheap or surround yourself in luxury in a full-service resort. This area was designed with families and couples in mind, with most resorts and hotels right on the beach to enhance leisure-time activities. Many visitors prefer the campground route, which shows off some of the area's many fine wooded areas. It's almost difficult to find accommodations that aren't on or near the water. The Panama City Beach area is blessed with an outstanding system of bays, bayous, lakes and inlets so that every visitor can take advantage of fishing, boating, swimming or just enjoying the incredible scenery in every direction.

One more note: Panama City Beach, more than any other resort area in Northwest Florida, is literally bursting with resorts, hotels, motels, townhomes, condominiums, cottages and campsites. There are hundreds of places to stay, so our list below barely scrapes the surface. What we've tried to do for you is give you a representative sampling of available accommodations in many different price ranges. And because of the number and variety of places to stay, rates are comparable with those in Pensacola — in other words, they're great!

Resorts/Hotels

Driving up and down the beach, you'd swear that every hotel chain in America is represented here. And that may be true. The 27 miles of beachfront is just the start. Many of the luxury resorts and condos front St. Andrew or one of the other bays and are every bit as scenic and accessible to restaurants, shopping and attractions. Below are top picks for the best Panama City Beach has to offer in all price ranges. Our price guide is for a double room for one night at the peak of the season; off-season rates can drop by as much as one third. Prices do not include tax.

$80 or less	$
$81-100	$$
$101-150	$$$
$151 or more	$$$$

BAY POINT YACHT & COUNTRY CLUB
100 Delwood Beach Rd.
Panama City Beach 235-6966
$$$ (800) 543-3307

Could there be a more perfect setting for this relative newcomer than on St. Andrew Bay, surrounded by water and shaded by tall pines? Bay Point is an all-inclusive 1,100-acre retreat from the workaday world with 36 holes of championship golf, a 147-slip marina, health club and swimming pools. Guests may choose from one-, two- or three-bedroom condos and villas on Bay Point's golf courses, on the marina or overlooking Grand Lagoon. All feature large balconies for a tranquil brunch and open living and dining spaces. Right there on the property are the Terrace Court and Greenhouse restaurants or the more casual Sunset Grill and Pub.

There's one thing you can get at Bay Point that you can't find much of on the beach: shade. If it's important to you, you'll love all the trees and gentle wooded setting. And that beach is never far away. There is a two-night minimum at Bay Point; weekly rates for a two-bedroom condo at Lagoon Towers run about $700.00.

HOLIDAY INN BEACH RESORT
11127 Front Beach Rd.
Panama City Beach 234-1111
$$$$ (800) 633-0266

Could be that this Holiday Inn is one of the nicest you've ever had the pleasure to stay in. All 342 rooms and suites overlook the turquoise waters and white sands of those famous Panama City Beaches. The resort doesn't just have a swimming pool, they've turned it into a tropical oasis with waterfalls, swaying palms and exotic flora of every description. Spacious rooms all have private balconies, ice makers, refrigerators and coffee makers (with coffee). There's a fitness center if you've just gotta pump iron while you're here. The steam room and sauna, though, make sweating worthwhile. The Blue Marlin Restaurant is a fine place to hang your hat after a hard day in the sun, or you might enjoy a cocktail at the Starlite Lounge, a local favorite. Sunsets are especially appealing over drinks and dinner at Charlie's Grill and the Oasis Bar.

EDGEWATER BEACH RESORT
11212 Front Beach Rd.
Panama City Beach 235-4977
$$$$ (800) 239-4853

A landmark in the Panama City area, Edgewater offers enough recreational activities, walking trails, pools and amenities to keep you within the confines of the resort property for a week! All studio, one-, two- and three-bedroom units are decorated in a tropical motif with full kitchens, living and dining areas, private baths for each bedroom and washers and dryers. Stay in the fancy waterfront towers on the gulf or one of the more private Caribbean-style golf villas along the golf course. On the 110-acre, $100 million property is a nine-hole, par 3 golf course, 12 all-weather tennis courts, 20 shuffleboard courts, three restaurants, a beauty salon, an arcade, and five heated spas. Wrapped around those niceties are fountains, ponds and enough tropical vegetation to make it feel like — well, like paradise! The nine pools include a lagoon pool — 11,500 square feet at the edge of the gulf! And just to wrap it all up in one incredible package are three restaurants on the property: the Bimini Sandbar Cafe, the Palapa Bar and Grill, and the Upstairs Clubhouse and Lounge.

Pleasure boats regularly ply the waters of the gulf.

PIER 99 BEACHFRONT MOTEL
9900 S. Thomas Dr.
Panama City Beach   234-6657
$$ (800) 874-6657

It's right on the beach, right next to the pier, right in the middle of everything. Rooms are not especially fancy, but you won't have much time to spend lazing away the days there with so much to do! This is a fine families-only motel, since location is everything and rates are fairly inexpensive. There's a two-night minimum stay at Pier 99, with a discount for your third through the sixth nights, and a seventh night free. Kitchen units are a little more expensive but well worth the extra ten or so dollars a night if you can make some meals in your room. Off the beach units save you even more. There's a gulf-front pool, a hot tub and Pineapple Willies Bar & Grill, serving up ribs, seafood and great entertainment nightly. If you stay here between Sunday and Thursday, Pier 99 will take $5 per night off the cost of a room.

HAMPTON INN
11004 Front Beach Rd.
Panama City Beach   234-7334
$$ (800) 426-7866

Hampton Inns do a fine job in every location and pride themselves on all the little extras that make a stay here so special. Start with gulf-view rooms (the inn is 75 yards from the beach), free HBO, no charge for kids, no-smoking rooms and free continental breakfast. This particular Hampton Inn also has an outstanding location just 10 miles from the airport, one-half mile from Miracle Strip Amusement Park and one mile from Hombre Golf Course. Double rooms have two double beds, and rooms with coffeemakers and refrigerators are $10.00 more per night.

PANAMA CITY BEACH — ACCOMMODATIONS

RAMADA INN BEACH
12907 Front Beach Rd.
Panama City Beach   234-1700
$$$ (800) 633-0266

The glitzy mirrored columns and reflective facade of the Ramada are right out of the '70s, but Ramada Inns grew by leaps and bounds during that decade, so many of the properties reflect the era of discos and mirror balls. But wait, there's more: the pool is something you'll want to photograph from all sides. Giant fake rocks create grottos, caves and waterfalls around the free-form gulf-front pool. And the lobby, well — but we should stop poking fun. Yes, there are aquariums built into the reception desk and some kind of nautical motif, but bear with us — the rooms are large and clean and comfortable, and they all have water views (that might mean pool views, but the pool's right on the gulf as well). There's a health club on site as well as the Crow's Nest Lounge with what else? A mirror ball on the dance floor!

PORTER'S COURT
17013 Front Beach Rd.
Panama City Beach   234-2752
$$ (800) 421-9950

This is a pretty little place with whitewashed single-story cottages and red roofs, or a three-story motel building by the pool and facing the gulf. Choose a one- or two-bedroom/one-bath unit featuring kitchen and dining areas, small kitchens and sofa sleepers. The larger cottages have porches facing the gulf, while some units face an open courtyard area. Efficiencies, though small, still pack in their own patios and refrigerators. Since the *two*-bedroom cottages are only $115 a night, a family could be very comfortable there, or even in a one-bedroom with a sleeper sofa. If you want the best at Porter's Court, there's a one-bedroom rooftop penthouse condo with its own private patio garden on the gulf.

Condominiums/ Townhomes/ Vacation Cottages

Some people just know how to live. Why *not* have all of the amenities of a resort, plus the privacy and space of a home? Bringing home fresh seafood from the market and cooking it yourself is a great vacation pastime, aside from eating it all up! Prices reflect the average weekly cost of a two-bedroom/two-bath condo or house during the peak summer season. Most rental agencies want a deposit up front which can be up to a third of the week's rental. Prices do not include tax.

$750-950	$
$951-1100	$$
$1101-1500	$$$
$1501 and over	$$$$

ABBOTT REALTY SERVICES, INC.
35000 Emerald Coast Pkwy.
Destin   837-4853, (800) 336-4853
$-$$$$

Abbott is one of the largest realty companies in the area, offering over 80 resort properties from high- and low-rise condominiums to townhomes and beach cottages. If you're unsure of where to start looking for your vacation retreat, Abbott can provide

Another spectacular sunset graces Panama City.

an excellent overview of the area and what's available.

SEACHASE CONDOMINIUMS
17351 Front Beach Rd., ¼ mile west of Hwy. 79
Panama City Beach   235-1300
$ (800) 457-2051

Seachase's reasonably priced condominiums directly overlook the gulf. Every unit, whether a condo or townhome, boasts a panoramic 60-foot-wide, floor-to-ceiling view. Twin high-rise towers have a gulfside pool and sundeck in between. Two-bedroom units have spacious 1400-square-foot floor plans. A $200 deposit is required at the time you make your reservation; nightly rentals are also available. All units have washers, dryers, microwaves, free local calls and HBO movies and cable. You must be 25 years old or older to rent (now hear this: no Spring Breakers!).

LARGO MAR
5717 Thomas Dr.
Panama City Beach   234-5750
$ (800) 645-2746

Although some of these units are set quite a ways back, the entire development is on the gulf. Largo Mar is another fine place to take the family; buildings are only three stories (you can request a ground-floor unit), there's lots of landscaped acreage for the kids to run around in and units are far enough from Thomas Drive so the sound of the surf will be louder than the blare of car horns. Every unit has its own washer and dryer, dishwasher, garbage disposal, fully equipped kitchen, cable and private deck. Outside, buildings are clustered around a large swimming pool. There's an outside Jacuzzi, a club room, saunas and barbecue grills. Most of the units overlook the pool.

PANAMA CITY BEACH — ACCOMMODATIONS

THE SUMMERHOUSE
6505 Thomas Dr.
Panama City Beach   234-1112
$ (800) 354-1112

These very nice, very comfortable condos are laid out in a series of three high-rises. From your private balcony, you can see out over the gulf or clear to Grand Lagoon. The views are spectacular. Inside, Summerhouse is designed with families and couples in mind. All units are two bedrooms and feature washers and dryers, a fully equipped kitchen for microwave popcorn and fresh coffee every day if you'd like, cable with HBO and everything to make your stay just as pleasant as can be. The two pools, hot tub and kiddie pool are nicely landscaped and center around a gazebo. Beach service is also available to guests — just ask for beach umbrellas, cabanas, water cycles, sail boats and more. For your littlest travelers, cribs and baby beds can be brought to your unit on request. Kids especially like the glass elevators and the game room! For a larger family, or one that likes its space, request one of the corner units. These are 1888 square feet with views all around.

PORTSIDE RESORT
17620 Front Beach Rd.
Panama City Beach   234-7157
$ (800) 443-2737

It's hard to imagine all this beauty, all this luxury, all these great amenities, and you're paying for a week what a two *night* stay would cost in South Florida! That's what so many people discover about this little corner of Florida... the most incredible resorts imaginable cost so little! Portside is one of the best. The development is long and skinny and spread out enough to make your unit very private. And since it isn't actually *on* the gulf, but across the street, they've made it up to you (!) by going overboard on amenities. Two-bedroom units are bedecked in casual Florida colors and furnishings that reflect the lifestyle so well. You can park right at your door. Palms, pampas grass, hibiscus and ginger surround the three pool areas (one is heated), and a giant Palapa overlooks the waterfall pool. Take advantage of the kiddie pool, the tennis courts, shuffleboard, a heated spa and the poolside clubhouse.

ST. ANDREW BAY RESORT MANAGEMENT, INC.
726 Thomas Dr.
Panama City Beach   235-4075; (800) 621-2462; (800) 621-2426; (800) 423-1889
$

These are the people who know Panama City Beach best, and prove it with an amazing assortment of accommodations all up and down the beach and five check-in offices. Take your choice from Ramsgate Harbour townhomes, offering the most privacy in their own "neighborhood," Endless Summer Condos, which are villas just steps from the beach; Premier Townhouses, low-rises with 2½ baths that sit right on the beach; Dunes of Panama on Thomas Drive with huge balconies on the gulf; Commodore Condominiums with a pool, a hot tub and within walking distance of St. Andrews State Park. Many other condos and beach houses are available with three bedrooms.

Campgrounds/RV Parks

ST. ANDREWS STATE RECREATION AREA
4415 Thomas Dr.
Panama City Beach 233-5140

"Back to nature" vacations are a trend throughout the United States, and St. Andrews is poised and ready to respond to eager campers. One hundred and seventy-six campsites were booked through April 11 of 1994, just to give you an idea of how popular eco-tourism has become. Waterfront sites on Grand Lagoon are $20.67 per night; non-waterfront go for $18.49. Obviously, reservations are recommended well in advance. For more information about St. Andrews, see the chapter on Panama City Beach Attractions.

PANAMA CITY BEACH KOA
8800 Thomas Dr.
Panama City Beach 234-5731

With something close to 300 campsites, KOA proves camping is as popular as ever. And to back that up (as if staying right on the Gulf of Mexico wasn't fun enough), KOA has a game room, a fishing lagoon, two pools, basketball, volleyball, a playground, picnic tables, a rec hall, a toy store and a gift shop! During the winter months, they add ping pong and shuffleboard to the lineup. Why, you can even have cable TV for an extra $2.00 a day! At the peak of the season, KOA still offers a 10% discount for staying a week (March 1 through Labor Day). The daily rate is $22.95 for a full hook-up (water, electric, sewer); $18.95 for primitive (tent) camping with water only; and if you don't wish to rough it, try one of the "Kamping Kabins," for $31.95 a night, year round. These have beds, kitchens, linens, heat, AC and just about everything you need to be comfortable except those little bottles of avocado body balm.

MAGNOLIA BEACH RV PARK
7800 Magnolia Beach Rd.
Panama City Beach 235-1581

This RV park is so pretty that many folks choose to stay here all year. Of course, those that do snatch up some of the tastiest sites, too, but there are plenty of others. If you're an RVer worth your salt, you'll know that the designation of a "Good Sampark" makes it top notch. Giant magnolia, yellow pine and oak dripping with moss make the park a cool respite even in the heat of July. It may be one of the *only* shady places to hang out at the beach in the heat of July! The St. Andrew Bay location means the water's usually warmer than the gulf, and the waves are easy to handle, even for the little ones. On the grounds are a rec room, air conditioned showers and baths, picnic tables and barbecue grills, a pier, a pool and a grocery store with camp supplies. For all this excitement, you pay about $20.00 a night during peak season (with cable!); about $125 if you stay all week.

RACCOON RIVER RESORT
12405 Middle Beach Rd.
Panama City Beach 234-0181

This is another "Good Sampark," but it's got to be an older one, first, because a raccoon probably hasn't been spotted on Panama City Beach since the '50s, and second, because it has all these "cutesy" names that somebody's grandpa probably named like "Turtle Turn," "Possum Pond," "Alligator Alley" and "Hoot Owl Hollow." The tent camping sites go by such monikers as "Hawk Heights," "Otter Alley" and "Beaver Bend." But it's within walking distance to the beach, there's a pond to fish in, a pool and playground, lots of shade trees and log cabin restrooms and a general store. Besides, the days-gone-by monikers are appealing in a comfortable sort of way. Primitive sites go for $14.00 in the peak season; sites with full hookups (that's with cable, too) are $19.50 per night; $117.00 per week. Would you feel sheepish about telling someone you were staying on "Porcupine Path?" Not I!

Panama City Beach Area
Shopping

T-shirt, beachwear and souvenir shops are crammed into every available space along the beach for take-home memories, so only a few of those are listed here. For more serious buyers, look into downtown for everything from imported tobacco to English bone china and original objets d'art.

On the Beach

ALVIN'S BIG ISLAND TROPICAL DEPARTMENT STORE
Across from Miracle Strip Amusement Park and twelve other locations all up and down Panama City Beach   234-3048

It's pretty hard to have a corner on the T-shirt and beachwear market in a place as huge as Panama City Beach, but it seems Alvin's tries very hard to do just that with an amazing array of stores. The big one's the most fun, though, and could almost be considered a tourist attraction. Delightfully tacky and whimsical, Alvin's Big Island seems to be poking fun at itself with its fake rock exterior, cavernous interior (complete with stalactites and stalagmites), a tank of small sharks, cages of tropical birds and an outdoor alligator exhibit. It is somehow dismaying to find giant macaws, parrots and cockatiels shoved in among T-shirt racks, too accessible to the whims of mean-spirited tourists. The alligator "farm" does a pretty good job; at least the creatures are somewhat distanced from passersby by fencing. An aquarium of small sharks is set in the middle of the sales floor, too, with shell nightlights, shell sculptures, caricature artists, coffee mugs and huggies all around.

You could call the stuff they have for sale beach junk, and they might even agree with you, but it sells like crazy! Who wouldn't want to take home a key chain with a tiny scene of *real* water and *real* sand and *real* shells encased in it? Or a visor sporting "I Survived Spring Break"? Alvin's has hundreds of top-name swimsuits, bikinis and other types of beachwear, but most of it is, well, beach junk. We can almost guarantee you can't walk out of there without buying *something*. Open daily from 9 AM to 6 PM.

TRADER RICK'S SURF SHOP
12208 Front Beach Rd. at the pier
Panama City Beach   235-3243

If you need *stuff* for the beach, for surfing, for skating, for volleyball, skateboarding or just for looking good, Trader Rick's is the beach authority. Beach gear, beachwear, beach equipment and most everything in between to outfit you for a great vacation is here. Open in the

• 259

off-season from 9 AM until 11 PM; in-season hours are 8 AM until midnight. Yep, people really *do* buy surfboards at midnight!

SHIPWRECK SHIRTS
10570 Front Beach Rd.
Panama City Beach   233-6750

By a Shipwreck Shirt, we don't mean they're all dirty and torn, but, hey, if they were, some people would still buy them (grunge is still "in," at least for this month). Shipwreck has plenty of shirts, but also swimwear, sportswear and gifts to bring home. Open every day from 9 AM to 11 PM; Sundays from 9 AM until 10 PM.

NIGHT MOVES
9526 Front Beach Rd.
Panama City Beach   234-5223

Somewhere on the beach there *had* to be somebody who sells more than just beachwear and T-shirts and souvenirs, and we finally found one. Night Moves sells sexy lingerie, dancewear, legwear, accessories, jewelry, adult toys, novelties and games. Oh, and that goes for men, too. Night Moves puts on a fashion show every week — if you're interested in seeing how this stuff looks on a real person, call for times. Open Monday through Saturday from 10 AM until the Night Moves, or about 10 or 11 PM; Sundays in season.

THE BOOK WAREHOUSE
Holiday Plaza Shopping Center
6646 W. Hwy. 98
Panama City Beach   235-2950

Come pick up a little light summer reading for the beach with 50 to 90 percent off suggested retail. The Book Warehouse carries an assortment of children's books, cookbooks, craft books, how-to's, computer books, fiction and scads of books in other categories. Bring your postcards and letters here, too; there's a post office inside the shop. Open 8:30 AM to 7 PM Monday through Saturday.

QUICK SNAPS
553 Shoppes at Edgewater, Front Beach Rd.
Panama City Beach   234-7160

Look just across from the Holiday Inn to have your precious vacation photos processed in just one hour at no extra charge. Quick Snaps offers same day service on enlargements, slides and reprints. They're open every day from 9 AM until 8 PM; 11 to 6 on Sunday.

THE JOINT, KILLER BEADS AND THE T-SHIRT CELLAR
14600 Front Beach Rd.
Panama City Beach   233-2752, 234-6361

We promise, it's one of the brightest shops you'll find anywhere on the beach. You can't miss this bizarre 1960s-style mural splashed in Day-Glo colors across the front of the store. Inside, things get even stranger. Buy beads, T's, beachwear, tobacco pipes and accessories, jewelry and some of the very finest airbrush work in the county. The Joint would be worth stopping into just to admire the work of airbrush artist Troy Pierce — it's truly spectacular. Open 9 AM to 9 PM daily; until 11 PM on the weekends.

BARRON'S ANTIQUE MALL
1½ miles west of the Hathaway Bridge, 8010 Front Beach Rd.
Panama City Beach   230-0612

More than 100 dealer room settings in a 20,000-square-foot, air-

A couple takes time out to laze along the white shores and dunes of Shell Island.

conditioned showroom feature fine antiques and collectibles of all descriptions. You could lose yourself (and your spouse), but the Antique Mall has a place for you to find each other again, the "Husband Recovery Room." Barron's accepts layaways, and will deliver locally or long distance. They're open daily ("We doze, but we never close") from 10 to 6 Monday through Saturday and Sunday 1 to 6.

Panama City

THE BRITISH PANTRY AND GIFT SHOPPE
In the Olde Towne Mini-Mall on Grace Ave.
Panama City   763-9781

Dearie, this is a proper British invasion of foods, gifts and English bone china, Crabtree & Evelyn soaps and bath accessories, and everything just as English as it comes. What fun to stroll around this little shop with all its cubbyholes and tiny displays! Collect all the accoutrements for a proper British "high tea," try some English candies (*much* different than ours, to be sure!), or a handcrafted British pipe. Open Monday through Friday 10 to 5; Saturdays 10 to 2.

CORNING REVERE FACTORY STORE
105 23rd St., one mile west of Hwy. 231 in the Manufacturer's Outlet Center
Panama City   784-0288
950 Prim Ave. at the Factory Stores of America
Graceville   263-3277

If you'd like a little variety in your shopping, then you'll just have to cross the bridge into town (or make the trek to Graceville), where you can pick up on some incredible bargains at Corning Revere. Look for more than just the famed Corning Ware — there's Visions cookware, Pyrex and Revere Ware,

• 261

Corelle dinnerware, lots of open stock dishes and glassware, plus kitchen gadgets and accessories. Open Monday through Saturday from 9 to 9; Sundays 10 to 5.

MANUFACTURER'S OUTLET CENTER
105 W. 23rd St., Panama City

For serious bargain hunters, here's true outlet shopping from about a dozen of your favorite name brands like Russell, Van Heusen, Capezio, Bass, Polly Flinders, London Fog and Corning. Heck, you can save up to 70% just by crossing the bridge — what a deal! Open every day.

PANAMA CITY MALL
2150 Cove Blvd., Hwy. 77 at Hwy. 231 and 23rd St.
Panama City 785-9587

More than 90 stores including JCPenney, Gayfers and Sears plus lots of eateries, puppet shows, a four-screen cinema and a game room make for a pleasant day's wandering. Shop in air-conditioned comfort seven days a week from 9:30 to 9 Monday through Saturday and 12:30 to 6 on Sundays.

PAUL BRENT STUDIO AND GALLERY
413 W. 5th St., Panama City 785-2684

Here's one of the best Insiders' tips you'll get this year: Go visit Paul Brent's studio and take home *one* souvenir. It is something you will always treasure after you learn that Paul Brent is a local artist and his works are displayed all over the world! You may already have seen some of his work, although you might not have known you were looking at a *local* artist's work; Brent's colorful watercolors are on display at Busch Gardens, Sea World and Disney World, as well as many other offices and galleries in exotic locales such as Australia, South Africa and the Caribbean. Now his designs have been transferred to linens, placemats, shower curtains, greeting and playing cards, and many other items. This is a gallery, so of course you can still buy his original works, prints and works by other artists. If you happen to catch him at the gallery, he won't mind you asking him to autograph your print. Brent is still very active in the local community, providing T-shirt and poster art for many worthwhile causes. Stop in Monday through Friday between 8 and 5 or on Saturday from 10 to 5.

FLORIDA LINEN OUTLET
At Stanford Station on 23rd St.
Panama City 769-0950

Walk in with an idea, walk out with a carload of bargains on curtains, comforters, sheets, towels, placemats, napkins and accessories for your home! Martex, Fieldcrest, Kirsch and other name brands are there for the picking in over 6,000 square feet of floor space. Coordinate an entire bath in the time it takes to pull the stuff off the shelves ... tissue holders, towel racks, toothbrush holders, matching picture frames, hampers, wicker shelves and baskets, rugs, everything! Open 9 AM to 7 PM weekdays; 9 to 6 Saturdays and 1 to 5 Sundays.

Panama City Beach Area
Attractions

Like the bumpers in a pinball game, visitors to Panama City Beach can bounce from one diversion to the next and never miss a beat; amusements rub elbows with outdoor activities all up and down the beach. Attractions that are most fun for families and kids are so noted by an asterisk (*), while museums, art galleries and more tranquil pursuits await discovery inland. Be sure to check the chapters on Panama City Beach Area Recreation and Shopping for more to do!

*St. Andrews State Recreation Area
4415 Thomas Dr.
Panama City Beach   234-2522

This 1000-plus-acre jut of land surrounded by water on three sides might seem at first to be a private island paradise. Just when you think you're really starting to commune with nature one-on-one, ten people pass you on the nature trail and scare off the raccoon you were watching. Not that you won't find places to be alone, but St. Andrews is one of Florida's most popular state parks, so prepare to share. Pine forests, marshes, flatwoods and great lines of white sand dunes characterize the terrain. Near Grand Lagoon, visit a reconstructed "Cracker" turpentine still, a remembrance of this area's once-thriving lumber industry. Cannon platforms still exist from World War II when the park was part of a military reservation. One of the platforms is now a pavilion; the other lies on the beach, a victim of constant buffeting by wind and waves.

Camping, picnicking and concessions are all available in the park, as are a number of water-related leisure activities. Fishing is probably the number one attraction at St. Andrews, since there are so many opportunities to wet a line — from the surf, the two piers, the jetties and freshwater fishing in Gator Lake or one of the other small ponds. Take your boat out (the boat ramp is on Grand Lagoon near the fishing pier) for some deep sea excitement. Boats can be rented by the hour during the summer months.

The park's nature trail may take you past alligators or wading birds, but for up-close marine life study, check out the jetties. Fish, crabs and other creatures love to congregate around the huge rocks. Please remember that all plant and animal life in the park is protected (yes, that includes the water). Please do not remove or disturb any living thing. Feeding the animals is also prohibited.

PANAMA CITY BEACH — ATTRACTIONS

Is this Zoo World camel being friendly or merely looking for a handout?

PANAMA CITY BEACH — ATTRACTIONS

Right across the thin stretch of beach is the Intracoastal Waterway, and beyond that, Shell Island, three miles of totally undeveloped solitude, accessible only by boat. Daily trips to the island are $66.00 for four hours. Call 234-2522 and talk to Captain Black about trip times. Many other boat cruises offer trips to the island as well. Entry fee to the park for one day is $3.25, which will admit up to eight people in one vehicle. For campground information, see the chapter on Panama City Beach Area Accommodations. St. Andrews is open from 8 AM until sunset all year.

*Cypress Springs
Hwy. 79
Vernon   535-2960

Just 30 minutes from the fury of Panama City Beach is one of Florida's many natural wonders, carved from a landscape inhabited by Native Americans thousands of years ago. The water is some of the purest and clearest in the world. Just reach your hand down and scoop some up. You've never tasted water so sweet and cold (68 degrees year round). Visibility is over 200 feet, just perfect for underwater photography and spelunking (cave diving).

You must be a certified spelunker to enter the underwater cavern through an oval-shaped vent. The flow of water is quite strong here, so be sure to wear a weight belt. The cave opens onto a room about 40 feet wide with a ceiling 14 feet high. Even at its deepest point, divers can see the surface, some 70 feet above!

Cypress Springs pumps out close to a million gallons of fresh water daily. Tubing and canoeing are leisurely ways to tour the adjoining creeks and springs for a few hours, or stay in the nearby RV park to explore the scenic wonders at your own pace. Call for information on float trips, dive trips, and RV park sites.

Ebro Dog Track
Off Hwy. 20
East of Freeport 234-3943, (800) 345-4810

Bursting out of the starting gate with lightning speed, the greyhounds take center stage every night but Sunday year round. Over a million dollars are paid out each week, and if you'd like to get in on some of that action, bring a friend, buy a tip sheet and get anxious with the rest of the crowd. Dine on prime rib, stuffed shrimp or Grecian Grouper in the Ebro Dining Room overlooking the action. The restaurant opens at 6 PM, and reservations are required. Just a little helpful hint on betting: Don't bring any more money than you can afford to lose! Ebro brings you continuous action in the off-season with simulcast wagering on greyhounds and thoroughbreds on tracks a bit farther south. Live racing goes on rain or shine every night at 7 PM with matinees at 1 PM (no racing Sunday). General admission is $1.00; children are free when accompanied by a parent. To get to Ebro from Panama City Beach, take Highway 79 north to Highway 20 and follow the signs.

*The Glass-Bottom Boat
Treasure Island Marina, 3605 Thomas Dr. behind the Treasure Ship
Panama City Beach   234-8944

Take a cruise through gentle bay waters and out into the emerald gulf

• 265

PANAMA CITY BEACH — ATTRACTIONS

while your captain fills you in on the scenery, the bird life, and what you're about to encounter. Feed friendly dolphins and pesky pelicans, look for unusual marine life through the huge underwater viewing windows, visit scenic and protected Shell Island, and try to identify the creatures captured in the Glass Bottom Boat's shrimp net! Snacks are served inside the air conditioned cabin. Bring your camera and a good pair of binoculars for an adventure you'll treasure. The Sea School trip just described runs from 9 AM until noon or 1 to 4 PM daily all year long. Prices may vary a bit from time to time, but are regularly $9.00 for adults, $6.00 for kids 3 to 12, and 2 and younger free.

Also docked at the marina is a 40-passenger catamaran to take you on a super shelling safari. Explore remote sand bars off the end of Shell Island and comb the beaches for shells and sand dollars. Prices for this trip are $11.00 for adults and $7.00 for kids. Call for times, since the trip depends so much on the weather and time of year.

*Sea Screamer
Treasure Island Marina, 3605 Thomas Dr.
Panama City Beach   233-9107

It's the world largest speedboat, and after one ride, you'll swear it's also the world's fastest! Climb aboard this 73-foot twin turbocharged cruiser for a nice, calm narrated tour of Grand Lagoon, Shell Island and the pass. Once the Sea Screamer hits open water, though . . . HANG ON!!! You'll blast off into the Gulf of Mexico for the wettest, most exhilarating ride of your life! Yes, you *will* want to wear your swimsuit. Or perhaps your wetsuit. Adult tickets are $8.00; $5.00 for children; younger than 6, free. The Sea Screamer departs at 10 AM, noon, 2, 4 and 6 PM daily.

*Gulf World
Front Beach Rd., 15412 W. Hwy. 98-A
Panama City Beach   234-5271

Ever see a dolphin hula? Hear a sea lion applaud? Or feel the rough surface of a stingray? All this and much more kicks into high gear at Gulf World, one of Florida's most popular attractions. The action never stops with continuous dolphin, sea lion and dive demonstration shows. While you enjoy the antics, you'll also learn something about dolphins and sea lions from their trainers. After the show, you might even get a chance to pet one of the dolphins!

At the Coral Reef Theater, a diver plunges into a giant tank filled with creatures of the deep such as sharks,

---

Insiders' Tips

In 1942, just off the coast of St. George Island, a German U-boat sank a British tanker, the HMS *Empire Mica*. Only 14 of 47 crew members survived the two torpedo blasts. The *Empire Mica* still lies 24 miles southwest of Cape St. George. Fishing there is terrific, and divers report it is one of the most popular dive spots on the Gulf Coast.

PANAMA CITY BEACH — ATTRACTIONS

Ever see eye-to-eye with a giraffe?

rays, barracuda and giant sea turtles. Although you may gasp in amazement when the diver grabs hold of a fierce-looking shark, he's really in no danger, since all of the marine life are well-fed before the show (we hope!).

Colorful tropical parrots squawk and talk and put on quite a performance of their own, then pose for pictures with visitors. Don't miss Gulf World's other star attractions — penguins, alligators, ducks and tropical fish of every description. Open rain or shine between February 1 and October 31; also open for a few days around Thanksgiving and Christmas. Gates are open from 9 AM until 3 PM, but to see all of the shows and attractions here, you should allow about 2½ hours. Admission prices are $13.95 plus tax for adults; children 5 to 12 $7.95; 4 and younger are free.

*EMERALD FALLS FAMILY ENTERTAINMENT CENTER
8602 Thomas Dr. at Joan Ave.
Panama City Beach   234-1049

You'll never hear the kids complain that there's nothing to do on the beach when they can spend a day at Emerald Falls. With *four* go-cart tracks, there's almost no waiting. Bumper boats are for everyone in the family — even the tiniest tots get excited about getting splashed ... and splashing back! The two 18-hole mini-golf courses wind through mysterious caverns, over bridges and past thundering waterfalls to keep things lively. If you get caught in one of the frequent summer showers here, don't worry; they rarely last long, and, hey, the kids can head to the arcade to play over 40 games, and parents can get some well-deserved down time over ice cream or cool drinks.

• 267

PANAMA CITY BEACH — ATTRACTIONS

The Ocean Opry provides good family fun every night.

Kid's Kingdom is an extravaganza for your little curtain climbers. Rides like the Red Baron Airplane Ride, the Spinning Top or the Rio Grande Express are low-key and high-flying pint-sized fun. Emerald Falls is open every day from 10 AM until around midnight. Ticket prices range from $2.25 for kiddie rides to $4.50 for adults; all rides require just one ticket. Ticket packages are available, which brings the cost per ticket down a bit. Pick up an Emerald Falls brochure from one of the Visitors Centers to get $1.00 a person off a game of mini-golf.

*MIRACLE STRIP AMUSEMENT PARK
12000 Front Beach Rd.
Panama City Beach   234-5810
This is the biggie . . . the one that's been here over 30 years, and is *still* one of the area's best family attractions. Be sure you don't try the 2000-foot roller coaster on a full stomach! The same goes for the Sea Dragon, a ride reminiscent of a Viking ship rocking on the "waves" up to 70 feet in the air! With more than 30 rides in all, an all-new arcade and favorite kid foods like Domino's Pizza, TCBY Yogurt and funnel cakes right here in the park, you may not see the kids until the vacation's over! But of course, you'll probably be right there with them chowing down on greasy, sticky foods and indulging your childlike tendencies with a corn dog and three trips on the ferris wheel! Shipwreck Island Water Park is operated by the same folks that run Miracle Strip, so they offer a special deal: Double Park tickets may be purchased at either park for $25.00 per person. The tickets may be used on separate days. Season passes are also available. Miracle Strip Amusement Park is closed all winter and reopens in late spring (too late for those Spring Breakers!) on Fridays from 6 to 11 PM and Saturdays from 1 to 11 PM. It's open daily during the summer season. Prices are $16.00 for those folks 50 inches tall and over; $13.00 for kids under 50 inches.

*SHIPWRECK ISLAND WATER PARK
12000 Front Beach Rd.
Panama City Beach   234-0368
Next to the Gulf of Mexico, you may not have seen this much water all in one place! Shipwreck Island is the largest water park within 300 miles and has become something of a landmark with its giant sunken "wreck" as the park's centerpiece. Around that, splash, squirt, shoot and squeal on six acres of waterlogged madness! Fly down the Speed Slide at 35 miles per hour, ride the waves in the Wave Pool, shoot down the Rapid River's cascades or cruise along the Lazy River in a giant inner tube. Grab a rope and swing off the ship's bow into the pool or jump the waves in Ocean Motion, recreating the wave action in the Gulf! The Tadpole Hole is, you guessed it, for the pre-swim set, as are the Elephant Slide and the Kid Car Wash, but any age will find enough ways to get wet to make the trip worth their while.

Closed during the winter months, the park reopens in late spring on weekends between 10:30 and 5 PM. It's open daily in the summer months. Tickets are $16.00 for visitors 50 inches tall and over; under that height, it's $13.00; ages 2 and

PANAMA CITY BEACH — ATTRACTIONS

Get acquainted with these friendly dolphins at Gulf World on Panama City Beach.

younger are free. Seniors get in for just $5.00. A pass to both Shipwreck Island and Miracle Strip Amusement Park is $25.00.

*ZooWorld
9008 Front Beach Rd.
Panama City Beach   230-0096

Years ago, the place where ZooWorld now stands was a kind of funky, tacky, old Florida attraction, but you couldn't beat the name: The Snake-A-Torium. Thank goodness a local veterinarian took it over, cleaned it up, and turned it into one of the area's nicest family attractions. Panama City Beach can be proud of this effort, a real first-class operation with more than 350 animals including orangutans, alligators and camels. A Petting Zoo with chickies and lambies and horsies will delight any preschooler, and the 250 different species of flora in the Botanical Gardens are lush, gorgeous and unusual at any time of year. A few of the former occupant's slinky reptilians may still be around, but the glitzy snake charmers and snake wrestlers were packed off to South Florida long ago. ZooWorld stays open all year from 9 AM until dusk; longer hours in the summer. Adults get in for $8.50; kids younger than 12 for $6.00, and kiddies 3 or younger get in free.

*Pirate's Island Adventure Golf
9518 W. Hwy. 98
Panama City Beach   235-1171

Well, go ahead and swash your buckles or whatever it takes to set out on the path to high adventure! Pirate's Island is one of several mini-golf courses along the beach, so the more lavish, the better. Look for the tilted mast sticking out of the water and the overall nautical theme of

270 •

these two 18-hole courses. You'll encounter Captain Kidd's Original Adventure (a par 42 course) and Blackbeard's Challenge (par 52) with a maze of caves, waterfalls, lagoons and islands. Mini-golf takes no particular skill to play, so even if you've never swung a club before, you'll thoroughly enjoy the challenge. Children as young as 3 can play with a small fry club of their own.

Admission to the Blackbeard's Challenge course is $6.00; Captain Kidd's Original Adventure costs $5.00. If you want to play both courses, it's $8.00 for all day. Kids five and younger play free. Look for coupons good for $1.00 off in motel racks, *SEE* magazine, and *Best Buys*. The coupon is good for a buck off for each member of your party. Pirate's Island is open all year, usually from 9 AM until 11 PM; midnight on the weekends. During the winter, hours are 10 to 10.

AIR BOINGO
Thomas Dr. across from Emerald Falls
Panama City Beach   230-9200

This is madness, but if you're looking for a thrill, you've certainly found it. Bungee cords are attached to your person, then you hurl yourself off a huge tower into mid-air. That's right, no one pushes you, no one *makes* you, you do this to yourself. And for about 15 seconds of sensation, you get to pay them $18.00 — *payable in advance*. Air Boingo, being a permanent structure, is safer than the giant cranes of a few years back, and there's a huge inflated cushion below you . . . in case. If you don't want to jump, it's still fun to congregate around the tower and watch other crazies do it. Thrill-seekers seem to enjoy the rush even more at night, when the tower is awash in electric lights and the spotlight is on the jumper! Videos of your jump are available at extra cost.

*OCEAN OPRY
8400 Front Beach Rd.
Panama City Beach   234-5464

No need to pack the kiddies off to the hotel after dark, the Ocean Opry provides good-time, clean family entertainment just about every night. It's knee-slappin', hand-clappin' lighthearted down-home fun featuring the best (or worst) of the South, depending on your point of view. Comedy bits, gospel, country and plenty of sing-a-longs to get everyone in on the show. No tellin' what kind of show you'll see, but the Rader family promises some favorite tunes, color and spectacle, a little humor, and smiles all around. Reservations are recommended for these popular shows, but are not necessary. Most

---

Insiders' Tips

One of the first projects undertaken by Claude Willoughby, the first park manager at St. Andrews, was creating Gator Lake by dredging a deep, round area in a marsh, replacing the original lake destroyed by channel dredging. In the middle of the island, Willoughby pumped in an island of sand for the alligators.

PANAMA CITY BEACH — ATTRACTIONS

Nothing is more refreshing on a steamy July afternoon than a cool dunk in Shipwreck Island's giant pool.

shows are $11.95 for adults; $5.00 ages 5 to 11; 4 and younger free. Open every night except Sunday at 8 PM during the summer months; open at 7:30 PM at other times. Ticket office opens at 9 AM daily.

*Museum of Man in the Sea
17314 Back Beach Rd.
Panama City Beach   235-4101

Here's a fascinating look back at man's final frontier. Exhibits cover topics such as the first diving bell (1690), sponge divers of the 19th century, Florida's many shipwrecks and rare diving equipment like inflated animal skins and breathing tubes. Outside, take a look at some of the unusual vessels used by the Navy and others to learn more about life under the sea. A favorite part of the museum is the video on Mel Fisher's successful attempt, after 20 years and many tragedies, to recover the tremendous wealth from the Spanish galleon *Atocha.* Admission is $3.50 for adults, $1.50 for children 6 to 16; there's a 10% discount for seniors. Open every day from 9 AM until 5 PM.

*Grand Oaks Ranch
Hwy. 79
Vernon   535-2101

The Camps own this 96-acre ostrich ranch out in the sticks north of Panama City (see sidebar). They'll be happy to have you visit, personally show you around, offer some good investment advice and provide you with literature on the big birds to take home. To get to Vernon from Panama City, go north on Highway 77 to Highway 279 at Greenhead. Turn left. Highway 279 dead-ends at 79. Turn right and go north 2½

The Big Venture in Tiny Vernon

Charles and Glenda Camp took a ranch over from A.D. Whitehurst not too long ago, but it isn't your typical ranch. Grand Oaks Ranch raises ostriches. Okay, go ahead and snicker if you want, but the big birds are BIG money. A good breeding pair is worth $50,000! The Camps have about 86 birds on their 96 acres, with more chicks hatching now through the end of September. Besides their own birds, they board birds for other folks throughout the region. And Glenda Camp says that although they get to be rather large (one of the roosters is nine feet tall!), they're not dirty or smelly "except maybe after a rain," she says.

Most folks get into the bird biz as an investment. Bird pairs 3 to 6 months old go for about $7,000. The Camps started their business with two trios of ostriches, a rooster and two hens for $12,000 per trio. Once the hens lay an egg, the Camps whisk it away to the warm and secure confines of the incubator. Taking the eggs away also keeps the birds breeding. Ostriches will lay for 30 to 40 years and live to be 60 to 70 years old.

Visitors flock to see these big birds at the Grand Oaks Ostrich Ranch in Vernon.

Photo: Grand Oaks Ostrich Ranch

---

miles from the caution light. Look for the Grand Oaks Ranch sign, the huge house and the giant oaks that are over 400 years old. There's no admission, but the Camps request that you please call ahead.

*BAY COUNTY JUNIOR MUSEUM
1731 Jenks Ave.
Panama City   769-6128

Just a short drive from the beach is a place where kids can feel, hear, see and participate in science, art and nature. They'll have so much fun they'll never realize they're actually learning! Exhibits, puppet shows, classes and traveling displays are geared to young scientists. Explore a life-sized tepee or a hardwood swamp, or feed chickens and ducks in an authentic pioneer village. Admission is free, but donations are accepted and appreciated. The museum is open Tuesday through Friday from

PANAMA CITY BEACH — ATTRACTIONS

9 AM to 4:30 PM, and Saturdays from 10 AM to 4 PM.

*COCONUT CREEK MINI-GOLF AND GRAN-MAZE

*9807 Front Beach Rd.
Panama City Beach   234-2625*

Although playing one of the two 18-hole mini-golf courses is great family fun, Coconut Creek's real lure is its giant-sized human maze, the Gran-Maze, which spans the length of a football field to give you plenty of opportunities to lose yourself. Get a time card, then time yourself, stopping at four check points along the way to get your card stamped. Look in *SEE* magazine for a coupon good for $1.00 off on a game of mini-golf or a trip through the Gran-Maze. Prices depend on what you'd like to do.

One round of golf for one person is $6.00; it's $5.00 for a ticket to the bumper boats; $9.00 for the bumper boats and the maze; a combination of golf and bumper boats is $9.00; tickets for the maze and a game of golf is $10.00. Kids five and younger are free. Coconut Creek is open 9 AM to 11 PM every day.

LAGOON CRUISE LINES M/V STARDANCER

*5325 N. Lagoon Dr. at Passport Marina
Panama City Beach 233-SHIP, (800) 355-SHIP*

It's a bit of Las Vegas right here in Florida. Take a cruise out into open waters on a daily brunch or dinner cruise, then enjoy a full run of casino games: 124 slot machines, blackjack, roulette, craps and oasis and video poker. Not enough excitement for you yet? Add to that live entertainment, dancing, bingo, karaoke, three lounges, a gift shop and shipboard lotto. It's an exotic and very romantic way to spend a day or an evening out. The season runs May 1 to October 31. Brunch cruises are Monday through Saturday for $39.95 per person for six hours; Sunday brunch cruise (11 AM to 5 PM) is $49.95. Dinner cruises from Monday through Thursday are $49.95; Fridays and Saturdays the price is $59.95. All night cruises are from 6:30 PM to 12:30 AM. Prices are all-inclusive — port charge, tax and meals. Advance reservations are requested.

Panama City Beach Area
Festivals and Special Events

If you want to know where the action is in the Panama City Beach area, all you need to do is look at a map. There almost seems to be more water than land — water for boating, water for building a home near, water for surfing and swimming and, most of all, for fishing. There's the occasional festival or parade or fishing tournament, but mostly Panama City Beach is about recreation, doing your own thing for as long as you're here. The events listed below occur *annually*, but there are a number of other events, such as concerts in McKenzie Park, lectures on marine life at the community college, and theatrical performances you might also enjoy. To find out more, call the Panama City Beach Convention & Visitors Bureau at 234-6575.

March

NIKE TOUR PANAMA CITY BEACH GOLF CLASSIC
Hombre Golf Club
Panama City Beach   233-8282

On the PGA tour, young professionals earn their stripes here first in order to compete with the big boys in upcoming tournaments. The Golf Classic raises $25,000 for charity and $10,000 for scholarships.

SPRING BREAK
Panama City Beach   (800) PCBEACH

Maybe you don't think this should be listed as a special event, but we'll bet there are thousands of college students who would heartily disagree. They look forward to their week in the sun like no other — and Panama City Beach is the quickest beach to get to from most points north. It's just sand, surf, sun and suds for the throngs that clog the hotels and T-shirt shops for about a month and a half each spring. MTV (Music Television) calls Panama City Beach "Spring Break Central," and shows up at various places around the beach to broadcast live. To be sure everybody has a safe and enjoyable time, you must be 21 to purchase or consume alcohol. Now get out there and have fun!

April

GULF COAST OFFSHORE POWERBOAT RACES
St. Andrews Marina, 3151 W. 10th St.
Panama City   785-2605

The week-long event not only attracts tens of thousands of spectators and competitors for the onslaught of races, regattas, parades and parties, but it serves to raise thousands for a local charity. Hydro-

PANAMA CITY BEACH — FESTIVALS AND SPECIAL EVENTS

Spring Break on Panama City Beach is the season for watching and being watched!

plane racing is one of the first events at Carl Gray Park, followed by a race boat parade and show, a race of radio-controlled race boats (how'd that slip in here?), and an air show, among many others. Parties thrown for the year's chosen charity go on all week!

SPRING FESTIVAL OF THE ARTS
McKenzie Park
Panama City 747-0102

The Junior Women's Club sponsors this yearly spring fling, inviting artists in a variety of media to apply for a space in this juried show. The Spring Festival is primarily a fine arts festival, so you won't find the usual band of peddlers and homemade crafts. Look for watercolors, acrylics, ceramics, photography and much more original works on display and for sale. About $4,000 in prize money is awarded to artists in various categories. As many as 30,000 people come through to browse and to buy over the two weekends of the show.

May

GULF COAST TRIATHLON
Various locations around
Panama City Beach 234-6575

Something like 800 professional and amateur athletes from the United States and several other countries compete for trophies, the Ironman World Championship qualification, and way more than $30,000 in cold cash. Now before you sign up, here's what's expected of you: Begin with a 1.2-mile swim in the gulf (fortunately all warmed up by this time of year), a 56-mile bicycle course around St. Andrew and North Bays, and a 13.2-mile marathon around Panama City Beach. Still sound fun? Well, it certainly *is* fun to watch.

June

ANCHORAGE LADIES BILLFISH TOURNAMENT
Bay Point Marina, 100 Delwood Beach Rd.
Panama City Beach 769-8321

Can female anglers (well, *any* angler, probably) be lured into competing in their own tournament without the temptation of big bucks? What if the top prize were a fishing trip for two — to Venezuela? That seems to do the trick, and thirty boats (with an average of four anglers apiece) are expected for the fourth annual tourney in 1994. Besides the big trip, second- and third-place winners receive exquisite pieces of jewelry or crystal. The contenders: blue marlin, white marlin, tuna, sailfish, dolphin and wahoo. Junior anglers have their own division with prizes, too.

July

BAY POINT INVITATIONAL BILLFISH TOURNAMENT
Bay Point Marina, 100 Delwood Beach Rd.
Panama City Beach 235-6911

The first 70 boats to enter the tournament at the stiff $5,000 entry fee vie for $300,000 in cash prizes. Not a bad deal. Nightly weigh-ins draw 10,000 spectators. For noncompetitors, there's plenty to do on shore; barbecues and live entertainment take place Thursday through Sunday evenings.

TURTLE WATCH
St. Andrews State Recreation Area 233-5140
Panama City Beach

This watchdog volunteer group monitors nesting loggerhead sea turtles from July through August. The tiny newborns are subject to predators, vandals and a host of other dangers. Anyone spotting a nest or an egg-laying female is encouraged to report it to one of the park rangers immediately so protective measures can be taken.

SHARK TOURNAMENT
Half Hitch Tackle Co., 2206 Thomas Dr.
Panama City Beach 234-2621

You may *possibly* be aware that there are (gulp!) sharks in our beautiful gulf waters, and here's a safe way to see them up close! (*Most* of these are harmless to humans.) This individual tournament breaks shark catches into two divisions: pier fishing and boat fishing. Besides the daily prizes, there's a $3,000 savings bond for the person bringing in the largest shark overall, and a first, second, and third place prize in each

PANAMA CITY BEACH — FESTIVALS AND SPECIAL EVENTS

division. We're not talking Great White here. Five species are in the running, including tiger, bull, dusky, sandbar and those really strange looking hammerhead sharks. Between 100 and 125 anglers compete each year.

August

PANAMA CITY BEACH FISHING CLASSIC
Half Hitch Tackle Co., 2206 Thomas Dr.
Panama City Beach   769-2536

Local tackle shop owners, charter boat captains and restaurateurs are also savvy business people, and sponsor this six-week event so they can sell more stuff. Great for them, great for anglers, great for you as a spectator. Competitors try their luck on private boats, on the jetties, in the surf and from the pier to snag a King Mackerel, Spanish Mackerel, barracuda, marlin, flounder or cobia (19 species in all) that will net them $10,000 bucks. And if that's not enough incentive, somebody could hook a mystery tagged fish and win ONE MILLION DOLLARS! They've got plenty of time to try, since the tournament lasts for 47 days!

September

BEACH AND SHORE CLEAN-UP
St. Andrews State Recreation Area
Panama City Beach   233-5140

Dedicated volunteers arrive at various coastal locations throughout Northwest Florida to pick up trash and learn more about the preservation of our delicate coastal environment. It may not sound like much fun, but it really can be. The park rangers keep track of how many bags of trash are collected and from where, what are the most unusual items collected, etc. The media almost always shows up to talk with volunteers and park rangers, and a very upbeat, positive atmosphere prevails. It's a great way for children to learn about ecology and how to preserve our most precious natural resource.

SHELL ISLAND STEAKS AT SUNSET
St. Andrews State Recreation Area
Panama City Beach   233-5140

What more fun and fascinating way to learn about natural Northwest Florida than a yacht cruise to a barrier island! This is an annual fundraiser the park staff and its volunteers put on each year. Board a private yacht at the park for the scenic half-hour trip over to Shell Island, where one of the park rangers fills you in on a little history and area lore. Next is an outdoor cookout as you watch a colorful Florida sunset accompanied by live music. Space is limited and reservations are necessary. Tickets are $27.50 per person.

TREASURE ISLAND KING MACKEREL TOURNAMENT
Treasure Island Marina, 3605 Thomas Dr.
Panama City Beach   234-6533

Always held the last full weekend in September, this tournament awards $10,000 in cash prizes. First place, for largest king mackerel overall, nets $4,000; second place, $2,000, $1000 for third. The winnings are split between two divisions, both private and charter boats. Even with the $150 entry fee, the tourney usually gets about 100 boats participating. On Friday, join the captains and crews for a kickoff party at the marina. Sunday, there's a fish fry to cook up all of that gooood fresh fish caught by *all of those boats*! That's open to the public, too, as are the nightly public weigh-ins.

October

INDIAN SUMMER SEAFOOD FESTIVAL
Aaron Z. Bessant Park (formerly Wayside Park), across from the Dan Russell City Pier
Panama City Beach 234-6575
(800) FAST-FLA

We're not sure the Gulf Coast ever really experiences an Indian Summer like up north, but it's an absolutely perfect time of year to be here. Tourist traffic has thinned considerably (the kids are back in school), the days are warm and sunny, and the gulf — well, the gulf just couldn't be prettier or clearer. So bring along a few of your friends to munch on scrumptious delights like grilled shark, broiled shrimp, Apalachicola oysters on the half shell (yep, they're raw), seafood gumbo and fried mullet (a Southern favorite). Of course you need something else to keep you there besides just eating your way through the weekend. The festival coordinators comply in abundance with more than 100 arts and crafts booths, a sky diving exhibition, a parade, fireworks and great, continuous, live entertainment. Advance three-day tickets are $13.00 ($15.00 at the gate); daily tickets are $5.00, with children younger than 12 admitted free.

BAY COUNTY FAIR
Bay County Fairgrounds, 15th St. at Sherman Ave.
Panama City 769-2645

This six-day fair may be more like the fairs of your childhood than the star-studded, thrill-a-minute fairs now common in most larger cities. Several midway rides are set up to entertain kids and teens, there are lots of candy apples and popcorn and cotton candy, but the main attraction is still the exhibits, spread out in several buildings around the grounds. You guessed it — prize roses and pies, girl and boy scout displays, raffles for TVs and the big cattle show in the fair arena. Fairs are still big business — 40,000 attended last year. Admission is $3.00 for adults; $1.00 for children, and parking is free.

"BLAST TO THE PAST" CLASSIC CAR SHOW
Holiday Inn Beach Resort/Shoppes at Edgewater
Panama City Beach 234-6575

How old does your car have to be to be considered a "classic"? Some cars from the '70s have snuck in here, but perhaps it has more to do with style than age. More than 200 classic and antique cars will be on display from 9 AM until 5 PM at the two locations above. Do you like those "muscle cars" from the '60s? Hot rods from the '50s? It's a festival of fins and flames (the painted-on kind), spoilers and sheepskin-covered steering wheels, mag wheels and fuzzy dice. On Saturday night, there's a benefit concert with some well-known "flashback" band at the Ramada Inn Beach Convention Center.

November

BOAT PARADE OF LIGHTS

On St. Andrew Bay between Panama City and Panama City Beach 785-2554

It's the one time of the year to really let your lights shine—on your boats, that is! The parade of gaily decorated fishing boats, yachts and charters winds its way along St. Andrew Bay with waving, cheering spectators on both the city and the beach side of the bay. The parade is sponsored by local marinas.

December

CHRISTMAS PARADES

Panama City and Panama City Beach 234-3193

These parades are a wonderful complement to all of the Christmas festivities in town and on the beach, guaranteed to make you feel all warm and mushy inside. Sometimes it's hard to get into the spirit when it's 70-plus degrees, there's no snow and you're wearing shorts, but most of the locals have been doing it for years, so the absence of bad weather doesn't concern them much. You'll see hordes of little ones lining the streets with shopping bags, knapsacks, and grocery bags, and if you're from the north, you may wonder why. It's to catch all of those great parade throws! It doesn't matter *what* is being thrown, the fun is in the *acquiring*. Watch out for strings of colorful beads, plastic cups and hard candy (especially when you get hit in the head by it!). Prized possessions are Moon Pies, those foil-wrapped chocolate-coated food products with something white in the middle that you can't identify. Get into the holiday spirit with marching bands, dance classes, Brownies, floats and, as the grand finale — Santa Claus! (Does he use a sleigh with wheels in the South? . . .)

Panama City Beach Area
Parks and Recreation

Perhaps no other area in Northwest Florida is as full of the party spirit as Panama City Beach, with an emphasis on beach recreation. Fishing, volleyball, outdoor concerts and nature trails through the Florida wilderness accent the temperate climate, warm gulf waters and sun-filled, fun-filled days and nights.

Golf

BAY POINT YACHT & COUNTRY CLUB
100 Delwood Beach Rd.
Panama City Beach   234-3307

One of Bay Point's two courses was rated one of North America's top golf resorts by *Golf Illustrated* magazine in 1990 and remains as scenic and challenging today. The two semiprivate 18-hole, par 72 courses are aptly named Club Meadows and Lagoon Legend, which characterize the terrain. Club Meadows is a kinder, gentler course and an all-time Florida favorite. With a slope rating of 152 and water on 16 of 18 holes, Lagoon Legend received a USGA rating as the second most challenging course in America by *Golf Digest* magazine in 1990. Ask about special rates for visitors.

HOLIDAY GOLF & TENNIS CLUB
100 Fairway Blvd. on Back Beach Hwy. 98
Panama City   234-1800

The 18-hole, semiprivate course is one of the area's oldest (1964), but recent renovations keep it on a par with many "just built" courses. You may find it to be one of the most enjoyable courses you've ever played with its bunkers of pure white sand. Tee times up to five days in advance may be required. The par 72 course features a lighted driving range, clubhouse and pro shop.

HOMBRE GOLF CLUB
120 Coyote Pass
Panama City Beach   234-3673

With some of the best scenery Northwest Florida has to offer, this semiprivate, par 73 championship course is adorned with lakes, dogwoods and azaleas, with 15 of 18 holes bringing water into play. Hombre is home to the PGA's Nike Panama City Classic. Besides its Florida-style clubhouse, Hombre has its own pro shop, lounge, driving range and golf instructors. Hole #2 will tend to stick with you; it's "one tough Hombre."

MAJETTE DUNES GOLF AND COUNTRY CLUB
5304 Majette Tower Rd.
Panama City   769-4740

Majette is a semiprivate city

Water traps are almost as common as sand on Panama City Beach courses.

course featuring 18 holes, a lighted driving range, putting green and practice holes. Drive six miles north of Panama City Mall, then two miles west to get here.

SUNNY HILLS GOLF COURSE
1150 Country Club Blvd.
Panama City   773-3619
Not much water, but the sand traps make up for it! Sunny Hills' 18 holes are open to the public. The course is located on Highway 77 between I-10 and Highway 20.

PELICAN POINT GOLF COURSE
On St. Andrew Bay at Tyndall Air Force Base
283-2565
This is a semiprivate, 18-hole, par 72 course with mature trees and sweeping bay views all around. Pelican Point sponsors more than 30 tournaments each year.

Golf Shops

FLORIDA GOLF OUTLET
Hwy. 98 (Back Beach Rd.) across from Holiday Golf Course
Panama City Beach   235-0391
Get 'em while they last — more than 1,000 pairs of golf shoes for men and women, custom clubs, a thousand shirts and other sportswear, all at up to 60% off retail! There's one-day service on custom clubs; regripping service while you wait. Florida Golf Outlet will be discounting prices every day from 8:30 until 5; on Sundays, 12:30 to 5.

GOLF DISCOUNT CENTER
501 Hwy. 231, Panama City   769-4745
Let the Golf Discount Center put more than two decades of experience to work to make your game. All types of equipment, top name brands, apparel and accessories will not only make you play better, but look better on the course. If you need club repair, Steve offers prompt and professional service. They're open 9 to 6 Monday through Saturday; you'll find them just one mile west of Panama City Mall.

BAY GOLF CLINIC
2521-A Thomas Dr.
Panama City Beach   235-0927
The doctor is in for sick and injured golf clubs. Regripping service is offered while you wait in addition to any type of club repair. Custom clubs can be made to fit your swing; Bay also offers new and used clubs for sale. The doctor will be seeing patients from 9 to 5:30 Monday through Friday; 9 AM until noon on Saturday. Look for the Bay Golf Clinic at the entrance to Bay Point Country Club.

Watersport/Beach Rentals

SCOTTYBOAT RENTALS INC.
5611 W. Hwy. 98 at the foot of the Hathaway Bridge
Panama City Beach   872-1714
Do your *own* cruise, make your own fun with a pontoon boat (up to 15 people) or a small five-person runabout. The friendly staff will show you the ropes before you head out to fish, picnic, snorkel or dive. Call early to reserve your boat. Scottyboat Rentals is located behind the Ashley Gorman Shell Island Cruise. Boat rental rates are $70.00 for three hours with 12 gallons' worth of fuel; four hours, $80.00; five hours, $95.00; and

all day is $120. Fuel is included with the pontoon boat rental; you pay for the fuel you use with the runabout. Open every day around 6:30 or 7:00 AM until around dark.

GREAT ADVENTURE WATER SPORTS
6426 W. Hwy. 98
Panama City Beach   234-0830

Great Adventure is your parasailing headquarters, if you're brave enough. Parasailing combines the fun of waterskiing with the thrill of skydiving, where a boat actually pulls you along on water skis until you become aloft! Enjoy fabulous beach views only seen by airplane banner pilots! If you've had either water skiing or skydiving experience previously, then you'll most likely be a natural for parasailing. For newcomers, though, it can be a little tricky. Great Adventures also rents waverunners and pontoon boats. They're located beachside of the Hathaway Bridge, behind Hathaway's Landing Bar & Grill.

ISLAND WAVERUNNER TOURS & LAGOON RENTALS
Next door to the Sea Screamer or behind Hamilton's on Thomas Dr.
Panama City Beach   234-SAIL

There isn't a sail in sight at this rental place, but maybe they just like the phone number. Rent a waverunner (same as a jet ski, which is like a motorcycle on water) and take the 20-mile trip around Shell Island. The "tour" consists of a bunch of these machines going to the island en masse, then all stopping to play and comb the remote beaches for shells, or do whatever people do on a remote island. If it's your first time (for renting a waverunner, that is), maybe the calmer one-hour tour is in order, or just take the waverunner anywhere you like around Grand Lagoon. The two-hour trip costs $69.00; bring an extra person for $10 more (waverunners fit two people comfortably). One-hour trips are $49.00. Open 8 AM to 6 PM every day.

JIMBO'S BEACH SERVICE
145 Christopher Dr. just before City Hall
Panama City Beach   234-2122

Rent all your basic beach equipment here, like beach umbrellas and lounge chairs. Jimbo's also has waverunners, torpedo tube rides, jet skis, sailboats and parasails, plus trips to Shell Island, dolphin feeding excursions and snorkeling and fishing trips. Jimbo's is open every day from 7 AM to 5 PM.

Insiders' Tips

The unusual sculptures on the jetties at St. Andrews State Recreation Area are the work of artist Gerald Thompson, who saw gigantic, multi-ton slabs of white marble back in 1972 and promptly began carving with his chisel, drawing on sand and sea for inspiration. What you'll find are "St. Andrew," a wrinkled man of the sea with flowing white locks, and perhaps the most beloved sculpture, a mermaid lying atop the jetties.

A gulf sunset illuminates the day's last cast.

Dive Shops

EMERALD COAST DIVER'S DEN
Panama City Marina on the water
Panama City   769-6621
On the east side at Tyndall Pkwy.
Parker   871-2876

Dive charters go out to many wreck sites in the bays. Emerald Coast Diver's Den also sells a full line of dive equipment. Air, rentals, service and instruction are offered.

PANAMA CITY DIVE CENTER
4823 Thomas Dr. on the curve
Panama City Beach   235-3390

Diving and snorkeling equipment is for sale or rent, plus they offer daily dive charters. Get your beginning instruction in one week sessions. Even if you're not certified, you can take a half-day diving excursion with a certified diving instructor just to see if you like it, or a snorkeling trip for which no particular skill is required (except maybe holding your breath!). For those who are already certified, PCDC offers daily dolphin excursions and four- and six-hour scuba trips.

HYDROSPACE DIVE SHOP
3605-A Thomas Dr. next to the
Treasure Ship   234-9463
6422 W. Hwy. 98 by the Hathaway Bridge,
Panama City Beach   234-3063
Toll free   (800) 874-3483

With a full range of diving and snorkeling equipment and services, Hydrospace is one of the Gulf Coast's largest dive operations. Especially for visitors, there's a half-day resort scuba course so you can experience what diving is like without having to go through certification. Daily snorkeling trips to the jetties are fun for everybody. Of course, the Hydrospace crew offers open water

---

Swimming Sense

BEFORE you hop into the surf, check the flag at the Lifeguard Station:
A BLUE flag means calm water. Swimming is generally safe.
A YELLOW flag means use caution when you swim. Some undertows and/or riptides may be present.
A RED flag means absolutely NO SWIMMING. Stay out of the water when you see this flag, which means strong undertows and riptides are present.

Please remember the rules for safe swimming:
ALWAYS swim with a buddy.
NEVER mix swimming and alcohol.
EVEN if waters are calm, DON'T assume you cannot encounter some danger. Be AWARE of your surroundings, keep your eye on the shore, and WATCH for changing weather conditions.

The best tip of all: USE COMMON SENSE!!

scuba classes and home study courses for those who want to experience the joy and excitement of diving.

CAPTAIN BLACK'S
Inside St. Andrews State Park
Panama City Beach 233-0504

This is a fairly new facility where divers and snorkelers can rent gear and take courses. The four-hour resort course is offered here, too, as well as more specialized courses for certification. Night dives are a specialty! Ask about Shell Island snorkel trips, too.

Charter Fishing/ Sightseeing Cruises

CAPT. ANDERSON'S PIER
5550 N. Lagoon Dr.
Panama City   234-3435, (800) 874-2415

The Anderson fleet may be the originators of the charter fishing craze, but don't hold us to that. What we *can* say about them is that they've been in business a very long time and have the charter boat business down to a science. Start with charters for deep sea fishing, offering three trips on six vessels, accommodating up to 68 passengers. If you're a seasoned angler, you might opt for the 15-hour trip, from 2 AM until 5 PM, for around $43.00 per person with an electric reel. There's a 10-hour trip (7 AM until 5 PM) for $32 (electric reel) or $25 (manual reel). Riders are $12.50 and kids younger than 12 who want to fish are $12.00. Half-day trips are $16.00 (7 AM until noon) with riders just $9.00. All boats are fully equipped (like with restrooms). They furnish equipment and bait, and you can buy beer and soda on board. Not all trips are available all year, so please call to inquire about a particular trip.

Next, spend a night out on the Capt. Anderson dinnerboat. It's a three-hour inland cruise on St. Andrew Bay while you enjoy the scenery, the sunset, your choice of five dinner entrees and a three-piece band for dancing. The triple-decker boat provides plenty of room to move around if you want to bring the kids, but it may also be your only opportunity for a little private romancing. Monday through Saturday cruises are from 7 until 10 PM; prices for one adult are $18.95 ($22.50 on Saturdays) and $16.95 for kids ($20.00 on Saturdays). All prices include taxes and tip. Reservations are recommended for this delightful cruise. Please call 234-5940.

Take a cruise to undeveloped Shell Island, where you'll disembark for a brief time to wade in the clear water and look for shell souvenirs. Aboard the boat, sailing at 9 AM and 1 PM, your captain narrates a bit of history and humor about the area, while you keep a sharp eye out for dolphins, seabirds and marine life. Sandwiches and snacks are all available on board. Adult tickets are $9.00; children 6 to 11 are $5.00; ages 2 to 5 are $4.00. A separate Dolphin Feeding Cruise, sailing daily from 5:15 to 6:30 PM, is $6.00 for adults and $4.00 for children.

BAY POINT'S ISLAND QUEEN
On the boardwalk at Marriott's
Bay Point Resort
100 Delwood Beach Rd.
Panama City Beach   234-3307 ext. 1816

Take a calm and scenic Missis-

PANAMA CITY BEACH — PARKS AND RECREATION

Rent a bike by the hour, the day or the week to explore Panama City Beach at a more leisurely pace.

sippi Riverboat ride out on St. Andrew Bay on this magnificent paddlewheeler. Shell Island Shuttles depart at 9 AM and 1 PM for a three-hour trip to this unique barrier island. Snacks, drinks and sandwiches are available to passengers, or you can bring your own picnic. Tickets are normally $10.00, $5.00 for kids 5 to 12 and $2.00 for 4 and younger. Pick up a Shell Island Cruise brochure for a 40% discount. A dinner cruise leaves the dock around 7:30 every evening for a Southern-style feast of Cajun seafood, fresh salads, pastas, cheeses and some kind of Old South dessert like plantation coconut pecan cake, strawberry bread pudding with whiskey sauce or pecan pie. Cocktails are available throughout the cruise, as is live entertainment topside. Cost is $24.95 per passenger, which is all-inclusive, except for cocktails. Tickets are available at Teddy Tuckers Gift Shop behind the Marriott.

DESTINY SAILING CHARTERS
8013 Thomas Dr.
Panama City Beach   234-5127

A sailboat cruise sounds so romantic, so intimate, so uncrowded. For sunset and moonlight cruises, it just doesn't get any better. The *Destiny* is a Morgan 41-foot Ketch, fully equipped with snorkel and fish gear. Bring your own food and drink. The sunset cruise, departing at 6 PM for two hours, provides wine, cheese and soft drinks for $12.00 a person. The two-hour moonlight cruise provides the same foodstuffs, but leaves at 8 PM; it's $12.00 a person also. Three-hour cruises leave at 9 AM and 1 PM every day for $20.00 a head.

Adventure Sailing Cruises
Treasure Island Marina, 3605 Thomas Dr. Panama City Beach   233-5499, 832-1454

Look at Slip #40 at the marina for *Glory Days*, a 51-foot ocean sailing yacht that will take you out into the gulf by the hour (there's a two-hour minimum), a half day, full day, weekend, week or more. Take an entire vacation aboard *Glory Days*, if you wish! The yacht is equipped with three private cabins, a 15-foot-wide main salon, seven feet of headroom, three TVs, a stereo and VCR, icemaker, freezer, fridge, two dinghies for exploring and a Coast Guard-licensed captain. Prices start at $20.00 per person plus tax for a two-hour cruise.

Parks

Bay Memorial Park
Garden Club Dr., Panama City

For those who like to keep in shape, this 13-acre nature park has a walking trail and 13 fitness stations.

Frank Nelson, Jr. Park
23rd St. and Mound Ave., Panama City

Eleven acres of park features a playground, a community building and three ball fields.

Truesdell Park
10th St. and Chestnut Ave., Panama City

Truesdell is a small park with a small playground, two tennis courts and a community building for square dancing and community activities.

Glenwood Recreation Center
14th Court and Palo Alto Ave., Panama City

The rec center has something for everybody with a playground area, basketball courts and a community building on 2½ acres.

Daffin Park
Everitt and Draft Avenues at 3rd St., Panama City

Ball fields, a playground, community building and tennis courts are just part of this 12-acre park.

Bob George Park
East Ave. and First Plaza, Panama City

One of the city's neighborhood parks, this one sports a playground area and picnic shelters.

McKenzie Park
Oak Ave. and Park St., Panama City

This shady and scenic nature park in the heart of downtown features a succession of outdoor concerts during tourist season.

Oakland Terrace Park
11th St. and Flower Ave., Panama City

One of the largest city parks, Oakland Terrace has ball fields, a playground area, six tennis courts, a picnic area and a community building.

Joe Moody Harris Park
2300 E. 8th Court, Panama City

One of the most popular city parks, Joe Moody features a community building, picnic shelters, a large playground area and a nature trail.

Hathaway Bridge Park
Collegiate Dr. and Hwy. 98, Panama City

The one-acre park near the bridge on the water has good fishing and natural areas. Gulf Coast Community College and the Panama City Branch of Florida State University are adjacent.

Rent yourself a sailboat or catamaran to tour Panama City Beach's many waterways.

HENTZ PARK
19th St. and Wilmont Ave., Panama City

Some parts of Hentz Park are left wild for your exploration; others provide playground equipment and picnic areas.

LAKE HUNTINGTON PARK
3504 W. 15th St., Panama City

This is a small park on three-quarters of an acre with a clubhouse fronting Lake Huntington.

FRANK G. BROWN PARK
On Back Beach Rd., ½-mile east of Hwy. 79, Panama City Beach

This extensive public beach park features a community center with an indoor gym, a picnic area and pavilion with grills and a fireplace, a softball complex, lighted tennis courts, a kid's playground and a fitness trail.

Panama City Beach Area
Arts and Culture

Panama City is gaining a reputation as an artist's community, thanks in part to the Bay Arts Alliance, the city's umbrella arts agency, which incorporates visual arts, music, dance, and theater groups. The Alliance is responsible for bringing in nationally known performing groups and arts events, opening up a world of experiences to locals without having to leave the area. Made up of more than 500 individual supporters, the Bay Arts Alliance serves to enhance the area's cultural upbringing by lending educational and financial support to talented area groups and individuals.

Literary

NORTHWEST REGIONAL LIBRARY SYSTEM
Headquarters, Bay County Public Library
25 W. Government St.
Panama City   872-7500

The network of community libraries in the Bay County area works to promote community needs and support through library materials and services. Other branches are on Panama City Beach (110 S. Arnold Road) and in Springfield (408 School Avenue).

THE PANHANDLE WRITERS' GUILD
P.O. Box 1691, 231 Harrison Ave.
Panama City   763-2022

This group provides instruction and development of the writing craft. They publish an annual literary magazine, *Pelican Tracks*, and offer workshops and lectures on literature and writing to the community. The Guild meets at the above address the second and fourth Tuesday of the month. Membership is $15.00 per year.

Music

BARBERSHOP HARMONY CHORUS
4630 Cato Rd.
Panama City   763-3200

Barbershop is one of the last vestiges of a cappella singing, and these gentlemen preserve it with a vengeance, performing anywhere they can and entering numerous competitions.

BAY ARTS STRING QUARTET
2508 Country Club Dr.
Lynn Haven   265-4937

The quartet, consisting of a violin, viola, cello and bass, performs at group functions, receptions and weddings.

PANAMA CITY BEACH — ARTS & CULTURE

Photo: Robin Rowan

Paul Brent, a local artist and interior designer, is responsible for restoration of the Martin Theatre into an art deco showplace.

BAY WIND BAND
1603 Maine Ave.
Lynn Haven   265-9028

This 50-piece community band plays at festivals, community events and as part of a performing arts series in the Panama City area. It is open to all comers, all ages, and performs between six and eight concerts every year, among them, a 4th of July concert at the Civic Arena, concerts at Tyndall Air Force Base and at the Automotive Extravaganza in McKenzie Park. The band rehearses at Mowat Middle School twice monthly on Thursdays.

HARMONY SHORES CHORUS OF SWEET ADELINES INTERNATIONAL
4035 Torino Way, Panama City   265-8402

This barbershop-type group exists solely to educate and entertain. The group performs publicly, and will even do private parties or sing greetings for birthdays and anniversaries.

PANAMA BRASS QUINTET
343 N. Star Ave., Panama City   871-1767

This rather loose-knit group, consisting of two band directors, one FSU student musician, one mathematician and one firefighter, mostly plays for its own gratification. Jazz, ragtime, Bach and wedding music (i.e. "Here Comes the Bride" and "There Goes the Bride") make up this group's repertoire.

PANAMA CITY YOUTH ORCHESTRA
329 Alexander Dr., Lynn Haven   265-3834
872-4570

Here's a chance for all budding violinists, violists, cellists and bass players to get some sound experience. Classes and lessons are also

• 293

offered through Community Education of Bay County Schools.

POLYTACTYL JAZZ COMBO
329 Alexander Dr., Lynn Haven   265-3834

The five piece combo performs traditional and contemporary jazz styles and pieces, plus some that haven't even been invented yet. They do parties and school programs, but particularly enjoy giving demonstrations on their various instruments and letting go during improvisational sessions.

Museums

JUNIOR MUSEUM OF BAY COUNTY
1731 Jenks Ave., Panama City   769-6128

The Junior Museum provides a terrific "hands-on" educational experience for youngsters. Kids and teens learn about the arts and sciences in creative and interactive exhibits, with guided tours available. It's especially great for ages 2 and up, but *all* ages can benefit. The museum is open 10 AM to 4:30 PM Monday through Friday; 10 AM to 4 PM on Saturday. A $1.00 donation is requested.

THE MUSEUM OF MAN IN THE SEA
17314 Back Beach Rd.
Panama City Beach   235-4101

Historical exhibits, artwork, photography and graphics tell the story of how people have lived, played and worked underwater for more than 5,000 years. The extensive collection of old diving equipment and an explanation of how it was used is really fascinating, even to the layperson. The museum is open 9 to 5 daily. Admission charge is $4.00 for adults; $2.00 for children 6 to 16; younger than 6 free.

Theater

KALEIDOSCOPE THEATRE
207 E. 24th St.
Lynn Haven   265-3226, 769-2653

The theater, offering live stage drama, comedy and music, has been around now for more than two decades. Audiences are larger than ever with a succession of sure hits such as *The Sound of Music* and Neil Simon plays. Each December, *A Christmas Carol* is performed at the Martin Theatre on Harrison Avenue.

MARTIN THEATRE
409 Harrison Ave.   763-8080
Panama City   763-8900

Recently renovated by local artist/designer Paul Brent, the 1935 Martin Theatre started life as the Ritz movie house, spent some time as the Martin Theatre in the 1950s, closed down during the '70s, then opened in the '80s as an indoor target range! Finally, in 1990, the Martin Theatre, restored to its original Art Deco glory, opened for live performances, children's shows, one-person traveling shows, concerts and Broadway plays.

Productions are staged by several local groups, including the School of Performing Arts, the Bay High School Drama Department, Mosley High School, and the Kaleidoscope Theatre. Season ticket holders will be treated by touring companies to shows such as *Stephen King's Ghost Stories*, *Conversations with Joan Crawford*, and *My Fair Lady's Men: A Visit with Lerner & Loewe*. The Green-room, a separate annex for meetings and receptions, has recently been completed with art deco furnishings, lots of plants and a wall mural by local artist Charles Wilson. Tickets are available only at the Martin Theatre box office, open Monday through Friday from 9 to 4. Season tickets are $60.00 and should be purchased in September. Write to the address above to be put on the Martin Theatre's monthly newsletter mailing list.

Visual Arts

GALLERY IN GADSDEN
14 E. Washington St., Quincy   875-ARTS

This gallery is an artists' cooperative of between 13 and 17 members featuring rotating displays of their own fine art as well as visual arts and crafts by other artists. Pottery, ceramics, watercolor, oils and works in other media can be purchased from the artists. The gallery is free and is open Wednesday 10 to 2, Thursday 10 to 5, Friday and Saturday 10 to 6, and Sunday 1 to 4.

VISUAL ARTS CENTER OF NORTHWEST FLORIDA
19 E. Fourth St., Panama City   769-4451

Like the Pensacola Museum of Art, the Visual Arts Center also occupies the old City Hall and Jail. (Could it be a trend?) The Arts Center promotes local artists at the gallery as well as in the new arts "district" downtown, and gets involved with the Gallery Night exhibition, a "tour" of downtown art shops and galleries held three times yearly (see below). Admission is free to both the Arts Center and the gallery tour. Gallery hours are 9 to 4 Tuesday through Saturday, Thursdays 9 to 8, and Sundays 1 to 4.

PANAMA CITY DOWNTOWN ARTS DISTRICT
Downtown Panama City   769-4451

The district is a cooperative effort between the city and several downtown galleries to breathe new life into support for the arts. If you're a return visitor, you may have noticed some changes downtown — renovation of the Martin Theatre, awnings, tree plantings, carriage lamps, free concerts in McKenzie Park. The atmosphere is conducive to strolling, browsing and, hopefully, buying. Each of the galleries sports a bright magenta flag:

The Visual Arts Center of Northwest Florida at 19 E. Fourth Street;

State of the Art Gallery at 537 Harrison Avenue;

Under Glass Framery at 28 W. Beach Drive;

Chip Lloyd's Photography at 28 W. Beach Drive;

Bayou Gallery, 125 E. Beach Drive;

Lyn's Fine Arts Gallery, 214 Harrison Avenue;

The Academy on Grace, 714 Grace Avenue;

the Paul Brent Design Studio and Gallery at 413 W. 5th Street; and;

the Bay Arts Alliance/Marina Civic Center at 8 Harrison Avenue.

In March, July and November each year, these galleries team up for a gallery "tour," where they showcase their own gallery work and put on special exhibits and demonstrations for guests. Call the number above or the Bay Arts Alliance (769-1217) for information.

Panama City Beach Area Higher Education

What could be more idyllic than going to school in one of the top beach resort areas in the country? It's a tempting prospect, with all of the area amenities at your disposal, and equally tempting when you look a little closer to the meat-and-potatoes of higher education. Schools here rank consistently well in academic excellence, turning out well-rounded students ready to face the tough job market with high hopes and impressive educational credentials.

GULF COAST COMMUNITY COLLEGE
5230 W. U.S. Hwy. 98
Panama City   769-1551

More than 8,000 students are enrolled in this small and specialized community college, ranked among the top 10 in Florida. Choose from 82 Associate degrees in the Arts and Sciences and five certificate programs. A good community college serves the needs of its residents well, and in that respect, GCCC gets high marks. The school offers traditional and nontraditional courses, flexible class hours and special courses for businesspeople needing a refresher in an aspect of sales, marketing or some other facet of business; students returning to the workplace after a long hiatus; residents desiring a handle on new technology; or seniors wanting to

Palms blend with live oaks and magnolias to create this Southern scene along St. Andrew Bay.

increase their personal or professional goals.

For students wishing to receive four-year or graduate degrees, Florida State University's Panama City Campus is adjacent to GCCC. The campus's location on North Bay makes it a startlingly scenic environment for recreation, meditation and learning.

FLORIDA STATE UNIVERSITY
Panama City Campus
4750 Collegiate Dr.
Panama City 872-4750

This offshoot of Florida State's main campus in Tallahassee was created in 1982 to provide opportunities for upper division (that is, juniors and seniors) undergraduate and graduate study. In other words, you need at least an Associate degree or enough credits from another college or university to transfer to FSU.

What makes the Panama City campus unique is its small classes and individualized instruction, a situation more difficult to obtain at the main campus in Tallahassee with more than 28,000 students.

Bachelor's programs are available in business, communications, criminology, elementary education, nursing, psychology, social science and social work. Master's programs, beginning in August of 1994, include an M.S. in business management, five different advanced education degrees, electrical or mechanical engineering, nursing and applied psychology.

FSU's 40-acre wooded campus on North Bay, surrounded by cultural and recreational offerings, provides the best of the main campus's educational opportunities but with a small-town flavor. Students here seem to like the fact that instructors know who they are and can dedicate themselves to their professional goals while enjoying all the finer offerings of this beautiful area.

Panama City Beach Area
Real Estate

In town or on the beach, single-family housing and investment property is affordable and selling fast! Who wouldn't want a piece of this beautiful beach to call her own? Literally thousands of cottages, condos, townhomes and timeshare properties stretch out along the beaches like a strand of glittering beads. Everything from studio apartments to grand four- or five-bedroom beach homes beckon vacationers to invest in Panama City Beach's little slice of heaven.

There's no shortage of waterfront property even in the city. Older homes lining Beach Drive are packed with history and character, and are unmatched for sunset viewing. Bunker's Cove Road lines the bay with the most fantastic assortment of private homes and gated estates anywhere in the area. Both are packed with mature and shady live oaks and palms, and a short distance from Panama City's charming small-town downtown.

Photo: Robin Rowan

Old estate homes rub elbows with newer residences along St. Andrew Bay.

Resort/Residential Communities

Panama City Beach

THE GLADES AT HOMBRE GOLF CLUB
120 Coyote Pass   235-6752
Panama City Beach   (800) 327-8686

This residential development built up around the golf course is close enough to the beaches to be a perfect spot for a vacation home, but private and secluded enough to live here all year long. Patio homes are currently available, or choose a homesite and build your own custom-designed single family home along the fairways, near a green or with a water view. And remember, one of the area's best courses is just a few steps from your back door.

PORTSIDE RESORT
17620 Front Beach Rd.   234-6696
Panama City Beach   (800) 277-1773

Packed with amenities, Portside is just the ticket for family vacationers who want their own getaway or couples ready to enjoy resort living. Each spacious townhome has two bedrooms and 1½ baths, balconies or patios, and offers parking right at your door. Enjoy two free-form pools on site and one more convenient to the property. Three tennis courts, shuffleboard courts, a poolside clubhouse and a heated spa surrounded by a Polynesian-style palapa hut and cascading waterfall are just part of the Portside package.

EDGEWATER BEACH RESORT
11212 Front Beach Rd.   235-6752
Panama City Beach   (800) 327-8686

Edgewater could be the Big Kahuna of the beach . . . it's 110 acres of lush grounds, stunning views and some of the prettiest condominiums you've ever had the pleasure to lay eyes on. A nine-hole, par 3 golf course is situated around 12 lakes, small islands and unusual layouts. Twelve two-tone, all-weather Plexicushion tennis courts are lit for night play, and to improve your game, there's a staff of resident pros offering programs, lessons and clinics all year long. At the golf and tennis pro shop are 20 shuffleboard courts, where residents and guests gear up for matches almost every day. The lagoon pool is Edgewater's masterpiece, set in the center of the property facing the gulf. Its 11,500 square feet incorporate exotic blooming plants and trees, a tropical island with a palapa hut, waterfalls and giant rocks. One-, two- or three-bedroom condos, penthouses and golf or tennis villas offer plenty of choices and great views. It's all surrounded by a privacy wall with white stucco columns and hundreds of lights. Three gatehouses provide for easy access and security.

LANDMARK HOLIDAY BEACH RESORT
17501 Front Beach Rd.   233-1500
Panama City Beach   (800) 456-0009

Another impressive beachfront condo, Landmark is accessible to the best of the beach while offering owners the chance to enjoy it all whenever they choose. One-, two- and three-bedroom condos provide gulf views, washers and dryers, fully

• 299

equipped kitchens, color cable TV with HBO and air conditioning, which in Florida is as much of an understatement as saying this condo comes with walls. For residents and guests, tennis courts, an indoor heated pool, a spa and sauna, a clubhouse and a barbecue grill area are right on the grounds. Golf privileges are a short drive away.

Sugar Beach Condominiums
8727 Thomas Dr.   *234-2102*
Panama City Beach   *(800) 457-8427*

These one-, two-, three- and *four-*bedroom low-rise units make Sugar Beach seem more like its own little neighborhood on the beach. Besides your own private 450 feet of "sugar beach," the condos have a gulfside pool, two lighted tennis courts, a clubhouse, game room and a private lake. If you tend to shy away from the cookie-cutter condos on the gulf-front, Sugar Beach may be a good solution for families.

Dunes of Panama
7205 Thomas Dr.
Panama City Beach   *234-8839*

It's all right here, and right on the beach: three gulfside pools, two lighted tennis courts, 1,500 feet of beachfront, two volleyball nets (exclusively for use by Dunes of Panama residents and guests), a game room and a deli and grocery store! Student groups are not permitted to stay at the Dunes of Panama, so if you're looking for a little tranquility or a nice family escape, the Dunes is a good choice. Units have either two bedrooms and two full baths or three bedrooms and two baths and are all individually furnished.

Watercrest
6201 Thomas Dr.   *234-7668*
Panama City Beach   *(800) 768-4528*

One of those fabulous high-rises right on the gulf, Watercrest is also on the high side price-wise but has some nice features to make life here infinitely more livable. All residents and guests have a spacious clubhouse, indoor racquetball, separate exercise facilities for women and men (is that considered a plus?) and steam rooms available to them, as well as two large atriums, large open rooms and five floor plans.

Harbour Towne
Wildwood Dr., one mile north of
Back Beach Rd.   *233-2321*
Panama City Beach   *(800) 762-3585*

Look for Harbour Towne, a new residential community just behind the new Kmart, for plenty of neighborhood extras. Residents may take advantage of two pools, a covered picnic/barbecue area and tennis courts. Nearby are shopping centers and a private marina. Choose from two- or three-bedroom floor plans with many custom features.

Pinnacle Port
23223 Front Beach Rd.
Panama City Beach   *234-2827*

Pinnacle Port is your first taste of Panama City Beach entering Bay County from the west. It's huge (23 acres), but the advantage here is that you've got water views on both sides, the gulf on one and Phillips Inlet on the other. At night, the lights at Pinnacle Port reflected in the Inlet are a picture postcard. One-, two- and three-bedroom units start as low as $69,500, and that's

Fast and flashy, the Panama City Beach strip will lure you back again and again.

totally furnished! On the property are two heated pools (one is indoors), four tennis courts, saunas, a game room, a playground, a private dock and boat ramp, a Tiki Bar and 24-hour security.

PEACHTREE PLACE
17680 Front Beach Rd.   233-7466
Panama City Beach   (800) 719-2689

If you love the architecture of Old Key West but don't want to live on such a remote (and tourist-laden) island, then come to Peachtree Place. Wrapped porches, a tin roof and pastel colors are reminiscent of the Conch style. Being right across from the gulf, you can enjoy resort living at a fraction of the gulf-front cost — prices start in the low $50s for a one-bedroom unit. There's a private pool on the property and, of course, beach access.

THE PRESERVE
3111 Delwood Beach Rd.
Panama City Beach   234-7111

Better hurry if you want to get in on some prime waterfront property! This gorgeous new development is still in its infancy, located right on St. Andrew Bay across from the Bay Point Resort entrance. That means that you'll not only be just minutes from the State Park, but that your home will sit in the midst of a lush wilderness. The Preserve strives to promote restrictive, earth-friendly development, blending with the natural landscape and preserving trees and natural beauty. Wake up to some of the beach's best views while having the advantage of shade and protection from storm winds that batter the beachfront.

PANAMA CITY BEACH — REAL ESTATE

Panama City

PINE TREE PLACE
17th St. and Everitt Ave.
Panama City   769-5555, 234-2426
Not far from the downtown hub, Pine Tree Place is a good neighborhood for young families. Homes and lots are priced affordably, all have garages, large lots and underground utilities. Choose from two- or three-bedroom plans.

Real Estate Companies

CENTURY 21 BEACH REALTY, INC.
11 Miracle Strip Loop   234-9865
Panama City Beach   (800) 225-4868
Two offices on the beach serve your needs for single-family homes and condos, plus long-term and vacation rentals. The East End office on Middle Beach Road can be reached at the above number. The West End office on Back Beach Road can be reached at 234-8444 or (800) 851-5321. A free relocation package plus a beaches and county map are waiting for you.

RESORT WORLD REALTY
6104 Thomas Dr.
Panama City   234-1418, (800) 752-7111
Does a cozy cabin with a fireplace sound good to you? Or a 10th-floor penthouse suite with a Jacuzzi and panoramic view? There's a vacation rental for every taste and budget in beach homes, townhouses, condos or something off the beach.

SAND DOLLAR
Surf 'n Sand Properties, Inc.
9722 S. Thomas Dr.
Panama City Beach   235-2205
Besides resort property management, Surf 'n Sand offers real estate sales at several of the beach's best condos: the Summit, Regency Towers, Sunbird, Sun Swept, Top of the Gulf, Edgewater and many others. All properties are gulfside with pools, dishwashers, icemakers and fully equipped kitchens. From there, the choice is up to you as to location, high- or low-rise, or any number of other amenities. Sand Dollar can also help with single-family homes, mobile homes or lots anywhere in the Bay County area.

SUNSPOT REALTY
16428 Front Beach Rd.   234-7151
Panama City Beach   (800) 423-8367
It's the beach, the beach, the beach, that people hunger for, so if you're looking for the best of the beach, these are the people to call. They deal ONLY in beach property, mostly gulf-front, which includes condos, single-family homes and villas.

ST. ANDREW BAY REAL ESTATE, INC.
111 W. 23rd St., Panama City   769-1484
2112 S. Hwy. 77, Panama City   265-3099
702 S. Tyndall Pkwy., Panama City   769-8971
726 Thomas Dr., Panama City Beach   234-6696
With its four locations in town and on the beach, you can imagine that they've got listings all over Bay County, which of course they do. St. Andrew Bay Real Estate specializes in single-family homes throughout the area and provides relocation assistance as well. Call them 24 hours a day.

Panama City Area
Retirement

It won't be too many years before the hundreds of thousands of family vacationers, honeymoon couples and empty nesters who have enjoyed Panama City Beach for decades start thinking about their own retirement. And why wouldn't they think about retiring in one of their favorite places on earth? Retirement communities bring people together from all over the United States to enjoy meals and activities, to make lasting friendships and maybe, too, to reminisce about *their* best vacation on Panama City Beach.

MARY ELLA VILLA RETIREMENT CENTER
526 N. Mary Ella Ave.
Callaway   871-1611

This facility began its life as a private, single-family home, albeit a rather large and fancy one. Eighteen bedrooms were added to the back of the house, and Mary Ella Villas began serving the ever-growing population of local retirees. Both private and semiprivate rooms are available (with shared baths), and all residents receive three full meals each day. Transportation for shopping and outside activities is part of the monthly fee, as is laundry service and supervision of medications. But one of the stand-out features of the newly remodeled facility is the private zoo out back. Right. A private zoo — with a llama, peacocks, turkeys, Shetland ponies, foxes, turkeys, deer and who knows what. It is actually a home for injured wildlife, but has collected an assortment of other exotic creatures over the years. The residents love it.

COVE MANOR RETIREMENT CENTER
521 E. Beach Dr.
Panama City   763-3655, 784-1203

Waterfront retirement living could be just a dream unless you're a resident of Cove Manor. Besides being just five blocks away from the Civic Center, McKenzie Park and the downtown area, you've got your own private view of St. Andrew Bay. Spacious units provide complete comfort in a cozy and relaxed setting. Residents enjoy delicious meals with each other, learn painting or pick up a new hobby with the many class offerings every month, or simply enjoy a quiet stroll along the waterfront or a chat with friends while soaking up some of that warm Florida sunshine. Cove Manor respects your privacy, but is always available to offer assistance any time you need it.

Who needs a boat? Just tossing a line into the surf yields some fine catches.

THE RETIREMENT CENTER OF PANAMA CITY
1313 E. 11th St.
Panama City   785-1651

The Retirement Center provides a more structured climate for those who may need a higher level of care. Staff members are always available to assist or supervise residents with medications, grooming or whatever need may arise. Three balanced meals are served daily. Residents may choose from a spacious private room with its own bath, or semiprivate lodging. Apart from strolling the landscaped and fenced grounds, visiting with friends or gathering in the living room to watch television, residents may visit the on-site library, play the piano or shoot a game of pool, or participate in one of the many regularly scheduled activities such as singing groups or Bible study. The Retirement Center offers a free two-day get-acquainted weekend for you and one guest. Call for reservations.

SUMMER'S LANDING
615 Florida Ave.
Lynn Haven   265-9829

This is a friendly retirement community where people *check* on you, but don't *check up* on you. And there's a big difference in those terms. As a resident of Summer's Landing, you're free to come and go as you please, entertain when you like, travel when you like, just as if you lived in your own private home. Because for the most part, that's what's most closely associated with living at Summer's Landing. But unlike living in a private home, you have friends and staff people who care about you. You're encouraged to participate in the full schedule of recreational activities offered every month. You may be invited to dine with neighbors or sit in on a friendly game of poker. The joy of living at Summer's Landing comes with the peace of mind of a secure environment, maintenance-free landscaping around your one-story unit, and the convenience of living near Panama City and its numerous recreational and cultural offerings.

Senior Support Services

BAY COUNTY COUNCIL ON AGING
1116 Frankford Ave.
Panama City   769-3468

The Council on Aging provides myriad services for both elderly and low-income residents of Bay County. In-home services offer Homemaking (assistance with housekeeping), Personal Care (assistance with hygiene, bathing and dressing) and Respite Care (to relieve the caregiver). Meals on Wheels, transportation to medical appointments, socialization, fellowship and Weatherization (weatherizing a resident's home) are other services provided by the Council.

LIFE MANAGEMENT CENTER OF NORTHWEST FLORIDA, INC.
525 E. 15th St., Panama City   769-9481

The Center provides Senior Adult Specialization in a variety of areas including counseling, mental health services and employee assistance. They also provide 24-hour emergency service.

Panama City Beach Area Health Care

The Bay County community of more than 150,000 year-round residents is well cared for through two excellent hospitals, more than 225 physicians, outpatient clinics and a variety of top-quality counseling centers. Older residents can feel secure in the knowledge that home health care can keep them in their own homes longer. Visitors to the area even have their own center for urgent medical needs.

Hospitals/Medical Centers

BAY MEDICAL CENTER
615 N. Bonita Ave.
Panama City   769-1511

Bay offers services and procedures you might have thought you had to go to a larger city to get, such as heart surgery, cancer treatment, kidney dialysis and lithotripsy. The hospital has its own Sleep Lab for patients with sleeping disorders, home health care nurses for post-surgery or longer-term care, radiation oncology, hospice care and a dedicated pediatric unit. The hospital has been accredited by the Joint Commission on Accreditation of Healthcare Organizations. The center is located 1.6 miles south of Panama City Mall on Highway 77.

HCA GULF COAST HOSPITAL
449 W. 23rd St.
Panama City   769-8341

Although it's smaller than Bay Medical Center, this 176-bed facility thrives on its commitment to patient care through wellness programs, a physician referral service and special services like outpatient surgery and cardiac catheterization.

The Wellness Center (785-8855) provides programs and services to keep you and your family in good health, such as stop smoking programs, parenting classes and cooking up heart-healthy meals.

Support Services

AMERICAN HOMEPATIENT
412 W. 15th St.
Panama City   769-7631, (800) 637-5103

Sales, service and rentals of all home-based medical equipment and supplies such as wheelchairs, home oxygen, hospital beds and rehab equipment are offered through American. An on-staff RN provides in-home IV therapy. Open Monday through Friday 8 to 5; the phone is answered 24 hours a day. They will bill Medicare and private insurance companies direct.

West Florida Home Health Care
2195 Jenks Ave.
Panama City 769-5688

This organization offers free delivery for in-home medical equipment and supplies, including 24-hour service for oxygen. They bill Medicare, Medicaid and other insurance plans direct. Open Monday through Friday 8 to 5; Saturday 9 to 1; they're located just south of 23rd Street.

Beach-Bay Health Star, Inc.
Off Middle Beach Rd. at
Two Miracle Strip Loop, Ste. 1
Panama City Beach 233-5432

Beach-Bay provides nursing services for in-hospital, private home and nursing home patients who are under the care of a physician. Professional nurses provide restorative nursing care, diabetic teaching, pediatric care, private duty nursing, terminal care and more.

Seawind Medical Clinic
4121 W. Hwy. 98
Panama City 872-9701

Seawind is known as the visitors' and travelers' clinic, but many locals have used its services for urgent medical needs as well. Now if you've run out of your prescription medicine, have a painful case of sunburn with fever, an itchy skin rash or some other malady, the hospitals' overcrowded emergency rooms are no longer your only alternative. Seawind takes patients with or without appointments and accepts most insurance and major credit cards. Open seven days from 9 AM to 9 PM Monday through Saturday and 10 to 6 on Sundays. They're conveniently located just 1½ miles east of the Hathaway Bridge.

Substance Abuse/ Psychiatric Counseling/ Mental Health Services

Rivendell
1940 Harrison Ave.
Panama City 763-0017, (800) 543-2919

Programs are set up for both young people and adults such as residential treatment, acute inpatient services, eating disorders, school or behavior problems and sexual trauma. Marital and family counseling is also provided. Call Rivendell to schedule a free assessment; referrals are taken 24 hours a day, seven days a week. Champus and most major insurances are accepted.

Twelve Oaks
2068 Healthcare Ave.
Navarre 763-6340, (800) 622-1255

Twelve Oaks Alcohol and Drug Recovery Center is located in Navarre, about 80 miles from Panama City, although the center provides a local phone number. Programs are designed for both adults and teens, with both inpatient and outpatient programs and adult partial hospitalization. Free confidential consultations are offered by appointment. A crisis line is staffed 24 hours a day.

Panama City Counseling Center
400 W. 11th St.
Panama City 785-1979

Four area professionals provide marriage and family therapy, mental health counseling, psychiatry, alcohol and drug therapy, and divorce mediation. Champus and other medical insurances are accepted.

LIFE MANAGEMENT CENTER OF NORTHWEST FLORIDA INC.
525 E. 15th St.
Panama City   769-9481
The Life Management Center offers comprehensive, professional counseling to get you, your family or a loved one back on track. The staff of psychiatrists, psychologists, counselors, nurses and social workers can offer the best options for your particular situation. A special emergency service hotline is staffed 24-hours a day (769-9481).

BAY VIEW CENTER
629 E. Business Hwy. 98
Panama City   784-1230
A complete mental health center, Bay View provides five specialists on staff to assist with learning disabilities, behavioral problems, marriage, family, child and teen counseling, anxiety and depression disorders, and a number of others. Evening and weekend appointments are available; Champus and most major insurances are accepted.

Panama City Beach Area
Military

To the casual visitor, it may seem that the military keeps a low profile in Panama City. Residents know that's just not the case. Tyndall Air Force Base might not have a museum, but there are several units and squadrons assigned there. Just look to the skies, where you can see and hear pilots going about their business.

And while the Coastal Systems Station doesn't allow visitors at all, everyone who lives in Panama City knows that's because of the highly-classified work conducted there.

The impact of these facilities on the local economy, however, is something everyone notices. Current estimates gauge that impact at over half a billion dollars, a figure that's hard to ignore.

TYNDALL AIR FORCE BASE

Tyndall Field, named after World War I aviator Lt. Francis B. Tyndall, was established by the Army just in time for American's entry into World War II. In fact, the first troops arrived at the newly completed Army facility on December 7, 1941, the day the Japanese attacked Pearl Harbor. Thousands of men were trained here as gunners, including actor Clark Gable.

After World War II, the Air Force became a separate branch of the armed forces and the field's name was changed to Tyndall Air Force Base. It sits about 12 miles southeast of Panama City and currently occupies nearly 30,000 acres in Bay County. The base has an estimated economic impact of over $280 million, employing over 5,000 military personnel and nearly 2,000 civilians. Over 7,000 military retirees from all branches are also served by the base facilities.

Some of the units assigned here include the 325th Fighter Wing, whose history dates back to World War II, as well as the 325th Operation Group, the 325th Logistics Group and the 325th Support Group. Other units assigned to Tyndall Air Force Base include the 1st Air Force Headquarters, the Southeast Air Defense Sector, the North American Aerospace Defense Command System Support Facility, Detachment 1 of the 148th Fighter Group, the 475th Weapons Evaluation Group, the 84th Test Squadron and the 3625th Technical Training Squadron. Needless to say, these units and many others keep the skies around the base fairly busy.

Unlike Ft. Walton Beach's Eglin Air Force Base, Tyndall Air Force Base doesn't have a museum for the public to inspect. But there are several planes and jets parked along Highway 231 as you approach the base, and many drivers pull over to snap pictures and inspect the aircraft. There are tours of Tyndall Air Force Base that are open to the public, and you can call 283-2983 for more information.

Coastal Systems Station

The Coastal Systems Station was established during World War II after the U.S. Navy field station in Solomons, Maryland, outgrew its Chesapeake Bay location. This field station was instrumental in mine and undersea countermeasure development, and Panama City's easy access to the Gulf of Mexico made it the most appealing candidate host for this station.

By the mid-1950s, the station's research and training mission had grown to include such naval weaponry as torpedo countermeasures, helicopter mine countermeasures and mine-hunting.

The station's mission and name have changed over the years, and currently the Coastal Systems Station conducts key research and training in fields such as surface and airborne mine countermeasures, Marine Corps systems development and support, naval special warfare, amphibious warfare and diving and salvage operations. These operations are carried out at the station's various facilities and state-of-the-art laboratories. Over 1,000 divers train here each year, and the station can confidently claim responsibility for much of the naval technology currently in the field.

The Coastal Systems Station employs over 3,000 people, and fiscal year 1992 figures show that figure is split almost evenly among civilian and military personnel. The total economic impact of the station is estimated at over $320 million.

Because most of the research and training conducted at the Coastal Systems Station is highly classified, no public tours are available. However, group tours for organizations closely related to the station's mission are granted. To see if your group or organization qualifies for such a tour, contact the station's public affairs office at 234-4803.

Inside Florida's Forgotten Coast

Look at any map of Northwest Florida and you'll see that the Gulf Coast would make an almost perfect arc from Pensacola to the peninsula — if it weren't for that great mass of land just east of Panama City Beach that juts out into the water. On the map, it looks like the crook of an elbow, as if the panhandle is just sitting back and trying to relax.

And when you look at what sits down there just east of Panama City Beach, you realize that this area — Florida's Forgotten Coast, as locals refer to it — is truly a hidden treasure, one that not many tourists know about. One recent incident illustrates this perfectly: When a major metropolitan Southeastern newspaper (we won't name names) did a supposedly "comprehensive" travel story on Northwest Florida, they skipped over this area *entirely*. Not a mention, not even a rumor that something wonderful existed down in these parts. Needless to say, the residents here were not amused. And as for any visitor unfortunate enough to use that newspaper article as a travel guide — well, we sincerely hope they had a nice trip, anyway.

It's time to let the rest of the world in on a little secret: The coastal area from Mexico Beach down to Apalachicola and on up to Carrabelle is unlike anywhere else in Florida. The history of the state is not found on the peninsula, which wasn't developed until the turn of the century. The history of Florida is here in the northwest, and you've got tons of it packed into this little stretch.

You've also got some of the most beautiful coastline in the nation. Florida's Forgotten Coast sports miles and miles of unspoiled, pristine landscape, much of it preserved so carefully it looks exactly as it must have hundreds of years ago.

The people here love to share their little secret. Friendly and personable, they've been waiting years for people to discover this special part of Florida. They've even tried calling it a number of catchy names over the years, none of which have really stuck.

No matter what you call it, it's a heavenly place to be. Take our word for it — go see for yourself.

Mexico Beach

You won't hear much Spanish spoken here, but you might feel like you're in another country because of the strangely calm waters that rest like a comfy blue shroud just off the fine beaches. Mexico Beach is fronted by a peninsula that extends

FLORIDA'S FORGOTTEN COAST

The Miss Dorothy is one of many shrimp boats that ply the waters off Florida's Forgotten Coast.

like a curled finger off Cape San Blas, and this natural barrier keeps the Gulf waters quiet and steady. There's practically no undertow here at all, and that's one reason why it's such a popular family beach. The other reason is the beautiful white sand, another facet that might make you think of Mexico.

It's strange to think that less than 20 years ago, Mexico Beach didn't see a lot of action — people usually passed through it on their way to somewhere else. Now that Florida's northwest Gulf Coast has become more developed, not so many people are taking its relatively unspoiled beauty for granted anymore.

The beach offers accommodations such as waterfront rentals and campgrounds, and if you need help finding a place just contact **Gulfaire Realty of Bay County, Inc.** (820 Highway 98, 800-872-2782), or **Fantasy Properties, Inc.** (Highway 98 and 12th Street, 800-458-7478). Other places to stay include the **Surfside Inn** (Highway 98 and 39th Street, 648-5771) and the **El Governor Motel and Campground** (Highway 98, 648-5432).

If you're looking to sample some of the local seafood, consider heading to **Toucan's** (812 Highway 98), whose menu also offers great alternate fare for landlubbers. And when you've had your fill, be sure to poke your head upstairs at the great second-floor gift shop.

Wander out on the city-owned fishing pier, stroll through Canal Park or just rent a boat — you'll discover why so many people who live here are peaceful and easygoing. It's quite contagious.

Mexico Beach is a few miles west of Port St. Joe on Highway 98. Contact the **Mexico Beach Chamber of Commerce** (800-239-9553) for more information.

Port St. Joe

This is a very small town, and when you know its history you'll understand why. Though at one time, Port St. Joe — known initially as St. Joseph — was the site of Florida's first Constitutional Convention, and at one point in the early 1800s it was the sixth largest city in the state. The reason? You guessed it: its proximity to the Gulf of Mexico. The 1835 construction of a railroad here allowed cotton from Georgia and Alabama to be easily shipped through here to Apalachicola.

No one expected St. Joseph to disappear completely, but that's exactly what happened when this growing boom town was shattered early on by the one-two punch of first a powerful hurricane and then a deadly yellow fever epidemic.

All that was a long time ago, and the town's recovery has been slow and steady. Port St. Joe is now a deep-water port, but its shallow bay waters produce some of the best scallops in the Gulf. They thrive here so well that, during certain summer months, visitors can wander out into the bay and harvest their own scallops.

As with most places along the coast, charter fishing boats are widespread and recommended. If you don't want to catch your own dinner, let others do it for you and

Come See Florida's Best Beach!

CAPE SAN BLAS • INDIAN PASS
ST. JOE BEACH
MEXICO BEACH • PORT ST. JOE

SALES • BEACH RENTALS

Tom Todd Realty, Inc.
HC 1 Box 150, Port St. Joe, FL 32456
904-227-1501
800-876-2611

---

cook it up right. **J. Patrick's Restaurant** (412 Reid Avenue, 227-7400) is a popular local spot, as is the **Sand Dollar Restaurant** (222 Reid Avenue, 229-8900). If you're looking for a place to sleep after you eat your fill, the **Motel St. Joe & Restaurants** (501 Monument Avenue, 229-8512) can take care of you on both counts.

Ever wonder what it's like to scuba dive? If you've never done it before, the beautiful waters off Port St. Joe might entice you. Two of the most popular and compelling underwater sights are a sunken lighthouse and a World War II-era British tanker. **Captain Black's Marine Boat Rentals and Dive Shop** (Highway 98, 229-6330) can outfit you and help you plan a charter expedition.

Stop and see the **Constitution Convention State Museum** (see the Parks and Recreation section at the end of this chapter) to get an idea of what this town once was—and might have been. Then you can really appreciate just how special it is right now. We don't know about you, but despite Port St. Joe's turbulent and tragic past, we wouldn't change a thing about it.

Port St. Joe is located on Highway 98 between Mexico Beach and Apalachicola, just across the bay from Cape San Blas. For more information, contact the **Port St. Joe Chamber of Commerce** at 227-1223.

Insiders' Tips

Incredible sunsets are viewed from Cape San Blas, which *mostly* faces due west.

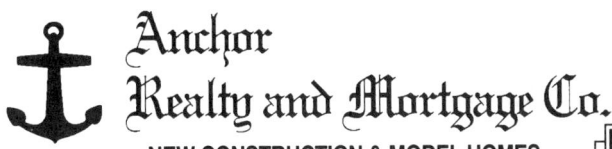

Anchor Realty and Mortgage Co.

NEW CONSTRUCTION & MODEL HOMES
Sales: A sales team of qualified professionals.
Beach Rentals: Over 200 of the best vacation rentals to choose from.

CAPE SAN BLAS:

PRIVATE BEACHFRONT & BAYFRONT ESTATES
"BARRIER DUNES" TOWNHOMES
(Pool, Tennis, Beach Club, Exercise Room)
"SEA CLIFFS" TOWNHOMES
(Pool, Beach Club)

LOCAL	**(904) 229-2777**
Housekeeping/Emergency 24 Hour	(904) 227-5555
Facsimile (FAX)	(904) 229-6556
TOLL FREE RENTALS & SALES	**(800) 624-3964**

(At Barrier Dunes Security Gate By State Park)
SR 1 Box 223, Port St. Joe, Florida 32456

Cape San Blas

We've got some of the best beaches in the nation along the coast of Northwest Florida, and most people agree that Cape San Blas is as good a place as any to enjoy sugar-white sand and sparkling blue water. Here you can enjoy sunbathing, swimming, shelling, snorkeling and one other important word that starts with the letter 's' — solitude.

There's plenty of beach for everyone, nearly 20 miles' worth. This beach, along with St. George Island to the east, has been ranked as one of the nation's best beaches for many years in a row. That's no surprise at all to residents of Northwest Florida.

There are two parks on the cape, St. Joseph Peninsula State Park (see the Parks and Recreation section in this chapter for more information) and Salinas Park, a new public park that features elevated boardwalks, picnic areas and a gazebo that lets you enjoy the coastal scenery.

You can also visit the site of the **Old Confederate Salt Works** — this facility was once a major saltworks plant until 1862 when it was destroyed by Union troops during the Civil War. And don't forget to check out the fascinating **San Blas Lighthouse** at the Coast Guard Station; this is one structure with a lot of history behind it. If you don't mind the 90-foot climb to the top, you can

---

COLDWELL BANKER

COLDWELL BANKER SUMMER PROPERTIES

REALTOR®

Serving Cape San Blas, Port St. Joe, Mexico Beach

SALES & RENTALS
1-800-261-1892

NUMBER ONE IN CUSTOMER SERVICE

---

check out the light's Fresnel lens — the cracks there were reportedly caused by Confederate musket balls fired during the Civil War.

If you want to stay overnight on Cape San Blas, there's the state park as well as **Ski Breeze Campground** (227-2136) off County Road 30. The cape also offers a wide selection of rental properties to choose from — just contact **Anchor Realty** (800-624-3964) or **Tom Todd Realty** (800-876-2611), both on the cape's County Road 30, for more information. There's also **Summer Properties of Cape San Blas, Inc.** (227-1892) in Cape San Blas near the entrance to the St. Joseph Peninsula State Park.

Cape San Blas sports only one restaurant, the **Cape Cafe** (229-8688), just a half-mile from the state park on County Road 30. Like most dining establishments in the area, the specialty is seafood. And most people say that the food alone is well worth the trip.

You can reach Cape San Blas by taking County Road 30 from Highway 98, between Port St. Joe and Apalachicola.

The **Gulf County Chamber of Commerce** has an excellent information package they'll gladly send you. Call them at 227-1223. Tell them we sent you.

St. Vincent Island

The western-most island in the barrier chain that sits off Franklin County's coastline, St. Vincent Island is a lush green wedge jutting out of Apalachicola Bay. It's home to the **St. Vincent National Wildlife Refuge**, and while this is a highly protected area, it doesn't mean visitors can't enjoy its beauty firsthand.

There are 14 miles of sandy white beach available for public use during the year. You have to hire your own boat to get out there, and visitors are welcome during daylight hours except during planned hunt-

FLORIDA'S FORGOTTEN COAST

This scenic palm grove is just one of the natural features preserved on St. Vincent Island.

ing or burning periods, which take place sporadically throughout the year. The interior of the island sports freshwater lakes and ponds as well as an abundance of wildlife. No camping is allowed on the island unless it's in conjunction with an overnight managed hunt approved by the Refuge Manager. The Manager also grants permits to those who merely wish to explore the island's interior.

Don't fool with Mother Nature — the island features an abundance of wildlife such as wild pigs and snakes, and an encounter with either of these can certainly pose a bit of a problem with even the most hardened tourists. If you come out here, you'd best be prepared to rough it a bit. It's certainly beautiful on the island, but its a beauty that demands great respect.

For more information, contact the St. Vincent National Wildlife Refuge office and tourist center in Apalachicola at 653-8808.

Apalachicola

The town of Apalachicola was established during the early part of the 1800s and provided the cotton plantations and lumber yards of Tallahassee and its environs with a convenient port — at the time, the third largest on the Gulf Coast.

Walk through the historic downtown district and you'll see plenty of evidence that industries such as cotton, lumber and seafood have been the backbone of this area. The breathtaking antebellum mansions you see in the old neighborhood also hint at the town's prosperous years before the Civil War. Just like so many other cities and towns

• *317*

FLORIDA'S FORGOTTEN COAST

Apalachicola Bay's oyster industry works overtime and still can't fill the world's demand.

ESCAPE TO BEAUTIFUL APALACHICOLA EAST BAY
Reasonable Rates • Daily, Weekly, Monthly • Charter Boats

Sportsman's Lodge
AAA APPROVED

(904) 670-8423 • P.O. Box 606 • Eastpoint, FL 32328

Sportsman's Lodge Motel and Marina is Bob and Edda Allen's quiet and restful sanctuary, tucked among the oaks on an oyster-strewn, high, sandy bluff on East Bay, part of the famous Apalachicola Bay. The Lodge has spacious units including bayfronts and kitchenettes. The Allen's make you feel right at home!

---

throughout the panhandle, Apalachicola was hit hard by this war and its aftermath. A blockade by Union naval forces ensured that virtually nothing could get out of Apalachicola during the war, and the shipping industry suffered greatly.

Apalachicola slowly built up its other industries, and it wasn't long before it established a solid reputation as the seafood capital of Florida. It's something that residents are certainly proud of, and if you're in town during November, you can let them show you why.

Apalachicola sits just off Highway 98 between Port St. Joe and Eastpoint, across the bay from St. Vincent and St. George islands.

Of course, traffic will be a lot heavier during the **Florida Seafood Festival**, but Insiders say it's worth it. Sometime around the turn of the century, the residents began having huge seafood celebrations which have given rise to the Florida Seafood Festival held each year in downtown Battery Park on the first Saturday and Sunday in November. Be ready to rub elbows with plenty of people, as this event usually attracts 20,000 or so seafood-loving individuals. Visitors can sample the best of Apalachicola Bay, including oysters, shrimp, crab and fish. There are plenty of booths offering enough food to feed an army.

If you're really, really hungry, consider entering the festival's Oys-

---

Insiders' Tips

There are no stoplights in all of Franklin County (west of Apalachicola to Alligator Point), only a flasher in downtown Apalachicola.

Experience the Picturesque Beauty of Historic

Ever Discovered A Pearl?

The Newly-Restored Bed & Breakfast

THE COOMBS HOUSE INN is the Gem of Apalachicola. Pamper yourself in an elegant Victorian mansion with airy, spacious, rooms furnished with beautiful antiques.

RATES: $59 - $95
PHONE: (904) 653-9199

For complete festival, fishing, fun, sun and real estate news on Florida's Forgotten coast... pick up your free copy of

Chuck Spicer's
Coast Line
Shopping Guide

and be sure to visit...
COAST LINE UNIQUES & ANTIQUES
Visitor Welcome Center
Historic Downtown

The Gibson Inn
Apalachicola, Florida

Restored Turn-of-the-Century Victorian Inn with all the Charm of the Era

We're proud to have been rated.

😊 😊
😊 😊

A Full Service
Four Hat Restaurant
by the *Tallahassee Democrat*
For reservations and information call
(904) 653-2191
(Be sure to ask about our riverboat cruises available on the *Apalachicola Belle*)

BEACHFRONT!

If you thought all of the best beaches were already "gone", THINK AGAIN!
Beachfront...
Creekfront...
Bayoufront...
We have it all!
Big, beautiful, pristine homesites that will knock you out.
Located between Carrabelle and Apalachicola on Florida's Forgotten Coast.
YENT BAYOU PROPERTIES
904/697-3133

Apalachicola

GALLERY 75

Painting
Sculpture
75 Commerce St.

653-2172

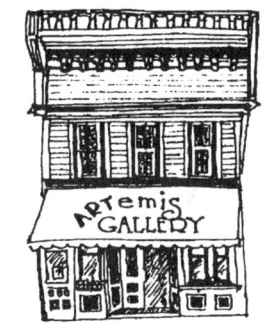

ARTemis Gallery
67 Commerce St. - Apalachicola

653-8304

Specializing in
Florida Landscape Paintings,
Fine Art Photography
and Children's Art.

PIED PIPER
Ladies Boutique

49 Market Street
Apalachicola, FL 32320

(904) 653-8196

Debra Stewart, Owner

LONG DREAM GALLERY

- Jewelry · Glass · Textiles · Iron
- Pottery · Wood · Paintings
- Sculpture · Local Illustrations &
Photography · Contemporary
· Handmade

FINE WORKS FOR YOU TO LIVE WITH FROM
THE HANDS OF LIVING ARTISTS

· LIV ART · LIV ART · LIV ART · LIV ART ·

SHAUN S. DONAHOE
Licensed Real Estate Broker

Investment Properties
Historic Apalachicola
St. George Island • Carrabelle
Dog Island • Cape San Blas

904/653-8330
17 1/2 Avenue E • Box 666 • Apalachicola, Fl 32329

---

ter Eating Contest. You get fifteen minutes to toss back all the bivalves you can hold. Contestants might want to skip meals for a couple of days prior to the event, because a recent winner consumed over 300 oysters to take first prize. The competition is certainly stiff and, when the buzzer sounds, well-stuffed.

Need to work off some of that extra weight you're sure to gain during the festival? Try the **Redfish Run**, a 5,000-meter event that's open to people of all ages. Or you can just stroll through several maritime heritage exhibits that feature boat building and net making. There's also a popular arts and crafts show, and evening festivities usually include plenty of live music and dancing.

Even if you can't make this well-attended festival, Apalachicola on a quiet day is still a treat. Apalachicola has managed to preserve much of its historic architecture, which includes antebellum homes, large brick warehouses and other buildings of interest. The downtown district provides history buffs and sightseers with the chance to experience the port's past firsthand.

This three-square-mile section features many important historic buildings and sites, some dating back over 150 years. Take the walking tour — it's the perfect way to spend the day here. When you've walked your shoes off, relax at either of two waterfront parks, Lafayette Park and Battery Park.

Insiders' Tips

Apalachicola is home to the largest estuarian reserve in the United States — over 200,000 acres.

FLORIDA'S FORGOTTEN COAST

This historic marker tells of a time when the Apalachicola River made the port one of the busiest in the world.

Senior Care Properties

Our facilities offer 24 hour skilled and intermediate health care services. We have structured restorative and rehab programs designed to maximize each individual resident's opportunity for maintaining quality of life during their convalescence. For more information on locations and available services, call (904) 653-9080 or come by our offices located at 82 6th Street in the historical Chapman House, Apalachicola, FL, 32320.

Main Office
82 6th Street
P.O. Dr. 70
Apalachicola, FL 32320
(904) 653-9080

Bay St. George Care Center
Hwy. 98 & Begonia
Eastpoint, FL 32328
(904) 670-8571

Bay St. Joseph Care Center
220 9th Street
Port St. Joe, FL 32456
(904) 229-8244

Apalachicola Health Care Center
150 10th Street
Apalachicola, FL 32320
(904) 653-8844

We are a drug free work place.

NIGHTINGALE & ASSOCIATES

PROFESSIONAL HOME HEALTH SERVICES

24 HOUR NURSING SERVICES
MEDICAL SUPPLIES
DIETARY COUNSELING
SOCIAL SERVICES

PHYSICAL THERAPY ARRANGEMENTS AVAILABLE
PRIVATE PAY · MEDICAID · MEDICARE

Debra Stewart, R.N.C., President/Administrator
Chai Sereebutra, M.D., Medical Director
Debbie Cooper, Assistant Administrator

NIGHTINGALE & ASSOCIATES
82 6TH ST. · APALACHICOLA, FL 32320
(904) 653-8551

FLORIDA'S FORGOTTEN COAST

You're sure to notice that many of these historic buildings are now home to various business, including a highly concentrated smattering of antique and gift shops. Here's a sampling of what you'll find there:

The **Gibson Inn** (653-2191), a 31-room hotel featuring a popular restaurant and bar, was built in 1907 and is one place you don't want to overlook during your visit. Furnishings are reminiscent of the Victorian era, and the atmosphere is quietly elegant without being pretentious. Rooms feature beds of either antique white iron or wooden four-posters along with modern amenities of full baths and television. The inn is located at 51 Avenue C downtown. Be sure to drop by the great bookstore, aptly called **Hooked on Books**, in the Gibson Inn annex.

The **Riverlily** is an off-center little shop featuring sundry items like scented soaps and incense. It's near the intersection of Avenue D and Market Street (their phone number is 653-8304), just around the corner from ERA Apalach Real Estate.

Gorrie Square is located just off Highway 98 in Apalachicola and is named after Dr. John Gorrie, who invented the ice machine in the mid-19th century. There's a museum there documenting Gorrie's various achievements (see the sidebar in this section). The next time you cool your jets in front of an air conditioner, you'll know who to thank.

The **Candy Kitchen Building** at the intersection of Market Street and Avenue G dates back over 100 years, and served much of that time as a general store and candy emporium. It was closed from the 1950s until recently, and currently houses **Uniques and Antiques**, which is jam-packed with antiques and collectibles. It also houses the offices of the popular *Coast Line Shopping Guide*. You can pick up copies of this free publication just about anywhere you look in these parts, and Insiders know it's a great place to find information about Apalachicola and neighboring towns. Stop by for a free issue and be sure to hit the **Visitor Welcome Center**, also in the same building, which offers dozens of free pamphlets and guides to the area.

This charming, picturesque little town is also becoming known as an artist community. Since 1985, many artists have renovated property downtown and set up their workshops and showrooms. Truly fine,

> **Insiders' Tips**
>
> Apalachicola is home to the *Governor Stone*, the oldest operational sailing vessel in the deep South. It is a national historic landmark. For more information on sailing schedules — offered are daily two-hour sails, sunsets sails, weddings, reunions and other special group events — call The Apalachicola Maritime Museum at 653-8708.

Apalachicola Realty, Inc.

Your Real Estate Specialists Serving All Of Franklin County

Leon R. Bloodworth, Broker
Al Mirabella, Jr., Associate

1-800-239-8990
1-904-653-8990
FAX: 1-904-653-9887
After Hours: 904-653-9860

COLDWELL BANKER

P.O. Box 684
18 Seventh Street
Apalachicola, Florida 32329-0684

The Chapel Home, a private residence, is a striking example of the Queen Anne-style architecture that can be seen in downtown Apalachicola.

one-of-a-kind items are available, so don't miss a visit. A few of our favorites are the **Long Dream Gallery** (32 Avenue D, 653-2249), the **Palmyra Gallery** (25 Avenue D, 653-9090), **Artemis Gallery and Cultural Center** (67 Commerce Street, 653-8304), and **Gallery 75** (75 Commerce Street, 653-2172).

There are other wonderful stores, inns and restaurants in the downtown area, including the **Coombs House Cottages** (94 5th Street, 653-2215), the **Coombs House Inn** (Highway 98 and Sixth Street, 653-9199), the **Rancho Inn** (240 Highway 98, 653-9435), **Dolores' Sweet Shoppe** (17 Avenue E, 653-9081), the **Apalachicola Seafood Grill and Steakhouse** (100 Market Street), **The Anchor Room**, which locals refer to as The Breakaway Lodge Restaurant (200 Waddell Road, 653-9988), **The Camouflage Shop** (75 Market Street, 653-9797), **Seahorse Gift and Florist** (87 Market Street, 653-8745), the **Rainbow Inn** and the **Riverfront Restaurant** (both on the waterfront at Water Street, 653-8139).

If you're smitten by the area (as most are) and want to buy property here, you'll have several reputable companies to contact. Apalachicola real estate brokers can help you, including **Apalachicola Realty** at 18 Seventh Street (653-8990), **Shaun S. Donahoe Realty** at 17½ Avenue E (653-8330), **ERA Apalach Real Estate** at 71 Market Street (653-2555), and **Marks Realty** (a Century-21 office) at 61 Avenue E. (653-2161).

If you're visiting and you have special health needs, consult with the staff of **Nightingale & Associ-**

Discover beautiful Eastpoint...
nestled between Apalachicola
East Bay & St. George

SHARON'S PLACE
RESTAURANT & SEAFOOD MARKET

GREAT FOOD AT GREAT PRICES!

COY & SHARON SHIVER
Owners/Operators
(904) 670-8646

Highway 98 • Eastpoint, FL
HOURS OPEN:
Restaurant 11-10 • Market 8-8

Purchase Fresh Seafood from our Market too!

The Painted Pony

Custom Braided Rugs
& Accessories
Made On-Site
Custom Colors & Sizes

"A room without a rug
is like a kiss
without a hug!"

All braided items are made in
Franklin County, Florida by
NATIVE AMERICANS.

HIGHWAY 98, EASTPOINT

Bill Bailey Realty

Located on Highway 98 between Historical Apalachicola and Beautiful St. George Island.

*Bay, River or Gulf…
We have some beautiful
homesites for you to
choose from. Call us.
Let us walk you around.*

P. O. Box 926
Eastpoint, FL 32328
904 · 670-8662

Apalachicola Bay CAMPGROUND

Full Hook-Ups
RV's • Pull Thru's
Pool • Laundry • Cable

Nightly ~ Weekly ~ Monthly

904-670-8307

"Eastpoint at the Bridge"

ates, Inc., at 82 Sixth Street (653-8551). They offer comprehensive home health care services and physical therapy. Associated business **Senior Care Properties** (653-9080), at the above address, manages convalescent homes in Eastpoint, Apalachicola and Port St. Joe.

And we haven't even scratched the surface with these listings. Our best advice for you is to simply get out there and explore. If you'd like to know more, the **Apalachicola Bay Chamber of Commerce** can provide you with a complete listing of what you'll see as you walk around. You can call them at 653-9419. The **Apalachicola Maritime Museum** is located in the same office as the chamber, and they can be reached at 653-8708.

Eastpoint

Just over the bridge east of Apalachicola lies Eastpoint, a fishing village in the truest sense of the word. Located right on Apalachicola Bay, Eastpoint was settled at the turn of the century, and the two miles of St. George Sound just off its coast are home to some of the best-tasting oysters in the entire world. Tons and tons of oysters are shipped each year from these waters to restaurants across the nation. Needless to say, the small town of Eastpoint is home to many fishing boats and their crew. The fish houses and docks along the waterfront always stay busy. Hang out in the afternoon and watch the oyster boats coming in and the shrimp boats preparing to head out for the night's catch.

John Gorrie State Museum

Dr. John Gorrie only meant to cure yellow fever patients, but he ended up changing the course of Florida history.

Yellow fever, sometimes called "Yellow Jack," was quite a problem in Florida during the mid-1800s, especially around port towns like Apalachicola, where sailors would spread the disease from town to town. Gorrie, a young physician who also found time to become postmaster, city councilman and treasurer, decided to try a new treatment against this deadly scourge. Many patients seemed to improve at night when the temperatures dropped, so Gorrie set about devising a way to cool their rooms on a permanent basis.

The success of his invention led Gorrie to develop the very first ice machine in 1845, and it's generally acknowledged that he paved the way for modern air conditioning, which many Florida residents and visitors couldn't imagine living without.

The John Gorrie State Museum contains a replica of his first ice machine, as well as many other exhibits pertaining to the history of Apalachicola. It's on Sixth Street downtown, just off Highway 98, 653-9347, and admission is free.

And, yes, the place is air-conditioned.

FLORIDA'S FORGOTTEN COAST

Florida's Forgotten Coast offers easy living — just ask these pelicans.

Here you can learn more than you ever thought possible about the oyster. The friendly locals are more than willing to let you see how the oysters are harvested and prepared for market. It's a Zen-like process, one they speak of reverently, and many of the harvesters and fishers have willingly given themselves over to this way of life.

The **Sportsman's Lodge Motel & Marina** (670-8423) sits right on Apalachicola Bay and is a convenient place to stay while visiting. You can rent a room or just hook up your RV or camper. There's also the **Apalachicola Bay Campground** (670-8307), which has an RV park and also sells plenty of camping supplies for travelers who belatedly discover they didn't pack everything they need.

If you need information on real estate in these environs, a good place to check is **Bill Bailey Realty** (670-8662), which sits just off Highway 98 in Eastpoint.

Be sure to scope out the scene for some of the small, quaint gift shops and galleries in Eastpoint. Don't miss the **Painted Pony** on Highway 98, right next door to Bill Bailey Realty, which offers a fine selection of custom rugs, woven and braided, as well as a wide selection of other assorted gifts. **Bayside Gallery**, also right in this area, features art, cards, gifts and flowers (this is an FTD Florist shop). The owner, Joyce Estes, is also the author of a cookbook called *Seafood the Apalachicola Way* that all good cooks will want to get (get one even if you're a bad cook and maybe it'll help!).

For good fresh seafood, check out **Sharon's Place** (670-8646), just off Highway 98. These people get it off the boats as soon as they come in, and it goes fast.

FLORIDA'S FORGOTTEN COAST

Beach erosion may soon claim the Cape St. George Lighthouse, but for now it still stands tall and proud as it has since the 1800s.

Anchor Realty and Mortgage Co.

NEW CONSTRUCTION & MODEL HOMES
Sales: A sales team of qualified professionals.
Beach Rentals: Over 200 of the best vacation rentals to choose from.

ST. GEORGE ISLAND:

PRIVATE BEACHFRONT & BAYFRONT ESTATES
"ST. GEORGE PLANTATION" MANSIONS
(Luxury, 24 Hour Security, Privacy, Tennis, Pool)
"300 OCEAN MILE" TOWNHOMES
(2 Pools, Volleyball, Mini Putting Green)
"VILLAS OF ST. GEORGE" (Pool)

LOCAL	(904) 927-2625
Housekeeping/Emergency 24 Hour	(904) 927-2849
Facsimile (FAX)	(904) 927-2735
TOLL FREE RENTALS & SALES	**(800) 824-0416**

(2nd bldg. on the left when driving onto the island.) • 212 Franklin Blvd., St. George Island, FL 32328

Nearby is the boundary for the Apalachicola National Forest, which contains Fort Gadsden. If you've got the time, it's a beautiful complement to friendly Eastpoint. See the Parks and Recreation sections in this chapter and in Tallahassee for more information.

If you need more information on Eastpoint, contact the **Apalachicola Bay Chamber of Commerce** at 653-9419.

St. George Island

There are four barrier islands that sit just off Franklin County's coastline. St. George Island is the largest in the chain and the only one accessible by automobile. It sports several permanent and rental residences as well as the Dr. Julian G. Bruce **St. George Island State Park** (for more information, see the Parks and Recreation section of this chapter), which features nearly 2,000 acres of sensitive, unspoiled beach landscape.

You'll see a lot of houses on the island, but also evidence that the growth here is carefully controlled and regulated. The residents have overall shown great consideration for the island's ecosystem and appearance, and it's something they love to share with visitors.

The state park is a lovely attraction. There's a free public beach visible as soon as you reach the is-

The Island Gathering Place

HARRY A's Porch Club

Island Entertainment Center-And Sports Bar

ST. GEORGE ISLAND'S OLDEST TAVERN & PACKAGE

...where strangers become friends...
#1 Bayshore Drive · St. George Island, FL 32328
Your Hosts, The Cates · **904-927-9810**

---

land. You'll see beachcombers, sun-worshippers and bird-watchers out here, but you'll probably be most impressed with the size of the beach; it's so large that people like to spread out and claim their own little private chunk of sand. In fact, it's easy to feel like you're the only person on the entire island. Locals say that's why they live here, and visitors say it's why they return again and again.

But you're sure to get hungry for the company of others as well as food. There are also several fine places to eat on St. George Island. The **Happy Pelican Restaurant** (49 W. Pine Avenue, 927-9826), is one of the best-kept secrets on the island.

The atmosphere is fun and casual, the food as fresh as you'll get and all cooked to order. Check them out for their daily lunch specials. The locals flock to this place. **Harry A's Porch Club** (10 Bayshore Drive, 927-9810), the island gathering place is, as they say, where strangers become friends. Your hosts, the Cates, will make you feel like a true islander. While their food is a good draw, one of the best things about Harry A's is the fact that any time you go, you'll find a friendly group of folks playing pool, shooting basketball out back or watching the big-screen TV. They also help sponsor a lot of good causes, like the annual Bow Wow Ball.

Insiders' Tips

Every spring the St. George Island causeway is home to several species of nesting birds. Because of this, the causeway is deemed a critical wildlife area. Do your part for nature and slow down as you drive through; the birds will appreciate it, and you might just get an audubon lesson to boot.

FLORIDA'S FORGOTTEN COAST

St. George Island has one of the most beautiful and carefully preserved beaches in the world.

> **RESORT REALTY**
> **OF ST. GEORGE ISLAND, INC.**
>
> *Your Beach Property Specialists*
>
> **VACATION RENTALS and SALES**
>
> Homes • Homesites • Townhomes
> *Residential • Commercial • Investment*
>
> HCR Box 108 • 120 Gulf Beach Drive W • St. George Island, FL 32328
> **800/332-5196 • 904/927-2666**

Other great spots include the **Paradise Cafe** (West Gorrie Drive at the public beach, 927-3300), **Island Oasis** (Gulf Beach Drive, 927-2639), the **East End Deli** (Gulf Beach Drive, 927-3474), **B.J.'s Pizza**, located in the Pine Street Mini-mall (927-2805), and **Oyster Cove Seafood Bar & Grill and Cajun Cafe** (East Pine at 2nd Street, 927-2829). And, if you're a chili lover, you'll definitely want to be here in March for the **St. George Island Chili Cookoff** (see the Tallahassee Festivals and Special Events chapter for more information).

If you need help in planning your outdoor excursions, **Jeanie's Journey Travel & Adventure Company** (927-3259) is just the ticket. Owner Jeanie McMillan organizes canoe trips, nature expeditions and re-

> **Insiders' Tips**
>
> St. George Island (recently honored by the Department of Commerce as a Florida Rural Community of the Year) is home of the largest regional chili cookoff in the nation, held the first Saturday in March.

> New owners Joe & Bobbie Felice have made this St. George Island's best kept secret. Relaxed casual atmosphere, friendly service, and all food cooked to order. Open daily for breakfast, lunch & dinner. Featuring seafood, fried, grilled or steamed. Steaks, pasta, homemade soups, gumbos, salads & munchies. See why the locals have made this their favorite place to eat. **Take outs (904) 927-9826.**
> # The Happy Pelican

cently started an environmental summer camp for kids.

The island also offers a few wonderful gift shops. **Two Gulls Two** (927-2044) has gifts, cards, T-shirts, beachwear — all one of a kind items that you won't see repeated in other shops in the area. They're located at the Pine Street Mini-mall. **Island Emporium** (927-2622), is another great little shop you'll want to visit, also on Pine Street, as is the **Island Shirt Company** (216 W. Gorrie Drive, 927-2044). You may come here for the great outdoors, but don't be surprised if you end up spending a few hours browsing through the wares found in these and other shops.

Needless to say, land is at a premium on St. George Island. There are plenty of vacation rental properties for visitors to choose from, no matter what your budget. **Anchor Realty and Mortgage Co.** (800-824-0416), **Resort Realty** (800-332-5196) and **Lighthouse Realty** (927-2821) handle many fine properties on the island, both sales and rentals. **Suncoast Realty** (927-2282) and **Collins Realty** (927-2900) are also reputable companies handling sales and rentals. While we know it's an Insiders' prerogative to point you in specific directions, really all these companies are well-respected by locals and visitors alike. So, you can't go wrong no matter who you call.

Larry Troy's *Cool Change* charter fishing boat **always** returns with full fish boxes.

Insiders' Tips

TWO GULLS
A UNIQUE SHOPPING EXPERIENCE

GIFTS, CARDS, OBJECTS AND ARTWORK

TWO GULLS	TWO GULLS TWO
Hwy. 98	Pine St. Mini Complex
Carrabelle, FL 32322	St. George Island, FL 32328
(904) 697-3787	**(904) 927-2044**

If you need a place to stay on this side of the bay, you can't miss **the St. George Inn** (927-2903), a wonderful abode that sits just off to your left as you come onto the island. The rooms and beds are big and comfortable, and there's also a lounge and restaurant in the building. The **Buccaneer Inn** (927-2585) is the oldest hotel on the island and sits right on the beach — it's truly a breathtaking view. Amenities include a guest pool, and you can choose from either a kitchenette or regular room.

The Gibson Inn, built in 1904, is one of St. George Island's most elegant lodgings.

Jeanni's Journeys, Inc.
Travel and Adventure Company
WE'RE A TRIP!

Full Service Travel Agency & Adventure Company located on St. George Island

CANOE TRIPS
SAILING LESSONS
BARRIER ISLAND TREKS
ENVIRONMENTAL CAMP FOR KIDS
BOOKING AGENT FOR DIVE TRIPS
FISHING TRIPS
PHOTOGRAPHY EXCURSIONS

(904) 927-3259

If you're really adventurous you can hire a private boat to take you to **Little St. George Island**, also called Cape St. George, which sits just west of St. George Island. This island was once connected to St. George Island, but in the late 1950s the U.S. Army Corps of Engineers opened a pass for boaters between the two land masses. Little St. George Island features a lighthouse that was built in the mid-19th century — it's operational but not open to the public. There are places for camping, but you must notify the St. George Island State Park office if you want to camp there since the island is officially under their jurisdiction.

To reach St. George Island, which sits across the bay from Apalachicola, take Highway 98 to Highway 300 South. This puts you on the causeway across Apalachicola Bay and lands you smack dab on the island.

For more information, contact the **Apalachicola Bay Chamber of Commerce** (653-9419) or the **St. George Island Business Owners Association** (653-9419).

Carrabelle

Carrabelle, about 20 miles east of Apalachicola, is a port town of around 2,000 people, and on any given afternoon you can stand at the docks and watch the ships come in, their holds full of fresh fish.

They call this the "Pearl of the Panhandle," and when you sample the seafood you'll know why. Seafood is the cause for a lot of celebration in these parts. Carrabelle serves up the **Big Bend Saltwater Fishing Classic** and the **Carrabelle Waterfront Festival**, both on Father's Day weekend, and these always manage to attract a few thousand people. The festival is a jam-packed day of fun, food and sunshine.

There are plenty of things to see and do here. Check out the **Crooked River Lighthouse**, just west of

LIGHTHOUSE REALTY
of St. George Island

"Properties for every Budget"
BOTH Sales and Rentals!

*Come Explore Beautiful St. George Island . . .
The Uncommon Florida!*

(904) 927-2821
HCR Box 62, Box 126 • St. George Island, FL 32328

---

town and about a quarter of a mile from St. George Sound. Carrabelle's **Wayside Park** can be found with a minimum of effort — it's just off Highway 98 (as is most everything else in Carrabelle) and is a perfect spot to picnic before heading on down to the beaches and islands farther west.

Don't blink as you pass through town or you'll miss the **World's Smallest Police Station**, a well-marked telephone booth that sits just off Highway 98 as it passes through town. It's a tourist attraction that many magazines, newspapers and TV shows across the country have featured, but it's also quite functional. Don't be at all surprised if you see a patrol car parked nearby with an alert officer waiting for that phone to ring.

Need a place to stay? Not a problem with **Ell's Court On the Gulf**, which sits just off Highway 98. You can reach them at 697-2050 or (800) 647-2050. There's also the **Gulf Water Motel and Campground** off the same highway (697-2840).

If you want to stay permanently, call **Carrabelle Realty**, also on Highway 98 (697-2181). Their agents are all true locals so can show you this area from an "insider's" perspective. You can also check out **Yent Bayou Properties**, Inc. (697-3133), located on Highway 98 between Carrabelle and Eastpoint.

Florida Coastal Properties, on Highway 98 (697-2734), also has an office in Carrabelle. They specialize

---

Insiders' Tips

Famous treasure-hunter Mel Fisher sometimes visits Papa Pirates's Tiki Bar on Timber Island in Carrabelle.

CARRABELLE
Florida's Fishermen's Paradise
Beautiful White Sandy Beaches

JULIA MAE'S
SEAFOOD RESTAURANT

WATERFRONT DINING

"The South's Finest"

- Local Seafood
- Delicious Steaks
- Daily Specials
- Catering

(904) 697-3791
US Hwy 98 West
Carrabelle, FL 32322

ELL'S COURT
ON THE GULF
(US HWY 98)

Rooms - Kitchenettes - Cable TV
Nightly - Weekly - Monthly Rentals
RV Facilities - 220' Fishing Pier
Boat Rentals - Charters

Friendly Atmosphere & Service Oriented

STAR ROUTE BOX 4
CARRABELLE, FL 32322
(904) 697-2050 • (800) 647-2050

CARRABELLE REALTY

(our name says it ALL)

Coming our way?
Check with the
#1 Real Estate Office in
The Pearl of the Panhandle.

We are hometown professionals who can show you every *"nook & cranny"* of this wonderful place we call home.

Ruby J. Litton
Lic. Real Estate Broker
(904) 697-2181   (904) 697-3870
(904) 697-3188

Tracy Hardman	Gina Millender
670-8195	697-3114
Rene Topping	Deene Cook
697-2616	697-2360

DOWN UNDER DIVE CENTER

Pirates Landing Marina
Timber Island Road

Sales & Rental
Equipment Sales
Air • Boat Rentals • Tackle

Stop & rest a spell at our new Papa Pirates Tiki Bar on the waterfront along the Carrabelle River - feel the breeze, enjoy the view and our local seafood, oysters, munchies, subs, beer, wine & soda.
Happy Hour 5-7 Daily
Closed Monday

(904) 697-3204

in sales of homes and investment properties. Their real estate professionals can help you with properties from Tallahassee to Eastpoint. Other offices are located in Shell Point and Crawfordville.

There are a handful of great restaurants and eateries in Carrabelle, the foremost probably being **Julia Mae's Seafood Restaurant** (697-3791) on Highway 98 at the foot of the Carrabelle Bridge. The seafood here is among the freshest you'll find, and it's open all week long from 11 AM to 9:30 PM.

If you want to experience your seafood firsthand before you eat it, then the **Down Under Dive Center** (697-3204) on Timber Island Road sells and rents a large assortment of diving equipment. They also have **Papa Pirate's Tiki Bar**, overlooking the Carrabelle River and the bay, which is a favorite local watering hole. And, if you're in the mood for a party on the water, rent their pontoon boat.

And Carrabelle also sports several gift and antique stores that are well worth checking out. **Two Gulls Gifts** (697-3787), **Linda's Trading Post** (697-2547), **Bayou Art Gallery** (697-2363), and the **Whistle Stop Antiques and Collectibles** (697-3539) all make driving down Highway 98 a stop-and-go journey for the antique hounds and gift-seekers among us.

Just east of Carrabelle is the community of **Lanark Village**, and beyond that is **Alligator Point**. Lanark Village was once the site of Camp Gordon, a former training ground during World War II. Since that time, it's been slowly and carefully developed into a tasteful resort and retirement area. Alligator Point doesn't really have any alligators — well, hardly any — but takes its name (say the locals) from its shape. Pull down the highway a bit to a quiet beach spot called St. Teresa and look out across Apalachee Bay to Alligator Point. We did and, with a bit of help from some friendly locals, were able to see, sure enough, the shape of a big grinning alligator.

Lanark Village and Alligator Point are low-key resort and retirement areas that cater to visitors who want to slow down to a panhandler's pace. Each offers waterfront camping and hotels as well as rental properties, and there are some fine places to eat, too. We shouldn't have to tell you that fresh fish is the dish of choice here, so we won't.

If this still isn't secluded enough for you, then we've got the answer. Superman has his Fortress of Solitude to retreat to when things get rough, and if he lived in Florida he'd surely rather be at **Dog Island**, which sits just off the coast of Carrabelle. It's the smallest of four islands that sit off Franklin County's

---

Insiders' Tips

Carrabelle Beach is a great place for finding unusual driftwood and sponges.

Several boardwalks carry visitors through the dunes and over the marshes of St. George Island State Park.

coastline and can be reached only by a ferry that runs from Carrabelle. There are about 100 homes on the island and one hotel, the **Pelican Inn**. Most of Dog Island is a nature preserve, and in the fall and spring there are so many birds here you might not notice the beautiful water and sandy beaches. The island is known for its quiet, low-key residents and breathtaking landscape.

If you want more information on Carrabelle, just contact the **Carrabelle Area Chamber of Commerce** at 697-2585.

Parks and Recreation

CONSTITUTION CONVENTION STATE MUSEUM
200 Allen Memorial Way
Port St. Joe   229-8029

St. Joseph coulda been a contender. It was one of the fastest-growing boomtowns in the mid-1800s and gave more than a few neighboring port towns a run for their money. At its peak, it served as the site for Florida's first State Constitution Convention. At its lowest point, the place was practically wiped off the map by a combination of poor business, yellow fever and a raging hurricane.

The Constitution Convention State Museum is about two hours from Tallahassee on Highway 98, and it's a time capsule that holds the memories of a town long since gone. Oh, there's a town there now called Port St. Joe, and its relaxed beach-front lifestyle is something a lot of visitors find attractive, but as far as the original township goes, we're just fortunate to have found enough material in the aftermath to fill this museum.

Inside you can see exhibits not

only about the Constitution Convention, but about the town's brief history as well.

> The Florida Park Service is now issuing vacation passes good for up to 15 days. A Family Entrance Permit (up to eight people) covers admission to any of Florida's State Parks and costs $20.00. The new passes can be purchased at any Florida State Park.

DEAD LAKES STATE PARK
Wewahitchka   639-2702

Someone should film a horror movie at Dead Lakes, and they should film it entirely in daylight. Not that the place is at all scary or sinister, but it is rather entrancing in a macabre sort of way.

Dead Lakes is full of dead trees, and they stand like the stark skeletons of fantastic creatures. Here's how it happened: the currents of the Apalachicola River long ago created a sand bar that blocked the flow of the Chipola River. The water backed up and killed thousands of trees, and that's where the park gets its name.

You'd think that no one would have any use for a floodplain with a bunch of strange-looking dead trees, but think again. Some of the industries that made money off the park were quite innovative. There was a fish hatchery here at one time, and later a turpentine factory — you can still see markings that look like little cat faces where turpentine was drawn out of the trees. Even later, the place was one big moss factory — that's right, Spanish moss. People dried it out and used it for packing material and furniture stuffing back in the 1930s and 1940s. Ah, those were certainly the days. . . .

And while most people think that tupelo honey comes from Tupelo, Mississippi, Insiders know that that golden sweetness comes from none other than Wewahitchka. It's a century-old commercial industry most outsiders don't know about. If you see bees buzzing around, you'll know they're working hard to turn out that next batch of honey.

For twenty years now, the area has been a state park offering good fishing and some, well, interesting scenery. There are campgrounds with full-facility camping, boat ramps to the lakes as well as the Chipola River, and a nature trail. And the lakes as well as two ponds dug in 1936 offer plenty of bass, bream crappie, gar and carp for the anglers. Don't forget the Florida freshwater fishing license.

FORT GADSDEN STATE HISTORIC SITE
Sumatra   670-8988

Fort Gadsden is known to historians by another name: Negro Fort. During the war of 1812, this base was built by the British to recruit Indians and blacks in their efforts against the U.S. Territory some fifty miles to the north. The fort rested on Prospect Bluff above the Apalachicola River and was armed to the gills with guns, cannon and gunpowder.

The skirmishes between American and British forces continued, and this fort became a training ground and, after Andrew Jackson took Pensacola, a refuge for blacks as well as Creek and Seminole Indians. In December of 1814, records indicate that nearly three thousand men, women and children were living on or near Prospect Bluff.

The British finally withdrew after signing the Treaty of Ghent in 1815, but when it became clear that Jackson had no intentions of honoring the treaty's provisions that protected the Indians from loss of their land, Major Edward Nicholls of the Royal Marines was careful to leave behind as much weaponry and ammunition as possible.

The fort offered a free and independent environment for the blacks, many of whom were escaped slaves. Because of its renegade nature, the fort also offered a haven for cattle rustlers, thieves and murderers. Jackson finally ordered the destruction of the fort, and the battle that ensued was probably about as brief as the order itself.

On July 27, 1816, a handful of gunboats and schooners approached the fort from the south while a unit of British and friendly Creek Indians moved in from the north. These ground troops were needed only for cleanup, however. The fifth shot from the gunboats landed squarely in the fort's magazine, detonating the stockpile of gunpowder.

When the smoke cleared, Negro Fort and 270 of its inhabitants were gone. The British troops discovered only thirty people who survived the blast.

Today, Fort Gadsden offers a visitor's center that recounts the tragic history of the fort and contains a miniature replica of the fort as it must have appeared shortly before its destruction. There are picnic sites available, and a nature trail that wanders through the vibrant green landscape above the river.

To get to Fort Gadsden State Historic Site, take Highway 20 west from Tallahassee until you hit State Road 65 at Hosford, then drop south through the Apalachicola National Forest. State Road 65 is also accessible from Highway 98 and U.S. 319 to the south between Carrabelle and Eastpoint.

St. Joseph Peninsula State Park
Port St. Joe 227-1327

Every autumn there are two migrations to the St. Joseph Peninsula State Park on Cape San Blas. One brings nature and wildlife enthusiasts from near and far, and the other migration is what attracts them: the annual southern flight of the monarch butterfly.

The butterflies use this as a stopping point before heading to Mexico, and visitors have learned to take the time to observe the colorful

---

While getting all your fishing supplies and weather conditions, you can still get a 5¢ cup of coffee at the Village Fina in Lanark Village.

FLORIDA'S FORGOTTEN COAST

Sailing just seems like the right thing to do on a hot summer day.

spectacle. It's hard to think of something this remarkable park doesn't offer. It's got swimming and diving, some wonderfully white beaches, saltwater fishing (with license), boating and some leisurely hiking trails through the huge dunes which are home to thriving pine trees.

The 2,650-acre setting provides excellent viewing for bird-lovers, and it's one of the best places to observe the annual fall migration of hawks and other birds.

Nearby is Salinas Park, which offers surfside picnic areas and boardwalks that follow the dunes to an elevated gazebo that provides a grand view.

Also of note on Cape San Blas is the old Confederate Salt Works, which was destroyed during the Civil War. There's also the Cape San Blas Lighthouse, the sixth one to stand in that spot. Natural elements — everything from hurricanes to shifting sands — caused the collapse of the other five. This one's been standing for over 100 years, and should be with us for a long time to come.

The park offers furnished cabins and over 100 full-facility campsites, and there's a special area for camping by organized, nonprofit youth groups. For handicapped visitors only, there's a special beach and recreational area just south of this park.

To get to the park, take Highway 319 south from Tallahassee to Highway 98 and head west. It's just off State Road C-30 near Port St. Joe and Apalachicola, about a two-hour drive from Tallahassee.

ST. GEORGE ISLAND STATE PARK
St. George Island 927-2111

St. George Island is one of a chain of barrier islands along the Gulf Coast, and although development is taking its toll on the natural beauty, the St. George Island State Park is preserving a good-sized chunk of it for everyone to enjoy. The 1,962-acre park is nearly 10 miles long and features some gently rolling dunes and salt marshes highlighted with stands of oak and pine trees.

The island has a rich history, and there's a marker at the western end where William Augustus Bowles was shipwrecked in 1799. Bowles was a renegade, self-styled leader of the Cherokee nation and a constant thorn in the side of the Spanish, who simply could not establish a military stronghold over their territory. Bowles had been captured once and sent to Spain, but he escaped and made his way back here aboard the schooner *Fox*, which ran aground on the island. Apparently unfazed by this incident, Bowles salvaged what supplies he could and set out for the Apalachicola River, leaving behind the ships' crew who were later res-

---

A trip to Dog Island, accessible only by boat, requires you to take all your necessities with you, especially drinking water and sunscreen.

Insiders' Tips

Havana has quickly established a reputation as the antique capitol of north Florida.

cued. In an attempt to secure an independent Indian nation under British protection, Bowles led a small army of Indians to the Spanish fort at St. Marks and overtook it. This action embarrassed Spain greatly, because now it had no military fort between Pensacola and St. Augustine. Soon after, the British were not so interested in Bowles welfare and he was again captured by the Spanish, spending the remaining years of his life in a Cuban prison.

You'll agree that although Bowles met a tragic end, he couldn't have picked a better place to shipwreck.

There are several pavilions for picnics, two boat launches, hiking trails and full-facility as well as primitive camping areas.

The best way to get to St. George Island State Park from Tallahassee is via Highway 319 south to Highway 98 west, which goes to Eastpoint. From Eastpoint, take County Road 300 south across the causeway. Once on the island, take a left at Gulf Beach Drive. From Tallahassee, this is about a 1½-hour drive.

High Seas Adventure:
No Experience Necessary

Lifelong chums David Volk and Patrick Barnes.

Photo: Robin Rowan

It's another perfect day at the beach on St. George Island — a sunshine-drenched shoreline, gentle waves and a few puffy clouds just to make it pretty. The colorful sail of a Hobie Cat snaps to attention in the ocean breeze captained by . . . YOU! Here on the island, you'll be handed the helm of this 16-foot beauty and be under sail in *ten minutes!* David Volk and his partner Patrick Barnes, owners of St. George Island Beach Rentals, offer what could be the world's shortest sailing lesson.

"We have people rent the Hobie who've sailed before, but sometimes it's better if they don't know anything about sailing," says Volk, an affable fortysomething islander with a quick grin and a dark Florida tan. "Those are the people who listen to what you tell them. Not everything sinks in, but they hear enough to at least sail down the beach."

Volk stresses that conditions have to be just right to let somebody with no previous experience take control of a sailboat. Ideally, winds should be heading straight at the beach (or straight out) and the gulf should be fairly calm. "I tell 'em, just head up the beach for 30 minutes, turn the sail around, and come on back," says Volk. "Sometimes the wind quits on us, and we've got a couple of boats just sitting there in the water, but usually everything goes pretty smoothly."

For the last 13 years, Volk and Barnes have enjoyed instructing wanna-be sailors here on St. George Island, but the boyhood pals learned the art of sailing much earlier. Volk remembers sailing at the age of 6 when his dad built a homemade sunfish. In Redington Beach near St. Petersburg, the boys were sent to "pram school" when they were 7 or 8 years old. A pram is a square-bottomed wooden sailboat about eight feet long with two-foot sides. Back then, pram school was something of a rite of passage for young boys raised near the water.

"We can teach anybody to sail, even real little kids — if their parents go with them," Volk smiles. Hobie Cat rentals are $25 for an hour, $40 for two hours, $85 for a half a day, or $130 for all day. If you're new at it, though, an hour is about as long as you'll want to be at sea. Volk or Barnes can also take a group of four or five adults sailing for $30 an hour . . . the guys do all the work and you just sit back and enjoy the ride.

Tallahassee
History

Although there is evidence that people lived in Florida at least 12,000 years ago, the first written records of the land did not appear until 1513 with the arrival of Spanish explorer Ponce de Leon.

But de Leon isn't credited with being the first to actually explore inland Florida. That distinction goes to Panfilo de Narvaez, whose expedition landed near present-day Tampa Bay in 1528. Like de Leon and so many later explorers, de Narvaez was seeking gold. From the natives he encountered at Tampa came news of a city to the north called Apalachen, where gold was abundant.

Panfilo de Narvaez and his men made the long trek northward to the panhandle and then headed due west. They didn't find much gold but did encounter the Apalachee Indians, the earliest recorded inhabitants of the Tallahassee area. The territory the Apalachees occupied stretched as far west as Pensacola and was bounded to the east by the Aucilla River and the tribes of Timucuan Indians just beyond. The Apalachees were an agricultural society first and foremost — the wandering Spanish were amazed at the abundance of corn, beans and other vegetables growing along the well-worn path they traveled. But the Indians could also be fierce warriors when they felt threatened. Unfortunately for de Narvaez, he and his men were perceived as a threat and faced constant attacks while exploring the area. The expedition finally decided to build sea-going vessels and head for Mexico.

Eleven years later, Hernando de Soto reached the Tallahassee area, also in search of gold. He and his men had to fight their way in but apparently fared much better than the earlier expedition. They spent the winter of 1539 on a hill overlooking Tallahassee, marking the first known celebration of Christmas on the North American continent.

Hernando de Soto never returned to the area; he met his death the following year while exploring present-day Mississippi. In fact, for the next 100 years Spanish settlers generally ignored this area. They were busy establishing their Pensacola and St. Augustine missions, designed to import their religion and save the souls of the godless natives. It was only a matter of time before they trekked inland, and in 1633 two friars established the first mission in the red hills of present-day Tallahassee.

By 1647 there were eight

Herman the prehistoric mastodon was recovered from nearby Wakulla Springs and now greets visitors at the Florida Museum of History.

churches in the area, and all but one was destroyed by an uprising of Apalachees who rejected the joint yoke of brutal Spanish rule and Christian faith forced upon them. Undaunted, the Spanish rebuilt the churches and in 1656 moved the main mission, San Luis, to a hill only a couple of miles west of the present-day capital. At its height, this mission became the centerpoint of activity in the Big Bend area, with a population of at least 1,400 people. In 1677, the Spanish also constructed a fort called San Marcos de Apalachee in St. Marks, effectively claiming the all-important coastal area.

In spite of their strong foothold, however, the Spanish were eventually forced to abandon San Luis. By this time the English and Spanish settlers were grabbing madly for land, each side using the Native Americans as soldiers in their battles. In 1704, the San Luis Mission faced an impending attack by Governor James Moore of South Carolina. Moore had tried unsuccessfully to take the Spanish garrison at St. Augustine two years earlier, and he was so determined to make up for his failure that when the state legislature refused to fund his next attack, Moore financed it himself.

Moore's forces — 50 white men and over 1,000 Creek Indians — plunged south to destroy the Spanish mission of Concepcion de Aubale, about 20 miles east of San Luis. As his unstoppable forces advanced westward, so did news of Moore's brutal methods. The Spanish decided to burn San Luis to the

352 •

ground and abandon the area.

By the time it was all over, Moore's forces had tortured and killed hundreds of the Apalachee and were returning triumphantly to their home state with more than 3,000 Indian slaves in tow, most of them women and children. Moore's raid effectively depopulated the area, sending the remaining Indians either east to St. Augustine or west to Pensacola.

For many years Tallahassee was nothing more than a black slash on the quiet hills, a ravaged ghost town. This was only the first of many pivotal fires that would change the landscape and its inhabitants.

The Seminoles

The Seminole Indians were originally Creek Indians whose homeland covered areas of Alabama, Georgia, Mississippi and other states. Their migration here is something of a mystery because it is known that the Creeks held sacred "the land of the dead," and considered it bad luck to live in places where people had been killed. Some historians believe these Indians simply had no choice, considering the expansionist example set by such men as Governor Moore of South Carolina. In the end, the Creek Indians might have concluded that bad luck was better than no luck at all.

Why were these Creeks suddenly called Seminoles? The first instance we have of the word comes from an Englishman, John Stuart, who served as an American Indian agent in the 18th century. Stuart believed the word meant "wild ones," but it's also quite close to the Spanish *cimarron*, which means "runaways" — too close, in fact, for the many Indians who disliked being called cowards simply because they'd broken off from their main tribe. Nevertheless, the name stuck and has become the accepted term over the centuries.

At the time the first Seminoles appeared, northern Florida wasn't entirely unpopulated. There was still a sizable Spanish presence around, often aided by a tribe called the Yammassee that moved into the area from other parts of the territory. After many battles with the fierce Seminoles, the Spanish were pushed back to the coastal areas and the Yammassees were virtually wiped out.

In 1763, after signing the Treaty of Paris that ended its war with Spain, England took control of Florida and, for safety's sake, sought to work more closely with the Indians. The British Empire offered better trading conditions and treated the Seminoles with respect, honoring nearly every treaty it signed with them. This was particularly fortunate during the Revolutionary War, because friendly relations with the Indians meant that retreating British Loyalists could be guaranteed a safe haven if they could make it this far south.

Two Indian cities appeared on maps of the area for the first time in 1778: Tallahassee Town, from an Indian word that translates aptly into "old field" or, more loosely, "abandoned village." It was also known as "Tonaby's Town," named after the powerful chief who founded it. Although Indians fared better under British rule, Chief Tonaby boldly

• 353

Excavations continue every spring at the San Luis Archeological and Historic Site.

declared his loyalty to the Spanish, who had employed him for two decades as a messenger. During the American Revolution when other north Florida tribes were aiding Britain, Tonaby proudly broke rank and flew above Tallahassee the flag of Spain, which had recently joined the Americans in their revolution.

Britain's defeat in the American Revolution ushered in the second era of Spanish occupation, as Spain was rewarded the territory for its loyalty to Americans during the revolution. This time, however, Spain's grasp was even more tenuous as the Seminoles were by now used to the better trading conditions with the British. Friendly individuals like Chief Tonaby had disappeared from the scene and Spain was forced to contract with a British trading firm to handle the commerce with the Seminoles.

By this time, the Southern states of the United States were producing cotton and other crops using the plantation system. This entire economy hinged upon the use of African slaves as a cheap labor force. Although some slaves were treated well, most were horribly oppressed. And if they wanted to escape, there were really only two places to hide: to the relatively unexplored west, or down south to the Florida Territory.

The Indians were generally receptive to the escaped slaves, and often helped them establish their own towns and villages. Sometimes lone escapees would be captured by the Seminoles and forced into labor, although this form of slavery was far different from that of the white plantation owners to the north. The Indians not only allowed these blacks to marry into their tribes and live among them, but any children from those unions were born into freedom and not extended generational slavery. Before long, the racial mix was diverse for so small an area, with English, Spanish, Indian and Africans often in daily contact with each other.

Andrew Jackson

In Alabama there arose a violent Indian faction whose aim, however, was to divide the races. These Creek Indians called themselves Red Sticks, and they followed the teachings of Tecumseh, a Shawnee chief who preached that the white man must be driven from the land by any means necessary. In 1813, the Red Sticks slaughtered over 250 people at Fort Mims in Alabama.

Enter Andrew Jackson, general of the U.S. Army, diehard expansionist and something of a hero for his role in the Battle of New Orleans in 1814. Not long after the Fort Mims massacre, he and his troops — which included many Cherokee Indians — killed eight hundred Creeks in the Battle of Horseshoe Bend, while suffering only a handful of losses themselves. The defeated Creeks signed the Treaty of 1814, giving up over 20 million acres of land in Georgia and Alabama, and it was only a matter of time before other Indian territories would be claimed.

Some of the Red Sticks escaped Jackson's wrath and disappeared into the swamps and forests of Florida. Many of them continued their attacks and raids against white settlers, though often it was necessary to make deals with the British and Spanish to get the supplies they needed.

In 1818, Jackson single-handedly came close to starting a war with Britain. He captured and executed two British agents who had been charged with instigating Seminole hostility. While the arrests were understandable, the resulting trial was questionable and many historians agree that such punishment was probably illegal. To temper England's wrath over the incident, the U.S. House of Representatives passed a resolution condemning Jackson's actions.

Undaunted, Jackson moved to quell Indian resistance. In March of 1818, Jackson's advancing army reached Tallahassee, not long after the forewarned Indians there had abandoned it. He ordered all buildings burnt to the ground, and once again Tallahassee was reduced to a smoldering ruin.

The First Seminole War flared from 1818 to 1819, and Jackson's raids during the conflict eventually forced the Spanish to sell its terri-

---

Insiders' Tips

Five different flags have flown over Florida: Spanish, French, British, Confederate and, last but certainly not least, American.

• 355

Built in 1957, the Governor's Mansion is based on designs of Andrew Jackson's home, The Hermitage.

tory to the United States. Jackson was rewarded for his efforts by being named the Governor of the Florida Territory in 1821, and he in turn rewarded his many friends with comfortable jobs and insider advice on investing in the territory's economy.

But Jackson grew restless; Florida was not exactly a hotbed of activity, and he felt that he'd been given this post by influential enemies who wanted to keep him out of national politics. After only a few months he and his wife returned to their home in Tennessee. Florida, however, would feel the man's influence for years to come.

A New Capital

Now, one of Tallahassee's most prized assets is its location. History reveals, however, that this site was chosen not because of its north-south boundaries, but because of what lay directly east and west of it.

In 1821, when Florida became a Territory of the United States, the land was divided into two areas. During the 20 years of British rule, two capitals had been established. On the Atlantic coast was the historic settlement of St. Augustine, and nearly four hundred miles away on the Gulf of Mexico was the equally-historic settlement of Pensacola. Both functioned well as centers of trade and legislation for their respective regions, but when the time came to coordinate the eventual consolidation of the area, the 400 miles of undeveloped swamp and piney forests between the two capitals proved to be a daunting barrier.

After much discussion, the two capitals decided to find a midpoint on the Panhandle that would accommodate a yearly meeting of both lawmakers. By anyone's map, Tallahassee was the logical choice.

In 1824 the first white settlers moved into the red hills area and began cutting down trees for the first capital building, which was a log cabin.

For many years, Tallahassee was little more than a tiny town of log cabins and dirt roads. William DuVal was named Jackson's successor, and they were similar in their general and frank dislike for the territory. At one point, the Secretary of State had to order DuVal to return to the capital after the governor went to Kentucky for an extended stay.

DuVal returned to oversee the development of the Tallahassee area, and successfully avoided another Seminole confrontation through diplomacy rather than force. When a local chief complained bitterly that his people had been forced to give their land away for pennies, DuVal simply deposed the man as chief and assigned another less rebellious Indian to the post.

Tallahassee was little more than a frontier town at this point, although several rich families had moved here. Among them was Prince Achille Murat, the nephew of Napoleon Bonaparte and exiled crown prince of Naples, who married the great-grand niece of George Washington. Francis Eppes, the grandson of Thomas Jefferson, also relocated to the area to run a plantation.

Tallahassee was growing. Streets had been planned, plantations built and routes of commerce established with the nearby Gulf Coast as well as other cities and towns. There was a genteel aristocracy in place, one that delighted itself with ring tournaments straight out of the legends of King Arthur, complete with chivalric silk-clad knights on horseback, crowned ladies and splendid balls. Several long-lived celebrations were held by the citizens, including the Fourth of July, the anniversary of the Battle of New Orleans and the May Day Festival.

In spite of all this transplanted aristocracy, Tallahassee was still a rather primitive settlement, and not a very nice one at that. In 1827, writer Ralph Waldo Emerson visited the area and later wrote that this was "a grotesque place, selected three years since as a suitable spot for the capital, and since that day rapidly settled by public officers, land speculators, and desperadoes."

Indeed, this was sometimes a violent little town. For many years duelling was popular among the young men of the area, resulting in the deaths and maiming of so many quarrellers that a law was passed outlawing the ages-old practice. But the law was pretty ineffective as it also included a clause requiring a fine from those individuals who refused a challenge to duel. It would take many more years — and lives — for this law to be given any real teeth.

And as if duelling and drunken brawls weren't killing enough people, the Yellow Fever Plague of 1841 certainly made Tallahassee a risky environment. Over 10 percent of the city's 1,600 inhabitants died from this fever. So many people died that Tallahassee had to establish a new graveyard, now called the Old City Cemetery. Many of the markers there bear witness to this plague year.

Two years after the plague came another catastrophe, one that would again change the face of this young town: the fire of 1843. It started in the kitchen of a hotel called Washington Hall and raged for only three hours one hot May evening. As most of the town's closely-packed buildings were wood, Tallahassee was almost wiped off the map for the third time in its history. It was decreed — and smartly so — that all future buildings must be constructed of masonry.

Tallahassee was rebuilt, but not as quickly. The terrible fire had devoured the dreams of several settlers along with the buildings, and some hard-luck cases were drawn westward by the California Gold Rush.

Through it all, one aspect of life in Tallahassee became increasingly clear: whites and Indians could not live together. The settlers eagerly wanted as much land as possible and the Indians bitterly felt they had already given too much. Numerous meetings were held, promises and treaties were made and broken and the antagonism between the two sides inevitably led to the Second Seminole War.

This conflict lasted from 1835 to 1842 and was much more costly than the first. Led by famous warriors such as Osceola, the Seminoles inflicted heavy losses on the U.S. Army forces that moved in to quell uprisings. The Indians managed to hold out for as long as they did by retreating into the swamps, where they easily evaded the clumsy, ill-trained troops pursuing them. As Americans slowly realized the extent to which these Native Indians were dedicated to their land and freedom, the war began to seem useless and cruel. An army surgeon, Jacob Rhett Motte, would echo this sentiment years later in *Journey Into Wilderness*, an account of his experiences during the war: "Why not in the name of common sense let them keep it [the swamp]? Every day served but to convince us of their inflexible determination to fight or die in the land of their fathers." Historians such as Gene Burnett have even likened the unpopular conflict to Vietnam.

In the end, the Seminoles were defeated because of their limited resources and dwindling manpower. Almost all of them were shipped off to reservations, and all the escaped slaves captured with them were returned to slavery.

Although there really weren't any Indian attacks closer than 10 miles of Tallahassee, the Second Seminole War had been on everyone's mind. Citizens had watched as thousands of soldiers from Tennessee and Georgia marched southward, sometimes camping just outside of town. Now that the conflict was over, Tallahasseans could finally breathe a sigh of relief and return their attention to the landscape unfolding around them. Northern Florida had become a dynamic agrarian economy, producing cotton as well as other crops like tobacco — the

TALLAHASSEE — HISTORY

The Union Bank is the oldest surviving bank building in the state.

latter was introduced to the area by Governor DuVal.

The first real capitol building was completed in 1845, the year Florida became a state and William D. Moseley its first elected governor.

But not long after the end of the Second Seminole War, another racial problem loomed on the horizon: the abolitionist movement. In the 1860 presidential election, Abraham Lincoln received no votes at all from the state of Florida - that's because his name was not even allowed on the ballot. The southern states reverberated with speeches and literature demanding secession from the Union.

The Civil War

In 1861, South Carolina was the first state to break away, Mississippi was the second, and Florida was third. Out of all the Confederate states east of the Mississippi, Florida was the only one whose capital did not fall to Union forces.

Though most Floridians supported the decision to secede, there were a few bold citizens who made public their stand against it. Richard Keith Call, a former governor, is remembered by his daughter as saying to a group of secession-happy people: "You have opened the gates of hell, from which shall flow the curses of the damned."

The First Infantry Regiment of Florida Volunteers was pooled mostly from Leon County and its neighbors, Gadsden, Jackson, Jefferson and Madison counties. Colonel James Patton Anderson, a Jefferson County planter, was in command. They first marched to

• 359

TALLAHASSEE — HISTORY

The front porch of the Knott House has seen a lot of history over the years.

Pensacola and helped fend off attacks from Union forces at Fort Pickens. Later the First Florida fought in Tennessee at Shiloh, one of the most tragic battles of the war. They also saw action at the Battle of Perryville in Kentucky and Murfreesboro, Tennessee.

John Milton, a planter from Marianna, was elected governor during the Civil War, and his ideas concerning states' rights were even more radical than those who supported secession. Let the states stand entirely alone, he reasoned, dismissing the need even for a Confederacy, although he was more than willing to let them direct the war effort.

Milton didn't like it when Florida's First and other regiments were pulled out of the state to fight elsewhere, and his paranoia was well-founded. Not long after their departure, Federal troops seized Pensacola and St. Augustine, as well as several other port towns.

By 1863, the general attitude in Tallahassee and other parts of the state was similar to national reaction during the Second Seminole War. Confederate troops were deserting their posts in great numbers and hiding out in woods and swamps, where Union forces gave them food and shelter as they waited for the war to end.

It was an understandable reaction from the lower-class soldiers conscripted into battle. If you had an extra few thousand dollars in your pocket, you could simply buy your way out of service, hire someone else to do the dirty work for you. The poorer folk could only hide and hope they wouldn't be captured and executed for desertion.

The lack of soldiers in the Tallahassee area makes the Battle of Natural Bridge all the more incredible. Union forces — including many black soldiers — landed at St. Marks in March of 1865. They planned to proceed northward and take the capital city by surprise.

Tallahassee got word of the impending invasion, however, and mustered up as many able-bodied men as possible. Old men and young boys took up arms along with the remaining Confederate troops, and together they hurried the fifteen miles south to Natural Bridge, a spot on the St. Marks River where the river disappears underground for one hundred feet. When the Union forces attempted to cross here, they were repelled and forced to retreat back to their ships. This was a small victory for the Confederacy, but to Tallahassee it felt as if the war had been won. The soldiers received heroes' welcomes when they returned.

This joy was short-lived, however, as news of countless Southern defeats and Union advances reached the city. "Death would be preferable to reunion," Governor Milton told the legislature, and then proceeded to prove the point. On April 1, 1865, eight days before General Lee surrendered at Appomattox, Florida Governor John Milton shot himself dead.

Restoration

People struggled to survive in the aftermath of the Civil War. No matter who you were, things had changed drastically. Tallahassee was now the capital city of a state that had to restructure and rebuild itself.

Some of the area plantations offered to pay their former slaves to resume their jobs, but it was a tough sell. Many of the blacks felt they had to shed every aspect of their old lives in order to truly be free, and this sometimes included moving away and changing one's name, even leaving one's family. The Freedmen's Bureau was established to help the blacks assimilate themselves into society, but because of the lifelong hardships they had endured, many blacks simply preferred to "drop out" and enjoy their freedom 24 hours a day. By 1866, though, most blacks were working again on plantations under a contract system that was sometimes not much different than slavery.

Old habits die hard but they do indeed die, and many whites felt as if all they had known was crumbling around them. Agriculture quickly dwindled to a small fraction of what it had once been, and the cotton industry all but disappeared from the area.

Other industries sprang up: old plantations were turned into hunting preserves, peanuts and tobacco replaced cotton as major crops. Still, the sense of dislocation was numbing to many, and it's no surprise that Federal troops occupied Florida for over a decade after the end of the war.

There was happiness to be found on a small scale. The poet Sidney Lanier visited Tallahassee not long after the war and wrote in his 1875 book *Florida: Its Scenery, Climate and History*: ". . . no one has starved, and albeit the people are poor and the dwellings need paint and ready money is slow of circulation . . . it must be confessed that the bountiful tables looked like anything but famine, that signs of energy cropped out here and there in many places, and that the whole situation was but a reasonable one for a people who ten years ago had to begin life anew from the very bottom. . . ."

Into the 20th Century

The first two decades of this century were boom years for Florida, and it all boiled down to one word: land.

Florida seemed endless to investors and developers, and once the railroads and highways connecting southern Florida were in place, big money moved in. Two of the state's largest industries — citrus and tourism — were mostly established during this period.

Tallahassee itself was also modernized to a large extent. At the turn of the century there had been a fruitless attempt to relocate the capital to either Jacksonville, St. Augustine or Ocala. There were several powerful factions who felt that Tallahassee was too distant from the rest of the state, especially the burgeoning southern peninsula. This move never took place, of course, but the threat was something of a wake-up call to the citizens. The lawmakers soon approved funding to improve the existing Capitol, and the city decided to update its services and utilities. An electric power plant and sewer system were con-

The Walker Library, built in 1903, was the city's first public library.

structed to support the city's increasing population.

This boom period, which lasted from the turn of the century to the 1920s, helped revitalize the state's stricken economy. But all booms must bust. The Depression made things tough all over, and Florida felt the blow as much as any state.

People were desperate for money, and that included lawmakers. After the Stock Market Crash of 1929, over 150 cities and towns in Florida were in default on their debts and the state government was burdened with a huge deficit its constitution wouldn't allow.

Governor Doyle Carlton (1929 - 1933) couldn't have picked a lousier time to head the state government, but he buckled down and got to work anyway. His feuds with lawmakers are legendary, and while they did pass a controversial gambling bill that reportedly had the backing of some big-time underworld figures, Carlton fought them to the end. He also campaigned heavily for Franklin D. Roosevelt during his run for president, and was a presidential advisor for many years.

To make things worse, there was a Mediterranean fruit fly invasion the same year as the stock market crash, and that year's bountiful citrus crop was more than halved. You couldn't grow oranges in Tallahassee, but if you were a lawmaker you could look out over the rest of the state and sense the devastation.

During World War II, Florida's vast coastline and friendly climate made it a prime spot to train soldiers, and this helped the state's economy considerably. Governor Spessard Holland was instrumental

The Big Bend Farm at the Tallahassee Museum of History and Natural Science gives viewers a look at the lives of early settlers.

in attracting the military to the state, and Tallahassee's Dale Mabry Airport (now the Tallahassee Regional Airport) became an important air base.

The town opened a downtown USO Club and welcomed the hundreds of troops who came into the area. The female college students at Florida State College for Women (later Florida State University) and Florida Agricultural and Mechanical College outnumbered the men in town by a ratio of more than two-to-one, and when it was announced that over 800 servicemen would be stationed at this new base, the town's atmosphere got livelier.

Of particular note was a class of Chinese fighter pilots who received their final training at Dale Mabry Field. The Chinese soldiers did not adapt readily to the cockpit of American fighters, and as they learned the controls they would often zoom very low over Tallahassee. More than one of them crashed, and residents knew just by looking at a plane in the sky if a Chinese pilot was flying it.

When the war was over, the resulting boom had a great impact on Florida. More people began to visit and relocate here than ever before. In fact, many of these people had been stationed here during the war and were returning for the state's climate and landscape.

But by the mid-1950s, Tallahassee seemed out-of-step with the rest of the state. Public transportation, health care and segregation were issues that needed to be addressed, and LeRoy Collins, elected as the state's thirty-third governor, was in-

TALLAHASSEE — HISTORY

Tallahassee's canopy roads are specially protected paths from the past.

strumental in bringing about many needed changes in Florida.

All was not peaceful in paradise, however. Beneath the formica veneer of the 1950s lurked renewed racial tension. Governor Collins was an important player during this era, and so were the students at Florida A&M University.

In 1956 there was a massive bus boycott in Tallahassee. Blacks refused to ride the city bus line because they were forced to sit in the back. Their unified actions brought about a permanent change in policy.

In 1960, FAMU students staged a sit-in at Woolworth's lunch counter in protest of segregated dining facilities. Three years later, blacks cleverly protested at the Florida Theatre, which admitted whites only. They formed a huge line to purchase tickets, and as each one was turned away they'd return again to the end of the line.

This was a turbulent decade for the nation and Tallahassee, which was quite resistant to change. The race issue was so controversial that when President John F. Kennedy was assassinated, many opponents of his civil rights policies could be heard openly laughing and joking throughout the city. And many agree that Collins lost his 1968 bid for re-election because of his work on the civil rights issue. His opponents simply handed out photos of the governor standing beside Martin Luther King, Jr., in Selma, Alabama.

One of the most violent and tragic racial episodes happened in April of 1968, after the assassination of King. Riots erupted on the FAMU campus, and the entire area was cordoned off by police following mob attacks on motorists. FAMU was closed down for over a week to allow tensions to subside. In the midst of it all, there was a peaceful march past the state Capitol to mark King's funeral.

This decade also saw the national space program take root in Florida, and it has remained a vital industry and tourist attraction. The first of Florida's many theme parks also began construction, and corporations continued their relocation here to take advantage of Florida's business-friendly environment and growing work force.

Florida has grown and changed considerably in the last quarter-century, and the Capital City has remained at the center of it all. Its citizens take pride in the fact that this old town on a hill still serves as the focal point for state politics. Tallahassee today is more diverse than it ever was, and yet there's also a sense of unity among its residents. It has passed from a rural agricultural center to a growing urban city, and since 1980 its population has almost doubled to over 200,000.

Often in the city's past, its residents have been afraid of the uncertain future. But they learned that the best way to overcome their fear was to remain in touch with their colorful, violent and often inspiring past.

Inside
Tallahassee

What's a city like Tallahassee doing in a state like Florida? That's the big question a lot of visitors ask themselves after paying us a visit, and it just goes to show that you can't always trust a preconceived notion.

When most people think of Florida, they usually picture what the peninsula has to offer from Orlando on down: wide sunny beaches, crowded theme parks and a sense of hustle-and-bustle that is notably absent from life in the northwest part of the state.

The capital city of Tallahassee is found at the thinnest point of Northwest Florida — fifteen miles to its north lies the Georgia state line, and twenty-five miles due south is the Gulf of Mexico. This geographic midpoint affords its inhabitants the best of both worlds, from tropical beaches normally associated with south Florida to the hilly pine forests one might encounter in the Deep South.

When people spend time in Tallahassee, they are always struck by how Southern the city seems. Unlike the more populous parts of the state, Tallahassee is a place where time seems to slow down a bit. People are more easygoing here than in, say, Miami or Tampa. There's an almost genteel sensibility in the air, one that captures the best aspects of Southern tradition.

Visitor Information

**TALLAHASSEE
CHAMBER OF COMMERCE**
100 N. Duval St.   224-8116

CONVENTION & VISITORS BUREAU
200 W. College Ave.   681-9200

VISITOR INFORMATION CENTER
The Capitol
Monroe St. and Apalachee Pkwy.   681-9200
                            (800) 628-2866

Another facet that sets Tallahassee apart from the rest of the state is the landscape, rippled with hills and winding rivers. Face it, in south Florida, the only hills you'll encounter are the on-ramps and off-ramps of interstate highways. There are palm trees all over Florida, but here they grow side-by-side with forests of pine and oak.

But while life is certainly paced leisurely in these parts, residents never forget that Tallahassee is the focal point of state politics, and the decisions made here affect every

TALLAHASSEE — INSIDE

county, town, city and person in Florida. For all its small-town charm, you can't deny the fact that the buildings of the Capitol Complex are what gives the city its skyline.

Tallahassee is a city that looks and feels young. Leon County is home to over 200,000 people, and the biggest chunk of them are between their late twenties and early forties. Not surprisingly, the largest local employer is the government, whose state and local jobs employ nearly one-third of the civilian labor force. And one-fifth of the residents work in the service industry that in no small part supports the government.

Economically, the area is fairly stable. The median family income is around $37,000 annually, and the unemployment rate is consistently under five percent. The cost of living is not much less than in other areas of the state, but keep in mind that the relaxed lifestyle is a big plus to most people.

A good portion of Leon County residents have been here a long time and can trace their roots back for generations. But most people you meet are from elsewhere. People from south Florida move here to get away from the hectic and harried pace of things, and residents of neighboring states like it here because the city has many of the features found in other Southern cities.

Tallahassee's a good place to raise children. Most parents feel that the city offers a good, safe environment, and the school system gets generally high marks. Part of that

Insiders' Tips

One way to tap into Tallahassee is through the FreeNet, a public computer bulletin board that offers free connections to the worldwide Internet. Residents use it as a springboard onto the Internet, but they also participate in many public forums concerning local and state issues. It's a great way for out-of-towners to check and see what's happening in Tallahassee.

For instance, visitors can sign onto FreeNet and type "visitors" or "attractions," and you'll see a menu offering information on these and many other aspects of Tallahassee life. Type "historic" and you'll get a listing of many historic sites and attractions around town.

Getting onto FreeNet is easy. If your town doesn't have a FreeNet that offers a gateway to the Tallahassee FreeNet, just have your modem dial **488-5056**. There's no charge; you'll only pay for any long-distance charges. The system is menu-driven, user-friendly and, as its **22,000** uses can attest, quite popular.

Moving To Tallahassee?

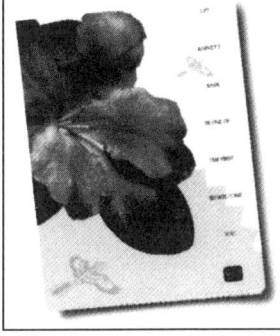

The Barnett Newcomers Guide to Tallahassee is loaded with all the information you'll need if you decide to make Tallahassee your new home. Everything from arts and entertainment to facts on taxes, licenses and financial services. There's even a map to help you get around Tallahassee.

So call us today at 1-800-386-8580 for your free newcomers guide. It may be the best move you'll ever make.

Barnett Bank **Your Bank For Life. Since 1877.**
All Barnett Banks are insured by the FDIC. ©1992 Barnett Banks, Inc.

IG

---

might have to do with the fact that, on the average, there is one teacher for every twenty students, and this lessens the chance of someone being overlooked in class. And nearly sixty-five percent of the high school graduates continue their education at either college or technical schools.

With the exception of screaming football and basketball fans, the biggest noisemaker in town is the state government. The legislature can sometimes get things cranking in late fall if there's a special session. Then in spring the lawmakers come to full session, and Tallahassee's downtown sidewalks are filled at lunchtime not only with elected officials but also small armies of lobbyists and journalists. For a few weeks it seems like all eyes of the state are on us, and we don't mind it one bit.

That could be because summertime is near, and that's when life here slows almost to a halt. The heat and humidity rise considerably. The oppressive air just doesn't move, and if you're not headed for a nearby lake or the Gulf of Mexico, then you really don't want to stray too far from the air conditioner.

Tallahassee's a big college town, too, and every summer two-thirds of the city's nonpermanent student population of 48,000 depart for vacation. The downtown strip of student-oriented businesses is so empty that you could fire a cannon right down the middle and not hit a soul.

Just when it seems that everyone is going to melt like the Wicked Witch from "The Wizard of Oz," the first cool snap of fall gives residents reason to hold out. Towards the end of September the temperatures have cooled quite a bit, especially at night, and the city comes to life again.

Driving through the remote areas of Tallahassee, you can see beautiful landscape that was probably once part of an old plantation being developed into housing tracts and subdivisions. The city must perform a tricky balancing act so its steady growth does not get out of hand.

There are plenty of leisure-time activities to do here, and people love to be outdoors enjoying the natural beauty around them. But even if you get bored, there's a major city only a few hours away in any direction. To the north, Birmingham and Atlanta are each about a five-hour drive away. Jacksonville is about three hours to the east and Pensacola is about three hours west, and is the halfway-point if you're heading for New Orleans' French Quarter. Head south for five hours and you're in the Orlando / Tampa area.

But for most folks, there's no real need to travel that far. From the hilly pine forests on down to the warm waters of the Gulf of Mexico, Tallahassee has just about everything you could need.

It's a growing city, but thank goodness it still feels like a small town.

Tallahassee
Getting Around

Tallahassee rests gently in what is known as Florida's Big Bend. It's easy to get to, and once you're here it's relatively simple to find your way around.

If you're driving, you'll probably be arriving by one of four major routes — Interstate 10, Highway 27, Highway 90 or Highway 319.

Commercial transportation is a growing business in town. Tallahassee Regional Airport features daily service from several national and regional airlines, and Greyhound-Trailways Bus Lines offers service from its downtown terminal. And after a long hiatus, the Amtrak Sunset Limited recently resumed passenger service through Tallahassee, with routes east to Jacksonville and as far west as Los Angeles.

The city itself is bisected quite neatly from north to south by Monroe Street, and from east to west by Tennessee/Mahan streets. This more or less splits the city into four easily navigable areas. An old truck route, Capital Circle, encircles the city and has been upgraded to handle much of the traffic around Tallahassee's perimeter.

The city's bus line, TalTran, provides service throughout the city., and the Dial-A-Ride service provides transportation for the elderly and disabled.

The Old Town Trolley offers free trolley rides and historical tours throughout the downtown area.

Airports

TALLAHASSEE REGIONAL AIRPORT
Capital Circle 891-7800

The Tallahassee Regional Airport currently offers air service through five national and regional carriers. The airport is located just six miles south of the city on Capital Circle and also hosts several car rental agencies. Need a taxi or limo instead? Just check the listings later in this section, as all of them offer service to and from the airport.

Airlines
Atlantic Southeast Airlines	1-282-3424
Comair	(800) 354-9822
Delta	(800) 221-1212
US Air	(800) 428-4322

Airport Automobile Rental
Alamo	(800) 327-9633
Avis	(800) 831-2847
Budget	(800) 527-0700
Dollar	(800) 800-4000
Hertz	(800) 654-3131
National	(800) 227-7368

TALLAHASSEE COMMERCIAL AIRPORT
Hwy. 27 562-1945

This is the only private airport in

Tallahassee

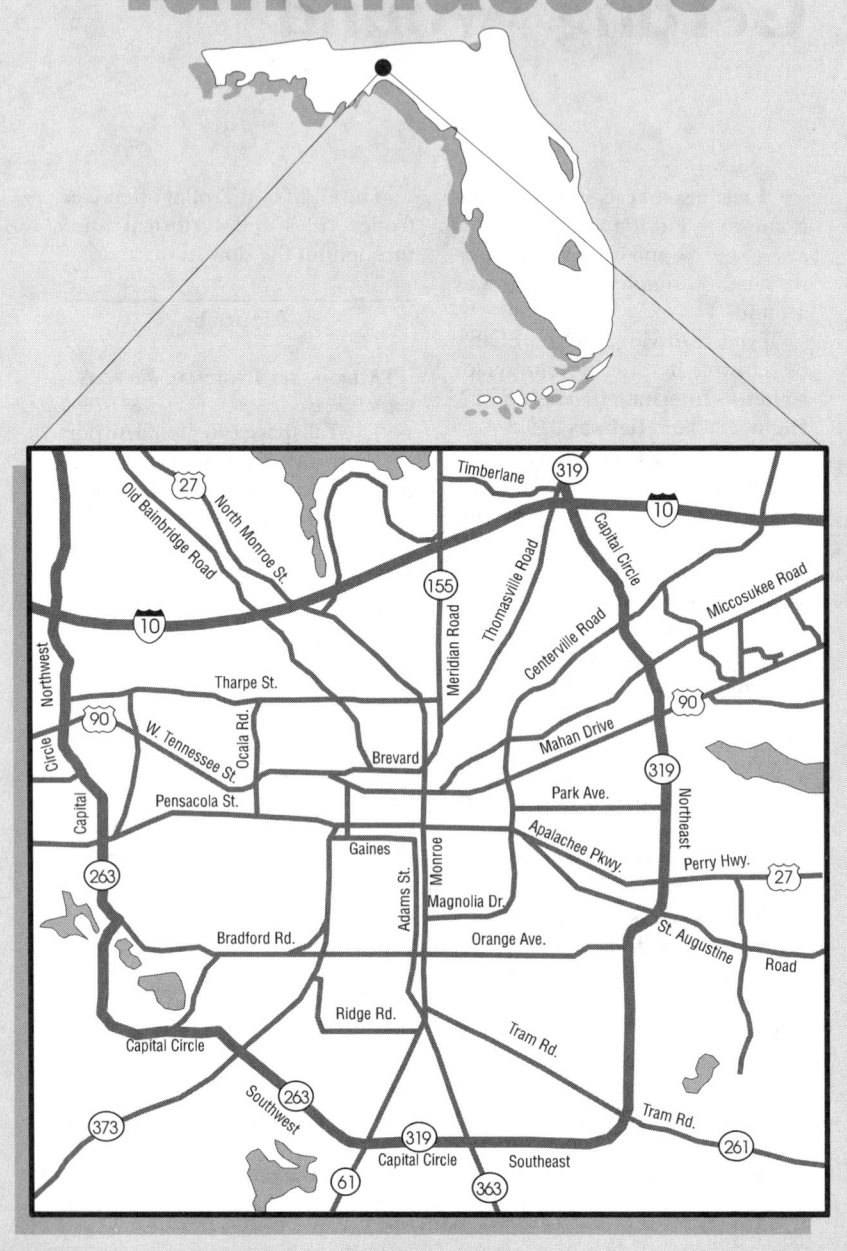

TALLAHASSEE — GETTING AROUND

The Old Town Trolley is a fast and free way to see downtown Tallahassee.

Leon County, and it sits one mile north of Old Bainbridge Road on Highway 27 (N. Monroe Street).

General Automobile Rentals

Tallahassee's population fluctuates wildly during the year. You've got lawmakers, lobbyists and news media in town during the legislative session, not to mention the 50,000 or so college students who come and go during the year. Needless to say, not everyone brings their own car, so car rental agencies are fairly numerous around here.

Agency	576-0196
Alamo	(800) 327-9633
Avis	(800) 831-2847
Budget	(800) 527-0700
Dollar	(800) 800-4000
Enterprise	(800) 325-8007
Hertz	(800) 654-3131
Honey-Bee	575-9175
Lucky's	575-0632
National	(800) 227-7368
Sears Rental	575-8238
Snappy	575-8808
Ugly Duckling	574-0400

Bus Service

For those who love riding the bus, take heed: you can not only ride the bus into town, but once here you can ride TalTran, the city bus line, all over town. The Greyhound-Trailways bus station is open 24 hours, seven days a week.

Riding the TalTran bus line will get you most anywhere you want to go within Tallahassee city limits, and it's generally 75¢ a ride. The TalTran bus routes usually begin around 7 AM and run until 10 PM, but check each route before riding because the hours do vary for each route. TalTran buses are not 100 percent handicapped accessible, but some

• *373*

TALLAHASSEE — GETTING AROUND

do have special wheelchair lifts. Contact the TalTran office ahead of time for more information.

The Old Town Trolley isn't really a trolley at all; it's a bus that looks a heckuva lot like a trolley. It's a fancy little commuter service that zips through the downtown area, and best of all, it's free. The trolley runs from 7 AM to 6 PM Monday through Friday, and no matter which of the dozen or so stops you're at downtown, the trolley will usually come chugging along every 15 minutes or so.

Greyhound-Trailways Bus Lines	222-4240
Old Town Trolley	574-5200
TalTran Bus Line	891-7800

Train Service

Amtrak recently resumed service through Tallahassee, including stops in the nearby towns of Chipley and Crestview. There's a newly refurbished train station here that's open from 9 AM to 5 PM, but you won't see much of it if you are leaving Tallahassee headed west. That's because Amtrak's current schedule has westbound trains arriving in Tallahassee usually after 1 AM, long after the station has closed. So if you're leaving Tallahassee and headed west, be sure to keep this in mind. East-bound travelers can usually expect their trains to depart Tallahassee around noon. Please note that these schedules are subject to change, and it's a good idea to contact Amtrak yourself concerning actual dates and times for train service.

Amtrak	(800) 872-7245
Tallahassee Amtrak Station	224-2779

Taxicabs and Limousine Service

Ambassador Limousines	942-2200
Capital Limousine	574-4350
City Taxi	893-4111
Elite Street Limousine Service	222-7006
Yellow Cab	222-3070

Tallahassee Restaurants

If you think that most Florida cuisine is based on seafood . . . well, you're not too far off the mark there. Residents will readily admit that we'd all be fools not to take advantage of the excellent fishing waters that surround most of the state.

But Floridians are also risk-takers, see. How else can you explain the fact that so many of us have chosen to live in a geographic region frequented by hurricanes? We like challenges and diversity, and that's definitely reflected in the culinary heritage of the state's melting-pot population.

If you love seafood, you've come to the right place. If you're looking for other kinds of cuisine, you won't be disappointed. Tallahassee is home to a wide variety of fine restaurants whose offerings range from the strictly Southern down-home cookin' to more exotic and adventurous international dishes.

There are plenty of restaurants in Tallahassee, and new ones open each year. Keep in mind that the following is only a partial listing. We don't include the many national chain restaurants you'll find in most any town, because you already know what to expect from these places. Rest assured that Tallahassee is well-served by these popular establishments.

The following list contain information on credit cards and pricing. The price guidelines are, of course, subject to change but are based on a basic dinner for two (without all the fancy extras like wine or double-decker desserts). Be sure to check out the chalkboard as you enter a restaurant; often the nightly specials will match or even beat regular menu items in both price and palatability.

Under $20	$
$21 to $35	$$
$36 to $50	$$$
More than $51	$$$$

ANDREW'S
228 S. Adams St.   222-3446
$$ All major credit cards

Tallahassee's skyline might not impress city slickers — and they'll forgive us if we're more proud of the landscape than the buildings. But if you feel the urge to look at architecture while you dine, Andrew's has the best view of downtown Tallahassee and some of the best food, as well. This two-story restaurant offers something different at every level. The downstairs restaurant offers mostly contemporary American fare, and the best bets are any of the pasta, chicken or seafood dishes. There's a popular jazz lounge upstairs (called, naturally, Andrew's Upstairs) where music aficionados can usually be found sampling the cold buffet, salad bar and appetizers. And diners can also opt for the outdoor dining courtyard during warm summery nights (this is Florida, and we get a lot of 'em around here).

Annella's
1400 Village Commons   668-1961
$$ All major credit cards

This is one of those places that's hard to find but well worth the search. Tucked back in a shopping plaza amidst several department stores, Annella's is an elegant little restaurant whose seasonal menu never fails to surprise or impress diners. You'll find an array of succulent styles, from French flourishes to Italian innovations. A popular dish is the Shrimp and Cornbread with Roasted Red Pepper Sauce, and many people swear that the meatloaf here is the best they've ever had. Other specialties include steaks, seafood and escargot.

Anthony's
Betton Place, 1950 Thomasville Rd.   224-1447
$$ All major credit cards

No offense to Anthony, but we think this place should really be called Eddies — plural because chefs Eddie Davis and Eddie Hogan are mostly responsible for the fine, traditional Italian fare served here. From the Eggplant Parmesan to the elegant veal dishes, you'll truly think you've taken a trip to rural Italy. Anthony's also serves up some other fine dishes, such as steaks — especially the New York strip — and the seafood (our favorite's the grouper).

Bahn Thai Restaurant
1319 S. Monroe St.   224-4765
$$ MC, VISA

There are only two Thai restaurants in Tallahassee, and both are so popular it's a wonder there aren't three or four of them — perhaps there will be by the time you read this. Bahn Thai sits less than a half-mile south of the Capitol Building, but one bite of the food and you're in another world. The chefs here create some of the spiciest fare in town. Even the most devoted heat-seekers usually settle for "medium" when specifying how hot they prefer a dish, because they know it'll come out scorching. Recently the dining room was renovated and now sports an Eastern decor that perfectly complements the food.

Barnacle Bill's Seafood Emporium
1830 N. Monroe St.   385-8734
$ All major credit cards

The atmosphere here is casual, but the seafood is dressed to kill. Barnacle Bill's trucks in it fresh daily

---

Insiders' Tips

Andrew's in downtown Tallahassee wasn't always such a lively hot spot — this fun, upscale restaurant and lounge sits on the former site of a tranquil 1870s mansion built by Dr. James Randolph, who served as a surgeon in the Confederate army.

and serves it up steamed, smoked or grilled. We recommend you stick around long enough to try it all three ways. Sit at the oyster bar and you'll find a fourth way: raw. Seafood's not the only reason to come here — the menu also sports hamburgers, chicken wings, pasta and vegetables — but it's the best reason. The place can get pretty packed on football weekends, but if standing room only is your bag, by all means do attend.

CAFE DI LORENZO
1002 N. Monroe St.   *681-3622*
$$ *All major credit cards*

This exciting Italian restaurant recently moved to a new location, but wisely kept the core of its mouthwatering menu. There are over a dozen thoughtfully prepared pasta dishes to choose from, as well as veal and seafood favorites. Owner Lorenzo Amato has a flair for decorating as well, and the rich surroundings here are almost as enjoyable as the food. There's a good wine selection to choose from, too.

CHEZ PIERRE
115 N. Adams St.   *222-0936*
$$ *MC, VISA, Discover*

This charming and affordable bistro has been serving excellent French cuisine for nearly two decades now, and it's only getting better with age. Quiche and crepes dominate the lunch menu, while dinners are usually fish or fowl. There are some tantalizing desserts and pastries (of course) and a wine and espresso bar. To top off the French cafe motif, the owners are currently displaying the work of local artists on the walls. You'd have to travel someplace very, very far away to get French fare this authentic. We'll give you one guess.

CHINA GOURMET
2580 N. Monroe St.   *385-1124*
$$ *All major credit cards*

China Gourmet continues to receive high ratings from residents as well as the local restaurant critic. These folks must know *something*, right? Eat a meal here and you too can be "in the know." The China Gourmet stands above many other Chinese restaurants because they go that extra mile to ensure that a dish is extra-flavorful and cooked to perfection. Their not-to-be-missed buffet line is designed to feed the masses but the items are prepared with individual attention.

EASTSIDE MARIO'S
2756 N. Monroe St.   *385-1774*
$$ *All major credit cards*

This American-Italian eatery is one of Tallahassee's latest culinary additions but has already established quite a reputation based on its pizza alone. The flavorful pie is baked New York-style in a wood-burning brick oven, and if you've never tried it this way, it does make a difference. Other zesty pasta, seafood and meat dishes fill out the impressive menu. The atmosphere is fun and casual, even though you'd normally expect formal wear to accompany cuisine this superb.

FOOD GLORIOUS FOOD
1950 Thomasville Rd.
(Betton Place)   *224-9974*
$ *All major credit cards*

If there's one restaurant in town whose name perfectly embodies the concept of "truth in advertising," then this is the place. Residents call it "FGF" for short, and its rotating menu is tantalizing and surprising. Fresh salads and gourmet entrees are the specialty here, along with sandwiches and croissants. Be sure to save room for the homemade desserts, which seem to quickly disappear with the lunch crowd. Seating can sometimes be at a premium, but they don't take reservations. Outdoor seating was added last year to great acclaim, and it offers some much-needed space. Your best bet is to take an early or late lunch. Even if you show up with the crowd, however, you're sure to agree that it's worth the wait.

Golden East
2696 N. Monroe St.   422-2881
$$ All major credit cards

This is a very popular Chinese restaurant, and you need look no further than its impressive lunch and dinner buffets to understand why. There are always at least 12 main courses offered on the line, as well as several appetizers and delicious soups. The specialty here is the Mongolian barbecue—it's heavenly. Choose from these and many other items on the menu, because it's darned near impossible to go wrong. Just head east and you'll do fine.

Kitcho
Market Square
1415 Timberlane Rd.   893-7686
$$ MC, VISA

The master chefs here serve up a variety of traditional Japanese dishes and adventurous specials. Kitcho also sports one of the Tallahassee's few sushi bars, giving those in the north end of town a convenient place to toss back raw delicacies. The place fills up quickly on weekend evenings, so call ahead or hit it on a weeknight. The lunchtime sushi roll buffet usually packs them in, too.

La Fiesta
911 Apalachee Pkwy.   656-3392
$ All major credit cards

This is one of the most authentic Mexican restaurants in town, and that's because the fare is good, cheap and plentiful. If you've ever been down to Mexico, you'll know what we're talking about here. Tacos, enchiladas, burritos and other specialties keep the masses satisfied. You can wash it all down with a good selection of Mexican beer and tequila. It's just off a major parkway through the city, and it's no wonder that traffic here is sometimes pretty heavy.

The Lieutenant Governor's Public House and Grill
1215 Thomasville Rd.   222-4547
$$$ All major credit cards

OK, this is a little joke that may need explaining. This new and elegant restaurant takes its name as a jibe to a private club in the downtown district. That one is called — you guessed it — the Governors Club. The Lieutenant Governor's Public House and Grill has quickly surpassed the amusing novelty of its name and established a reputation for some truly innovative American cuisine. Chef Bryant Withers assembles a new handwritten menu daily, featuring a wide range of sea-

THE SIGHTS, SOUNDS & FLAVORS OF MANHATTAN'S "LITTLE ITALY"

Enjoy great Italian and American grill favorites in a fun atmosphere reminiscent of Manhattan's famous "Little Italy" district. You must experience it to believe it!

★ Wood-burning brick oven pizza
★ Pasta favorites
★ Rotisserie roasted chicken
★ American grill favorites

**Happy Hour
Hungry Hour**
Party outdoors in Central Park!

An American Italian Eatery
385-1774 · 2576 N. Monroe St.

EAST SIDE MARIO'S

food and steak meals. He also serves several crepe dishes that will literally melt in your mouth. If you can, save room for the delicious desserts. This place may not be a private club, but they sure treat you special anyway.

LUCY HO'S BAMBOO GARDEN
2814 Apalachee Pkwy.   *878-3366*
$$ *All major credit cards*

Lucy Ho's gives us the best of two worlds: Japanese and Chinese. Their menu offers great selections from both cuisines. There's a popular dinner buffet as well as an elegant sushi bar. For the purist, you can even shed your shoes and dine in the tatami room. There's usually weekend entertainment in the adjoining lounge, which also boasts a karaoke machine.

THE MELTING POT
1832 N. Monroe St.   *386-7440*
$$ *All major credit cards*

This Swiss fondue restaurant keeps 'em dipping around here. There's a wide range of tableside fondues to choose from, as well as what to dip: chicken, seafood and meat. You should know that this kind of food can be quite rich and filling, so plan to go on an empty stomach. Trust us, you'll have no trouble reversing the trend. Reservations are recommended, especially on weekends.

The Mill Bakery and Eatery
2136 N. Monroe St.   386-2867
2329 Apalachee Pkwy.   656-2867
$ All major credit cards

With two locations, the Mill has Tallahassee well covered when it comes to thick sandwiches, gourmet pizzas (especially the pesto chicken), vegetarian chili and some of the biggest fresh-baked muffins you've ever seen. The Mill is a small southeastern chain that also brews its own beer. There are four kinds of ale, each highly recommended. Weekends can get a little crowded, as students pile in for live music and drink specials. So if you can, plan dinner a bit on the early side of the evening.

Mounir's
1000 W. Tharpe St.   422-0816
$ No credit cards

This is probably the only Tallahassee restaurant with professional belly dancing — hey, accept no substitutes. Mounir's is known for its tasty and tangy Middle Eastern fare. There are so many great dishes that newcomers might not be able to choose, so the best bet is to order one of the appetizer samplers that contains a little bit of everything. Some people claim it's a meal all unto itself. We'd agree. Currently, belly dancing is featured on Saturday nights only, so make your plans accordingly.

The Mustard Tree
Market Square
1415 Timberlane Rd.   893-8733
$$ All major credit cards

Formerly the Mustard Seed, this place changed its name to reflect its popularity — and growth. The Mustard Tree serves exceptional American cuisine with a flair for the Cajun. The menu features standard fare as well as more adventurous seafood dishes — and if you like spicy adventures, any of the blackened offerings should please you. The Mustard Tree recently reopened for lunch service with outdoor terrace dining.

The Nicholson Farmhouse
S. R. 12   539-5931
$$$ MC, VISA

Sitting about 15 miles north of Tallahassee in Havana, the Nicholson Farmhouse serves some of the best steaks in the area. Owner Paul Nicholson's great-great grandfather built the house in 1828, and it's been beautifully restored. The dining area spills out into three other houses on the property, one of which was the farm's original smokehouse. All have been renovated and offer a unique rustic country setting. Although they serve fine fish and fowl, the seasoned and aged steaks are the prime dishes here. An evening at the Nicholson Farmhouse is a fascinating and gastronomically pleasing trip back in time.

Nino's
6497 Apalachee Pkwy.   878-8141
$$ All major credit cards

Nino's is a Tallahassee favorite — a friendly Italian restaurant whose fine food is something you'd easily pay twice as much for in a big city. Here, it's cheap and plentiful and prepared with a gourmet touch. You can come as casual or as dressy as you like; as long as you're ready for some good food, you'll fit right in. Note that Nino's serves dinner only and is not open for lunch.

THE OLD TOWN CAFE
1415 Timberlane Rd. 893-5741
$$ All major credit cards

The Old Town prides itself on knowing how to cook prime rib and baby back rib, but they're pretty good at seafood and burgers, too. This may sound fairly standard but it's the special flourishes that count here — Caribbean and Cajun, in particular. They also make excellent salads that are meals unto themselves. The walls are muted pastels, but the food is colorful and distinctive. Be sure to save room for the homemade desserts.

THE PARADISE GRILL & BAR
1406 Meridian Rd. 224-2742
$ MC, VISA

If good food and a friendly crowd is your idea of paradise, then look no further. The Paradise Grill & Bar's active social setting should serve as an indicator of the quality of food here. On weekends and during football season, the place can be standing room only. If you don't want to rub elbows, however, pick most any night during the week and sample the delicious Cajun-style seafood and Jamaican jerk chicken. If your palate is more conservative, there are some sizzling hamburgers and hot dogs that come highly recommended. The Paradise has a glassed-in porch and open-air deck. There's plenty of room here, and it's easy to see why they need it.

POSEY'S OYSTER BAR
St. Marks 925-6172
$ No credit cards

This modest seafood shack is known for its smoked mullet and fresh raw oysters. The weekend lunch and dinner crowds can be intimidating, and Sunday nights are usually the busiest as Tallahassee residents flock down for an evening of food and karaoke before the work week starts up again. It's in St. Marks about 15 miles south of Tallahassee; just take Monroe Street south out of town. It turns into Highway 363, which dead ends at Posey's.

THE SHELL OYSTER BAR
114-A E. Oakland St. 224-9919
$

These people do raw oysters and that's about it. For years this tiny oyster bar just south of the capitol was housed in a former gas station, and all it offered was a bench, a bar, Apalachicola oysters and sliced lemons. You brought your own drinks. The amiable no-frills atmosphere made it an instant classic with residents and visitors alike. It's moved back half a block to slightly larger digs, and the owners smartly haven't messed too much with the menu. This is about as casual as you can get.

THE SILVER SLIPPER
531 Scotty Lane 386-9366
$$$ All major credit cards

The Slipper has been around for half a century, and it's still going strong. The reason? The thick and juicy Angus steaks, not to mention the appetizing seafood and Greek dishes. There's an adjoining lounge with weekend entertainment, and private dining rooms are available. During the legislative session, those private rooms are usually filled with lawmakers and lobbyists. But no matter what time of year, you shouldn't take any chances on this venue, folks: make reservations.

THE WHITE SWAN CAFE

The Verandas, 1355 Market St.   668-2812
$$$ All major credit cards

Master Chef Tim Waingraw has served his delectable dishes to U.S. Presidents and foreign heads of state, and most Tallahasseans feel lucky he moved here after leaving Washington, D.C. The White Swan has quickly established a reputation of offering classic American cuisine at very affordable prices. The Steak Alexander and Beef Wellington are hard to pass up, and the roast duck and Salmon Moussileine also come highly recommended. The lunchtime crowd moves steadily enough to accommodate most everyone, but reservations for dinner are almost mandatory here.

Tallahassee
Nightlife

Believe it or not, Tallahassee has an active nightlife that goes back well over a hundred years.

During the antebellum years, as Tallahassee grew from a frontier village to a small town, recreation and relaxation became something of a fine art. This was mostly due to Southern aristocracy's penchant for dignified and extravagant spectacles. Local history books are filled with accounts of genteel garden parties, gallant ring tournaments in the tradition of English royalty as well as brash and sometimes deadly duels.

One can of course still find an abundance of lawn parties and modern-day chivalry. As far as duelling goes, the city forefathers were wise enough to outlaw gun duels in 1840, thereby helping Tallahassee's image in no small manner.

Today, Tallahassee caters to a large and sometimes fluctuating population of fun-seekers and party-lovers. During the fall, students back from summer break eagerly fill the warehouses, bars and dives that cater to the younger set by offering cheap beer and loud bands. This continues into winter, which leads to spring, when the more upscale places are filled with lobbyists and lawmakers in town for the legislative session, either making complex deals or taking breathers from such hot-bed activity.

Summer offers a brief and welcome respite for locals, as students and politicians retreat for a few months. The sun is sweltering and nobody moves very much. Depending on the time of day, summer visitors might think they've stepped into a ghost town, but all they have to do is find where everyone is cooling down. If it's not at a lake or the beach, then it just might be at one of the following places.

Usually, there's a core cross-section of bars and nightlife spots that operates year round. Things may slow down a bit at times, but they never come to a complete stop. And when things are moving, you'd best be assured that they can move mighty fast.

As we said, this kind of thing has been going here on for a long time. Practice certainly makes perfect.

THE ABBEY
2425 Spoonwood Dr.   *386-3000*

What sets The Abbey apart from other nightclubs is the fact that it's a nonalcoholic party place. They offer over 100 different drinks, and people still manage to look like they're having a great time. There's food and dancing and a spacious outdoor deck. Mostly The Abbey is reserved for the use of church and civic organizations, but Friday nights find the place open to a receptive public.

Andrew's Upstairs
228 S. Adams St. Commons   222-3444

Above Andrew's Street Cafe sits this prime nightspot, Andrew's Upstairs. It's a class act that likes its patrons to dress and act casual. This is mostly for the Baby Boomers and above who like their jazz intimate and hot. On the weekends, the place can really get jumpin'. During the week, the music's a bit more refined and quiet, though it too can sometimes perk up your ears. Andrew's Upstairs also sports a great view of the downtown Tallahassee skyline. Kick back with a cold one, enjoy the music and for a few hours pretend you're in a big city.

Barnacle Bill's Half Shell Lounge
1830 N. Monroe St.   385-8734

Some say the drinking side of this restaurant is just as good as the eating side, but we've never seen the difference. If you want, you can sit in the Half Shell Lounge and toss back buckets of oysters, even order from the menu if you want your seafood cooked. There's usually live entertainment on weekend evenings — rock and blues and country, the standard Tallahassee mix. There's no cover charge. If there's a game on, the band may have to really vie for the crowd's attention. Sometimes they'll play it smart and wait until it's over so people will notice them. Hours are Sunday to Thursday, 11 AM to 11 PM; Friday and Saturday, 11 AM to midnight.

Buffalo's Wings and Rings
1904 W. Pensacola St.   574-9464

Here is where the wings are hot and the beer is cold. Buffalo's serves up fried food and burgers with plenty of gusto, but it's the weekend evenings that really get this place cooking. There's usually no cover charge to hear some of the local bands blaring blues and rock into the night. The crowd is mostly students, but they're often having so much fun that many "adults" infiltrate the place with ease. Hours are Sunday to Wednesday, 11 AM to 10 PM; Friday and Saturday, 11 AM to 11 PM.

Bullwinkle's
620 W. Tennessee St.   224-0651

This is the ultimate college bar because it concentrates nearly all of its energies in one area: cheap drinks. Aside from that, there's really not all that much to Bullwinkle's. They play lots of loud music, of course, and some of it ain't bad at all. Many students swear religiously by this place, and during Parents' Weekend or graduation, a lot of the bolder ones drag their parents down here for a look-see. It's quite a sight when that happens.

The Cab Stand
1019 N. Monroe St.   224-0322

One of the newest bars in town, the Cab Stand has quickly established itself as a rockin' good place to have a drink. The crowd varies widely from the marginal to the very upscale, especially on weekends. There's live music during much of the week, most of it in the classic rock or blues vein. When the patrons stop chatting long enough to take a sip of something cold, they seem to enjoy the tunes.

CHARLEY MAC'S RESTAURANT & LOUNGE
Oak Lake Village
1700-3 Halstead Blvd.   *893-0522*

This upscale but highly casual place is a favorite hangout for Baby Boomers trying to relax after a hard day's work. The restaurant's good enough to recommend on its own — the seafood and steak are excellent, and the Sunday brunch is a popular attraction — but it's the lounge here that really adds some life to the proceedings, in our opinion. There's a Happy Hour each night from 4 to 7 PM that usually gets things going. Weekends see the place sometimes jumping till around the midnight mark. They close when they close, and that's the way it's always been.

CLYDE'S & COSTELLO'S
210 S. Adams St.   *224-2173*

This is a cool, casual place where college students rub elbows with professionals, good cheap drinks are hoisted, and if there's not a live band playing raucous rock then the DJ is spinning something that's best left in the background. Clyde's & Costello's sounds like two places but it's only one — unless you're seeing double (in which case, take a taxi home, please). It's a cut above most places in Tallahassee, but it doesn't have any pretensions. It's a popular downtown spot where you come to relax and enjoy yourself. Hours are Monday, Tuesday and Thursday, 4 PM to 10 PM; Wednesday and Friday, 4 PM to 2 AM; Saturday and Sunday, 8 PM to 2 AM.

THE COW HAUS
836 Lake Bradford Rd.   *574-2697*

This is one of the most recent additions to the student-oriented university scene. It's not known for its atmosphere, which is best described as no-frills, but it does feature some very interesting, often very good music. You can see bands with memorable monikers such as Frankenfinger and Doomed Clowns, or you can catch one of the more well-known acts that pass through town. Recently blues great Bo Diddley played a scorching show here.

Insiders' Tips

What's the singles scene like in Tallahassee? It can be frustrating if you don't know the hangouts, which include the Cab Stand, the Mill and the Paradise Grill & Bar (the latter is listed in the Restaurants section, but it has a popular bar). The Moon can be a hot meetin' spot on weekends when it features country line dancing, because a whole heap of people sign up for the early evening lessons. Then they hang out 'till the wee hours to strut their stuff. Lookin' for a dance pardner? Hop to it.

TALLAHASSEE — NIGHTLIFE

Doc's
1921 W. Tennessee St.   *224-5946*

This is one of the largest and most popular sports bars in town, and for over one dozen very good reason (here's a hint: all of them are very large TV sets). Doc's packs 'em in during game time year round and keeps them there with good drinks, great food and plenty of fun. If you're looking for a dimly lit, quiet place to enjoy a brief repast, this is not the place. Practice your tomahawk chop and get ready to roar.

Dooley's Downunder
2900 N. Monroe St.   *386-1027*

Yes, this Australian-themed bar is tucked away inside a Ramada Inn, but you shouldn't dismiss it just for that. Dooley's is actually a tasteful little nightspot that has made a name for itself by offering some of the best stand-up comedy and live jazz music in town. Comedy Zone nights sometimes bring nationally known stand-up comedians. Jazz nights get very hot, especially when featuring national recording artist Marcus Roberts, a hometown talent who plays a few of shows here each year. Other artists of note to appear here are Lynee Arriale and Travis Shook. It's a long list, one that grows each year. Check it out — no joke.

Fat Tuesday
101 S. Adams St.   *224-5000*

One of the newest bars in town, Fat Tuesday bills itself as a taste of New Orleans in The Sheraton in downtown Tallahassee. They've certainly got the exotic drinks to prove it, from a heady concoction called Swampwater to another life-threatening conviviality known as the Triple-Bypass. It's loud and bright and weekends usually find it full of laughing, dancing people.

The 4th Quarter
2033 N. Monroe St.   *385-0017*

Like all good sports bars, this one is most fun when there's a good game on. Otherwise, people just stand around quoting stats and watching ESPN—which is still pretty fun for sports fans, mind you, though others may balk and head for more exciting venues. Because of its somewhat limited seating capacity, the 4th Quarter is never as wild or raucous as Doc's, but it can still pull a good crowd when game time rolls around.

The Palace Saloon
1303 Jackson Bluff Rd.   *575-3418*

This friendly, low-key tavern is a favorite gathering spot for many residents. On game days, sports fans crowd around the big screen TV to cheer on their favorite teams. On weekend evenings, there's usually live music, everything from good old boys playing Jimmy Buffett to hungry rock 'n' roll bands trying to bring down the roof.

Silks Food and Spirits
3425 Thomasville Rd.   *893-4161*

Silks is the hot nightspot adjoining a rather upscale restaurant named Courtney's, and the two go well together. Silks offers a fun, elegant setting where professionals — many of whom come straight from work with power suits and briefcases — gather to appreciate the finer subtleties of life, such as mixed drinks, good food and live jazz. It's a bit formal for some tastes, but just right for others.

THE WAREHOUSE
706 W. Gaines St.   *222-6188*

This old converted warehouse has proven to be a popular hangout for residents and students alike. It sports what many claim to be the best pool tables in Tallahassee, and the weekend musical acts always draw crowds, as well. The crowd's interesting, the beer is cold and the restrooms are well marked; what more can you ask of a good watering hole?

THE WATERWORKS
104 S. Monroe St.   *224-1887*

There's not a lot of room at this downtown Tallahassee gathering spot, but some say it's the intimacy that makes it cool. Although the scene caters mostly to the college crowd, it's upscale and smart enough to feature live jazz music at least one night each weekend. Monday nights usually see an "open mike" night where aspiring poets and singer/songwriters can be heard. Depending on your frame of mind, the slick pastels and neon lighting just might prove to be the perfect backdrop for some loud music and people-watching.

YIANNI'S CAFE
646 W. Tennessee St.   *681-9565*

Yianni's at one point was actually a cafe, complete with private nooks and a menu featuring cappuccino and pastries. These days it's virtually indistinguishable from many of the other college-oriented bars, but that's not all bad. There's plenty of good beer and weekend music here as well as a great extra: each Tuesday, Yianni's hosts poetry and fiction readings sponsored by the FSU Department of English. These are usually well-attended, standing-room-only events.

Tallahassee
Accommodations

Tallahassee plays host to thousands of visitors each year, and it knows how to take care of them. Whether they're in town for a Seminole game, the legislative session or any of the other myriad events that take place here, people find that Tallahassee has plenty of accommodations for everyone.

The city's 56 hotels and motels provide over 5,000 rooms for the city's visitors, and during peak periods — championship sports events or the legislative session, for example — things can get very crowded in these parts. Most of the time, however, visitors can be assured of finding a place to stay with minimal difficulty. Any and all tastes can be met, from quaint bed and breakfast inns to no-frills economy lodging to upper-crust corporate hotels.

The following is a random sampling of some of the accommodations Tallahassee has to offer. Note that rates are subject to change, and when making reservations always remember to ask if there are any special rates available. Sometimes you'll find prices so low you'll be tempted to extend your trip for a couple of days. The codes below are for a one-night stay for two adults.

$60 or less	$
$61 - 85	$$
$86 - 99	$$$
$100 or more	$$$$

Bed & Breakfast Inns

Tallahassee only has one bed and breakfast inn. This is amazing, especially when you realize how many historic downtown homes would make perfect spots for such a venture. Thankfully, the nearby communities of Quincy, Monticello and Thomasville provide nearly one dozen additions to the city's short list. If Tallahassee's Riedel House is full, you can try any of the others and rest assured that, for the cost of a short drive, you can have that homey, personalized atmosphere bed and breakfast inns are known for.

Tallahassee

THE RIEDEL HOUSE
1412 Fairway Dr.   222-8569
$$

Built in 1937, the stately Riedel House sits on an acre of land in the Myers Park area of town, only a few blocks down the hill from the Capitol. Owner Carolyn Riedel opened it up as a bed and breakfast less than a decade ago and never seems to have much trouble keeping its two guest

> **The style and intimacy of a French Country Inn in downtown Tallahassee.**
>
> **GOVERNORS INN**
>
> Come enjoy our weekend "Escape" package. Starting at $99.
>
> 209 SOUTH ADAMS STREET • TALLAHASSEE, FLORIDA 32301
> 904-681-6855 • TOLL FREE IN FLORIDA 1-800-342-7717

rooms and one suite filled. There are private baths and, of course, breakfast. Many weekends find the downstairs part of the house rented out for parties and wedding receptions.

Havana

GAVER'S BED AND BREAKFAST
301 E. 6th Ave.　　　　539-5611
$$

This well-preserved 1907 house was remodeled in the mid-1980s and is a great place to stay, whether you're visiting Tallahassee (only 12 miles down Highway 27) or just shopping for antiques in any of downtown Havana's numerous stores. It sports private baths, pine walls and restored antique furniture. Innkeepers Bruce and Shirley Gaver provide a continental breakfast and airport service. The back porch swing is always rocking gently with visitors who know when to slow down and appreciate the finer things in life.

Monticello

SOMEWHERE ELSE
625 E. Washington St.　　　997-1376
$$

Fewer than 25 miles from downtown Tallahassee rests Somewhere Else, a historic bed and breakfast in Monticello. Built in 1888, this renovated house is owned by Alex DiMuro, a Certified Public Accountant who offers special "Tax Break" weekend specials for those who need to hole up somewhere peaceful and fill out those IRS forms. Even if you've already done your taxes, however, this is still a great place to stay. The house, which boasts an impressive assortment of antique music boxes, sits on an acre of land that features fig, peach, pear and walnut trees. There are four guestrooms which share a common bath.

Quincy

THE ALLISON HOUSE
215 N. Madison St. 875-2511
$$

This is truly a house with two stories — the first floor was built in 1925, the second in 1843. How the heck did that happen? The second floor was originally a one-story house on brick pilings. When it was moved from an adjacent lot in the 1920s, it was decided another floor should be added, and it was simply easier to build up than down. Originally that old one-story house was the home of Governor A.K. Allison, who served as Florida's governor after John Milton killed himself at the end of the Civil War in 1865.

Innkeepers Clay and Kate Ingram tend to the many travelers who stay in the Allison House. Its Greek Revival-style architecture and charming antique furnishings make it a special place to stay, and it's only 20 miles from downtown Tallahassee.

Thomasville, Georgia

1884 PAXTON HOUSE
445 Remington Ave. (912) 226-5197
$$-$$$$ (800) 278-0138

This Victorian Gothic house is a wonder to look at, with a circular staircase, one dozen fireplaces, rich pine floors and a neoclassical porch. You can bet it's also pretty pleasant to stay here, too. There are several suites and rooms to choose from, and basic amenities include a gourmet breakfast, private baths, bedside chocolates or fruit and turndown service. Located in the heart of downtown Thomasville's historic district, the 1884 Paxton House is a grand place to spend your time.

DEER CREEK BED & BREAKFAST
1304 Old Monticello Rd. (912) 226-7294
$$

Deer Creek Bed & Breakfast operates two houses, the one listed here and another on South Dawson Street. Both houses have been beautifully restored and feature huge windows with impressive views of trees and the surrounding landscape. If you're a gourmet chef, they'll even let you cook your own breakfast (though theirs is pretty good and shouldn't be passed up so easily).

THE EVANS HOUSE
725 S. Hansell St. (912) 226-1343
$$

The Evans House is lucky to be here. Ten years after its construction in 1898, the house suffered a fire that caused extensive damage. Thankfully the local fire department wasted no time in saving this Victorian-style home. Innkeeper Lee Puskar says the inn offers four guest rooms with private baths, all furnished with turn-of-the-century antiques. The Evans House offers visitors a full continental breakfast and bicycles for those who wish to tour the nearby 27-acre Paradise Park or, just a few blocks farther, downtown Thomasville. Commercial and long-stay rates are available upon request.

THE GRAND VICTORIA INN
817 S. Hansell St. (912) 226-7460
$$

Built in 1893, this Victorian house offers a quartet of large guest rooms and is conveniently located across

Executive Suite Motor Inn

★ Jacuzzi Baths in Most Rooms ★

(904) 386-2121
FLORIDA 1-800-386-2121
522 Scotty's Lane • Tallahassee, FL

from Paradise Park and just a few blocks from downtown Thomasville. Innkeeper Ann Dodge not only serves up a full breakfast but provides an afternoon tea as well. The antique furniture is complemented by plenty of books, fresh flowers and a resident black cat whose path only brings good luck when crossed. The backyard offers a pond and rock garden for strolling and relaxation.

OUR COTTAGE ON THE PARK
801 S. Hansell St.   (912) 227-0404
$$

Almost every bed and breakfast inn here in Thomasville has a wide, spacious porch with rockers or swings, and this quaintly named inn is no exception. The house was built by George Cox in 1893, when a big porch ensured shade and air circulation during the hottest months of the year. Proprietor Constance Clineman also runs the Cottage Shoppe out of the Cox House; this is one gift shop you'll want to visit even if you're not staying overnight.

SERENDIPITY COTTAGE
309 E. Jefferson St.   (912) 226-8111
$$

What some people call a cottage, others would call a very large house. That's the case with this beautiful home, which was built in 1906. Innkeepers Kathy and Ed Middleton offer an irresistible full course breakfast that features their delicious homemade jams, jellies and breads. Each room has a private bath and, if you desire, you might get a visit from any of the resident cats and dogs. The library not only offers books for relaxation but a selection of movies, as well.

SUSINA PLANTATION INN
Hwy. 155   (912) 377-9644
$$$$

As inns go, the Susina Plantation is the cream of the crop. Located 12 miles south of Thomasville and 18 miles north of Tallahassee, this magnificent antebellum mansion was built in 1841 by the noted architect John Wind. It rests on 8,000 acres of rolling green countryside, an area roughly half of the plantation's original size. The eight rooms are breathtaking, with four-poster beds and private baths that feature claw-footed tubs. Completing the plantation atmosphere are tennis courts, a swimming pool, walking trails, ponds and croquet court. Even if the Susina weren't an inn, the gourmet food that comes out of its kitchen would certainly ensure its continued popularity. Lunch is served for groups of 10 or more.

Hotels and Motels

GOVERNOR'S INN
209 S. Adams St.   681-6855
$$$$ (800) 342-7717

This is *the* downtown place to stay for the upscale movers and shakers and power players — and those who want to rub elbows with them. Only a five-minute walk from the Capitol complex, Governor's Inn is elegant and extravagant without going overboard; there's a sense of refinement in the air. There are 40 tasteful, friendly rooms and eight suites, and these fill up quickly when the politicians flock to town. The inn features a fitness facility, continental breakfast, in-room refrigerators, dry cleaning service, morning newspaper and copier and fax facilities. There's also a complimentary airport shuttle that runs whenever you need it.

RAMADA INN TALLAHASSEE
2900 N. Monroe St.   386-1027
$$ (800) 228-2828

Less than four miles from the Capitol on N. Monroe Street, the Ramada Inn Tallahassee is the second largest motel in the area, sporting nearly 200 rooms and half a dozen suites. Like any Ramada Inn, it's great value for the cost and features a fitness facility and walking trail, on-site restaurant, swimming pool, cable TV and computer, copier and fax services. Their lounge, Dooley's, is a popular night spot for many Tallahasseans (see its entry under the Nightlife section).

SHERATON TALLAHASSEE
101 S. Adams St.   224-5000
$-$$$$ (800) 325-3535

The Sheraton is the area's largest motel, with nearly 250 rooms and half a dozen suites available. As you can see from its price rating, the Sheraton can accommodate any and all travelers, no matter how large or small their budget. The Sheraton sits downtown only a couple of blocks from the Capitol and features indoor parking, in-room refrigerators, microwaves, dry cleaning and fax and copier services. There's an on-site restaurant and lounge, too.

RADISSON HOTEL
415 N. Monroe St.   224-6000
$$-$$$$ (800) 333-3333

The Radisson's spacious rooms, reasonable rates and close proximity to the heart of town are big attractions for people with business in downtown Tallahassee — the walk to the Capitol is only half a mile and carries you through the historic downtown district and past the Park Avenue chain of parks. The Radisson's 116 rooms and eight suites are usually jam-packed during the legislative session and football

TALLAHASSEE AT ITS BEST!
RAMADA INN
TALLAHASSEE
2900 N. Monroe St. Tallahassee, FL 32303

NEWLY RENOVATED

AWARD-WINNING RESTAURANT AND LIVE-ENTERTAINMENT LOUNGE FEATURING WEEKEND COMEDY CLUB

- 200 Guest Rooms
- Ample Free Parking
- Shopping Nearby
- Non-smoking Rooms
- Outdoor Swimming Pool
- Jogging Trail
- Business Center/Fax
- Conference Rooms
- Evening Security Provided
- Complimentary Cribs Available

RELOCATION AND EXTENDED STAY RATES AVAILABLE

I-10 (Exit 29) and U.S. 27 • (904) 386-1027

---

season (two sporting events that draw tons of people around here), and it effortlessly hosts those seeking business as well as pleasure. There's a restaurant and lounge in the lobby, not to mention a fitness facility, whirlpool and sauna. Copier and fax services are well-used by lobbyists and business people.

HOLIDAY INN UNIVERSITY CENTER
316 W. Tennessee St. 877-3141
$-$$$$ (800) 465-4329

You can always trust a Holiday Inn to deliver spacious, clean rooms in a convenient setting. There are three Holiday Inns in Tallahassee, but we choose this one because of its close proximity to the Capitol — about half a mile. If you're driving, then by all means check out the other two — there's the Holiday Inn Parkway on the Apalachee Parkway about a mile from the Capitol, and the Holiday Inn Northwest about five miles from downtown. Their rooms top out a bit cheaper, too. But if you're walking — and this is a walking town — this is the place to be. There are 174 rooms to choose from, with a restaurant and lounge on the premises. You'll also enjoy a swimming pool, fitness facility, dry cleaning, copier and fax services.

CABOT LODGE NORTH
2735 N. Monroe St. 386-8880
$-$$ (800) 223-1964

There are two Cabot Lodges in Tallahassee, and both are popular because they offer more of a relaxed and secluded setting than is found in most roadside motels. Their sign claims they're a "bed and breakfast," but don't expect an inn. This is simple, spacious and clean lodging with several pleasant extras. The Cabot Lodge East, with its Executive Floor offering many business-oriented amenities, is more suited for visiting professionals. The Cabot Lodge North is the larger of the two — 160 rooms — but both are equidistant from the Capitol (about four miles) and the airport (around nine miles). There are several restaurants within walking dis-

TALLAHASSEE — ACCOMMODATIONS

tance, and Tallahassee Mall is only a few blocks away. The Cabot Lodge North offers dry cleaning, fax and copier services, as well.

COURTYARD BY MARRIOTT
1018 Apalachee Pkwy. 222-8822
$$-$$$$ *(800) 321-2211*

Visitors who commute by car are likely to be found at the Courtyard by Marriott, which meets the high standards set by the nationwide chain. It sits on the Parkway about a mile from the Capitol, but unfortunately it's not a place for people who prefer to walk to their destination. Still, its 154 rooms and 13 spacious suites attract their fair share of visitors. You'll probably enjoy the quiet seclusion, and the on-site restaurant, lounge and fitness and swimming facilities should please you. Special rooms for the disabled are available upon inquiry.

TALLAHASSEE MOTOR HOTEL
1630 N. Monroe St. 224-6183
$ *(800) 251-1962*

The Tallahassee Motor Hotel has been around for over 60 years and looks it — we say this in all sincerity, because it's a great-looking hotel, an honest-to-gosh glimpse of days past when inexpensive, no-frills hotels of this sort studded the landscape. You know the sort: colorful, friendly and with a lot of character. The Tallahassee Motor Hotel is wonderfully preserved and offers over 90 very large rooms as well as a swimming pool. There's no need for a walking trail with Lake Ella just across the street where, sunup to sundown, walkers and joggers rule. The Cottages on Lake Ella offer several great specialty shops for browsers, too. The Tallahassee Motor Hotel is about two miles from the Capitol.

Tallahassee
Shopping

Tallahassee is truly a shopper's paradise. It boasts two large malls, several shopping centers and enough eclectic boutiques, crafts and antique shops to whet anyone's appetite.

And even if you just can't find that special item here, try the neighboring towns of Quincy, Havana, Monticello or Thomasville. All are less than an hour's drive from Tallahassee.

Please note that this list doesn't include many of the standard stores you'll find across the nation. What you'll find here are some of the individual stores that make Tallahassee a unique and exciting place to go shopping.

GOVERNOR'S SQUARE MALL
1500 Apalachee Pkwy.   671-4636

In addition to anchor stores such as Burdines, Dillard's, JCPenney and Sears, Governor's Square mall offers over 150 specialty stores. For those who like to shop till they drop, the central food court, which seats 500, offers a great place to relax and recharge. Open Monday through Saturday 10 AM to 9 PM; Sunday 12:30 to 5:30 PM.

TALLAHASSEE MALL
2415 N. Monroe St.   385-7145

The recently remodeled and expanded Tallahassee Mall features three main anchor stores — Parisian, Gayfers and Montgomery Ward — as well as dozens of other specialty stores, a new food court and a two-screen movie theater. Open Monday through Saturday from 10 AM to 9 PM; Sunday 12:30 to 5:30 PM.

CARRIAGE GATE SHOPPING CENTER
3425 Thomasville Rd.

This shopping center has a whole lot for everyone, no matter what your age or interest. Kids really flip over the new Discovery Zone, a gigantic indoor playground with enough tunnels, obstacle courses and games to keep them busy for hours. Adults, on the other hand, will probably want to slow down and browse the fine clothing at such stores as Fletcher-Cantey, Tails & Tweeds and Jason's & Jason's Petites. But everyone can enjoy the fine food at Georgio's & Filks. Hours vary.

THE PAVILIONS
1410 Market St.

There are plenty of ways to look and feel good at the Pavilions. This shopping plaza lets you choose from Chelsea Hairsmith Salon, Career Woman Fashions, Arthur Murray Dance Studio, Narcissus Swimwear and Lingerie, Peggy's Fine Arts, Wallpaper It Now, the Mandarin Chinese Restaurant and Nu-Life, a ladies-only fitness center. Hours vary.

Bradley's Country Store hasn't changed much since it opened in 1927, and that's one reason for its success.

TALLAHASSEE — SHOPPING

THE VERANDAS
1355 Market St.

Talbots is the anchor store at this north Tallahassee shopping plaza, but you can also say that the gourmet dining at the White Swan Restaurant is another big draw. These two establishments rub elbows with such shopping attractions as Oldfield Interiors, Someone's In the Kitchen, Cotton, Etc. and many others. Hours vary.

PARKWAY SHOPPING CENTER
Apalachee Pkwy. and Magnolia

This popular shopping plaza is almost 30 years old but you wouldn't know it from looking. It sports a wonderful bookstore, Books-A-Million, Spec's Music, and several clothing stores. If you're hungry, try the Italian fare at the Olive Garden, the fine Mexican offerings from Cabo's Tacos, or some healthy and delicious food from the New Leaf Cafe. Hours vary.

BETTON PLACE
1950 Thomasville Rd.

This plaza bills itself as "a delightful shopping place," and we can't argue. Nestled within this small but spacious plaza are nearly a dozen excellent shops and boutiques, such as A Stitch In Time, the Museum Shop, Ivy Rose Garden and Gifts, Strauss Gallery and Planned Furnishings. Food Glorious Food offers elegant and inexpensive dining on the lower level. Hours vary.

VILLAGE COMMONS
1400 Village Square Blvd.

At first glance, this is just another strip shopping centers with anchor stores such as Wal-Mart and Rheinauer's clearly visible. But look closer and you'll find an exciting collection of most uncommon shops such as the Wildlife Gallery, My Favorite Things, Lissie Petites, Eleni's Coffee & Tea Company and restaurants such as Annella's and Applebee's. Hours vary.

MARKET SQUARE SHOPPING CENTER
1415 Timberlane Rd.   893-8287

This spacious shopping plaza features over two dozen specialty shops and restaurants as well as an open square that features a farmer's market each weekend. After seeing the wares at stores like Festivity Factory, Designs & More, Art House and Lamb's & Ivy, you can catch your breath at eateries such as Kitcho, Au Piche Mignon French Pastry Shop, the Phyrst Grill. Hours vary.

PEDLERS ANTIQUE MALL
660 Capital Circle NE   877-4674

There are plenty of places to hunt for antiques, and this is one of the most popular ones. Not only do they feature a great assortment of antiques and collectibles, but Pedlers is also known for its gifts, quality wood furniture and accessories. Open Monday through Saturday from 10 AM to 5:30 PM, and Sunday from 1 PM to 5 PM.

FLEA MARKET TALLAHASSEE
200 SW Capital Circle   877-3811

This is one of the largest flea markets in northwest Florida, covering over 22 acres and featuring over 500 covered booths. You can find just about anything here: antiques, collectibles, clothes, furniture, fresh vegetables and more. Admission and parking are free. Open Saturdays and Sundays from 9 AM to 5 PM.

Specialty Stores

RUBYFRUIT BOOKS
666-4 W. Tennessee St.   222-2627

This eclectic bookstore has a wide range of new, used and out-of-print books, and they're well-known for catering to the smaller presses. They also sport a fine assortment of magazines, cards, jewelry, music and children's books. Open Monday to Saturday from 10:30 AM to 6:30 PM; open Thursdays until 8 PM.

TRAIL & SKI
2020 W. Pensacola St.   576-6225

This store can outfit you for the outdoors no matter what you want to do. They've got a great selection of camping gear, athletic shoes, sportswear and many other items. Chances are if they don't have it, you really don't need it. Hours are Monday to Thursday 10 AM to 8 PM, Friday and Saturday 10 AM to 6 PM, and Sunday noon to 5 PM.

NICE TWICE
931 N. Monroe St.   224-5435

This popular consignment shop is aimed at women, and many say it hits the mark. Nice Twice has been around for over a dozen years, so you can bet that their inventory and selection has gotten pretty good over that time. They usually rotate their merchandise for the winter and spring seasons accordingly. Some of their clothes look brand new. If you don't tell, no one will know — but finding a great bargain is something worth shouting about. Hours are Monday to Friday, 9 AM to 6 PM, Saturday 10 AM to 4 PM.

MOON'S
536 N. Monroe St.   224-9000

If you're looking for jewelry, this is the place. Moon's has been a rather opulent fixture in Tallahassee for many, many years now. Their reputation rests solely on the beauty, selection and affordability of their jewelry. They've got a great staff that can help you pick out the perfect gift no matter what the occasion. Hours are Monday to Friday 9:30 AM to 5:30 PM, closed weekends.

INDIAN NOTIONS
4176 Apalachee Pkwy.   942-0582

Looking for some authentic Indian arts and crafts? This is the place. Indian Notions carries a great assortment of handmade drums, pipes, rugs and other crafts, and they freshen up their shelves with new inventory each month. Hours are Tuesday to Saturday, 10 AM to 6 PM.

Insiders' Tips: Are you an antique hound? The nearby towns of Quincy, Havana, Monticello and Thomasville, Georgia, all sport excellent antique shops, but don't forget about Tallahassee. At last count there were over one dozen excellent antique stores in town, with rumors of several more on the way. During the weekend exodus to out-of-town antique shops, smart residents and visitors-in-the-know might do well to check out the antique scene here in town first.

THE COSMIC CAT
1907 W. Pensacola   574-1487
220 W. Tharpe   386-5551

Much more than just another bookstore, the Cosmic Cat is a vital focal point for the dissemination of alternate cultural artifacts. Translation: Not only do they have a great selection of comic books and graphic novels, but they also have interesting and eclectic clothing, artwork, foreign animation videos and other assorted items. It's the kind of store that big bustling cities take for granted. Here, it's a counter-cultural oasis. Students are the main customers, but grown-ups in-the-know are found here, too. Hours are Monday to Saturday, 10 AM to 8 PM, Sunday noon to 6 PM.

VINYL FEVER
2033 W. Pensacola St.   576-4314

This independent music store offers a great selection of new and used CDs, cassettes and albums (yes, there are still a few of the latter in existence). All styles of music are given ample shelf space, from alternative rock to zydeco. The knowledgeable staff is always ready to offer assistance. Open Monday to Saturday from 10 AM to 9 PM; Sunday 11 AM to 5 PM.

AGYEIWA'S AFRICAN BOUTIQUE
1429 S. Monroe St.   656-2700

Plenty of African arts and crafts await you at this boutique, including beautiful handcrafted wooden carvings. The bright and cheerful clothing is another attraction, and there's plenty of uncut fabric for those who wish to sew their own creations. Open Monday to Saturday, 9 AM to 6 PM.

THE COTTAGES ON LAKE ELLA
1600 Block of North Monroe St.

Several cottages line Monroe Street on Lake Ella, and they've been turned into a delightful assortment of specialty shops. Among them are tantalizing names such as The Quarter Moon Import Shop, Tabanelli & Lee (jewelry and watchmaking), the Blind Pig Antique Shop and Cornhusk & Creations. Hours vary.

HEPBURN'S
119 S. Monroe St.   222-2234

The antiques and gifts alone are good reasons for browsing at Hepburn's. When you throw in the wonderful and sometimes startling antique furniture the owners manage to procure, Hepburn's proves itself to be a must-see on the list of any antique hound. Open Monday through Friday 10 AM to 6 PM; Saturday 10 AM to 3 PM.

AMEN-RA'S BOOKSHOP
1326 S. Adams St.   681-6228

The shelves of this bookshop are lined with great works of literature by and about African-Americans. There's also a fine selection of cards, poster and photographs to choose from. Open Monday to Saturday from 8 AM to 7 PM.

CARE PACKAGES
112 E. College Ave.   224-8727

If you're buying gifts for those hard-to-buy-for people, let Care Packages solve all your problems. They've got an incredible collection of items to spur your instincts, from handmade chocolates to stained glass ornaments to delicate wind chimes. Open Monday through Friday 10 AM to 5:30 PM; Saturday from 10 AM to 3 PM.

Tallahassee
Kidstuff

What's a kid got to do in Tallahassee? *Plenty.*

Here's a short list of things that should please even the most stubborn and hard-to-please kids visiting the Tallahassee area.

The following items have been thoroughly tried, tested and found true by the various children of friends and relatives. These kids are highly trained professionals in the art of having fun and staving off boredom, and their following recommendations are guaranteed to satisfy kids of all ages.

1. Go to the top of the Capitol — it's a great view and most kids just love heights. Thunderstorms and lightning look great from way up here.

2. Hit the Tallahassee Museum of History and Natural Science — where else can you see panthers, alligators and bald eagles?

3. Get out that frisbee and head to any of the city's beautiful parks — there's a complete listing in the Parks and Recreation chapter of this book.

4. If it's a weekend, head on down to the Flea Market Tallahassee, where there's always plenty of booths that offer comics, toys and other things kids can't live without. See the Shopping section for more information.

5. Got a computer and modem? Dial up Tallahassee FreeNet at 488-5056, a public computer bulletin board that features a special forum where kids can exchange ideas about everything from the newest Nintendo game to more serious issues like peer pressure and summer school.

6. Go to the Museum of Florida History in the R.A. Gray Building — we've yet to see a kid who wasn't wowed by the standing skeleton of Herman, the resident mammoth.

7. Head out to the popular Discovery Zone at the Carriage Gate

---

Insiders' Tips

It's not here yet, but very soon youngsters of all ages will be able to go on a true odyssey when visiting Tallahassee. The Odyssey Science Center, scheduled to open in 1995, will be a 24,000-square-foot facility that lets kids explore science and technology with numerous hands-on experiments and participatory exhibits. We're sorry to tease you with this wonderful news, but it's something Tallahasseans are pretty excited about.

TALLAHASSEE — KIDSTUFF

Tallahassee parks offer families many beautiful picnic sites.

Shopping Center, a pretty awesome indoor playground that features giant tubes and tunnels, an obstacle course, snack bar and enough games to keep you busy for hours! The rules say you have to bring a grown-up along, but that doesn't mean you can't have gobs of fun anyway.

8. Take the boat tour at Wakulla Springs State Park a few miles south of Tallahassee — one look at the thick forest and huge alligators and you'll see why they filmed the classic horror movie *Creature From the Black Lagoon* here!

9. Take an hour's drive west to the Florida State Caverns where you can walk hundreds of feet below the earth and see some pretty amazing — not to mention creepy — rock formations.

10. Head for the beach! The Gulf Coast is only 30 minutes away and makes for a perfect daytrip.

• 401

Tallahassee
Historic Sites and Attractions

The major difference between Tallahassee and almost every other vacation spot in northwest Florida is the beach. Granted, the capitol city is only 30 miles from the nearest stretch of sand, so it's really no big deal. But when people think about Tallahassee's major attractions, they usually think of what the city means in terms of politics and history.

Some folks say the only real way to understand history is to experience it. That may be true, but it's pretty darned difficult to do unless you've got a time machine.

Tallahassee's history is special, and some of the best attractions around not only entertain you but tell a story, as well. We're not talking freeze-fried exhibits here; there are plenty of attractions, such as the Tallahassee Museum of History and Natural Science, which bring history to life and make you a part of it.

Ask around and you'll discover that Tallahasseans are pretty proud of their city's heritage. To residents, the word "history" doesn't mean anything passive. We know that this area's rich history is alive all around us — noted by inclusions not only in this chapter's listings but in others, such as the Arts and Parks and Recreation sections, as well.

This isn't the beach, and it's certainly no tourist trap. The attractions here offer exciting experiences that cannot be mass-produced and sold in stores. And that's what makes them special.

Like they say, the best way to know history is to experience it firsthand. So, here are a few special time machines offering you fun-filled trips that rival those of any theme park.

BLACK ARCHIVES RESEARCH CENTER AND MUSEUM
Florida A&M University   *599-3020*

This is just one of many national treasures Tallahassee can boast as its own. The Black Archives Research Center and Museum documents vital chapters in the history of African-Americans with a series of exhibits and an exhaustive library of rare books and maps, as well as artifacts such as slave irons. It's located in the recently refurbished Carnegie Library, which is the oldest building on the FAMU campus. The Museum is open Monday through Friday from 9 AM to 4 PM. Guided tours should be scheduled in advance. Admission is free.

BROKAW-MCDOUGALL HOUSE
329 N. Meridian St.   *488-3901*

This handsome house is a magnificent example of Classic Revival architecture. Built in the 1850s, it's now used as a conference center and as home to the Historic Preservation Board. And these people know how to take care of it. The house is open Monday through Friday from 9 AM to 5 PM. Admission is free.

CANOPY ROADS

Just what and where are these? Canopy roads are lined with live oak trees so huge and thick that they create a lush green canopy. The five canopy roads — Centerville, Meridian, Miccosukee, Old Bainbridge and Old St. Augustine — were once major transport routes for cotton and others crops. Once the crops were harvested from area plantations, they were sent to the center of town and prepared for transport down to the Gulf for shipping. These beautiful moss-draped trees make travels along the roads cool and pleasant even in the hottest part of summer. Now they're specially protected parts of the environment.

THE COLUMNS
100 N. Duval St.   224-8116

Built in 1830 by banker William "Money" Williams (who's also responsible for the Union Bank building listed below), this is the oldest surviving building in the city. The house gets its name from the thick Greek-style pillars featured prominently on its porch. Over the years it's been a bank, a boarding house, a doctor's office and a restaurant. The house was almost demolished in 1971 to make way for newer buildings, but many citizens rallied behind the Tallahassee Chamber of Commerce and managed to move the stately manor across the street, where it now rests. It currently serves as the Chamber's headquarters, and they are working to restore the Columns to its original splendor. Even though the restoration has a long way to go, this beautiful house is still worth a look.

The Columns is open Monday through Friday from 9 AM to 4:30 PM. Admission is free.

FIRST PRESBYTERIAN CHURCH
110 N. Adams St.   222-4504

This is the oldest church building in Tallahassee. Built in 1838, it is notable for being one of the few churches that allowed slaves to become members, even without the consent of their masters. Inside one can still see the narrow balconies where blacks were allowed to sit. Today the church has over 500 members and is a registered historic site.

The church is open Monday through Friday from 9 AM to 4:30 PM. Admission is free.

FLORIDA VIETNAM VETERANS MEMORIAL
S. Monroe St. and
Apalachee Pkwy.   487-1533

Twin granite slabs face each other like giant soldiers standing at attention. Between them hangs a massive, 40-foot American flag. The Vietnam Veterans Memorial is stark and simple and powerfully moving. Carved into the base of each slab are the names of the Florida soldiers who died or are still missing in Vietnam.

Standing at the Memorial, you can look across the street at the Old Capitol and see a small black flag flying beneath the stars and stripes on the cupola there. That's the official emblem for those soldiers listed as missing in action, and it's a symbol that the state hasn't forgotten about them. Judging from the flowers, notes and other tokens you'll sometimes see at the Memorial, many citizens also remember those same soldiers.

GOVERNOR'S MANSION
700 N. Adams St.   488-4661

Florida's first family lives less than a mile away from the Capitol. This Georgian-style mansion has a portico similar to that of the Hermitage, Andrew Jackson's heavily-columned manse. Inside it's just as resplendent, with several rooms featuring antique furniture and gifts from around the world.

Tours are available Monday through Friday from 9 AM to 4:30 PM. The Governor's Mansion is closed to the public during the summer months. Admission is free.

KNOTT HOUSE MUSEUM
301 E. Park Ave.   922-2459

In the introduction we claim there's no such thing as a time machine, but the historic Knott House might be an exception. This grand old house was designed and constructed in 1843 by George Proctor, a free black man who built half a dozen homes in the area. It's a fitting irony that this particular house was built by a black man because of the historic events that would later unfold in the shade of its porch.

In May of 1865, the Civil War came to a close. Union General Edward McCook took possession of Tallahassee and set up his headquarters in the house. On May 20 of that year, all enslaved blacks were freed as the Emancipation Proclamation was read aloud from the front steps of the Knott House.

Sometime after the Civil War, the house fell into the hands of Tallahassee physician Dr. George Betton, whose buggy driver was a black man named William Gunn. In time, Betton realized that his driver had higher dreams and aspirations and paid to put him through medical school. Although he was born into slavery, William Gunn later became Florida's first black physician.

Currently the Knott House has been frozen at a specific moment in time during the 1930s. That's when State Treasure William V. Knott and his family were in residence there and the house was at the height of its splendor. His wife, Luella Pugh Knott, wrote poems for nearly every piece of furniture in the house and tied them all to their respective subjects with bits of ribbon. When you hear people refer to this as "the house that rhymes," you'll know what they mean.

Mrs. Knott was a forceful, strong-willed and very religious woman. While her husband was helping guide the state through its most serious financial difficulties, she was working hard to ban the legal sale of alcohol in Tallahassee — and she succeeded, for over fifty years.

Out back there's a daylily garden which blooms frequently during the year, and during the holiday season there are special evening candle-light tours of the house, decked out for a very Victorian Christmas.

TALLAHASSEE — HISTORIC SITES AND ATTRACTIONS

Insiders' Tips

Tallahassee is a prominent stop along the Florida Black Heritage Trail, which was created by a Department of State commission in 1990 to highlight the contributions of African Americans to Florida's history. There are over 140 sites along this trail, which stretches from Pensacola to key West. Here's what you'll find in Tallahassee:

Florida A&M University on South Adams Street, the oldest historically black university in the state.

FAMU's Black Archives Research Center and Museum in the university's Carnegie Library Building, whose collection of early African American artifacts is among the most comprehensive in the nation.

First Presbyterian Church at 102 N. Adams Street, a church built in the 1830s that allowed slaves to become members, although they were required to sit in the north gallery.

The Gibbs Cottage on South Adams Street, home of lawmaker Thomas Van Renssalaer Gibbs who worked to establish the Florida State Normal and Industrial School for Negroes, which is now FAMU.

The Knott House at 301 E. Park Avenue, from whose steps Union General Edward M. McCook read aloud Abraham Lincoln's Emancipation Proclamation in 1865.

The John Gilmore Riley house at 419 W. Jefferson Street, home to Riley, a noted educator and civic leader who became the first principal of Tallahassee's first high school for blacks, Lincoln Academy.

St. James C.M.E. Church at 104 N. Bronough Street, the oldest black church structure still standing in Tallahassee.

continued on next page

TALLAHASSEE — HISTORIC SITES AND ATTRACTIONS

> **Insiders' Tips**
>
> The C.K. Steele Memorial at 111 W. Tennessee Street, a civil rights activist who organized a bus boycott in Tallahassee that helped to end segregated public transportation.
>
> The Union Bank Building at the corner of the Apalachee Parkway and Calhoun Street, which housed the National Freedman's Bank for newly freed slaves after the Civil War.

The Knott House Museum is open Wednesday through Friday from 1 PM to 4 PM, and on Saturday from 10 AM to 4 PM. It is closed during the month of August. Admission is $3 for adults, $1.50 for children. There's a special Family Rate of $7.00.

MUSEUM OF FLORIDA HISTORY
R.A. Gray Building
500 S. Bronough St. 488-1484

Come say hello to Herman — he's certainly no pee-wee! Herman is the skeleton of a prehistoric mastodon that was dredged out of nearby Wakulla Springs in the 1930s, and he serves as the official mascot of the Museum of Florida History. You'll find a lot of fascinating history here, including treasure recovered from a sunken Spanish galleon, a reconstructed steamboat, a homemade Depression-era mobile home and a four-foot armadillo who was probably good friends with old Herman.

Guided tours are available, and the museum gallery also hosts several traveling exhibits during the year. There's a great gift shop and special programs for kids.

The Museum is open Monday through Friday from 9 AM to 4:30 PM, on Saturday from 10 AM to 4:30 PM, and on Sunday from noon to 4:30 PM. Admission is free.

OLD CITY CEMETERY
Park Ave. and
Martin Luther King Blvd. 599-8712

The oldest public cemetery in Tallahassee is located downtown just west of the Park Avenue Chain of Parks. Established in 1829, this was the only public cemetery for decades, and its markers, gravestones and monuments relate Tallahassee history in a unique way. Sooner or later everyone comes here, so you have governors and slaves, Union and Confederate troops, old people and infants all buried within a stone's throw of each other.

Here you can see the final resting places of several movers and shakers, including Dr. William J. Gunn, Florida's first black physician, and Thomas Vann Gibbs, founder of the Florida State Normal Industrial School (now FAMU). You'll also notice the number of markers for citizens who died during the yellow fever epidemic of 1841.

Across the street is St. Johns Cemetery, which was established in 1840 for the church's congregation. Some

TALLAHASSEE — HISTORIC SITES AND ATTRACTIONS

of the graves you'll find there are those of Prince Achille Murat, nephew of Napoleon Bonaparte, and the Prince's wife, Madame Catherine Murat, the great-grandneice of George Washington. Governor William D. Bloxham is also buried there.

The years haven't been kind to the Old City Cemetery, and recently some of the gravestones were restored due to damage from vandalism and weathering. Because of their delicate condition, visitors are not allowed to make stone rubbings of the markers. The cemetery is open daily from sunrise to sunset.

SAN LUIS ARCHAEOLOGICAL AND HISTORIC SITE
2020 W. Mission Rd. 487-3711

Long before the Spanish erected their mission here in the mid-15th century, the Tallahassee area was populated by tribes of Apalachee Indians. When the Spanish arrived and decided to build a mission and fort here, there were some Indians who chose to live with them, and they erected a massive council house and plaza. In 1704, however, the Spanish and many of the Indians abandoned San Luis rather than face the threat of advancing British soldiers and Creek Indians. The fort and village were burned to the ground.

In 1983, the state bought the land containing the buried ruins of San Luis and began excavations. For four months each spring, archaeologists descend on the site and spend the rest of the year studying the artifacts and structures they've dug up. This means that each year something new could be uncovered at the site, making this one museum that *really* changes its exhibits on a regular basis.

The San Luis Archaeological and Historic Site offers guided tours on weekdays at noon, on Saturday at 11 AM and 3 PM, and on Sunday at 2 PM. Tours for large groups should be arranged prior to visit. The site is open Monday through Friday from 9 AM to 4:30 PM, on Saturday from 10 AM to 4:30 PM, and on Sunday from noon to 4:30 PM. Admission is free.

TALLAHASSEE MUSEUM OF HISTORY & NATURAL SCIENCE
3945 Museum Dr. 576-1636

This used to be called the Tallahassee Junior Museum, but that name really didn't do this place justice. Everyone agreed that by calling the museum "junior," visitors might think the facility was meant only for children.

Well, kids love it but so do the adults. It's hard not to feel young at heart when you visit the Tallahassee Museum of History and Natural Science because the best parts of this 52-acre museum are outdoors. You can wander a raised wooden walkway and see red wolves, alligators, Florida panthers and bald eagles roaming their in their natural habitat.

The museum's aim is to present an accurate depiction of early life in Florida, and needless to say those beautiful animals, many of them endangered, do the trick. There's also the Big Bend Farm, an authentic 19th-century farm where visitors can get an up-close look at how early settlers lived.

• *407*

TALLAHASSEE — HISTORIC SITES AND ATTRACTIONS

Also on the museum grounds is the Bellevue Plantation House, which was the home of Madame Catherine Murat, wife of Prince Achille Murat and great-grandneice of George Washington. The Bellevue House was her home after the Prince died and has been restored to its original beauty.

The museum is open Monday through Saturday from 9 AM to 5 PM, and on Sunday from 12:30 PM to 5 PM. Admission is $5 for adults, $4 for seniors, $3 students and kids ages 4 to 15 years; children younger than 4 years are free.

UNION BANK BUILDING
Apalachee Pkwy.   *487-3803*

This small blue stone structure sits across from the Capitol next to the Florida Vietnam Veterans Memorial, and is the oldest bank building in the state. It was constructed in 1840 by William "Money" Williams, who also built the Columns (see above). Over the years the bank has probably seen more bad luck than good, and its history gives us rare glimpses into Tallahassee's past. The bank was forced to close just three years after its opening due to the rotten financial climate brought about in no small part by the Second Seminole War. After the Civil War, the bank housed the National Freedman's Bank, and was later used as a shoe factory, beauty shop and bail-bond office.

The building originally sat next to the Columns on Adams Street, and in 1971 both structures faced demolition to make room for new construction. Thankfully the Columns was lifted and moved across the street, while the Union Bank Building found safe berth here.

The Union Bank Building is open Tuesday through Friday from 10 AM to 1 PM, and on weekends from 1 PM to 4 PM. Admission is free.

WALKER LIBRARY
209 E. Park Ave.   *224-5012*

This charming building housed Tallahassee's first public library. Now it serves as the headquarters for Springtime Tallahassee, but you wouldn't know it from looking. The well-preserved interior sports fine woodwork as well as a collection of rare books and historical items. It's open to the public from September through May every year. The hours are Monday through Friday from 8:30 AM to 1 PM. Admission is free.

Tallahassee
Festivals and Special Events

The year-round good weather in these parts means that people who like to enjoy the outdoors will seize upon almost any chance to do so. Tallahassee's got a long history of sponsoring well-attended events and celebrations, one that stretches all the way back to the old May Day Festivals, which were the oldest annual events in the state.

Whether you're looking for high-brown culture or down-home fun, there are happenings for all age groups. Some of them are just plain dumb fun, while others may be associated with a cause or charity.

Tallahassee is known for its friendly and fun-loving people, and the only way to meet them is to go where they go. And right here is a good listing of when and where to find them.

January

RATTLESNAKE ROUNDUP
Whigham, Georgia   (912)762-4215

Needless to say, if you don't like snakes, don't come here. This annual festival usually attracts a lot of attention because where else can you see a bunch of people who like to hunt snakes? Prizes are awarded for the biggest and longest snake, and over the years this roundup has produced some whoppers. There's also an arts & crafts show, animal rides for the kiddies and lots of good food. And yes, you can even eat snake if you want to. This cultural gem is found 40 miles north of Tallahassee on U.S. Highway 84.

February

HARAMBEE ARTS AND CULTURAL HERITAGE FESTIVAL
Tallahassee/Leon County
Civic Center   656-8388

This black culture and arts festival is always fun, lively and well-attended. You can browse the arts and crafts booths for African-American jewelry and wares, or just listen to some of the good and diverse musical offerings.

TALLAHASSEE KENNEL CLUB DOG SHOW
North Florida Fairgrounds   877-6795

Sanctioned by the American Kennel Club, this show brings out the beast in everyone. Actually, you'll be amazed at the beautiful and well-trained dogs that come here to compete for prizes and titles. Tallahasseans love animals of all kinds, and here's where you can see some of the best dogs in town.

Ice skating in Florida? You bet! The Winter Festival gives Tallahasseans the chance to hit the ice for a few days.

BIG BEND CARES ANNUAL AIDS WALK
St. Pauls Methodist Church   656-2437

This walk benefits Big Bend CARES, an agency that provides services to people with HIV and AIDS in the Big Bend area. Hopefully one day walks like this won't be needed; until then, Tallahassee has proven that it can get out there and offer its support in large numbers.

March

NATURAL BRIDGE BATTLEFIELD HISTORIC SITE
Natural Bridge Road
Woodville   922-6007

This re-enactment of the famous Civil War battle gets bigger and better each year. Come and see the decisive victory that made Tallahassee the only Confederate capital east of the Mississippi that did not fall to Federal troops. Authentic uniforms and weapons are used.

WALKAMERICA
422-3152

Held at a park across from the Department of Transportation downtown, this national event benefits the March of Dimes Birth Defects Foundation.

ANTIQUE SHOW AND SALE
Tallahassee Museum of History & Natural Science   576-1636

Tallahasseans love their antiques, so this annual event is always a big draw. The proceeds from the event go to the Tallahassee Museum of History and Natural Science. Call for each year's exact location.

TALLAHASSEE — FESTIVALS AND SPECIAL EVENTS

SPRINGTIME TALLAHASSEE
Downtown and Vicinity   224-1373

This is a biggie. Spring is one of the most beautiful seasons in Tallahassee, and this festival gives everyone a chance to get out there and soak up some sunshine among the blooming flowers. Some of the many events include the Andrew Jackson Breakfast in the Park, the Springtacular Children's Parade, the Annual Arts and Crafts Jubilee and the American Indian Cultural Society's Annual Pow-wow.

JAZZ & BLUES FESTIVAL
*Tallahassee Museum of
History & Natural Science   576-1636*

Come hear some soulful music in a comfortable, woodsy environment. This festival features lots of musical acts throughout the day as well as good food and fun for the kids.

ST. GEORGE ISLAND CHILI COOKOFF
St. George Island   927-2396

This is one of the tastiest annual events in Florida's great northwest, and for over a decade it's made St. George Island a hot spot during the first weekend in March. Featuring more chili than you can shake a spoon at, the benefits from this cookoff and auction go to Gulf Coast Regional Charity. These people are serious about chili and use the rules of the International Chili Society, and the winner advances to the World Championship Cookoff. This stuff is good and a lot of it is *hot hot hot*. You have been warned.

To reach St. George Island, take Highway 319 south out of Tallahassee. Head west on Highway 98 and take Highway 300 south across the causeway. Total driving time from Tallahassee is about an hour-and-a-half.

April

FLORIDA STATE UNIVERSITY FLYING HIGH CIRCUS
*Jack Haskin Circus Complex
W. Pensacola and Chieftain Way   644-4874*

And you thought all students cared about was football. These students will have you thinking otherwise as they fly, flip, tumble and swing from the trapeze and perform other amazing airborne feats. Kids love it and so do the adults who bring them.

SPRING FARM DAYS
*Tallahassee Museum of
History & Natural Science   576-1636*

So you think your mornings are hectic, hard and fast-paced? Well, come and see what early Tallahassee settlers had to do each morning. You'll see a demonstration of spring farm chores at the restored, turn-of-the-century farm buildings on the museum grounds. And you'll be so exhausted from just watching that you'll need to stay around for the pioneer breakfast they offer.

EASTER EGG HUNT
Wakulla Springs Park   224-5950

Open to the public, this Easter egg hunt is as much fun for the parents as it is the children. Sit back and watch the little ones search through the park's beautiful greenery for hidden eggs and treats.

• 411

TALLAHASSEE — FESTIVALS AND SPECIAL EVENTS

The Rattlesnake Roundup in Whigham, Georgia, is not for the squeamish or faint-of-heart.

City-wide Easter Egg Hunt
Myers Park   891-3866

If you can't get down to Wakulla, then head for Myers Park, only a few blocks from downtown. Toddlers and older children through the age of 10 have five different areas in which to hunt for eggs. There are games and prizes and more, all courtesy of the Easter Bunny.

Thomasville Rose Festival
Thomasville, Georgia   (912) 225-5222

A rose by any other name would still get its own festival, according to our friends in nearby Thomasville. They grow some of the prettiest roses around and they love to show them off. Some of the festivities include a parade, county fair, juried rose show as well as golf and soccer tournaments.

Stephen C. Smith Memorial Regatta
Shell Point Beach   921-3816

The Steven C. Smith Memorial Regatta is one of the largest sailing events in the region. Catamarans, rowing shells and sailboards (and their occupants) show up in this benefit for the American Cancer Society to memorialize Steven C. Smith, a local sailor who died of a rare form of leukemia. Take Highway 363 south from Tallahassee to Highway 98, go west and take County Road 365 south, which eventually branches off onto County Road 367.

May

Blue Crab Festival
Wooley Park, Panacea   681-9200

There's plenty of good crabbin' in these parts, and this is the time of year when resident fisherfolk and chefs like to show you why. This well-attended festival also has a parade, music, entertainment, an arts and crafts show, a road race and, of course, plenty of great food. Skip breakfast and head down there.

DANCE FOR SPRING
Ruby Diamond Auditorium, FSU   222-1287

Want to see another way to think about Tallahassee's favorite season? Come watch the agile and fluid dancers of the Tallahassee Ballet Company.

FLORIDA FOLK FESTIVAL
White Springs
Stephen Foster State Folk
Culture Center   397-2192

About an hour-and-a-half east is one of the biggest folk festivals in the southeast. People from all over come to hear the dozens of musical artists who perform. There's also dancing, storytelling and down-home-style food.

June

PLANET PARTY
Tallahassee Museum of
History & Natural Science   576-1636

Other people call it Earth Day, but here it's known as Planet Party, and it's a festive occasion indeed. There are plenty of environment-related activities for kids and adults, and there's no better place to appreciate the Earth's beauty than here at the museum's wonderfully wooden site.

WATERMELON FESTIVAL
Monticello   997-5552

How far can you spit a watermelon seed? If you're good, you can enter the seed-spitting contest here. But you'd better practice because some of the entrants have probably broken world records. There's also a horse show and many arts & crafts booths.

BIG BEND SALTWATER CLASSIC
Carrabelle   697-2800

This big fishing tournament always takes place on Father's Day weekend, and it's a doozy. The proceeds go to the Organization for Artificial Reefs and other nonprofit organizations. The fun begins at The Moorings in Carrabelle. From Tallahassee, take Highway 363 south to Highway 98 and head west.

July

FOURTH OF JULY CELEBRATION
Tom Brown Park   891-3866

This celebration is one of the city's largest, and rightly so. Thousands of people sprawl out across the park to enjoy music, theater productions, a road race, arts & crafts booths and what is definitely the most spectacular fireworks around.

SUMMER SWAMP STOMP
Tallahassee Museum of
History & Natural Science   576-1636

Local and regional artists highlight this popular folk and bluegrass festival.

August

"TELL" AHASSEE TALE-TELLIN' TIME
Tallahassee Museum of
History & Natural Science   576-1636

Oral history is an ages-old tradi-

TALLAHASSEE — FESTIVALS AND SPECIAL EVENTS

tion in the South, and leave it to Floridians to throw in some tall tales for good measure. This festival features several well-honed storytellers who never fail to captivate and entertain.

September

NATIVE AMERICAN HERITAGE FESTIVAL
Tallahassee Museum of
History & Natural Science   576-1636
For a taste of Tallahassee before settlers arrived, come to this festival. There are numerous American Indian exhibits, crafts, tribal dances and authentic period music.

"AN EVENING OF MUSIC AND DANCE"
Opperman Music Hall, FSU   222-1287
They've been practicing all summer, and now you can see why. This dance showcases members of the Tallahassee Ballet Company and is always a popular event.

October

QUINCYFEST
Quincy   627-2346
This is a down-home family festival that features good music, a fine arts & crafts show, several international food booths and a special children's section for the little ones.

OLD TIME/BLUE GRASS FESTIVAL
Tallahassee Museum of
History & Natural Science   576-1636
The museum continues its tradition of mixing music and the outdoors in this fun, foot-stompin' fest. The old-time country music you'll hear is some of the best around, and really takes you back to another era.

NORTH FLORIDA FAIR
North Florida Fairgrounds   671-8400
This large agricultural fair features many exhibits from nearly two dozen North Florida counties. There's a livestock shows, rides for the kids, entertainment nightly.

GREEK FOOD FESTIVAL
Holy Mother of God
Greek Orthodox Church   878-0747
Southern food is mighty fine around here, but if you're looking for a change of pace, try this festival. It offers an amazing and tasty assortment of traditional Greek dishes.

SAN LUIS HERITAGE FESTIVAL
San Luis Archaeological
and Historic Site   487-3711
This festival commemorates the Spanish settlers who came here in the 17th century. You can see how they lived back then, as well as examples of their crafts, music and food.

November

FLORIDA SEAFOOD FESTIVAL
Apalachicola   653-8051
Fishing is a big industry down on the coast, and one plate of food from this big festival will tell you why. There's plenty of good eatin' and usually plenty of evening activities, such as concerts and dances. Insiders usually diet a few days in advance because they know they'll soon be happily stuffed to the gills.

414 •

The annual Springtime Tallahassee Parade brings out the clown in everyone.

Bradley's Old Fashioned Fun Day
Bradley's Country Store
Centerville Road   893-1647

Take a trip back in time as this popular country store pulls out all the stops to show you how country folk used to have fun. This all-day celebration includes a cane grinding (they even use a friendly old mule to pull the grinding wheel), syrup cooking, free wagon rides, free Model-A Ford rides, a country band, arts and crafts and plenty of smiling faces. Thousands of people wait all year long for the chance to ride this time machine. One visit and you'll see why.

Mule Days
Calvery, Georgia   (912)377-6853

This mule show and beauty contest (yes, they're separate events) takes place about 20 miles northwest of Tallahassee on Georgia State Road 111. It also offers an arts & crafts show and a big parade.

Market Days
North Florida Fairgrounds   576-1636

Sponsored by the Tallahassee Museum of History & Natural Science, this easygoing fair has plenty of food booths, arts & crafts displays, handmade toys and ceramics.

Swine Times
Climax, Georgia   (912)246-0910

Oink! This hog-heaven festival is plenty of backwoods fun. There's a contest for the best-dressed pigs, and the highlight is probably the greased pig contest. Yes, they still do that around here. There's also an arts & crafts show and parade. It's about 35 miles north of Tallahassee on U.S. Highway 84.

December

A CHRISTMAS CAROL "ON THE AIR"
Location announced each year 847-3479
The Charles Dickens classic is presented by the Nucleus Group, and it's staged as an old-time radio show complete with music, sound effects and audience participation. The old story of Scrooge really comes to life under the direction of this talented and innovative group.

WINTER FESTIVAL: CELEBRATION OF LIGHTS
Downtown 891-3866
This is the biggest fall festival by far. Winter Festival signals the beginning of the Holiday season. Over 100,000 people fill the downtown area to see the Park Avenue Chain of Parks set ablaze with miles of Christmas lights. Kids love the parade and the giant animated toys and candy-makers. Ice skating is big on the list for both kids and adults (isn't it wild to think of *that* cold-weather sport in Florida!). There's plenty of good food and music, too. And don't miss the Jingle Bell Run, either — participants each get a red cap with a bell on it, and there's probably nothing more surreal than seeing thousands of joggers clad in Santa hats running through the downtown streets.

DECEMBER ON THE FARM
Tallahassee Museum of
History & Natural Science 576-1636
We only *think* that getting up on cold winter mornings and cranking up the heater is a pain! You should come and see what early settlers and pioneers had to go through. Several farm chores are demonstrated here, and afterward everyone gets to sidle up to the breakfast table for a country breakfast.

QUINCY'S VICTORIAN CHRISTMAS STROLL
Quincy 627-2346
This very popular holiday extravaganza features old-time carriage and hay rides, Santa's Secret Shop, strolling carollers and plenty of great holiday goodies.

THOMASVILLE'S VICTORIAN CHRISTMAS
Thomasville, Ga.
Though we mention this event under the Thomasville section of our Tallahassee Daytrips chapter, we want to make sure you don't miss it, so here's another reminder.

NUTCRACKER BALLET
Ruby Diamond Auditorium, FSU 222-1287
This timeless favorite is staged by the Tallahassee Ballet Company in association with the Tallahassee Symphony Orchestra.

HOLY COMFORTER EPISCOPAL SCHOOL ANNUAL TOUR OF HOMES & HOLIDAY CRAFT SHOW
877-2126
And if you think the name of this festival is a mouthful, just wait until you see the sights. This open house tour through four of Tallahassee's historic homes, all of them beautifully decorated for Christmas, can really put you in the spirit. There's also a craft show at the Dorothy Oven Park.

Tallahassee
Parks and Recreation

Parks

When most people think of Florida, they usually picture white sandy beaches — with a condo or theme park always lurking in the background.

Florida's climate and landscape presented great challenges to early settlers and pioneers, but progress prevailed and the state is one of the fastest-growing in the nation. Unfortunately, such progress also threatens much of the remaining unspoiled landscape.

While things might be getting a little crowded down on the peninsula, the Florida's Northwest sports many undeveloped areas, and several key places are thankfully preserved as parks. In fact, there are over 100 state parks throughout Florida, and some of the best are located in the Tallahassee area, which boasts many fine city parks as well.

With all that beautiful scenery and warm weather out there, why are you sitting there reading this book? Pick a park, put the book down and just get out there.

National Parks

APALACHICOLA NATIONAL FOREST
942-9300

Florida has three national forests, and insiders tend to think that we've got the best one right here. If you fly into Tallahassee, you'll get a bird's-eye view of this forest because Tallahassee Regional Airport sits right on the northeastern edge of the Apalachicola National Forest.

The forest is huge, made up of more than 600,000 acres of pristine woodland covering several counties. Needless to say, there's a lot to see and do out there.

The wildlife, for example, is incredibly diverse. Black bear, deer, wild pigs and more make their home in the forest.

The recreation area nearest to Tallahassee is Silver Lake, a few miles outside of town on Highway 20 west. This beautiful lake offers swimming, camping and hiking and is pretty popular during spring and summer.

Another hot spot is Camel Lake on the northwestern edge of the forest. This beautiful lake has a campground, swimming beach and picnic area and is popular with boaters and anglers. From Tallahassee there are two routes. Take Highway 20 west to Hosford, where you drop south for a few miles on State Road 647 to State Road 12. Or just take Interstate 10 west about 25 miles to the State 12 exit, and drop south. It's a bit of a drive, but well worth it.

TALLAHASSEE — PARKS AND RECREATION

Beautiful Lake Ella is ringed with a paved walking path that is popular with walkers, joggers and bicyclists.

TALLAHASSEE — PARKS AND RECREATION

The Ochlockonee River snakes along two lake areas, Whitehead Lake and Hitchcock Lake. Both of these parks offer primitive camping areas and are greatly enjoyed by boaters and anglers. To reach them, take highway 319 south out of Tallahassee to Crawfordville, where you'll go west on State Road 12. This quiet and lovely drive will take you out through the middle of the huge forest. You'll cross the Ochlockonee River after about 25 miles, and just beyond it you'll head south on State Road 67. Whitehead Lake is only a couple of miles down the road, and Hitchcock Lake just a few miles beyond that.

About 20 miles south of the above-mentioned Camel Lake is Cotton Landing, which also offers primitive camping, fishing and boating along Kennedy Creek. And just southeast of Cotton Landing are Wright Lake and Hickory Landing, either of which would make a great sidetrip while visiting Fort Gadsden State Historic Site (see the Florida's Forgotten Coast chapter).

One of the more impressive geological features is Leon Sinks, a chain of sinkholes that were formed when the underlying limestone was dissolved by rainwater made acidic by carbon dioxide and decaying vegetation. There are three walking trails through the Leon Sinks area. To get there, take Highway 319 south out of Tallahassee. The sinks are about five miles past Capital Circle. Though these sinks are often filled with water, swimming is not allowed in them.

St. Marks National Wildlife Refuge
St. Marks   925-6121
$4.00 per vehicle

Along with the Apalachicola National Forest, the St. Marks Wildlife Refuge preserves two important facets of Florida history: wildlife and landscape. This 63,000-acre refuge was established in 1931 and was one of the first such refuges created. It's about a half-hour's drive from Tallahassee down Highway 363 to Highway 98. Head east for a few miles and you reach the entrance to this sight-filled preserve.

You'll want to stop by the Visitor Center to orient yourself to the wildlife refuge. It's got several educational displays about what you can expect when you enter the area. There's also the Plum Orchard Pond Trail behind the center, which offers a 1/3-mile trail with interpretive markers that highlight some of the local plants and trees found in the refuge.

If you don't want to hike either of the walking trails (one's seven miles and the other is about 13), then stick to your wheels. The main road through the refuge is County Road 59, a seven-mile stretch that curves through the wilderness and stops at the St. Mark Lighthouse. There are several places where you can pull off and do some wildlife watching. There's a picnic area about five miles into the refuge, and you'll also pass several dikes that allow you to get off the beaten path a bit.

Keep your eyes open, because you never can tell what might cross your path. Deer, foxes, raccoons and armadillos can sometimes appear

• *419*

out of nowhere, and if you're a birdwatcher, be sure to pick up the free guide to birds in the refuge Visitor Center.

You can't camp at St. Marks Wildlife Refuge, but just across from the entrance is the Newport Recreation Area, which has camping facilities. On the other end of the park is the Ochlockonee River State Park (see below), which also has campgrounds.

There's good fishing in these parts. Cast a line and find out why it's still a booming industry around here. Boats can be launched from the Lighthouse, but aren't permitted in the refuge pools except from March 15 to October 15, and leave the big outboard at home because boat motors can't be more than 10 horsepower. Canoeing remains a popular way to see the sights from the water.

There's good crabbing too, but the refuge warns you to watch out for alligators that may try to steal your bait. And they know what they're talking about.

Hunting is allowed on a select basis in fall and spring. You should contact the refuge for dates, regulations and permits.

State Parks — Tallahassee

Not only can you spend days wandering through the wonderfully varied landscape in the local state parks, but they also present plenty of activities. There's a free *Florida State Parks Guide* available for residents and visitors. All you have to do is ask for one. Write the Florida Department of Environmental Protection, Division of Recreation and Parks at 3900 Commonwealth Boulevard, Mail Stop 525, Tallahassee, Florida 32399-3000. Or you can call at 488-9872.

All Florida State Parks are open from 8 AM until sundown, 365 days a year. State museums are open from 9 AM to 12 noon, and again from 1 PM to 5 PM. Many museums and historic sites are closed two days each week, so be sure to contact the park before you visit.

Enjoy these parks, but also treat them with respect. The natural resources within state parks are protected, and rightly so. Any hunting, livestock grazing or timber removal could severely damage the ecosystems. You'll probably see some amazing wildlife, but don't feed the animals. And don't drink — alcoholic beverages are a no-no. The same goes for firearms.

Pets aren't allowed in camping areas, bathing beaches or concession areas, but are generally welcome anywhere else. Leashes are required. Guide dogs for the deaf and blind are, of course, welcome in all park areas.

Handicapped persons should note that not all state parks are readily accessible — it's something the park system is certainly working towards, but it's not there yet. Accommodations can be made, however, in parks where access is not permanently available. For more information, just call the individual park office at least ten days before your visit.

Campers have a lot of sites to choose from. Some parks offer modern facilities, while others are strictly "primitive" camping.

TALLAHASSEE — PARKS AND RECREATION

Many state parks offer some great fishing, so pack your rod and reel. Note that saltwater and freshwater fishing licenses are required for those 16 years and older. Licenses are available for a fee at county tax collector offices and at most bait and tackle shops. And keep in mind that some parks do have size and species limits. For a free copy of the pamphlets "Know Your Limits" and "Go Fish . . . But First Get A License," in either English or Spanish, write the Department of Environmental Protection, Office of Fisheries Management & Assistance Services, Mail Station #240, 3900 Commonwealth Boulevard, Tallahassee, Florida 32399-3000, or call 922-4340.

Unless otherwise stated, here's the fee structure for Florida state parks:

Per vehicle (8 passengers max.)	$3.25
Pedestrians, Bicyclists, Extra Passengers	$1.00
Museum/Visitor Center Fee	$1.00

Camping fees vary from park to park. It's a good idea to call ahead prior to any park visit to check the fees.

The Florida Park Service is now issuing vacation passes good for up to 15 days. A Family Entrance Permit (up to eight people) covers admission to any of Florida's State Parks and costs $20.00. The new passes can be purchased at any Florida State Park.

LAKE JACKSON MOUNDS STATE ARCHAEOLOGICAL SITE
1022 DeSoto Park Dr. 922-6007

This park is located just a few miles north of I-10, just off U.S. 27 and down Indian Mound Road. From 1200 A.D. to 1500 A.D., this area near Lake Jackson was a major trading, religious and social center for early Indians in the area. Archaeologists and historians generally agree that these Indians were part of a complex Indian society knows as the "Southeastern Ceremonial Complex," or "Southern Cult." Among the many artifacts and remains unearthed here was evidence that these Indians had extensive contact with tribes all over the southeast.

There are six earthen mounds here, but only three are accessible to visitors. There's a large picnic area bisected by a small stream that feeds into the nearby lake, and a nature trail through the woods displays an abundance of plant life.

Each October the mounds are alive with the sound of music during "Sounds of the Mounds," a free outdoor concert designed to promote environmental awareness of the area. The actual date changes each year, so if you want to attend, call the park office for the schedule.

LAKE TALQUIN RECREATION AREA
Hwy. 20 576-8233

The Lake Talquin Recreation Area is a very popular outdoor attraction. One look at the beautiful pristine waters and surrounding forest and you'll understand why. This 10,000-acre lake sits just 10 miles west of Tallahassee on the northeastern edge of the Apalachicola National Forest and offers plenty of outdoor activities.

This lake was created in 1927 when the Jackson Bluff Dam was thrown up across the Ochlockonee

TALLAHASSEE — PARKS AND RECREATION

River. There's no single park here, but rather a seamless integration of several smaller parks and recreational areas. Although the state owns nearly 20,000 acres of land around the lake, the only park they run is the River Bluff Picnic Site, which is operated during the same hours as all other state parks (see this chapter's introduction). It's the perfect place to spread out with a blanket and enjoy a leisurely lunch while enjoying the great view. The River Bluff Picnic Site sports a pavilion and barbecue pit, as well as a boardwalk tour that shows off the remarkable landscape.

In addition to the good fishing — largemouth bass and speckled perch are abundant here — there's a wide variety of birds and other wildlife. Patient birdwatchers (are there any other kind?) can be rewarded with excellent views of wild turkeys and bald eagles.

The other parks and landings are managed by Leon and Gadsden counties and offer various camping, picnic and boating facilities. There are six landings — Williams, Coe, Lewis Hall, Wainwright, Vause and Elkhorn — offering boat ramps. Of these landings, Coe's offers recreational vehicle and tent camping, while Hall's offers only primitive camping.

Pat Thomas Park recently underwent a facelift, and now its camping, picnic and boat launch facilities are better than ever, ready to handle the crowds.

There are several fish camps dotted along Lake Talquin, a testament to the good fishing that goes on here year round. Blount's Fish Camp rents cabins and has boat launch facilities. Ingram's Marina has full camper hookups, camping sites and storage facilities. Gainey's Talquin Lodge offers motel rooms as well as camp sites.

To go to Lake Talquin, take Highway 20 west out of Tallahassee.

Several numbers to keep handy are:

River Bluff Picnic Site	922-6007
Pat Thomas Park	875-4544
Blount's Fish Camp	576-4301
Ingram's Marina	627-2241
Gainey's Talquin Lodge	627-3822

MACLAY STATE GARDENS
3540 Thomasville Rd.   487-4556

New York financier Alfred B. Maclay loved flowers, and he'd probably be proud this his name is connected with one of the most beautiful sculpted gardens in the South. When his estate was donated to Florida in the early 1950s, it quickly became a notable tourist attraction that even the locals can't get enough of.

Located just one mile north of I-10 on Thomasville Road, Maclay State Gardens is home to hundreds of varieties of plants. There are over 100 varieties of camellias alone, and each week from January on into summer a different variety reaches full bloom. Along with the other plants, this creates a never-ending festival of color that many residents return to witness each year.

The Maclay house sits atop gently rolling hills that feature great pine and live oak trees. The house appears as it was furnished when the Maclays lived there, and is well worth a tour for its preserved history.

Down the hill rests Lake Hall,

TALLAHASSEE — PARKS AND RECREATION

The Maclay Gardens feature a colorful, neverending festival of flowers and plants.

which is home to fish, turtles and alligators. Along its banks can be seen many birds and, if you're lucky, an occasional bobcat or fox.

The surrounding area is accessible by way of the Big Pine Nature Trail and makes for a brisk walk. There are spots for picnics, including a large pavilion that's available for rental, and the lake is open for swimming and boating — no motors are allowed, however. Bring your own sailboat or canoe, or just rent a canoe from the park. Also note that the opposing shoreline of the lake is private property and the last thing its owners want are boatloads of visitors coming ashore.

The fishing is excellent. Local anglers report great success in catching largemouth bass, bream and bluegill. Just don't forget your Florida freshwater fishing license.

Each December "Camellia Christmas" is a hot ticket in town. The lanes through the park are lit for special nighttime tours and the air is filled with Christmas carols. This usually takes place the first weekend in December as part of the city's Winter Festival, so call ahead to check the actual date.

The gardens are free except during the peak bloom season which officially runs from January 1 through April 30. Then the gardens admission fee is $3.00 for adults, $1.50 for children. Guided garden tours are usually offered in mid-March, and special tours may be booked with a three-week advance notice.

The Maclay Home is open only during those same peak bloom months, from January until April.

If you've got a green thumb, you might want to note that a special seminar on ornamental plant care is offered on the first Saturday of each month, and is taught by the Maclay State Gardens landscape gardener.

NATURAL BRIDGE BATTLEFIELD STATE HISTORIC SITE
Natural Bridge Rd., Woodville   922-6007
Free Admission

During the Civil War, Tallahassee was the only Confederate state capital east of the Mississippi that did not fall to Union forces. The reason for this can be found in a tiny town called Woodville that sits nine miles south of the city on State Road 363 (South Monroe Street). Six miles east of Woodville is Natural Bridge, an area along the St. Marks River where the water flows through an underground cavern for a brief stretch, creating a natural crossing.

In early March of 1865, a joint Union Army and Navy force sailed into Apalachee Bay some 25 miles south of the capital. Their mission was to land and take the St. Marks

Insiders' Tips

Johnny Weissmuller and Maureen O'Sullivan spent a lot of time in the 1930s filming *Tarzan* movies at Wakulla Springs.

TALLAHASSEE — PARKS AND RECREATION

Every March the Battle of Natural Bridge is re-enacted with authentic Civil War costumes and weapons.

Lighthouse. After that, they planned to move north and destroy unsuspecting Confederate forces in a sneak attack that would culminate with the taking of Tallahassee.

The Confederate forces got wind of the invading troops and tried to halt the Union forces at Newport. They could not gain a foothold, however, and were forced to retreat. The Confederate troops were at least able to channel the Union forces towards Natural Bridge, the only safe crossing at the St. Marks River. Because the Confederate ranks were thin, several young boys, old men and even wounded soldiers from the area found themselves pressed into service, and they all waited for the Union troops to begin their assault.

At 4 AM on March 6, 1865, the attack began. The Union forces — reportedly made up of many black soldiers — were swift and strong, but the Confederates were braced for the attack. After repelling three powerful charges over a 10-hour period, the Confederates themselves advanced and eventually forced the Union troops back down the river to St. Marks, where they took to their ships and departed. The Union dead numbered 21, and the Confederates lost three.

Today the pivotal battle site is marked by a huge obelisk monument to the troops who fought and died there. Each year this historic battle is re-enacted by volunteers sporting authentic uniforms and firearms. The re-enactment takes place on a weekend close to the actual date of the battle. Call the park for the actual date each year.

Picnic tables are available, and park admission is free.

• 425

The St. Marks Wildlife Refuge is a thriving haven for many birds and animals.

TALLAHASSEE - ST. MARKS HISTORIC RAILROAD STATE TRAIL
State Rd. 363 & Capital Circle 922-6007
Free Admission

In the early 1800s, Tallahassee planters and merchants needed a railroad to ship their wares down to ports at St. Marks, and then bring supplies and passengers back. It took a long time and a lot of hard work, but the Tallahassee - St. Marks Railroad was completed in 1837. Of course this was a great convenience at the time, but one must remember that passengers and freight rode in open wooden box cars. And it's not like there was a good breeze to cool things down, because the first few trains were pulled slowly by oxen, and it took them nearly half a day to make the 16-mile journey.

Even after the addition of a nice new engine, things were only moderately better. Writer Bradford Torrey, in his 1894 book *Florida Sketchbook*, rode the train and wrote, "I could never have imagined the possibility of running trains over so crazy a track."

These days that crazy track has been replaced by a smoothly-paved trail and you can make the journey at your own speed, whether it's by foot, skates, bicycle or horseback. In 1987 the Florida Rails-to-Trails Program was established and this, its first completed project, runs from just south of Tallahassee all the way down to St. Marks.

When it ceased operating in 1984, the railroad was the oldest one in the state. Now it can thankfully enjoy many more years as a unique and historic nature trail.

Water fountains are dotted along this piney path and there are several places to stop and picnic, so it's a good idea to pack a meal. If you're

TALLAHASSEE — PARKS AND RECREATION

The St. Marks Trail offers great bicycling through unspoiled landscape.

bold and want some good seafood, however, you can take the entire trail down to St. Marks, where it empties out practically at the doorstep of several good restaurants. If you eat or drink your fill, you've got a 16-mile bike ride back to Tallahassee that'll help you work it all off.

Also nearby is San Marcos de Apalache State Historic Site, if you want to do some sight-seeing. It's only about a mile from the end of the trail.

If you want to take your horse along the trail, there's a separate path that runs parallel to the paved trail. If you're accompanying persons on foot or bike, you're asked to keep your horse on the shoulder to protect the pavement. Note that proof of a recent negative Coggins test for sleeping sickness is required of all horses that enter the trail.

Bike and skate rentals are available at the beginning of the trail.

As the Tallahassee - St. Marks Trail crosses over several streets and state roads, you should always be alert for cross-traffic. The crossings are well-marked for drivers, but play it safe and treat it like any other crossing. It shouldn't break your stride too often.

EDWARD BALL WAKULLA SPRINGS STATE PARK

Wakulla Springs 922-3633

This is probably the busiest, hardest-working park in the region, possibly even the state, and one look tells you why: it's got one of the largest and deepest freshwater springs in the world. This beautiful spring is the centerpiece of an unspoiled natural habitat that sprawls for nearly 3,000 acres.

Boat tours take you out over the spring and down the river a bit, where

• 427

The Wakulla Springs Lodge Restaurant offers fine dining with
a great view of the springs.

TALLAHASSEE — PARKS AND RECREATION

you can observe wildlife such as alligators, anhinga birds, wild turkeys and turtles. And though the springs have a depth of 185 feet, the waters are so clear that most of the underwater plant and animal life is easily visible.

We know that the Apalachee Indians greatly valued this area as a hunting ground and fresh water source, but its history goes even further back than that. Several pre-Ice Age bones and fossils have been discovered by dive teams in the underwater cave from which the spring flows. In fact, a mastodon skeleton retrieved from this very spring in 1930 now stands in the Museum of Florida History.

It's only 20 minutes from downtown Tallahassee, but you feel like you've stepped into another world, another era. The lush jungle-like setting has attracted many filmmakers, and the park's tropical beauty can be seen in such flicks as *The Creature From the Black Lagoon*, *Airport '77* and several of the old Johnny Weissmuller *Tarzan* films of the 1930s.

The Wakulla Springs Lodge and Conference Center was built in 1937 as a private hunting lodge. It has overnight accommodations, a restaurant, snack bar and gift shop. Conference rooms are also available, and you might see several attendees ducking out of busy meetings for a quiet stroll along the river.

There are spots for picnics, and several nature and hiking trails through the park. Swimming is allowed only within the designated area near the spring.

There are so many monthly activities at the park that to list them all would probably take another book or two, but note that there are regular tours, hikes and lectures as well as seasonal activities such as night cruises and sunrise boat tours. Call ahead for a current schedule.

To get to Wakulla Springs State Park and Lodge, take State Road 267 south for 14 miles.

Other Area State Parks

FALLING WATERS STATE RECREATION AREA
Chipley   638-6130

Whoever names the Florida state parks usually gets them right, and this park is no exception. Yes, there is a waterfall here, a 70-footer that falls into a deep sink, or cylindrical pit in the limestone aquifer upon which Florida sits.

There's camping here, nature trails and spots for picnics. It's about 90 miles west of Tallahassee. Take I-10 west to State Road 77A and drop south about three miles.

FLORIDA CAVERNS STATE PARK
Marianna   482-9598

For many years, people knew about the caves in Marianna. Indians were living in them when the first settlers arrived, and many early explorers also used them for shelter. Historians believe that many Indians hid in these caves during Andrew Jackson's brutal raids in the early 1800s.

But in the early part of this century, a hurricane swept across the Panhandle and uprooted a huge tree near the caves. Beneath its exposed root structure was a huge dark cav-

• 429

TALLAHASSEE — PARKS AND RECREATION

The popular Florida Caverns are just an hour west of Tallahassee in Marianna.

ern, one the Indians hadn't discovered because until the hurricane there had been no opening.

The current irony here is that this latter cave is the only you can visit. The other caves have been closed to the public due to misuse and abuse. Park officials still justly grumble about the graffiti that constantly appeared on those ancient walls.

While that important bit of history is now lost to visitors, the good news is that these more recently discovered caverns are open to the public. What's more, they offer some fascinating and beautiful rock formations. Tours take about half an hour (after you sit through a sleep-inducing short video about the history of the park, or something) and the park guides are knowledgeable enough to explain the difference between stalactites and stalagmites, which everyone seems to forget as soon as they hear it.

The formations are caused by carbonic acid in the rainwater washing over the limestone hollows, which are usually filled with water. This residue is called calcite and it builds up slowly over the years. The resulting formations — which bear exotic and apt names such as rimstone, flowstone and draperies — are thousands, even millions, of years old, and a truly amazing sight to behold.

Those who suffer claustrophobia probably wouldn't go inside a cave in the first place, but here's an official warning anyway: some parts of the cave are really tight. You wander 65 feet below the surface, and are asked to navigate passages with names like Fat Man's Squeeze, where the ceiling hangs at about four feet.

Even if you can't do that, the

1,280-acre park still has a lot to offer. There are plenty of full-facility campsites for those who wish to explore the swimming, canoeing, fishing and hiking. There are also horse trails and stables. Be sure to check out the natural bridge where the Chipola River dips underground for a few hundred feet.

Ponce de Leon Springs State Recreation Area
Chipley   836-4281

There's a sardonic joke about Ponce de Leon that sums up a lot of attitudes about Florida. If the famous Spanish explorer had actually found his Fountain of Youth and achieved immortality, then one look at today's endangered Florida environment would have the old-timer desperately seeking the services of one Dr. Jack Kevorkian.

Okay, maybe it's not as bad as all that, but it's often useful and refreshing to retreat to a state park to see some unspoiled natural landscape. This park is one good place to do just that. The park is named after Ponce de Leon because its several crystal-clear springs probably attracted his attention during his exploration of the panhandle. Maybe he didn't acquire much longevity from drinking their waters, but then again, a good cold drink on a hot day can certainly make you feel born again.

The park offers swimming in the year round 68-degree springs, picnic areas, hiking trails and fishing. Due to state restrictions on empty promises, however, the park management cannot guarantee immortality to those who drink from the springs.

Ponce de Leon Springs State Recreation Area is about 100 miles west of Tallahassee on Interstate 10.

Ochlockonee River State Park
Sopchoppy   962-2771

There's plenty of camping and hiking do to in this 400-acre park, but the real reason to come is the 50-mile Ochlockonee River, which winds through the nearby Apalachicola National Forest. It's great for swimming and just perfect for boating and canoeing.

In fact, the water probably provides the best view of the surrounding forest, which is home to abundant wildlife such as deer, bobcats and foxes. The birdwatching is excellent, so don't forget your binoculars and Audubon guide.

To get to the park from Tallahassee, take Highway 319 south for 22 miles. The park is four miles south of Sopchoppy.

San Marcos de Apalache State Historic Site
St. Marks   922-6007

For nearly five hundred years, this historic site has been the setting for some of the most pivotal, dramatic and tragic events in the history of Florida. The Spanish explorer Panfilo de Narvaez arrived here in 1528, having walked his expedition up the peninsula from present-day Tampa. Narvaez should have stayed around to enjoy life a bit more, but he insisted on building wooden boats and sailing to Mexico. He and his 300 men were lost at sea not long after.

Originally a wooden fort stood on this wedge of land where the Wakulla River joins the St. Marks

River as they flow southward. Erected by Spanish explorers, this structure was destroyed in a hurricane in 1758. The following year a masonry fort was built, and ownership passed from the Spanish to the local Indians to the Spanish again.

The fort was briefly held by William Augustus Bowles, an Indian sympathizer who wished to establish an independent Indian nation. He held it for less than a month at the turn of the 19th century before Spanish forces drove him away.

General Andrew Jackson claimed the Spanish fort in 1819 and it became an army outpost from which Jackson dealt severe blows to the Indians. When Jackson caught two British citizens among the Indians, he tried and executed them on the spot, and to soften the outcry from Britain, the U.S. Congress passed a resolution condemning Jackson's misguided actions.

Jackson withdrew and the fort returned to Spanish rule for two years. Then Florida was ceded to the United States. In 1830, the nearby town of St. Marks was created and became a bustling port town. The fort was again pressed into military service during the Civil War and called Fort Ward. Its formidable presence discouraged forces from the ever-present Union blockade from landing.

The museum, which stands on the foundations of a pre-Civil War hospital for yellow fever victims, has a fascinating exhibit about the history of the fort. There are self-guided walking tours through the site featuring the remains of Confederate earthworks, bastion walls, Spanish moats and other features. There is also a picnic area available.

Each May the park plays host to HuManatee, a small but heartfelt festival that welcomes the manatees back to the immediate area.

To get to the San Marcos de Apalache State Historic Site from Tallahassee, take State Road 363 south for 16 miles.

THREE RIVERS STATE PARK
Sneads 482-9006

Two's company and three's a crowd, goes the old saying. Whoever coined that phrase obviously never visited Three Rivers State Park, where the Apalachicola, Chattahoochee and Flint Rivers meet near Lake Seminole.

Needless to say, activities here are geared for maximum use of the available water resources. There's excellent swimming, fishing, canoeing and boating to be done here.

But don't ignore the surrounding terrain. The hilly pine forests and hardwood hammocks are great for hiking and camping.

From Tallahassee, take Interstate 10 west to State Road 271, about 45 miles. Head north for 10 miles and there you are.

TORREYA STATE PARK
Bristol 643-2674

Torreya State Park might take its name from a tree, but the park is perhaps best known for its magnificent 150-foot bluffs overlooking the Apalachicola River.

Which is too bad, considering that the rare Torreya trees might be on the verge of extinction. In the 1960s, a disease practically wiped out the species, and the few remaining ones in this park may not survive.

There are several other rare species of plant and animal in the park, and quite a bit of history. Indians once lived along the banks of this river. Later it was an important waterway for settlers and early industry.

Along one of the bluff's hiking trails can be seen the huge pit where a six-cannon battery once stood, designed to keep Union ships from passing during the Civil War.

The park also sports the Gregory House, a mid 19th-century plantation house. The house was built by Jason Gregory, a cotton farmer, and is furnished with articles from that time period. The Gregory House is open for tours on weekdays at 10 AM and on weekends and state holidays at 10 AM, 2 PM and 4 PM. A fee of $1.00 per adult and 50¢ per child younger than 13 years of age is charged.

There are several nature trails, including a seven-mile hiking trail that displays most of the park's features. There are also picnic areas as well as full-facility and primitive campsites.

To get to Torreya State Park from Tallahassee, take Interstate 10 west for about 45 miles and take the State Road 12 exit.

Tallahassee City Parks

The city park system is an active one, and there's a special hotline for events and programs. Call 891-3866 for more information.

A.J. HENRY PARK

Just south of Killearn Estates in the northern part of town. There's a place for picnics, a playground and walking trails through this 70-acre park.

CAMPBELL POND

Located just south of Four Points, this park features a 24-acre lake, picnic pavilions and a playground.

CAPITAL PARK

Down Old Tram Road, this park features a youth baseball field, a picnic area and playground.

CARTER-HOWELL-STRONG PARK

Located in Frenchtown, bordered by Georgia, Copeland, Deqey and Virginia streets, this is one of the city's newest parks.

CHAPMAN POND (SYLVAN LAKE)

Located on Circle Drive, this 5.2-acre park is perfect for picnics and bird-watching.

Insiders' Tips

Wakulla Springs is a nesting ground for many anhinga, or "snake birds," as they are often called. These agile birds can swim effortlessly, and the manner in which they hold their long, thin heads above the water makes them look like snakes at first glance. Chance are you'll see an anhinga perched gracefully on a log or rock, wings outspread in the sun to dry them off from a recent splash.

Country Club Park
There are three softball fields at this park, which is found at the intersection of Magnolia Avenue and Golf Terrace Drive.

Dorothy B. Oven Park
3205 Thomasville Rd.
Impressive flower gardens and a classic manor-style home are the two main reasons to visit this park.

Indianhead Acre Park
Indianhead Drive is home to this 30-acre park that offers walking and open grounds.

John G. Riley Park
Just off Indiana Street, this park offers five acres of passive park land.

Koucky Park
This three-acre park has a playground and a picnic area, and is found on Chowkeebenee Drive.

Lake Ella
This midtown lake just off North Monroe Street is a popular walking spot.

Levy Park
At Tharpe Street and Gibbs Drive, this park has a swimming pool, baseball fields and a picnic area.

Myers Park
Forty acres of hilly wooded land make for a brisk hike through this park, which also features a playground, youth baseball field, tennis courts and a year round swimming pool.

Old Fort Park
Just a few blocks from Myers Park on Old Fort Road is this one-acre Civil War site, which features a historic earthen fort.

Optimist Park
Just off East Indianhead Drive, this park has a picnic area, playground, softball field, basketball court and volleyball field.

Park Avenue Chain of Parks
As a safeguard against Indian attacks and wild animals, early settlers in Tallahassee cleared out a northern buffer zone known as 200-Foot Street. As the township grew it eventually extended beyond this swath, which exists today as a downtown chain of seven parks along Park Avenue. Cherokee Park, E. Peck Green Park, McCarty Park, Ponce de Leon Park, Bloxham Park, Lewis Park and Genevieve Randolph Park all offer downtowners the chance to relax and enjoy the sunshine among live oaks, thick grass and several historic markers.

In Lewis Park, for example, you can visit the gigantic stump where Tallahassee's May Oak once stood. For over 100 years, this great tree was the site of the May Day Festival, one of the oldest annual celebrations in Florida. The aging tree collapsed in the mid-1980s, but its huge flat stump is a historic marker in its own right.

A few blocks west, in McCarty Park, you can see the camellias bloom from December on into summer at the William Lanier "Red" Barber Memorial Garden. The flowers were favorites of the legendary sports broadcaster, and he spoke of them often during his heartwarming, wise and popular commentaries on National Public Radio. Locals like to think that Red is looking down on his flowers and smiling broadly.

Some of the historic structures you'll see on a stroll through the parks are the Knott House (open for tours), Tallahassee's first library (now headquarters for Springtime Tallahassee — duck inside for a look at its magnificent woodwork), the Lewis Home (main offices for the Florida Council for Community Mental Health, Inc.), the Murphy House (shops and offices), the Columns (Tallahassee Chamber of Commerce), the U.S. District Courthouse and the First Presbyterian Church, the oldest public building in Tallahassee.

Springtime Tallahassee and the Winter Festival are just two of the many events that make use of this beautiful stretch of greenery. You're encouraged to explore all of the parks — and heading from east to west lands you at the Old City Cemetery, which is also a fascinating place to spend a couple of hours.

SAN LUIS MISSION PARK

Located on San Luis Road, this 70-acre park has picnic pavilions, walking trails and a boardwalk around Lake Esther.

SOUTHSIDE PARK

A 50-acre park on Paul Russell Road with basketball, tennis and volleyball courts and a picnic area.

SWEETBAY SWAMP

This five-acre field is found at the intersection of Yaupon Street and Redbud Avenue.

TOM BROWN PARK

On Easterwood Drive just off Capital Circle, this sprawling park has picnic pavilions, playgrounds, baseball, soccer and softball fields, tennis and racquetball courts, bike tracks, walking trails and even a track for remote-control toy vehicles.

WAVERLY POND PARK

This seven-acre park on Waverly Road has a pond and picnic area.

WINTHROP PARK

This park, at the intersection of Betton Road and Mitchell Avenue, offers a picnic area, playground and softball field.

Community Centers

Whether you want to chop onions with a knife or break boards with your bare hands, Tallahassee's Community Centers can help you sharpen your skills. The city's Parks and Recreation Department has established six community centers in neighborhoods throughout Tallahassee, and these support a wide range of participatory programs and classes.

What are some of the things you can do? Martial arts and cooking are two popular classes we've already mentioned. There's also belly dancing and several art classes, as well as participatory sports programs such as swim teams, football (touch and tackle), volleyball, soccer and basketball.

TALLAHASSEE — PARKS AND RECREATION

The community centers are open six days a week, Monday through Saturday. Each center has its own schedule of classes and programs, so it's advisable to check with each one to find out what's going on.

DADE STREET COMMUNITY CENTER
1115 Dade St.   891-3910

**FOURTH AVENUE
RECREATION CENTER**
Fourth Avenue at Macomb   891-3930

JAKE GAITHER COMMUNITY CENTER
801 Tanner Dr.   891-3940

**LAFAYETTE PARK
COMMUNITY CENTER**
403 Ingleside Dr.   891-3946

**PALMER MUNROE
COMMUNITY CENTER**
1900 Jackson Bluff Rd.   891-3958

WALKER FORD COMMUNITY CENTER
2301 Pasco St.   891-3970

Tallahassee
Golf and Hunting

Let's face it, golf and hunting aren't for everybody.

Avid fans often lapse into Zen-like trances when speaking of the pleasures found in either sport. The rest of us just sit there nodding calmly, waiting for the whole episode to pass.

Golfers say that there are some mighty fine holes to played in these parts. And hunters claim that there's nowhere to go but Myrtlewood Plantation, up the road in Thomasville, Georgia.

Here's where you'll find the people who take such endeavors very, very seriously.

Golf

There are plenty of private golf clubs in Tallahassee and its environs, but we list only the ones that will allow members of the public to play without being accompanied by a member.

Don't let the silly stigma of playing a public course affect you. Tallahassee golfers we know and trust say that some of the courses are every bit as well-maintained and challenging as the private courses.

HILAMAN PARK MUNICIPAL GOLF COURSE
2737 Blairstone Rd.   891-3850

This 72-par course offers a driving range and putting green. It's open from 7 AM until sunset all week long. Green fees with cart are $22.38 weekdays, $27.82 weekends.

JAKE GAITHER GOLF COURSE
801 Tanner Dr.   891-3942

This 9-hole municipal golf course is open from 7:30 AM until sunset every day of the week. Green fees with cart are $11.70 for nine holes, $14.98 for 18 holes.

PLAYERS CLUB AT SUMMERBROOKE
7505 Preservation Rd.   894-4653

One of Tallahassee's newest golf clubs, Summerbrooke is a semiprivate club that welcomes the public. It's open from dawn to dusk, all week long. Green fees with cart are $30 weekdays, $35 weekends.

SEMINOLE GOLF COURSE AND COUNTRY CLUB
2550 Pottsdamer St.   644-2582

This public course allows walking anytime after 4 PM. It's open from 7:30 AM until dark every day each week. Green fees with cart are $25 weekdays, $29.96 weekends.

TALLAHASSEE — GOLF AND HUNTING

KILLEARN COUNTRY CLUB AND INN
100 Tyron Circle   893-2186
(800)476-4101

The Killearn Country Club and Inn is a private club, but there's something you should know: if you stay at the inn then you can play the 27-hole golf course. The inn itself is worth the trip – and don't miss the wonderful food in the Oak View Dining Room. An overnight stay gets you access to the swimming pool and tennis courts, too. You'll see plenty of out-of-towners here, as well as a healthy smattering of residents hiding out for the weekend. The 72-par course is open from 7 AM to 6:30 PM all week long. Green fees with cart are $41 weekdays, $46 weekends. Cart rentals are required on weekends.

Hunting

MYRTLEWOOD PLANTATION
P.O. Box 32
Thomasville, Ga.   (912) 228-6232

Thomasville has always been known for its fine quail hunting, and Myrtlewood Plantation is where some of the finest happens.

The beautiful house that lords over these 3,300 acres of prime forest was built in 1887 by John Masury of New York. Masury was among the many wealthy Northerners who spent winters in rustic Thomasville because of its climate and scenery.

Masury built a popular hotel that was later torn down, but his lasting achievement was this impression mansion, which was acquired by R.C. Balfour, Jr. in the 1930s. Balfour was an avid hunter and wildlife enthusiast who turned Myrtlewood into the hunting preserve you see today.

This is truly a hunter's paradise. It's not cheap, but those who come here seem very satisfied with what their money buys them.

Fall season brings deer and quail hunting, and there's plenty of good blue gill bream and largemouth bass fishing from March through October of each year.

Whether you want a full-blown classical quail hunt or just a little practice time shooting the sporting clays, Myrtlewood has a national reputation that's sure to please even the most discriminate hunter.

Myrtlewood Plantation is located in Thomasville, Georgia, on Campbell Road, just 3.5 miles off Highway 319.

Tallahassee
Spectator Sports

If you're looking for year-round spectator sports, you need look no further than Tallahassee. With two state universities and one large community college in the area, residents and visitors have quite a lineup to choose from.

And there's much more to come. In late fall of 1994, Tallahassee will become the home base for a new ice hockey team in the East Coast Hockey League. This late-breaking development has a lot of people in town smiling broadly — those who have worked hard to bring the team here, and those who can't wait to go cheer the team to victory.

Tallahassee's great climate means that plenty of people like to get outdoors and soak up some action with their sunshine. Be warned that some sporting events are so popular that tickets are often impossible to find. Then again, if you're a die-hard Seminole or Rattler fan, you're not gonna listen anyway.

FLORIDA A&M UNIVERSITY

Everyone knows that rattlesnakes are things to be avoided. That's the image that the FAMU Rattlers like to convey, and most of the time they live up to it. The Rattlers and the Rattlerettes have broken several impressive sports records over the years and show no signs of slowing down.

Neither do the fans. Excited residents crowd the bleachers along-

---

Insiders' Tips

Where the heck is Florida State University's Doak Campbell Stadium? Oh, it's still there just off Pensacola Street west of campus, but over the past couple of years, it's gotten quite a facelift. Once the big concrete and steel bowl was all girders and walkways. Now the stadium is ringed by a thick, rather imposing layer of faculty offices and classrooms. It's an attempt on FSU's part to make the sports complex more integrated with the rest of campus life. One thing's for sure: the stadium now looks like a modern castle, and the legions of fans who cheer on the team's shining knights are sure to approve.

side screaming students and alumni, and sometimes you'll leave a game with your ears literally ringing from the roar.

Take earplugs. The next scream you hear might be your own.

For information on FAMU athletics, call 599-3200.

FLORIDA STATE UNIVERSITY

Just say Seminoles.

It's a magic word in these parts, and most of the time it works wonders. If you haven't heard about the recent achievements of the Seminole football team, you've obviously had your head under a rock and probably aren't reading this chapter anyway. It's a popular team right now, and some folks get downright rabid about it.

But residents are careful not to forget the other fine Seminole athletes, although hysteria over football can sometimes get a little out of hand. Doak Campbell Stadium is always packed for home games, but you'll also be impressed by the energetic, supportive fans who crowd into the Tallahassee/Leon County Civic Center for basketball and Dick Howser Stadium for baseball.

It's all just a matter of how you get your kicks. Some people retreat to sports bars and sit in air-conditioned comfort. Others paint their faces garnet and gold and spend hours screaming their throats raw and doing the tomahawk chop. When it comes right down to it, it's the game that matters most. And the FSU Seminoles play a lot of good games. If you're in town, you might want to catch one.

For more information on FSU Seminole Football, call 644-1830

For information on FSU Men's Basketball, call 644-1461.

For information on FSU Lady Seminole Basketball, call 644-1091.

For information on FSU Baseball, call 644-1073.

TALLAHASSEE COMMUNITY COLLEGE

Okay, these aren't the biggest games in town. With FSU and FAMU taking up most of the athletic horizon, it's only expected that TCC sports might not generate the excitement and crowd-base they deserve.

But it's understood that many excellent athletes often start their collegiate careers at community colleges, and TCC has certainly been a helpful stepping stone for many of them. There are a number of reasons why the college has been able to build and maintain a steady support base among Tallahassee residents.

One big plus at TCC is the addition of women's sports, specifically baseball, softball and basketball. Another big attraction is the new EagleDome, a modern sports arena recently constructed on the campus.

For more information on TCC sports, call 922-0230 (baseball); 922-8201 (basketball); and 922-8200 (softball).

Tallahassee
Arts and Culture

Tallahassee's vibrant cultural scene is just as diversified as its surrounding landscape, and you'll see that reflected in the fine arts and attractions offered here.

Recently there's been a lot of public discourse on the arts and its role in Tallahassee's future. Residents last year voted down a tax that would have funded a new arts center in the downtown district. The debate was active and lively, reflecting the community's strong interest in its economic and cultural future. It's still a hot issue, and if it doesn't lead to another referendum, it may at least stoke some fires under various arts group in the area.

The presences of Florida State University, Florida A&M University and Tallahassee Community College contribute greatly to Tallahassee's arts scene. You'll find listings for their many programs and galleries as well as in this book's Inside Tallahassee Colleges and Universities chapter.

One big problem is how to keep up with everything. There have been a variety of arts-oriented publications over the years, but the place where most people turn to is the city's major daily newspaper, the *Tallahassee Democrat*, which does a fine job of keeping its readers abreast of current cultural happenings. The arts listings in the newspaper's "Limelight," a weekend pullout section, are highly recommended for residents and visitors alike.

Dance

FLORIDA STATE UNIVERSITY SCHOOL OF DANCE
644-6500

The renowned FSU School of Dance is one of the nation's most respected programs. Its faculty and students offer several performances during the year. Each November the school presents the popular "Twelve Days of Dance" program, with all works choreographed and danced by students, faculty and guest artists. Most performances are held in the Dance Theater of the Montgomery Gym, which faces Landis Street in the center of the FSU Campus.

TALLAHASSEE BALLET COMPANY
Tallahassee Community College   222-1287

The city's own regional ballet company, led by artistic director Joyce Straub, serves as the official "Dance Company in Residence" at Tallahassee Community College. The Tallahassee Ballet Company presents several programs each year, as well as its annual major performances of *The Nutcracker* (with the

The FSU School of Dance stages several popular performances each year.

Tallahassee Symphony Orchestra) and *Dance for Spring.*

Exhibits and Galleries

THE NEW CAPITOL
Monroe St. and Apalachee Pkwy.   488-6167

There's a rotating exhibit of work by Florida artists in the Capitol Gallery, located on 22nd Floor observation deck. The New Capitol is open Monday through Friday from 8 AM to 5 PM, and on weekends and holidays from 8:30 AM to 4:30 PM (with access from the West Plaza entrance only). Weekend visitors must be accompanied to the observation deck by a tour guide. Admission is free.

FLORIDA STATE UNIVERSITY GALLERY AND MUSEUM
Tennessee and Copeland Sts.   644-6836

The works of local and national artists are displayed here in a two-story gallery and museum. FSU has several permanent works that it keeps in rotation, while simultaneously offering student artists a space to exhibit their work. Many traveling national and regional exhibits are also displayed here.

FOSTER TANNER FINE ARTS GALLERY
Florida A&M University Campus   599-3161

This impressive gallery features both permanent and rotating works of regional and national artists. FAMU art students also present shows and programs here throughout the year.

LEMOYNE ART FOUNDATION
125 N. Gadsden St.   222-8800

This is Tallahassee's premier visual arts gallery, located in the historic George Meginniss House that was constructed in 1853. The center offers several well-attended exhibitions, educational programs and special events each year. There's also a gift shop and a beautifully sculpted garden. 1994 marks the center's 30th anniversary.

The LeMoyne Art Foundation is open Tuesday through Saturday from 10 AM to 5 PM, and on Sunday from 2 PM to 5 PM; closed Mondays and holidays. The Gallery is usually closed during the last two weeks of July.

LEROY COLLINS LEON COUNTY PUBLIC LIBRARY
200 W. Park Ave.   487-2665

There are several places in the library where the works of local artists are featured. Downstairs in the children's section you can see artwork from area schools. The three-story building can at any time feature dozens of diverse exhibits. Call ahead or just take a stroll and see for yourself.

THE MUSEUM OF FLORIDA HISTORY
R.A. Gray Building
500 S. Bronough St.   488-1673

The Museum of Florida History's main gallery offers several rotating exhibits each year, all of them pertaining to some element of the state's history. There's an annual Quilt Show that displays modern and antique quilts, and one recent exhibit consisted of early photographs of Seminole and Miccosukee Indians. There's also a great permanent exhibit of items and artifacts from the state's history — see the Inside Historic Tallahassee chapter for more details.

The Museum of Florida History is open Monday through Friday from 9 AM to 4:30 PM, on Saturday from 10 AM to 4:30 PM, and on Sunday from noon to 4:30 PM. Admission is free.

NOMADS
508 W. Gaines St.   681-3222

Nomads bills itself as an "eclectic emporium," and we'd agree with that label. This little gallery midway between Florida A&M and FSU just celebrated its first anniversary. It features rotating exhibits by local artists, but also specializes in art you can wear. They have a unique display of jewelry fashioned by area artists.

Nomads is open Tuesday through Saturday from 11 AM to 6 PM. Admission is free.

OLD ARMORY GALLERY
1400 N. Monroe St.   891-6800

The Old Armory Gallery features a changing exhibit of work by members of the Tallahassee Senior Center. The Old Armory Gallery is open Monday through Friday from 9 AM to 5 PM. Admission is free.

THE OLD CAPITOL
Monroe St. and Apalachee Pkwy.   487-1902

The lower level rotunda of the Old Capitol features occasional exhibits from Florida artists across the state. The Old Capitol is open on Monday through Friday from 9 AM to 4:30 PM, on Saturday from 10 AM to 4:30 PM, and on Sundays and holidays from noon to 4:30 PM. Admission is free.

621 GALLERY
Railroad Square Industrial Park
621 Industrial Dr.   224-6163

Railroad Square is quickly becoming a hotbed for local artists. This collection of renovated warehouses and buildings serves as work space and gallery space for a number of visual artists in the area. The 621 Gallery is a good place to sample

---

Insiders' Tips

Several well-known artists make their homes in Tallahassee, including filmmaker Victor Nunez, whose 1993 independent feature motion picture *Ruby in Paradise* starred Ashley Judd and garnered great critical acclaim. Performance artist Terry Galloway, who performs regularly in New York City, sometimes debuts new material on Tallahassee stages. There's also writer Bob Shacochis, one of America's best short story writers, and Marcus Roberts, a piano genius whose handful of excellent recordings merely hint at the greatness yet to come. Perhaps one reason why Tallahassee's arts culture is so active is because residents never know who's going to be the next big player on the cultural horizon.

TALLAHASSEE — ARTS AND CULTURE

The Tallahassee-Leon County Civic Center stages several major concerts and events every year.

some of the latest contemporary and often experimental efforts. It's open from Wednesday through Friday from 11 AM to 2 PM, and on weekends from 2 PM to 5 PM. Admission is free.

TOWNE GALLERY
410 E. 6th Ave.   222-8565

This traditional gallery usually displays a strong exhibit of watercolors and prints, as well as pottery, sculpture and handmade toys. They are open Monday through Saturday from 10 AM to 6 PM. Admission is free.

Music

There's plenty of music to be heard in Tallahassee, and up front we thought we'd clue you in to a couple of the larger-sized venues the city sports.

The **Tallahassee-Leon County Civic Center** is the grandaddy of them all, with an arena that can seat 14,000 people. It hosts sporting events and conventions during the year, but also several major musical events. Hot stars of all sorts have packed the arena: Janet Jackson, Garth Brooks, Metallica and Nirvana are but a few of the diverse stars who have found enthusiastic reception at the civic center. It sits at 505 W. Pensacola Street, and the box office can be reached at 222-0400.

Another, somewhat smaller venue is **The Moon**, an entertainment facility at 1105 E. Lafayette Street. The Moon has been around for nearly a decade, and in that time its stage has been graced with musicians as diverse as Bonnie Raitt, the Neville Brothers, B.B. King, Los Lobos, Leo Kottke and the Dead Milk-

• 445

TALLAHASSEE — ARTS AND CULTURE

The Tallahassee Symphony Orchestra presents several well-attended concerts each season.

men. It holds about 1,500 people and also hosts several other public and private events during the year. Friday nights are usually given over to live country music, while Saturday evenings feature dance music. The box office can be reached at 878-6900.

FLORIDA STATE UNIVERSITY SCHOOL OF MUSIC
Ruby Diamond Auditorium,
Westcott Building
Opperman Music Hall, Kuersteiner
Music Building   644-6500

The FSU School of Music is a large and well-respected program that has been turning out top-notch musicians for almost a century. They don't show any signs of slowing down, either. Each year they present approximately 350 concerts and recitals, most of which are free to the public. During any given season, you'll hear symphonies, jazz, opera and other styles of music. The annual fall Prism concert series, which features dozens of FSU performers playing a wide and often unexpected range of material, is just one of the school's major events. They also sponsor a Summer Music Camp Program, where FSU faculty offers instruction to young musicians between the ages of 12 and 18.

TALLAHASSEE BACH PARLEY, INC.
1127 Victory Garden Dr.   386-3812

This group is dedicated to the preservation and public performance of music from the Baroque period. They usually produce four concerts a year — three with local musicians and one featuring a special guest from out of town. Often these concerts are performed with actual period instruments, and some shows also feature guest lectures about Baroque music.

The organ-based compositions and performances are held at the First Presbyterian Church at 110 N. Adams Street because it sports a wonderful handmade Taylor and Boody organ. Other instrumental works are usually performed at the Epiphany Lutheran Church, 3208 Thomasville Road.

TALLAHASSEE COMMUNITY CHORUS
P.O. Box 11295   539-8959

In the first year of the Tallahassee Community Chorus' existence, there were only 35 members. The following year there were over 200. The chorus is now in its sixth year and it just keeps on growing. They perform a handful of concerts each year, including a Spring Pops Concert every April. They also perform classical and larger choral works with the Tallahassee Symphony Orchestra.

TALLAHASSEE MUSIC GUILD
2311 Ellicott Dr.   877-2878

Since 1958 this guild has been promoting the appreciation of music through its FSU School of Music scholarships. Their major fund-raiser for this worthy effort is the annual sing-along *Messiah* held the first Tuesday in December at Faith Presbyterian Church at N. Meridian Street and John Knox Road. Here voices and musicians from all over the community gather for a spirited performance of Handel's holiday classic. They welcome any and all voices, and appreciate listeners, as well.

TALLAHASSEE — ARTS AND CULTURE

TALLAHASSEE SYMPHONY ORCHESTRA
203 N. Gadsden St.   224-0461

The city's symphony orchestra presents seasonal concerts throughout the year. Every December the orchestra teams up with the Tallahassee Ballet for a spirited and graceful performance of the perennial favorite, Tchaikovsky's *The Nutcracker*. Music director and conductor David Hoose fills out the rest of the concert season with a fine roster of guest musicians and conductors. Concerts are held in FSU's Ruby Diamond Auditorium at the corner of College and Copeland streets.

Theater

FAMU ESSENTIAL THEATRE
Charles Winter Wood Theatre   561-2524

The FAMU Theatre Department gives black playwrights and actors their due through the Essential Theatre. Several times a year they showcase the works of new playwrights such as Judy Ann Mason (who currently scripts the PBS drama "I'll Fly Away") as well as the classics — a recent all-black production of Shakespeare's *Hamlet* drew large, enthusiastic crowds of all color. Recent graduates of the FAMU Theatre Department include Meshach Taylor, who has appeared on several sitcoms including "Designing Women," and T'keyah Keymah, who can be seen on the hit comedy show "In Living Color." If you're looking for innovative, exciting and often ground-breaking theater, check out the Essential Theatre. Tickets are available on a per show basis.

FSU SCHOOL OF THEATER
Fine Arts Building
Call & Copeland Sts.   644-6500

The School of Theater at FSU has a long tradition of excellence. Several of its former students have gone on to great success in the performing arts. The University's Mainstage program always features a strong offering of classic and contemporary plays and musicals. It pays to check out a show, because you never know who will be the next big star from FSU

TALLAHASSEE COMMUNITY COLLEGE WEST END PLAYERS
444 Appleyard Dr.   488-9200

The TCC West End Players serve up an annual offering of dramas, comedies and musicals. These energetic and well-honed student productions always draw crowds, so it's advisable to get your tickets early if you plan to attend.

THE TALLAHASSEE-LEON COUNTY CIVIC CENTER BROADWAY SERIES
505 W. Pensacola St.   222-0400

This popular series trucks in some of the most extravagant Broadway road shows that tour the Southeast. Everything from the recent revival of the musical *Grand Hotel* to Neil Simon's recent comedy *Lost in Yonkers* has been staged here. Each season brings half a dozen impressive and professional Broadway shows to the civic center stage.

TALLAHASSEE LITTLE THEATRE
Thomasville & Betton Rds.   224-8474

This active community theater has been staging solid shows for nearly 50 years. They display a penchant for including modern Broadway fare such as Alfred Uhry's *Driving Miss Daisy* with traditional dramas like *The Little Foxes* by Lillian Hellman, as they did during one recent season. They usually stage five or six shows per season, which runs from September to May.

QUINCY MUSIC THEATER
118 E. Washington St., Quincy   875-9444

Established in 1983, this group makes its home in downtown Quincy in the refurbished Leaf Theatre, a charming 1940s-era movie house. Each year they stage a handful of dramas and musicals, and the rest of the season the stage is given over to various local music and choral ensembles.

THE NUCLEUS GROUP
P.O. Box 15391   847-3479

The Nucleus Group is a versatile company that breaks from traditional theater and puts on entertainment of a different sort. Their most popular offering is *A Christmas Carol on the Air*, where audiences get to watch — and participate in — an old-fashioned radio drama version of Charles Dickens' classic holiday story. The Nucleus Group also stages murder mystery dramas and comedy shows.

YOUNG ACTORS THEATRE
609 Glenview Dr.   386-6602

This active troupe usually performs around five shows per season, all of them featuring local performers from kindergarten to high school. This may not be the most sophisticated theater fare in town, but give them a chance and these youngsters will certainly surprise and entertain you when they hit the stage.

Other Activities

FSU DISTINGUISHED LECTURE SERIES
Leon County Civic Center   644-3801

Sponsored by the Florida State University Center for Professional Development and Public Services, this annual lecture series brings acclaimed writers, artists, scientists and others to Tallahassee. Past speakers include Dr. Carl Sagan, columnist William Raspberry, filmmaker Spike Lee and writer Joyce Carol Oates. The lectures are held at Leon County Civic Center. The season runs from September to April.

Tallahassee
Higher Education

One reason that Tallahassee's median age is so low might be because of the large number of students in the area. There are two universities and one community college in town, with the total student population approaching the 50,000 mark and rising.

And these are remarkably good schools. They rank nationally in dozens of areas, and their alumni are often as distinguished as the faculty and administrators that graduate them. Surprisingly, there's not much real competition or rivalry. Certainly there's a little healthy friction from time to time, but overall each has managed to carve out its own specialty niches, while at the same time providing a solid core curriculum.

Needless to say, there aren't nearly as many students in Tallahassee over the summer. They make quite an impact on the local economy, and while the town doesn't exactly roll up the sidewalks during the warmest months of the year, things do slow down a bit, particularly with the restaurants, bars and shops that cater almost exclusively to the student population. But some of these merchants actually welcome the slow pace because during the regular school year the business is brisk and hectic. Summer's a chance for everyone to reenergize and prepare for fall.

FLORIDA A&M UNIVERSITY
Visitor Center/Public Affairs
103 Lee Hall   599-3000

Florida Agricultural & Mechanical University (FAMU) is one of the nation's premier historically black colleges, boasting fine programs in pharmacy, journalism, engineering and business, among others. Established by the Florida Legislature in 1887 as the Florida State Normal and Industrial School for Negroes, the university now boasts a student population of over 9,000 and has seen steady increases in enrollment over the past several years.

The stately campus sits just south of the capitol. While its faculty and student makeup are multiracial, FAMU still plays an important role in minority issues. One recent study, for example, found that the university's College of Education produces nearly half of Florida's minority teachers. As FAMU is one of 28 institutions of higher education with teacher education programs, that's an impressive and important figure.

There are guided tours of the

TALLAHASSEE — HIGHER EDUCATION

Seminole football is one of Tallahassee's major sporting events.

campus, and the Black Archives Research Center and Museum is one of the high points. Pivotal chapters in African-American history are recorded in the museum's voluminous collection of books, photographs and artifacts. The Research Center and Museum is located in the Carnegie Library Building, and is open from 9 AM to 4 PM.

Then there are the FAMU Rattlers, whose records in football, baseball, basketball, track and other sports have gained them a loyal legion of fans. The popularity of men's and women's sports here is matched only by that of the FAMU Marching "100" Band, whose electric halftime shows and parade appearances always bring crowds to their feet.

FAMU has a lot to offer visitors. Guided tours are available upon request. The campus is open to the public from 8 AM to 5 PM weekly.

FLORIDA STATE UNIVERSITY
Visitor Information Center
100 S. Woodward Ave.   644-33246

Established in 1857 as the Seminary West of the Suwannee (how's that for a site-specific name?), Florida State University (FSU) is the second-oldest institution of higher learning in the state. Its name was changed in 1905 to the Florida State College for Women, and it remained as such until 1947 when it went coed as FSU.

The handsome campus sits on several hills just west of the capitol, and for the better part of each year it's filled with nearly 30,000 students. They make a sizable impact on the city's social, cultural and economic scene. Some residents liken Tallahassee in the summer to a ghost town, and it's got nothing to do with the absent legislators.

FSU has more than a dozen schools and colleges, including arts and sciences, business, education,

TALLAHASSEE — HIGHER EDUCATION

The campus of Florida State University sits just west of the Capitol.

law and social sciences. The university is also a big player in the field of research. After a white-hot contest with other universities (including the Massachusetts Institute of Technology), FSU was recently named as the site of the ultra-high-tech National High Magnetic Field Laboratory. The lab (operated by a consortium composed of FSU, the University of Florida and Los Alamos National Laboratory) will usher in the coming age of high field magnetics, an area that many forecasters say will be every bit as important and earth-changing as electricity was at the turn of the century. This facility hosts the world's fastest supercomputer and has already attracted a great deal of attention and funding.

But not everything here is bookish and scholarly. Needless to say, men's and women's sports also feature prominently on FSU's landscape. During football season, things can get positively insane as the championship Seminole football team takes to Doak Campbell Stadium. Basketball, baseball, track and other events also draw crowds and awards. See the Tallahassee Spectator Sports section of this book for more information.

The FSU campus welcomes visitors Monday through Friday from 8 AM to 5 PM, and on Saturday from 9 AM to 1 PM. There's a free one-hour guided tour available three times a day during the week at 11 AM, 1 PM

> **Insiders' Tips**
> The Florida A&M University's "Marching 100" was the only American group asked to perform in the recent Bicentennial Bastille Festival in France.

Quality live-in child care...

with a special European *flair*.

- carefully screened European au pairs
- about $170/week for any size family
- AuPairCare counselors in your area

800-4-AUPAIR

AuPairCare

A U.S. Government-designated program.

and 3 PM. From September through April, this tour is also available on Saturdays at 10 AM only. For more information, contact the Visitor Information Bureau at 644-3246.

TALLAHASSEE COMMUNITY COLLEGE
444 Appleyard Dr.   488-9200

Sometimes community colleges can seem invisible, especially in a city like Tallahassee, which is not only the state capitol but also home to the above-mentioned high-profile universities.

So credit is due to the students, faculty and administration at Tallahassee Community College (TCC) for not disappearing into the background. With an enrollment of just under 10,000 students and a newly refurbished campus, TCC manages to make its presence known on an almost daily basis.

Established in 1966, this is primarily a transfer institution and serves as a primary feeder school for FSU. Although its core student base comes from Leon, Gadsden and Wakulla counties, students from all over the state are enrolled here.

TCC's major programs include two-year degrees in such areas as nursing, criminal justice technology, computer programming, business administration, emergency medical services technology and legal assisting.

The athletic program has expanded rapidly over the last few years. Initially, men's basketball and baseball were the major sports here, but recently women's teams were added. There's lots of action in the college's modern EagleDome arena, with the men's basketball team ranking among the top 10 of the state and the women's softball team taking the panhandle conference title in its first year of existence.

There are also several arts groups and organizations, including the West End Players, who stage theater productions during the year.

The TCC campus welcomes visitors and is open to the public from 8 AM to 5 PM. Guided tours can be arranged by contacting the Counseling Department at 922-8128.

Tallahassee
State Government

The presence of state government in Tallahassee is reflected in the city's skyline. Were it not for the dominant buildings of the capitol complex, the hilly terrain would be filled with modest two- and three-story structures, the kind you'd expect to find in any small city. But with the 22-story obelisk of the New Capitol building towering over the landscape, it's clear that this city owes most of its heritage to palm tree politics.

If you are a political junkie, this is the epicenter of governmental power-shifting. The regular legislative session gets underway in late winter and lasts until spring. During this time Tallahassee is filled with legions of lawmakers and lobbyists, armies of activists and aides. The media arrives *en masse*, as well, armed with cameras, tape recorders and laptop computers.

It's quite a transition. Tallahassee awakens from its seasonal slumber and suddenly the downtown sidewalks are crowded, the local eateries are standing room only during lunchtime and the city literally buzzes with a nervous and somewhat contagious energy. Things can get going much earlier, too, if a special session is called in late fall.

And each session is different in its own way, the issues and policies shaped by a constantly rotating cast of people and events across the state. Recently, the high crime rate has been the subject of several bill and measures, with legislators regularly delivering tough sound-bites over the airwaves. Florida is also spearheading a bold and controversial state-level health care program that may very well serve as a model for national reform somewhere down the road. Environmental issues always loom large on the state's political horizon as Florida struggles to encourage growth while maintaining and preserving its valuable and irreplaceable natural resources.

Needless to say, it's an exciting place to be. If you want an up-close look at how state government operates, then the legislative and special sessions offer invaluable lessons. If you just want to take advantage of the visitor sites that some buildings host, then sit out the session and dodge the crowds. There's plenty of parking spaces if you know where to look — if the streetside metered parking spaces are all filled, be sure to check out the various parking decks in the vicinity, as many of them have metered spaces that aren't visible from the outside.

Not every building in the capitol

complex is really worth the attention of visitors. Most simply serve as office space for the various state agencies. The ones listed below offer special attractions for visitors. For more information about any of the state agencies, call 488-1234.

THE OLD CAPITOL
Monroe St. and Apalachee Pkwy.   487-1902

Constructed between the years 1839 to 1845, this proud and impressive building has seen several additions and renovations over the years. There's plenty of history here beneath the stained-glass cupola and candy-striped awnings, so it's no surprise that the building is now a museum. There are self-guided tours available, so at your own pace you can wander through the old Senate and House chambers and inspect intriguing displays of political memorabilia. The original capitol building was a log cabin; thankfully, this one was built soon thereafter to stand the test of time. There's a gift shop downstairs and exhibits detailing the history of Florida politics. It's the sensible starting point on any tour of the capitol complex.

The Old Capitol is open on Monday through Friday from 9 AM to 4:30 PM, on Saturday from 10 AM to 4:30 PM, and on Sundays and holidays from noon to 4:30 PM. Admission is free.

THE NEW CAPITOL
Monroe St. and Apalachee Pkwy.   681-9200

If you approach the capitol from the Apalachee Parkway, the towering New Capitol seems to sprout majestically out of the Old Capitol that sits at its base. Constructed in the 1970s, the 22-story building is the center of political action (or inaction, depending on the issue). The setting is at once user-friendly and highly functional. On the first floor, or plaza level, you'll find the Tallahassee Area Visitor Information Center, where you can pick up information about the area or sign up for a free guided tour of the building.

The fifth floor sports special viewing galleries of the House and Senate chambers, and these are open during the legislative and special sessions. Many visitors find it fascinating to sit in for a bit and see how state government operates. Often you'll see field trips from state and local schools getting a close-up civics lesson. Free copies of House and Senate agendas are available from the information desk at the fourth floor rotunda. If you really want to match lawmakers' names with their faces, you can order a copy of the annual *Pocket Guide to Florida's Government* which is published by the Florida Chamber of Commerce. They can be reached at (800) 204-6002. The price of the guide is around $8, and it's money well-spent if you need a comprehensive listing of who's who in the Florida Legislature.

Continue upward in the elevator until you reach the 22nd floor observation deck, which offers a spectacular 360-degree bird's-eye view of the city and its surrounding environs, especially the nearby campuses of Florida State and Florida A&M universities. There are plenty of seats here, and not a one of them has a bad view. Be sure to turn your view

TALLAHASSEE — STATE GOVERNMENT

The Old and New Capitol Buildings stand at the center of downtown Tallahassee.

away from the windows long enough check out the art gallery on the observation deck, which features rotating exhibits from Florida artists across the state.

Back down the elevator to the lower-level plaza and you'll find the capitol cafeteria, which offers a good cheap lunch, as well as a gift and snack shop. If you don't stop to gawk at the lawmakers for too long, you can get through the New Capitol in an hour or so.

The New Capitol is open Monday through Friday from 8 AM to 5 PM, and on weekends and holidays from 8:30 AM to 4:30 PM (with access from the West Plaza entrance only). Admission is free.

Insiders' Tips

So where do you park when you want to see the Capitol? That's a tough one. Most of the parking decks you'll see aren't available for the public. There are many metered spaces along downtown streets, but depending on the time of year, they can stay filled all day long.

There's a metered lot across from the Capitol at the corner of Monroe Street and Apalachee Parkway, next to the Vietnam Memorial. Unless the lawmakers are in session, there's usually plenty of room to park here. The lot is accessible from Calhoun Street.

A wise note: don't try to cross Monroe Street at this point. There's no crosswalk and the traffic can sometimes be very heavy. You'll probably see others — mostly harried state workers — making a mad dash for the safety of the thin yellow median in the middle, but take it from us and walk down one block to the crosswalk.

There is one public parking deck you should also consider, next to the R.A. Gray Building at 500 S. Bronough Street (the Museum of Florida History is housed here). Along with spaces reserved for state employees, there are a couple of levels of public metered spaces, too. The ones along the lower level are metered for one hour, with two-hour spaces available on the higher level. This will put you behind the Supreme Court Building a couple of blocks from the Capitol, and it's an uphill walk, but insiders know the deck rarely, if ever, fills up.

The Ralph D. Turlington Florida Education Center
325 W. Gaines St.   487-1785

Although the Commissioner of Education's office resides in the New Capitol, this sleek, modern structure a few blocks south houses much of the agency's administrative staff. Visitors are encouraged to visit the first-floor lobby where the visual artwork of students from across the state is often displayed. On the 17th floor of the Turlington Center there's an observation deck that offers a stunning view of the capitol complex. It also sports a gallery with rotating exhibits as well as sculpture.

The Turlington Building is open Monday through Friday from 8 AM to 5 PM; closed weekends. Admission is free.

State Supreme Court
500 S. Duval St.   488-8845

Sitting just behind the New Capitol, the State Supreme Court building is an impressive sight. Its thick marbled columns and great doors hint at the sophisticated proceedings that go on inside its chambers. The Supreme Court was originally located in the south wing of the Old Capitol. This building was completed in 1949, and extensive renovations were completed in 1991.

This is primarily an appeals court for cases across the state. Oral arguments are usually held during the first week of each month, and the public is welcome to attend. Sometimes you can catch students from local schools holding mock trials in its hallowed chambers; these trials are often more interesting than the actual cases presented here.

Tours are available, and group tours should be scheduled in advance. The State Supreme Court is open Monday through Friday from 8 AM to 5 PM. Admission is free.

Tallahassee
Real Estate

Almost everyone agrees that Tallahassee's most valuable asset is its landscape. The sprawling green countryside offers a breathtaking glimpse into the city's past, as well as its future.

The historic downtown area has remained pretty much the same size for decades now. Several of the great old houses here have been lovingly renovated and preserved and mostly serve as space for law firms, museums, galleries and the like. In the meantime, Tallahassee's outskirts have been growing — mostly northward, as the southern border is formed by the lush Apalachicola National Forest. New housing subdivisions and neighborhoods are going up at a rapid pace.

A community called Killearn sits just north of the city and each day seems to edge just a little bit closer to Thomasville, Georgia. Southeast of Tallahassee sits Buck Lake Road, along which many popular subdivisions have taken seed. And the newest hot spot for growth is found northwest of town, towards nearby Havana.

Once plantations lorded over this landscape. Now many of these great old houses are gone. Their meadows and pastures have been sold and parceled and, in a number of cases, carefully preserved as much as possible. Homeowners have generally shown great restraint when building in unspoiled countryside. After all, nature's solitude is what attracts them to these areas in the first place.

Potential home-seekers should know that prices vary widely throughout Tallahassee. There's a lot of construction going on to the north and east of the city, and new home prices there often top the $120,000 mark. That's quite a contrast with the prices just to the southwest, where an older home with the same square footage can be had for less than $50,000. In other parts of town, there's a lot of action in between. Needless to say, Tallahassee is a volatile and ever-changing market, and it certainly pays to look around.

The Tallahassee Board of Realtors (1029 Thomasville Road, 224-7713) has over 800 members, and you can contact them for a free listing. The Tallahassee Builders Association (2522 NE Capital Circle, 385-1414) also offers many helpful services to new home builders.

Rental properties are plentiful throughout Tallahassee, many of them playing host to the large student population that flocks here each fall and departs in the spring. Others serve the more affluent state workers and other professionals. Many of these management companies are aware that since Tallahassee is a hub for many state and regional activities, there's a sizable number of visitors staying here for a short indeterminate period. These visitors don't necessarily want to spend weeks here living out of a suitcase in a motel, so many of them find furnished rental properties available for short-term rentals.

Rental prices vary widely, depending on the area. Near either the FSU or FAMU campus, a modest two-bedroom can run anywhere from $300 to $500 per month. Expect to pay more if you're renting short-term without a lease.

The best thing to do to find out about available properties is obtain copies of the many real estate guides — they're free and can be found at practically any newsstand in town. These offer clear and concise information on the real estate scene in Tallahassee. The *Rental Guide of Tallahassee* is one such publication, and if you need to obtain a copy before you get to town just call (800) 277-7800. The *Homes & Land of Tallahassee* guide, aimed at homebuyers, is published by the same company, and they'll also provide a free copy for the asking.

The *Real Estate Book of Tallahassee* covers not only Leon County but also Franklin, Gadsden, Jefferson and Wakulla counties. You can get a free copy by request at (800) 841-3401.

One of the most popular real estate publications is the Homes Section of the *Tallahassee Democrat*, published each Sunday. Each issue usually profiles a neighborhood or subdivision in Tallahassee, and the listings are as up-to-date as you'll find.

Whether you want to live in Tallahassee or just visit for a few days, you'll find plenty of real estate companies willing to accommodate you. We've listed some of the bigger and/or well-known ones here, but be advised that there are lots and lots of reputable companies in the area. Get your start here, and happy hunting!

Real Estate Companies

ARMOR REALTY
1519 Killearn Center Blvd.   893-2525

Armor Realty is a full-service real estate company that has been in Tallahassee for five years now. Its 13 full-time agents handle primarily residential properties, with most of their action located in the northeast part of town. A separate sister company handles many rental units in the area.

Insiders' Tips

The Homes Section of the *Tallahassee Democrat* is a good reason to pick up a copy of the Sunday paper, but the supplement is also available free at many newsstands around town. And be warned: whenever a neighborhood or community is profiled, Sunday afternoons will often see heavy traffic in that area as readers like to get out and see homes for themselves.

TALLAHASSEE — REAL ESTATE

BOUTIN BROWN & BUTLER REAL ESTATE SERVICES
822 N. Monroe   681-6332

This full-service real estate firm has been around since the early 1960s and handles residential and commercial properties throughout Tallahassee. They offer appraisal brokerage and consulting.

COMMUNITY REALTORS OF KILLEARN, INC.
2707 Killearney Way   893-2115

Killearn is a fast-growing subdivision just north of Tallahassee, and this is one realty company that stays on top of the action up there. Community Realtors of Killearn has a separate New Homes Division that can be reached at 668-7929.

COASTAL PROPERTY SERVICES, INC.
926 N. Gadsden St.   224-3253

If you're looking to rent in Tallahassee, you'd best start with one of the largest firms in town. Coastal Property Services, Inc. manages well over 500 rental homes and a number of large apartment complexes. They've got everything from secluded houses to popular apartment communities.

COLDWELL BANKER HARTUNG AND ASSOCIATES, INC.
3303 Thomasville Rd.   386-6160

This full-service national firm has been in Tallahassee since 1979, and in that it's grown to command the biggest market share in town. Their 32 full-time real estate professionals handle mostly residential properties, with some commercial and acreage properties. They publish their very own real estate guide (it's free),

and also run a property management division.

FEZLER & RUSSELL REAL ESTATE, INC.
3360 Capital Circle N.E., Ste. B   385-4646

This full-service real estate company has been around for seven years. Although they handle primarily residential property, including several Tallahassee subdivisions, they also represent some commercial properties. Their 12 real estate professionals handle properties throughout the Tallahassee area.

INVESTORS REALTY OF TALLAHASSEE, INC.
3531 Thomasville Rd.   224-6900

This is another large real estate firm offering full services for residential, commercial, acreage and investment properties. They also run a separate property management division that handles nearly 40 apartment communities in Tallahassee.

MILLARD J. NOBLIN REALTY, INC.
1300 Metropolitan Blvd. 385-1400

Noblin Realty is a full-service firm with plenty of years of experience in Tallahassee real estate. They handle properties in all areas of the city and also several surrounding counties, such as Jefferson and Wakulla. The 21 full-time salespersons on Noblin's staff are a pretty active bunch.

MONTGOMERY & ASSOCIATES, INC.
3370 Capital Circle, N.E.   386-3721

Montgomery & Associates, Inc. is a real estate company handling only residential properties in Tallahassee, so they know the market well. Established about three years ago, they represent properties throughout the area. They are a full-service company, with nine full-time agents.

RE/MAX REALTY
2804-B Remington Green Circle   385-6936

This full-service real estate company has been in Tallahassee for just over eight years, and already they've established themselves as one of the top three companies in town. Their 15 full-time real estate professionals handle commercial and residential properties throughout the Tallahassee area, as well as in many surrounding areas.

Tallahassee Retirement

Tallahassee's social makeup reflects much about Florida in that a sizable number of its residents have relocated here from other parts of the country. But it differs from the rest of Florida in one important aspect: its long-term residents are overwhelmingly young and mobile.

Not too many people retire to Tallahassee. A recent Quality of Life Report from the Tallahassee Chamber of Commerce reveals that Leon County has the second youngest median age of any county in the state. Only 7.7 percent of the city's population is over 65 years old, while the rate for the entire state is 17.6 percent.

We can look at the area's two largest employers to find reasons for this. The state government and educational systems provide employment for much of the area's white-collar workers, and working life in the city can be quite active and hustle-bustle. Chances are that when a worker retires, the last thing they want to do is remain in a relatively fast-paced environment with a high turnover rate.

Nonetheless, there are indeed some people who retire to this area. Some have family here while others just prefer its dual blend of city life in a country setting. Those retirees who still love Tallahassee but want to back off a bit are finding calm havens in nearby Quincy, Monticello and Thomasville.

There are eight adult retirement communities in Tallahassee and, along with six nursing homes, they easily provide quality living for the area's senior citizens.

Adult Retirement Communities

CASA CALDERON APARTMENTS
800 W. Virginia St.   222-4026

Established in 1981, this 111-room apartment complex houses persons 62 and older capable of functioning independently. The carpeted, unfurnished apartments afford elderly citizens the luxury of private living with round-the-clock security.

GEORGIA BELL DICKINSON
301 E. Carolina St.   224-8021

This is a federally subsidized, independent-living unit for elderly persons 62 or older. There are 49 one-bedroom units and 101 efficiency units. The complex offers plenty of activities, and Elder Care provides lunch during weekdays.

"FOR THOSE WHO AREN'T READY YET"
WESTMINSTER OAKS

Tallahassee's Premier Continuing Care Retirement Community

Located on 96 wooded and beautiful landscaped acres

Enjoy a carefree and active independent lifestyle with Assisted Living and Skilled Nursing available if needed.

4449 Meandering Way • Tallahassee, FL 32308
(904) 878-1136

Owned an operated by Presbyterian Retirement Communities, Inc. Westminster Oaks Continuing Care Retirement Community is accredited by the Continuing Care Accreditation Commission sponsored by the American Association of Homes for the Aging.

LAKE ELLA MANOR
1433 N. Adams St.   224-1341

This HUD-subsidized apartment complex is for low-income and mobility impaired low income senior citizens. The 72-unit complex was established nine years ago and sits conveniently next door to the Senior Citizens' Center.

MEADOWBROOKE TERRACE
1978 Village Green   385-4533

Meadowbrooke Terrace is a private, assisted living complex. It was established five years ago, and its private and semiprivate rooms have a capacity of 120 residents.

MABRY VILLAGE APARTMENTS
315B Mabry St.   576-1188

Mabry Village isn't really a retirement community — most of its units are open to the public — but it does have a special block of apartments for elderly and handicapped persons who can live independently.

MICCOSUKEE HILLS
3201 Miccosukee Rd.   878-5844

Miccosukee Hills, a subsidized retirement community established in 1979, rests on several acres of wooded landscape. Its 106 units accommodate senior citizens capable of unassisted living.

OAK RIDGE TOWNHOUSES
4704 Warehouse Rd.   878-5612

This 16-year-old apartment complex offers independent living for senior citizens. Its 60 units afford ambulatory residents the privacy and comfort of one- and two-bedroom apartments.

WESTMINSTER OAKS
4449 Meandering Way   878-1136

Westminster Oaks sits on 96 heavily wooded acres of land, and this vibrant setting provides the backdrop for its apartments, duplexes and single-family dwellings. This continuing-care facility host around 350 residents and offers independent and assisted living as well as a health center.

TALLAHASSEE — RETIREMENT

WOODMONT RETIREMENT COMMUNITY
3207 N. Monroe St.   562-4123

This adult congregate living facility was established eight years ago. Its 102 units exist in a homey atmosphere that features a community courtyard. Two full-time activities directors ensure that the residents are never bored.

Nursing Homes

CAPITAL HEALTH CARE CENTER
3333 Capital Medical Blvd.   877-4115

Established 15 years ago, this is the second-oldest nursing home facility in Tallahassee. This skilled nursing facility provides 24-hour care, and its rehabilitation team offers several therapy programs for the 156-bed center. It has received a superior rating from the state for several years in a row.

CENTERVILLE CARE CENTER
2255 Centerville Rd.   386-4054

The seven-year-old Centerville Care Center is a skilled nursing facility with 120 beds and 24-hour care. Its rehabilitation team provides many services, including subacute care.

HERITAGE HEALTH CARE CENTER
1815 Glonger Dr.   877-2177

Heritage Health Care Center is a skilled nursing facility with rehabilitation programs in physical, speech, occupational and respiratory therapy, among others. Established 11 years ago, it currently has 120 beds.

TALLAHASSEE CONVALESCENT HOME
2510 Miccosukee Rd.   877-3131

This is the oldest nursing home in Tallahassee, having been established in 1966. It's a skilled nursing facility offering 72 beds and the full range of rehabilitation programs.

TALLAHASSEE MEMORIAL REGIONAL MEDICAL CENTER LONG-TERM NURSING
1609 Medical Dr.   681-5440

This skilled nursing care facility is affiliated with Tallahassee Memorial Regional Medical Center, whose resources it can tap whenever needed.

MIRACLE HILL
1329 Abraham   224-8486

Established 26 years ago, this skilled nursing facility is owned by the Florida Primitive Baptist Association. It offers 24-hour nursing care and rehabilitation programs and has received a superior rating from the state for the last five years.

Tallahassee Medical Care

Tallahassee's a great place to be healthy. If you're ill, well, it's still a pretty good place to be because the city's telephone directory lists over 20 pages of physician listings, and it boasts one major regional medical center and a well-established community hospital to boot. Walk-in family medical clinics are also plentiful.

Finding a Physician or Dentist

There are three major referral lines offering assistance in finding a physician or dentist. Two are sponsored by Tallahassee's general hospitals, while the third is operated by the Capital Medical Society, a professionally-affiliated medical society providing referrals for Leon, Jefferson, Wakulla and Gadsden counties. A fourth line, Telephone Counseling Referral Service, can offer assistance for those in need of any counseling or mental health services. Because Tallahassee has so many medical facilities to choose from, these services provide valuable help to visitors and new residents.

Capital Medical Society	877-9018
Tallahassee Community Hospital	656-3627
Tallahassee Memorial Regional Medical Center	681-5063
Telephone Counseling Referral	224-6333

General Hospitals

TALLAHASSEE MEMORIAL REGIONAL MEDICAL CENTER
Magnolia Dr. & Miccosukee Rd.   681-1155

Established in 1948, this is the area's oldest hospital, serving northwest Florida, south Georgia and southeast Alabama. This 771-bed hospital is one of nine designated acute head and spinal cord injury centers in the state. It also features a specialized diabetic program and serves the area with its Life Flight emergency helicopter service. It also hosts the only neonatal center in the region.

Some of the important phone numbers are:

Patient Room Information	681-1111
Ambulance/Paramedic Emergency	911
Non-Emergency	681-5400
Life Flight	681-5000
Diabetes Center	681-5403
Heart Institute	681-5022

TALLAHASSEE COMMUNITY HOSPITAL
2626 Capital Medical Blvd.   656-5000

This community hospital was established in 1979 and has grown to a 180-bed medical-surgical facility. Its case management program, designed to coordinate and expedite in-patient care, has been used as a model nationwide. The hospital operates a 24-hour emergency room

• 467

No Advance Reservations Needed...

Call our Emergency Department at 904/681-5411 or Dial 911

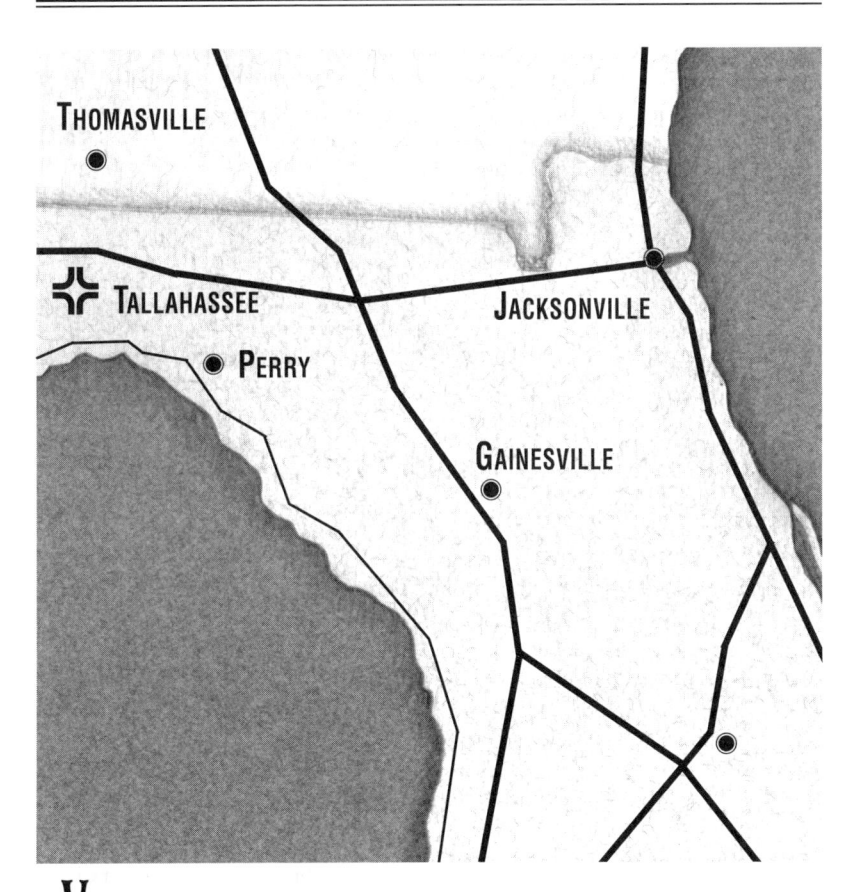

Visitors like to go where the "locals" go. And for health care, "locals" in this part of Florida count on Tallahassee Memorial.

The seventh largest hospital in Florida, Tallahassee Memorial provides not only primary care service but also the highly advanced and sophisticated services not found elsewhere in the region.

For accident victims or patients with cardiac emergencies, our Life Flight emergency helicopter service makes it possible for skilled treatment to begin immediately.

For medical treatment of any kind during your stay, call or ask to be referred to Tallahassee Memorial. The "locals" count on us. You can, too!

TALLAHASSEE MEMORIAL
REGIONAL MEDICAL CENTER

TALLAHASSEE — MEDICAL CARE

and recently acquired two area walk-in clinics. The Physician Care Clinics (see listings below) offer the convenience of a walk-in clinic with the full resources of the hospital, if needed. The hospital serves Tallahassee and the immediate vicinity.

Some of the important phone numbers are:

Emergency Room	656-5090
Addiction Recovery Center	656-5112
Admitting	656-5045
Back Rehabilitation Center	656-5199
Childbirth Classes	656-5361

Walk-in Clinics

Visitors who need non-emergency medical attention usually search the telephone directories for the nearest "doc-in-a-box." In Tallahassee, there's a fine assortment of clinics to choose from. These clinics aren't just for visitors, either; many local residents turn to them when such treatment is needed. They offer the convenience of flexible hours, little to no waiting and reasonable fees and rates. For out-of-towners, many clinics will also consult with your hometown physicians regarding treatment, when necessary. The two Physician Care clinics listed below boast the added bonus of being affiliated with Tallahassee Community Hospital.

SHERMAN WALK-IN CENTER AND SKIN CLINIC
3721 North Monroe St.   562-1128

MAHAN MEDICAL WALK-IN
1705 East Mahan Dr.   877-7164

PATIENTS FIRST MEDICAL CENTERS
2907 Kerry Forest Pkwy.	668-3380
3258 North Monroe St.	562-2010
1160 Apalachee Pkwy.	878-8843

PHYSICIAN CARE
1690 North Monroe St.	385-2222
3401 Northeast Capital Circle	386-2266

TALLAHASSEE WALK-IN MEDICAL CENTER
2451 Centerville Rd.   386-6000

Specialty Hospitals and Clinics

When a person is in pain, it sometimes takes a specialist to offer proper curative treatment. These Tallahassee area hospitals, clinics and centers offer treatment and therapy for a wide range of specific illnesses, diseases and disorders.

CAPITAL REHABILITATION HOSPITAL
1675 Riggins Rd.   656-4800

This medical rehabilitation hospital provides physical and occupational therapy through a dozen different programs. Please note that all patients must be referred by outside physicians.

EASTSIDE PSYCHIATRIC HOSPITAL
2634 Capital Circle NE   487-0300

Although primarily a treatment center for major mental illnesses, this 24-bed private hospital also counsels substance abuse patients. Programs here provide individual and group counseling, as well as daily individual therapy.

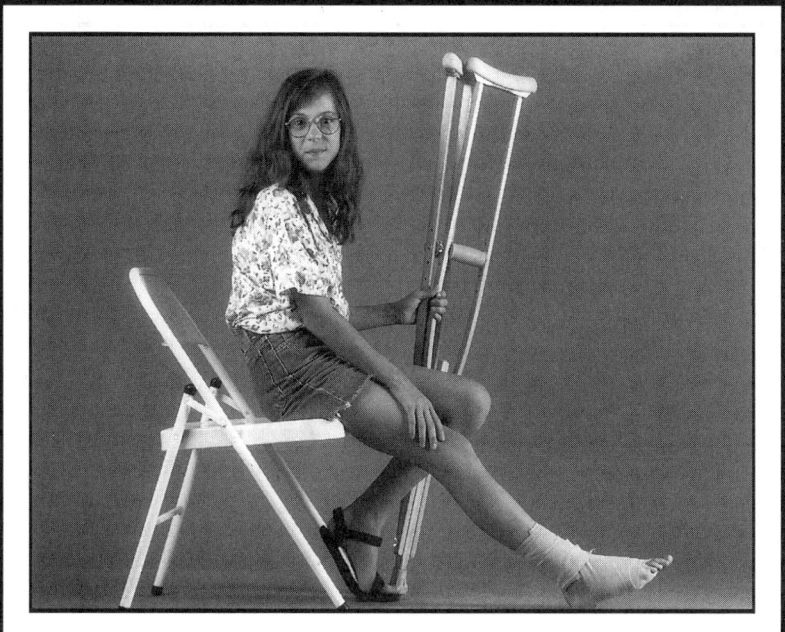

Accidents Happen.

Whether you're sizzled by the mid-afternoon sun, hobbled by an injury or can't escape the flu, Physician Care can help with your minor medical emergencies.

And when you need emergency care after hours, turn to Tallahassee Community Hospital.

Convenient hours, quality care. When you need it the most.

Physician ✚ Care

N. Monroe, just south of Tharpe St. ■ 385-2222
Open 8 am-8 pm seven-days-a-week.
Capital Circle N.E., just south of the I-10 overpass. ■ 386-2266
Open 8 am-8 pm Monday-Friday, 9 am-6 pm on weekends.

TALLAHASSEE — MEDICAL CARE

TALLAHASSEE CATARACT SURGERY CENTER
3411 Capital Medical Blvd.   878-3834

Affiliated with Dr. James R. Copeland's Eye Center, this ambulatory surgery center has provided total eye care since 1989. Eye surgery is performed here, and there is an optometrist and optical shop on-site.

TALLAHASSEE ORTHOPEDIC CENTER
3334 Capital Medical Blvd.   877-4688

This 50,000 square-foot medical complex provides physical therapy and rehabilitation, an orthopedic clinic, an outpatient surgery center and other facilities. The doctors here serve as team physicians for the athletic departments of Florida State University, Florida A&M University, Tallahassee Community College and over 80 high schools.

Tallahassee Daytrips

Repeat after us: you must take daytrips, you must take daytrips, you must take daytrips . . .

Don't get us wrong here — Tallahassee offers plenty of things to see and do. But one of its best facets is its close proximity to places like Havana, Monticello and Thomasville, Georgia.

It's very simple. All you have to do is pick a direction. Any one will do. From Tallahassee, you can drive north for 15 minutes and spend the day in a thriving community of spectacular antique shops. Or go east for 20 minutes and enjoy a concert in a magnificent turn-of-the-century opera house.

Ask almost anyone you meet in Tallahassee about Havana or Thomasville. They'll readily tell you what's special about each place, and they'll even offer directions out of town.

Here's what they'll say, in a nutshell. Pick a place and go. Chances are you'll see plenty of Tallahasseans out there, too.

Havana

Havana, just 20 miles north of Tallahassee, is a phoenix that has risen from the ashes twice in its lifetime. It's grown from a tobacco boomtown to a popular antique district in fewer than 100 years.

Established at the turn of the century, Havana and its sister town, nearby Quincy, were prime places to grow tobacco. Quincy had already risen to prominence once as a tobacco producer, but after the Civil War the town fell on hard times. Havana was established thanks to a "second wind" that had to do with a unique new method of tobacco farming.

Growers discovered that tobacco grown in the shade had a texture and flavor vastly different from that of normal tobacco. As farmers realized this, the national rail systems were slowly extending into north Florida, providing the perfect pipeline into the lucrative cigar market.

Quincy recovered to some extent, and Havana literally exploded. Huge brick warehouses were constructed to cure and store all that tobacco. Farmers became rich and built amazing houses in fields where shacks once stood. A lot of money came into this area — and when tobacco farming eventually moved to climates farther south, a lot of money abruptly left this area, too. For many years, downtown Havana was practically deserted, its once-grand brick buildings suddenly empty and shuttered.

Havana

A Renaissance in Progress

Stroll the charming tree-lined streets of this fast growing Art & Antique center. Enjoy browsing in the relaxed atmosphere of a quaint old-style community.

Explore more than two dozen renovated buildings and shops featuring exquisite antiques, fine art, specialty decor items, rare books, collectibles of all types.

Havana is conveniently located on U.S. Highway 27 just 10 minutes north of Interstate 10 and Tallahassee, FL

North Florida's Antique & Art Capital

Over 30 Shops

Antiques
Art & Collectibles

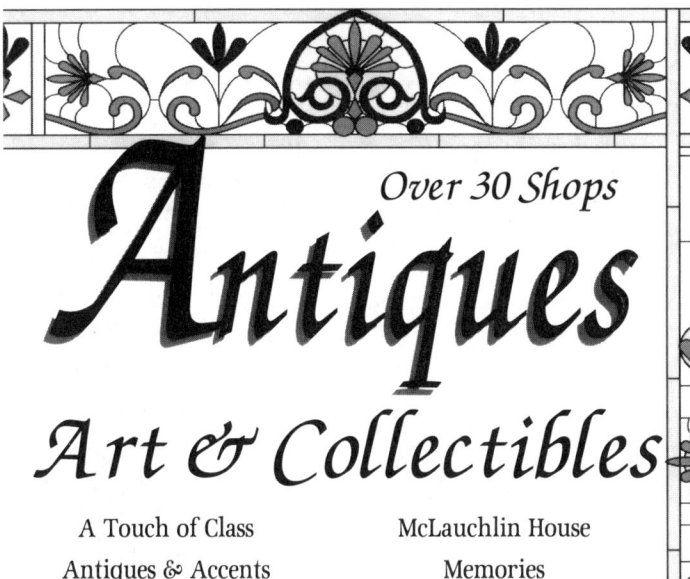

A Touch of Class
Antiques & Accents
Antique Center
Barn Door Gift Shop
Carol's Christmas Shop
Florida Art Center & Gallery
H & H Antiques
Hancock's Antiques
Helen's Hallway Annex
Historical Bookshelf
Jackie's
Lenora Charles Courtyard Cafe
Main Street Market
McLauchlin House
Memories
Mirror Image
My Secret Garden
The Nice Picture Gallery
Rescued Relics
Fig Tree Productions
Specialty Design
Sticks 'n Stitches
Susanne's
Village Market
Wanderings

Most Shops Open Wed. Thru Sun.

Explore Havana
Discover A Treasure

Several antique shops and galleries fill the old tobacco warehouses of downtown Havana.

In the mid-1980s, however, Havana began its comeback, thanks to a small but dedicated group of artists and merchants who realized that the buildings would be perfect as studios, galleries and shops.

Now you'll wonder how these buildings ever could've stood empty. During the week these new shops and galleries don't see much traffic, but you'd better show up early on the weekends. Art and antique lovers throughout the southeast make a point to visit Havana, and with very good reason: it's a shopper's paradise.

It seems as if there are new stores and shops opening every season in Havana. If you're looking for antiques, you'll want to search them all, including The **Antique Center** (102 E. 7th Avenue, 539-0529), **H&H Antiques** (302 N. Main Street, 539-6886), **Havana Daydreamin', Inc.** (308 N. Main Street, 539-6889), **Lenora Charles Antiques** (211 1st Street, 539-0073), **My Secret Garden** (108 E. 7th Avenue, 539-8729) and the **Antique Corner** (302 N. Main Street, 539-8399), among others. Art lovers will find plenty to consider at galleries and showplaces such as the **Nice Picture Company and Art Gallery** (100 W. 7th Avenue, 539-5952).

You can safely plan to spend an entire day in Havana and not have to worry about meals. Tucked away in the downtown district are such eateries as the **Old Thyme Cafe** (Highway 27, 539-1828), the **Lenora Charles Cafe** (211 1st Street, 539-0073) and the **Gazebo Cafe** (310 N. Main Street, 539-6285). And if you're aching for a full-fledged country-style meal, you'll want to try the

Nicholson Farmhouse (539-5931), four miles west of Havana on State Road 12. This 1828 farmhouse is well-known for its steaks, chicken and seafood served with all the old-time trimmins'.

If you're going to be in town on the second Saturday in May you'll want to mark **Old Time Havana Day** on your calendar. This is when town residents celebrate their town's history with a costume dinner, a dessert contest and a street dance. The streets are opened up for special booths and tables from Havana merchants, and there's also plenty of home-cooked food and hot live music to enjoy.

To get to Havana from Tallahassee, take Monroe Street (Highway 27) north out of the city for about 15 miles. The highway cuts right through downtown Havana.

For more information, contact the **Gadsden County Committee of 100** at 627-9231.

Monticello

Monticello is located in nearby Jefferson County, the only Florida county that stretches from the Georgia state line all the way south to the Gulf of Mexico. It's not only a very long county, it's also oddly shaped. For example, when you drive to Monticello from Tallahassee along Highway 90, you'll hit a stretch just below Lake Miccosukee where you weave in an out of both Jefferson and Leon counties.

Getting to Monticello currently requires a drive across some beautiful country landscape, but the trip was once even more spectacular, especially if you were a Northerner heading south. In the late 1800s, many vacationers spent the winter in nearby Thomasville, Georgia, and often stopped off in Monticello on their way south to the Gulf of Mexico. The county had been named in honor of Thomas Jefferson in 1827, and the county seat was suitably named for his famous residence. For a while, Monticello was frequented by a large number of tourists who readily appreciated and supported the local economy.

But after the turn of the century more and more railroads began extending from the northern part of Georgia, and soon there was no longer any need for visitors to pass through Monticello on their way to Thomasville. The area suffered greatly because of this disruption, but many insiders think it's lucky that things worked out this way. If Monticello had kept on growing, it certainly wouldn't be the picturesque town we see today.

As you approach Monticello from Tallahassee along Highway 90, your first sight of the town will be of the county courthouse, a stately turn-of-the-century structure at the end of a broad, tree-lined avenue. While other counties feature extravagant homes that were built on cotton and tobacco money, many of Monticello's regal homes were constructed by northern businessmen who wintered here. The town's tree-lined skyline is highlighted by dozens of such houses, many of which are open for tours. At the least, Monticello is worth driving through just to sample the amazingly varied architectural styles.

• 477

One shining example that will impress anyone is the **Monticello Opera House** (W. Washington Street, 997-4242). Built in 1890 by local merchant John H. Perkins, the building was designed to house businesses on the lower levels while the upper level contained an ornate and acoustically perfect opera house. Perkins' daughter wanted to be a singer and Perkins himself hoped that the stream of tourist traffic through town would readily support his venture. Unfortunately this was not the case, and later attempts at transforming the opera house into a movie theater were quashed by residents who feared the advent of such newfangled technology. While the first floor played host to several business ventures over the years (including the town post office and the original furniture shop of well-known woodworker Homer Formby), the upstairs opera house stood empty for several decades and vandalism took its toll. Thankfully, the opera house has been rescued and restored by a dedicated band of residents, and if you're in town you may want to see if they're putting on a show. So far they've showcased everything from popular jazz to country to classical music, and everyone agrees that the Perkins Building, which sits across from the courthouse, is a vital cornerstone in the downtown district.

There are over two dozen historic homes in the downtown area, some of which are open to the public. These include the **Wirick-Simmons House**, built in 1833 and now housing the **Jefferson County Historical Society and Museum** (Pearl Street, 997-2565). There's also the **Simon-Ridgeway House**, built in 1888 and now operated as **Somewhere Else** (625 E. Washington Street, 997-1376), a bed and breakfast inn.

The downtown area is undergoing a period of rejuvenation due in no small part to the number of antique and thrift shops that have taken root there. Stores such as **The Chinaberry Tree** (1485 N. Jefferson Street, 877-7342), **Collectors Quarters** (150 Dogwood Street, 997-4649), **Courthouse Antiques** (205 E. Washington Street, 997-8008) and **Bush Baby** (280 N. Cherry Street, 997-6108) have all attracted collectors and antique enthusiasts, and there are many more shops within a few blocks' radius.

Several restaurants have established themselves in the area, as well, including **Mary's Place** (1305 W. Washington, 997-6707) and the **Rendezvous Restaurant** (175 N. Railroad Street, 997-8476).

The annual **Jefferson County Watermelon Festival** is a big event for Monticello and area residents, one that dates back almost 50 years. The festival is held each year during the last week in June, and events include a parade, golf tournament, street dance, rodeo, softball tournament and the crowning of the Watermelon Queen. Needless to say, there are also about a million melons to help you keep cool. If you're of the mind, you can even compete in the watermelon seed-spitting contest, but you'd best be warned that there are some real professionals who turn out for this heated event.

To get to Monticello from Talla-

Until Pebble Hill Plantation opened in 1984, the public had no idea of the splendor to be found behind its closed doors.

hassee, just take Tennessee Street (Highway 90) east out of the city for 25 miles until you reach Monticello.

For more information, call the **Monticello-Jefferson County Chamber of Commerce** at 997-5552.

Quincy

Quincy was named in 1825 after then-president John Quincy Adams. The town was the seat of a county that featured many successful cotton and tobacco plantations. To say that this area flourished would be an understatement. At one point just before the Civil War, Quincy was the second largest city in Florida in terms of population.

The Civil War cut deep and wide into the area's prosperity. These plantations were forced to abandon their more lucrative crops in order to grow food needed by Confederate troops. After the war ended, a raging fire blazed through the downtown district and most of the wooden buildings were destroyed. Along with the poor postwar economic situation, this signalled the beginning of a recession that was to last until the turn of the century, when tobacco — grown under shady trees this time — again proved to be a popular crop.

As Quincy slowly recovered its economic power base, the nearby community called Havana sprang up, and the industry was strong enough to support both places. Just after the turn of the century, Quincy State Bank president Mark W. "Pat" Monroe talked several residents into purchasing stock in the fledgling Coca-Cola Company. When this company took off just before World War II, two dozen Quincy residents suddenly found themselves to be millionaires, and the town was briefly the wealthiest town per capita in the nation.

Quincy was once again a boomtown, and much of its growth from this period has been preserved in the historic downtown district. At its center is the Gadsden County Courthouse, built in 1913, and it proudly presides over the 36-block downtown area that has been designated as an official Nationally Registered Historic District.

Bring an extra pair of shoes if you want to see everything, because you'll just about wear out a pair. There's a great little booklet available from the Gadsden County Chamber of Commerce that details over 50 of historic buildings and houses in downtown Quincy. Some of the highlights include the **Allison House**, home of General A.K. Allison who became governor of Florida when Governor John Milton killed himself at the end of the Civil War. The Allison House (215 N. Madison Street, 875-2511) is now a charming bed and breakfast inn.

There's also the **Owl Cigar Company Shade Leaf Building** (404 N. Madison Street), a brick warehouse used to cure tobacco during the turn-of-the-century boom. Now it houses a furniture business, a stained-glass studio, several apartments and office space. And the well-hoofed stage of **Leaf Theatre** (118 E. Washington Street, 875-9444), an excellent example of 1940s-era movie theater design, now features the daring dramatics of the **Quincy Music Theatre**.

Downtown Quincy can wear down even the most energetic of history buffs, so please note that there are also plenty of antique stores and art galleries where you can chill your hot heels. And if you're hungry you need look no farther than a block in either direction to find a suitable place to eat.

If you visit the area in September you may have the pleasure of attending Quincyfest, a huge festival that features art, food, music and fun. This event sometimes attracts more than 10,000 people, and insiders seem certain that those numbers will certainly climb as more and more people find out about this not-so-secret secret.

To reach Quincy from Tallahassee, the easiest route is to take Tennessee Street (Highway 90) west for 20 miles; this takes you right into the downtown area. Or you can take Monroe Street (Highway 27) north to Interstate 10, then take I-10 west

---

Insiders' Tips

Country music sensation Billy Dean is one of Quincy, Florida's, most profitable and popular exports.

Historic downtown Thomasville is a beautiful place for shopping and strolling.

for eight miles to the Highway 90 exit. Go west for 10 miles until you reach Quincy.

Contact the **Gadsden County Committee of 100** at 627-9231 for more information.

Thomasville, Georgia

Northwest Florida offers so much to see and do that you really don't need to leave the state at all — but we'd be terribly remiss if we didn't let you know about the wonderful town of Thomasville, just beyond the Georgia state line to the north. It's a special place where many Tallahasseans head for the weekend, and just for the record, we think you should know why.

Thomasville was established in the 1820s and, like other area communities, much of its initial success was founded in farming. Unlike much of northwest Florida, however, Thomasville sits on higher ground and is therefore a bit cooler and drier. This was something to consider if you were a Northerner vacationing in the 1800s, as yellow fever and malaria epidemics routinely claimed hundreds, even thousands, of lives.

From the end of the Civil War to just after the turn of the century, Thomasville became a booming resort town known for its appealing countryside and clean air. Many wealthy families built winter homes there, but some moved there permanently. Most of the opulent and elegant houses built during this period still stand, and they form the core of the town's historic district.

What ruined Thomasville's reputation as a resort town? Believe it or not, it was the Panama Canal, whose construction proved that swamp

• *481*

The Ransom Reid House, constructed in 1857, has changed greatly over the years but still exhibits the Victorian influences that were so prevalent in Thomasville.

drainage over large areas was feasible and effective. As a result South Florida, once shunned by those fearing death by germ-carrying insects, was suddenly flooded with wealthy vacationers, and towns like Thomasville and nearby Monticello, Florida, lost their seasonal residents.

Over 70 of these plantation homes still exist, but until 1984 the public really had no idea what they were like on the inside. That was the year that **Pebble Hill Plantation** opened for public tours. This huge Georgian and Greek Revival-style mansion was built years before the town was even established, and its unique exhibits and meticulously kept grounds afford us a crystal-clear view of Thomasville's amazingly ornate past. Pebble Hill was originally a working plantation but over the years was transformed into a classy hunting and sporting lodge. One-hour tours are available (and highly recommended), or you can just spend time wandering the grounds. Pebble Hill Plantation (912-226-2344) sits just off Highway 84 about 5 miles east of Thomasville.

Another fascinating house is the **Lapham-Patterson House** (626 N. Dawson Street, 225-4004), whose history is as odd as its design. Charles Lapham was a shoe manufacturer from Chicago who just barely survived that city's great fire of 1871. His lungs were severely damaged from smoke inhalation and he chose Thomasville as a fresh-air winter resort for his health. Lapham decided to build a house here, and from its design we can surmise that the fire must've instilled a deep fear in his mind. His three-story house has the distinction of having 19 rooms, 45 doors — and absolutely no right angles. Poor old Lapham was so deathly afraid of being trapped in a burning building again that he built his house with as many escapes and safeguards as possible. All the windows slide up into the wall, for example, becoming instant doors in case of emergency. All doors were also designed to allow smoke to rise and exit the house so no one would be trapped in a smoke-filled room. Lapham's concerns were understandably well-founded. Thomasville is fortunate that fire never threatened the man again. This incredible house, open for tours, is one of the town's major attractions.

There's so much history here that a visit to the **Thomas County Historical Museum** is doubly recommended. The strange and colorful history of Thomasville is presented here through several exhibits and photographs, and it certainly helps new visitors get a handle on some of the amazing sights that await them. The museum is open from 2 PM to 5 PM every day except Friday.

When you're in town, be sure to stop by and say hello to Thomasville's oldest living resident: "**Big Oak.**" This oak tree is estimated to be over three hundred years old, has a limbspan of over 160 feet, a trunk circumference of 24 feet and a height of almost 70 feet. Located on a plot of land at the corner of North Crawford and East Monroe streets, this giant tree looms over Thomasville like a trusty and steadfast soldier — albeit an elderly one, as evidenced by the support cables and struts that help stabilize the oak against high winds.

• 483

The Lapham-Patterson House is just one of the architectural wonders to be found in Thomasville.

One of the city's biggest annual attractions is the **Rose Festival**, held each April. Thomasville is known as the rose capital of the world, and this festival, dating back to 1921, justifies that reputation splendidly. Don't keep your nose buried in the flowers for too long, however, or you'll miss all the other events like the various sports tournaments, animal shows, parades, balls, dances and fairs. In other words, this is a huge week-long celebration you don't want to miss.

Another annual celebration that packs them in is the **Holiday Homecoming**, held during the first week in December. This features candlelight tours of Pebble Hill Plantation, a live nativity scene, a Victorian reader's theater and a historic walk through Thomasville during the **Downtown Victorian Christmas**. Wrap a scarf around your neck, pocket that shopping list and get in the spirit.

It probably makes you hungry just reading about all these activities. Fear not, for Thomasville can satisfy your tastes, no matter how picky your palate may be. The historic Neel House is now home to the **Grand Old House Restaurant** (502 S. Broad Street, 227-0108), and its menu is as elegant and refined as its name. There's also the **Market Country Restaurant** (Farmer's Market at Smith Avenue, 225-1777), featuring vegetables and produce from the nearby Farmer's Market. **Mom & Dad's Italian Restaurant** (1800 Smith Avenue, 226-6265) can take you back to Italy for cheaper than you can buy a plane ticket, and **Melissa's** (134 S. Madison Street, 228-9844) always offers piquant, tantalizing fare. If these don't grab your taste buds, there are plenty of other places to check out.

What else is there to do in Thomasville? We haven't yet mentioned the **Thomasville Rose Test Garden**, the **Cultural Center**, **Foxfire Hunting Preserve** or **Myrtlewood Plantation** (actually, the latter is mentioned in the Tallahassee Golf and Hunting chapter of this book). Nor have we had time or space to go into the downtown shopping district and the wonders found there. Let's put it this way: you can easily spend a weekend in Thomasville. Use Tallahassee as your home base, or grab a room at any of Thomasville's bed and breakfast inns, all of which are found in historic houses. For a complete listing of Thomasville inns, see the Tallahassee Accommodations chapter of this book.

Thomasville is about 40 miles north of Tallahassee. Take Thomasville Road (Highway 319) north out of town. Depending on traffic, the drive can take about an hour. Note that northbound traffic on Thomasville Road is usually jam-packed during rush hour, and there's a bottleneck just past I-10 north of town that can often bring traffic to a standstill. If you can't leave before 4:30 PM on a weekday, consider waiting until after 6 PM before you depart.

If you need more information on Thomasville, you can get a free *Visitor's Guide* from the **Destination Thomasville Tourism Authority** at (912) 225-5222.

Wakulla County

Crawfordville is the seat of Wakulla County, which also plays home to the towns of St. Marks, Panacea and Sopchoppy. The towns are so small and the county so big that when you talk about any one of the towns, you may as well be talking about all of them. So here we'll take the opportunity to tell you not only about Crawfordville, but about all of Wakulla County as well.

There's a lot of history in this rich landscape that sits just a few miles south of Tallahassee. It is believed that when Ponce de Leon first ventured into the area in 1521, he walked ashore at nearby St. Marks in the southern part of the county. In the early part of the 1600s, the Spanish erected San Marcos de Apalache, a fort that has been restored and preserved as a state park (see the Parks and Recreation chapter for more details).

As American settlers moved into north Florida, they came to rely heavily on access to the Gulf of Mexico to import supplies and export their

---

America's largest concentration of plantations — over 70 of them — lies in the 28-mile stretch between Tallahassee and Thomasville.

valuable cotton. In 1836, railroad tracks were laid down from St. Marks to Tallahassee, thus allowing a greater supply of goods and visitors through the Wakulla County area. This track has since been paved over and serves as the Tallahassee - St. Marks Historic Railroad State Trail (see the Tallahassee Parks and Recreation chapter for more information).

Crawfordville became the county seat shortly after the Civil War, when resident Noah Posey deeded some land to the county on the condition that the courthouse be moved to Crawfordville, which is named after Dr. John Crawford, Florida's Secretary of State from 1881 to 1902. The original courthouse burned down and was rebuilt at the turn of the century, and currently the stately white building serves as the Wakulla County Library.

Crawfordville is a little town, and the piney woods and vibrant landscape that attracted its early inhabitants are still easy to find. People come to Wakulla County when they want to get back to nature. Here you not only have the **St. Marks Wildlife Refuge** (detailed in Parks and Recreation), but also the **Gulf Specimen Marine Lab** in Panacea (Rock Landing Road and Clark Drive, 984-5297). Crawfordville's **Lost Creek Stables** (off Arran Road, 926-3033) offers horseback riding through the Apalachicola National Forest, while St. Marks' **TNT Hideaway** (Highway 267, 925-6412) rents canoes for unforgettable trips up and down the Wakulla River, which teems with a wonderful assortment of wildlife. The county's three other rivers — St. Marks, Sopchoppy and Ochlockonee — are also popular waters for rowers and boaters. Be advised that the wildlife here requires and demands *mucho* amounts of respect. It's not dangerous if you're careful and sensible. But if you feel uneasy seeing alligators and snakes up close, let the tour guides of the Edward Ball Wakulla Springs State Park, Lodge & Conference Center (see Parks and Recreation) introduce you to such reptiles from a safer distance.

There's plenty to do outdoors in Wakulla County, but indoors is where some of the best eating takes place. **Posey's Oyster Bar** sits in St. Marks at the end of Highway 363 (and the Tallahassee - St. Marks Historic Railroad Trail) and serves up some of the best seafood around. It's not to be confused with **Posey's Beyond the Bay Motel and Restaurant** in Panacea (Highway 98, 984-0180), which definitely gives the other Posey's a run for its money. In Crawfordville, **Myra Jean's** (Highway 319, 926-7530) is the friendliest hamburger joint in town, with an

---

Insiders' Tips

Academy award-winning actress Joanne Woodward spent much of her childhood in Thomasville and started her acting career on the stage of the East Side School Center, which is now the Thomasville Cultural Center.

old-fashioned soda fountain that'll take you back to simpler times.

There are plenty of places to stay in Wakulla County, including the **Shell Point Resort** (Highway 365, 926-7163), which, at a distance of 30 miles, is the closest beach to Tallahassee. The resort also sports a restaurant and marina that come highly recommended. There are plenty of campgrounds, too, including the **Newport Recreation Area** (at the entrance to the St. Marks Wildlife Refuge, 925-6171) and **Ochlockonee River State Park** in Sopchoppy (Highway 319, 962-2771).

If you're looking for rental properties in Wakulla County, call **Florida Coastal Properties** in Crawfordville (926-7811). They have a wide range of rental townhomes, condos and houses.

For more information, contact the **Wakulla County Chamber of Commerce** at 926-1848.

Many of Mobile's historic homes are open to the public.

Daytrips
Mobile

Although only 50 miles separate Mobile from Pensacola, the two cities remain vastly dissimilar in landscape, in long-held traditions, in the forces driving their economies. While many may know of Pensacola for its beautiful beaches and strong military presence, Mobile's recognition stems from its many gracious Southern homes and thriving port.

This bustling city by the bay introduced azaleas to the United States in the mid-1700s. The roots of Mardi Gras come not from New Orleans, but right here in Mobile, starting with the "Cowbellions" some time around 1830. And while so much of the South has become "homogenized," where cities lose their character and become no more than strings of condominiums and fast food restaurants, Mobile has retained much of its Southernness, highlighted in events like the Azalea Trail Festival, the Blessing of the Fleet, and the Historic Homes Tour.

Getting Around

Quick, before you come, you've got to learn to say it correctly: mow-BEEL. Now you're talking like a native. From Florida, I-10 will bring you right into the heart of the city. While you will be traveling almost due west, you'll find yourself quite a ways inland from the Gulf of Mexico. The City of Mobile is built at the headwaters of Mobile Bay and on the Mobile River. The bay is nearly shallow enough to walk across at the point where the eight-mile-long Jubilee Parkway (I-10) crosses it. If you're just passing through, I-10 is the quickest way through town, but you won't see much. Take the exit at Government Street if you're planning to stop and explore. Both routes take you through tunnels *under* the Mobile River.

Once you get through the Bankhead Tunnel (named for Tallulah's daddy), you'll be right downtown on Government Street. Take a quick left onto Royal Street and stop first at the Fort Conde' Welcome Center to pick up brochures, ask directions, and get a tour of the fort. But more on that later. Since some of the area's best attractions are outside the city limits, it's best to have your own car to get to those. But in town, there are a few alternate modes of transportation you may wish to try. Note: The area code for the entire state of Alabama is 205. Please remember to use the area code when calling from Florida.

Gulf Coast Carriage Service (433-8601) will pick you up right at the

Any time of year you'll find a flowering spectacle at Bellingrath Gardens.

front door of Fort Conde' from 9 AM until 5 PM for a 35-minute tour through Mobile's historic downtown district. The tour is $30.00 per couple, or $40.00 for a family of four.

Gray Line Tours (432-2228/ (800) 338-5597) provides four different scenic tours where they do the driving and you relax in air-conditioned comfort! A tour of Historic Mobile is $15.00 (two hours) and includes one historic home tour. A one-hour Historic Districts tour is $8.00 per person; it's $12.00 for a tour of the battleship U.S.S. *Alabama*; and to tour the Bellingrath Gardens and Home, you'll pay $26.00 ($18.50 for the gardens only). All tours depart from Fort Conde' at 10:30 AM and 2 PM (Sundays 2 PM only). Children are half price.

The Mobile Bay Ferry [(904) 434- 7345 in Florida; (205) 421-6420 or (800) 634-4027] takes you and your car from Dauphin Island south of Mobile Bay to Fort Morgan, built on a peninsula between the bay and the gulf. Ferry service began in 1979 after Hurricane Frederic wiped out the old drawbridge connecting Dauphin Island with the mainland. There's a new bridge now, so the ferry provides a pleasurable shortcut across the bay. Cost to ride is $12.00 for trucks and cars; motorcycles cost $5.00; and walk-ons are $1.00. Ferries leave every hour and twenty minutes from 8 AM until 7:20 PM.

Attractions

In town, Mobile's focus is on history in its many museums, walking and driving tours, and grand houses.

Discover famous forts, verdant gardens, rural wilderness and Gulf Coast beaches within a short drive. Mobile Bay's eastern shore offers pleasures aplenty for yet another day's outing.

THE DE TONTI SQUARE HISTORIC DISTRICT

Bounded by Adams, Claiborne, St. Anthony and Conception Sts.   438-7011

This nine-block historic district is just three blocks north of the central business district and is the oldest residential area in Mobile. All buildings are antebellum, from the 1830s through the 1850s. Most of these homes were built by cotton brokers, river pilots and traders in maritime supplies. Look for the architectural detailing of Italianate and Victorian styles as well as the classic lines represented by Gulf Coast, Greek Revival and Federal architecture.

CHURCH STREET EAST HISTORIC DISTRICT

Bounded by Broad, Canal, Conti, Eslava, Church and Royal Sts.   438-7011

Fifty-nine buildings of historical significance are found within this neighborhood, surpassed in age only by the De Tonti Square district. The buildings here serve many purposes — civic, commercial and religious as well as residential. Among these are the 1857 City Hall at 111 Royal Street, which began life as a one-story open market. A second story was designed in the Italianate style featuring bracketed cornices and the unusual polygonal cupola (in regular people's language, that's the round thing at the top with all the windows). This building is one of just a handfull of city halls in the country still used for its original purpose.

The European influences of earlier neighborhoods were lost to fires in 1827 and 1839, replaced by American Federal, Greek Revival, Italianate, Queen Anne and Victorian. The district remains the largest and one of the most architecturally diverse of all the city's historic districts.

OAKLEIGH GARDEN HISTORIC DISTRICT

Bounded by Ann, Government, Texas and Broad Sts.   438-7011

Most of the 41 buildings in this mainly residential district are post-Civil War, reflecting a surge of new growth and economic prosperity in the South in the last quarter of the 19th century. Besides the magnificent architecture, what is striking about this area is the abundance of live oaks, planted some 135 years ago, which now form shady canopies over the streets.

OAKLEIGH MANSION

350 Oakleigh Pl.   432-1281

This simple yet striking 1833 home is the focal point of the Oakleigh Garden Historic District (above). During the spring, the blush of azaleas combines with the majesty of the live oaks to produce a real Southern spectacle. The interior curving stairway is unique in Mobile homes. Currently operated as a house museum by the Historic Mobile Preservation Society (its headquarters are in the house), tours operate Monday through Saturday between 10 AM and 4 PM; and Sundays between 2 and 4 PM. Admission charge is $5.00 for adults, $4.50 for seniors 65 and older, $3.00 for ages 12 to 18, and $2.00 for ages 6 to 11. You may also purchase an admission pass to all four of the house museums for $10.00. These are available at any of the houses.

THE RICHARDS - DAR HOUSE
256 N. Joachim St.   434-7320

Inside the De Tonti Square district, this 1860s Italianate townhome stands out for its iron lace detailing. Steamboat Captain Charles G. Richards built the house with Neoclassic figurines of the Four Seasons worked into the intricate arabesques and scrolls of the ironwork. Inside adornments show off the almost overdone tastes of the period: brass and bronze chandeliers sporting mythological figures, ruby Bohemian glass, Carrara marble mantels, silver bell pulls for calling servants, and a garish crystal chandelier in the hexagonal dining room.

Open Tuesday through Saturday, 10 AM to 4 PM; Sundays 1 to 4 PM. A $3.00 donation is requested for adults; $1.00 for children.

CONDE'-CHARLOTTE MUSEUM HOUSE
104 Theatre St.   432-4722

The house, built as Mobile's first official jail around 1822-24, is considered Mobile's oldest. It stands adjacent to the Fort Conde' Welcome Center in the Church Street East Historic District. About 10 years before Mobile joined the Confederacy, the jail was converted to a residence, now owned by the National Society of Colonial Dames of America in the State of Alabama (did you get all that?). This society took it upon themselves to decorate the rooms in this house to reflect periods and nationalities — French Empire, 18th-century English, American Federal and the Confederate room (a Southern parlor, of course). Tour the house between 10 AM and 4 PM Tuesday through Saturday; Sundays by appointment. Adult admission is $3.00; children are $1.00.

THE BRAGG-MITCHELL MANSION
1906 Springhill Ave.   471-6364

This 20-room showplace of the Old South is part of the Explore Center, which includes one of Alabama's oldest schoolhouses and the Exploreum/Museum of Discovery science museum. Judge John Bragg built the residence in 1855, a combination of Greek Revival and Italianate styles. During the Civil War, all the massive oaks around the property were cut down allowing the Confederate artillery a clear shot at Federal troops. Following the war, Judge Bragg replanted all of the oaks from acorns he'd saved from the original trees. During the home's renovation in 1986, workers discovered elaborate Victorian stenciling beneath layers of paint on the crown moldings. Every room in the house was then restored using the brilliant colored moldings. The Bragg-Mitchell Mansion is open for tours Monday through Friday from 10 AM until 4 PM; Sundays 1 to 4. Admission is $4.00 for adults; $2.00 for students.

FORT CONDE'
150 S. Royal St.   434-7304

This French fort, reconstructed from original plans in 1975-76, is the

The reconstructed Fort Condé serves as one of Mobile's visitor centers.

third fort to be built on this site. The first Fort Conde' was a 1711 wooden stockade, but it must not have held up well since another French fort, this made from brick and mortar, went up between 1724 and 1735. It is this second Fort Conde' that has been recreated (and somewhat adapted into a welcome center).

The French, the English and the Spanish all laid claim to the fort at one time. In 1813, American troops bullied their way in to capture the fort from the Spanish. Just seven years later, Fort Conde' was declared surplus by the government; its walls were blasted, its brick sold at public auction, and its rubble used as fill for low-lying streets in the city. As you tour the fort, look for costumed guides and bits of 1720s fort life. Admission to the fort is free.

Magnolia Cemetery
Virginia and Ann Sts.

Cemeteries seem to be the best place for people looking for clues to their past. This 120-acre cemetery, established in 1836 and listed on the National Register of Historic Places, is the final resting place of many notable Mobilians. Look for Confederate generals, Alabama governors, Civil War-era writers, Apache Indians and Coca-Cola magnates Walter D. and Bessie Morse Bellingrath. Gravestone architecture is appealing here as well with Victorian funerary art, unusual styles of mausoleums and intricately sculpted cast and wrought ironwork.

FINE ARTS MUSEUM OF THE SOUTH (FAMOS)
4850 Museum Dr. off Springhill Ave. in Langan Park, or at 300 Dauphin St. 343-2667, 694-0533

Two thousand years of cultural history are depicted in 4,500 works of art. Prestigious museums across the country provide the museum with traveling exhibits, strengthening and expanding the works on display. The 19th- and 20th-century exhibits of American art and Southern decorative art are some of the museum's best. FAMOS is open between 10 and 5, Tuesday through Sunday and is always free. The downtown museum is open 8:30 to 4:30 Monday through Friday.

MUSEUM OF THE CITY OF MOBILE
355 Government St. 434-7620

Showcased inside an 1872 Italianate townhouse, this history museum thoroughly details Mobile's heritage, beginning with its river-dwelling Indian tribes to today. Of special note are the Colonization Room, covering French, English, Spanish and American rule; the Civil War Room, with its mostly Confederate relics; the Rutherford Carriage Room's fine collection of horse-drawn buggies; the grand and glorious women's fashions in the Hammel Collection; and the unforgettable Staples Gallery tracing Mardi Gras' history in costumes and float designs. The City Museum is absolutely free (!) and open from 10 to 5 Tuesday through Saturday.

EICHOLD HEUSTIS MEDICAL MUSEUM OF THE SOUTH
In the lobby of the Lafayette St. entrance at the University of South Alabama - Springhill Ave. campus 434-5055

Two hundred years of medical history are traced in this free museum, which contains the largest collection of medical artifacts anywhere in the Southeast. Gaze in awe at the curious assortment of old machines and instruments, read about primitive techniques for treating tuberculosis and the ghastly practice of blood-letting, or recreate a Civil War battlefield scene with photographs and a set of Army surgical instruments. Although quite fascinating, we recommend not doing this museum before lunch! Open Monday through Friday from 8 until 5.

THE EXPLOREUM MUSEUM OF DISCOVERY
2½ miles east of the Springhill Ave. exit off I-65 476-MUSE

The Exploreum is a hands-on science museum geared to fun and learning. Send a message in the "whispering" chamber that a friend can hear from 50 feet away... build an arch like an ancient engineer and learn the secrets of defying gravity... or watch the movement of the earth "draw" a picture! These plus many other stimulating exhibits teach youngsters and grown-ups about the laws of physics, the world of nature and our fascination with the humanities. Come and discover Tuesday through Friday from 9 to 5 or weekends 1 to 5. There's a $3.00 admission for adults; $2.00 for children 2 to 17.

Phoenix Fire Museum
203 S. Claiborne St.   434-7554

Imagine the scene of bells clanging, horse hooves pounding and the cries of men dressed in fire gear racing to the scene of a fire. Even now, the sight of a shiny red engine with its tense and stern-faced crew, its sirens and lights shouting out a warning to motorists, still plays out a thrilling drama for many.

The fire museum is actually in the old Phoenix Steam Fire Company No. 6's station house, built in 1859. Inside are old horse-drawn and steam fire engines and artifacts dating back to Mobile's first volunteer companies in 1819. The museum is free and open from 1 to 5 Tuesday through Saturday; Sundays 1 to 5.

USS Alabama Battleship Memorial Park
East on I-10 to Exit 27 at U.S. 90 (Battleship Pkwy.)   433-2703

Ready for inspection! The giant battleship floating in Mobile Bay once held a 2,500-member crew in the Pacific during World War II. Even after shooting down 22 enemy planes and earning nine battlestars, the USS *Alabama* remained untouched. You can tour both the battleship and the USS *Drum* submarine, then visit the other military exhibits, which include a B-52 bomber, a gull-winged Corsair, and the P-51 "Mustang" WWII fighter planes in the 100-acre park. On the grounds, too, are a nature observatory, where a boardwalk and a two-story observation deck provide views of natural wetlands; a snack bar, and a display of 1,700 varieties of roses. The tours and the park are free to the public, which is open every day but Christmas from 8 AM until sunset.

Alabama Cruises
At Battleship Memorial Park   433-6101

What a way to see the bay! The *Commander* takes visitors out on either a 1½-hour harbor tour or a 2 ½-hour dinner cruise nearly every month (no cruises in January). The first trip, the sightseeing cruise, leaves its dock at Battleship Park and slowly cruises by the USS *Alabama* for a view you can't get on land! Your captain will narrate local stories and folklore as you cut by Little Sand Island and enter Mobile Harbor. Ships from all over the world await entry into the Port of Mobile. There's a snack bar on board and no reservations are necessary (for the cruise, not the snack bar!). Cruises run daily at 1 PM in November, December and February; 11 AM and 1:30 PM March through May and September and October; and during the summer months at 10:30 AM and 1 and 3:30 PM. Tickets are $7.00 for each adult; children 3 to 12 are $3.50.

Dinner cruises offer a spectacular glimpse of Mobile's downtown skyline and the majesty of bay sunsets. You'll have your choice of three entrees in a large buffet, frosty cocktails and live entertainment for listening or dancing. The dinner cruise schedule is a little easier to follow (all cruises are at 7 PM): During November, December and February there's one cruise every Saturday. March through May, and again in September and October, the *Commander* departs Monday, Friday and Saturday. Summer months schedule is every day but Monday. Ticket prices, which include all taxes, but not cocktails, are $24.95 for adults and $14.95 for children 3 to 12.

BELLINGRATH GARDENS AND HOME
West of Mobile off I-10, 12401 Bellingrath Garden Rd., Theodore   973-2217

A most spectacular showplace, Bellingrath Gardens is one of the area's finest attractions. It's *way* out in the boonies, but if you follow the signs, you'll get there eventually. A tour of the 65-acre floral and landscaped paradise is worth a trip in itself. Seasonal flowers are in bloom all year long, but nothing compares with the spring azaleas. During springtime, too, is a showing of more tulips and daffodils than you may have ever seen all in one place. At every turn is another incredible view eliciting gasps, squeals or shutter clicks from the entourage. There's the Oriental American Garden, the Bridal Garden, the Rose Garden, the Exotica Conservatory and Mirror Lake, among many other sights. The home is built along the Fowl River, and a roofed pavilion with big porch swings affords cooling breezes all year. Still to come is a wildlife exhibit and a hummingbird garden.

The Bellingrath home is grand as well, with a superb collection of antiques, but if you only have a few hours, spend it in the gardens; the rewards are great. Open every day from 7 AM until sunset. Admission to the gardens only is $6.50 per person; ages 6 to 11 $3.25; younger than 6 free. Tickets to both the gardens and the home are $14.00 for adults; $11.00 for children 6 to 11; and younger than 6 $8.15. Ask about special senior prices.

WILDLAND EXPEDITIONS
Hwy. 43 at the Chickasaw Marina, Chickasaw   460-8206

Captain Gene Burrell invites visitors out on his custom-built 22-passenger boat, the *Gator Bait*, for a tour of the swamps, tidal marshes and bayous of the Mobile-Tensaw Delta. Prepare yourself for adventure throughout the largest inland delta in the United States. Bring along a camera and a pair of binoculars to capture the flight of one of 250 species of birds or 200 species of fish and wildlife. You may even be fortunate enough, if the time is right, to spot a black bear munching clumps of palmetto. Other endangered species can be found in the dense woodlands including the bald eagle and the osprey, whose giant nests of twigs perch atop cypress trees.

It wouldn't be an adventure without an alligator or two . . . or two dozen, and Capt. Gene can almost promise that some of the leathery reptiles will surface for your cameras. Tours leave at 9 AM and 2 PM and take about two hours and fifteen minutes. Prices for the expedition are $20.00 for large gator bait; $10.00 for bite-sized bait. Take I-10 west to I-65 north. Take Exit 13 (Highway 158) west for two miles. It intersects with Highway 43.

South of Mobile

DAUPHIN ISLAND
Off Hwy. 193 south of Mobile   861-5525

Dauphin Island suffered a direct hit from Hurricane Frederic back in 1979 but has come back to life with many fine public areas island-wide. There are a couple of nice little

The Blessing of the Fleet at Bayou La Batre kicks off the fishing season along the Gulf Coast.

shopping areas with restaurants, a marina and charter boat cruises, six public boat ramps, two fishing piers, a 150-site campground, a pre-Civil War fort, the Dauphin Island Sea Lab, an 18-hole public golf course, the 160-acre Audubon Bird Sanctuary, and an Indian shell mound, besides miles of white-sand beaches along the 15-mile-long island.

FORT GAINES
Exit I-10 at 193 south to
Dauphin Island 861-6992

This 1821 fort marks the place where Admiral David Farragut shouted the oft-quoted command: "Damn the torpedoes. Full speed ahead!" during the Civil War Battle of Mobile Bay. Early French explorers dubbed the island "Massacre Island" for a curious pile of human skeletons they found there. The first wooden fort was built by the French in 1717 on the far eastern tip of the island.

It was 1813 when the Americans moved in to capture the island from the Spanish and establish a fort on this strategic spot of land guarding the entrance to the bay. The five-pointed design has walls 22½ feet high and 4½ feet thick. Soldiers lived and worked at Fort Gaines from the early 1800s up to 1946, when it became a historic site. The fort is open every day but Christmas and New Year's Day from 9 to 5. Admission is $2.00 for adults; $1.00 for ages 7 to 12.

FORT MORGAN
Hwy. 180 at the tip of Pleasure Island
Fort Morgan 540-7125

It's a day trip all by itself; the drive

• 497

over to Fort Morgan is as much fun as being there. Our recommendation is to head out to Perdido Key from Pensacola, and keep on going west along Highway 292 into Alabama. You'll pass by the famous Flora-Bama Lounge at the state line, then on into the scenic coastal resort towns of Gulf Shores and Orange Beach. The trip to Fort Morgan will take about 1½ hours from Pensacola, but there's much to see and do along the way. You may want to stop for lunch in Gulf Shores or Orange Beach, since the Gulf Shore peninsula is rather devoid of commercialism. At the tip of the island (also known as Pleasure Island) is the fort, built between 1819 and 1834, which was one of the last Confederate forts to fall to Union forces in the Battle of Mobile Bay. Every fort seems to get in on the action with Admiral David Farragut's famous line (see Fort Gaines).

There's a controversy afoot with the old fort, stemming from new plans to build more houses, an inn, a restaurant and a marina on the 450-acre park site. The Fort Morgan Civic Association has other ideas, and is talking to another developer about erecting replicas of a barracks, a hospital, a quarantine pier and officers' houses that were once at the fort. Right now, the area is rather development deficient, with a few beach cottages and the undeveloped Bon Secour Wildlife Refuge along the two-lane road. Fort Morgan is open weekdays from 8 to 5 and weekends 9 to 5 year-round except for Thanksgiving, Christmas and New Year's Day. People younger than six get in free to the fort; ages 7 to 12 pay $1.00; older than 12, it's $2.00. Seniors pay $1.00, and if you're 100 years old and have a note from your mom, you get in free.

Restaurants

Although it really isn't far enough away from Pensacola to have to spend the night, you will need sustenance to get you through the day. Whether beachside, bayside, islandside or on the bayous, restaurants throughout the Gulf Coast almost always offer some type of seafood fare, so dig in and savor the flavor of the Gulf Coast's best catches!

Price code for Alabama restaurants follow for a dinner for two with beverage and dessert (no tax, tip or cocktails). All restaurants accept major credit cards unless otherwise noted.

Under $20	$
$21-40	$$
$41-60	$$$
More than $60	$$$$

ROUSSOS SEAFOOD RESTAURANT & CATERING
166 S. Royal St. in the
Fort Conde' Village   433-3322
$$

The first Roussos on Battleship Parkway was obliterated by 1979's Hurricane Frederic, but the new restaurant is still making old favorites such as Hot'n Spicy Cajun Shrimp, Sauteed Crabmeat, Fried Baby Squid (squid?) and fresh seafood cooked your way. Come on back to the kitchen to watch the preparation, ask questions and talk to one of the seven family members who work here. Roussos can be a romantic night-out place or an in-and-out family spot — you choose. Kid's plates start at just $1.95. Roussos is open 11 to 11 every day but Sunday, when the hours are 11:30 to 9:30.

Korbet's Restaurant of Mobile
At the loop in midtown Mobile
2029 Airport Blvd.   471-1000
$$$

Warm, comfortable surroundings are the hallmark of Korbet's, which has been here for decades. Just about every kind of food imaginable is served at Korbet's, so nobody gets left out and everybody goes home happy. Soups, salads, specialty sandwiches, burgers, steaks and chops, chicken entrees, eggs and omelettes, seafood and spaghetti round out the list of tempting delights. Ever try a lump crab omelette sandwich? This may be your only opportunity. How about a fresh Florida Lobster stuffed with crabmeat dressing and served with lemon butter sauce ... mmmmmm. You'll get your fill here, and then some, with sweet endings like homemade pies, strawberry shortcake and hot fudge sundaes. The landmark restaurant is open every day from 7:30 AM until 10 PM; weekends it stays open until 11 PM.

Weichman's All Seasons Restaurant
168 S. Beltline Hwy.   344-3961
$$$

Okay, it's pretty hokey, and we hope some high-priced advertising exec didn't come up with it, but the All Seasons' slogan is: "The Quality is Rare, the Prices are Medium, and the Service is Well Done." Kind of makes you cringe, doesn't it? All that aside, the fresh seafood, prime rib, aged steaks, lamb, pasta and chicken specialties are absolutely first class, especially when served with one of the many fine wines offered by Weichman's. Be sure to try their gumbo. Dinners start at just $7.95. Open for lunch and dinner every day but Saturday, which is only open for dinner. Hours are 11 AM to 3 PM, then 5 to 10 PM.

Wintzell's Oyster House
605 Dauphin St.   433-1004
$$

Fried, stewed and nude, get your oysters here. Just be careful about those raw ones — warnings should now be placed in every restaurant still serving raw oysters. But Wintzell's knows oysters, probably better than anybody around here, since they've been here longer than just about everybody (1938). This is a suck-n-slurp, good-times place; just looking at the walls as you come in will tell you that. It will take your entire visit here to read just the sayings within eyeshot. When you come back, ask to sit in a different spot so you can read something new! You don't have to be an oyster aficionado to eat here; Wintzell's promises some of the best fresh seafood on the Gulf Coast will be cooked any way you like it. Open Monday through Saturday 11 AM until midnight; Sunday 11 to 5.

The Pillars
1757 Government St.   478-6341
$$$$

Another gourmet restaurant with a sterling reputation for quality, The Pillars' romantic setting in an antebellum Southern mansion exudes charm, style and a fairly steep price tag. The 12 dining rooms are each decorated with period antiques, fireplaces, chandeliers and candlelight. Chef Tim Ward is sometimes helped in the kitchen by the owner, Filippo Milone, who also likes to run quality control. Milone was trained in Europe as a chef himself, so he knows the business from the kitchen to the food selection to the impeccable service to the extensive selection of wines from The Pillars' own cellar. Choose thick, sizzling steaks, fresh seafood, veal, lamb and pasta creations.

Menu specialties change daily; your server will be happy to explain the preparation of each. Dining hours are 5 to 10 PM Monday through Saturday.

Historic Downtown Dauphin Street

Dauphin St.
$

From Royal Street to Hamilton, several little eateries and food boutiques are making news. They're fun, trendy, and inexpensive. **G.T. Henry's** at Dauphin and Hamilton (432-0300) is a good local watering hole, featuring live music Wednesday through Saturday. Across the street, **South Side** (438-5555) features blues, Cajun, reggae and rock, mixed with muffelattas, po-boys and pizza. Head three blocks west for a lively game of darts, foosball, cold beer and good company at **Hayley's** (433-4970), where there's never a cover charge. Hayley's is open seven days from 3 PM to 3 AM.

Within every large city, there seems to be at least one great chocolatier, and **Three Georges Southern Chocolates** is it in Mobile (433-6725). Free samples, gift boxes and special offers make it a great souvenir (and dessert) stop. Open Monday through Saturday between 9 and 5; closed Saturdays during the summer. **Port City Brewery & Eatery** (438-2739) actually has its own micro brewery on the premises. So try a local brew and top it off with one of their great specialty sandwiches. Where would any tourist town be without its own Subway? This one, at Dauphin and Joachim, is called **Subway Bienville** (433-0571), most likely for the historic district.

Cafe au lait (half chickory coffee and half hot milk), bagels, beignets (French doughnuts), lunch specials and sandwiches are all made fresh at **Bagel Fanagle, Inc.** at 107 Dauphin (694-0900). They also specialize in low fat and no fat cooking, then they go and make fattening gourmet desserts. Go figure. Buy bagels Monday through Friday from 7 AM until 4 PM every day. **Mostly Muffins** (433-9855) is *mostly* muffins, but also croissants, cookies, coffee beans, shakes, yogurts and specialty coffees. Drink it there or take some home! Open every day from 7:30 AM to 3:30 AM.

Shopping

Factory outlets, antique stores and specialty boutiques are all the rage in the Mobile area; down south along the gulf, shops selling sundresses, floppy hats and resort-type beachwear line the shore. Flea markets are big business everywhere, and who knows what you'll uncover!

**ROBERT MOORE & CO.
CHRISTMAS TOWN & VILLAGE**
4213 Halls Mill Rd.   661-3608, 661-3693
If you just can't wait until Christmas, stop in here for that holiday feeling all year long. Beautifully decorated "themed" trees are everywhere, as are tiny lighted villages, creches, beautiful doll displays and more lights and ornaments than you'll know what to do with! Also in the village are a candy shop, a deli, a wine and cheese shop and a coffee and tea shop to make a day of it. Located half a mile west of Azalea Road, just 10 minutes off I-65 or I-10. Christmas Town and Village is open Monday through Saturday from 10 to 6; Sundays 1 to 6. Closed New Year's Day, Mardi Gras Day, Easter, 4th of July, Thanksgiving and — yes — Christmas! The little elves who work here can only take so much holiday spirit, you know.

RIVIERA CENTRE FACTORY STORES
2601 S. McKenzie St., Hwy. 59 S.
Foley   943-8888, (800) 5-CENTRE
People drive for hours to get here, so the savings and the selection must be worth the trip. Save as much as 70% every day from 85 manufacturers. A small sampling: Arrow Shirts, Bugle Boy, Calvin Klein, Oshkosh B'Gosh, Oneida, West Point Pepperell, Bass, Reebok, American Tourister, Carter's, Ruff Hewn, L'eggs . . . you get the idea. Seven food court merchants provide quick lunches and dinners (so you can get back to shopping). Open Monday through Saturday 9 to 9; Sunday 10 to 6 daily except Easter, Thanksgiving, and Christmas.

FLEA MARKET MOBILE
401 Schillinger Rd. N.   633-7533
You won't have time to look at everything with 700 — that's right, 700 booths under cover. Besides what people have dug out of the attic or the root cellar, there are fair-type foods (you know, like Auntie Peg's jams and Sister Lil's 'maters), fresh produce, fine and not-so-fine antiques, and the catch-all "collectibles," meaning everything from "Z-Man" comics to Hummel figurines. Up to 40,000 people pass through here every week! The Flea Market is on Schillinger Road just off Airport Boulevard. Market hours are Saturday and Sunday 9 AM to 5 PM.

COTTON CITY ANTIQUE MALL
2012 Airport Blvd. at the Loop   479-9787
Ninety dealer spaces showcase period furniture, accessories, glassware, jewelry, silver and more. The mall is open Monday through Saturday, 10 to 5; Sunday 1 to 5.

VICTORIAN ROSE ANTIQUES
450 Dauphin Island Pkwy.
at the Loop   479-9119
Victorian Rose Antiques is not huge, but the priceless store of antiques makes up for volume. Shop, deal and haul it away Monday through Saturday from 9 to 5; Sundays 1 to 5.

... And yet another Alabama day trip

We can't leave you day-tripping through Mobile without telling you about one more wonderful route. Pick up Highway 98 west in Pensacola

• **501**

(the same one that stretches through most of Northwest Florida) and follow it into Alabama over the Lillian bridge. Pass through the tiny German community of Elberta, then on into historic Foley (where the Riviera Centre factory stores are), through scenic **Magnolia Springs**, where the mail is still delivered by boat, then swing northward into **Point Clear**. Stop at the **Punta Clara Kitchen** to watch wonderful candies and sweets being made, have lunch, and don't forget to pick up some souvenirs in the 1897 Victorian home. You really owe yourself a trip to **Marriott's Grand Hotel** in Point Clear to see what a real genteel Old South hotel is like. The grounds are immaculate (there may be a few folks playing croquet on the lawn), the view is lovely (right on Mobile Bay), and the hotel, which was first built in 1847, is a tribute to tradition and service. Continue north into the pretty little town of **Fairhope**, site of numerous arts and crafts festivals and historic homes along the waterfront.

Index of Advertisers

Abbott Realty	163	Julia Mae's	341
Anchor Realty, Cape San Blas	315	Kokomo Motel and Marina	161
Anchor Realty, St. George Island	333	Lenora Charles Courtyard Cafe	474
Antiques & Accents	474	Lighthouse Realty	340
Antique Center	474	Long Dream Gallery	321
Apalachicola Bay Campground	329	Main Street Market	474
Apalachicola Realty	327	McLauchlin House	474
A Touch of Class	474	Memories	474
AuPairCare	453	Mirror Image	474
ARTemus Gallery	321	My Secret Garden	474
Barn Door Gift Shop	474	Nightingale & Associates	325
Barnett Bank	369	Northwest Florida Tourism Council	
Beaches of South Walton	145		Inside Front Cover
Beach TV/The Visitors Information		Painted Pony	329
Center Inside Back Cover		Pensacola Beach	25
Bill Bailey Realty	329	Physician's Care	471
Carol's Christmas Shop	474	Pied Piper Ladies Boutique	321
Carrabelle Realty	341	Ramada Inn	393
The Coombs House Inn	320	Resort Realty	336
Chuck Spicer's Coast Line Shopping		Rescued Relics/Fig Tree	
Guide and 'Uniques & Antiques	320	Productions	474
Down Under Dive Center	341	River Plantation Inside Front Cover	
dune-Allen Realty	223	Senior Care Properties	324
East Side Mario's	379	Sharon's Place	329
Ell's Court	341	Shaun Donahoe Realty	322
Executive Suite Motor Inn	391	Shell Point Beach Inside Front Cover	
Florida Art Center & Gallery	474	Specialty Design	474
Florida Coastal Property		Sportsman's Lodge	319
Inside Front Cover		Sticks 'N Stitches	474
Gallery 75	321	Summer Properties	316
Governor's Inn	389	Susanne's	474
The Gibson Inn	320	Tallahassee Community Hospital	471
H&H Antiques	474	Tallahassee Memorial Regional	
Hancock's Antiques	474	Medical Center	468, 469
Happy Pelican	337	The Nice Picture Gallery	474
Harry A's	334	Tom Todd Realty	314
Helen's Hallway Annex	474	Two Gulls	338
Historical Bookshelf	474	Village Market	474
Innovation Park Inside Front Cover		Wanderings	474
Jackie's	474	Westminster Oaks	465
Jeannie's Journeys	339	Yent Bayou	320

• 503

Index

Symbols

1 First Choice Realty of Pensacola 120
1884 Paxton House 390
1913 Exchange Hotel 66
4 Kids 178
4th Quarter 386
621 Gallery 444

A

A Christmas Carol "On the Air" 416
A Highlands House 169
A Stitch In Time 397
A.J. Henry Park 433
Abbey, The 383
Abbott Realty Services, Inc. 166, 170, 223, 226, 229, 254
Academy on Grace 295
Accommodations, Fort Walton Beach Area 159
Accommodations, Panama City Beach Area 251
Accommodations, Pensacola Area 43
Accommodations, Tallahassee 388
Admiral Mason Park 96
Adventure Sailing Cruises 289
Adventure Watersports 202
Adventures on the Kokomo 208
Adventures Unlimited 48, 68, 92, 203
African-American Heritage Society, Inc. 100
Agency Car Rentals 373
Agyeiwa's African Boutique 399
Air Boingo 271
Air Force Armament Museum 184
Air Force Development Test Center 239
Air Force Enlisted Widows Home Foundation 232
Airlines 371
Airports 2, 371
AJ's Seafood & Oyster Bar 150
Alabama Cruises 493
Alamo Car Rentals 371
Ale House 32
Allan Davis Seashells & Souvenirs 53
Alligator Point 342
Allison House 390, 478
Alvin's Big Island Tropical Department Store 50, 174, 176, 259

Ambassador Limousines 374
Amen-Ra's Bookshop 399
American Association of Retired Persons 124
American Homepatient 234, 306
American Indian Cultural Society's Annual Pow-wow 411
American Indian Spring Festival 191
American Realty of Northwest Florida, Inc. 223
American Theatre Organ Society 101
Amtrak Station 4, 374
Amtrak Sunset Limited 371
Amusement Centers 92
An Evening of Music and Dance 414
Anchor Realty and Mortgage Co. 316, 337
Anchor Room 328
Anchorage Ladies Billfish Tournament 277
Andrew Jackson Breakfast in the Park 411
Andrew's 375
Andrew's Upstairs 376, 384
Ann L. Baroco Center for Women's Health 125
Annella's 376, 397
Annual Events, Fort Walton Beach Area 191
Annual Events, Panama City Beach Area 275
Annual Events, Pensacola Area 73
Annual Events, Tallahassee Area 409
Anthony's 376
Antique Center 474
Antique Corner 474
Antique Show and Sale 410
Antiques 397, 399, 474, 478
Apalachee Indians 351, 429
Apalachicola 317
Apalachicola Bay Campground 331
Apalachicola Bay Chamber of Commerce 330, 333, 339
Apalachicola Maritime Museum 330
Apalachicola National Forest 333, 417, 484
Apalachicola Realty 328
Apalachicola Seafood Grill and Steakhouse 328
Apple Annie's 32
Applebee's 397
Aquanaut Scuba Center, Inc. 208
Aquatic Realty 114
Arcadia Mill 109
Area Codes 9

504 •

INDEX

Armament Museum, Eglin 239
Armor Realty 461
Art House 397
Artel Gallery 106
Artemis Gallery and Cultural Center 328
Artesana Inc. 51
Arthur Murray Dance Studio 395
Artist's Showroom 217
Arts & Crafts 409, 413, 414, 415, 416
Arts & Design Society 217
Arts and Culture,
    Fort Walton Beach Area 216
Arts and Culture, Panama City 292
Arts and Culture, Pensacola 98
Arts and Culture, Tallahassee 441
Arts and Crafts Jubilee 411
Arts Council of Northwest Florida 98
Artz 178
Association of Volleyball Professionals
    Miller Lite 78
Attractions, Fort Walton Beach 181
Attractions, Panama City Beach Area 263
Attractions, Pensacola 55
Attractions, Tallahassee 402
Au Piche Mignon French Pastry Shop 397
Audubon Bird Sanctuary 495
Audubon Society 73
Automobile Rental 371
Avis Car Rentals 3, 371
Azalea Trace 121
Azalea Trail Festival 487
Azure 179

B

B.J.'s Pizza 336
Back Door Poets 101
Back Porch 151
Bagdad Historic District 67
Bagel Fanagle, Inc. 498
Bahama Bay Club 116
Bahn Thai Restaurant 376
Ballet Pensacola 99
Baptist Hospital 125
Bar-B-Q Rib Burnoff 82
Barbershop Harmony Chorus 292
Barkley House 61
Barnacle Bill's Half Shell Lounge 384
Barnacle Bill's Seafood Emporium 376
Baroco Center for Science
    and Advanced Technology 110
Barron's Antique Mall 260
Bartram Park 97
Baseball 433, 434, 435
Basketball 289, 434, 435
Basmati's 157
Battle of Horseshoe Bend 355
Battle of Mobile Bay 496

Battle of Mobile Bay Reenactment 81
Battle of Natural Bridge 361
Bay Area Vocational-Technical School 220
Bay Arts Alliance 292
Bay Arts Alliance/Marina Civic Center 295
Bay Arts String Quartet 292
Bay Bluffs Park 65, 97
Bay Breeze Nursing & Retirement Center 122
Bay County Council on Aging 305
Bay County Fair 279
Bay County Junior Museum 273
Bay County Tourist Development Council 243
Bay Golf Clinic 283
Bay Heritage Nursing
    and Convalescent Center 236
Bay Medical Center 306
Bay Memorial Park 289
Bay Point Invitational Billfish Tournament 277
Bay Point Yacht & Country Club 251, 281
Bay Point's Island Queen 287
Bay Towne Biathlon 198
Bay View Center 308
Bay Wind Band 293
Bay Window Deli 37
Bay Woods 117
Bayou Art Gallery 342
Bayou Bill's Crabhouse 155
Bayou Chico 55
Bayou Country Store 51
Bayou Gallery 295
Bayou Hills Run 87
Bayou Texar 55
Bayou Villas 123
Bayside 227
Bayside Gallery 331
Baytowne Marina 196
Bayview Community Center 94
Bayview Park 96
Bayview Senior Citizens Center 94
Beach and Shore Clean-up 83, 278
Beach Ave. T-Shirt Factory 175
Beach Barbecue and Dance Party 197
Beach Bums 178
Beach Rentals 211
Beach-Bay Health Star, Inc. 307
Beaches, General Information 5
Beaches of South Walton 142, 144
Beachmark Inn 160
Beachside Towers 166
Beacon Club 94
Beatles on the Beach Fall Festival 85
Beaux Arts Ball 218
Bed and Breakfast Inns 46, 388
Behavioral Medicine Center 129
Bellevue Plantation House 408
Bellingrath Gardens and Home 494
Bellissimo Pasta & Pizza 149
Betton Place 397

• 505

INDEX

Biathlons 198
Big Bend CARES Annual Aids Walk 410
Big Bend Saltwater Fishing Classic 339, 413
Big Kahuna's Waterpark 187
Big Lagoon State Recreation Area 58
Big Pine Nature Trail 424
Biking 56, 94, 198, 211, 427, 435
Bill Bailey Realty 331
Billy Bowlegs Festival 191
Bimini Sandbar Cafe 252
Birding 422
Black Archives Research Center
    and Museum 402, 451
Blackbeard Sailing Charters 206
Blackwater Bay 67
Blackwater Canoe Rental 92, 204
Blackwater Heritage Tour 87
Blackwater River State Park 69
"Blast to the Past" Classic Car Show 279
Blind Pig Antique Shop 399
Blount's Fish Camp 422
Bloxham Park 434
Blue Angel Marathon 74
Blue Angels Homecoming Air Show 81, 86, 132
Blue Crab Festival 412
Blue Marlin Restaurant 252
Bluewater Bay 221
Bluewater Bay Golf Club 200
Bluewater Bay Resort 160, 162
Bluewater Bay Tennis Center 202
Boar's Head 248
Boat Parade of Lights 280
Boating 69, 263, 344, 347, 349, 417, 422,
    424, 431, 432
Boating Safety 10
Bob George Park 289
Bob Hope Village 230
Bob Sikes Airport 3
Bob's Canoes 92, 204
Bodenheimer's 31
Boggy Bayou Mullet Festival 192
Bohemia 65
Bon Appetit Cafe & Bakery 44
Bon Secour Wildlife Refuge 496
Boogie's Watersports 209
Book Warehouse 260
Books-A-Million 397
Boutin Brown & Butler
    Real Estate Services 462
Bowles, William Augustus 347, 432
Boy On A Dolphin 37
Brackin Wayside Park 214
Bradley's Old Fashioned Fun Day 415
Bragg-Mitchell Mansion 490
Breakaway Lodge Restaurant 328
Breakers 245
Breakfast in the Park 411
Briarwood Park 214

Bridge to the Beach Run 74
Bridgeway Center 236
British Car Show 76
British Festival 79
British Pantry and Gift Shoppe 261
Brokaw-McDougall House 402
Buccaneer Inn 338
Bud & Alleys 156
Budget Car Rentals 371
Buffalo's Wings and Rings 384
Bullwinkle's 384
Bumin' in the Sun Beachwear 176
Bungee Jumping 210
Burdines 395
Burnt Pine Golf Club 228
Bus Service 4, 373
Bush Baby 476
Bushwacker Festival 82
Buster's Oyster Bar & Grill 155

C

Cab Stand 384
Cabana Man 211
Cabo's Tacos 397
Cabot Lodge North 393
Cafe di Lorenzo 377
Call Sacred Heart 128
Camel Lake 417
Camellia Christmas 424
Camoflauge Shop 328
Camp Seaside Adventure Program 195
Camp Walton 142
Campbell Pond 433
Campbell Town 65
Campfire Program 79
Camping 48, 56, 58, 69, 172, 173, 189,
    203, 238, 257, 265, 313, 331, 339,
    342, 344, 347,349, 417, 420, 422,
    429, 431, 432, 433
Candy Kitchen Building 326
Candymaker, The 177
Canoeing 68, 69, 92, 203, 238, 265, 420,
    424, 431, 432, 484
Canopies 249
Canopy Roads 403
Cantonment Family Medical Center 127
Cape Cafe 316
Cape San Blas 315, 347
Cape San Blas Lighthouse 347
Capital Health Care Center 466
Capital Limousine 374
Capital Medical Society 467
Capital Par 433
Capital Rehabilitation Hospital 470
Capt. Anderson's 246
Capt. Anderson's Pier 287
Capt. Dukes Party Boat 206

506 •

INDEX

Captain Black's 287
Captain Black's Marine Boat Rentals
 and Dive Shop 314
Captain Dave's on the Gulf 153
Captain Dave's Restaurant
 & Marina on the Harbor 153
Captain Davis Dockside Restaurant
 & Lounge 247
Car Rentals 373
Car Show 76
Care Packages 399
Career Woman Fashions 395
Carlton, Governor Doyle 363
Carpenter's Creek Community 122
Carrabelle 339
Carrabelle Area Chamber of Commerce 343
Carrabelle Realty 340
Carriage Gate Shopping Center 395
Carriage Hills Family Care Center 126
Carriage Hills Realty, Inc. 222
Carriage Hills Realty South, Inc. 229
Carter-Howell-Strong Park 433
Casa Calderon Apartments 464
Casa de Cosas 106
Casino Beach 73
Casino Restaurant 46
Cassine Gardens 212
Cecil T. Hunter Municipal Pool 96
Center for Cancer Care 125
Center for Diagnostic Services 125
Centerville Care Center 466
Central Square 179
Century 21 Beach Realty, Inc. 302
Century 21 Four Winds Realty 117
Chapman Pond 433
Charley Mac's Restaurant & Lounge 385
Charlie's Grill 252
Charter Boats 90, 205
Charter Fishing 287
Chautauqua Festival 145, 195, 218
Chautauqua Vineyards 189
Cheese Barn 250
Chelsea Hairsmith Salon 395
Cherokee Park 434
Cherokee Reservation 191
Chester Pruitt Park 215
Chester Pruitt Recreation Center 213
Chez Pierre 377
Children's Parade 411
Children's Treasure Hunt
 and Sandcastle Contest 80
China Gourmet 377
Chinaberry Tree 476
Chip Lloyd's Photography 295
Chipley, W.D. 17
Choral Society of Northwest Florida 216
Choral Society of Pensacola 101
Christmas by Candlelight 199

Christmas By The Sea Program 199
Christmas Festival 193
Christmas on the Island 87
Christmas Parades 87, 88, 193, 199, 280
Christmas Walk 88
Chuck's Dive World 202
Chulamar 91
Church Street East Historic District 489
Cinco de Mayo 79
City Taxi 374
City-wide Easter Egg Hunt 412
Civil War 15, 142, 315, 359, 432, 433,
 434, 477, 479, 495, 496
Civil War Soldiers Museum 62
Clarion Suites Resort & Convention Center 45
Cleland Antiques 52
Clement's Antiques 179
Club at Hidden Creek 89, 118
Club Destin Resort 165
Clyde's & Costello's 385
Coast Line Shopping Guide 326
Coastal Property Services, Inc. 462
Coastal Systems Station 310
Coconut Bay Lounge 44
Coconut Creek Mini-Golf and Gran-Maze 274
Coconuts Comedy Club 44
Coffee Cup 35
Coldwell Banker Hartung
 and Associates, Inc. 462
Collectors Quarters 476
Colleges and Universities,
 Fort Walton Beach Area 219
Colleges and Universities,
 Panama City Beach Area 296
Colleges and Universities, Pensacola Area 110
Colleges and Universities, Tallahassee 450
Collins, Governor LeRoy 364
Collins Realty 337
Colonial Archaeological Trail 26, 61
Columns, The 403
Comedy Zone 250, 386
Comfort Inn 43
Commodore Condominiums 256
Community Centers 94, 212, 435
Community Realtors of Killearn, Inc. 462
Concert Tickets 94
Conde'-Charlotte Museum House 490
Condominiums 162, 254
Condos 47, 165
Confederate Salt Works 347
Connell & Manziek Realty Inc. 120
Conquistador Inn 160
Constitution Convention State
 Museum 314, 343
Coombs House Cottages 328
Coombs House Inn 328
Cordova Mall 50
Cordova Park 119

• 507

INDEX

Corinne Jones Center 95
Cornhusk & Creations 399
Corning Revere Factory Store 261
Cosmic Cat 399
Cottage Shoppe 391
Cottages 162, 165, 254
Cottages on Lake Ella 399
Cotton City Antique Mall 499
Cotton, Etc. 397
Cotton Landing 419
Country Club Park 434
Courthouse Antiques 476
Courtney's 395
Courtyard by Marriott 394
Cove Manor Retirement Center 303
Cow Haus 385
Crab Trap 151
Crafts 98
Crawfish Festival 97
Crawfordville 483
Creative Guild 108
Creative Senior Center 214
Creek Indians 353
Creekside Golf 89
Crestview Area Chamber of Commerce 143
Crestview Senior Center 232
Crestview Vocational-Technical Center 220
Criolla's 155
Crisis Lines 236, 307, 308
Crooked River Lighthouse 339
Crow's Nest Lounge 254
Crystal Cove at Sandestin 230
Cultural Arts Association 218
Cultural Center 483
Curiosity Rentals 93
Cypress Springs 265

D

Dade Street Community Center 436
Daffin Park 289
Dale Mabry Airport 364
Dance 98
Dance Classes 94
Dance for Spring 413
Dauphin Island 494
Dauphin Island Sea Lab 495
Days Inn - Destin 163
Daytrips, Tallahassee 473
de Galvez, General Bernardo 14
de Leon, Ponce 351
de Luna, Don Tristan 13, 27
de Luna Landing, Fiesta of Five Flags 80
de Narvaez, Panfilo 351, 431
de Soto, Hernando 351
De Tonti Square Historic District 489
Dead Lakes State Park 344
December on the Farm 416

Decemberfest 88
Deer Creek Bed & Breakfast 390
DeFuniak Springs 145
Delta Med of Florida 235
Depot Days 86
Designs & More 397
Destin 142, 144
Destin Beach Club Condominium 226
Destin Bridge Catwalk 210
Destin Diner 154
Destin Fireworks 193
Destin Fishing Museum 187
Destin Fishing Rodeo 194
Destin Holiday Beach Resort 166
Destin Hospital 234
Destin Ice Seafood Market 177
Destin King Mackerel Tournament 194
Destin Medical Center 234
Destin Racquet & Fitness Center 205
Destin Realty Inc. 227
Destin Seafood Festival 194
Destin Shark Fishing Tournament 194
Destin T-Shirt & Supply Co. 176
Destin White-Wilson Medical Center 234
Destination Thomasville Tourism Authority 483
Destiny Sailing Charters 288
Diablo Point 65
Dial-A-Ride 371
Dick Howser Stadium 440
Dillard's 395
Discovery Zone 395, 400
Dive Shops 286
Do It In The Sand Volleyball 76
Doak Campbell Stadium 440
Doc's 386
Dog Island 342
Dollar Car Rentals 3, 371
Dollarhide Music Center 103
Dolores' Sweet Shoppe 328
Dolphin Feeding Cruise 287
Donut Hole II Cafe & Bakery 158
Dooley's 392
Dooley's Downunder 386
Doolittle Memorial 183
Dorothy B. Oven Park 434
Dorr House 61
Down Under Dive Center 342
Downtown Arts District Association 108
Downtown Victorian Christmas 482
Dunes of Panama 256, 300
Dunes, The 45
DuVal, William 357

E

E-CHOTA Cherokee Reservation 191
E. Peck Green Park 434
E.S. Cobb Community Center 94

INDEX

Eagle Horizons, Inc. 205
EagleDome 440
Early Music Consort 102
Earth Day Celebrations 77, 78, 413
East End Deli 336
East Hill 119
East Pensacola Heights Center 95
Easter Egg Hunt 76, 94, 411
Eastpoint 330
Eastside Mario's 377
Eastside Psychiatric Hospital 470
Ebro Dog Track 265
Eden 113
Eden Condominium 48
Eden State Gardens 145, 189
Edgewater 302
Edgewater Beach Condominium 170, 225
Edgewater Beach Resort 166, 252, 299
Edgewater Services, Inc. 166
Edgewood Terrace 231
Edward Ball Nature Preserve 65
Edward Ball Wakulla Springs
    State Park 427, 484
Edwin Watts Golf Shop 90
Eglin Air Force Base 200, 238
Eglin Air Show 191
Eglin Reservation 204
Eichold Heustis Medical Museum
    of the South 492
El Governor Motel and Campground 313
Elberta, Ala. 500
Elberta Sausage Festival 75, 84
Eleni's Coffee & Tea Company 397
Elephant Walk 156
Elephant Walk Triathlon
    & Bay Towne Biathlon 198
Elite Guest House 121
Elite Street Limousine Service 374
Ell's Court On the Gulf, 340
Emerald Bay 224
Emerald Bay Golf & Country Club 204, 211
Emerald Coast Chef's Tasting 195
Emerald Coast Concert Association 216
Emerald Coast Convention
    & Visitors Bureau 143
Emerald Coast Diver's Den 286
Emerald Coast RV Resort 172
Emerald Coast Scuba School 208
Emerald Falls Family Entertainment Center 267
Emerald Isle Condominium 162
Emerald Surf 47
End O' the Alley 32
Endless Summer Condos 256
English Point 64
Eppes, Francis 357
ERA Apalach Real Estate 326, 328
Escambia Amateur Astronomer's
    Association 104

Escambia Bay 55
Escambia County Council on Aging, Inc. 123
Escambia County Transit System 4
Escape to Create 195
Estates at Hidden Creek 118
Ethnic/Cultural Arts 100
Evans House 390
Evenings in Olde Seville Square 80
Exchange Park 97
Executive Inn 44
Explore Center 490
Exploreum Museum of Discovery 490, 492
Expressions in Dance 98

F

Fairhope, Ala. 500
Falling Waters State Recreation Area 429
Family Expo 83
FAMU Essential Theatre 448
Fantasea Scuba Headquarters 208
Fantasy Properties, Inc. 313
Farley's Old and Rare Books 53
Farmer's Market 397
Fast Eddies Fun Center 92
Fat Tuesday 386
Fernleigh Ltd. 179
Ferry Park 214
Festa Italiana 192
Festivals and Special Events,
    Fort Walton Beach Ar 191
Festivals and Special Events,
    Panama City Beach Ar 275
Festivals and Special Events, Pensacola 73
Festivals and Special Events, Tallahassee 409
Festivity Factory 397
Fezler & Russell Real Estate, Inc. 462
Fiesta of Five Flags 80
Fine Arts Museum of the South 492
Firematics Competition 79
First Night Pensacola 108
First Presbyterian Church 403
First Seminole War 355
Fish Heads 154
Fishing 144, 185, 204, 210, 238, 263, 287,
    313, 344, 347, 417, 420, 421,
    422, 424, 431, 432, 438
Fishing, Charter Boats 287, 313
Fishing, Sport 144
Fishing Tournaments 80, 277
Five Flags Speedway 59
Flea Market 53
Flea Market Mobile 499
Flea Market Tallahassee 397, 400
Fletcher-Cantey 395
Florida A&M University 439, 450
Florida Caverns State Park 429
Florida Coastal Properties 340, 485

• *509*

INDEX

Florida Five   106
Florida Folk Festival   413
Florida Golf Outlet   283
Florida Linen Outlet   262
Florida Rails-to-Trails Program   426
Florida Seafood Festival   319, 414
Florida State Caverns   401
Florida State College for Women   364
Florida State Parks Guide   420
Florida State University   297, 440, 451
Florida State University Flying High Circus   411
Florida State University Gallery
 and Museum   443
Florida State University School of Dance   441
Florida State University School of Music   447
Florida Vietnam Veterans Memorial   403
Florida's Forgotten Coast   311
Flounder's Chowder & Ale House   40
FOCUS Center   181
Folk Festivals   413
Food Glorious Food   377, 397
Football   435
Fort Barrancas   57, 140
Fort Conde'   490
Fort Conde' Welcome Center   487
Fort Gadsden State Historic Site   344
Fort Gaines   495
Fort George   97
Fort McRee   15, 138
Fort Morgan   495
Fort Pickens   15, 56, 138
Fort Pickens Museum   56
Fort San Carlos de Barrancas   15
Fort Walton Beach   142
Fort Walton Beach Art Museum   184
Fort Walton Beach Care Center   236
Fort Walton Beach Chamber of Commerce   143
Fort Walton Beach Civic Auditorium   213
Fort Walton Beach Community Chorus   216
Fort Walton Beach Medical Center   233
Fort Walton Beach Municipal Course   201
Fort Walton Beach
 Municipal Tennis Center   202
Fort Walton Beach
 Senior Citizen's Center   231
Fort Walton Landing   214
Fort Walton Racquet Club   202
Fort Walton Yacht Club   196
Foster Tanner Fine Arts Gallery   443
Founaris Bros. Greek Restaurant   35
Fourth Avenue Recreation Center   436
Fourth of July Celebrations   81, 196, 413
Foxfire Hunting Preserve   483
Foxwood Country Club of Crestview   200
Frank Brown International
 Songwriters' Festival   87
Frank G. Brown Park   290
Frank Nelson, Jr. Park   289

Fred B. Hedrick Recreation Center   213
Freedmen's Bureau   362
FreeNet   368
Friary of Baptist Health Care   129
Fricker Center   95
Friends of the Library Book Sale   77
Friends of the Pensacola Public Library   101
Fritz, Nina   179
FSU Distinguished Lecture Series   449
FSU School of Theater   448
Fudpucker's Beachside Bar & Grill   146, 149

G

G.T. Henry's   498
Gaberonne Point   65
Gadsden County Committee of 100   475, 479
Gadsden County Courthouse   478
Gainey's Talquin Lodge   422
Gallery 75   328
Gallery in Gadsden   295
Gallery Nights   75, 81, 86, 295
Gallery of Fine Art   177
Garden, The   204, 211
Garnier's Beach Park   214
Garth's Antiques & Auction Gallery   106
Gaver's Bed and Breakfast   389
Gayfers   395
Gazebo Cafe   474
Genevieve Randolph Park   434
George Meginniss House   443
George Stone Area
 Vocational-Technical Center   111
Georgia Bell Dickinson   464
Geriatric Services   128
German-American Society of Pensacola   100
Geronimo   19
Gibson Inn   326
Glades at Hombre Golf Club   299
Glass Bottom Boats   185, 265
Glenwood Recreation Center   289
Goatfeathers Raw Bar & Restaurant   158
Golden East   378
Golf   89, 200, 204, 210, 281, 437
Golf Discount Center   283
Golf Shops   283
Golf Supplies and Equipment   90
Gorrie Square   326
Government   455
Governor Stone   326
Governor's Inn   392
Governor's Mansion   404
Governor's Square Mall   395
Grand Festival of Art   85
Grand Lagoon   55
Grand Oaks Ranch   272
Grand Old House Restaurant   482
Grand Victoria Inn   390

INDEX

Gray Line Tours 488
Grayton Beach 145
Grayton Beach Fine Arts Festival 196, 218
Grayton Beach State Recreation
    Area 173, 189, 212
Grayton Corner Cafe 158
Great Adventure Water Sports 284
Great Gulfcoast Arts Festival 85, 97, 108, 110
Great Southern Gumbo Cook-Off 195
Greek Food Festival 414
Greenhouse Restaurant 249, 252
Gregory House 433
Greyhound-Trailways Bus Lines 4, 371, 374
Guitar Association 103
Gulf Breeze 24, 55, 116
Gulf Breeze Area Chamber of Commerce 26
Gulf Breeze Arts, Inc. 106
Gulf Breeze Family Medical Center 127
Gulf Breeze Hospital 126
Gulf Coast Carriage Service 487
Gulf Coast Chorale 102
Gulf Coast Community College 296
Gulf Coast Immediate Care Center 235
Gulf Coast Offshore Powerboat Races 275
Gulf Coast Triathlon 277
Gulf Coast Weavers Guild 98
Gulf Convalescent Center 236
Gulf County Chamber of Commerce 316
Gulf Front Realty 229
Gulf Islands National Seashore 22, 56, 135
Gulf Shores Shrimp Festival 84
Gulf Specimen Marine Lab 484
Gulf Water Motel and Campground 340
Gulf Winds 47
Gulf World 266
Gulfaire Realty of Bay County, Inc. 313
Gulfarium 143, 181
Gull Point Center 95
Gull Point Performing Dancers, Inc. 98
Gymnastics 94

H

H&H Antiques 474
Hamilton's Seafood Restaurant & Lounge 244
Hampton Inn 253
Hang Gliding 238
Hansa Club 100
Happy Pelican Restaurant 334
Harambee Arts and
    Cultural Heritage Festival 409
Harbor Cove Charters 209
Harbor Docks 150
Harbor Docks Summer Open 193
Harbor Oaks Hospital 236
Harbour Towne 300
Harmony Shores Chorus of Sweet Adelines
    International 293

Harry A's Porch Club 334
Harry T's Boathouse 149
Hathaway Bridge Park 289
Haunted House Walking Tour
    of Seville Square 85
Havana 473
Havana Daydreamin', Inc. 474
Hayley's 498
HCA Gulf Coast Hospital 306
HCA Twin Cities Hospital 233
Health Care, Fort Walton Beach Area 233
Health Care, Panama City Beach Area 306
Health Care, Pensacola 125
Health Care, Tallahassee 467
Health Performance Center 127
Henderson Beach State Park 187
Henderson Park Inn 165
Henderson Park Townhomes 166
Hentz Park 290
Hepburn's 399
Heritage Health Care Center 466
Hertz Car Rentals 3, 371
Hickory Landing 419
Hidden Dunes 166, 170, 211, 225
Higher Education 110, 219, 296, 450
Hightide Restaurant,
    Lounge & Oyster Bar 148
Hiking 56, 173, 212, 263, 347, 349, 417,
    429, 431, 432, 433
Hilaman Park Municipal Golf Course 437
Hispanic Heritage Festival 84
Historic Downtown Dauphin Street 498
Historic Homes Tour 487
Historic Pensacola Preservation Board 104
Historic Pensacola Village 61
Historic Preservation Board 403
Historic Sites, Tallahassee 402
Historical Society Museum 183
History, Fort Walton Beach Area 142
History, Panama City 241
History, Pensacola 13
History, Tallahassee 351
Hitchcock Lake 419
Hog's Breath Saloon & Cafe 148
Holiday Golf & Tennis Club 281
Holiday Homecoming 482
Holiday Inn 159
Holiday Inn - Okaloosa Island 160
Holiday Inn Beach Resort 252
Holiday Inn Navarre Beach 46
Holiday Inn Northwest 393
Holiday Inn Parkway 393
Holiday Inn Pensacola Beach 46
Holiday Inn University Center 393
Holiday Inn University Mall 44
Holiday Isle Properties, Inc. 226
Holiday Travel Park 173
Holland, Governor Spessard 363

• 511

INDEX

Holley By The Sea 118
Hollywood & Memorial Park 214
Holt 69
Hombre Golf Club 281
Homes & Land of Tallahassee 461
Homestead Village 123
Honey-Bee Car Rentals 373
Hooked on Books 326
Hopkins House 29
Horse Shows 413
Horseback Riding 69, 427, 431
Horseback Trails 212
Hospitality Inn 44
Hospitals 233, 306, 467
Hotlines 236, 307, 308
HuManatee Festival 432
Hunting 69, 238, 420, 437, 438
Hurlburt Air Force Base 201
Hurlburt Field 239
Hydrospace Dive Shop 286

I

Ice Hockey 439
Ice Skating 416
iii s 179
Immediate Care Centers 126
Imogene Theatre and Milton Opera House 67
Indian Bayou Golf and Country Club 204
Indian Notions 398
Indian Shores 222
Indian Summer Seafood Festival 279
Indian Temple Mound Museum 183
Indianhead Acre Park 434
Ingram's Marina 422
International Billfish Tournament 82
International Fall Festival 85
Intracoastal Waterway 4, 55, 58
Inverness 120
Investors Realty of Tallahassee, Inc. 462
Island Echos Condominium 222
Island Emporium 337
Island Golf Center
    & Lost Lagoon Mini-Golf 201
Island Oasis 336
Island Shirt Company 337
Island Waverunner Tours & Lagoon Rentals 284
Islander's Surf & Sport 175, 177, 178
Italian Cultural Society
    of Northwest Florida, Inc 100
Ivy Rose Garden and Gifts 397

J

J. Patrick's Restaurant 314
J.W. Renfroe Pecan Company 51
Jackson, Andrew 355
Jake Gaither Community Center 436
Jake Gaither Golf Course 437
Jamie's French Restaurant 31
Japan Cultural Society
    of Northwest Florida, Inc. 100
Jason's & Jason's Petites 395
Jazz & Blues Festival 411
Jazz Jam 77
Jazz Society of Pensacola, Inc. 102
Jazzfest 110
JCPenney 395
Jeanie's Journey Travel
    & Adventure Company 336
Jefferson County Historical Society
    and Museum 476
Jefferson County Watermelon Festival 476
Jerry's Cajun Cafe & Market 36
Jerry's Drive Inn 33
Jet Drive Park 214
Jimbo's Beach Service 284
Jingle Bell Run 416
Joe Moody Harris Park 289
Joe Occhipinti's Big Band 102
Joe Patti's Seafood Co. 52
John Beasley Wayside Park 214
John G. Riley Park 434
John Hitzman Park 97
Joint, The 260
Joseph M. Endry Realty Company 120
Josephine's Bed and Breakfast 169
Josephine's Dining Room 157
Jubilee Beachside 40
Jubilee Lobster Fest 84
Jubilee Topside 38
Jubilee's Lobster Fest 79
Judy's Garden Cafe 147
Julee Cottage 61
Julia Mae's Seafood Restaurant 342
Junior Museum of Bay County 294

K

Kaleidoscope Dance Theatre 99, 294
Karate 95
Keeping Room 179
Kennel Club 59
Key Concepts 115
Key Sailing 93
Kidstuff 400
Killer Beads 260
Kitcho 378, 397
Knott House 435
Knott House Museum 404
Korbet's Restaurant of Mobile 497
Koucky Park 434

L

L. Pizitz & Co. 179

INDEX

La Fiesta 378
Labor Day Fireworks 82
Lads & Lassies Consignment 54
Lady Eventhia 205
Lafayette Park Community Center 436
Lagoon Cruise Lines M/V Stardancer 274
Lake Ella 434
Lake Ella Manor 465
Lake Huntington Park 290
Lake Jackson Mounds
        State Archaeological Site 421
Lake Miccosukee 475
Lake Talquin Recreation Area 421
Lakeview Center Inc. 129
Lamb's & Ivy 397
Lanark Village 342
Landmark Holiday Beach Resort 299
Land's End 113
Lapham-Patterson House 481
Largo Mar 255
Laura's Point 65
Lavalle House 61
Leaf Theatre 449, 478
Lear House 61
LeBleau's Cajun Kitchen 158
Leeside Inn & Marina 161
Leib & Associates Realty 114
LeMoyne Art Foundation 443
Lenora Charles Antiques 474
Lenora Charles Cafe 474
Leon Sinks 419
Leroy Collins Leon County Public Library 443
Levy Park 434
Lewis Home 435
Lewis Park 434
Lieutenant Governor's
        Public House and Grill 378
Life Management Center
        of Northwest Florida, Inc. 305, 308
Lifeguards 5
Lighthouse Realty 337
Lighthouses 57
Limousine Service 374
Lin-C-Ann 206
Linda Watson Realty Inc. 226
Linda's Trading Post 342
Lindz's A Place of Christmas 176
Lissie Petites 397
Little League 214
Little St. George Island 339
Liza Jackson Park 214
Lo-Baby 91
Long Dream Gallery 328
Lost Creek Stables 484
Lost Lagoon Mini-Golf 201
Louisiana Lagniappe 153
Lucky's Car Rentals 373
Lucy Ho's Bamboo Garden 379

Lyn's Fine Arts Gallery 295

M

Mabry Village Apartments 465
Maclay State Gardens 422
Magnolia Beach RV Park 257
Magnolia Bluff and Beach 65
Magnolia Cemetery 491
Magnolia Springs, Ala. 500
Mahan Medical Walk-In 470
Majette Dunes Golf and Country Club 281
Malcolm Yonge Center 96
Mandarin Chinese Restaurant 395
Manufacturer's Outlet Center 174, 262
Marathons 74
Marcus Pointe Golf Club 89
Mardi Gras 74
Mardi Gras Celebration 74
Marier Memorial Park 214
Marina Cafe 151
Marina Civic Center 295
Marina Oyster Barn 34
Marine Life 6
Marine Supplies 208
Market at Sandestin 179
Market Country Restaurant 482
Market Days 415
Market Square Shopping Center 397
Marketbasket 87
Marks Realty 328
Marriott's Grand Hotel 500
Martha Green Gallery 179
Martial Arts 435
Martin Luther King Jr. Parade 74
Martin Theatre 294
Mary Ella Villa Retirement Center 303
Mary's Place 476
Maxine's of Destin 175
Mayfest 193
McCarty Park 434
McGuire's Irish Pub and Brewery 33
McKenzie Park 289
MDLine 128
Meadowbrooke Terrace 465
Meals on Wheels 123, 305
Medical Care, Fort Walton Beach Area 233
Medical Care, Panama City Beach
        Area 306
Medical Care, Pensacola 125
Medical Care, Tallahassee 467
Medical Center Clinic 126
Medical Center Clinic, P.A. 128
Medical Centers 233, 306
Melissa's 482
Melting Pot 148, 379
Memorial Day Sailing Regatta 196
Mental Health Services 128, 307

• 513

INDEX

Mesquite Charlie's 35
Mexico Beach 311
Mexico Beach Chamber of Commerce 313
Miccosukee Hills 465
Milestone 119
Military, Fort Walton Beach Area 238
Military, Panama City 309
Military, Pensacola 130
Mill Bakery and Eatery 380
Millard J. Noblin Realty, Inc. 462
Miller Lite Pro-Beach Volleyball Tournament 78
Milton 24, 55
Milton Depot 67
Milton Historic District 66
Milton L&N Depot 109
Milton Opera House 109
Mimosa Park 215
Mini-Masquers, Inc. 105
Miracle Hill 466
Miracle Strip Amusement Park 242, 269
Miracle Strip Aviation 3
Misty 206
Mobile, Ala. 487
Mobile Bay Ferry 488
Mobile Historic Homes Tour 74
Mole Hole 175
Mom & Dad's Italian Restaurant 482
Monarch Butterfly 198, 345
Monarch Realty at Seaside 170, 229
Montage 119
Montego Bay 247
Montgomery & Associates, Inc. 462
Montgomery Realtors 117
Montgomery Ward 395
Monticello 475
Monticello Opera House 476
Monticello-Jefferson County Chamber of Commerce 477
Moody's 205
Moon, The 445
Moon's 398
Moore, Governor James 352
Moors, The 89, 120
Mostly Muffins 498
Motel St. Joe & Restaurants 314
Mounir's 380
Movie Theaters 395
Mule Days 415
Mullet Toss 78
Murat, Prince Achille 357
Murphy House 435
Museum of Commerce 61
Museum of Florida History 400, 406, 443
Museum of Industry 61
Museum of Man in the Sea 272, 294
Museum of the City of Mobile 492
Museum of the Sea and Indian 186

Museum Shop 397
Music 101
Music at Christ Church 87, 102
Music Study Club of Pensacola 102
Mustard Tree 380
Mutual UFO Network 70
My Bookstore 51
My Favorite Things 397
My Secret Garden 474
Myers Park 434
Myra Jean's 484
Myrtlewood Plantation 438, 483

N

Narcissus Swimwear and Lingerie 395
National & U.S. Open Water Ski Tournament 197
National Car Rentals 3, 371
National High Magnetic Field Laboratory 452
National Museum of Naval Aviation 57, 104, 131
National Parks 417
National Society of Colonial Dames of America 490
Native American Heritage Festival 414
Natural Bridge Battlefield State Historic Site 410, 424
Naval Air Station Pensacola 18
Naval Air Station, Pensacola 130
Naval Aviation Depot 132
Naval Live Oaks Area 56, 138
Navarre Agency, Inc. 47
Navarre Beach 24, 117
Navarre Beach Chamber of Commerce 26
Navarre Beach Family Campground 49
Navarre Family Medicine Center 127
Navarre Villas 47
Negro Fort 344
New Age Shop 53
New Capitol 455, 456
New Leaf Cafe 397
New World Landing 29, 44
Newbill Collection by the Sea 179
Newman-Dailey Resort Properties, Inc. 226
Newport Recreation Area 420, 485
Nice Picture Company and Art Gallery 474
Nice Twice 398
Niceville-Valparaiso-Bay Chamber of Commerce 143
Niceville/Valparaiso Christmas Parade 193
Niceville/Valparaiso Fireworks Display 192
Nicholson Farmhouse 380, 475
Night Moves 260
Nightingale & Associates, Inc. 328
Nightlife, Fort Walton Beach Area 146
Nightlife, Panama City Beach Area 244
Nightlife, Pensacola 28

514 •

INDEX

Nightlife, Tallahassee 383
Nightown 154
Nike Tour Panama City Beach Golf Classic 275
Nino's 380
Nomads 444
Norma's Cafe 30
North Davis Family Medicine Center 127
North Florida Fair 414
North Florida Surgery Center 128
North Hill Hideaway 46
North Hill Preservation District 17, 21, 63
North Okaloosa Medical Center 233
Northwest Florida Ballet 216
Northwest Florida Creek Indian Council 100
Northwest Florida Home Health Agency 235
Northwest Florida Porcelain Artists 106
Northwest Florida Symphony Orchestra 217
Northwest Regional Library System 292
Nu-Life 395
Nucleus Group 449
Nursing and Convalescent Centers 236
Nursing Homes 466
Nutcracker Ballet 88, 416

O

Oak Ridge Townhouses 465
Oakland Basin 67
Oakland Terrace Park 289
Oakleigh Garden Historic District 489
Oakleigh Mansion 489
Oasis Bar 252
Ocean Opry 271
Ochlockonee River State Park 420, 431, 485
Okaloosa Coordinated Transportation 232
Okaloosa County Air Terminal 3
Okaloosa County Council on Aging 232
Okaloosa Film Commission 218
Okaloosa Island 138, 159
Okaloosa Island Pier 204
Okaloosa Symphony Orchestra 213, 217
Okaloosa-Walton Community College 110, 219
Okaloosa-Walton Historical Society 191
Oktoberfest 192
Old Armory Gallery 444
Old Brick Road 67
Old Capitol 444, 456
Old City Cemetery 406
Old Confederate Salt Works 315
Old Destin Post Office Museum 187
Old Fort Park 434
Old Spanish Trail Festival 191
Old Thyme Cafe 474
Old Time Havana Day 475
Old Time/Blue Grass Festival 414
Old Town Cafe 381
Old Town Trolley 374

Old World Folkdancers 99
Oldfield Interiors 397
Olin Marler's Charter Service 206
Olive Garden 397
Optimist Park 97, 434
Orange Beach Marina 82
Our Cottage on the Park 391
Owl Cigar Company Shade Leaf Building 478
Oyster Cove Seafood Bar & Grill and Cajun Cafe 336

P

Page & Palette 51
Painted Pony 331
Palace Saloon 386
Palafox Place Historic and Business District 21, 62
Palapa Bar and Grill 252
Palm Beach Club 116
Palmer Munroe Community Center 436
Palmyra Gallery 328
Panacea 483
Panama Brass Quintet 293
Panama City Beach Fishing Classic 278
Panama City Beach KOA 257
Panama City Counseling Center 307
Panama City Dive Center 286
Panama City Downtown Arts District 295
Panama City Mall 262
Panama City Youth Orchestra 293
Panama City-Bay County Municipal Airport 3
Panhandle Writers' Guild 292
Papa Pirate's Tiki Bar 342
Parade of Homes 79
Parades 411, 413, 415
Paradise Cafe 336
Paradise Grill & Bar 381
Paradise Scooter & Bicycle Rental 94
Paradise Watersports 202, 210
Parisian 395
Parks and Recreation, Fort Walton Beach Area 200
Parks and Recreation, Panama City Beach Area 281
Parks and Recreation, Pensacola Area 89
Parks and Recreation, Tallahassee 417
Parkway Shopping Center 397
Pastel Society of North Florida 218
Patchouli's 179
Patients First Medical Centers 470
Patrone's 179
Paul Brent Design Studio and Gallery 262, 295
Pavilion, The 126, 129
Pavilions, The 395
Peachtree Place 301

• 515

INDEX

Pebble Hill Plantation 481, 482
Pebble Ridge 120
Pediatric Extra Hours at Sacred Heart 127
Pedlers Antique Mall 397
Peggy's Fine Arts 395
Pelican Inn 343
Pelican Point Golf Course 283
Pensacola 24, 118, 356
Pensacola & Atlantic Railroad 64
Pensacola Area Chamber of Commerce 26
Pensacola Aviation 3
Pensacola Bay 55
Pensacola Beach 24, 55, 73, 115
Pensacola Beach Air Show 81
Pensacola Beach Chamber of Commerce 26
Pensacola Beach Fishing Pier 64
Pensacola Beach Properties, Inc. 47
Pensacola Beach Realty, Inc. 47, 116
Pensacola Big Game Fishing Club 80
Pensacola Boulevard Family Care Center 126
Pensacola Christian College 111
Pensacola Convention
  & Visitor Information Center 73
Pensacola Fiesta Barbershop Chorus 102
Pensacola Grand Hotel 44
Pensacola Greyhound Track 58
Pensacola GuitarEnsemble and Society 103
Pensacola Heritage Foundation 21, 109
Pensacola Historic Village 104
Pensacola Historical Museum 63
Pensacola Historical Society 21, 105
Pensacola International Billfish Tournament 80
Pensacola Interstate Fair 85
Pensacola JazzFest 77, 102
Pensacola Junior College 110
Pensacola Junior College Dance Theatre 99
Pensacola Junior College Guitar Association 103
Pensacola Junior College Lyceum 109
Pensacola Little Theatre, Inc. 105
Pensacola Mining
  and Water Ballet Authority 105
Pensacola Museum of Art 63, 107
Pensacola Music Teachers Association 103
Pensacola Naval Air Station 132
Pensacola Opera, Inc. 105
Pensacola Regional Airport 2
Pensacola Special Steppers, Inc. 99
Pensacola Sports Association 74
Pensacola Summer Music Festival 102
Pensacola Symphony Children's Chorus 103
Pensacola Symphony Orchestra 104
Pensacola Tourism and Convention Center 55
Penthouse Lounge 46
Per-spi-cas-ity 179
Perdido Bay Family Care Center 126
Perdido Bay Resort 90
Perdido Key 24, 55, 113, 136
Perdido Key Area Chamber of Commerce 26

Perdido Key State Recreation Area 57
Perdido Pass Marina 91
Perdido Sun 114
Perdido Sun Condominiums 48
Perri's Italian Restaurant 147
Perry's Seafood House
  and Gazebo Oyster Bar 35
Philippine Cultural Society, Inc. 100
Phineas Phoggs 32
Phoenix Fire Museum 493
Phyrst Grill 397
Physician Care 470
Physician Referral Services 128, 235, 236, 467
Physicians' Home Care 235
Picnic Areas 345, 347, 349, 417, 425, 429, 431, 432, 433, 434, 435
Picnics in the Park 77
Picnics in the Plaza 96
Pier 99 Beachfront Motel 253
Pillars, The 497
Pine Forest Family Care Center 126
Pine Tree Place 302
Pineapple Willies Bar & Grill 248, 253
Pinnacle Port 300
Pirates' Bay Condo & Hotel Marina 160
Pirate's Island Adventure Golf 270
Planet Party 413
Planned Furnishings 397
Play It Again Sports 90
Players Club at Summerbrooke 437
Playgrounds 433, 434, 435
Playwright's Repertory Festival 106
Plaza Ferdinand 96
Pleasure Island Waterpark 185
Poarch Creek Indians
  Thanksgiving Day Pow Wow 86
Point Clear, Ala. 500
Point Washington 145
Polar Bear Dip 73
Polytactyl Jazz Combo 294
Ponce de Leon Springs
  State Recreation Area 431, 434
Pontoon Boat Rentals 203
Port City Brewery & Eatery 498
Port St. Joe 313, 343
Port St. Joe Chamber of Commerce 314
Porter's Court 254
Portside Resort 256, 299
Portside Villas 47
Posey's Beyond the Bay Motel
  and Restaurant 484
Posey's Oyster Bar 381, 484
Pre-Easter Egg Hunt 76
Premier Townhouses 256
Preserve, The 301
Professional Realty of Pensacola Beach 48
Psychiatric Counseling 307
Punta Clara Kitchen 500

INDEX

Puppet Factory 105

Q

Quail Ridge Landing 117
Quarter Moon Import Shop 399
Quayside Market 54
Quick Snaps 260
Quietwater Beach 6, 73
Quina House 61
Quincy 473, 477
Quincy Music Theatre 449, 478
Quincyfest 414, 478
Quincy's Victorian Christmas Stroll 416

R

Raccoon River Resort 257
Racquetball 435
Radisson Hotel 392
Rainbow Inn 328
Ralph D. Turlington
    Florida Education Center 459
Ramada Bayview 45
Ramada Beach Resort 161
Ramada Inn Beach 254
Ramada Inn Tallahassee 392
Ramada Resort 159
Ramsgate Harbour 256
Rancho Inn 328
Rape Crisis Center 129
Rattlesnake Roundup 409
Re/Max Realty 463
Readers Showcase 101
Real Estate Book of Tallahassee 461
Real Estate Companies 114, 116, 117, 120, 222, 226, 229, 302
Real Estate, Fort Walton Beach Area 221
Real Estate House Inc. 116
Real Estate, Panama City Beach Area 298
Real Estate, Pensacola Area 112
Real Estate, Tallahassee 460
Realty One Services Inc. 227
Recreation, Fort Walton Beach Area 200
Recreation, Panama City Beach Area 281
Recreation, Pensacola 89
Recreation, Tallahassee 417
Red Sticks, Creek Indians 355
Redfish Run 322
Regattas 196, 412
Regency Towers 302
Rehabilitation Institute of West
    Florida 126, 128
Rendezvous Restaurant 476
Rental Guide of Tallahassee 461
Resort Realty 337
Resort World Realty 302
Restaurants, Fort Walton Beach Area 146
Restaurants, Moblie 496
Restaurants, Panama City Beach Area 244
Restaurants, Pensacola 28
Restaurants, Tallahassee 375
Retirement Center of Panama City 304
Retirement, Fort Walton Beach Area 230
Retirement, Panama City Beach Area 303
Retirement, Pensacola 121
Retirement, Tallahassee 464
Reynalds Music House 103
Rheinauer's 397
Richards - DAR House 490
Riedel House 388
Rivard of South Walton 170
Rivendell 236, 307
River Gardens 65
Riverfest 81
Riverfront Restaurant 328
Riverlily 326
Riverwalk Fine Arts Show 107
Riviera Centre Factory Stores 50, 499
Robert Moore & Co.
    Christmas Town & Village 499
Rock Point 65
Rocky Bayou State Recreation Area 183
Rocky Top 92
Rose Festival 482
Rosie O'Grady's 32
Roussos Seafood Restaurant & Catering 496
Rubyfruit Books 398
RV Parks 48, 172, 257

S

Sabine Yacht & Racquet Club 116
Sacred Heart Hospital 125
Sacred Heart Surgical Center 127
Sailing South 205
Salinas Park 347
San Blas Lighthouse 315
San de Luna 115
San Dollar 47
San Luis Archaeological and Historic Site 407
San Luis Heritage Festival 414
San Luis Mission Park 435
San Marcos de Apalache 483
San Marcos de Apalache
    State Historic Site 427, 431
Sand Dollar 302
Sand Dollar Restaurant 314
Sandcastle Shores 231
Sandcastle Shores at Sandestin 237
Sanders Beach Center 95
Sandestin 228
Sandestin Beach Hilton Golf
    & Tennis Resort 168, 196, 210
Sandestin Beach Hilton Resort Rentals 212
Sandestin Bike Rental 212

• 517

INDEX

Sandestin Cup 196
Sandestin Professional Grass Court
    Tournament Cham 196
Sandestin Resort 168
Sandestin Resort Rentals 212
Sandestin Tennis Center 211
Sandestin Wine Festival 196
Sandpiper Cove 167, 225
Sandshaker Lounge,
    Package Store & Sandwich Shop 38
Sans Souci 47
Santa Fe Depot 177
Santa Rosa Art Association 107
Santa Rosa County Chamber of Commerce 26
Santa Rosa Fair 82
Santa Rosa Golf & Beach Club 210, 211
Santa Rosa Historical Society, Inc. 67, 109
Santa Rosa Island 56, 73, 136, 145
Santa Rosa Mall 174
Saturday in the Park
    Concert Series 76, 79, 191
Scenic Highway Family Medicine Center 127
Scenic Highway Historic Trail 64
Scenic Hills Country Club 90
Scholarship Arts and Crafts 218
Schooner's 246
Science & Space Theatre 104
Scott Tennis Center 96
Scottyboat Rentals Inc. 283
Scratch Ankle Festival 75
Scuba 202, 208, 286
Scuba Shack Charters 90
Scuba Tech 209
Sea Oats Condominium 162
Sea Screamer 207, 266
Seabreeze Park 215
Seachase Condominiums 255
Seafood Festival 84
Seafood the Apalachicola Way 331
Seagrove Beach 144
Seagrove Villas Bike Rental 212
Seahorse Gift and Florist 328
Sears 395
Sears Rental (Cars) 373
Seascape Golf & Racquet Club 211
Seascape Resort & Conference Center 169
Seaside 144, 159, 172, 178, 195, 211, 229
Seaside Beach Rentals 212
Seaside Bike Rental 212
Seaside Concert Series 198
Seaside Institute 198
Seaside Writer's Conference 198
Seaspray Condominiums 162
Seaweed 7
Seawind Medical Clinic 307
Second Seminole War 358
Seeing Red Weekend 198
Seminole Golf Course and Country Club 437

Senior Care Properties 330
Senior Support Services 123, 231, 305
Serendipity Cottage 391
Sertoma's July 4th 81
Seville Historic District 61
Seville Quarter 32
Seville Square 96
Shades 156
Shalimar Pointe Golf and Country Club 201
Shalimar Pointe Tennis Center 202
Shark Tournament 277
Sharon's Place 331
Shaun S. Donahoe Realty 328
Shell Island 265, 287
Shell Island Steaks at Sunset 278
Shell Oyster Bar 381
Shell Point Resort 485
Sheraton Tallahassee 392
Sherman Walk-In Center and Skin Clinic 470
Ships Chandler 178, 208
Shipwreck Island Water Park 269
Shipwreck Shirts 260
Shoal River Country Club 201
Shopping, Fort Walton Beach Area 174
Shopping, Moblie 498
Shopping, Panama City Beach Area 259
Shopping, Pensacola 50
Shopping, Tallahassee 395
Shoreline Towers 166
Shoreline Village Mall 175
Showtown Swap Shop & Flea Market 175
Shuffleboard 95
Sightseeing Cruises 287
Silks Food and Spirits 386
Silver Bucket 157
Silver Lake 417
Silver Sands Factory Stores 176
Silver Slipper 381
Simon-Ridgeway House 476
Ski Breeze Campground 316
Skopelos On the Bay 29
Smith's 175
Snappy Car Rentals 373
Snorkeling 202, 208
Snow Ball Derby 59
Snow Fest 73
Soccer 435
Society for Creative Anachronism 109
Softball 97, 289, 434, 435
Someone's In the Kitchen 397
Somewhere Else 389, 476
Sopchoppy 483
Sound Restaurant and Lounge 147
Soundside Holiday Beach Resort 48
South Santa Rosa Welcome Center 26
South Side 498
South Walton 142, 144
South Walton Sportfest Weekends 198

INDEX

Southside Park 435
Spanish Trail Family Medical Center 127
Spec's Music 397
Spectator Sports, Tallahassee 439
Spelunking 265
Spinnaker 248
Sport Fishing 144
Sportfest Weekends 198
Sports, Spectator 439
Sportsman's Lodge Motel & Marina 331
Spring Break 74, 275
Spring Farm Days 411
Spring Festival of the Arts 276
SpringFest 76, 110
Springtacular Children's Parade 411
Springtime Tallahassee 411, 435
St. Andrew Bay Real Estate, Inc. 302
St. Andrew Bay Resort Management, Inc. 256
St. Andrew's Society
    of Pensacola, Florida, Inc. 100
St. Andrew's Society
    of Pensacola Scottish Country 100
St. Andrews State Recreation Area 6, 257, 263
St. Anne's Round-Up 84
St. Augustine 356
St. George Inn 338
St. George Island 333
St. George Island Beach Rentals 349
St. George Island
    Business Owners Association 339
St. George Island Chili Cookoff 336, 411
St. George Island State Park 333, 347
St. Johns Cemetery 406
St. Joseph Peninsula State Park 345
St. Mark Lighthouse 419
St. Marks 483
St. Marks National Wildlife Refuge 419, 484
St. Martin Beachwalk Villas 224
St. Mary's Productions 106
St. Michael's Cemetery 61
St. Patrick's Day Celebration
    and Kite Contest 75
St. Vincent Island 316
St. Vincent National Wildlife Refuge 316
Starboard Village 115
Starlite Lounge 252
State Government 455
State of Florida Aging and Adult Services 232
State Supreme Court 459
Stateline Bungee 210
Stephen C. Smith Memorial Regatta 412
Storybook Gallery 52
Strauss Gallery 397
Streetwear 176
Strega Nona's Bakery & Cafe 28
Student Writer's Network 101
Substance Abuse Services 128, 307
Subway Bienville 498

Sue Vaneer's 178
Sugar Beach Condominiums 300
Summer Music Camp Program 447
Summer Properties of Cape San Blas, Inc. 316
Summer Swamp Stomp 413
Summerhouse 256
Summer's Landing 304
Summerspell 165
Summit 302
Sun Dunes 47
Sun Swept 302
Sunbird 302
Suncoast Realty 337
Sundance Agency Inc. 223
Sundestin 166
Sundog Books 178
Sunny Hills Golf Course 283
Sunset Grill and Pub 252
Sunset Limited Amtrak Service 4, 371
Sunspot Realty 302
Surf Dweller Condominium 222
Surfside Inn 313
SurgiCare 128
Susina Plantation Inn 391
Sweet Jody 5 207
Sweetbay Swamp 435
Swimming 347, 417, 424, 429, 431, 432,
    434, 435
Swine Times 415
Sylvan Lake 433

T

T-Shirt Cellar 260
T.T. Wentworth, Jr. Florida State Museum 61
Tabanelli & Lee 399
Taekwondo 94
Tails & Tweeds 395
Talbots 397
Tallahassee - St. Marks Historic
    Railroad State Trail 426, 484
Tallahassee Area Visitor
    Information Center 456
Tallahassee Bach Parley, Inc. 447
Tallahassee Ballet Company 441
Tallahassee Board of Realtors 460
Tallahassee Builders Association 460
Tallahassee Cataract Surgery Center 472
Tallahassee Chamber of Commerce 367
Tallahassee Commercial Airport 371
Tallahassee Community Chorus 447
Tallahassee Community College 440, 454
Tallahassee Community College
    West End Players 448
Tallahassee Community Hospital 467
Tallahassee Convalescent Home 466
Tallahassee FreeNet 400
Tallahassee Kennel Club Dog Show 409

• 519

INDEX

Tallahassee Little Theatre 448
Tallahassee Mall 395
Tallahassee Memorial
    Regional Medical Center 466, 467
Tallahassee Motor Hotel 394
Tallahassee Museum of History and Natural
    Science 400, 407, 410
Tallahassee Music Guild 447
Tallahassee Orthopedic Center 472
Tallahassee Parks
    and Recreation Department 435
Tallahassee Regional Airport 364, 371
Tallahassee Symphony Orchestra 448
Tallahassee Walk-In Medical Center 470
Tallahassee-Leon County Civic Center 445
Tallahassee-Leon County Civic Center
    Broadway Series 448
Tallahassee/Leon County Civic Center 440
TalTran Bus Line 371, 374
Tanning Tips 6
Taxi Service 3, 374
Taxi's Diner 250
Telephone Counseling Referral 467
"Tell"Ahassee Tale-Tellin'Time 413
Tennis 96, 196, 202, 205, 211, 289, 434, 435
Tennis Tournaments 196
Teresa Village 230
Terrace Court Restaurant 252
Texas Saloon and Dance Hall 146
Thanksgiving Day Pow Wow 86
Theo Docie Bass Recreation Center 213
Thomas County Historical Museum 481
Thomasville, Georgia 479
Thomasville Rose Festival 412
Thomasville Rose Test Garden 483
Thomasville's Victorian Christmas 416
Thompson's Bayou 65
Three Georges Southern Chocolates 498
Three Rivers State Park 432
Thunderbirds 250
Ticketmaster Outlets 94
Tides 5
Tiger Point Family Care Center 126
Tiger Point Golf & Country Club 90
Time Zones 9
Timucuan Indians 351
TNT Hideaway 484
Tom Brown Park 435
Tom Todd Realty 316
Tomahawk Landing 69
Tooley Street 176
Top of the Gulf 302
Tops'l Beach and Racquet Club 170, 211
Tops'l Beach Manor 225
Torreya State Park 432
Toucan's 313
Tour of Homes & Holiday Craft Show 416

Tours, Boat 427
Town & Country Plaza 50
Towne Gallery 445
Townhomes 47, 162, 165, 254
Track Family Recreation Center 186
Trader Jon's 32
Trader Rick's Surf Shop 259
Trail & Ski 398
Train Service 374
Transportation, Beaches Area 1
Transportation To Tallahassee 371
Trauma Recovery Center 129
Treasure Island King Mackerel Tournament 278
Treasure Ship 245
Treaty of 1814 355
Treaty of Ghent 345
Treaty of Paris 14
Triathlons 192, 198
Tristan Realty, Inc. 116
Tristan Towers 47, 115
Troy State University 219
Truesdell Park 289
Tubing 92, 203, 265
Turtle Watch 197, 277
Twelve Oaks 128, 307
Two Gulls Gifts 342
Two Gulls Two 337
Tyndall Air Force Base 309

U

U.S. Coast Guard Station 133
U.S. Navy Demonstration Squadrons 132
UFOs 70
Ugly Duckling Car Rentals 373
Under Glass Framery 295
Undertows 5
Union Bank Building 408
Uniques and Antiques 326
Universities, Fort Walton Beach Area 219
Universities, Panama City Area 296
Universities, Pensacola Area 110
Universities, Tallahassee 450
University Mall 50
University of West Florida 65, 106, 110, 219
University of West Florida Art Gallery 107
University Theatre 106
Untitled II 108
Upstairs Clubhouse and Lounge 252
USS *Alabama* Battleship Memorial Park 493

V

Vacation Cottages 47
Valparaiso Senior Center 232
Verandas, The 397
Vesta Heights Park 215
Veterans' Day Parade 86

INDEX

Veteran's Memorial Park   60
VF Factory Outlet   175
Victorian Rose Antiques   499
Villa Russ Park   215
Village at Sandestin   236
Village Commons   397
Village Realty East   223
Vinyl Fever   399
Visitor Information   143, 367
Visual Arts   106
Visual Arts Center of Northwest Florida   295
Vocational-Technical Schools   219
Volleyball   76, 78, 434, 435

W

Wakulla County   483
Wakulla County Chamber of Commerce   485
Wakulla Springs Lodge
    and Conference Center   429
Wal-Mart   397
WalkAmerica   410
Walker Ford Community Center   436
Walker Library   408
Walking Tours   322
Wall South   60, 96
Wallpaper It Now   395
Walters, Ed and Frances   70
Walton County Fourth of July   197
Walton County Vocational-Technical
    School   220
War of 1812   14
Warehouse, The   387
Warrington Family Medical Center   127
Warrington Primary Care   127
Water Ski Tournaments   197, 198
Watercrest   300
Watermelon Festival   413
Watersport Rentals   93, 202, 209
Watersport/Beach Rentals   283
Waterworks, The   387
Waverly Pond Park   435
Waverunner & Jet Ski Rentals   93
Weaver's Cottage   61
Weichman's All Seasons Restaurant   497
West East Hill Preservation District   64
West End Players   454
West Florida Advertising Council   108
West Florida Cancer Institute   126
West Florida Home Health Care   307

West Florida Literary Federation, Inc.   101
West Florida Railroad Museum   67, 86
West Florida Regional Library   101
West Florida Regional Medical Center   126
West Pensacola Medical Center   127
West Side Family Medicine Center   127
Westminster Oaks   465
Westwood Retirement Communities   230
Whistle Stop Antiques and Collectibles   342
White Sands Manor   230
White Swan Cafe   382
White Swan Restaurant   397
White Wine and Music Festival   196
White-Wilson Medical Center   234
Whitehead Lake   419
Whiting Field   133
Wildland Expeditions   494
Wildlife Gallery   397
Wildlife Rescue and Sanctuary   59
William Lanier "Red" Barber
    Memorial Garden   434
Wine Festival   82
Winston Cup All-Pro   59
Winter Bird Count   73
Winter Festivals   416, 424, 435
Winthrop Park   435
Wintzell's Oyster House   497
Wirick-Simmons House   476
Women's Resource Center   125
Woodmont Retirement Community   466
World's Smallest Police Station   340
Wright Lake   419
Writers in Service to Education   101
Writer's Workshop   101

Y

Yacht Restaurant   34
Yachties'   178, 208
Yammassee Indians   353
Yellow Cab   374
Yellow Fever   17, 330, 357
Yent Bayou Properties   340
Yianni's Cafe   387
Young Actors Theatre   449

Z

Zoos   65, 270

• 521

ORDER FORM
Fast and Simple!

Mail to:
Insiders Guides®, Inc.
P.O. Drawer 2057
Manteo, NC 27954

Or:
for VISA or
Mastercard orders call
1-800-765-BOOK

Name _____
Address _____
City/State/Zip _____

Qty.	Title/Price	Shipping	Amount
	Insiders' Guide to Richmond/$12.95	$2.50	
	Insiders' Guide to Williamsburg/$12.95	$2.50	
	Insiders' Guide to Virginia's Blue Ridge/$12.95	$2.50	
	Insiders' Guide to Virginia's Chesapeake Bay/$12.95	$2.50	
	Insiders' Guide to Washington, DC/$12.95	$2.50	
	Insiders' Guide to Charlotte/$14.95	$2.50	
	Insiders' Guide to North Carolina's Triangle/$14.95	$2.50	
	Insiders' Guide to North Carolina's Outer Banks/$12.95	$2.50	
	Insiders' Guide to Wilmington, NC/$12.95	$2.50	
	Insiders' Guide to North Carolina's Crystal Coast/$12.95	$2.50	
	Insiders' Guide to Charleston, SC/$12.95	$2.50	
	Insiders' Guide to Myrtle Beach/$12.95	$2.50	
	Insiders' Guide to Mississippi/$12.95 (8/94)	$2.50	
	Insiders' Guide to Orlando/$12.95	$2.50	
	Insiders' Guide to Sarasota/Bradenton/$12.95 (8/94)	$2.50	
	Insiders' Guide to Northwest Florida/$12.95 (7/94)	$2.50	
	Insiders' Guide to Lexington, KY/$12.95	$2.50	
	Insiders' Guide to Louisville/$12.95 (12/94)	$2.50	
	Insiders' Guide to the Twin Cities/$12.95 (12/94)	$2.50	
	Insiders' Guide to Boulder/$12.95 (11/94)	$2.50	
	Insiders' Guide to Denver/$12.95 (11/94)	$2.50	
	Insiders' Guide to The Civil War (Eastern Theater)/$12.95	$2.50	
	Insiders' Guide to Western North Carolina/$12.95 (2/95)	$2.50	
	Insiders' Guide to Atlanta/$12.95 (2/95)	$2.50	

Payment in full(check or money order) must accompany this order form.
Please allow 2 weeks for delivery.

N.C. residents add 6% sales tax _____

Total _____

Who you are and what you think is important to us.

Fill out the coupon and we'll give you an Insiders' Guide® for half price ($6.48 off)

Which book(s) did you buy? _____

Where do you live? _____

In what city did you buy your book? _____

Where did you buy your book?   ( ) catalog   ( ) bookstore   ( ) newspaper ad   ( ) retail shop   ( ) other

How often do you travel?   ( ) yearly   ( ) bi-annually   ( ) quarterly   ( ) more than quarterly

Did you buy your book because you were   ( ) moving   ( ) vacationing   ( ) wanted to know more about your home town   ( ) other

Will the book be used by a   ( ) family   ( ) couple   ( ) individual   ( ) group

What is your annual income?   ( ) under $25,000   ( ) $25,000 to $35,000   ( ) $35,000 to $50,000   ( ) $50,000 to $75,000   ( ) over $75,000

How old are you?   ( ) under 25   ( ) 25-35   ( ) 36-50   ( ) 51-65   ( ) over 65

How often has your family moved?   ( ) never   ( ) once   ( ) twice   ( ) three times   ( ) more than three times

Did you use the book before you left for your destination?   ( ) yes   ( ) no

Did you use the book while at your destination?   ( ) yes   ( ) no

Is there anything you would like to tell us about Insiders' Guides? _____

_____

_____

Name_____   Address_____

City _____State_____Zip_____

We'll send you a voucher for $6.48 off any Insiders' Guide® and a list of available titles as soon as we get this card from you. Thanks for being an Insider!

No Postage
Necessary
if Mailed in the
United States

BUSINESS REPLY MAIL
FIRST CLASS   PERMIT NO. 20   MANTEO, NC

POSTAGE WILL BE PAID BY ADDRESSEE

The Insiders' Guides®, Inc.
PO Box 2057
Manteo, NC 27954